Kaplan Publishing are constantly finding
difference to your studies and our exciti
offer something different to students loo

C000299820

This book comes with free MyKaplan onl
study anytime, anywhere. **This free onli**
separately and is included in the price or the book.

Having purchased this book, you have access to the following online study materials:

CONTENT	ACCA (including FBT, FMA, FFA)		FIA (excluding FBT, FMA, FFA)	
	Text	Kit	Text	Kit
Electronic version of the book	✓	✓	✓	✓
Knowledge checks with instant answers	✓		✓	
Material updates	✓	✓	✓	✓
Latest official ACCA exam questions*		✓		
Pocket Notes (digital copy)	✓		✓	
Study Planner	✓			
Progress Test including questions and answers	✓		✓	
Syllabus recap Videos		✓		✓
Revision Planner		✓		✓
Question Debrief and Walkthrough Videos		✓		
Mock Exam including questions and answers		✓		

* Excludes BT, MA, FA, FBT, FMA, FFA; for all other papers includes a selection of questions, as released by ACCA

How to access your online resources

Received this book as part of your Kaplan course?
If you have a MyKaplan account, your full online resources will be added automatically, in line with the
information in your course confirmation email. If you've not used MyKaplan before, you'll be sent an activation
email once your resources are ready.

Bought your book from Kaplan?
We'll automatically add your online resources to your MyKaplan account. If you've not used MyKaplan before,
you'll be sent an activation email.

Bought your book from elsewhere?
Go to **www.mykaplan.co.uk/add-online-resources**
Enter the ISBN number found on the title page and back cover of this book.
Add the unique pass key number contained in the scratch panel below.
You may be required to enter additional information during this process to set up or confirm your account
details.

This code can only be used once for the registration of this book online. This registration and your online
content will expire when the examinations covered by this book have taken place. Please allow one hour from
the time you submit your book details for us to process your request.

Please scratch the film to access your unique code.

Please be aware that this code is case-sensitive and you will need
to include the dashes within the passcode, but not when entering
the ISBN.

KAPLAN
PUBLISHING

ACCA

Paper SBL

Strategic Business Leader

Study Text

KAPLAN PUBLISHING'S STATEMENT OF PRINCIPLES

LINGUISTIC DIVERSITY, EQUALITY AND INCLUSION

We are committed to diversity, equality and inclusion and strive to deliver content that all users can relate to.

We are here to make a difference to the success of every learner.

Clarity, accessibility and ease of use for our learners are key to our approach.

We will use contemporary examples that are rich, engaging and representative of a diverse workplace.

We will include a representative mix of race and gender at the various levels of seniority within the businesses in our examples to support all our learners in aspiring to achieve their potential within their chosen careers.

Roles played by characters in our examples will demonstrate richness and diversity by the use of different names, backgrounds, ethnicity and gender, with a mix of sexuality, relationships and beliefs where these are relevant to the syllabus.

It must always be obvious who is being referred to in each stage of any example so that we do not detract from clarity and ease of use for each of our learners.

We will actively seek feedback from our learners on our approach and keep our policy under continuous review. If you would like to provide any feedback on our linguistic approach, please use this form (you will need to enter the link below into your browser).

https://docs.google.com/forms/d/1Vc4mltBPrfViy8AhfyKcJMHQKBmLaLPoa_WPqFNf4MI/edit

We will seek to devise simple measures that can be used by independent assessors to randomly check our success in the implementation of our Linguistic Equality, Diversity and Inclusion Policy.

British library cataloguing-in-publication data

A catalogue record for this book is available from the British Library.

Published by:

Kaplan Publishing UK
Unit 2 The Business Centre
Molly Millars Lane
Wokingham
Berkshire
RG41 2QZ

ISBN 978-1-83996-369-8

© Kaplan Financial Limited, 2023

Printed and bound in Great Britain

Acknowledgements

These materials are reviewed by the ACCA examining team. The objective of the review is to ensure that the material properly covers the syllabus and study guide outcomes, used by the examining team in setting the exams, in the appropriate breadth and depth. The review does not ensure that every eventuality, combination or application of examinable topics is addressed by the ACCA Approved Content. Nor does the review comprise a detailed technical check of the content as the Approved Content Provider has its own quality assurance processes in place in this respect.

We are grateful to the Association of Chartered Certified Accountants and the Chartered Institute of Management Accountants for permission to reproduce past examination questions. The answers have been prepared by Kaplan Publishing.

Contents

KAPLAN PUBLISHING

Introduction

How to use the Materials

These Kaplan Publishing learning materials have been carefully designed to make your learning experience as easy as possible and to give you the best chances of success in your examinations.

The product range contains a number of features to help you in the study process. They include:

1 Detailed study guide and syllabus objectives

2 Description of the examination

3 Study skills and revision guidance

4 Study text

5 Question practice

The sections on the study guide, the syllabus objectives, the examination and study skills should all be read before you commence your studies. They are designed to familiarise you with the nature and content of the examination and give you tips on how best to approach your learning.

The **Study Text** comprises the main learning materials and gives guidance as to the importance of topics and where other related resources can be found. Each chapter includes:

- The **learning objectives**, which have been carefully mapped to the examining body's own syllabus learning objectives or outcomes. You should use these to check you have a clear understanding of all the topics on which you might be assessed in the examination.

- The **chapter diagram** provides a visual reference for the content in the chapter, giving an overview of the topics and how they link together.

- The **content** for each topic area commences with a brief explanation or definition to put the topic into context before covering the topic in detail. You should follow your studying of the content with a review of the illustration/s. These are worked examples which will help you to understand better how to apply the content for the topic.

- **Test your understanding** sections provide an opportunity to assess your understanding of the key topics by applying what you have learned to short questions. Answers can be found at the back of each chapter.

- **Summary diagrams** complete each chapter to show the important links between topics and the overall content of the paper. These diagrams should be used to check that you have covered and understood the core topics before moving on.

KAPLAN PUBLISHING

Quality and accuracy are of the utmost importance to us so if you spot an error in any of our products, please send an email to mykaplanreporting@kaplan.com with full details, or follow the link to the feedback form in MyKaplan.

Our Quality Coordinator will work with our technical team to verify the error and take action to ensure it is corrected in future editions.

Icon Explanations

 Definition – Key definitions that you will need to learn from the core content.

 Key point – Identifies topics that are key to success and are often examined.

 Illustration – Worked examples help you understand the core content better.

 Test your understanding – Exercises for you to complete to ensure that you have understood the topics just learned.

 Supplementary reading – These sections will help to provide a deeper understanding of core areas. The supplementary reading is **NOT** optional reading. It is vital to provide you with the breadth of knowledge you will need to address the wide range of topics within your syllabus that could feature in an exam question. **Reference to this text is vital when self-studying.**

On-line subscribers

Our on-line resources are designed to increase the flexibility of your learning materials and provide you with immediate feedback on how your studies are progressing.

If you are subscribed to our on-line resources you will find:

1   On-line reference ware: reproduces your Study Text on-line, giving you anytime, anywhere access

2   On-line testing: provides you with additional on-line objective testing so you can practice what you have learned further

3   On-line performance management: immediate access to your on-line testing results. Review your performance by key topics and chart your achievement through the course relative to your peer group.

Ask your local customer services staff if you are not already a subscriber and wish to join.

ACCA Performance Objectives

In order to become a member of the ACCA, as a trainee accountant you will need to demonstrate that you have achieved nine performance objectives. Performance objectives are indicators of effective performance and set the minimum standard of work that trainees are expected to achieve and demonstrate in the workplace. They are divided into key areas of knowledge which are closely linked to the exam syllabus.

There are five Essential performance objectives and a choice of fifteen Technical performance objectives which are divided into five areas.

The performance objectives which link to this exam are:

PO1 Ethics and professionalism (Essential)

PO2 Stakeholder relationship management (Essential)

PO3 Strategy and innovation (Essential)

PO4 Governance risk and control (Essential)

PO5 Leadership and management (Essential)

PO6 Evaluate investment and financing decisions (Technical)

PO7 Identify and manage financial risk (Technical)

PO8 Evaluate management accounting systems (Technical)

PO9 Plan and control performance (Technical)

PO10 Review and report on the finding of an audit (Technical)

The following link provides an in depth insight into all of the performance objectives:

https://www.accaglobal.com/content/dam/ACCA_Global/Students/per/PER-Performance-objectives-achieve.pdf

Progression

There are two elements of progression that we can measure: first how quickly students move through individual topics within a subject; and second how quickly they move from one course to the next. We know that there is an optimum for both, but it can vary from subject to subject and from student to student. However, using data and our experience of student performance over many years, we can make some generalisations.

A fixed period of study set out at the start of a course with key milestones is important. This can be within a subject, for example 'I will finish this topic by 30 June', or for overall achievement, such as 'I want to be qualified by the end of next year'.

Your qualification is cumulative, as earlier papers provide a foundation for your subsequent studies, so do not allow there to be too big a gap between one subject and another. We know that exams encourage techniques that lead to some degree of short-term retention, the result being that you will simply forget much of what you have already learned unless it is refreshed (look up Ebbinghaus Forgetting Curve for more details on this). This makes it more difficult as you move from one subject to another: not only will you have to learn the new subject, you will also have to relearn all the underpinning knowledge as well. This is very inefficient and slows down your overall progression which makes it more likely you may not succeed at all.

In addition, delaying your studies slows your path to qualification which can have negative impacts on your career, postponing the opportunity to apply for higher level positions and therefore higher pay.

You can use the following diagram showing the whole structure of your qualification to help you keep track of your progress.

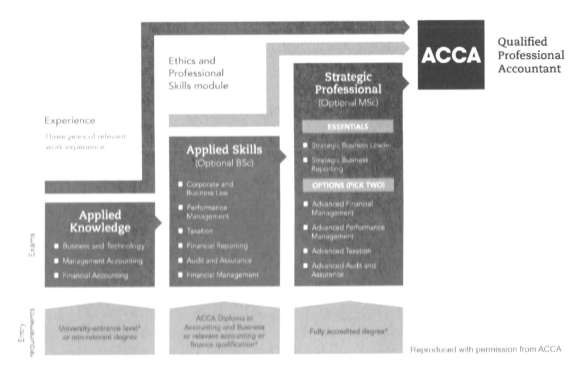

Reproduced with permission from ACCA

Syllabus

AIM

To demonstrate organisational leadership and senior consultancy or advisory capabilities and relevant professional skills, through the context of an integrated case study.

MAIN CAPABILITIES

On successful completion of this paper, candidates should be able to:

A   Apply excellent leadership and ethical skills to set the 'tone from the top' and promote a positive culture within the organisation, adopting a whole organisation perspective in managing performance and value creation.

B   Evaluate the effectiveness of the governance and agency system of an organisation and recognise the responsibility of the board or other agents towards their stakeholders, including the organisation's social responsibilities and the reporting implications.

C   Evaluate the strategic position of the organisation against the external environment and the availability of internal resources, to identify feasible strategic options.

D   Analyse the risk profile of the organisation and of any strategic options identified, within a culture of responsible risk management.

E   Select and apply appropriate information technologies and data analytics, to analyse factors affecting the organisation's value chain to identify strategic opportunities and implement strategic options within a framework of robust IT security controls.

F   Evaluate management reporting and internal control and audit systems to ensure compliance and the achievement of organisation's objectives and the safeguarding of organisational assets.

G   Apply high level financial techniques from the Applied Skills exams in the planning, implementation and evaluation of strategic options and actions.

H   Enable success through innovative thinking, applying best in class strategies and disruptive technologies in the management of change; initiating, leading and organising projects, while effectively managing talent and other business resources.

I   Apply a range of Professional Skills in addressing requirements within the Strategic Business Leader examination and in preparation for, or to support, current work experience.

J   Demonstrate other employability and digital skills in preparing for and taking SBL examinations

DETAILED SYLLABUS AND STUDY GUIDE

We have reproduced the ACCA's syllabus below, showing where the objectives are explored within this book. Within the chapters, we have broken down the extensive information found in the syllabus into easily digestible and relevant sections, called Content Objectives. These correspond to the objectives at the beginning of each chapter.

Syllabus learning objective and Chapter references

A   LEADERSHIP

1   Qualities of leadership

(a)   Explain the role of effective leadership and identify the key leadership traits effective in the successful formulation and implementation of strategy and change management.[3] **Ch.10**

(b)   Apply the concepts of entrepreneurship and 'intrapreneurship' to exploit strategic opportunities and to innovate successfully.[3] **Ch.10**

(c)   Apply in the context of organisation governance and leadership qualities, the key ethical and professional values underpinning governance.[3] **Ch.10 and 17**

2   Leadership and organisational culture

(a)   Discuss the importance of leadership in defining and managing organisational culture.[3] **Ch.10 and 24**

(b)   Advise on the style of leadership appropriate to manage strategic change.[2] **Ch.24**

(c)   Analyse the culture of an organisation, to recommend suitable changes, using appropriate models such as the cultural web.[3] **Ch. 24**

(d)   Assess the impact of culture on organisational purpose and strategy.[3] **Ch.24**

3   Professionalism, ethical codes and the public interest

(a)   Critically evaluate the concept of responsible leadership and the creation of public value by acting in the public interest.[3] **Ch.17**

(b)   Assess management behaviour against the codes of ethics relevant to accounting professionals including the IESBA (IFAC) or professional body codes.[3] **Ch.17**

(c)   Analyse the reasons for and resolve conflicts of interest and ethical conflicts in organisation.[3] **Ch.17**

(d)   Assess the nature and impacts of different ethical threats and recommend appropriate safeguards to prevent or mitigate such threats.[3] **Ch.17**

(e)   Recommend best practice for reducing and combating fraud, bribery and corruption to create greater public confidence and trust in organisations.[3] **Ch.17**

B **GOVERNANCE**

1 **Agency**

(a) Discuss the nature of the principal-agent relationship in the context of governance.[3] **Ch.7**

(b) Analyse the issues connected with the separation of ownership of an organisation and control over its activities.[3] **Ch.7**

2 **Stakeholder analysis and social responsibility**

(a) Discuss and critically assess the concept of stakeholder power and interest using the Mendelow model and apply this to strategy and governance.[3] **Ch.9**

(b) Evaluate the stakeholders' roles, claims and interests in an organisation and how they may conflict and be resolved.[3] **Ch.9**

(c) Explain social responsibility and viewing the organisation as a 'corporate citizen' in the context of governance and sustainability.[2] **Ch.9**

3 **Governance scope and approaches**

(a) Analyse and discuss the role and influence of institutional investors in governance systems and structures.[2] **Ch.8 and 12**

(b) Compare rules- versus principles-based approaches to governance and when they may be appropriate.[3] **Ch.8**

(c) Discuss different models of organisational ownership that influence different governance regimes (family firms versus joint stock company-based models) and how they work in practice.[2] **Ch.8**

(d) Apply general principles of International corporate governance network (of ICGN) codes to organisations' corporate governance.[2] **Ch.8**

4 **Reporting to stakeholders**

(a) Discuss the factors that determine organisational policies on reporting to stakeholders, including stakeholder power and interests.[3] **Ch.12**

(b) Assess the role and value of integrated reporting and evaluate the issues concerning accounting for sustainability.[2] **Ch.12**

(c) Advise on the guiding principles, the typical content elements and the six capitals of an integrated report, and discuss the usefulness of this information to stakeholders.[3] **Ch.12**

(d) Describe and assess the social and environmental impacts that economic activity can have (in terms of social and environmental 'footprints' and environmental reporting).[3] **Ch.12**

(e) Describe the main features of internal management systems for underpinning environmental and sustainability accounting including EMAS and ISO 14000.[2] **Ch.12**

(f) Examine how the audit of integrated reports can provide adequate assurance of the relevance and reliability of organisation reports to stakeholders.[2] **Ch.12**

5 The board of directors

(a) Assess the duties and roles of directors and functions of the board (including setting a responsible 'tone' from the top and being accountable for the performance and impact of the organisation).[3] **Ch.11**

(b) Evaluate the case for and against, unitary and two-tier board structures. [3] **Ch.11**

(c) Describe and assess the purposes, responsibilities and performance of Non-Executive Directors (NEDs). [3] **Ch.11**

(d) Describe and assess the importance of, induction performance appraisal and the continuing professional development of directors on boards of directors.[3] **Ch.11**

(e) Explain the meanings of diversity and critically evaluate issues of diversity on boards of directors.[3] **Ch.11**

(f) Assess the importance, roles purposes and accountabilities of the main committees within the effective governance.[3] **Ch.11, 14 and 16**

(g) Describe and assess the general principles of remunerating directors and how to modify directors behaviour to align with stakeholder interests.[3] **Ch.11**

(h) Explain and analyse the regulatory, strategic and labour market issues associated with determining directors remuneration.[3] **Ch.11**

6 Public sector governance

(a) Discuss public sector, private sector, charitable status and non-governmental (NGO and quasi- NGOs) forms of organisation, including agency relationships, stakeholders aims and objectives and performance criteria.[2] **Ch.7**

(b) Assess and evaluate the strategic objectives, leadership and governance arrangements specific to public sector organisations as contrasted with private sector.[3] **Ch.7**

(c) Explain democratic control, political influence and policy implementation in public sector organisations.[3] **Ch.7**

(d) Discuss obligations of the public sector organisations to meet the economy, effectiveness, efficiency (3'E's) criteria and promote public value.[3] **Ch.7**

C STRATEGY

1 Concepts of strategy

(a) Explain the fundamental importance of strategy and strategic decisions within different organisational contexts.[2] **Ch.2**

(b) Apply the Johnson, Scholes and Whittington of strategic management – the strategic analysis, strategic choices and strategic implementation.[3] **Ch.2**

2 Environmental issues

(a) Assess the macro-environment of an organisation using appropriate models such as PESTEL.[3] **Ch.3**

(b) Assess the implications of strategic drift.[3] **Ch.2**

(c) Evaluate the external key drivers of change likely to affect the structure of a sector or market.[3] **Ch.3**

(d) Apply Porter's Diamond to explore the influence of national competitiveness on the strategic position of an organisation.[3] **Ch.3**

(e) Assess scenarios reflecting different assumptions about the future environment of an organisation.[2] **Ch.3**

3 Competitive forces

(a) Evaluate the sources of competition in an industry or sector using Porter's five forces framework.[3] **Ch.3**

(b) Analyse customers and markets including market segmentation.[2] **Ch.21**

(c) Apply Porter's value chain to assist organisations to identify value adding activities in order to create and sustain competitive advantage.[2] **Ch.3**

(d) Advise on the role and influence of value networks.[3] **Ch.3**

(e) Evaluate the opportunities and threats posed by the competitive environment of an organisation.[2] **Ch.3**

4 The internal resources, capabilities and competences of an organisation

(a) Identify and evaluate an organisations strategic capability, threshold resources, threshold competences, unique resources and core competences.[3] **Ch.3**

(b) Discuss the capabilities required to sustain competitive advantage.[2] **Ch.5**

(c) Discuss the contribution of organisational knowledge to the strategic capability of an organisation.[2] **Ch.3 and 5**

(d) Identify and evaluate the strengths and weaknesses of an organisation and formulate an appropriate SWOT analysis.[2] **Ch.3**

5 Strategic choices

(a) Assess and advise on the different strategic options to an organisation.[3] **Ch.5**

(b) Assess the opportunities and potential problems of pursuing different strategies of product/market diversification from a national, multinational and global perspective.[3] **Ch.5**

(c) Advise on how the 7 'P's, including price-based strategies, differentiation and lock-in can help an organisation sustain its competitive advantage.[3] **Ch.5 and 21**

(d) Apply the Boston Consulting Group (BCG) and public sector matrix portfolio models to assist organisations in managing their portfolios.[3] **Ch.6**

(e) Recommend generic development directions using the Ansoff growth vector matrix.[2] **Ch.5**

(f) Assess how internal development, or business combinations, strategic alliances and partnering can be used to achieve business growth.[3] **Ch.6**

D RISK

1 Identification, assessment and measurement of risk

(a) Discuss the relationship between organisational strategy and risk management strategy.[3] **Ch.15**

(b) Apply the enterprise risk management (ERM) approach to risk management and for establishing risk management systems.[2] **Ch.15**

(c) Identify and evaluate the key risks including environmental and climate related risks and their impact on organisations and projects.[3] **Ch.15**

(d) Distinguish between strategic and operational risks.[2] **Ch.15**

(e) Assess attitudes towards risk and risk appetite and how this can affect risk policy.[2] **Ch.15 and 16**

(f) Discuss the dynamic nature of risk and the ways in which risk varies in relation to the size, structure and development of an organisation.[2] **Ch.15 and 16**

(g) Assess the severity and probability of risk events. [2] **Ch.15**

(h) Explain and evaluate the concepts of related and correlated risk factors.[3] **Ch.15**

2 Managing, monitoring and mitigating risk

(a) Explain and assess the role of a risk manager.[2] **Ch.16**

(b) Evaluate a risk register and use heat maps when identifying or monitoring risk.[3] **Ch.15**

(c) Evaluate the concept of embedding risk in an organisation's culture and values.[3] **Ch.15 and 16**

(d) Explain and analyse the concept of diversifying risk and when this would be appropriate.[2] **Ch.15 and 16**

(e) Advise on risk management strategies, including the use of the TARA model. [3] **Ch.16**

(f) Explain and assess the benefits of incurring or accepting some risk as part of competitively managing an organisation referring to the 'as low as reasonably practicable' (ALARP) principle.[2] **Ch.16**

(g) Apply the concept of assurance mapping to modern risk management using the 'four lines of defence'.[3] **Ch.16**

E TECHNOLOGY AND DATA ANALYTICS

1 Cloud and mobile technology

(a) Discuss from a strategic perspective the need to explore opportunities for adopting new technologies such as cloud, mobile and smart technology within an organisation.[3] **Ch.20**

(b) Discuss key benefits and risks of cloud, mobile and smart technology [2] **Ch.20**

(c) Assess and advise on using the cloud as an alternative to owned hardware and software technology to support organisation information system needs.[3] **Ch.20**

2 Big data and data analytics

(a) Discuss how information technology and data analysis can effectively be used to inform and implement organisation strategy.[3] **Ch.20**

(b) Describe big data and discuss the opportunities and threats big data presents to organisations.[2] **Ch.20**

(c) Identify and analyse relevant data for strategic decisions about new product developments, marketing and pricing.[3] **Ch.20 and 21**

3 Machine learning, AI and robotics

(a) Explain the potential benefits of using artificial intelligence (AI), robotics and other forms of machine learning to support strategic decisions and the pursuit of corporate objectives.[2] **Ch.20**

(b) Assess the risk, control and ethical implications of using (AI), robotics and other forms of machine learning.[3] **Ch.20**

4 E- business: value chain

(a) Assess the organisation's approach to delivering e-business. [3] **Ch.19**

(b) Assess and advise on the potential application of information technology to support e-business.[3] **Ch.19**

(c) Explore the characteristics of the media of e-marketing using the 6 'I's of Interactivity, Intelligence, Individualisation, Integration, Industry structure and Independence of location.[2] **Ch.21**

(d) Assess the importance of on-line branding in e-marketing and compare it with traditional branding.[2] **Ch.21**

(e) Explore different methods of acquiring and managing suppliers and customers through exploiting e-business technologies.[2] **Ch.20 and 21**

5   IT systems security and control

(a)   Discuss from a strategic perspective the continuing need for effective information systems control within an organisation.[3] **Ch.19**

(b)   Assess and advise on the adequacy of information technology and systems security controls for an organisation.[3] **Ch.19**

(c)   Evaluate and recommend ways to promote cyber security.[3] **Ch.19**

(d)   Evaluate, and if necessary, recommend improvements or changes to controls over the safeguard of information technology assets, to ensure the organisation's ability to meet business objectives.[3] **Ch.19**

F   ORGANISATIONAL CONTROL AND AUDIT

1   Management and internal control systems

(a)   Evaluate the key components or features of effective internal control systems such as those included under the COSO framework.[3] **Ch.13**

(b)   Assess whether information flows to management are adequate for the purposes of managing internal control and risk.[3] **Ch.13**

(c)   Evaluate the effectiveness and potential weaknesses of internal control systems.[3] **Ch.13**

(d)   Discuss and advise on the importance of sound internal control and compliance with legal and regulatory requirements and the consequences to an organisation of poor control and non-compliance.[2] **Ch.13**

(e)   Recommend new internal control systems or changes to the components of existing systems to help prevent fraud, error, waste or harmful environmental impacts. [2] **Ch.13**

2   Audit and compliance

(a)   Examine the need for an internal audit function in the light of regulatory and organisational requirements.[3] **Ch.14**

(b)   Justify the importance of auditor independence in all client-auditor situations (including internal audit) and the role of internal audit in compliance.[3] **Ch.14**

(c)   Justify the importance of having an effective internal audit committee overseeing the internal audit function.[2] **Ch.14**

(d)   Assess the appropriate responses to auditors' recommendations.[3] **Ch.14**

3   Internal control and management reporting

(a)   Justify the need for reports on internal controls to shareholders.[3] **Ch.13**

(b)   Discuss the typical contents of a report on internal control and audit including the environmental and sustainability audit.[2] **Ch.13**

(c)   Assess how internal controls underpin and provide information for reliable financial and sustainability reporting.[3] **Ch.13**

G FINANCE IN PLANNING AND DECISON MAKING

1 Finance transformation

(a) Discuss how advances in information technology is transforming the finance sector and the role and structure of the finance function within organisations [2] **Ch.23**

(b) Evaluate alternative structures for the finance function using business partnering, outsourcing and shared or global business services.[3] **Ch.23**

2 Financial analysis and decision – making techniques

(a) Determine the overall investment requirements of the organisation.[2] **Ch.23**

(b) Assess and advise on alternative sources of short and long-term finance available to the organisation to support strategy and operations. [3] **Ch.23**

(c) Review and justify on decisions to select or abandon competing investments or projects applying suitable investment appraisal techniques.[3] **Ch.23**

(d) Justify strategic and operational decisions taking into account risk and uncertainty.[3] **Ch.23**

(e) Assess the broad financial reporting and tax implications of taking alternative strategic or investment decisions.[2] **Ch.23**

(f) Assess organisation performance and position using appropriate performance management techniques, key performance indicators (KPIs) and ratios.[3] **Ch.4**

3 Cost and management accounting

(a) Discuss from a strategic perspective, the continuing need for effective cost management and control systems within organisations.[3] **Ch.23**

(b) Evaluate methods of forecasting, budgeting, standard costing and variance analysis in support of strategic planning and decision making.[3] **Ch.23**

H ENABLING SUCCESS AND CHANGE MANAGEMENT

1 Enabling success: organising

(a) Advise on how an organisation structure and internal relationships can be re-organised to deliver a selected strategy.[3] **Ch.18**

(b) Advise on the implications of collaborative working and partnering such as franchising, organisation process outsourcing, shared services and global business services.[3] **Ch.18**

2 Enabling success: disruptive technology

(a) Identify and assess the potential impact of disruptive technologies such as Fintech, including cryptocurrencies.[3] **Ch.20**

(b) Assess the impact of new product, process, and service developments and innovation in supporting organisation strategy.[2] **Ch.5**

3 Enabling success: talent management

(a) Discuss how talent management can contribute to supporting organisation strategy.[3] **Ch.24**

(b) Analyse opportunities for organisational improvement using the four view POPIT (people, organisation, processes and information technology) model.[3] **Ch.24**

4 Enabling success: performance excellence

(a) Apply the Baldrige model for world class organisations to achieve and maintain business performance excellence.[3] **Ch.4**

(b) Assess and advise on how an organisation can be empowered to reach its strategic goals, improve its results and be more competitive focusing on its critical success factors.[3] **Ch.4**

5 Managing strategic change

(a) Evaluate the effectiveness of current organisational processes.[2] **Ch.18**

(b) Evaluate different types of strategic change and their implications.[2] **Ch.24**

(c) Establish an appropriate scope and focus for organisation process change using Harmon's process-strategy matrix.[3] **Ch.18**

(d) Assess and advise on possible redesign options for improving the current processes of an organisation. [2] **Ch.18**

(e) Recommend an organisation process redesign methodology for an organisation.[2] **Ch.18**

(f) Manage change in the organisation using Lewin's three stage model.[2] **Ch.24**

(g) Assess the implications of change in an organisation using Balogun and Hope Hailey's contextual features.[3] **Ch.24**

6 Leading and managing projects

(a) Determine the distinguishing features of projects and the constraints they operate in.[2] **Ch.22**

(b) Discuss the implications of the triple constraint of scope, time and cost.[2] **Ch.22**

(c) Prepare a business case document and project initiation document.[2] **Ch.22**

(d) Analyse, assess and classify the costs and benefits of a project investment.[3] **Ch.22**

(e)   Establish the role and responsibilities of the project manager and the project sponsor.[2] **Ch.22**

(f)   Assess the importance of developing a project plan and its key elements.[3] **Ch.22**

(g)   Monitor and control project risks and slippages recommending improvements [2] **Ch.22**

(h)   Discuss the benefits of a post- implementation and a post-project review.[2] **Ch.22**

I   PROFESSIONAL SKILLS

1   Communication

(a)   **Inform** concisely, objectively, and unambiguously, while being sensitive to cultural differences, using appropriate media and technology.[3]

(b)   **Persuade** using compelling and logical arguments demonstrating the ability to counter argue when appropriate.[3]

(c)   **Clarify** and simplify complex issues to convey relevant information in a way that adopts an appropriate tone and is easily understood by the intended audience.[3]

2   Commercial acumen

(a)   **Demonstrate awareness** of organisational and wider external factors affecting the work of an individual or a team in contributing to the wider organisational objectives.[3]

(b)   **Use judgement** to identify key issues in determining how to address or resolve problems and in proposing and recommending the solutions to be implemented.[3]

(c)   **Show insight** and perception in understanding work-related and organisational issues, including the management of conflict, demonstrating acumen in arriving at appropriate solutions or outcomes.[3]

3   Analysis

(a)   **Investigate** relevant information from a wide range of sources, using a variety of analytical techniques to establish the reasons and causes of problems, or to identify opportunities or solutions.[3]

(b)   **Enquire** of individuals or analyse appropriate data sources to obtain suitable evidence to corroborate or dispute existing beliefs or opinion and come to appropriate conclusions.[3]

(c)   **Consider** information, evidence and findings carefully, reflecting on their implications and how they can be used in the interests of the department and wider organisational goals.[3]

4   Scepticism

(a)   **Probe** deeply into the underlying reasons for issues and problems, beyond what is immediately apparent from the usual sources and opinions available.[3]

(b)   **Question** facts, opinions and assertions, by seeking justifications and obtaining sufficient evidence for their support and acceptance.[3]

(c)   **Challenge** information presented or decisions made, where this is clearly justified, in a professional and courteous manner; in the wider professional, ethical, organisational, or public interest.[3]

5   Evaluation

(a)   **Assess** and use professional judgement when considering organisational issues, problems or when making decisions; taking into account the implications of such decisions on the organisation and those affected.[3]

(b)   **Estimate** trends or make reasoned forecasts of the implications of external and internal factors on the organisation, or of the outcomes of decisions available to the organisation.[3]

(c)   **Appraise** facts, opinions and findings objectively, with a view to balancing the costs, risks, benefits and opportunities, before making or recommending solutions or decisions.[3]

J   OTHER EMPLOYABILITY AND DIGITAL SKILLS

(a)   Use computer technology to efficiently access and manipulate relevant information.**Ch.25**

(b)   Work on relevant response options, using available functions and technology, as would be required in the workplace.**Ch.25**

(c)   Navigate windows and computer screens to create and amend responses to exam requirements, using the appropriate tools.**Ch.25**

(d)   Present data and information effectively, using the appropriate tools. **Ch.25**

The examination

NB: From September 2023, ACCA have introduced changes to the Strategic Business Leader (SBL) exam.

ACCA has introduced <u>pre-seen information</u> that will be released two weeks in advance of the SBL exam session.

The purpose of the pre-seen is to reflect real business life, where appropriate advice and recommendations are offered in the workplace only after a broader understanding of the industry and the organisation has been established.

Additionally, the pre-seen will help support those students who have English as a second language, have limited business experience, or have had minimal exposure to the industry on which the SBL exam is based.

Since much of the background information is now provided in advance, the <u>SBL exam duration has been reduced</u> from 4 hours to 3 hours and 15 minutes.

<u>Format of the SBL exam</u>

The SBL exam will contain further new information in the form of exhibits, which students should focus on in answering the requirements.

The total number of exhibits has been significantly reduced to reflect the introduction of the pre-seen information.

The exhibits in the exam may take a variety of forms including memos, emails, briefing notes, interview extracts, web pages, financial reports etc.

The SBL exam will now have <u>three compulsory tasks</u>, with each task having a varying numbers of parts and total marks.

There are three key changes as detailed below:

The three key changes are:

1. Pre-seen information

The primary aim of the pre-seen is to enable students to become familiar with the business activities of the case study organisation and the industry in which it operates. Familiarity with this important contextual information will help students to better understand and apply the further information that will be provided via exhibits in the SBL exam.

The pre-seen is designed to provide background and context only and will purposefully not signal areas of the syllabus or tasks to be assessed in the exam.

Students **will not be allowed** to take into the exam their own annotated copy of the pre-seen, since SBL will remain a closed book exam. A copy of the pre-seen will be available to students for reference purposes during the exam.

2. Duration of the SBL exam

The SBL exam time has been reduced from 4 hours to 3 hours and 15 minutes to reflect the fact that students will already be familiar with the background information and the context of the case study through the pre-seen.

The new exam length will bring SBL in line with other ACCA Strategic Professional exams.

3. Format of the SBL exam

The SBL exam will contain further new information in the form of exhibits, which students should focus on in answering the requirements.

The total number of exhibits will be significantly reduced from the current format to reflect the introduction of the pre-seen information. The exhibits in the exam may take a variety of forms including memos, emails, briefing notes, interview extracts, web pages, financial reports etc.

The SBL exam will now have three compulsory tasks, with each task having a varying numbers of parts and total marks.

All five professional skills will continue to be tested and will be worth 20 marks in total. However, due to the reduced number of tasks and exam time, each professional skill will be tested only once and will be worth four marks. There will no longer be two- and three-mark professional skills requirements.

The SBL exam will no longer be answered as a single requirement in one word processer document. Each task (or part of the task requirement, where appropriate) will be completed as a separate requirement in a separate response option or options.

As a result, the exam workspace area will look slightly different in that only one task will be shown at a time, and it will no longer be possible to view all tasks together.

The examination will continue to be based on an integrated case study containing a number of assignments which will vary at each examination.

These assignments or tasks may require the candidate to take on different roles, depending on the situation. The number of marks allocated to all these assignments or the sub-parts of these will add up to 100 in total.

Within the total marks available, there are 20 Professional Skills marks. Usually each task will contain some professional skills marks which may vary by examination, depending on the requirements. All tasks must be completed.

As previously stated, the examination is of 3 hours and 15 minutes duration, which includes Reading, Planning and Reflection time (RPRT). This time can be used flexibly at any time during the exam.

	Number of marks
Three tasks with multiple parts	**100**
Total time allowed: 3 hours 15 minutes	

Examination tips

Note: make sure you read the ACCA's Strategic Business Leader – Examiner Approach Article.

The SBL exam is different from any other exam that you have sat before and good exam technique is vital for success. In particular you should use this time to ensure that you understand the requirements, highlight key verbs, consider which parts of the syllabus are relevant and plan key calculations.

Time management

You will have 3 hours and 15 minutes (195 minutes) to read and analyse the case study and requirements, plan your approach to answering each of the tasks, and produce full answers to them all.

A recommended approach is that you allocate <u>at least</u> **35 minutes to RPRT** – reading, annotating and planning your answers to the requirements, leaving <u>approximately</u> **160** minutes for writing up your answers.

Given the 20 professional marks are earned how you write your answers (rather than writing anything extra), this means 160 minutes for 80 technical marks, or 2.0 minutes per technical mark.

Using the reading time effectively

Your objective here is to read and understand the scenario and requirements fully within 35 minutes. This may take longer than you first think so be prepared to spend a maximum of 45 minutes

Start by reading the requirements, so that when you read through the pages of exhibits, you can evaluate the information and link all pieces of relevant information to the requirements. As you do this, start thinking about the implications of what you are reading, and mentally compile a big picture of the organisation and the issues it is currently facing.

The exam you will be sitting is computer – based so you should highlight and annotate those areas of text that you consider useful to answering the questions, linking them to the different requirements.

Note: be sure to read the ACCA's Strategic Business Leader – SBL CBE Introduction article.

Weaker candidates annotate far too much, so try to be selective and prioritise issues as you go along.

Planning answers

Start by analysing the requirement itself:

- What role are you adopting?
- Who is the task addressed to and what do they want?
- What verbs have been used to express the requirement?
- Are there any limitations of scope highlighted?
- Are there any key issues mentioned that need addressing?
- Which professional skill(s) is being explicitly tested?

Next you could assess what approach you will take:

- Are any calculations, ratios or other quantitative analysis required?
- Does the question lend itself to the use of a specific theoretical model?

  The SBL syllabus has many frameworks and models that were developed to make analysis more focussed and effective, and to help develop strategic responses. The exam task will not specify which model to use (if any), so you need to decide which is/are the most useful. It is also perfectly reasonable to use parts of models if some aspects are less relevant – it is not an "all or nothing" decision.

  NB – detailed knowledge of these models is not required, you need to be able to apply the key concepts.

Given the above, you are now in a position to start writing up a plan:

Planning your answers – When the exam starts spend a few minutes skimming through each question to get a feel for what is included.

This will include a number of **exhibits** breaking down the scenario into relevant sections and including the detailed requirement. It will also include a list of the summarised **requirements** and an option to complete your answer in a **word processing** document and/or a **spreadsheet** document.

You can move around and resize the windows that you open to lay the screen out in a format that suits you.

Now copy and paste the specifics of the requirement into your answer document, perhaps highlighting in bold the different parts of the requirement and the verb used. Once complete review the exhibits in detail, highlighting and making notes as you do so and copy and pasting any relevant information to your answer document. These steps will help with your planning and structure but will also enable you to minimise the number of windows you have open.

Completing your answers – Start by revisiting the relevant exhibits for each requirement. Remember that the aim is to produce a professional and easy to read answer.

For calculations and numerical work, use a logical and well laid out structure in a spreadsheet. Calculations should be labelled and referenced in to any relevant discussion in the word processor.

For discursive answers, the word processing format should be used and answers should include bold headings and sub-headings and professional language. Ensure all aspects of the requirement are addressed in a sensible and balanced way. It is vital that you relate your answer to the specific circumstances given.

You may be required to produce a report, briefing note, presentation slides or any form of business communication. Head up your answer as appropriate and use the requirements as a basis for your introduction.

NB Some students write too much detail on their plans, wasting time, whereas others do not have sufficient information in order to take the plan and write up an answer. You will only find this balance through practice and experimentation.

Finally, leave enough time to read through the answers, ensuring they are clear and organised, and to make any necessary changes.

Earning professional skills marks as you write up your answers

To demonstrate professionalism and earn skills marks you need to do the following:

- Address the requirements as written, taking particular notice (again!) of the verbs used.

- Make sure you include the most important, relevant and crucial points relating to the requirement.

- Only make relevant points and try not to include superfluous information or make unsupported points.

- Show deep/clear understanding of underlying or causal issues and integrate or link different sources of information from various parts of the scenario or different exhibits to make points.

- Avoid repeating points already made.

- Show your ability to prioritise and make points in a logical and progressive way, building arguments rather than using a random or 'scattergun' approach to answering the question.

- Structure and present your answers in a professional manner through faithfully simulating the task as would be expected of the person being asked to carry it out and always have a clear stakeholder focus in mind when constructing the answer.

- Demonstrate evidence of your knowledge from previous learning or wider reading and apply this knowledge appropriately to strengthen arguments and make points more convincing.

- In addition to being clear, factual and concise, you should express yourself convincingly, persuasively and with credibility.

Note: be sure to watch the ACCA Strategic Business Leader – short videos on professional skills for SBL.

The use of theories or models in the Strategic Business Leader exam

The Strategic Business Leader exam set by the ACCA Examining Team is a practical exam and, unlike other exams, will **not** test individual theories or models in isolation or require for these theories or models to be quoted in answers to exam questions.

However, understanding the technical theories, models and knowledge is essential as these provide a framework for students to help them approach the practical tasks that they will need to complete in the Strategic Business Leader exam.

The use of models in the exam will be a judgement made by students and is part of the ACCA Professional Skills for analysis and evaluation. Students are advised to use models which they judge to be relevant for a particular task or scenario to generate the scope of their answer. There is not a prescriptive list of theories and models, however, so this textbook focuses on the models that it considers to be most relevant to the syllabus and to aid students in being successful in Strategic Business Leader.

Study skills and revision guidance

This section aims to give guidance on how to study for your ACCA exams and to give ideas on how to improve your existing study techniques.

Preparing to study

Set your objectives

Before starting to study decide what you want to achieve – the type of pass you wish to obtain. This will decide the level of commitment and time you need to dedicate to your studies.

Devise a study plan

Determine which times of the week you will study.

Split these times into sessions of at least one hour for study of new material. Any shorter periods could be used for revision or practice.

Put the times you plan to study onto a study plan for the weeks from now until the exam and set yourself targets for each period of study – in your sessions make sure you cover the course, course assignments and revision.

If you are studying for more than one paper at a time, try to vary your subjects as this can help you to keep interested and see subjects as part of wider knowledge.

When working through your course, compare your progress with your plan and, if necessary, re-plan your work (perhaps including extra sessions) or, if you are ahead, do some extra revision/practice questions.

Effective studying

Active reading

You are not expected to learn the text by rote, rather, you must understand what you are reading and be able to use it to pass the exam and develop good practice. A good technique to use is SQ3Rs – Survey, Question, Read, Recall, Review:

1   **Survey the chapter** – look at the headings and read the introduction, summary and objectives, so as to get an overview of what the chapter deals with.

2   **Question** – whilst undertaking the survey, ask yourself the questions that you hope the chapter will answer for you.

3   **Read** through the chapter thoroughly, answering the questions and making sure you can meet the objectives. Attempt the exercises and activities in the text, and work through all the examples.

4   **Recall** – at the end of each section and at the end of the chapter, try to recall the main ideas of the section/chapter without referring to the text. This is best done after a short break of a couple of minutes after the reading stage.

5   **Review** – check that your recall notes are correct.

You may also find it helpful to re-read the chapter to try to see the topic(s) it deals with as a whole.

Note-taking

Taking notes is a useful way of learning, but do not simply copy out the text. The notes must:

*   be in your own words

*   be concise

*   cover the key points

*   be well-organised

*   be modified as you study further chapters in this text or in related ones.

Trying to summarise a chapter without referring to the text can be a useful way of determining which areas you know and which you don't.

Three ways of taking notes:

Summarise the key points of a chapter.

Three ways of taking notes:

(1) **Make linear notes** – a list of headings, divided up with subheadings listing the key points. If you use linear notes, you can use different colours to highlight key points and keep topic areas together. Use plenty of space to make your notes easy to use.

(2) **Try a diagrammatic form** – the most common of which is a mind-map. To make a mind-map, put the main heading in the centre of the paper and put a circle around it. Then draw short lines radiating from this to the main subheadings, which again have circles around them. Then continue the process from the sub-headings to sub-sub-headings, advantages, disadvantages, etc.

(3) **Highlighting and underlining** – you may find it useful to underline or highlight key points in your study text – but do be selective. You may also wish to make notes in the margins.

Revision

The best approach to revision is to revise the course as you work through it. Also try to leave four to six weeks before the exam for final revision. Make sure you cover the whole syllabus and pay special attention to those areas where your knowledge is weak. Here are some recommendations:

Read through the text and your notes again and condense your notes into key phrases. It may help to put key revision points onto index cards to look at when you have a few minutes to spare.

Review any assignments you have completed and look at where you lost marks – put more work into those areas where you were weak.

Practise exam standard tasks under timed conditions. If you are short of time, list the points that you would cover in your answer and then read the model answer, but do try to complete at least a few questions under exam conditions.

Also practise producing answer plans and comparing them to the model answer.

If you are stuck on a topic find somebody (a tutor) to explain it to you.

Read good newspapers and professional journals, especially ACCA's Student Accountant – this can give you an advantage in the exam.

Ensure you know the structure of the exam – how many tasks and of what type you will be expected to answer. During your revision attempt all the different styles of tasks you may be asked.

Further reading

You can find further reading and technical articles under the student section of ACCA's website.

KAPLAN PUBLISHING

Introduction to the strategic business leader exam

Chapter learning objectives

Upon completion of this chapter you will be able to:

- understand the aims and structure of the Strategic Business Leader (SBL) exam and how it is marked

- understand what it means to be a "strategic leader"

- understand the professional skills required in the SBL exam and how they are examined

1 Introduction

The aim of the exam

The aim of the Strategic Business Leader (SBL) exam is to demonstrate organisational leadership and senior consultancy or advisory capabilities and relevant professional skills, through the context of an integrated case study.

The examination requires candidates to demonstrate a range of professional skills demanded by effective leaders or in advising or supporting senior management in directing organisations.

Role play

The basic structure of each exam will require the candidate to take the **role** of an organisational leader or as a consultant or adviser to senior management.

For example, in specimen exam 1, candidates were asked to adopt the role of an independent business analyst employed by PSS to advise the PSS board of directors on various strategic projects and initiatives.

Whereas in specimen exam 2, Yexmarine is seeking advice on a number of issues from Tranart Consultants. You work for Tranart Consultants, and you have been assigned to Yexmarine.

In each scenario candidates were expected to "get into character" and be very careful to consider who they were working for and who the report was for and what they required.

2 The strategic leader

Being a leader

Increasingly the role of accountants is that of professional advisors and leaders within business.

A leader is expected to be able to

- analyse a business situation and

- provide and implement appropriate, effective and sustainable solutions.

This means that they can

- be clear and focused, identifying the key issues in any situation

- analyse and address ethical concerns

- use technical models and quantitative analysis to draw out key issues, establish causality and integrate a wide range of factors into a coherent argument

- make clear recommendations that meet and exceed the needs of users and are 'fit for purpose'.

The SBL exam will test the extent to which you can fulfill this role and demonstrate this skill set.

Thinking strategically

Strategic analysis is covered in great depth within the strategic business leader syllabus but at this stage it is sufficient to remind you of the key characteristics of thinking strategically.

Having a strategic perspective means the following:

- Taking a **long-term perspective**.

  In the exam you could be presented with a problem and a potential solution but are expected to ascertain that the solution is nothing more than a short-term 'fix' and fails to address the longer term issues facing the firm, such as a decline in its main markets.

- Looking at the **whole organisation** as well as individual products/divisions/strategic business units (SBUs).

  For example, suppose a division is looking to introduce a new low-cost product – how could this affect sales of other company products that are currently marketed as high-quality, luxury items? Could the low cost item erode the existing brand name? Should the new product be sold under a different brand name?

- Setting the **direction** of the whole organisation and integrating its activities.

  A new strategy could require a change in the firm's organisational structure, governance structures and IT systems. All of these will need to be integrated to ensure success.

- Considering the views of **all stakeholders**.

  A project may create wealth for shareholders but would pollute the environment – would you accept it?

- Analysing the organisation's **resources** and defining resource requirements.

  For example, a company that has previously sold mainly to middle-aged consumers is considering targeting teenagers. Is the company's brand name strong enough to move into the new market?

- Relating the organisation to its **environments**.

  All strategies need to be 'positioned' in respect of what is happening within markets, key trends, the activities of competitors and so on.

- Looking at gaining a sustainable **competitive advantage**.

  How is the firm currently competing – is it on the basis of low cost, high quality or a strong brand name? Does the new strategy ensure a sustainable competitive edge going forwards?

In the exam most, if not all, of the questions will have a strategic context, so pitch your answer accordingly.

Test your understanding 1 – MacDonald Farm Ltd

The company

The entire share capital of MacDonald Farm Ltd is owned by Ken MacDonald and his wife, Jane. Their business consists of owning and running a 1,200 hectare farm, with land split between rearing lambs and growing a range of fruit and vegetables, including sugar beet.

MacDonald Farm Ltd is in the country of Florentinia, which is currently part of an economic union that includes the following systems and rules:

- There are no trade barriers or tariffs for the sale of goods between member states.

- There is a uniform, high level of tariffs that countries outside the union have to pay. This means for example, that there are few imports of African cane sugar and that imported New Zealand lamb is relatively expensive for consumers.

- Farmers within the union receive subsidies based on how large their farms are.

Recent events

Most of MacDonald Farm Ltd's produce is sold to large supermarket chains, who have been exerting more pressure on the farm to reduce prices. As a result the farm has started to see a decline in its annual trading profits, which in recent years have averaged $180,000 per annum.

In a recent referendum the people of Florentinia voted to leave the economic union with the "Flexit" scheduled to take place within the next two years. At this stage it is unclear what type of trading deals (and associated rules and restrictions) will be negotiated between Florentinia and the economic union and between Florentinia and other countries outside the union.

Proposal

Ken MacDonald is worried about the future and is therefore investigating using 200 hectares to set up a new exclusive 18-hole golf course.

Preliminary research suggests that planning permission will be forthcoming and demand projections are encouraging, given that membership waiting lists at the two existing golf clubs in the area exceed 350. If the project goes ahead, the new golf club is expected to be much better appointed than the two existing courses nearby.

Advantages and disadvantages

Ken has discussed the golf club idea with Jane and their sons, Rory and Callum, and they have together drafted the following list of advantages and disadvantages:

Advantages	Disadvantages
• Golf club income could help replace lost farm subsidies • Stable source of income • Could sell farm produce to the golf club restaurant generating extra income	• The family has no experience of running a golf club • The club could adversely affect the farm – e.g. extra noise during lambing season • Lost income from the land currently used for other purposes • Will need to build additional gates for access • Weedkiller used on golf putting greens could get blown onto vegetables • Damage to roads and farm tracks from additional cars

Required:

You have been appointed as a management consultant by Ken MacDonald to advise the family.

Briefly explain the most important strategic issues this case presents.

3 Professional skills

3.1 Overview

Employability and professional skills

Employers have consistently informed the ACCA and other professional accountancy bodies that their employees need to possess certain professional and ethical skills, in addition to the technical knowledge and skills that they expect of a qualified accountant.

The main capabilities that employers are seeking in qualified accountants are the ability to communicate appropriately, demonstrate commercial acumen, deploy analytical skills, adopt a sceptical stance and evaluate data and business information effectively.

These form the basis of the professional skills listed in the syllabus:

- Communication
- Commercial acumen
- Analysis
- Scepticism
- Evaluation

How the skills are examined

Depending on the particular professional skill being examined in the requirement, the examiner will be looking for that skill to be evident in how you answer the question in respect of the technical points you make. Demonstrating professional skills should therefore not be viewed as a distinct exercise separate from earning technical marks but rather as influencing how you answer the requirement.

The exam will contain 20 professional skills marks in total, distributed across the different tasks and be subject to the following:

(1)   All five professional skills must be tested in each exam.

(2)   Only one professional skill will be tested per requirement or part requirement.

(3)   The marks per professional skill tested will always be 4 marks.

(4)   When awarding professional skill marks, markers will use a professional skills grid, which will be consistently applied to the skill concerned on a sliding scale as follows:

Total marks for skill in this requirement	Skill demonstrated "not at all"	Skill demonstrated "not so well"	Skill demonstrated "quite well"	Skill demonstrated "very well"
4	0	1.33	2.66	4

Within each box, the answer will give further guidance to help assess the extent to which skills have been demonstrated.

It is extremely important that you understand what these professional skills are in more detail so that you know what is being expected of you.

Professional skills – Marking guide

For example, in specimen exam 2, Task 3 (a) candidates were asked to

(a) Prepare a report for the chief executive which:

- Evaluates the adequacy of the risk mitigating activities for each risk; and

- Recommends any further mitigating activities, which may be required.

This was to provide Yexmarine's chief executive independent assurance that the company is taking sufficient steps to effectively manage significant risks

Within this – Task 3 (a) evaluate the adequacy of the risk mitigating activities and recommend any further mitigating activities that nay be required for 16 marks. The professional skills aspect, for 4 marks, was given as follows:

"Professional skills marks are available for demonstrating *scepticism* skills by questioning the adequacy of the risk mitigation activities that have been suggested by the operations director"

The marking guide for this explained how marks were awarded as follows:

How well has the candidate demonstrated professional skills as follows:	Not at all	Not so well	Quite well	Very well
3a *Scepticism skills* By questioning the adequacy of risk mitigation activities. REPORT	The candidate has failed to challenge the current risk mitigation activities. The answer is purely descriptive. No attempt has made to suggest improvements in risk mitigation activities	The candidate has made a limited attempt at challenging the adequacy of Yexmarine's current risk mitigation activities. There is limited evidence of evaluating the effectiveness of the operations director's risk mitigation activities, but the opinions given and the challenges made are mostly not justified.	The candidate has made a good attempt at challenging the current risk mitigation activities. Most of the answer attempts to evaluate the operations director's suggestions of risk mitigation activities. The opinions given and the challenges made are mostly justified. Most of the challenges relate to significant concerns. The candidate has presented the answer in a report format.	The candidate has made an excellent attempt at challenging the current risk mitigation activities. The whole answer is an evaluation of the operations director's suggestion for risk mitigation activities. All the opinions given and the challenges made have been justified. The challenges reflect significant concerns. The candidate has presented the answer in a report format.
	0	1.33	2.66	4

3.2 Communication

Definition

(a) **Inform** concisely, objectively, and unambiguously, while being sensitive to cultural differences, using appropriate media and technology.

(b) **Persuade** using compelling and logical arguments demonstrating the ability to counter argue when appropriate.

(c) **Clarify** and simplify complex issues to convey relevant information in a way that adopts an appropriate tone and is easily understood by the intended audience.

In the ACCA's Strategic Business Leader – Examiner Approach Article, this is summarised as meaning that you have to express yourself clearly and convincingly through the appropriate medium while being sensitive to the needs of the intended audience.

The appropriate medium

You need to be able to present using a range of formats – reports, slides, letters, briefing documents etc. – so it is important to be aware what is considered to be best practice for each.

For example, in sample assessment 1, one requirement asked for slides with supporting notes. The expectation was that students would select key points, prioritise them and then present them in a logical order with a maximum of five points per slide. The accompanying notes were key as well as it was here that further detail and explanations could be added.

The intended audience

It is vital that you are aware of the recipient of the communication, so you can produce "the right message for the right person".

Key questions to consider are the following:

- who is the recipient?
- why have they requested the report (or slides or...)? Is there a key underlying question that they want an answer to?
- what are their key concerns likely to be?
- what arguments are more likely to persuade them?
- what level of technical discussion is appropriate?
- what do they already know?

This is also known as having "user focus".

3.3 Commercial acumen

Definition

In the syllabus, having commercial acumen is described as the ability to:

(a) **Demonstrate** awareness of organisational and wider external factors affecting the work of an individual or a team in contributing to the wider organisational objectives.

(b) Use **judgement** to identify key issues in determining how to address or resolve problems and in proposing and recommending the solutions to be implemented.

(c) Show **insight** and perception in understanding work-related and organisational issues, including the management of conflict, demonstrating acumen in arriving at appropriate solutions or outcomes.

In the ACCA's Strategic Business Leader – Examiner Approach Article, this is summarised as meaning that you have to show awareness of the wider business and external factors affecting business, using commercially sound judgement and insight to resolve issues and exploit opportunities.

Acquiring commercial acumen

In an ideal world you will have worked within a number of different industries and gained valuable experience and insight as a result. However, this will not be the case for the vast majority of students, so the required acumen needs to be gained in other ways.

Some aspects of commercial acumen can be learnt. For example, when you study franchising, licencing and joint ventures as possible business vehicles you will see that a key issue in 'the real world' is often how risks and returns are shared out among the different parties.

However, the best way to acquire the required insights is to do wider reading, whether through newspapers, journals or other sources. The examiners have made it clear that students will be rewarded for demonstrating wider reading by bringing real life examples into their answers.

When reading articles you should ask the following:

- What influenced the decisions made by the company concerned?

- What influenced whether those decisions turned out to be successful or not?

The aim of the pre-seen information is to provide students with more time to become familiar with the business activities of the case study organisation and its industry. This reflects real life, where advice and recommendations are only offered in the workplace when a broader understanding of the organisation has been established.

The pre-seen therefore provides important contextual information that will help students to better understand the further information provided in the exam.

3.4 Analysis

Definition

In the syllabus, analysis is described as the ability to:

(a) **Investigate** relevant information from a wide range of sources, using a variety of analytical techniques to establish the reasons and causes of problems, or to identify opportunities or solutions.

(b) **Enquire** of individuals or analyse appropriate data sources to obtain suitable evidence to corroborate or dispute existing beliefs or opinion and come to appropriate conclusions.

(c) **Consider** information, evidence and findings carefully, reflecting on their implications and how they can be used in the interests of the department and wider organisational goals.

In the ACCA's Strategic Business Leader – Examiner Approach Article, this is summarised as meaning that you have to thoroughly investigate and research information from a variety of sources and logically process it with a view to considering it for recommending appropriate action.

Another way of understanding this is to recognise that to analyse something is to examine it in detail in order to discover its meaning or essential features. This will usually involve breaking the scenario down and looking at the fine detail, possibly with additional calculations, and then stepping back to see the bigger picture to identify any themes to support conclusions.

Requirements may be unstructured but your analysis should be structured and have purpose

You will not be given a specific framework to work with in the requirement but will be expected to identify key data and use appropriate metrics and models, where useful, to analyse it.

The exam will be written to ensure that key data is spread across more than one exhibit and/or that key issues require some "digging" to unearth them, particularly when presented with large amounts of raw numerical data.

There should always be a purpose to the analysis – e.g. to identify reasons for a problem, to assess an opportunity or to generate solutions. It is therefore important to ask yourself why you are doing a particular calculation or using a specific framework – what will this reveal? Will it help answer the key questions?

'Analyse' does not mean 'describe'

A common complaint by examiners of higher level papers is that students are asked to analyse something but weaker answers merely describe the scenario without really adding any additional insight.

For example, if asked to **describe** a company's organisational structure, then you might comment that it has a basic functional structure. However, if asked to **analyse** the structure, then you might consider:

- **causes** – why has it got a functional structure? Has it been this way for years? What advantages does/did it gain from this? Are these arguments still valid?

- **context** – consider the wider picture. For example, maybe the structure was developed when the company had a more limited product range but now there is a strategic need to diversify the product portfolio and enter new markets.

- **consequences** – perhaps the company has outgrown its current structure and needs to adopt, say, a divisional approach to enable its new strategies?

Numerical analysis

If asked to analyse a set of financial statements, the end result will be a set of comments about the performance of the business with supporting evidence.

This could involve the following:

(1) You could break down your analysis into areas of profitability, liquidity, gearing and so on, depending on the requirement. You may not have time to calculate every possible ratio, so decide which areas are more likely to help.

(2) Under each heading look at key figures in the financial statements, identifying trends (e.g. sales growth) and calculating supporting ratios (e.g. margins).

(3) Try to explain what the figures mean and why they have occurred (e.g. why has the operating margin fallen?).

(4) Start considering the bigger picture – are the ratios presenting a consistent message or do they contradict each other? Can you identify common causes?

(5) Finally you would then seek to pull all this information together and interpret it to make some higher level comments about overall performance.

The main error students make is that they fail to draw out any themes and conclusions and simply present the marker with a collection of uninterpreted, unexplained facts and figures.

3.5 Scepticism

Definition

In the syllabus, scepticism is described as the ability to:

(a) **Probe** deeply into the underlying reasons for issues and problems, beyond what is immediately apparent from the usual sources and opinions available.

(b) **Question** facts, opinions and assertions, by seeking justifications and obtaining sufficient evidence for their support and acceptance.

(c) **Challenge** information presented or decisions made, where this is clearly justified, in a professional and courteous manner; in the wider professional, ethical, organisational, or public interest.

In the ACCA's Strategic Business Leader – Examiner Approach Article, this is summarised as meaning that you have to probe, question and challenge information and views presented to you, to fully understand business issues and to establish facts objectively, based on ethical and professional values.

Responsible accountants and auditors need to probe into issues, to question assumptions, scrutinise what is presented to them and challenge the status quo. These skills are also important for accountants in other functions. For example management accountants, particularly in relation to the budgetary planning and control process, will need to exercise scepticism where careful scrutiny of variances and their causes is concerned.

Not taking things at face value

Scepticism means not accepting things at face value.

For example:

- Looking for weaknesses in governance structures.

- Not believing something just because a director said it – many students are reluctant to challenge directors, even when they express very debatable viewpoints!

- Questioning data and how it was put together:

  - Who prepared it?

  - How competent are they?

  - Is there anything missing – what additional information is required?

  - Why did they produce it – what are they trying to achieve?

  - Could this result in bias?

  - What assumptions have they made and are they realistic?

  - Has the data been verified?

Ethical perspectives

Ethics is developed in great detail in later chapters. However, based on your earlier studies it is worth noting that potential solutions and strategies should be assessed against ethical frameworks, the public interest and professional codes.

The need for tact

For example, suppose a senior manager has presented a proposal for a new project. It is more tactful to suggest that forecast growth rates may be too 'optimistic' (coupled with arguments relating to industry growth, actions of competitors, etc.), rather than claiming that the manager concerned was trying to deceive the board to get funding.

Test your understanding 2 – Scepticism

You work in the mergers and acquisitions division of Global Foods Inc, a multinational group that specialises in food and drink products. The company has grown primarily through acquisition targeting smaller businesses that have high quality products but lack the financial, managerial and marketing resources to fully exploit them.

Kanter Ice Cream is a small ice cream manufacturer set up by George Kanter, a nutritional biologist. George has developed a way of making low fat, non-dairy ice cream that tastes just as good as traditional dairy high-fat products. George has financed the company through its first year from personal savings and by taking out a second mortgage on his home and has had some success in winning sales contracts from local health food shops. He is now considering selling the company to release equity.

George has approached you to discuss a potential valuation and has provided the following details:

	Forecast for next year $000	First year of trading (actual) Unaudited $000
Sales	60	30
Cost of sales	(15)	(10)
Gross Profit	**45**	**20**
Distribution costs	(10)	(5)
George's salary	–	(10)
Net profit	**35**	**5**

Required:

Explain five reasons why you should exercise scepticism regarding the figures presented by George.

3.6 Evaluation

Definition

In the syllabus, evaluation is described as the ability to:

(a) **Assess** and use professional judgement when considering organisational issues, problems or when making decisions; taking into account the implications of such decisions on the organisation and those affected

(b) **Estimate** trends or make reasoned forecasts of the implications of external and internal factors on the organisation, or of the outcomes of decisions available to the organisation

(c) **Appraise** facts, opinions and findings objectively, with a view to balancing the costs, risks, benefits and opportunities, before making or recommending solutions or decisions.

In the ACCA's Strategic Business Leader – Examiner Approach Article, this is summarised as meaning that you have to carefully assess situations, proposals and arguments in a balanced way, using professional and ethical judgement to predict future outcomes and consequences as a basis for sound decision-making.

Having a balanced argument

A key aspect of evaluation involves demonstrating **balance**, taking into account a broad range of issues, such as the following:

- Looking at both financial and non-financial indicators.

   For example, project A may have a higher NPV than project B but that does not necessarily mean that it should be preferred. What if project B has a more positive impact on the company's "green credentials" due to having a less damaging impact on the environment – would that make the directors choose project B instead?

- Looking at the needs of wider stakeholders and not just shareholders.

   For example, in an attempt to reduce costs and boost profits, a car manufacturer is considering using cheaper components in its engines. These are expected to fail after 4 years whereas the current components usually last the life of the car. Should the needs of shareholders be prioritised over those of customers?

- Balancing both risk and return.

   There are many ways of measuring the "return" of a proposal, ranging from profit-based metrics such as ROCE to cash-based approaches, such as NPV. However, return cannot be viewed in isolation but rather the risk-return trade off should be considered – does the extra return on one proposal outweigh the additional risks? How has risk been incorporated into the decision-making – for example, using different discount rates when calculating NPVs.

- Incorporating implementation aspects.

  A project may look attractive in terms of risk and return but that does not mean that it would be feasible for this company to undertake it – does it have sufficient resources, can it raise the finance required, can it achieve key deliverables in the timescales needed?

Prioritisation

Another key aspect of evaluation is that points are weighed and prioritised so that the most important issues are developed and discussed. Quality is more important than quantity in the SBL exam.

In prioritising points you could consider the following:

- Is the issue a strategic one or operational?

  For example, a new rival entering the market with a superior product (strategic threat) is more serious than problems with the air-conditioning in one of the firm's offices (operational issue).

- How urgently is a response needed?

  For example, the resignation or death of the CEO would require immediate action to reassure shareholders.

- What is the potential impact or materiality of the issue?

  For example, a company is considering a product recall due to safety concerns. How much will it cost to rectify and what is the possible cost if nothing is done and customers end up suing the company for injuries received?

- How likely is the issue to materialise?

  With the product recall issue mentioned above, how likely is it that customers will be injured and to what extent? If sued, then what are the chances of the company winning?

- Do not under-estimate the importance of ethical issues.

  Suppose in the product recall example it would be cheaper for the company to ignore the problem, even taking into account the costs of being sued. You could argue that the company should go ahead with the recall as that would be the ethically responsible thing to do.

- What is the relevance of the issue to the key question that is being addressed?

  For example, suppose the key issue at the heart of the question is declining quality and that the directors are looking for ways to improve quality and remain competitive. If discussing outsourcing as a possible solution, then quality-related issues should be seen as more important than, say, cost ones, although (obviously) a balance must be struck between these.

> ## Test your understanding 3 – Expected Values
>
> XYZ plc is a large manufacturing company that specialises in the innovative use of new technologies. Forecast results for the next year are as follows:
>
> - Revenue – $100m
>
> - Profit – $20m
>
> Unfortunately both of these are around 10% lower than the actual results for last year so the Directors are looking for new investment opportunities.
>
> One new possibility is project FG4526, which involves the use of a pioneering new composite material with exciting properties that are still being researched. The cash flows for the new project are estimated to be:
>
> - Probability of 40%: NPV = $30m
>
> - Probability of 50%: NPV = $2m
>
> - Probability of 10%: NPV = ($120m)
>
> The expected value of the above outcomes is $0.4 \times 30 + 0.5 \times 2 + 0.10 \times (120) = +\$1m$
>
> **Should the company proceed with the project?**

3.7 Summary

In summary, to demonstrate professionalism and earn skills marks you need to do the following (based on the ACCA's *Strategic Business Leader – Examiner Approach Article):*

- Make sure you include the most important, relevant and crucial points relating to the requirement.

- Show deep/clear understanding of underlying or causal issues and integrate or link different sources of information from various parts of the scenario or different exhibits to make points.

- Only make relevant points and try not to include superfluous information or make unsupported points.

- Avoid repeating points already made.

- Address the requirements as written, taking particular notice of the verbs used.

- Show your ability to prioritise and make points in a logical and progressive way, building arguments rather than using a random or 'scattergun' approach to answering the question.

- Structure and present your answers in a professional manner through faithfully simulating the task as would be expected of the person being asked to carry it out and always have a clear stakeholder focus in mind when constructing the answer.

- Demonstrate evidence of your knowledge from previous learning or wider reading and apply this knowledge appropriately to strengthen arguments and make points more convincing.

- In addition to being clear, factual and concise, students should express themselves convincingly, persuasively and show credibility in what they say and how they express themselves.

 Test your understanding 4 – MacDonald Farm Ltd – Continued

Recap

The entire share capital of MacDonald Farm Ltd is owned by Ken MacDonald and his wife, Jane. Ken and Jane are concerned about the future impact of Flexit and growing supermarket power and are investigating using 200 of their 1,200 hectares to set up a new exclusive 18-hole golf course. Preliminary research suggest that planning permission will be forthcoming and demand projections are encouraging, given that membership waiting lists at the two existing golf clubs in the area exceed 350.

The golf club company

It is proposed that MacDonald Farm Ltd will sign a 100-year lease with a new company, Calum Golf Club Ltd, which will pay an annual rent of $50,000 to MacDonald Farm Ltd for use of the land.

The issued capital of the golf club company will be two $1 ordinary shares, owned by Mr and Mrs MacDonald, and the remainder of its initial funding will be $2 million in the form of 15% per annum irredeemable loan stock. Fifty local business men, including Mr MacDonald, have each agreed to purchase $40,000 of this stock. The terms of the debenture loan stock issue prohibit a dividend being paid on the two ordinary shares so that any surplus is applied for the benefit of the club and its members.

Of the funds thus raised, $450,000 will be spent on converting farmland to become a landscaped golf course. A further $50,000 will provide working capital.

The club house company

The remaining $1,500,000 will be used to purchase a 25% stake in a separate company, Tarpon Club House Ltd, which will develop and operate a club house. This will have conference facilities, a sports hall, two bars and a restaurant. A local property company will subscribe the other 75% of the share capital of Tarpon Club House Ltd.

Calum Golf Club Ltd will pay an annual rent of $50,000 for the use of the club house, but Tarpon Club House Ltd will manage and run all facilities offered there, taking the profits that will be earned.

When ready to commence business in January 20X6, the new golf club will be much better appointed than the two existing local courses.

Costs and revenues

Annual operating expenses of Calum Golf Club Ltd are budgeted at $900,000.

On the revenue side, Calum Golf Club Ltd's share of profits on the investment in Tarpon Club House Ltd is expected to total $200,000 in 20X6, the first year of operations. Green fees, chargeable to non-members using the golf course, are expected to amount to an additional $100,000 a year.

On the assumption that target membership levels are achieved, annual subscriptions are initially to be set at $1,000 for each member. This will be $200 less than for full membership at the two rival golf clubs in the area. In addition, no joining fees will be payable in the first year of operation, but thereafter (as with the other two clubs) they will be equal to one year's subscription.

Break-even analysis

Based on the above data the break-even point for Calum Golf Club Ltd has been estimated at 600 members:

Expected fixed costs	$900,000
Income from Club House	$200,000
Green Fees Income	$100,000
Net costs to be covered	$600,000
Membership fee	$1,000
Break-even membership	600

Task

You are a management consultant advising the MacDonald family.

Prepare slides for use in a presentation to the family that addresses risk and return. There is no need for accompanying notes.

Test your understanding answers

Test your understanding 1 – MacDonald Farm Ltd

The key strategic issues facing the MacDonald family are both external environmental factors:

Flexit

There is huge risk and uncertainty relating to the post-Flexit trading environment:

- How much trade will MacDonald Farm Ltd continue to do within the economic union or will new tariffs price its products out of current markets?

- Will new trade rules with countries outside the economic union result in increased imports of African sugar and New Zealand lamb?

- If so, then will there be a system of new tariffs or will imported goods be cheaper than those produced by MacDonald Farm Ltd?

- Presumably MacDonald Farm will lose existing farming subsidies but will the Government of Florentinia replace this with anything to support domestic farmers?

The power of supermarkets

Large supermarket chains have been exerting more pressure on the farm to reduce prices. Even without the problems that may arise due to Flexit, MacDonald Farm is facing a major strategic threat here:

- Will supermarkets continue to squeeze prices as they appear to have the power to do so?

- Could MacDonald Farm find other retailers to use as an alternative to the larger supermarkets?

- Could MacDonald Farm offset the power in some way, such as building its own brand strength or specialising in a niche with less competition, such as producing organic foods?

Implications

Both of these factors mean that there is considerable uncertainty whether MacDonald Farm Ltd has a sustainable competitive strategy over the longer term.

The key issue facing the family is therefore how to reduce this uncertainty and develop a less risky income stream going forwards.

(Note: issues such as noise, new gates and weedkiller are all operational matters rather than strategic ones)

Test your understanding 2 – Scepticism

1   George's expertise and experience

George may be an expert biologist but there is no indication that he has any experience or expertise in accounts preparation and/or forecasting. Now it may be the case that he has had help from a professional accountant but we should not assume either the completeness or accuracy of the figures presented. Furthermore we should not assume that his lack of experience means that he has over-estimated the forecasts – it may be that George has under-estimated how desirable his new ice cream might be to major supermarket chains, for example.

2   George's motivation and interest

George is keen to sell the business to "release equity", so may, either consciously or unconsciously, be over-optimistic in his expectations regarding future success. He wants Global Foods to make an offer so wishes to make Kanter Ice Cream more attractive as a potential target. Furthermore, he will understand that higher forecast profits are likely to result in a higher offer price, so, again, may try to make the results look better to boost his return.

3   Unaudited accounts

While not a point to be laboured, there is the possibility that an audit might find errors in the actual results for the first year, resulting in a different profit figure.

4   Problems with figures that have been included

Some key figures are given without supporting assumptions and evidence. For example, is there any evidence, say in terms of commitments from new customers, to justify the 100% increase in revenue? Other figures seem too low – for example, a salary of $10,000 would not reflect market rates for a senior manager or director. For next year there is no salary at all – in both cases profit would need adjusting to reflect a more realistic figure.

5   Categories that appear to be missing

A final area of concern is that certain key costs appear to be absent altogether – for example, in order to penetrate the competitive, brand-conscious ice cream market significant expenditure on marketing would be required. No costs have been included for this.

Test your understanding 3 – Expected Values

Based on your knowledge of expected values from FM, you could have answered the question as follows:

The expected NPV is positive, so the project should be accepted. This would be expected to boost shareholder wealth, thus helping to meet the company's primary objective of maximising shareholder value. However the use of expected values can be criticised on the following grounds:

- *The expected value represents a long term average so may not be appropriate for a one-off decision*

- *The use of expected values loses the information regarding the spread of possible outcomes, so may not reflect the risks concerned*

- *The decision rule does not fully incorporate the risk aversion of key stakeholders.*

While this is all correct, the answer is limited in as much as it does not really **evaluate** the information fully and misses the key point:

- There is a 10% of a negative NPV of $120m, probably sufficient to bankrupt the company based on its forecast results.

- While the expected NPV is positive, there is a 10% chance of destroying shareholders' investments.

- This is very unlikely to be acceptable to shareholders – the risks are too great.

Test your understanding 4 – MacDonald Farm Ltd – Continued

Tutorial note:

*The key professional skill here is **communication** – in particular the idea of **user-focus** – you are asked to discuss risk and return from the **MacDonald's** perspective, rather than the golf club or the debenture holders or the property company or risks in general. The investment proposed should give them reliable income of $56,000 per annum unless the golf club performs very badly.*

SLIDE 1

Introduction/objectives

- To analyse risk/return for the MacDonald family from the Calum Golf Club

- Key question: Does the golf club provide a low risk source of income?

SLIDE 2

Context – 1 – Flexit

Significant uncertainty!

- Tariffs
- Access to markets
- Competition
- Loss of subsidies

SLIDE 3

Context – 2 – Increasing supermarket power

Increasing pressure on margins

- Pressure on prices
- Difficult to counter
- Likely to get worse

SLIDE 4

Scenario 1: the golf club is extremely successful:

You will receive an annual rent of $50,000 and interest of $6,000 on the debentures.

- No dividends can be paid on profits.
- You will also have a 100% equity stake in a successful golf company.

SLIDE 5

Scenario 2: the golf club just hits its BEP:

- You will still receive an annual rent of $50,000 and interest of $6,000 on the debentures.
- No dividends can be paid on profits.

SLIDE 6

Scenario 3: the golf club fails to attract enough members to hit BEP

- Unless the situation is particularly bad, you will still receive rent of $50,000 and interest of $6,000

- No additional liability on shares

- If interest cannot be paid, then the debenture holders may insist on a receiver. Uncertainty

- If rent cannot be paid, can the farm reclaim the land? Uncertainty

SLIDE 7

Conclusion and preliminary recommendations

Unless the golf club does very badly, you should receive a steady income of $56,000 per annum.

The investment gives a higher return than farming and at a lower risk, and is thus recommended on financial grounds.

However, before proceeding, we recommend that you seek to clarify/address the following risk areas:

- What is the legal position concerning the land and club house should rent not be paid?

- What assets are the debentures secured on, if any, as this will affect possible outcomes should interest not be paid?

Concepts of strategy

Chapter learning objectives

Upon completion of this chapter you will be able to:

- understand the common vocabulary of strategic management and why strategic management is important

- describe the different levels of strategic planning for an organisation

- explain the fundamental importance of strategy and strategic decisions within different organisational contexts

- apply the Johnson, Scholes and Whittington model for strategic management – strategic analysis, strategic choices and strategic implementation

- assess the implications of strategic drift and how it might be avoided

PER

One of the PER performance objectives (PO3) is that you contribute to the wider business strategy of your organisation through your personal and team objectives. You identify innovative ways to improve organisational performance – which may include making or recommending business process changes and improvements. Working through this chapter should help you understand how to demonstrate that objective.

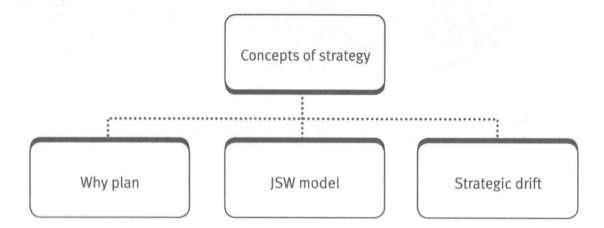

1 The nature of strategic decisions

We introduced the idea of thinking 'strategically' in chapter 1. This chapter explains in more detail what is meant by strategic planning and some of the different approaches that are taken to achieve strategic goals. By the end of the chapter you should be familiar with many of the common terms in the strategic vocabulary.

Strategic planning

'Strategic planning' can also be known as 'long-term planning' or 'corporate planning'. Those alternative names give some insight into the nature of strategic planning. It:

- considers the longer term (think of a time-horizon of about five years or beyond)
- considers the whole organisation.

Other characteristics of strategic planning are that:

- it gives direction to the whole organisation, and integrates its activities
- it considers all stakeholders
- it looks at how to gain a sustainable competitive advantage
- it relates the organisation, its resources and competences to its environment.

There is no universally accepted definition of strategy, and the word is used in different contexts to mean different things. The following definition is as useful as any.

 '**Strategy** is a pattern of activities that seeks to achieve the objectives of the organisation and adapt its scope, resources and operations to environmental changes in the long term.'

Why bother?

Studies show that companies that plan are more successful than those that do not. Strategic planning can have the following potential advantages and disadvantages:

Advantages	Disadvantages
• forces organisations to look ahead	• can be time consuming and expensive
• improved fit with the environment	• may be difficult in rapidly changing markets
• better use of resources	• can become a straightjacket
• provides a direction/vision	• some unplanned for opportunities may be missed
• helps monitor progress	• can become bureaucratic
• ensures goal congruence	• is less relevant in a crisis

Strategic planning is particularly important when:

- there are long lead times,

- the business needs to be turned around,

- there is high capital expenditure and

- many stakeholders are affected.

Test your understanding 1

How important is strategic planning likely to be to the following organisations?

(a)   A health service.

(b)   A small building contractor.

Levels of strategic planning

There are three levels of strategic planning:

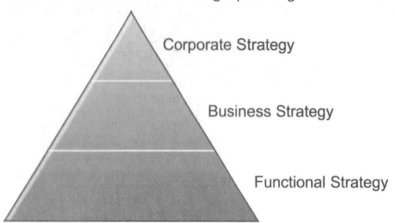

Corporate Strategy

This looks at the organisation as a whole and considers:

- the firm's orientation toward growth (also known as its directional strategy)

- the level of diversification in the company's products and markets (also known as its portfolio strategy)

- the manner in which management coordinates activities and transfers strategic capabilities between business units (also known as its parenting strategy).

Business Strategy

This examines each individual business unit and focuses on:

- actions taken to provide value to customers and gain a competitive advantage by exploiting core competencies in specific, individual product or service markets.

- the firm's position in an industry, relative to competitors and to the five forces of competition.

Functional or Operational Strategy

Functional strategy relates to a single functional operation (such as purchasing, marketing, human resource management etc.) and the activities involved therein. Decisions at this level within the organisation are often described as tactical.

They are much more detailed and specific than corporate and business level strategies and deal with areas such as:

- allocation of resources among different operations within that functional area

- coordination between functions for optimal contribution to the achievement of the SBU and corporate-level objectives

- gaining, retaining and developing resources and capabilities into ones which can give strategic advantages and support the business level strategy.

Consistency

The strategies at the different levels should be consistent. There is no point having a corporate strategy that says that the organisation should move up-market, if the business strategy is to stay in cheap markets and functions provide low-quality resources.

Strategic choices need to be made at every level, though obviously choices made at any particular level can influence choices at other levels.

Illustration – Levels of strategic planning

Gap is an international clothing retailer. Classification of different levels of strategic planning could be:

Corporate

- Should another range of shops be established (as Gap did with Banana Republic, a more up-market chain)?

- Should the company raise more share capital?

Business

- How will the company beat rivals and gain market share in Australia?

Functional/operational

- How will suitable premises be found and fitted out for the new range of shops?

Test your understanding 2

A full-service airline is making the following decisions.

(a) Should a 'no-frills', low-fare subsidiary be set up?

(b) If it is set up, how should cabin staff be recruited?

Are these likely to be corporate, business or operational decisions?

2   An approach to strategic planning

 The Johnson, Scholes and Whittington (JSW) model of strategic planning consists of three elements:

The strategic position/analysis

Strategic choices   Strategy into action (implementation)

Interdependencies between the elements

The model is shown in a way that recognises the interdependencies between the elements of strategic planning. For example, it might only be at the strategy into action (implementation) stage that an organisation discovers something that sheds light on its strategic position.

Also, Johnson, Scholes and Whittington argue that strategic planning can begin at any point. For example, firms might decide that they will launch an internet sales division without first carrying out any strategic analysis or choosing how the new strategy might compete. Once the division has been put into action it might then become clearer about what its position is relative to rivals or customer needs and how a strategy can be chosen to put the division into a better strategic position.

The strategic position/analysis

Assessing the strategic position consists of analysing:

- the environment (competitors, markets, regulations, discoveries, etc), helping identify opportunities and threats

- the strategic capability of the organisation (resources and competences), helping identify strengths and weaknesses

- the culture, beliefs and assumptions of the organisation

- the expectation and power of stakeholders (what do the shareholders want? Will employees co-operate?).

The aims of strategic analysis

The aim of strategic analysis is to form a view of the main influences on the present and future well-being of the organisation. This will obviously affect the strategy choice.

Strategic analysis would cover the following areas.

- The PESTEL environmental variables – political, economic, social, technological, environmental and legal as well as competitive factors and how they will affect the organisation and its activities.

- The resource availability and its relative strengths and weaknesses.

- The aspirations and expectations of the groups that have an interest in the organisation, e.g. shareholders, managers, owners, employees and unions.

- The beliefs and assumptions that make up the culture of the organisation will have an effect because they are the means of interpreting the environment and resource influences.

The environmental variables – Since strategy is concerned with the position a business takes in relation to its environment, an understanding of the environment's effects on an organisation is of central importance to strategic analysis. The historical and environmental effects on the business must be considered, as well as the present effects and the expected changes in environmental variables. This is a major task because the range of environmental variables is so great. Many of those variables will give rise to opportunities of some sort, and many will exert threats upon the organisation. The two main problems that have to be faced are, first, to distil out of this complexity a view of the main or overall environmental impacts for the purpose of strategic choice; and second, the fact that the range of variables is likely to be so great that it may not be possible or realistic to identify and analyse each one.

The resources of the organisation – There are internal influences as well as outside influences on the firm and its choice of strategies. One of the ways of thinking about the strategic capability of an organisation is to consider its strengths and weaknesses (what it is good or not so good at doing, or where it is at a competitive advantage or disadvantage, for example). Considering the resource areas of a business such as its physical plant, its management, its financial structure and its products may identify these strengths and weaknesses. Again, the aim is to form a view of the internal influences and constraints on strategic choice. The expectations of different stakeholders are important because they will affect what will be seen as acceptable in terms of the strategies advanced by management. However, the beliefs and assumptions that make up the culture of an organisation, though less explicit, will also have an important influence.

Expectations and influence of stakeholders – A stakeholder can be defined as someone who has an interest in the well-being of the organisation. A typical list of stakeholders for a large company would include shareholders, employees, managers, customers, locality, suppliers, government and society at large.

Strategic planning and management cannot be achieved without regard to stakeholders.

- In a profit-making organisation, management might have a choice of adopting a high risk/high return strategy or a low risk/low return strategy. It's important to know which the shareholders want.

- In a not-for-profit organisation, such as a hospital, managers need to know what the government and potential patients want. How much resource should go into heart operations, how much into hip replacement, etc.

The beliefs and assumptions within an organisation – affect the interpretation of the environmental and resource influences; so two groups of managers, perhaps working in different divisions of an organisation, may come to different conclusions about strategy, although they are faced with similar environmental and resource implications. Which influence prevails is likely to depend on which group has the greater power, and understanding this can be of great importance in recognising why an organisation follows, or is likely to follow, the strategy it does.

A consideration of all relevant features – the environment, resources, expectations and objectives within the cultural and political framework of the organisation – provides the basis for strategic analysis of that organisation. However, to understand its strategic position, it is also necessary to examine the extent to which the direction and implications of the current strategy and objectives that it is following are in line with, and can cope with, the implications of the strategic analysis.

Strategic choice

Strategic choice follows strategic analysis and is based upon the following three elements.

- Generation of strategic options, e.g. growth, acquisition, diversification or concentration.

- Evaluation of the options to assess their relative merits and feasibility.

- Selection of the strategy or option that the organisation will pursue.

  There could be more than one strategy chosen but there is a chance of an inherent danger or disadvantage to any choice made. Although there are techniques for evaluating specific options, the selection is often subjective and likely to be influenced by the values of managers and other groups with an interest in the organisation.

In addition to deciding the scope and direction of an organisation, choices also need to be made about how to achieve the goal. Broadly, there are two ways in which a strategy can be pursued:

- internal development (organic growth)

- external development – merger/acquisition, JV, franchising/licensing.

The generation of strategic options

Generation of strategic options

There may be several possible courses of action open to the organisation. For example, an international retailer may need to decide on areas such as:

- which areas of the world are most important to concentrate on

- whether it is possible to maintain a common basis of trading across all the different countries

- whether it is necessary to introduce variations by market focus

- what strategic directions are necessary for product development and product range

- should the company attempt to follow these strategies by internal development or joint venture activity through franchising?

All of these considerations are important and need careful consideration; indeed, in developing strategies, a potential danger is that managers do not consider any but the most obvious course of action – and the most obvious is not necessarily the best. A helpful step in strategic choice can be to generate strategic options.

Strategic options generation is the process of establishing a choice of possible future strategies. There are three main areas to consider.

- Porter describes certain generic competitive strategies (lowest cost or differentiation) that an organisation may pursue for competitive advantage. They determine how you compete.

- Ansoff describes product-market strategies (which markets you should enter or leave). They determine where you compete and the direction of growth.

- Institutional strategies (i.e. relationships with other organisations) determine the method of growth.

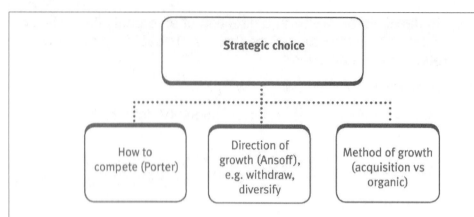

Evaluation of the options

Strategic options can be examined in the context of the strategic analysis to assess their relative merits. We will see in a later chapter that strategies are often assessed against three criteria – whether it is suitable, feasible and acceptable for the organisation.

In deciding on any of the options that they face, the organisation might want to know whether they are suitable to the firm's existing position. They need to know which of these options builds upon strengths, overcomes weaknesses and takes advantage of opportunities, while minimising or circumventing the threats the business faces. This is called the search for strategic fit or suitability of the strategy. However, a second set of questions is important:

* To what extent could a chosen strategy be put into effect?

* Could require finance be raised, sufficient stock be made available at the right time and in the right place, staff be recruited and trained to reflect the sort of image the organisation is trying to project?

These are questions of feasibility.

Even if these criteria could be met, management would still need to know whether the choice would be acceptable to the stakeholders.

A variety of techniques are used to assess the value of strategies. Some strategies will be assessed on financial criteria (such as net present value). Where this is not possible, or where the uncertainty in the environment is great, more sophisticated models are used.

Selection of the strategy or option

This is the process of selecting those options that the organisation will pursue. There could be just one strategy chosen or several. There is unlikely to be a clear-cut 'right' or 'wrong' choice because any strategy must inevitably have some dangers or disadvantages. So in the end, choice is likely to be a matter of management judgement. It is important to understand that the selection process cannot always be viewed or understood as a purely objective, logical act. It is strongly influenced by the values of managers and other groups with interest in the organisation, and ultimately may very much reflect the power structure in the organisation.

Strategy into action/implementation

Implementing a strategy has three elements.

- Organising/structuring. For example, should the organisation be split into European, US and Asian divisions? How autonomous should divisions be?

- Enabling an organisation's resources should support the chosen strategy. For example, appropriate human resources and non-current assets need to be acquired.

- Managing change. Most strategic planning and implementation will involve change, so managing change, in particular employees' fears and resistance, is crucial.

The implementation process

Structure

It is likely that changes in organisational structure will be needed to carry through the strategy and there is also likely to be a need to adapt the systems used to manage the organisation.

Organisation structure – lines of authority and communication must be established that are appropriate to the way the strategy is broken down into detailed targets. Systems are required to provide the necessary strategic information, as well as essential operational procedures. Control systems are used to assess performance. The type of questions that will need answering include:

- what will different departments be held responsible for?

- what sorts of information system are needed to monitor the progress of the strategy?

- is there a need for retraining of the workforce?

Implementation involves devising sub-strategies for products and markets, human resources and so on.

Resource planning

Resource planning covers finance, human resource management and physical resources such as land and buildings. It involves assessing the key tasks to satisfy the critical success factors, and the resources to be allocated to the key tasks. It is concerned with the following questions.

- What are the key tasks that need to be carried out?

- What changes need to be made in the resource mix of the organisation?

- By when?

- Who is to be responsible for the change?

Managing change

Successful implementation will rely on the successful management of the change to the new strategy. This will involve not only the management of the systems and structures of the organisation, but also the management of its people and routines. This will involve two elements:

- overcoming resistance to change from staff

- leading staff in a manner that encourages them to make the change successfully.

Illustration 1 – The JSW model of strategic planning

Illustration – Johnson, Scholes and Whittington model of strategic planning

A full-price airline is considering setting up a 'no frills', low-fare subsidiary. The strategic planning process would include the following elements.

Strategic position: An analysis will need to be made of areas such as expected competitor actions, oil price forecasts, passenger volume forecasts, availability of cheap landing rights, public concern for environmental damage, the strength of the airline's main brand.

Strategic choices: A number of options will need to be considered such as which routes to launch? Whether to set up a service from scratch or buy an existing cheap airline? Which planes to use, what on-board services to offer?

Strategic implementation: Once a decision has been made the best way to put that decision into practice will have to be considered and this will involve an assessment of areas such as how autonomous should the new airline be? How to recruit and train staff? Implementation of the internet booking system. Acquisition of aircraft. Obtaining landing slots.

Test your understanding 3

A health provider has only large, edge of town, hospitals. It is considering setting up additional small city centre clinics capable of treating less serious day cases.

Give examples of what the provider should consider under the headings of strategic position, strategic choices and strategic implementation.

Strategic management in different contexts

Type of organisation	Characteristics	Key strategic issues
Small businesses	• Likely to operate in a single market with a limited product range • Expectations/ views of founders dominate	• Dealing with pressure from larger competitors, e.g. by development of unique capabilities, niche strategies, etc. • Strategy choice may be limited by financing opportunities – relationship with banks is vital
Multinationals	• Likely to operate in many diverse markets with a wide product range	• Corporate strategy – control of diverse businesses is vital – e.g. relationship between head office and local subsidiaries/ divisions • Business unit strategy – resource allocation to business units and co-ordination between them (e.g. logistics)

Type of organisation	Characteristics	Key strategic issues
Public sector	• Significant government influence (e.g. may have to offer a universal service) • Planning horizons driven by political rather than market conditions	• Role of ideology • Competition for resources – e.g. have to demonstrate value for money to win funding • Strategic options limited by funding (e.g. tax implications) • Strategic alliances are often key (e.g. public and private partnerships)
Voluntary and not-for-profit sectors	• Key objectives non-financial • Funding often not linked to recipients of service	• Role of values/ ideology – key decisions are usually centralised • Competition for funds – e.g. meeting expectations of funding bodies

3 Strategic drift

When planned strategies are not realised it is often because events develop in unexpected ways:

- the organisation's underlying assumptions turn out to be invalid
- the pace of development overtakes it
- changes in the organisation's external environment, e.g. changes in the market for the goods and services that the firm produces and in the nature of the competition facing the company
- the organisation's internal environment changes.

If an organisation fails to keep up with the changes in its external environment it can lead to what is known as strategic drift.

Strategic drift

Strategic drift describes a situation where the organisation's strategy gradually, if imperceptibly, moves away from the forces at work in its environment.

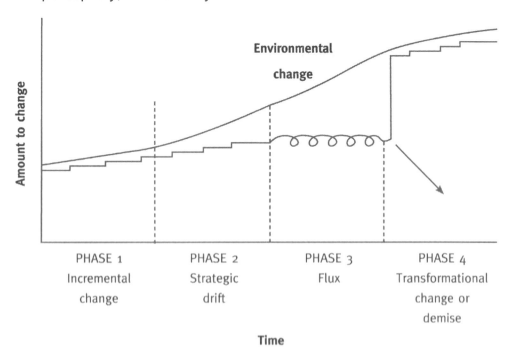

	Explanation of the stages in strategic drift

- Phase 1: The organisation takes a series of logical, incremental steps that were part of its plan to change ahead of the market and develop a competitive advantage.

- Phase 2: The rate of change in the market place speeds up, and the firm's incrementalist approach is not enough to maintain its advantage, and it is left behind.

- Phase 3: Faced with a stimulus for action, managers may seek to extend the market for their business, but may assume that it will be similar to their existing market, and therefore set about managing the new venture in much the same way as they have been used to.

  If this is not successful, strategy development is likely to go into a state of flux, with no clear direction, further damaging performance.

- Phase 4: Eventually transformational change is required if the demise of the organisation is to be avoided.

  Transformational change tends to occur when performance has fallen off significantly, i.e. in times of crisis.

Causes of strategic drift

The reasons for the drift can vary and can include rapid and unexpected changes in the environment through the discovery of, say, new technologies. The extent of drift can also be influenced by:

- cultural influences in maintaining strategic stability and sometimes resisting strategic change

- the power structure within the organisation

- the effect of politics and the relative influence on the decision-making of different individuals and groups.

These forces can work to create either a resistance to change or a lack of focus on the changes occurring in the external environment (or sometimes a lack of belief in the permanence of the changes in the environment). The organisation becomes too slow to react and drifts away from what the market wants.

Avoiding strategic drift

In order to avoid strategic drift it will be vital that an organisation

- regularly assesses its environment (both in its current state and its expected future state) for changes

- has flexible systems for reacting to changes in its environment

- breaks down barriers to change by having an organisational culture that successfully copes with change

- has a clear idea of its mission and objectives in order to understand where it wants to be in the future and to guide strategic choices

- has strong leaders who are willing and able to make changes to organisational direction and strategy.

These are ideas that are explored in other chapters within this study text.

Illustration 2 – Strategic Drift and Blockbuster

At the height of its success, Blockbuster had 60,000 employees across 9,000 stores and was worth around $8 billion. In 2000 Blockbuster took a staggering $800 million in late fees alone, accounting for approximately 16% of its total revenue.

Most would attribute the growth of the internet and Netflix as being the key factors in the destruction of this huge business but maybe a catastrophic ignorance of the increasing competitive threat and missed opportunities were also contributory factors. For example, dig a little deeper and we discover that Blockbuster decided against investing some of its huge financial resources to go online as well as declining several offers to buy Netflix (for a mere $50 million) believing that they had a fantastic business model which they didn't want to disrupt for a 'maybe business' in the online world.

4 Chapter summary

```
                    ┌─────────────────────────┐
                    │                         │
                    │   Concepts of strategy  │
                    │                         │
                    └─────────────────────────┘
```

Why plan
- Helps meet goals
- Avoids drift
- Provides direction

Levels:
- Corporate
- Business
- Functional

JSW model
- Analysis: understand position relative to the environment
- Choice: choose a strategy to close the gap with the environment
- Action: implement strategic choices

Strategic drift
- Continue to make incremental changes
- Environment has changed fundamentally
- Need transformation to close the gap

Test your understanding answers

Test your understanding 1

(a)   Health service

Strategic planning is vital. Hospitals are hugely expensive and take years to plan and build and their provision must be closely aligned with population trends and treatment advances. Training medical staff is also a long-term process. If hospital and other health service facilities are inadequate, many people will be adversely affected.

(b)   A small building contractor

Relatively little long-term planning is needed. If the builder buys and develops land, then some planning will be needed to ensure that land and planning permission can be acquired. Otherwise, many builders work from job to job using a high proportion of sub-contractors.

Test your understanding 2

(a)   There will be very high costs involved, careful planning is needed to ensure that the cheap flights do not cannibalise the expensive service. This is a decision that would be made by the main board and is a corporate level strategy.

(b)   The nature of this decision is most likely to be a functional level strategy. However, it will be important that the strategy is consistent with whatever business level strategy is being followed. If the company decides to offer a low level service as part of its business level strategy, then it will be important that the recruitment of staff supports this.

Test your understanding 3

Suggestions are:

Strategic position: likely demand. Some type of cost/benefit analysis to show that the strategy is worthwhile. Safety of patients being treated in less well-resourced environments. Acceptability to patients. Acceptability to staff.

Strategic choices: which illnesses to treat? Where should the clinics be? How should the clinics be staffed? Opening hours?

Strategic implementation: acquiring and fitting out clinics. Hiring and/or transferring staff. Publicity, so that patients know where and when to go. Liaison with general practitioners and the main hospitals.

Strategic analysis

Chapter learning objectives

Upon completion of this chapter you will be able to:

- assess the macro-environment of an organisation using appropriate models such as PESTEL

- evaluate the sources of competition in an industry or sector using Porter's five forces framework

- assess scenarios reflecting different assumptions about the future environment of an organisation

- apply Porter's diamond to explore the influence of national competitiveness on the strategic position of an organisation

- evaluate how external key drivers of change are likely to affect the structure of a sector or a market

- evaluate the opportunities and threats posed by the environment of an organisation

- identify and evaluate an organisation's strategic capability, threshold resources, threshold competences, unique resources and core competences

- discuss the contribution of organisational knowledge to the strategic capability of an organisation

- apply Porter's value chain to assist organisations to identify value adding activities in order to create and sustain competitive advantage

- advise on the role and influence of value networks

- identify and evaluate the strengths and weaknesses of an organisation and formulate an appropriate SWOT analysis

PER

One of the PER performance objectives (PO3) is that you contribute to the wider business strategy of your organisation through your personal and team objectives. You identify innovative ways to improve organisational performance – which may include making or recommending business process changes and improvements. Working through this chapter should help you understand how to demonstrate that objective.

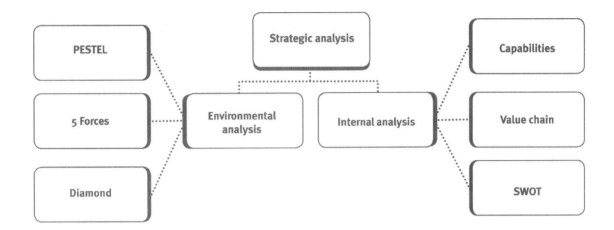

1 Introduction

This chapter explores some of the planning tools that can help to analyse an organisation's environment and its position within that environment. In order to avoid strategic drift and to ensure a proper fit with an organisation's environment, strategic planners need to understand the environment and the drivers for change that will come from it.

 ACCA Guidance on models and frameworks

The Strategic Business Leader exam set by the ACCA Examining Team is a practical exam and unlike other exams will not test individual theories or models in isolation or require for these theories or models to be quoted in answers to exam questions. However, understanding the technical theories, models and knowledge is essential as these provide a framework for students to help them approach the practical tasks that they will need to complete in the Strategic Business Leader exam.

The use of models in the exam will be a judgement made by students and is part of the ACCA Professional Skills for analysis and evaluation. Students are advised to use models which they judge to be relevant for a particular task or scenario to generate the scope of their answer.

There is not a prescriptive list of theories and models, however, the textbook and kit focuses on the models which it considers to be most relevant to the syllabus and which aid students in being successful in Strategic Business Leader.

Internal and external analysis tools

There are a number of key tools that can be used to perform strategic analysis. Key external analysis tools (i.e. those which look outside the organisation and focus on the potential changes in its environment) are:

- PESTEL
- Porter's 5 forces
- Porter's diamond

This should provide an organisation with some factors to consider with regard to where change in the environment may occur. To consider whether the organisation will fit with the environment and its expected changes some internal (company specific) analysis will be needed. Key internal analysis tools are:

- Porter's value chain
- Strategic capabilities
- SWOT

2 The PESTEL model

The **PESTEL** model looks at the macro environment, using the following headings:

- **Political.** The political environment includes taxation policy, government stability and foreign trade regulations.

- **Economic.** The economic environment includes interest rates, inflation, business cycles, unemployment, disposable income and energy availability and cost.

- **Social.** The social/cultural environment includes population demographics, social mobility, income distribution, lifestyle changes, attitudes to work and leisure, levels of education and consumerism.

- **Technological.** The technological environment is influenced by government spending on research, new discoveries and development, government and industry focus of technological effort, speed of technological transfer and rates of obsolescence.

- **Ecological/environmental.** The ecological environment, sometimes just referred to as 'the environment', considers ways in which the organisation can produce its goods or services with the minimum environmental damage.

- **Legal.** The legal environment covers influences such as taxation, employment law, monopoly legislation and environmental protection laws.

Overall, the model should allow a business to assess the **growth prospects** for the industry within which the organisation operates.

Further PESTEL examples

Social/cultural factors: include changes in tastes and lifestyles. They may also include changes in the demographic make-up of a population. For example in Western Europe people are living longer and in most countries the birth rate is falling, leading to an ageing population. This has obvious implications for the types of products and services which businesses and other organisations may plan to offer. Typical questions that need to be answered include:

- What are the current and emerging trends in lifestyles and fashion?

- What demographic trends will affect the size of the market or its sub-markets?

- Does the trend represent opportunities or threats?

Legal/political factors: the addition or removal of legislative or regulatory constraints can pose major strategic threats and opportunities. The organisation needs to know:

- What changes in regulations are possible and what will their impact be?

- What tax or other incentives are being developed that might affect strategy?

Economic factors: include interest rates and exchange rates, as well as the general state of the economy (e.g. entering or emerging from a recession). The organisation needs to know what the economic prospects and inflation rates are for the countries that it operates in and how will they affect strategy.

Technological factors: may include changes in retailing methods (such as direct selling via the Internet), changes in production methods (greater use of automation), and greater integration between buyers and suppliers via computer link-ups. The managers would need to know to what extent the existing technologies are maturing and what technological developments or trends are affecting or could affect the industry.

Environmental factors: include product stewardship, which considers all raw materials, components and energy sources used in the product and how more environmentally friendly substitutes could be used. They also include ways in which product and product waste could be more effectively recycled. Typical questions that need to be answered include:

- Are we adhering to the existing environmental legislation?

- Are there any new product opportunities that could be exploited that would have a favourable environmental impact on the market?

- What impact will future environmental legislation have?

Some of the **PESTEL** influences may affect every industry, but industries will vary in how much they are affected. For example, an interest rate rise is likely to affect a business selling cars (car purchase can be postponed) more than it will affect a supermarket (food purchase cannot be postponed). More detailed analysis of the environment and competitive forces will be focused on specific industries.

Illustration 1 – PESTEL for a newspaper

Illustration – The PESTEL model

A newspaper is planning for the next five years. The following would be some of the **PESTEL** factors it should consider:

- **Political influences:** tax on newspapers – many countries treat newspapers in the same way as books and have no sales tax (or value added tax) on their sales price. If government policies on the classification of newspapers were to change so that sales tax had to be charged, then sales of newspapers are likely to fall.

- **Economic influences:** exchange rates – most newspapers import their raw materials (paper, pulp etc.) and therefore they will suffer when their domestic currency weakens. Recession – in a recession buyers might move down market, so that cheap tabloids benefit, and more expensive broadsheets suffer. The opposite might apply as the economy recovers.

- **Social influences**: people want more up-to-date information – buyers are less inclined to wait for news than they were 20/30 years ago and may therefore switch to alternative sources of information. More ethnicity in countries – the increased social mobility around the world might actually open new avenues of growth for newspapers through launching, for example, different language versions.

- **Technological influences:** there are many alternative sources of information that are provided through technologies such as the internet, mobile phones and television – this is likely to adversely affect the sales of newspapers. At the same time, e-readers are becoming more popular – this might present an opportunity for newspapers to provide daily downloadable content to these devices.

- **Environmental/ecological influences:** concern about the impact of carbon emissions from the use and production of paper – newspapers may be seen as being harmful to the environment due to their use of natural resources, their high production volumes and large distribution networks. Buyers might abandon newspapers in favour of carbon neutral news via modern technologies.

- **Legal influences:** limits on what can be published – this will make it harder for newspapers to differentiate themselves from each other and therefore harm growth prospects

Overall, it would appear that growth prospects for newspapers are poor. The industry is more likely to decline than to grow. Existing rivals need to plan ahead for new products and new markets and perhaps focus on new technologies such as the provision of news via e-readers.

Note that it does not matter under which category an influence has been listed. Tax has economic, legal and political dimensions. All that matters is that tax has been considered in the environmental scan.

Test your understanding 1

Carry out a **PESTEL** analysis on a supermarket business. Try to get at least two items under each heading.

3 Porter's five forces model

Porter looked at the structure of industries. In particular, he was interested in assessing industry attractiveness, by which he meant how easy it would be to make above average **profits** (for shareholders and to fund adequate investment). He concluded that industry attractiveness depends on five factors or forces:

Force	Potential impact on attractiveness
Buyer power	Powerful buyers can demand discounted prices and extra services (which add costs to the organisation)
Supplier power	Powerful suppliers can demand higher prices for their product(s)
Competitive rivalry	High levels of competition can lead to price wars and high expenditure on marketing and innovation
New entrants	New entrants can increase the cost of resources as well as increasing the power of other forces
Substitutes	If an organisation has a lot of substitutes it will have to keep its prices low to deter customers from moving to these substitutes

As the forces become more powerful and prevalent the industry becomes less attractive (and the margins within the industry are likely to decline). The opposite applies if the forces are weak or absent.

Test your understanding 2

Consider the factors that might make each of these forces more powerful or weak.

Porter's five forces

Bargaining power of buyers

Powerful customers can force price cuts and/or quality improvements. Either way, margins are eroded. Bargaining power is high when a combination of factors arises.

Such factors could include where:

- a buyer's purchases are a high proportion of the supplier's total business or represent a high proportion of total trade in that market

- a buyer makes a low profit

- the quality of purchases is unimportant or delivery timing is irrelevant, and prices will be forced down

- there are similar alternative products available from other suppliers.

Bargaining power of suppliers

The power of suppliers to charge higher prices will be influenced by the following:

- the degree to which switching costs apply and substitutes are available

- the presence of one or two dominant suppliers controlling prices

- the extent to which products offered have a uniqueness of brand, technical performance or design not available elsewhere.

Competition/rivalry

Intensity of existing competition will depend on the following factors:

- Number and relative strength of competitors. The competition in a market can range from perfect competition through to monopoly.

- Rate of growth. Where the market is expanding, competition is low key.

- Where high fixed costs are involved companies will cut prices to marginal cost levels to protect volume, and drive weaker competitors out of the market.

- If buyers can switch easily between suppliers the competition is keen.

- If the exit barrier (i.e. the cost incurred in leaving the market) is high, companies will hang on until forced out, thereby increasing competition and depressing profit.

Threat of new entrants

New entrants into a market will bring extra capacity and intensify competition. The threat from new entrants will depend upon the strength of the barriers to entry and the likely response of existing competitors to a new entrant. Barriers to entry are factors that make it difficult for a new entrant to gain an initial foothold in a market. Major sources of barriers to entry are:

- **Economies of scale,** where the industry is one where unit costs decline significantly as volume increases, such that a new entrant will be unable to start on a comparable cost basis.

- **Product differentiation,** where established firms have good brand image and customer loyalty. The costs of overcoming this can be prohibitive.

- **Capital requirements,** where the industry requires a heavy initial investment (e.g. steel industry, rail transport).

- **Switching costs,** i.e. one-off costs in moving from one supplier to another (e.g. a garage chain switching car dealership).

- **Access to distribution channels** may be restricted (e.g. for some major toiletry brands in the UK 90% of sales go through 12 buying points, i.e. chemist multiples and major retailers). It is therefore difficult for a new toiletry product or manufacturer to gain shelf space.

- **Cost advantages of existing producers,** independent of economies of scale, e.g. patents, special knowledge, favourable access to suppliers, government subsidies.

- **Know-how.** It is much more difficult to penetrate a business where considerable know-how and skills are needed than to enter a simple, basic market.

- **Regulation.** Governments or professional bodies might supervise and limit new entrants.

Threat of substitute products

This threat is across industries (e.g. rail travel versus bus travel versus private car) or within an industry (e.g. long life milk as a substitute for delivered fresh milk). **Porter** explains that 'substitutes limit the potential returns … by placing a ceiling on the price which firms in the industry can profitably charge'. The better the price-performance alternative offered by substitutes, the more readily will customers switch.

Illustration 2 – Porter's five forces

Consider the attractiveness of the industry for a builder of commercial property:

Competitive rivalry

There are likely to be tens and perhaps hundreds of rival firms!

Within this, larger firms have some advantages.

1   Greater bargaining power when purchasing prime development sites.

2   Dealing with major customers.

3   Economies of scale (e.g. in using prefabrication building techniques).

4   Pursuing planning applications.

5   Better able to offset risk.

6   Better able to use sophisticated techniques such as critical path analysis need for larger developments.

7   More able to offer part-exchange deals to house buyers.

However, this must not be taken to extremes:

1   The individuality of each construction project limits economies of scale – especially in respect to materials.

2   It is difficult for firms to differentiate their product – basically make what the architect has designed.

3   Even small firms can benefit from learning effects.

Overall, this is likely to be a highly competitive market where price wars and industry consolidation are common.

Threat of entry

There are likely to be low barriers to entry through low capital requirements (equipment can be hired if necessary) and a potential high level of available, skilled labour. Working capital may be an issue but progress payments from buyers can be used to reduce this barrier. There are also likely to be few legal barriers as no formal qualifications are needed.

It will therefore be important to build a brand and a reputation (for example, based on reliability, quality, workmanship and efficiency) to ensure that a buyer chooses an existing builder over a new rival.

Threat of substitutes

The main threat is second hand property available for rent or purchase. There may be a lot of property available but high prices in some parts of the country might make new property more attractive. (However this will partly be offset by higher land prices in such areas.) But as governments continue to invest in regeneration initiatives there should still be a demand for new buildings.

This factor is likely to be closely linked to the PESTEL model for example, the threat will be highest when the economy is in decline, but it will be low when demand for housing is increasing.

Power of suppliers

There are likely to be numerous suppliers of materials selling an undifferentiated product. So suppliers should generally have low power and large builders should be able to demand bulk discounts and to achieve cost control.

Power of customers

Commercial buyers will have low switching costs, the product is undifferentiated and buyers may themselves be experiencing low profitability. This is likely to make them powerful and allow them to demand lower prices for work done.

Overall opinion

It would appear that margins in this industry are likely to be low. It is very competitive and buyers have lots of power (and lots of available substitutes). Commercial builders will have to rely on a high volume of work and will need to establish a reputation that ensures that buyers choose them over rivals

Test your understanding 3

Apply a five forces analysis to a company that does garden maintenance for households – cutting grass, removing weeds, pruning shrubs, etc.

4   Scenario planning

PESTEL and 5 Forces analysis often focus on the 'most likely' potential future market state. Scenario planning is therefore often employed by organisations in order to force managers to think about other potential future market positions. In scenario planning the key environmental factors are identified and the firm then considers how these might change in the future. Plans are then considered for each of these eventualities.

The number of scenarios to plan for

The most common approach to scenario planning is to create three potential future scenarios:

- The most likely scenario – this reflects the majority of managements' expectations of the future possibilities for the market.

- The best case scenario – this reflects a position where the key environmental factors move in a favourable direction for the organisation (for example, if the product becomes fashionable, the economy improves, competitors fail to react to changing technology etc.).

- The worst case scenario – this reflects a position where the environment turns against the organisation (for example, if there were more entrants into the market or if the economy were to suffer a period of recession).

The organisation can then evaluate how it might react to these changes. Plans should be put in place for all potential scenarios. The organisation should model how it would react to different scenarios and create key performance indicators or key risk indicators that indicate whether one scenario is becoming more likely than other expected scenarios.

However, many strategists suggest that having three alternatives, and in particular a most likely scenario, can render this analysis meaningless. They suggest that this will narrow managers' focus to the most likely scenario at the expense of the others. They therefore argue that it would be better to have only two potential future scenarios rather than distorting managers' mind-sets with a 'most likely' scenario.

Also, the scenarios should be plausible alternatives rather than a consideration of every potential eventuality that can be created by managers. Scenarios are also likely to consider the culmination (and interrelation) of changes in the environment rather than plan for each one discretely. For example, it may plan for a change which results in legislation on imports coming together with problems in achieving domestic supplier agreements occurring at the same time rather than examining these separately if separate changes are unlikely to cause business problems.

This approach is particularly useful in environments that are unpredictable or which change quickly and in unexpected ways. But that is not to say that the managers are aiming to predict the unpredictable. The aim here is to help managers become more aware of what the key environmental factors are and how they might influence the organisation in the future.

Benefits and problems of scenario planning

The key benefit of scenario planning is that it makes managers aware of what the key environmental factors for the organisation are. It also forces managers to have warning signs in place for potential scenarios that may cause problems for the organisation. Managers may also have created contingency plans for coping with different scenarios so that the organisation becomes more flexible at adapting to its environment. This last advantage may in turn lead to a strategic competitive advantage in the long term, especially in fast moving environments.

But scenario planning is time consuming and expensive to carry out. Also, care should be taken to avoid thinking of these scenarios as forecasts. These scenario plans should not be seen as a replacement for budgeting and control systems. The aim is to force management to consider and prepare for different scenarios, it is not to set these scenarios as targets as many best case scenarios, for example, will be unachievable and any target matched to this scenario is likely to be unattainable and demotivational for managers.

5 Porter's diamond

Porter tried to answer the following questions:

- Why does a nation become the home base for successful international competitors in an industry? Germany is renowned for car manufacture; Japan is prominent in consumer electronics.

- Why are firms based in a particular nation able to create and sustain competitive advantage against the world's best competitors in a particular field?

- Why is one country often the home of so many of an industry's world leaders?

Porter called the answers to these questions the determinants of national competitive advantage. He suggested that there are four main factors which determine national competitive advantage and expressed them in the form of a diamond.

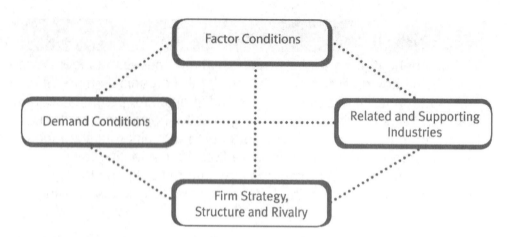

Further detail on Porter's diamond

(a) Favourable factor conditions:

    (i) physical resources such as land, minerals and weather

    (ii) capital

    (iii) human resources such as skills, motivation, price and industrial relations

    (iv) knowledge that can be used effectively

    (v) infrastructure.

Porter also found that countries with factor disadvantages were forced to innovate to overcome these problems, e.g. Japanese firms experienced high energy costs and were forced to develop energy efficient products and processes that were subsequently demanded worldwide.

(b) Demand conditions: there must be a strong home market demand for the product or service. This determines how industries perceive and respond to buyer needs and creates the pressure to innovate. A compliant domestic market is a disadvantage because it does not force the industry to become innovative and able to excel.

(c) Relating and supporting industries: the success of an industry can be due to its suppliers and related industries. Sweden's global superiority in its pulp and paper industries is supported by a network of related industries including packaging, chemicals, wood-processing, conveyor systems and truck manufacture. Many of these supporting industries have also achieved leading global positions.

(d) Firm strategy, structure and rivalry: organisational goals can be determined by ownership structure. Unquoted companies may have slightly longer time horizons to operate in because their financial performance is subject to much less scrutiny than quoted companies. They may also have different 'return on capital' requirements.

Porter found that domestic competition was vital as a spur to innovation and also enhanced global competitive advantage. Conversely, where governments have encouraged mergers to get the critical mass required to be a global player, these national monopolies have not, on the whole, been successful in establishing a global position.

Illustration 3 – Porter's diamond

Starbucks, a large American cafe chain, has been very successful when expanding overseas in areas such as Canada, Japan and the UK. To some extent this can be attributed to the following:

- **Factor conditions:** Starbucks were able to offer better-looking premises, which were more attractive to customers as a place to meet and mix than coffee shops previously established in these countries.

- **Demand conditions:** Starbucks had developed in a US market where customers were very demanding. Each customer wanted a bespoke/personal experience and Starbucks had to develop systems to cope with this (such as allowing customers to choose which bean to use, whether to use milk or cream, the size of the cup etc.). This allowed the company to easily adapt to new tastes and cultures in new overseas markets.

- **Structure and rivalry:** existing suppliers in these new countries were often small, local and undifferentiated. Starbucks were able to offer a branded experience with economies of scale which kept costs down. The skills it developed in achieving huge success in its domestic market were exploited to the full in these new markets.

The result is that Vancouver and London now have more Starbucks per person than New York.

However, Starbucks has been slow to expand into some markets such as Germany and France (which are much larger than other markets such as the UK and Japan).

This can be put down to:

- **Factor conditions:** these countries have established cafe cultures and consumers are already experiencing high quality environments in some instances.

- **Demand conditions:** consumers often have little diversity in their tastes in these countries and there is less demand for bespoke products. Existing domestic cafes have already developed systems to cope with this when necessary.

- **Structure and rivalry:** existing cafes have a built up reputation and loyalty that Starbucks might struggle to overcome. Whereas Starbucks is often seen as a differentiator in markets such as Japan and the UK, it is likely to be perceived as a low cost alternative in markets such as Germany and France.

So Porter's diamond can be used to choose between overseas destinations for expansion. It is important when choosing a country for overseas expansion that the elements of the diamond are considered and the chance of success assessed.

- **Firm strategy, structure and rivalry:** not much rivalry, so no structural advantages.

- Although factor conditions provide the right environment and home demand would be strong, the other elements of the diamond are missing.

Test your understanding 4

Apply **Porter's diamond** to the US personal computer (PC) industry.

---

6 Environmental opportunities and threats

So far, this chapter has looked at a number of tools (or models) that can be used to help to make sense of the environment. The results of these analyses can be classified as either an:

- opportunity or a

- threat.

Once categorised as an opportunity or threat the influences first need to be:

- prioritised, e.g. some will be much more important than others.

Then the organisation has to decide how to:

- grab the best opportunities

- defend against the most serious threats.

 There is absolutely no point in identifying opportunities and threats, but doing nothing about them.

Explanation of opportunities and threats

Opportunities are favourable conditions that usually arise from the nature of changes in the external environment, e.g. new markets, improved economic factors or a failure of competitors. Opportunities provide the organisation with the potential to offer new or to develop existing products, facilities or services.

Threats are the opposite of opportunities and also arise from external developments. Examples include unfavourable changes in legislation, the introduction of a radically new product by a competitor, political or economic unrest, changing social conditions or the actions of a pressure group. Threats can remove an organisation's competitive advantage or change the industry in such a way that the organisation's product or service is no longer valued. This can significantly hamper future growth prospects for the organisation.

It may be a little simplistic to assume that blame can be apportioned exclusively to the organisation's environment when, in fact, weaknesses in (say) the management team or the organisational structure may have led to a compounding of the problems arising externally. Indeed, throughout our analysis we must bear in mind the linkages between issues and the possibility that it may have been a combination of various internal and external factors that led to the problems being experienced.

Illustration of opportunities and threats

Opportunities are favourable conditions that usually arise from the nature of changes in the external environment. The following might represent some of the opportunities and threats identified for a commercial television station.

Opportunities	Threats
The internet, e.g. streaming programmes as viewers want to watch them.	Competing forms of entertainment, e.g. video games, programmes streamed on the internet, podcasts.
Increased monitoring of which programmes viewers watch.	Advertisers moving to more efficient channels, e.g. advertisements triggered by internet search activity.
Highly portable computers (the equivalent of audio MP3 players) on which programmes can be watched.	Public taste changes (eventually, after the 25th series of a reality TV programme, enthusiasm for reality TV might wane).
Set of back catalogue material.	Economic downturn reducing advertising revenue.

| TV acquisition by people in developing economies, e.g. China and India have high rates of economic growth. Purchasing a TV company, if permitted in those countries, could be a source of long-term growth. | Government imposing quality standards. |

Many of these influences arise from **PESTEL,** but **Porter's five forces** and the other tools can be relevant also.

Remember, it doesn't matter which model is used to identify an influence. All that matters is that it has been identified.

Test your understanding 5

Perform an opportunities and threats analysis on:

1   a passenger train service

2   a nuclear power station.

Once categorised as an opportunity or threat the influences first need to be:

*   prioritised, e.g. some will be much more important than others.

Then the organisation has to decide how to:

*   grab the best opportunities

*   defend against the most serious threats

The ability to do this will come from an organisation's strengths and weaknesses – these can be determined through internal analysis of the organisation itself.

7   Strategic capabilities, resources and competences

Strategic capability is the adequacy and suitability of the resources and competences an organisation needs if it is to survive and prosper.

Another way to look at CSFs is to examine an organisation's strategic capabilities. If a business can obtain unique resources and core competences this should lead to its success. This can be explained in the following table:

	Resources	Competences
Threshold capabilities • these are necessary for any organisation to exist and compete in an industry • they are likely to be common to most rivals and easily copied • they will not lead to success or competitive advantage.	**Threshold resources** Example: any daily newspaper has reporters, editors, printing staff etc.	**Threshold competences** Example: every consumer electronics firm will have capabilities in electrical engineering.
Strategic Capabilities • these are particular to an individual business • they will be hard to copy • they will be valued **by the customer (CSF)** • they will lead to competitive advantage.	**Unique resources** Example: A particular newspaper may be able to stand out from its rivals if it has an exclusive deal with the country's top sportstar who will write a daily column on his/her sport.	**Core Competences** Example: Sony believe they have core competences in design and user-friendliness that their rivals can't match.

So as part of an internal analysis a business should look for any unique resources that it may own or core competences that it has created. These would be significant strengths to any business.

More on strategic capabilities

Note that capability refers to resources and competences and their relationship can be shown as:

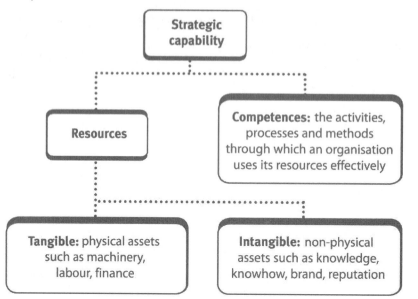

Strategic capability can also be divided into threshold capabilities and capabilities for competitive advantage.

- Threshold capabilities. These are the **minimum** capabilities needed for the organisation to be able to compete in a given market. They consist of threshold resources and threshold competences – the resources and competences needed to meet customers' minimum requirements.

- Capabilities for competitive advantage. The capabilities that allow an organisation to beat its competitors. These capabilities must meet the needs and expectations of its customers. Unique capabilities are not enough – they must be valued by the customers

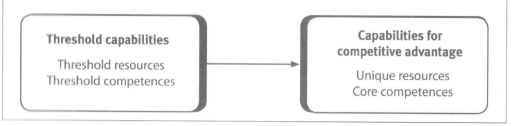

- Unique resources are those resources that create competitive advantage and that others **cannot imitate or obtain**. Examples of unique resources are:

    - brand

    - situation, for example, near a source of raw material or a source of cheap labour

    - sunk – competitors have to cover depreciation costs

    - right to use a patented process.

Note that if the unique resource is people-based, the people can move to competitors or start their own business.

- Core competences are the activities, processes and methods through which an organisation uses its resources effectively, in ways that others cannot imitate or obtain. Examples of core competences are:

    - sophisticated IT that, for example, enables complex and accurate demand forecasting

    - a corporate culture that fosters innovation

    - the ability to share and lever knowledge throughout the organisation.

Illustration 4 – Capabilities, resources and competences

The Coca-Cola Corporation has, for many years, maintained a very strong position in the soft drinks market. Consider its flagship product, Coca-Cola. This has largely survived competition from supermarkets' own-label colas. There is no great secret in how to make a reasonable imitation (though purists would maintain the imitations are not as good) and the resources needed are not demanding. The own-label colas sell at much lower prices, so high-volume production resources, capable of producing flavoured carbonated water do not seem to be important in keeping production prices down. So how has Coca-Cola managed to keep its dominant position?

It has been argued above that physical resources do not seem to be important. Therefore, the answer must lie in non-physical resources (such as a very powerful brand) and core competences. The core competences lie in managing the brand by producing memorable global advertising, global recognition, careful sponsorship, responding to customer requirements (diet/light products).

Test your understanding 6

Manchester United Football Club are one of the biggest sporting institutions in the world. Recent research has shown that they have over 600 million fans across the world, they hold a record number of English championships and have been crowned the best team in Europe many times. They are the most valued sporting franchise in the world (according to Forbes magazine in 2017) at over $3.5 billion and have shown revenue growth year on year for at least a decade.

Consider the strategic capabilities that contribute to the success of the football club.

Critical success factors

An important strength for any organisation will be the achievement of critical success factors. This should allow the organisation to cope better than rivals with any changes in its competitive environment.

What are critical success factors?

Critical success factors (CSFs) are the essential areas of the business that must be performed well if the mission, objectives and goals of the business are to be achieved.

Critical success factors (CSFs) are performance requirements that are fundamental to an organisation's success. In this context CSFs should thus be viewed as those product features that are particularly valued by customers. This is where the organisation must outperform competition.

Examples of CSFs for major industries include:

- in the automobile industry – styling, an efficient dealer network, organisation, performance

- in the food processing industry – new product development, good distribution channels, health aspects (e.g. low fat)

- in the life insurance industry – reputation, innovative new policies

- in the supermarket industry – the right product mix available in each store, having it actually available on the shelves, pricing it correctly.

Note: CSFs and competences are different. CSFs are what an organisation needs to be good at, while competences focus on what an organisation is good at. Strategies need to focus on maximising the correlation between the two.

Organisational knowledge as a strategic capability

Knowledge is a strategic capability. An organisation's knowledge of its environment (such as expected technological changes, changes in substitute availability etc.) can make it stand out from rivals. It can be more proactive towards its environment and also be in a position to react quicker to environmental changes when necessary.

Johnson, Scholes and Whittington define organisational knowledge as:

> 'the collective experience accumulated through systems, routines and activities of sharing across the organisation.'

Resources (such as staff skills, assets etc.) can be purchased but capabilities must be developed and grown. Organisations therefore need to work on this. It is not automatic and problems that are discovered too late can be difficult to rectify.

Organisational knowledge is cumulative in nature. It will be built up over time from past experience and actions. But it does not simply follow a learning curve effect (otherwise organisations of a similar 'mass' or history would have similar organisational knowledge – which is not often the case). Organisational knowledge can also be added to and improved. Environmental analysis, staff development, process improvement, organisational structure etc. (many of these areas are covered later in the syllabus) can all impact on and improve organisational knowledge.

Organisations must recognise that successful development of organisational knowledge can be a critical success factor. A key part of this can be knowledge management.

Knowledge management involves the processes of:

- uncovering, or discovering, knowledge

- capturing knowledge

- sharing knowledge

- distributing knowledge

- levering knowledge

- maintaining knowledge.

The growing importance of knowledge management

Knowledge management has become an important part of gaining and maintaining competitive advantage. Reasons for this are as follows.

- Both business and not-for-profit organisations are more complex than they were previously, so there is more knowledge to manage. For example, there are many more government regulations that have to be followed for health and safety. The government sets many more targets to monitor the performance of hospitals and schools.

- The environment, technology, competitors and markets are changing rapidly. Look at the pace of change in the broadcast/internet industry.

- The move from manufacturing to service industries means that a greater proportion of an organisation's knowledge is likely to be tacit. It is relatively easy to formally specify a product, but harder to specify everything that should happen in the successful delivery of a service.

- Greater job mobility means that, unless captured and recorded, valuable knowledge can be lost as staff move on.

Test your understanding 7

A barrier to knowledge management is that many people believe that keeping knowledge secret gives them unique power. Knowledge management, however, requires that knowledge is uncovered and shared.

What arguments could be used to encourage individuals freely to give up and share knowledge?

8 Value chain analysis

A key strength for any organisation will come from its competitive advantage. Porter suggests that competitive advantage means that an organisation can beat its rivals by either offering goods and services at a lower cost, or by being different (which means being perceived by the customer as better or more relevant) and by charging a premium for this difference. Success, both now and in the future, for an organisation will therefore often depend on the strength (or weakness) of its competitive advantage.

The best way to assess whether an organisation has achieved a competitive advantage is by examining its value chain.

The value chain

Porter developed the value chain to help identify which activities within the firm were contributing to a competitive advantage and which were not.

The approach involves breaking down the firm into five 'primary' and four 'support' activities, and then looking at each to see if they give a cost advantage or quality advantage.

Porter's value chain

Support or secondary value activities	Firm infrastructure				
	Human resource management				
	Technology development				
	Procurement				
	Inbound logistics	Operations	Outbound logistics	Marketing and sales	Service

Primary value activities

Explanation of the value chain activities

Primary activities:

- Inbound logistics – receiving, storing and handling raw material inputs. For example, a just-in-time stock system could give a cost advantage.

- Operations – transformation of the raw materials into finished goods and services. For example, using skilled craftsmen could give a quality advantage.

- Outbound logistics – storing, distributing and delivering finished goods to customers. For example, outsourcing delivering could give a cost advantage.

- Marketing and sales – for example, sponsorship of a sports celebrity could enhance the image of the product.

- Service – all activities that occur after the point of sale, such as installation, training and repair, e.g. Marks & Spencer's friendly approach to returns gives it a perceived quality advantage.

Secondary activities:

- Firm infrastructure – how the firm is organised. For example, centralised buying could result in cost savings due to bulk discounts.

- Technology development – how the firm uses technology. For example, the latest computer-controlled machinery gives greater flexibility to tailor products to individual customer specifications.

- Human resource management – how people contribute to competitive advantage. For example, employing expert buyers could enable a supermarket to purchase better wines than competitors.

- Procurement – purchasing, but not just limited to materials. For example, buying a building out of town could give a cost advantage over high street competitors.

All organisations in a particular industry will have a similar value chain, which will include activities such as:

- obtaining raw materials

- designing products

- building manufacturing facilities

- developing co-operative agreements

- providing customer service.

It is vital that the linkages between the different elements of a value chain are considered. Firstly this is to ensure consistency – for example, a differentiator will want to ensure that any cost advantages within the value chain do not compromise overall quality. Secondly it may be that through linking separate activities more effectively than competitors, a firm can gain a competitive advantage.

 Apply the value chain in a scenario

To gain a competitive advantage over its rivals a company must either:

- perform value creation functions at a lower cost than its rivals, or

- perform them in a way that leads to differentiation and a premium price.

Illustration 5 – Linking the value chain to competitive advantage

The value chain is a way of explaining and examining how and why an organisation has a competitive advantage. The value chain will differ depending on how the organisation chooses to compete.

For example, a manufacturing organisation that aims to beat rivals on price will need to keep its costs low. Therefore, in its primary activities it might have operations that have little flexibility and are geared towards bulk production. It is also likely to minimise the level of after-sales service provided. In support activities it might use low skilled labour, high levels of technology and have bulk procurement agreements with suppliers.

An organisation in the same industry which is looking to compete at the top end of the market might have operations that are more focused on producing a higher quality product with more variety and offer a more extensive service with, say, free installations and money back guarantees. In support activities it might use higher skilled labour and a wider range of quality suppliers. Note: as will be seen later in this chapter, these types of organisations are usually referred to as differentiators.

The competitive advantage will permeate all elements of the value chain:

Nature of competitive strategy:	Low cost, low selling price	High end (differentiator)
Primary activities		
Inbound logistics	Standardised components and materials with little customisation	Premium materials Selective sourcing
Operations	Bulk production Focus on efficiency High levels of standardisation	Flexible production Focus on quality Facilitation of customisation
Outbound logistics	Few outlets used Bulk delivery and careful management of delivery loads Minimal packaging	Use of premium distributors and retailers Flexible (possibly free) delivery Premium packaging

Marketing and sales	Minimal levels of marketing Sales focus is on quantity Standardised	High levels of promotion Lots of market research High levels of customer management and personalisation
Service	Very little	Extensive
Support activities		
HRM	Use low skilled staff Reduced training and staff development	Use higher skilled staff Encourage staff development See staff as a key resource
TD	Use e-procurement to reduce costs of procurement High use of technology to improve efficiencies and cut costs	Less use of technology in operations Greater use of technology in marketing in sales to facilitate high promotion levels High R&D Regular process redesign
Procurement	Seek out cheapest and most efficient supplies Use outsourcing when it reduces costs	Seek premium suppliers
Infrastructure	Functional structure Many centralised services A more global approach Produce in cheapest locations	Flexible structures Small span of authority Tall structures National independence

Note: These are simply examples to illustrate how companies with different competitive strategies will have different value chains. It does not mean that all low cost manufacturers or differentiators will have the characteristics illustrated above.

 In an exam situation you might use Porter's value chain analysis to decide how individual activities might be changed to reduce costs of operation or to improve the value of the organisation's offerings.

Test your understanding 8

Nicole has inherited a restaurant from her uncle. The restaurant had been underperforming and was closed six months ago. Nicole wants to begin a new restaurant in the premises, with a new name and a new cuisine.

She has performed some market research in the area and determined that there is a demand for a restaurant offering Mediterranean cuisine. There is little local competition for such cuisine but there are many other local restaurants offering a wide range of cuisines.

Nicole has decided to follow a differentiation strategy for her restaurant and to charge premium prices.

Required:

Consider how the activities in a value chain for the proposed restaurant could be used to create such a competitive position.

Professional skill:

Illustrate analysis skills in considering the restaurant's competitive advantage.

Value chain analysis

Value chain analysis looks at each of the processes that make up the chain of activity and:

- rates how important it is in a given company's production or service activity

- rates how the company compares to its competitors

- helps to decide how individual activities might be changed to reduce costs of operation

- helps to improve the value of the organisation's offerings.

Value networks

The organisation's value chain does not exist in isolation. There will be direct links between the inbound logistics of the firm and the outbound logistics of its suppliers, for example. An understanding of the value system and how the organisation's value chain fits in to it will therefore aid in the strategic planning process.

 Illustration of value chain analysis

A value network is a web of relationships that generates economic value and other benefits through complex dynamic exchanges between two or more individuals, groups or organisations.

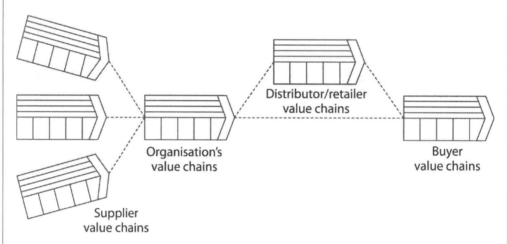

Distributor/retailer value chains

Organisation's value chains

Buyer value chains

Supplier value chains

- Tangible value exchanges – involve all exchanges of goods, services or revenue, including all transactions involving contracts and invoices, return receipt of orders, requests for proposals, confirmations or payment.

- Intangible knowledge exchanges – include strategic information, planning knowledge, process knowledge, technical know-how, collaborative design, policy development, etc.

Illustration

Amazon, for example, not only revolutionised the business model for selling books, but also formed an entire new value network of suppliers and buyers that redefined the value chain for acquiring books and music. Replacing the retail bookstore with a website and the 'over the counter' delivery process with FedEx and UPS delivery created a new value network that delivered customer convenience and an entirely different and lower-cost business model.

9   SWOT analysis

Strengths, weaknesses, opportunities and threats

A SWOT analysis can be used as an analysis tool in its own right or can be used as a summary sheet on which other results can be placed.

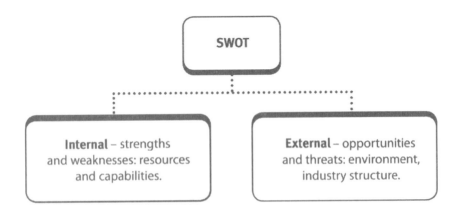

- Strengths and weaknesses relate to resources and capabilities: what is the organisation good at? What is it poor at? Where are resources in short supply? Where are resources excellent? Ultimately, strengths and weaknesses determine an organisation's ability to cope with the expected changes, opportunities and threats that will be occurring in its environment.

- Opportunities and threats relate to external factors: what will the effect on the organisation be of economic changes? Can the organisation make use of new technologies? Are new entrants likely to enter the market place? Can a powerful customer dictate terms?

The examination will feature scenarios detailing the history and current position of an organisation and possible future states. Candidates will probably have to analyse the organisation's strategic position, i.e. to carry out a corporate appraisal. It is possible to arrive at a reasonable analysis merely by producing a SWOT analysis, but it is likely to be more productive and impressive to use one or more of the other analysis tools, such as PESTEL, to help generate ideas for the SWOT analysis.

Using a SWOT analysis

The first step is to rank in order of importance the findings of the SWOT analysis.

- Strengths that match no opportunity are of little use without an opportunity.

- A distinctive competence is a strength that can be exploited.

Strategies can be developed which:

- neutralise weaknesses or convert them into strengths

- convert threats into opportunities

- match strengths with opportunities.

These are discussed in later chapters.

Illustration 6 – SWOT analysis

Consider the following SWOT for a small advertising agency:

It has 12 staff – 4 of whom are joint owners. It has a strong client base across many industries such as healthcare, training, publishing, sports and financial institutions. However, it has never taken working capital management and the financial side of the business seriously – even to the extent that it can never be sure that clients are being billed properly. It now has a chance to bid for a new large, national contract from a major company.

Its overall SWOT looks as follows:

Strengths	Weaknesses
• well diversified client portfolio	• high work-in-progress levels
• strong management team	• high levels of receivables
• profitable	• poor control of time allocation to clients
• listed on a stock exchange	• limited access to debt finance
• low gearing	• reached overdraft limit
• award winners	• lacks ability to service very large clients
• differentiated, personal service	• 40% of turnover from two clients
• established 60 years ago	• Recent complaint about tone of an advert

Opportunities	Threats
<ul><li>tender for a major contract</li><li>expand overseas</li><li>launch an internet marketing advisory service</li><li>buy a rival</li><li>move into film production</li></ul>	<ul><li>recession putting downward pressure on volume and prices</li><li>loss of bank support</li><li>loss of a major client</li><li>customers moving to e-marketing</li><li>loss of key staff</li><li>takeover by a rival</li></ul>

In an exam scenario, generating the SWOT should be relatively straightforward and all the necessary information would be provided in the scenario. This stage is unlikely to score many marks and is probably best considered as part of the planning phase of your answer.

Your task as a student is to then **analyse** this SWOT. This means we need to explain the importance of issues, prioritise them, spot linkages between them and consider implications for the business.

All of the issues generated by the SWOT are good, relevant points that can be explored in an exam answer. However, in an exam scenario you are unlikely to have enough time to discuss all of these. Therefore, we need to choose a selection of issues under each heading and focus on analysing these. The choice of issues to analyse is not greatly important, but you should try to focus on the more important ones.

From a time management point of view, it is important that you set yourself a deadline for these questions based on the marks available. It is very unlikely that you will be able to analyse every point in the SWOT in the time available to you.

Let's consider an analysis of the key strengths from the above SWOT:

Analysis of key strengths

A key strength of the company is that it has a wide portfolio of clients. The company will therefore not be reliant on one industry group for its revenue. This is likely to mean that if one industry type cuts back on advertising or moves to another form of marketing, the company will be able to continue to rely on other industries for income.

The company has won marketing awards. This is likely to attract potential customers to the company. It may also mean that existing customers remain loyal and resist switching to the company's rivals.

As a listed business the company may be able to raise external equity finance on the market. This may allow it to fund new strategies and partake in the opportunities that have been identified.

Test your understanding 9

Continuing on from the SWOT in the illustration just considered, analyse the weaknesses, opportunities and threats to the company.

Professional skill:

Illustrate analysis skills in considering the advertising agency's strategic position.

An organisation's SWOT analysis is likely to drive the need for change within the organisation. A lack of fit between the current strategic position and the organisation's environment will mean, for example, that new strategies will be required in order to avoid any further strategic drift.

Other key drivers of change

Much of this syllabus considers the changes that may be necessary or undertaken by a business. Examples of the key drivers of change are as follows:

- The change may come as a reaction to competitor actions or as a new deliberate change of competitive strategy.

- The change may be driven by changes in the organisation's environment (such as from the availability of new technology, changes in regulation or changes in taste and fashion that were covered in the PESTEL model). Often change is customer-led through changes in demographics or definitions of value.

- There may be internal drivers of change from a change in culture or changes in organisational missions and goals from redesigned and improved processes etc. Many of these topics are covered elsewhere in this text.

- The change may be market-led. Markets are becoming more global and organisations are having to create global strategies which are themselves driving changes within organisations. Declining barriers to international trade mean that many organisations are producing and selling in many more countries than they have in the past.

These changes may have a number of impacts on the organisation:

- The market sector is likely to change as rivals change and some rivals leave the sector and new rivals enter the sector. Collaborations between organisations may be necessary and the sector may even split into smaller strategic groups.

- Organisational structure will need to change as part of an overall change in the culture of the organisation.

- A new organisational mission and set of objectives may need to be considered.

- New monitoring and control tools will be needed to ensure strategic fit with the changing environment as well as fit with the organisational mission.

- Organisations may have to become more flexible and adaptable in order to be better prepared for further changes in the future.

These changes will also be explored across the syllabus/text.

10   Chapter summary

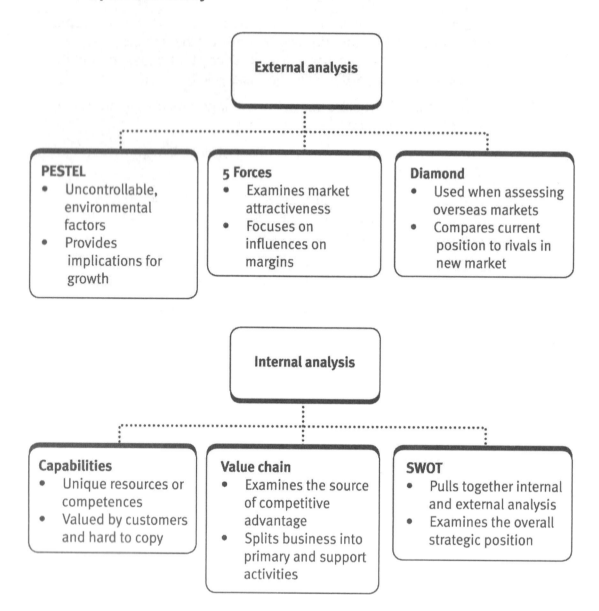

External analysis

PESTEL
- Uncontrollable, environmental factors
- Provides implications for growth

5 Forces
- Examines market attractiveness
- Focuses on influences on margins

Diamond
- Used when assessing overseas markets
- Compares current position to rivals in new market

Internal analysis

Capabilities
- Unique resources or competences
- Valued by customers and hard to copy

Value chain
- Examines the source of competitive advantage
- Splits business into primary and support activities

SWOT
- Pulls together internal and external analysis
- Examines the overall strategic position

Test your understanding answers

Test your understanding 1

Here are our suggestions. You might have other valid ones.

Political influences: planning policy on large out-of-town sites, competition policy.

Economic influences: unemployment rate, interest rates, taxation.

Social influences: changes in population sizes, changes in consumer taste (for example, possibly more health conscious).

Technological influences: the internet (internet ordering), sophisticated Just-In-Time systems, food packaging technology.

Environmental/ecological influences: use of land for building, sustainable resources, packaging, animal welfare.

Legal influences: health and safety regulations, consumer legislation, food packaging regulations, inclusion of additives in food.

Test your understanding 2

No answer provided. The factors are considered in the expandable text which follows the Test Your Understanding question.

Test your understanding 3

A garden maintenance company

Threat of entry: high. Only modest amounts of capital and know-how are needed. No regulations, hard to differentiate, and limited scope for economies of scale.

Threat of substitute products: low, except for householders who opt for a very low-maintenance garden and for customers who choose to look after their own gardens.

Bargaining power of customers: low. There will be many small customers so individual bargaining power will be low. Quality is perhaps not a vital component of the service.

Bargaining power of suppliers: low. The supplies needed are widely available.

Competition: high. The business is very easy to get into. There are negligible switching costs.

Test your understanding 4

Factor conditions: large population of well-trained engineers.

Demand conditions: large population of individuals and businesses who need or want PCs.

Related and supporting industries: many component manufacturers close by; large and well-endowed universities.

Firm strategy, structure and rivalry: an entrepreneurial economy allowed many start-ups and the best survive the intense rivalry.

Test your understanding 5

1   A passenger train service

Threats

–   losing the franchise or right to operate the service (if the service is provided by a private company)

–   underinvestment in the network infrastructure

–   terrorism

–   increased affluence in some countries leading to less use of trains as people acquire cars

–   competing services.

Opportunities

–   increasing cost of petrol making cars more expensive to run

–   environmental concerns and regulation

–   building customer loyalty, e.g. perhaps a scheme similar to air miles

–   innovative fares for different market segments

–   new routes which are very expensive to develop but once established might be barriers to entry of competitors

–   new technology, e.g. magnetic levitation; generally reduced journey times.

2   A nuclear power station

Threats

- environmental concerns about the nuclear industry

- terrorism

- theft of nuclear material

- accidental release of radioactive material

- alternative energy sources (e.g. biotechnology might provide a very efficient way of creating fuel from sunlight)

- global warming, e.g. less fuel needed to heat homes and offices.

Opportunities

- political risks associated with reliance upon Middle Eastern and Russian supplies of fossil fuels

- environmental concerns about greenhouse gas emission from fossil fuel use

- global warming, e.g. more fuel needed to cool homes and offices

- growing world demand for power

- new technology to deal safely, and permanently, with radioactive waste.

 Test your understanding 6

All football clubs will need certain types of resources such as:

- players

- a stadium

- a manager

- a fan base

- finances.

They will also need certain competences such as:

- tactical knowledge

- training methods

- youth development

- ability to attract sponsors.

For Manchester United to be successful they must therefore develop these in ways which are unique, valued by customers and difficult to copy. Some of the ways that Manchester United have achieved this are:

Resources

Manchester United have a bigger fan base than any other sporting franchise in the world. This allows them to garner more merchandising revenue than any other franchise and also to attract better deals from sponsors.

Manchester United have the biggest stadium in England (and one of the biggest in Europe). This allows them to maximise match day revenue and be one of the leaders from this source of income in Europe.

Competences

Manchester United are the leader in acquiring and interacting with fans on social networks – they have over 65 million fans on Facebook alone. This skill allows them to keep fans informed of new product offerings as well as sell events and broaden the club's brand image.

Manchester United were one of the first clubs in the world to obtain sponsorship for their training equipment. In 2013, AON agreed to pay the club around $20 million per season for the right to rename Manchester United's training complex – something that no other club had even considered as a marketable asset. The ability to attract such sponsorships is one of the things that makes the club stand out.

Manchester United seem to have a unique ability amongst the elite teams in England in developing youth players for the first team. For example, when Manchester United were crowned champions of Europe in 2008, 5 members of their cup final squad had come through the club's ranks as youngsters. By contrast, opponents Chelsea, another English club, didn't have any players in their cup final squad that had come through the club's youth ranks. This allows Manchester United to keep a local tradition, garner fan loyalty and reduce team development costs.

There are many other strategic capabilities at Manchester United but these examples should highlight some of the reasons why an organisation can be successful. It is not simply about having resources and competences that are necessary for existence in the industry, it is about developing and acquiring ones which can lead to competitive advantage. As can be seen in Manchester United's example, no one resource or capability might be the unique strategic capability of the club. But when they are put together, success becomes much more likely.

Test your understanding 7

The following arguments could be used to encourage individuals to share knowledge.

- If everyone shares their knowledge, each person should gain more than they give up.

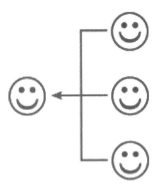

- Organisations are often so complex that it is rare that one person can achieve much alone. Teamwork and sharing knowledge is the best way of assuring a safe future.

- Knowledge is perishable – and increasingly so as the pace of change increases. If knowledge is not used quickly it is wasted. If knowledge is not shared the chances are that it becomes worthless before it can be used.

- Knowledge management is vital to the success of many businesses. If an organisation uses knowledge creatively the chances are that it will beat an organisation with poor knowledge management. Organisations compete with rivals; people within organisations should not be competing with each other at the organisation's expense.

Test your understanding 8

A differentiation strategy for a restaurant will be about creating a premium dining experience which allows the restaurant to charge premium prices. The strategy should be reflected in all of the primary activities of the supply chain and be supported by a differentiated approach to support activities.

Primary activities

Inbound logistics could be differentiated by the use of local, high quality produce for ingredients. This is likely to add costs and possibly bring diseconomies of scale, but it could be attractive to customers who want to know where their food has come from and who demand fresh ingredients.

Operations will concern the cooking and presentation of the food. Food should follow traditional Mediterranean recipes, be cooked on the premises and be cooked to the highest standard. It should be presented in surroundings that are upmarket, with a high investment in premium fixtures and fittings, expensive cutlery and tableware and well-spaced furniture.

Outbound logistics will consider the delivery of the food to tables. This should be efficient, staff should be pleasant and tables should only be served when all meals are ready.

Marketing should highlight the premium location and surroundings as well as the high quality cooking and presentation of meals. The restaurant should seek out positive reviews from local press. The menu should be kept simple and seasonal, and the restaurant could consider offering both an a la carte and fixed price option. A fixed price could be available as a business lunch option which might spread awareness and create some repeat business. Customers should have the opportunity to book tables in advance, either by phone or via the internet.

The service could be enhanced by the use of a sommelier who could recommend wines to match particular dishes. Waiters should be knowledgeable about both the menu and the source of ingredients. The restaurant should also offer a cloakroom service and parking and/or taxi ordering services.

Support activities

From a human resource perspective, an experienced, and ideally award winning, chef should be used to ensure food is cooked to the highest standard. Staff should be trained in the highest levels of service and uniforms provided that are clean and ironed. Ideally, both the chef and the staff should have Mediterranean backgrounds in order to support the focus and marketing of the restaurant's cuisine.

Procurement of produce should happen locally and a dedicated responsibility should be created for vetting suppliers. Suppliers should be carefully assessed and regular audits carried out. The restaurant should look to grow many of its ingredients itself if possible in order to ensure that ingredients are as fresh as possible.

Technology can be simple in the restaurant. There may be advanced cooking equipment required in order to create some dishes, but sales technology can be bought off-the-shelf and electronic procurement can be kept to a minimum due to the need to vet suppliers and maintain supplier flexibility.

The restaurant should be supported by an infrastructure that allows for different responsibilities to be performed efficiently. Separate roles should be created for procuring marketing, supplier vetting, staff training and appraisal etc. Some power should be decentralised so that, for example, the chef can determine the menu and ingredients and the sommelier can influence the wines purchased.

Professional skill:
The key analysis skill will be in linking the information to the competitive position. The aim here is not to come to one, definitive solution. Instead it is testing your understanding of the elements of the value chain. You may have very different ideas to those suggested in the solution but it is important that you have considered all of the activities in the value chain and that you have considered ways that these activities can be used to stand out from the activities of rivals. You are not looking for ways to cut costs – that would be a very different type of competitive strategy and the activities are likely to look very different.

Test your understanding 9

Analysis of key weaknesses

Having high levels of work-in-progress and receivables will tie up a lot of cash. This will limit the company's ability to finance new opportunities.

This issue is made more important by the fact that the company is nearing its overdraft limit. Not only will this limit the company's ability to take on new work and expand the business, but it might even put the company's entire existence at risk.

The company is also reliant on only two clients for 40% of its revenue. If one of these clients were to leave the company then, again, going concern could become an issue. It will be important that the business can expand its client base in order to reduce the reliance on these clients.

Analysis of key opportunities

There is an opportunity to tender for a major new client. This would reduce the reliance on existing powerful clients. However, it is likely to put further short-term pressure on work-in-progress and the overdraft and the company also needs to consider whether it has the resources and skills to meet the needs of a large client.

The company could start to offer e-marketing services to clients. This would allow them to 'follow the customer' and meet their needs. It would need an investment in acquiring the skills and resources to provide this service, however.

A move into film production would be a move towards backward integration. It might give the company control over a key cost and a key resource. But it is likely that this might restrict the company's ability to move into other areas and customers may no longer desire filmed adverts as a source of marketing.

Analysis of threats

In a recession customers are likely to cut back on discretionary expenditure such as marketing. They may also move 'downmarket' to lower cost rivals and move away from differentiated services on the basis of price.

Loss of key staff would be a major threat as staff are likely to be a key asset for the business. It will be important to tie-in staff through loyalty bonuses and strong reward schemes, as well as putting in protection clauses to contracts to stop them taking clients with them when they leave.

If customers move to e-marketing avenues and the company does not follow them it is likely to experience a steady decline in revenue. It will be important to make this switch in line with its environment and offer this service to customers.

Overall

The company is in a position where it needs to adapt to its changing environment. Its first priority needs to be to sort out its financial position and obtain the finance to secure its viability and to finance new opportunities. It then needs to consider offering e-marketing services to clients.

Professional skill:

Note how the points in the SWOT are not just regurgitated in the analysis. Instead, a further sentence or two is added to explain the relevance to the company, the importance of the issue, the implications for the future, links to other areas of the SWOT, etc. This is how we achieve the professional skills marks for analysis. It is acceptable to analyse these points in other ways and to write a very different answer. The examiners will be as concerned with your style and approach as they are with your content. The key to success will be to ensure that you are not simply regurgitating points.

Performance analysis

Chapter learning objectives

Upon completion of this chapter you will be able to:

- assess organisation performance and position using appropriate performance management techniques, key performance indicators (KPIs) and ratios

- apply the Baldrige model for world class organisations to achieve and maintain business performance excellence

PER

Two of the PER performance objectives (PO3) and (PO13) are that you contribute to the wider business strategy of your organisation through your personal and team objectives. You identify innovative ways to improve organisational performance and plan business activities and control performance, making recommendations for improvement. Working through this chapter should help you understand how to demonstrate these objectives.

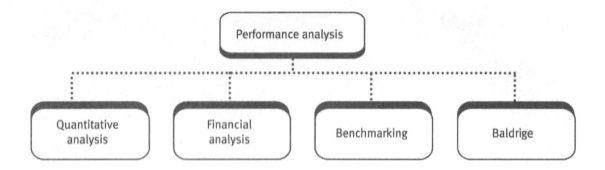

1 Quantitative analysis

 It is very likely in the exam that the examiner will provide tables and data in order to provide some of the information that is needed in order to properly perform the strategic analysis (both external and internal). It will be vital that students can both interpret and use this information in their answers.

This information might be provided using various methods and some of the key methods will be:

Tables of data

In order to reduce the amount of text in a scenario the examiner will often provide tables of data to provide part of the story. It will be important that a student can understand what the table is trying to explain, and that this part of the story is used in the answer to this part of the examination.

Test your understanding 1

The following data is given for sales of cinema tickets in a large country over the last two years.

Company	20X7 Sales ($bn)	20X8 Sales ($bn)
A	2.0	2.0
B	1.8	2.0
C	2.2	2.1
D	2.1	1.9
Others	1.6	1.7
Total industry sales	9.7	9.7

Required:

Analyse the competitive nature of the cinema industry in this country.

Professional skill:

Illustrate analysis skills in investigating the competitive nature of the cinema industry.

Financial statements

The examiner might provide sets of financial statements and a student must use these to pull out the key messages and issues. There will be some important technique points to this:

- choose three or four key ratios

- there is no need to illustrate the formula or the calculation

- only one comparator should be needed

- focus on the cause of any changes and what this might tell us about the organisation's position.

Explanation of the financial statement analysis technique

- choose three or four key ratios

The aim is to try to pick some ratios that best tell the organisation's "story". Key ratios might be its sales growth (which can be linked to the PESTEL), its margins (which can be linked to the 5 forces model), and its gearing (which will give an idea of the organisation's risk profile and its ability to raise finance for future opportunities).

Ratio analysis has already been examined at the fundamentals level and we are not trying to show how well we can calculate ten or twelve different ratios. A ratio should not be included if it adds nothing to the story (for example, there is little point in calculating receivable days if it has not changed during the year and the business does not have a problem with debt collection).

- there is no need to illustrate the formula or the calculation

This has been examined at the fundamentals level and would only waste time at this level. There is also no need to explain what the ratio means (for example, comments such as "The gross profit percentage shows how much profit the business makes per $ of turnover" are unlikely to gain any marks).

- only one comparator should be needed

The examiner will often provide four or five years' worth of financial statements. However, in order to get to the key messages for the company's story we do not need to calculate the ratios for every year. Normally we simply need to compare this year's results with last years, or occasionally this year's results to the first year's results if we're assessing how performance has changed over time.

- focus on the cause of any changes and what this might tell us about the organisation's position

The key to gaining any marks will be to analyse the data that has been calculated (simply performing the calculation and not discussing it will not achieve all of the marks that are available). So we need to explain why a ratio has changed (for example, is it due to changes in the external or internal environment) and what these changes mean for the business (for example, does it need to react to these changes or can the position be improved in the future).

Revision of financial ratios

Ratios

The mechanics of ratio analysis are repeated here for revision purposes.

Profitability ratios

- ROCE =   Operating Profit (PBIT)/Capital Employed   × 100
- Gross margin =   Gross profit/Sales   × 100
- Net margin =   Net profit/Sales   × 100
- ROE =   Profit after tax and preference dividends/Shareholders' funds   × 100

Efficiency ratios

- Asset turnover =   Sales/Capital Employed
- ROCE =   Net margin × asset turnover
- Receivables days =   Receivables balance/Credit sales   × 365
- Payables days =   Payable balance/Credit purchases   × 365
- Inventory days =   Inventory/Cost of sales   × 365
- Revenue per employee =   Sales/Number of employees

Liquidity ratios

- Current Ratio =   Current Assets/Current Liabilities
- Quick Ratio (acid test) =   Current Assets – inventory/Current liabilities

Gearing ratios

- Financial Gearing =   Debt/Equity

- Financial Gearing =   Debt/Debt + Equity

Investor ratios

Dividend Cover =	PAT/Total Dividend	
Interest Cover =	PBIT/Interest	
EPS =	Profit after tax and preference dividends/Number of shares	× 100
PE ratio =	Share price/EPS	

Inter-firm comparisons

Inter-firm Comparisons (IFCs) – as previously noted, it is possible (through use of financial ratios) to compare and contrast the performance of one entity within an industry with that of another within the same industry. It is also possible to compare and contrast the performance of one firm with that of the whole industry, or a large sample or particular segment of that industry. However, these comparisons may suffer from one or more of the following limitations.

- Different accounting methods may be used by individual firms making up the industry sample, or by the firm being compared.

- The industry figures may be biased by one or a few very large firms within the sample.

- Conversely, an industry mean may be misleading for a small or large firm being compared with the mean. Ratios may vary for different sizes of firms.

- The companies within the industry sample may span across more than one industry classification.

- The industry figures may be relevant for a different financial period, and could possibly be out-of-date.

Non-financial performance measures

Although profit cannot be ignored as it is the main objective of commercial organisations, performance analysis should not focus on profit alone. A range of performance indicators should be used and these should be a mix of financial and non-financial measures.

Examples of Non-financial CSFs and KPIs

The table below shows a number of non-financial performance indicators grouped against CSFs. The organisation will formulate its own, specific KPIs which best suit its business

CSFs	KPIs
Competitiveness	• sales growth by product or service
	• measures of customer base
	• relative market share and position
Resource utilisation	• efficiency measurements of resources planned against consumed
	• measurements of resources available against those used
	• productivity measurements
Quality of service	• quality measures in every unit
	• evaluate suppliers on the basis of quality
	• number of customer complaints received
	• number of new accounts lost or gained
Customer satisfaction	• speed of response to customer needs
	• informal listening by calling a certain number of customers each week
	• number of customer visits to the factory or workplace
	• number of factory and non-factory manager visits to customers
Quality of working life	• days absence
	• labour turnover
	• overtime
	• measures of job satisfaction
Innovation	• proportion of new products and services to old
	• new product or service sales levels

CSFs	KPIs
Responsiveness (lead time)	• order entry delays and errors • wrong blueprints or specifications • long set-up times and large lots • high defect count • machines that break down
Quality of output	• returns from customers • reject rates • reworking costs • warranty costs
Flexibility (ability to react to changing demand and a changing environment)	• product/service introduction flexibility • product/service mix flexibility • volume flexibility • delivery flexibility • time to respond to customer demands

Problems with non-financial performance indicators

The use of NFPI measures is now common place, but it is not without problems:

- Setting up and operating a system involving a wide range of performance indicators can be time-consuming and costly

- It can be a complex system that managers may find difficult to understand

- There is no clear set of NFPIs that the organisation must use – it will have to select those that seem to be most appropriate

- The scope for comparison with other organisations is limited as few businesses may use precisely the same NFPIs as the organisation under review.

Using Key Performance Indicators (KPIs) in scenarios

KPIs may be presented in the scenario (such as customer return rates, % of repeat business, market share, age of products etc.) alongside financial information (or in an accompanying exhibit).

It will be important to react to this data in the same way that you would react to data that is presented in tables or financial statements – that is, to interpret what they are trying to tell you, and to link these in to the analysis of the organisation's position.

Test your understanding 2

Explain in what ways your approach to performance appraisal would differ if you were asked to assess the performance of a not-for-profit organisation.

2 Benchmarking

Why benchmark?

Benchmarking is the process of systematic comparison of a service, practice or process. Its use is to provide a target for action in order to improve competitive position.

The strategic role of benchmarking

Benchmarking permeates the entire strategic planning process.

- In strategic analysis it can be used in value chain analysis to compare one company's values to another. A company's strengths can be garnered by comparing strategic capabilities to those of rivals, and the same can be said of rivals. For example, a company that recognises that staff are a key asset might examine their level of staff turnover and sick days to industry averages to determine whether a problem or weakness exists in this area.

- In making strategic choices we have seen in this chapter that a competitive advantage can be gained if a company has rarer strategic capabilities in areas such as innovation, cost efficiency and knowledge management. So a company might, for example, benchmark their production cost per unit if they are seeking a low cost strategy through cost efficiency.

- In putting strategy into action (explored in detail later in the text) benchmarking can be used in many ways to determine, for example, which processes need to be redesigned, whether staff are being utilised in the best way, setting budgets and targets, assessing the efficiency and effectiveness of IT solutions etc.

There will be links between benchmarking, critical success factors (CSFs) and key performance indicators (KPIs). Benchmarking can help decide which areas to measure and also in setting a target against which KPIs are measured.

Illustration 1 – Benchmarking

Xerox used process benchmarking in the early 1980s to help correct a serious cost deficiency. To obtain cost-reducing ideas, they attempted to identify organisations in other industries that were particularly good in functional areas similar to those at Xerox. For example, LL Bean, a sportswear retailer and mail order house, became one of the models for the warehouse operations because they also dealt with products that were diverse in shape, size and weight. Altogether Xerox made six warehouse benchmark studies, which helped it improve its annual productivity gains in the logistics and distribution area. Company-wide efforts of this type meant that Xerox overcame a cost gap with respect to Japanese manufacturers.

Types of benchmarking

There are various types of benchmarking such as:

- internal
- competitive/industry
- functional/activity
- generic

Types of benchmarks explained

Internal benchmarking

This method examines past performance over a period of time to determine trends and best performance. Alternatively, a range of processes might be assessed in order to determine internal best practice, which can then be used as the benchmark for other processes. There is a danger however that this will result in the continuance of poor habits and that competitors are ignored.

Competitive benchmarking

This method compares performance of the process against other firms in the same industry or sector. Major automakers, for example, will buy cars made by their competitors then reverse engineer those cars to see how to improve their own product. However, there is a danger that, if this is only carried out on a local level, it may not promote performance that is good enough to match wider (e.g. international) rivals.

Functional benchmarking

In functional benchmarking, comparisons are made with a similar function (for example selling, order handling, despatch) in other organisations that are not direct competitors. For example, a fast food restaurant operator might compare its buying function with buying in a supermarket chain.

Generic benchmarking

For some activities, the process might be so unique that there may not be competitive or activity benchmarks available. In these cases, a conceptually similar process is sought as a benchmark.

For example, when building a rail tunnel connecting Aomori Prefecture on the Japanese island of Honshū and the island of Hokkaidō which travels under sea, the construction company would have had no similar activities against which to benchmark (the under-sea tunnel between England and France was yet to be built). However, the tunneling was conceptually similar to explorations into volcanic crusts and this process was used as the benchmark.

Test your understanding 3

Outline the advantages of internal benchmarking compared with the other types.

Benefits and dangers of benchmarking

The main benefits include:

- improved performance and added value – benchmarking identifies methods of improving operational efficiency and product design and helps companies focus on capabilities critical to building strategic advantage

- improved understanding of environmental pressures

- improved competitive position – benchmarking reveals a company's relative cost position and identifies opportunities for improvement

- a creative process of change

- a target to motivate and improve operations

- increased rate of organisational learning – benchmarking brings new ideas into the company and facilitates experience sharing.

Dangers of benchmarking

- 'you get what you measure' – managers may learn to direct attention at what gets benchmarked rather than at what is important strategically.

- Benchmarking does not always reveal the reasons for good/poor performance.

- Managers need to be aware that a benchmarking exercise can appear to threaten staff where it appears that benchmarking is designed to identify weaknesses in individual performance rather than how the process itself can be improved. To alleviate this fear, managers need to be involved in the benchmarking exercise and provide reassurance to staff regarding the aims and objectives of benchmarking.

- In today's environment, the more innovative companies are less concerned with benchmarking numbers (for example, costs or productivity) than they are with focusing on the processes. If a company focuses on the processes, the numbers will eventually self-correct.

3 Multi variable performance analysis

Organisations should combine financial and non-financial performance measures in order to provide a broader view of the organisation's performance and position. There are a number of tools that can be used to do this. Two of these are explored below.

The balanced scorecard

The balance scorecard, developed by Kaplan and Norton, suggests that managers should appraise performance from four perspectives

- a financial perspective – this considers whether an organisation is achieving its financial targets and meeting the needs of shareholders

- a customer perspective – this considers the organisation from a customer point of view to determine whether the organisation is meeting customer needs

- an innovation perspective – this considers whether the organisation is continuing to improve and develop

- an internal business process perspective – this considers whether the organisation's processes are efficient as well as whether employees are satisfied and motivated

Further details

The aim of the model is to ensure that managers are only deemed to have been a success if they have succeeded from all of the perspectives. So, for example, a manager who has increased financial results (and thus scored well from a financial perspective) will not be rewarded if this success has been achieved by cutting back on staff training (a poor internal business perspective) or cutting back on research and development (a poor innovation perspective).

Critical success factors and associated key performance indicators (KPIs) will be attributed to each perspective. For example, from a customer perspective an organisation might want to ensure that it has a quick response to customer queries and might therefore measure the average response time. Benchmarking can be used to set targets for each KPI.

Successful organisations are likely to be those who have a good 'balanced' score across all of the perspectives. Scoring well in only one or two of the perspectives is likely to lead to longer term problems for the organisation which result in a poorer strategic position and a failure to meet strategic goals.

Baldrige performance excellence

An alternative approach is to use the Baldrige performance excellence model. This was developed by Malcom Baldrige as a way of measuring and rewarding those organisations that have performed better than their contemporaries. Baldrige developed criteria for performance excellence in the belief that organisations that incorporate them into their organisational practices can expect to achieve performance superior to their competitors.

The Baldrige model assesses an organisation across seven categories:

- Leadership – how the organisation's leadership guides, governs and sustains the organisation's performance.

- Strategy – the ability to successfully plan, develop and implement strategies.

- Customers – the success in building and sustaining strong, lasting relationships with customers.

- Workforce – how the organisation enables and empowers its workforce to achieve organisational goals.

- Operations – the design and effectiveness of organisational processes and whether these are improving and meeting strategic needs.

- Results – the performance and improvement of the organisation relative to competitors, in the key categories of the model.

- Measurement, analysis, and knowledge management – how data is stored, managed, analysed and used within the organisation.

Further details

Leadership will consider an organisation in areas such as:

- whether its leaders provide clear, well communicated goals and lead by example

- its corporate governance – for example, in whether best practice is being applied and all stakeholder views are considered

- whether it has considered its wider social responsibilities

Strategy will consider an organisation in areas such as:

- whether it has clear objectives

- its ability to create strategic plans

- whether strategic plans fit with the strategic objectives

- how strategies are developed and implemented

- whether suitable and sufficient resources are provided for strategic implementation

- whether it measures success or failure of strategic objectives

Customers will consider an organisation in areas such as:

- the level of customer support

- customer complaint management

- the level of customer interaction and engagement

- whether customers are segmented and products/services personalised to segments

Workforce will consider an organisation in areas such as:

- recruitment and retention

- workforce career progression

- workforce training and development

- reward schemes and controls

- appraisals

- workforce engagement

Operations will consider an organisation in areas such as:

- whether processes are reviewed and assessed

- whether processes are improved

- how effective processes are in delivering customer value and strategic value

Results will consider organisational improvement in all key areas such as:

product and process results

- customer results

- workforce results

- leadership and governance results

- financial and market results

The category asks about performance levels relative to those of competitors and other organisations with similar product offerings.

Measurement, analysis and knowledge management will consider an organisation in areas such as:

- whether organisational knowledge is managed and shared

- whether benchmarking is used

- which performance measures are used and how data is collected

- whether action is taken as a result of performance measurement

From this it can be seen that the Baldrige Values include:

- visionary leadership

- customer-driven excellence

- organisational and personal learning

- valuing employees and partners

- agility

- focus on the future

- managing for innovation

- management by fact

- social responsibility

- focus on results and creating value

- systems perspective

In some countries an award is given to those organisations that achieve performance excellence. Recipients include companies such as Motorola and Honeywell. Organisations that apply for the Baldrige Award are judged by an independent board of examiners. Recipients are selected based on achievement and improvement in seven areas, known as the Baldrige Criteria for Performance Excellence.

An organisation that scores well in the areas of the model should be better at

- achieving its strategic goals
- competing
- improving its results
- improving and learning
- meeting customer needs and retaining customers

Test your understanding 4

Two of the Baldrige values are valuing people and agility. Explain how these might contribute to the strategic success of an organisation.

Refer to the SBL article in ACCA study support resources **"Assessing Organisational Performance"**

4   Chapter summary

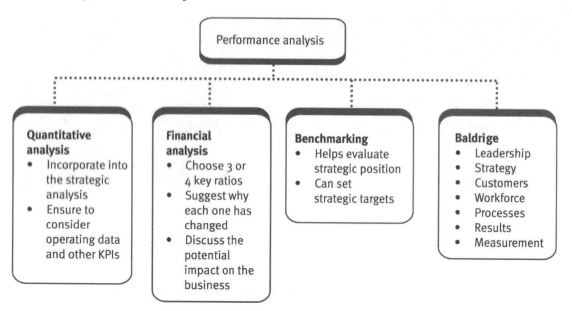

Test your understanding answers

Test your understanding 1

The table shows two things:

- the market overall is not growing

- no one company dominates the market.

Professional skill:

Simply identifying the issues is not enough. You need to investigate why the industry is competitive and what this might mean for the attractiveness of the industry.

The data provided on the industry would suggest that this is likely to be a competitive industry. No company has significantly better economies of scale in order to achieve cost leadership and marketing budgets and techniques are likely to be very similar which will make differentiation strategies harder. The companies will know that, in order to grow, there is unlikely to be new sales coming into the market and therefore they will have to tempt customers away from rivals – which will increase the competitive activities in the industry. This is likely to adversely impact on margins and make the industry less attractive for those organisations operating in it.

Note: The table might also provide information on the difficulty that new entrants into the market might have in overcoming the position of the four established providers.

Test your understanding 2

It is generally assumed that the objective of stock market listed companies is to maximise the wealth of their shareholders. This in turn places an emphasis on profitability and other factors that influence a company's share price. It is true that some companies have other (secondary) aims such as only engaging in ethical activities (e.g. not producing armaments) or have strong environmental considerations. Clearly by definition, not-for-profit organisations are not motivated by the need to produce profits for shareholders, but that does not mean that they should be inefficient. Many areas of assessment of profit-oriented companies are perfectly valid for not-for-profit organisations: efficient stock holdings, tight budgetary constraints, use of key performance indicators, prevention of fraud, etc.

There are a great variety of not-for-profit organisations; e.g. public sector health, education, policing and charities. It is difficult to be specific about how to assess the performance of a not-for-profit organisation without knowing what type of organisation it is. In general terms an assessment of performance must be made in the light of the stated objectives of the organisation. Thus, for example, in a public health service one could look at measures such as treatment waiting times, increasing life expectancy, etc. and although such organisations do not have a profit motive requiring efficient operation, they should nonetheless be accountable for the resources they use. Techniques such as 'value for money' and the three Es (economy, efficiency and effectiveness) have been developed and can help to assess the performance of such organisations.

Test your understanding 3

The main advantages of internal benchmarking are that access to sensitive data and information are easier; standardised data is often readily available; and, usually less time and resources are needed. There may be fewer barriers to implementation as practices may be relatively easy to transfer across the same organisation. However, real innovation may be lacking and best in class performance is more likely to be found through external benchmarking.

Test your understanding 4

Valuing people

An organisation's success depends on an engaged workforce that benefits from work which they feel is making a contribution to the organisation, a clear understanding of (and buy-in to) the organisational direction, the opportunity to learn, and accountability for performance. The workforce must be provided a safe, trusting, and cooperative environment. Particularly in service industries, the workforce is a key differentiator and source of competitive advantage. A better workforce leads to a better organisation.

But valuing people goes beyond the workforce. This includes anyone who has a stake in the organisation to include not only the workforce, but also customers, community members, shareholders, and other people and groups affected by the organisation's actions.

Organisational learning and agility

Agility is the capacity for rapid change and for flexibility in operations. Disruptive events occur more frequency in today's world; critical to success is the ability to make transformational change and manage risk. Organisations need to evolve quickly and have the ability to change as their environments change.

Organisational learning includes both the continuous improvement of existing approaches and significant change or innovation leading to new goals, approaches, products and markets. Learning must be embedded in the way the organisation operates. This supports agility.

Strategic choice

Chapter learning objectives

Upon completion of this chapter you will be able to:

- assess how an organisation may choose to compete

- discuss the capabilities required to sustain competitive advantage

- assess and advise on how an organisation can be empowered to reach its strategic goals, improve its results and be more competitive, focusing on its critical success factors

- recommend generic development directions using the Ansoff growth vector matrix

- assess the opportunities and potential problems of pursuing different organisational strategies of product/market diversification from a national, multinational and global perspective

- assess and advise on the different strategic options available to an organisation

PER

One of the PER performance objectives (PO3) is that you contribute to the wider business strategy of your organisation through your personal and team objectives. You identify innovative ways to improve organisational performance – which may include making or recommending business process changes and improvements. Working through this chapter should help you understand how to demonstrate that objective.

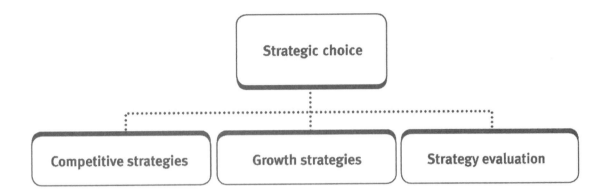

1 Introduction

Strategic choice aims to close the gap between where the organisation is at the moment (potentially determined by a strategic position analysis using a model such as SWOT) and where the organisation wants to be in the future (determined potentially by its mission and an analysis of expected changes in its environment). An organisation must choose the strategy that it feels best suits its mission, is feasible using its strategic capabilities and gives it the best fit with its environment.

This chapter examines three key elements of strategic choice:

- competitive strategies – how best to beat competitive rivals
- growth strategies – how to achieve growth in new areas
- strategy evaluation – choosing the best available option

 Competitive or growth strategies

At the end of the chapter we will illustrate how individual strategies can be evaluated in more detail. But as a general principle, competitive strategies are best employed when the organisation feels that it can improve its market share. This might be because the product, service or market is in the early stages of its life (such as the wearable technology industry) or because the market is continuing to grow and the organisation believes that its value chain can be improved (such as Chinese mobile phone manufacturers trying to take on the Apple iPhone).

Growth strategies are more likely to be employed when an existing market is mature or declining. For example, Apple may believe that it has a strong, defendable and high market share in the US mobile phone market. It would be difficult for the company to compete any better than it is already doing. But as the sales in this market slow down Apple should be looking for where its future growth will come from. It will therefore consider expanding into new markets, launching new products etc. These are growth strategies.

2 Competitive strategy options

Generic strategies: cost leadership, differentiation and focus

Professor Michael Porter identified three generic strategies through which an organisation can achieve competitive advantage.

	Cost Leadership	Differentiation	Focus
Aim	To cut costs of production/ purchasing/service and in turn cut selling prices	To offer a product that can't be matched by rivals and charge a premium for this "difference"	Position the business in one particular niche in the market
How (examples)	<ul><li>economies of scale</li><li>use of learning effects</li><li>large production runs</li><li>using cheaper labour and materials</li><li>moving to cheaper premises</li></ul>	<ul><li>branding</li><li>quality and design</li><li>innovation</li><li>knowledge management</li><li>control over suppliers</li><li>support</li></ul>	1 find a segment where the cost leader or differentiators have little or no presence and build business here 2 reduction in product range
Benefits	<ul><li>high volumes</li><li>creates a barrier to entry</li><li>can operate in unattractive segments</li><li>win price wars</li><li>reduced power of substitutes</li></ul>	<ul><li>builds brand loyalty and repeat purchases</li><li>higher margins</li><li>reduction in power of customers</li></ul>	<ul><li>develops brand loyalty</li><li>little competition</li><li>often a first step towards the other generic strategies</li></ul>

	Cost Leadership	Differentiation	Focus
Threats	<ul><li>no fallback position if leadership is lost</li><li>larger rivals (possibly from overseas) may enter the market</li><li>strong currency makes imports cheaper</li></ul>	<ul><li>perform badly in a recession</li><li>often easily copied in the long run</li><li>need to constantly innovate</li><li>needs much higher marketing than cost leadership</li><li>fewer barriers to entry</li><li>smaller volumes</li></ul>	<ul><li>low volumes</li><li>if successful, it attracts cost leaders and differentiators</li><li>few barriers to entry</li></ul>
Suitability	Large organisations with economies of scale	Innovative companies with large marketing budgets	Small businesses with entrepreneurial flair, strong market knowledge and a risk taking attitude (often new starts)

A business that fails to achieve one of these generic positions will be **stuck in the middle** – it will lose some customers who will move downmarket to the cost leader, other customers who will move upmarket to differentiators, and others will move to rivals who focus on their specialist needs.

Porter's generic strategies

Cost leadership

Set out to be the lowest cost producer in an industry. By producing at the lowest possible cost the manufacturer can compete on price with every other producer in the industry and earn the highest unit profits.

How does one become a cost leader?

- Decide whom you are competing against (e.g. Tesco, M&S or Harrods food hall)?

- Perform value analysis to determine why customers value the product – what are key features that have to be matched and which product attributes could be dropped or reduced?

- Understand your own costs and cost drivers.

- Try to make a product of comparable quality for a lower cost – this may involve a full analysis of the value chain.

Advantages

- Better margins through lower costs.

- Ability to undercut competitors on price, thus reducing competitive rivalry.

- Low costs act as a barrier to entry deterring new entrants.

- Low prices make substitutes less attractive.

- Better margins give more scope to absorb pressure from powerful buyers/suppliers.

- Low costs give a platform for expansion – both gaining market share and moving into new markets.

Drawbacks of such a strategy

- In industries that only require a low critical mass of production output to achieve economies of scale, cost leadership would be difficult to achieve, because many other firms would be able to match the costs. It is only when the critical mass of production is high that a cost leadership strategy is likely to be effective.

Other drawbacks

Only room for one cost leader – no fallback position if the cost advantage is eroded.

- Cost advantage may be lost because of inflation, movements in exchange rates, competitors using more modern manufacturing technology or cheap overseas labour, etc.

- Customers may prefer to pay extra for a better product.

Differentiation

Here the firm creates a product that is perceived to be unique in the market.

Consider the following case.

Suppose you wanted to develop a better coffee percolator. To decide what makes it 'better' you need to ask why people need a percolator rather than making instant coffee; the answer is taste.

The key issue is therefore to discover how the design of a percolator affects the taste.

1   The most important issue is the water quality. A 'better' percolator thus needs to remove chlorine in the water and ensure it is at the correct temperature when meeting the coffee.

2   Another key factor is the time between grinding the beans and pouring on the water. A 'better' percolator should thus grind the beans and control when the water is applied.

Ways of achieving differentiation

Quality differentiation

This has to do with the features of the product that make it better – not fundamentally different but just better.

Design differentiation

Differentiate on the basis of design and offer the customer something that is truly different as it breaks away from the dominant design if there is one.

Image differentiation

Marketing is used to feign differentiation where it otherwise does not exist, i.e. an image is created for the product. This can also include cosmetic differences to a product that do not enhance its performance in any serious way (e.g. packaging).

Support differentiation

More substantial, but still no effect on the product itself, is to differentiate on the basis of something that goes alongside the product, some basis of support, such as after-sales service.

Rewards of a differentiation strategy:

- better margins through being able to charge higher prices
- higher quality offsets competitive rivalry
- product uniqueness reduces customer power
- quality acts as a barrier to entry
- quality reduces the attractiveness of substitutes.

Risks of such a strategy:

- cheap copies
- being out-differentiated
- customers unwilling to pay the extra (e.g. in a recession)
- differentiating factors no longer valued by customers (e.g. due to changes in fashion).

Focus

Position oneself to uniquely serve one particular niche in the market. A focus strategy is based on fragmenting the market and focusing on particular market segments. The firm will not market its products industry-wide but will concentrate on a particular type of buyer or geographical area.

Cost focus

This involves selecting a particular niche in the market and focusing on providing products for that niche. By concentrating on a limited range of products or a small geographical area the costs can be kept low.

Differentiation focus

Select a particular niche and concentrate on competing in that niche on the basis of differentiation.

Reward

You become an expert in your field and understand the marketplace more.

Risks

The segment is not sustainable enough to provide the firm with a profitable basis for its operations.

Test your understanding 1

What types of generic strategies are the following companies adopting?

1   Walmart

2   Saga Holidays (specialises in holidays for those over 55)

3   Bang and Olufson

The strategy clock

 An alternative way of identifying strategies that might lead to competitive advantage is to look at 'market facing' generic strategies.

- This approach is based on the assumption that competitive advantage is achieved if a firm supplies what customers want better or more effectively than its competitors.

- Better could mean a more suitable product or service, or could mean a cheaper one of adequate quality.

- In effect, customers are looking for what they perceive as best 'value for money'.

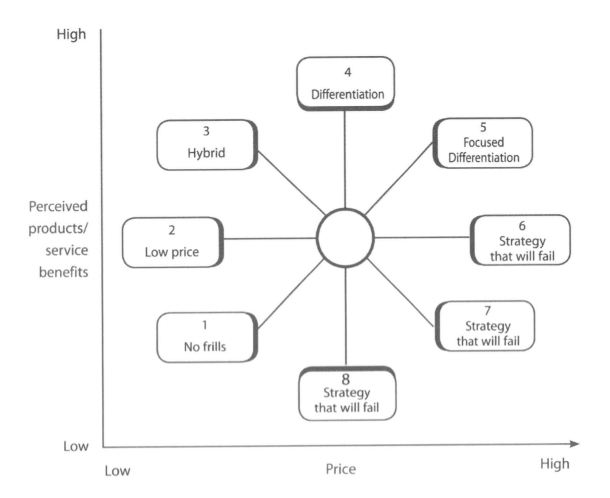

Explanation of the strategy clock strategies

(Adapted from the work of **C. Bowman and D. Faulkner** 'Competitive and Corporate Strategy' – Irwin – 1996)

Routes 1 and 2 are **price-based** strategies.

- 1 = no frills

  Commodity-like products and services. Very price-sensitive customers. Simple products and services where innovation is quickly imitated – price is a key competitive weapon. Costs are kept low because the product/service is very basic.

- 2 = low price

  Aim for a low price without sacrificing perceived quality or benefits. In the long-run, the low price strategy must be supported by a low cost base.

- 3 = hybrid strategy

  Achieves differentiation, but also keeps prices down. This implies high volumes or some other way in which costs can be kept low despite the inherent costs of differentiation.

Routes 4 and 5 are **differentiation** strategies.

- 4 = differentiation

  Offering better products and services at higher selling prices. Products and services need to be targeted carefully if customers are going to be willing to pay a premium price.

- 5 = focused differentiation

  Offering high perceived benefits at high prices. Often this approach relies on powerful branding. New ventures often start with focused strategies, but then become less focused as they grow and need to address new markets.

- 6, 7, 8 = failure strategies

  Ordinary products and services being sold at high prices. Can only work if there is a protected monopoly. Some organisations try option 8 by sneakily reducing benefits while maintaining prices.

A strategic business unit (SBU) is a part of an organisation for which there is a distinct external market. Different strategies can be adopted for different SBUs. For example, Toyota and Lexus (part of Toyota) operate as separate SBUs with different strategies. Some fashion businesses successfully separate their exclusive ranges of clothing from their diffusion lines.

Illustration on the strategy clock

Illustration – Competitive strategy options – strategy clock

No frills

Ryanair (a very successful, no-frills airline). Ferocious attention to keeping costs down: non-reclining seats (break, extra weight); no back-of-seat pockets (extra cleaning); discouraging checked-baggage (airport charges for loading/unloading baggage); use of cheap airports.

Low price

Dell computers. Good quality computers at low prices. Relies on very efficient production techniques to keep costs low to preserve a reasonable margin.

Hybrid

IKEA. Cheap furnishings, but smart design and large range of inventories. Costs are kept low by self-service, efficient production, high volumes and excellent logistics.

Differentiation

Full service airlines such as British Airways. Prices are usually higher, but there is in-flight service, more leg-room and customers are better looked after if there are scheduling problems.

Focused differentiation

Business/first class on full service airlines. Another example would be couture fashion – small markets, high prices, sustained by brand names.

Failing strategy

Consider the Apple iPad. This is typically sold at a premium price as a differentiated product – it has excellent features, market leading software and strong branding. Apple is effectively placing the product in position 4 of the strategy clock. There may also be companies who position themselves in, say, position two (low cost) on the clock by selling refurbished iPads. These have not got the quality of a new iPad but they are available at a lower price. Now consider a company who decides to place itself in position 8 on the clock. It does this by attempting to sell refurbished iPads at the same price as new iPads. This strategy should fail – it can either be beaten on price by those rivals in position two who offer the same product at a lower price, or it will be beaten by Apple (in position 4) who offer a better product at the same price.

Test your understanding 2

What position on the strategy clock might the following organisations have?

1   A company selling specialised planting consultation to new farmers in an area where the company has expertise in the local unusual soil

2   A large manufacturer selling unbranded copies of an old children's toy to low fixed priced retailers

3   A sole trader selling second hand tractors at the retail price of equivalent new tractors

---

3   Sustaining competitive advantage

Once a competitive advantage is achieved it will be important that it is sustained. Competitive advantage can best be sustained by strategic capabilities which are:

- valued

- rare, and

- robust

Further details

- **Value of strategic capabilities**. The strategic capability must be one that is of value to the customer. A distinctive capability is not enough: the strategic capability must be able to generate what customers value in terms of products or services.

- **Rarity of strategic capabilities**. Competitive advantage will not be attained if competitors have identical strategic capabilities. Unique or rare resources or competences are needed to allow the organisation to outperform its rivals.

- **Robustness of strategic capabilities**. Capabilities for competitive advantage should be robust, meaning that they are hard to imitate. Therefore, competitive advantage is not so often sustained through physical/tangible resources as these can be copied/acquired over time. More important is the way in which the resources are organised and deployed as these competences are, in general, more difficult to identify and imitate.

Test your understanding 3

In the early part of this century, companies from the US and UK flocked to India to outsource their call centre operations. This was due to the presence of cheap labour, a common language, cheap property prices and development of technology which facilitated the service. Also, domestic providers had often reached capacity and couldn't facilitate further growth or expansion.

However, in recent years this trend has been reversed. Consider reasons why US and UK companies may be repatriating their call centre services.

However, organisations can also take strategic steps to protect their competitive position through:

- price based strategies,
- further differentiation, or
- lock-in.

Price based strategies

An organisation that is pursuing a price-based strategy (such as a no-frills position on the strategy clock) may be able to sustain this position as follows:

- further cost efficiencies,
- winning price wars, or
- accepting lower margins.

Further details

- further cost efficiencies – as rivals try to catch up with the organisation's cost savings, the organisation should be looking for further ways to cut costs. For example, Ryanair are a leading no-frills airline in Europe. But they are constantly looking for new ways to cut costs such as putting pressure on governments to allow them to operate flights without a co-pilot and even going to the extreme of using less ice in drinks in order to slightly reduce the weight of the craft (and subsequently the fuel usage). Ryanair are so focused on cost reductions that they have stated that one of their missions is to be able to offer customers free flights in the future.

- winning price wars – reacting aggressively to new entrants by under-cutting their prices can force them to leave the market and allow the cost leader to restore margins again in the future. For example, News Corp is a multi-national media company selling products such as daily newspapers. One newspaper in one market was attacked by a new rival who wanted to provide better news analysis at the same selling price. So News Corp (who had lower production costs per unit due to its economies of scales) reduced their selling price by two-thirds for one month. This deterred their existing readers from trying out or moving to the new rival. By the end of the month the new rival had abandoned production as it had incurred unsustainable losses in the period.

- accepting lower margins – ultimately, low cost providers may have to reduce selling prices and lower margins in the light of new competition. They would hope however that this would be compensated by higher volumes. For example, the French company Societe Bic produced the Bic pen (known as the Biro or the Cristal) and achieved a low cost position in the 1960s. Over the last 50 years there have been many rivals who have been able to match the company's cost of production so that the margin per unit on the product has steadily eroded. However, Bic have still managed to make very large profits on the product overall on the basis that they continue to be the market leader in disposable pens and sell the product in large volumes (over 100 billion of the pens have been produced). So although margin per unit has fallen, Bic continue to make profits which are larger than all of their rivals.

Differentiation based strategies

These can be sustained through:

- creating difficulties in imitation,

- achieving imperfect mobility of resources, and

- re-investing margins.

> **Further details**
>
> - creating difficulties in imitation – this is about ensuring that strategic capabilities cannot be copied by rivals. Examples would be patent protection, unique production methods, ownership of technology, tying in suppliers etc.
>
> - achieving imperfect mobility of resources – this is about ensuring that the capabilities that create the difference cannot be traded to rivals. Examples would be to tie in key staff to long-term and non-competition contracts, protecting insider knowledge, creating intangible assets such as brand names etc.
>
> - re-investing margins – as seen in earlier segments, investing profits in areas such as innovation and knowledge management can sustain a competitive advantage. For example, Apple ensure that whilst rivals try to catch up with the latest innovations that Apple have made to the iPhone or iPad, Apple are busy working on the next innovation. It means that, by the time rivals have caught up with one innovation, Apple can still be differentiated by launching an updated phone or tablet with a new innovation.

Differentiation through innovation

Innovation is increasingly seen as important for strategic success. The reasons are:

- increased rate of technical advances
- increased competition
- increased customer expectations.

In all functions that serve to produce goods and services, achieving superior innovation, relative to competitors, can help the firm to acquire new customers. Superior innovation gives a company something unique, something that its competitors lack until they are able to imitate the innovation. By the time competitors succeed in imitating the innovator, the innovating company has already built up such brand loyalty that its imitating competitors will find it difficult to attack its position.

Innovation can apply to:

- the nature of the product or service being supplied
- how the product or service is produced and delivered
- operating the firm in a new or novel way.

Research and development

Research and development (R&D) can be defined as 'the organisation of innovation at the level of the firm'. R&D aims to satisfy a market need by developing new products and by improved methods of production. It must also find applications for scientific and technical developments. However, an R&D (innovation) strategy cannot sensibly be pursued in isolation from the rest of the organisation. The business strategy will concentrate on the broad range of products that the organisation wishes to have and the broad markets in which it wishes to compete. This strategy will be supported by the organisation's competence strategy, focused on the technologies the organisation needs if it is to pursue its business strategy successfully.

The R&D function should have a major innovative role in all organisations. The pressures to introduce new ways of doing things may be 'demand pulled', that is the innovation filling a market need, or it may be 'technology pushed', the innovation coming from the application of discoveries. In many organisations, there is a group of people, not necessarily called R&D, whose responsibilities include the creation of new business ideas and techniques.

An innovation strategy calls for a management policy of giving encouragement to innovative ideas. This has a number of aspects.

- Financial backing must be given to innovation, by spending on R&D and market research and risking capital on new ideas.

- Employees must be given the opportunity to work in an environment where the exchange of ideas for innovation can take place. Appropriate management style and organisation structure are needed.

- Management can actively encourage employees and customers to put forward new ideas. Participation by subordinates in development decisions might encourage them to become more involved with development projects and committed to their success.

- Development teams can be set up and an organisation built up on project teamwork.

- Where appropriate, recruitment policy should be directed towards appointing employees with the necessary skills for doing innovative work. Employees should be trained and kept up to date.

- Certain managers should be made responsible for obtaining information about innovative ideas from the environment, and for communicating it throughout the organisation.

The importance of innovation in strategy is one of the most hotly disputed questions in the subject. In many cases, the most innovative companies in an industry consistently fail to be among the most profitable. This creates a divergence of opinion over the role of innovation-based strategy.

A company that chooses not to be innovative is still influenced by the effect of innovation. It is innovation that frequently undermines the basis of competition in existing markets, and creates new markets that may supersede old ones. Firms must learn to innovate with greater commercial effectiveness than is the case at present, or learn to replicate innovations more quickly than they would choose to. The rate of innovation is often too quick for a balanced assessment of it to be carried out in a sensible time period.

Richard Lynch identifies three distinctive roles for innovation within a business level strategy:

- achieving new growth through entry into new products and markets

- retaining competitive advantage by strengthening the product offering

- achieving competitive advantage through jumping ahead of existing rivals.

The indications are that organisations with high market share develop strategies of higher price and/or higher quality than low-share competition. These organisations tend to be more profitable, thus providing the cash to invest in R&D to improve and differentiate products, enhancing their market position and also justifying higher prices.

Acquiring new technologies

New technologies often emerge in one of two ways. Technology-push is based upon an understanding of the technology, but a less well-developed idea of market-pull has important applications. A technology-push-based innovator always has difficulty in finding product/market applications for the discoveries he or she makes. Consequently, a firm using technology-push may frequently develop strategies by emergent processes to exploit the latest discoveries. The danger is that the new innovation might be ahead of complementary applications, and the advantage lost by the time other technologies catch up. It is possible to see this in the information technology business where hardware runs in excess of the specifications for existing software, and sellers find it increasingly difficult to justify margins at the high performance end of the market. On the other hand, breakthrough technologies are almost invariably of the technology-push kind.

New ideas frequently emerge through market-pull. In this case, new technologies are developed based upon a good understanding of customer requirements, or close collaboration with a customer. In such cases, finding a market for a new product is less problematic, but may still be fraught with difficulty.

These two approaches are not mutually exclusive, and frequently support each other. For example, an attempt to store films on a compact disc was an example of market-led innovation, but the technology was more effectively applied to data storage for computers after the failure of the original product. It is far better to think of these as the two complementary drivers to innovative activity.

Exploitation of existing technologies

An organisation that develops an advantage in a particular technology should consider a strategy of market development. That is, that the knowledge and competences can be applied to new markets. An illustration of switching from entertainment to data storage based upon knowledge of a particular technology is one such example. Where the company has a diversified product range, discoveries in one area can be readily applied to another.

Innovation and existing products

In certain stages of the product life cycle, innovation may be a threshold competence. For example, in mobile telephones and software it is vitally important to maintain product features at least as good as those of competing products. Technology-driven strategies tend to be more effective than market ones because many users will be unaware of the possibilities of the technology or the uses to which it might be put. Innovation plus good sales skills are threshold competences.

Overall

A successful company is one that:

- is outward-looking, has accepted the reality of constant change and reviews its product-market policy continuously

- is always looking to the future towards new markets, innovative products, better designs, new processes, improved quality, increased productivity

- has a structure designed for innovation in which management and staff are stimulated to think and act innovatively, which recognises potential 'intrapreneurs' and ensures that everyone (particularly senior people) welcome changes for the better

- stimulates creativity, and rewards ideas and supports individual and team abilities.

The impact of new product, process, and service developments and innovation in supporting organisation strategy

New developments will play an important role in supporting organisational strategy in a number of ways:

- They will help close the gap between the organisation's current strategic position and its desired position as defined by its mission and objectives.

- New launches can be a differentiator and innovative organisations can be more attractive to customers and investors.

- Many new developments fail and therefore launching more than one new development can diversify away some of this risk.

- As products and services age, new developments need to be found to replace them. This should happen before older products and services start to experience declining sales.

- New developments are often copied by rivals so that any competitive advantage is short-lived. Organisations therefore need to be thinking about their next development whilst rivals are busy catching up with existing developments.

- Developments encourage an organisation to be flexible and to learn. These can be critical success factors for future success (especially in changing environments).

- Organisations with a focus on quality see continuous improvement as core competency and organisational mission. New developments make the achievement of competitive strategies easier – either by cutting costs or by differentiating the business.

Illustration 1 – The importance of innovation

Amazon first appeared on the internet in 1995 selling books. It was a major innovator in the business of internet retailing and soon CDs and DVDs were added to its product lists. The website allowed customers to search a very extensive database and to order goods, which would normally be delivered by post in a few days. The website also allowed customers to write reviews about products, and informs customers about how consumers of a particular product also bought other products. Consumer goods such as electronics are now available from Amazon.

Although Amazon was preeminent in internet-based sales of books, CDs and DVDs, innovation in the industry provided further technological opportunities to stream music and video content over the internet rather than having them delivered by post. These development opportunities were also being exploited by the competitors of Amazon forcing the company to react and innovate accordingly.

> On-demand printing of books is particularly suitable for lower-volume books and those that would normally be regarded as out of print.
>
> The development of the Kindle and Kindle Fire were therefore essential to Amazon. Without these, Amazon risked losing customers to those who could offer an innovative alternative method of delivery for its products – rather like when Amazon itself attacked conventional book and music shops.

Lock-in

This approach can work for both price-based and differentiation-based strategies. It happens where a business' products become the industry standards. Examples are:

- Microsoft Windows
- Dolby
- Microsoft Edge or Google Chrome

These are not necessarily the best or cheapest products but have such market-dominance that competitors find it very difficult to break into the market because users are often locked in to the product and would find it expensive or inconvenient to switch to rivals. The major threat to such businesses is likely to be attention from anti-monopoly regulators.

4   Growth strategies

Introduction

 Growth strategies are explored through the use of the **Ansoff Matrix.** Ansoff suggested that growth strategies can fall into 4 categories.

The Ansoff Growth Vector Matrix

	Existing Products	**New Products**
Existing Markets	**Market penetration/growth.** • This typically involves the use of a new/improved competitive strategy. Key risks: • competitor reaction • can lead to stagnation	**Product development** • New products could arise from R&D, joint ventures, buying in other people's products, copying innovations of rivals or licensing. • It might also come from product augmentation (for example, by upgrading software capabilities). Key risks: • market size and demand are unknown • can lead to cannibalisation of existing products

New Markets	Market development	Diversification
	• This involves finding new markets for existing products. • These could be new segments in current markets (e.g. new age groups) or overseas markets. Key risks: • needs a new external analysis • puts a strain on existing strategic capabilities	• This involves moving away from existing core activities and offering a new product to a new customer. • More details are available elsewhere in this chapter. Key risks: • combines the risks of product and market development • need good corporate parenting skills (covered in detail in the next chapter)

More details on market penetration

Market penetration – existing markets and products

Market penetration involves some of the following:

- increasing the average spend per visit for existing customers
- increasing the frequency of visits for existing customers
- winning customers away from rivals
- encouraging non-users to buy.

Strategies used to penetrate a market include:

- Changes to the marketing mix. For example, spending more on sales promotion, changing the selling price of products or redesigning the product. The marketing mix is explored in more detail in a later chapter.
- Pursuing a new competitive strategy. This would involve moving positions on the strategy clock.
- Increasing the sales force.

The ease with which a business can pursue a policy of market penetration will depend on the nature of the market and the position of competitors. When the overall market is growing it may be easier for companies with a small market share to improve quality or productivity and increase market activity rather than in static markets, where it can be much more difficult to achieve. The lessons of the experience curve stress the difficulty of market penetration in mature markets where the cost structure of the market leaders should prevent the entry of competitors with lower market share.

A market penetration strategy would be contemplated for the following reasons.

- When the overall market is growing, or can be induced to grow, it may be relatively easy for companies entering the market, or those wishing to gain market share, to do so relatively quickly. (Some companies established in the market may be unable or unwilling to invest resources in an attempt to grow to meet the new demand.) In contrast, market penetration in static or declining markets can be much more difficult to achieve.

- Market penetration strategy would be forced on a company that is determined to confine its interests to its existing product/market area but is unwilling to permit a decline in sales, even though the overall market is declining.

- If other companies are leaving the market for whatever reasons, penetration could prove easy – although the good sense of the strategy may be in doubt.

- An organisation that holds a strong market position, and is able to use its experience and competences to obtain strong distinctive competitive advantages, may find it relatively easy to penetrate the market.

- A market penetration strategy requires a relatively lower level of investment with a corresponding reduction in risk and senior management involvement.

Even though market penetration is seen as the least risky of Ansoff's options, it should not be assumed that risk is always low. When Yamaha attempted to gain share over Honda, it provoked a retaliation that left Yamaha in a worse position than before. The example should serve to remind us that Ansoff's strategies still require a competitive advantage to be effective (a point Ansoff made many times, but one that is frequently forgotten). Also, if a company focuses purely on market penetration and rarely develops new products, then it runs the risk of stagnation and falling behind rivals who have better more innovative products. A good example of this would be Kodak. The company focused on building market share in traditional, high-end cameras. Rivals started to leave the market and move into digital photography. So when the traditional market went into decline, Kodak were too far behind rivals to catch up on digital photography which led the company to file for bankruptcy in 2012.

Where a company believes that the product is not performing as well as it could do, Ansoff suggests that, if penetration through an improved competitive strategy cannot be achieved, the organisation could instead consider.

- consolidation – acquire or merge with rivals in order to increase market share or obtain economies of scale

- efficiency gains – it will be important to reduce costs as much as possible and to improve processes to make them quicker, more effective and more attractive to customers

- withdrawal – if no obvious route for improvement is available it may be best to withdraw from the market entirely (for example, by selling out to rivals).

 More details on product development

Product development – existing markets and new products

This strategy has the aim of increasing sales by developing products for a company's existing market. For our purposes, new-product development is a generic term that encompasses the development of innovative new products and the modification and improvement of existing products. By adopting this strategy the company could:

- develop new product features through attempting to adapt, modify, magnify, substitute, rearrange, reverse or combine existing features

- create different quality versions of the product

- develop additional models and sizes.

A company might show a preference for product development strategy for the following reasons:

(a) it holds a high relative share of the market, has a strong brand presence and enjoys distinctive competitive advantages in the market

(b) there is growth potential in the market

(c) the changing needs of its customers demand new products. Continuous product innovation is often the only way to prevent product obsolescence

(d) it needs to react to technological developments

(e) the company is particularly strong in R&D

(f) the company has a strong organisation structure based on product divisions

(g) for offensive or defensive motives, for example responding to competitive innovations in the market.

However, product development strategy does have its down sides and there are strong reasons why it might not be appropriate for a company. For example, the process of creating a broad product line is expensive and potentially unprofitable, and it carries considerable investment risk. Empirical research reveals that companies enjoying high market share may benefit in profit terms from relatively high levels of R&D expenditure, while companies in weak market positions with high R&D expenditure fare badly.

There are reasons why new-product development is becoming increasingly difficult to achieve:

(a) in some industries there is a shortage of new product ideas

(b) increasing market differentiation causes market segments to narrow with the effect that low volumes reduce profit potential that in turn increases the risk of the investment involved

(c) a company typically has to develop many product ideas in order to produce one good one. This makes new product development very costly

(d) even when a product is successful it might still suffer a short life cycle with rivals quick to 'copycat' in the market but with their own innovations and improvements

(e) there is a high chance of product failure.

Success frequently depends upon stretching a brand further than the market is willing to take it. Also, there is a risk that this product will adversely affect the sales of existing products. For example, as Apple announced the launch of the third generation of its iPad, sales of second generation iPads fell dramatically. This is known as sales cannibalisation.

More details on market development

Market development – existing products and new markets

Market development strategy has the aim of increasing sales by repositioning present products to new markets. (Note: this strategy is also referred to as **'market creation'**.)

Kotler suggests that there are two possibilities:

(a) the company can open additional geographical markets through regional, national or international expansion

(b) the company can try to attract other market segments through developing product versions that appeal to these segments, entering new channels of distribution, or advertising in other media.

For example, during 1992 Kellogg's undertook a major television and promotion campaign to reposition Kellogg's Cornflakes (traditionally regarded as a breakfast cereal) to provide afternoon and evening meals. In the same way, the malt drink Horlicks had previously repositioned from a once-a-day product ('a night meal') to become a through-the-day 'relaxing drink' for young professionals. This was not successful. On the other hand, Lucozade has successfully moved its brand from a product associated with infirmity to a sports-related product.

Market development strategy would be contemplated for the following reasons:

(a) the company identifies potential opportunities for market development including the possibilities of repositioning, exploiting new uses for the product or spreading into new geographical areas

(b) the company's resources are structured to produce a particular product or product line and it would be very costly to switch technologies

(c) the company's distinctive competence lies with the product and it also has strong marketing competence (Coca-Cola provides a good example of a company that pursues market development strategies, as does the fast-food restaurant chain of McDonalds.)

The new market will need a new external analysis. The company will be coming up against new cultures, legal rules, competitors etc. so a new PESTEL and 5 Forces will be essential. It will also need to ensure it has the knowledge, expertise and resources to cope with the demands from a new market.

Often the risk of failure is perceived to be high and therefore strategic alliances (such as joint ventures, franchises and licensing agreements) are commonly used to reduce the risks from market development. These ideas are explored more in the next chapter.

More details on diversification

Growth by diversification – new products and new markets

Diversification is the deployment of a company's resources into new products and new markets. The company thus becomes involved in activities that differ from those in which it is currently involved. Diversification strategy means the company selectively changes the product lines, customer targets and perhaps its manufacturing and distribution arrangements.

The term 'diversification' actually covers a range of different techniques.

- **Conglomerate diversification** – a firm moves into markets that are unrelated to its existing technologies and products to build up a portfolio of businesses. Sometimes this is because the company has developed skills in turnaround or brand management, and can buy an ailing company very cheaply and quickly create value. Hanson have achieved great things in this way, based upon a nucleus of around 500 people. On other occasions, a company might use conglomerate diversification if it believes it has no real future in its existing product market domain. Finally, many entrepreneurial leaders move in and out of markets simply because of opportunities – Virgin being a good example.

- **Horizontal diversification** – synergy is highest in the case of horizontal diversification, especially if the technology is related, but the disadvantage is that little additional flexibility is provided. This type of strategy affects all parts of the value chain since fixed costs can be spread over an increased number of units. Most diversification strategies are of this type. The strategy is undertaken when a company extends its activities into products and markets in which it already possesses necessary expertise. For example, a manufacturer of televisions branching into the manufacture of DVD recorders, camcorders and hi-fi equipment.

- **Vertical integration** – this can take the form of forward or backward integration

    - **Forward integration** – moving towards the consumer – control of distribution, e.g. drinks manufacturers buying public houses.

    - **Backward integration** – moving away from the consumer – control of supplier, e.g. beer brewers buying hop growers.

    Suppose that a company currently manufactures cars. If the company were to buy a chain of car dealers, this would represent forward integration since it is moving towards the final consumer. If the company were to buy a manufacturer of car components (headlights, windscreens, etc.), this would represent backward integration.

Let's look at some of these strategies in more detail:

Unrelated/conglomerate diversification

- Diversifying into completely unrelated businesses.

- Not clear where added value comes from – except if an ailing business is turned round.

- Often leads to loss of shareholder value.

Advantages	Disadvantages
• Increased flexibility • Increased profitability • Ability to grow quickly • Better access to capital markets • Avoidance of anti-monopoly legislation • Diversification of risk	• No synergies • No additional benefit for shareholders • No advantage over small firms • Lack of management focus

Vertical integration

Advantages	Disadvantages
Cost • Economies of combined operations. • Economies of internal control. • Economies of avoiding the market. **Quality** • Tap into technology – enhanced ability to differentiate. **Barriers** • Assured supply/demand. • Defence against lock-out. • Create barriers by controlling supplies/distribution/retail outlets.	**Cost** • It may not be cheaper to do it oneself – especially if suppliers have economies of scale. • Increased operating gearing. • Dulled incentives. • Capital investment. • Reduced flexibility to switch to cheaper suppliers. **Quality** • Cut off from suppliers/customers. • Reduced flexibility to switch to better suppliers. • Differing managerial requirements. **Barriers** • Much more difficult to exit the industry.

Horizontal diversification

Horizontal diversification refers to development into activities that are competitive with, or directly complementary to, a company's present activities. There are three cases.

(a) Competitive products. Taking over a competitor can have obvious benefits, leading eventually towards achieving a monopoly. Apart from active competition, a competitor may offer advantages such as completing geographical coverage.

(b) Complementary products. For example, a manufacturer of household vacuum cleaners could make commercial cleaners. A full product range can be presented to the market and there may well be benefits to be reaped from having many of the components common between the different ranges.

(c) By-products. For example, a butter manufacturer discovering increased demand for skimmed milk. Generally, income from by-products is a windfall: any you get is counted, at least initially, as a bonus.

Advantages	Disadvantages
• Likely to be more synergies. For example, when Coca Cola moved into the production of other types of drinks such as bottled water and bottled tea, they could share bottling plants, staff and distribution networks.	• Selling to different customers against different rivals will require an understanding of the market.
• This can offer a defence against substitutes.	• Some new strategic capabilities will be needed.
• This can widen the company's product portfolio and reduce reliance on one product or on powerful customers.	• Synergies are not automatic and will need to be worked on.
• There is likely to be less risk than with vertical integration or conglomeratisation as some existing strategic capabilities can still be used.	• It can be more difficult to manage a diversified business. Many of these problems can be overcome by the use of strategic alliances and good corporate parenting and these ideas are explored in more detail in the next chapter.

Illustration 2 – Ansoff matrix

Tesco plc is a UK based supermarket. It has grown from a position where 30 years ago it had revenue of around $3 billion p.a. to a position today where revenue exceeds $90 billion p.a. and profits exceed $3 billion p.a. It is the third biggest retailer in the world (behind Walmart and Carrefour).

It has achieved this growth through a variety of strategies, many of which can be plotted onto the Ansoff matrix

	Existing Products	**New Products**
Existing Markets	24 hour opening Move from a differentiation to a hybrid strategy	Expansion into petrol sales Expansion into clothing and electrical sales
New Markets	Overseas expansion Tesco Express – smaller stores aimed at convenience shoppers	Launch of financial services Tesco Direct – selling its products over the internet

There are many other strategies that could be added to the matrix, but even in this simple form it can be seen that companies who grow successfully will often employ the full range of the Ansoff growth strategies.

Test your understanding 4

M Company, a clothes manufacturer, is considering vertical integration.

Discuss the advantages and disadvantages for M Company in integrating forwards by buying up a chain of retail outlets and integrating backwards by buying a company that manufactures cloth.

Achieving international growth

Market development and diversification can often lead to an organisation expanding internationally.

Reasons why companies pursue a strategy of international diversification

- There are increasing opportunities from global markets, either where products themselves are becoming global or where the organisation's customers operate on a global basis.

- If local markets are saturated or limited, it may be possible to sell products into new locations using existing skills and infrastructure.

- Risks may be spread as poor results in one market due to local economic conditions can be balanced against good conditions in another.

- It may be possible to take advantage of particular aspects of different locations and markets such as low labour costs.

Driving and restraining forces for international expansion

Driving forces:

- Technology
- Culture
- Market needs
- Cost
- Free markets
- Economic integration
- Peace/political stability
- Management vision
- Strategic intent
- Global strategy and action.

Restraining factors:

- Culture
- Market differences
- Cost
- National controls
- Nationalism
- War
- Management myopia/short-sightedness
- Organisation history
- Domestic focus.

Possible strategies for geographical diversification

- A multi-domestic strategy where products and services are tailored to individual countries and markets, with many activities specific to particular countries.

- A global strategy, where standard products are sold in different countries.

- A balance between the two above strategies, where products are largely global but have minor modifications to suit the requirements of individual countries. There will generally be a trade-off between scale economies and the need to tailor products or services to local markets.

The concept of globalisation

Globalisation, if it can be seen as a single concept at all, is a very complex one. The term provides a collective label for a whole series of trends and changes related to the significance of geography in shaping organisations and the interactions between them. For example, many local markets are globalising as their governments reduce import restrictions and tariffs, or as other countries re-open trade relationships. This not only means that goods and services become available from other parts of the world, but that the nature of competition changes from local to global, in turn affecting the way that local firms must operate in order to survive and thrive.

A somewhat different type of globalisation concerns the homogenising of tastes across geographies. Food, once highly local in style, has become more global in many respects. This is not simply what has been called the culinary imperialism of America being rolled out across the world via Coca-Cola and McDonalds. The changing economics of transportation and increased experience of foreign travel have enabled consumers to break away from largely national determinants of taste, and re-segment across countries on more individual lines. It is not that everyone is moving to a single global standard, but that shared tastes transcend national borders. Some consumers are moving towards a traditional Italian diet whether they live in London, Toronto or Stockholm, while others eat increasing quantities of Chinese style stir-fries, whether in New York, Adelaide or Madrid.

In this context globalisation simply means that geographic location is no longer the key determinant of behaviour.

Other forms of globalisation can also be distinguished. More and more firms have a presence in multiple locations across the world, rather than simply exporting from a home base. But, perhaps more importantly, as such firms seek to standardise approaches or gain purchasing economies, they increasingly demand co-ordinated, multi-country support from their suppliers. This requires the suppliers not only to be present in different parts of the world, but also to manage the relationships between their local units in new ways.

5 Strategy evaluation

So far, this chapter has provided a number of strategic options that an organisation can choose from. But not all of these will be successful for every organisation. The choices need to be evaluated to determine which is the best one for a particular organisation.

Johnson, Scholes and Whittington (JSW) argue that for a strategy to be successful it must satisfy three criteria:

- **Suitability** – whether the options are adequate responses to the firm's assessment of its strategic position.

- **Acceptability** – considers whether the options meet and are consistent with the firm's objectives and are acceptable to the stakeholders.

- **Feasibility** – assesses whether the organisation has the resources it needs to carry out the strategy.

 This criteria can be applied to any strategy choice such as the competitive strategies and the growth strategies assessed in this chapter, or even the methods of development considered in a later chapter.

Further explanation on each test

Suitability

Suitability considers whether the new strategy fits in with the organisation's environment and addresses its key issues. It means that in this test we should consider factors that may have arisen in the PESTEL and 5 Forces analysis (covered in chapter 2), for example. Suitability would therefore consider whether the strategy takes account of

- changes in technology

- the threat from substitutes

- the reaction of competitors

- where the business is in its life cycle

- support for overseas expansion

- the timing of the strategy

So the key focus is on whether the strategy solves the problems that the company is facing (and which you are likely to have identified from previous strategic analysis).

Suitability will also examine the 'cultural fit' of the strategy – this examines whether there would be resistance to change from staff, whether the organisational structure can incorporate the new strategy, whether suitable controls are in place etc. Culture is explored in detail in a later chapter.

Feasibility

Assesses whether the organisation has the resources it needs to carry out the strategy. It could be linked back to the resource audit and strategic capabilities covered in chapter 3. This would involve ensuring that

- the organisation has the right number of staff
- staff have the right skills
- adequate finance is available
- technology is suitable
- the organisation has appropriate skills in areas such as marketing and design
- the organisation has experience with this market and/or product.

Feasibility may also consider barriers to entry to ensure that the market can be accessed.

Acceptability

Acceptability concerns assessing risk, return and stakeholders' expectations.

Risk

Risk can be assessed through using:

- financial ratios to identify any problems. For example, a low operating margin and long cash operating cycle for the strategy might highlight that there will be a risk to the organisation's cash flows and that the project will put extra burdens on finances. Assessing the impact on capital structure through using gearing ratios could be equally important.

- sensitivity analysis. You should be aware from previous studies how sensitivity (or 'what if?') analysis can identify key assumptions and provide an indication of the margin of safety in assumptions.

A strategy that is deemed to be too risky may be rejected regardless of whether it is suitable and feasible.

Risk (and how to evaluate it) is covered in more detail in chapter 15 when we revise areas such as expected value and decision tree techniques.

Return

A project will only be acceptable if it meets the returns expected by key stakeholders. These returns may be both financial and non-financial and could include areas such as:

- the change in shareholder wealth (i.e. NPV)
- the accounting return (in terms of profits)
- impact on KPIs (such as customer satisfaction, market share gains etc.)

In chapter 4, we considered how financial ratios should be calculated and analysed and we also considered what KPIs might be important to an organisation. Later in the syllabus we will look at project appraisal techniques such as payback and NPV methods which would be appropriate here.

For non-profit organisations non-financial KPIs may take preference. But there would still be a need to assess the financial performance of any proposed strategy and techniques such as cost-benefit analysis are commonly used to achieve this.

Risk and return are typically linked together so that if one increases the other increases (i.e. taking more risks can often lead to greater returns). It will therefore be important to determine the risk attitude of key stakeholders. Risk-averse stakeholders will be willing to sacrifice returns in order to keep risk low, whereas risk seekers will aim to maximise returns irrespective of risk.

Stakeholder expectations

It will be important to consider the reactions to the strategy of all stakeholders (not just shareholders). We should consider areas such as:

- stakeholder attitudes to risk (as explained above)
- how customers will react (for example, how will the new strategy affect brand and reputation)
- whether there will be any resistance from staff and whether staff will continue to be motivated by any new strategic direction (this will be particularly important when staff are a key asset)
- whether the policy is ethical and how the wider community will react
- whether the strategy fits in with the overall vision, mission and objectives of the organisation
- whether the strategy meets any known goals set out by stakeholders (for example, if industry bodies are demanding that the organisation becomes less aggressive towards competition etc.)

Stakeholder mapping and analysis (covered in chapter 7) can be of great value here.

Test your understanding 5

Sarah Wu has set up and run her own bookstore for five years. She faces little local competition and has made strong financial returns from the store. She now has $15,000 available for investment and plans to open up a second store in a nearby town which currently does not have a bookstore.

Her friend, Misah, has just returned from completing a university course and has suggested that Sarah should instead invest in a website for her store. He has said that this will allow Sarah to sell her books worldwide and make a much quicker return on her investment than the new store opening.

Required:

Evaluate Misah's strategy.

Professional skill:

Illustrate evaluation skills in appraising the option from Sarah's point of view.

6   Chapter summary

```
                          ┌─────────────────────┐
                          │   Strategic choice   │
                          └─────────────────────┘
```

Competitive strategies
- No frills
- Low cost
- Hybrid
- Differentiation
- Focused differentiation

Growth strategies
Ansoff suggested:
- Market penetration
- Product development
- Market development
- Diversification

Strategy evaluation
- Feasibility – do we have the resources and skills?
- Acceptability – does it match our goals?
- Suitability – does it fit with the environment?

Test your understanding answers

Test your understanding 1

1   Walmart – cost leadership. The company is renowned for its attention to keeping costs low.

2   Saga Holidays – focus.

3   Bang and Olufson – differentiation. Upmarket, very stylish, home entertainment equipment.

Test your understanding 2

1   The specialised consultation service is likely to be in a position of focused differentiation. It will be focused on the local area and the unusual soil present in that area and it will be able to differentiate itself through its specialist knowledge.

2   The manufacturer is likely to be using a no frills position. It does not have the branding to offer a low cost or differentiated product.

3   The sole trader is likely to be in an uncompetitive position. It will not be able to compete on either price or quality and its strategy is likely to fail.

Test your understanding 3

Indian call service providers are struggling to sustain their international competitive advantage for the following reasons:

Robustness

The demand for call centre staff in India has made it a scarce resource. This in turn has pushed up wage rates – with annual wage inflation running at around 13% per annum in 2011. In contrast, wage inflation in the US and UK is falling and due to the economic recession call centre staff are no longer a scarce resource in these countries. Some companies are finding that domestic wage rates are coming to a par with rates in India.

Property and rent prices in India have also risen sharply over the past decade as call centres fight for an ever diminishing resource. This again has threatened the cost effectiveness of these centres.

Rarity

Domestic call centres had reached capacity by the late 1990s as demand for call centres grew beyond what they could cope with. However, over the last 10 years these companies have invested in extra capacity which has allowed them to satisfy the needs of domestic customers. The Indian service is now not as rare as it was ten years ago.

Value

Domestic consumers have started to complain about the quality of service from Indian call centres and this in turn leading to US and UK companies valuing the service less. In the US there has also been a political backlash against using foreign labour instead of domestic labour.

On top of this, staff turnover in Indian call centres has risen to epidemic levels as staff move on to seek higher salaries in a market where good staff are difficult to retain (recent reports show attrition rates of between 25 and 35% per annum). It is typically the better staff who are leaving and this is harming the value of the service provided.

The future

Already many small Indian call centres have closed down as they can no longer sustain their competitive advantage. Larger companies have so far managed to maintain the bulk of their customers. But they will need to focus on building value, rare and robust new strategic capabilities if they are to maintain this position in the future.

Test your understanding 4

There are several reasons why M Company might pursue forward integration. It will be easier for a chain of retail outlets to differentiate its clothes from those of its competitors through branding. This gives an opportunity for higher margins to be earned. M Company can produce clothes as the shops demand them (JIT), leading to reductions in inventory levels. They will also have a guaranteed customer for its output.

There are also reasons against this course of action. The reaction of the customers that M Company presently supplies may be hostile. If they stop stocking M Company's products, will the chain of retail outlets be able to sell enough to cover this fall in demand? What is the likely effect of the increased costs of distributing clothes to the shops, rather than to the depots of current customers?

A strategy of backward integration into the supply chain would give M Company a dedicated supplier with both guaranteed quality and price. The material could be manufactured when required by M Company, leading to lower inventory levels.

The downside to this course of action is that, if alternative cheaper suppliers become available, M Company will not be able to use them, since it will be committed.

There are also arguments against integration generally, whether forwards or backwards.

Being successful may require different skills from those presently possessed by the company. For example, M Company may know little about retailing or material manufacturing. To be successful, it will have to stretch its current competencies to cover these areas.

In addition, there may be a very different focus for each of the businesses. For example, the chain of retail outlets may well be successful if it can differentiate its products from those of its competitors using innovative colours and material, while the cloth manufacturer is likely to be successful by keeping its costs low by using basic materials and standardised colours. It will be difficult for M Company to maintain both of these at the same time.

Test your understanding 5

Johnson, Scholes and Whittington's tests will be used to evaluate the strategy:

Feasibility

A website may be cheap to set up and gaining a web presence is relatively easy. But designing the site and maintaining it will need technical expertise which Sarah is unlikely to possess.

Selling internationally will also require international distribution networks that Sarah will not possess. She may be able to outsource distribution, but the costs of this are likely to outweigh any benefits.

Therefore, this strategy may not be a feasible one for Sarah.

Acceptability

As a small, owner-managed business, Sarah is likely to be risk averse and may well want to focus on the area that she is comfortable with. She may decide that international expansion is too risky and difficult to control and lack the confidence necessary to run the business successfully.

She is therefore unlikely to find the strategy to be acceptable.

Suitability

There are already worldwide book selling companies on the internet such as Amazon. They are likely to have built up a reputation and supply chain that Sarah cannot overcome. They will also have economies of scale which enable them to sell books at a lower price than Sarah would find possible and therefore Sarah's website would struggle to gain any competitive advantage against these rivals.

Therefore the strategy is also unsuitable.

Overall

This is not a valid strategy for Sarah to pursue and she should instead evaluate the market development opportunity further.

Professional skill:
The key evaluation skills will be in considering the positive and negatives from Sarah's point of view. It will not be good enough to simply state or identify the issues. Likewise, few professional skills marks would be awarded for having an unsupported opinion. It is not good enough to state, for example, that the strategy is unsuitable. Instead this needs to be supported by an assessment of the relevant issues from either an external or internal perspective.

Methods of strategic development

Chapter learning objectives

- assess how internal development, or business combinations, strategic alliances and partnering can be used to achieve business growth

- describe the relationship between corporate parents and business units and how the corporate parent can create or destroy value

- apply the Boston Consulting Group (BCG) and the public sector portfolio matrix models to assist organisations in managing their organisational portfolios

PER

One of the PER performance objectives (PO3) is that you contribute to the wider business strategy of your organisation through your personal and team objectives. You identify innovative ways to improve organisational performance – which may include making or recommending business process changes and improvements. Working through this chapter should help you understand how to demonstrate that objective.

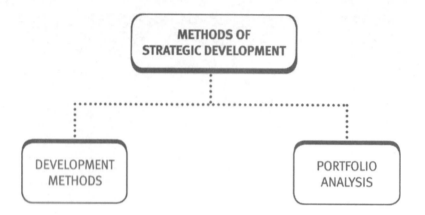

1 Introduction

This chapter looks at how some of the strategies discussed in the last two chapters might be developed. It looks at various types of business combinations. If the chosen method is to develop a strategy through acquisition, then an organisation must consider corporate parenting and portfolio analysis.

2 Alternative development options

There are many ways in which a strategy can be developed. Some of the key methods are explored in this section.

Acquisition

This chapter uses the term acquisition when referring to both acquisitions and mergers.

 Further details on the terminology

Technically, a merger is in essence the pooling of interests by two business entities which results in common ownership. An acquisition normally involves a larger company (a predator) acquiring a smaller company (a target).

A merger typically involves the creation of a new company with mutual decision making by each party entering into the agreement. All staff therefore feel that their views and culture will be expressed in the new venture. Acquisitions often experience more resistance from staff than mergers as the acquired business will be the less powerful partner and will have less influence on future decisions.

Acquisitions are usually easier to control as the predator can more easily and quickly dictate controls, working methods, power structures etc. There are also more opportunities to remove excess or inefficient senior management in the acquired business than would be possible with a merger.

The acquisition can also be quicker to complete as it involves an acquisition of the shares of the target company (though this can have a high cost and have a significant financial impact). Mergers do not often require an exchange of an 'acquisition price', but they do involve the creating of a new entity which can be slow and complex. Mergers will require new branding, for example, which an acquisition can avoid by simply using the branding of the predator.

But mergers provide a better pooling of skills and resources, with each party focusing on its core competences. A merger allows all parties to participate in future growth and synergies whereas an acquisition allows only the predator to receive these (although the target company sellers are often compensated for this in the acquisition price).

Acquisitions typically have the following issues

Advantages	Disadvantages
• it is a quick way to grow	• can be very expensive
• there can be synergistic gains	• synergies are not automatic
• acquire the necessary strategic capabilities	• can lead to cultural clashes
• overcomes barriers to entry	• there may be legal barriers to overcome (e.g. competition law)
• can choose a target that fits best (see portfolio analysis later)	• all parts of the target are acquired (including its problems)
• enhances reputation with finance providers	• requires good change management skills

Potential sources of synergy

"Synergistic gains" refers to a position where the combined entity is worth more than the sum of the value of the companies prior to acquisition. This can come from areas such as improved combined profitability, a better financial position or better market position.

Improved profitability

Combined profits can be higher due to:

- Sales synergies. These can come from sharing databases, selling products which are complementary, sharing distribution channels etc.

- Cost synergies. Combined costs may be lower through sharing staff (and making excess staff redundant), gaining economies of scale, sharing premises, sharing central services (such as accounting) etc.

Improved financial position

The financial position of the combined company may be better due to:

- sharing assets (and selling off excess assets)
- using assets better
- shared working capital management
- finding cheaper financing
- stabilising cash flows (e.g. removing seasonality).

Improved market position

This can come from:

- sharing skills or knowledge
- risk reduction from a portfolio effect
- improved management/better corporate parenting
- better focus.

Test your understanding 1

Blueberry is a quoted resort hotel chain based in Europe.

The industry

The hotel industry is a truly global business characterised by the following:

- Increasing competition
- An increasing emphasis on customer service with higher standards being demanded.
- In particular the range of facilities, especially spas, is becoming more important as a differentiating factor.

Performance

- Blueberry offers services at the luxury end of the market only, based on a strong brand and prestigious hotels – although its reputation has become tarnished over the last five years due to variable customer satisfaction levels.
- Despite a reputation for having the most prestigious coastal resort hotels along the Mediterranean in 20X0, Blueberry was loss-making in the financial years 20X4/5 and 20X5/6.
- To some extent this situation has been turned around in 20X6/7 with an operating profit of $11 million. However shareholders are putting the board under pressure to increase profits and dividends further.

- Management have responded to this by setting out an ambitious plan to upgrade hotel facilities throughout the company and move more upmarket. The bulk of the finance is planned to come from retained profits as Blueberry has historically kept its financial gearing low.

Acquisition opportunity

The management of Blueberry have been approached by the owner of 'The Villa d'Oeste', a luxury hotel on the shores of Lake Como in Italy, who is considering selling it. The hotel has an international reputation with world-class spa facilities and generates revenue throughout most of the year due to Lake Como's mild micro-climate. The asking price will be approximately $50m.

Required:

Outline the issues to be considered when assessing the acquisition.

Corporate parenting

Corporate parenting looks at the relationship between head office and individual business units. This will become more important if a business follows the route of growth through acquisitions – the aim will be to become a good "parent" to new subsidiaries.

Corporate parents do not generally have direct contact with customers or suppliers but instead their main function is to manage the business units within the organisation. The issue for corporate parents is whether they:

- add value to the organisation and give business units advantages that they would not otherwise have. This can be done, for example, through providing resources and skills or by sharing expertise.

- add cost and so destroy the value that the business units have created. For example, if central overheads are re-charged to business units.

Organic growth

Advantages	Disadvantages
• can spread the cost	• lack of experience in new areas
• no cultural clashes or control issues	• less attractive to finance providers
• can be set up in many ways – for example, through a new division	• there may be barriers to organic entry
• may get access to government grants	• it may be too slow
• easier to terminate	• no access to skills, reputation etc. or other strategic capabilities required for success
• can be developed slowly (less risk)	• managers may be spread too thinly

Joint venture

Advantages	Disadvantages
• can share the set-up and running costs	• can often lead to disputes
• can learn from each other	• may give access to strategic capabilities and eventually allow the partner to compete in core areas
• can focus on relative strengths	• there may be a lack of commitment from each party
• may reduce political or cultural risks	• requires strong central support which may not be provided
• it is better than going it alone and then competing	• transfer pricing issues may arise and performance appraisal can be complicated

Characteristics of a well-structured strategic alliance

A strategic alliance can be defined as a co-operative business activity, formed by two or more separate organisations for strategic purposes, that allocates ownership, operational responsibilities, financial risks, and rewards to each member, while preserving their separate identity/autonomy.

- Alliances can allow participants to achieve critical mass, benefit from other participants' skills and can allow skill transfer between participants.

- The technical difference between a strategic alliance and a joint venture is whether or not a new, independent business entity is formed.

- A strategic alliance is often a preliminary step to a joint venture or an acquisition. A strategic alliance can take many forms, from a loose informal agreement to a formal joint venture.

- Alliances include partnerships, joint ventures and contracting out services to outside suppliers.

Seven characteristics of a well-structured alliance have been identified

- **Strategic synergy** – more strength when combined than they have independently.

- **Positioning opportunity** – at least one of the companies should be able to gain a leadership position (i.e. to sell a new product or service; to secure access to raw material or technology).

- **Limited resource availability** – a potentially good partner will have strengths that complement weaknesses of the other partner. One of the partners could not do this alone.

- **Less risk** – forming the alliance reduces the risk of the venture.

- **Co-operative spirit** – both companies must want to do this and be willing to co-operate fully.

- **Clarity of purpose** – results, milestones, methods and resource commitments must be clearly understood.

- **Win-win** – the structure, risks, operations and rewards must be fairly apportioned among members.

Some organisations try to retain some of the innovation and flexibility that is characteristic of small companies by forming strategic alliances (closer working relationships) with other organisations. They also play an important role in global strategies, where the organisation lacks a key success factor for some markets.

Franchising

Advantages	Disadvantages
• receive an initial capital injection	• share profits
• can spread brand quickly	• may give access to strategic capabilities and eventually allow the partner to compete in core areas
• easy to terminate	• there may be a lack of goal congruence
• a good way to test the market before full investment	• there is a loss of control over quality, recruitment etc.
• franchisee may provide better local knowledge	• there may be a lack of consistency across franchises
• franchisor management can focus on strategic rather than operational issues	• it may be difficult to attract franchisees

 Further detail on franchising

Franchising

The mechanism

- The franchiser grants a licence to the franchisee allowing the franchisee to use the franchiser's name, goodwill and systems.

- The franchisee pays the franchiser for these rights and also for subsequent support services the franchiser may supply.

- The franchisee is responsible for the day to day running of the franchise. The franchiser may impose quality control measures on the franchisee to ensure the goodwill of the franchiser is not damaged.

- Capital for setting up the franchise is normally supplied by both parties.

- The franchiser will typically provide support services including: national advertising, market research, research and development, technical expertise, management support.

The advantages for the franchiser are as follows:

- Rapid expansion and increasing market share with relatively little equity capital.

- The franchisee provides local knowledge and unit supervision. The franchiser specialises in providing a central marketing and control function, limiting the range of management skills needed.

- The franchiser has limited capital in any one unit and therefore has low financial risk.

- Economies of scale are quickly available to the franchiser as the network increases. For example, with the supply of branded goods, an extensive advertising spend is justifiable.

The advantages for the franchisee are as follows.

These are mainly in the set-up stages where many new businesses often fail.

- The franchisee will adopt a brand name, trading format and product specification that has been tested and practised.

- The learning curve and attendant risks are minimised.

- The franchisee usually undertakes training, organised by the franchiser, which should provide a running start, further reducing risk.

Disadvantages

Note: most of these relate to clashes between the franchiser and franchisee

- A franchisee is largely independent and makes personal decisions about how to run his or her operation. In addition, the quality of product, customer satisfaction and goodwill is under his or her control. The franchiser will seek to maintain some control or influence over quality and service from the centre but this will be difficult if the local unit sees opportunities to increase profit by deviating from the standards which the franchiser has established.

- There can be a clash between local needs or opportunities and the strategy of the franchiser, for example, with respect to location.

- The franchiser may seek to update/amend the products/services on offer whilst some franchisees may be slow to accept change or may find it necessary to write off existing stock holdings.

- The most successful franchisees may break away and set up as independents, thereby becoming competitors.

Test your understanding 2

Which of licensing, joint venture, strategic alliance and franchising might be the most suitable for the following circumstances?

1　A company has invented a uniquely good ice cream and wants to set up an international chain of strongly branded outlets.

2　An oil company which, in common with its rivals, is under political pressure to develop alternative, renewable energy sources.

3　A beer manufacturer wants to move from its existing domestic market into international sales.

Business partnering

As we have noted above, partnerships between businesses have a long history and come in many forms, including strategic alliances and joint ventures (JVs).

Business partnering is the development of successful, long term, strategic relationships between, for example, customers and suppliers, based on achieving best practice and sustainable competitive advantage.

Why a partnership?

A recent PwC analysis of more than a quarter century of global data on alliances and JVs shows we're in another period of upswing when it comes to those partnerships. The combined number of alliances and JVs has increased in the past two years and is now at its highest level since the start of the century.

For example, the Amazon–Berkshire Hathaway – JPMorgan deal in 2018, which targeted waste in the current US healthcare system and improving patient service, shows how companies today, responding to technological disruption, geopolitical uncertainty, regulatory overhaul, and demographic shifts, are pushing such partnerships beyond their traditional limits.

The aim is often to bring together expertise to expand the companies' reach, drive growth, and cope with rising competition. Few companies can afford to follow their previous deal blueprints if they want to respond to the disruptions and risks in today's markets. More important, the traditional lines between industries are blurring, with consumers increasingly expecting goods and services to be interconnected, and businesses seeking to make their supply chains more efficient and effective.

Similarly, co-branding is a strategic marketing and advertising partnership between two brands wherein the success of one brand brings success to its partner brand, too. Co-branding can be an effective way to build business, boost awareness, and break into new markets, and for a partnership to truly work, it has to be a win-win for all players in the game. Both partners need to find value in the future relationship.

Whatever the path the partnership takes, success usually hinges on trust and good management. Building trust early on is important in managing an alliance or JV. It can enable partners to set big long-term goals while celebrating small wins along the way. Companies that manage partnerships well also design agreements that are flexible, coordinate planning and budgeting with each other, and follow strong governance processes and principles. When partners work to be agreeable, collaborative, and responsible, alliances and JVs can thrive.

3 Portfolio analysis tools

The use of portfolio analysis

An organisation may have to make investment decisions such as whether to add a company to its existing portfolio or whether to divest of an existing subsidiary. One technique that can be used to perform this task is portfolio analysis, which determines the fit between the business unit and other business units held by the organisation.

More on portfolio analysis

Portfolio analysis:

- is designed to reveal whether the organisation has:

    - too many declining products or services

    - too few products or services with growth potential

    - insufficient product or service profit generators to maintain present organisation performance or to provide investment funds for the nurturing of tomorrow's successful ventures

- portfolio analysis can be very valuable in assessing how the balance of activities contributes to the strategic capability of the organisation

- should be applied to SBUs, that is units dealing with particular market segments not whole markets

- will result in different targets and expectations for different parts of the organisation, which will impact on the resource allocation processes – both capital and revenue budgets

In this section the BCG matrix is discussed in detail and alternatives in outline. The ACCA has stated that it will not explicitly ask for a specific portfolio tool but will expect you to use whichever models are most useful in the scenario given.

The Boston Consulting Group (BCG) matrix

- This two-by-two matrix classifies businesses, divisions or products according to the present market share and the future growth of that market.

- Growth is seen as the best measure of market attractiveness.

- Market share is seen to be a good indicator of competitive strength.

BCG measurement issues

Assessing the rate of market growth as high or low is difficult because it depends on the market. A useful tool for assessing growth is the PESTEL model studied in chapter 3. In an exam scenario, this would be a good tool to use alongside the BCG in order to assess whether a market has good growth prospects.

Relative market share is defined by the ratio of market share to the market of the largest competitor. The log scale is used so that the midpoint of the axis is 1.0, the point at which an organisation's market share is exactly equal to that of its largest competitor. Anything to the left of the midpoint indicates that the organisation has the leading market share position.

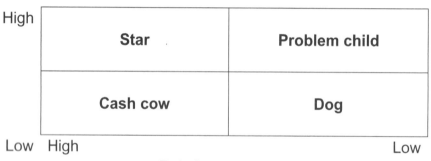

An organisation would want to have the following in a balanced portfolio:

- cash cows of sufficient size and/or number that can support other products in the portfolio

- stars of sufficient size and/or number that will provide sufficient cash generation when the current cash cows can no longer do so

- problem children that have reasonable prospects of becoming future stars

- no dogs or – if there are any – there would need to be good reasons for retaining them.

BCG decision making aspects

Decision-making implications for different quadrants in the matrix

A **cash cow** has a high relative market share in a low-growth market and should be generating substantial cash inflows. The period of high growth in the market has ended (the product life cycle is in the maturity or decline stage), and consequently the market is less attractive to new entrants and existing competitors. Cash cow products tend to generate cash in excess of what is needed to sustain their market positions. Profits support the growth of other company products. The firm's strategy is oriented towards maintaining the product's strong position in the market.

A **star** has a high relative market share in a high-growth market. This type of product may be in a later stage of its product life cycle. A star may be only cash-neutral despite its strong position, as large amounts of cash may need to be spent to defend an organisation's position against competitors. Competitors will be attracted to the market by the high growth rates. Failure to support a star sufficiently strongly may lead to the product losing its leading market share position, slipping to the right in the matrix and becoming a problem child. A star, however, represents the best future prospects for an organisation. Market share can be maintained or increased through price reductions, product modifications, and/or greater distribution. As industry growth slows, stars become cash cows.

A **problem child** (sometimes called 'question mark') is characterised by a low market share in a high-growth market. Substantial net cash input is required to maintain or increase market share. The company must decide whether to do nothing – but cash continues to be absorbed – or market more intensively, or get out of this market. The questions are whether this product can compete successfully with adequate support and what that support will cost.

A **dog** product has a low relative market share in a low-growth market. Such a product tends to have a negative cash flow, that is likely to continue. It is unlikely that a dog can wrest market share from competitors. Competitors, who have the advantage of having larger market shares, are likely to fiercely resist any attempts to reduce their share of a low-growth or static market. An organisation with such a product can attempt to appeal to a specialised market, delete the product or harvest profits by cutting back support services to a minimum.

Options for the future can be plotted onto a BCG matrix and the long-term rationale of business development can be highlighted by the matrix. Using the original matrix a strategist could address the following issues.

- Which strategies are most suitable to move products from question marks through to stars and eventually to cash cows? In other words, will the strategy move the organisation to a dominant position in its market?

- Will there be sufficient funds from cash cows to provide the necessary investment in stars? Many bankruptcies have occurred because firms have invested heavily in the promotion of products in rapid growth without profitable and well-established products from which it can fund these new ventures.

- Does the portfolio have a balance of activities that matches the range of skills within the organisation? Unless a balance is achieved certain groups are overstretched while others remain underemployed. In general, question marks and stars can be very demanding on the time of management.

- Is the organisation thinking about an acquisition strategy? Firms that embark on acquisition programmes often forget that the most likely targets for acquisition are not the cash cows and stars of the business world but the question marks and dogs. There may be logic in acquiring a question mark if an organisation has the resources to move it towards stardom.

 Strategic movements on the BCG matrix

A product's place in the matrix is not fixed forever, as the rate of growth of the market should be taken into account in determining strategy.

- Stars tend to move vertically downwards as the market growth rate slows, to become cash cows.

- The cash that they then generate can be used to turn problem children into stars, and eventually cash cows.

The ideal progression is illustrated below:

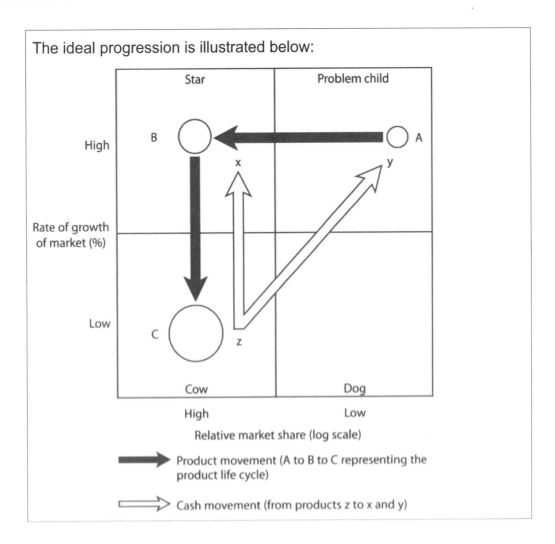

Product movement (A to B to C representing the product life cycle)

Cash movement (from products z to x and y)

 ## Evaluating BCG strategies

The BCG matrix suggests what appear to be very prescriptive strategies for each position in the box. For example, it suggests that all cash cows should be exploited and that all dogs should be disposed of.

But this is not always the case. It may be that some cash cows cannot be exploited if, say, the market has remained competitive, rivals have not left the market and large cash surpluses are not possible. For example, the New York Times could be classed as a cash cow in the BCG matrix but it has been reporting net losses in recent years. For other cash cows it may be inappropriate to 'milk' them for cash if doing so would jeopardise the strategic position of the product or business unit.

Likewise, not all dogs should be removed from the portfolio. Some dogs may support other products and act as a 'loss leader', whilst other dogs can continue to generate a positive contribution for many years. A major customer might, for example, require sales of two products, one of which is a dog and the other is a cash cow. But if the dog is not supplied sales of the cash cow would also be lost and the business would be much worse off.

This is why in an examination you should not simply state that 'dogs', for example, should be removed from the portfolio. Instead you need to evaluate the suggested BCG strategy. This means you need to justify why you think it should be removed or perhaps justify why it should instead be retained within the business portfolio. It usually doesn't matter which way you suggest that the business should proceed as long as you have a structured argument for doing so.

Test your understanding 3

Fruity Drinks provides fruit juices to a number of supermarket chains, that sell them under their own label. Its marketing manager explains, 'We've got a large number of products. Our freshly squeezed orange juice is doing fine. It sells in the same huge quantities now as it has done for a number of years. Although margins are low, we have sufficient economies of scale to do very nicely in this market. We've got advanced production and bottling equipment and long-term contracts with some major growers. No problems there. We also sell freshly squeezed pomegranate juice: customers loved it in the tests, but producing the stuff at the right price is a major hassle – all the seeds get in the way. We hope it will be a winner, once we get the production right and start converting customers to it. After all, the market for exotic fruit juices generally is expanding fast.'

Required:

Analyse the position of each of Fruity Drinks products in its portfolio.

Professional skill:

Illustrate analysis skills in considering each product.

The public sector portfolio matrix

The BCG is aimed primarily at commercial, private sector organisations. The public sector portfolio matrix adapts the BCG idea to public sector organisations and the axes are "public need and funding effectiveness" and "value for money".

Expandable Text

The dimensions of the matrix are:

- value for money – this considers whether the service can be provided effectively

- the desirability of the service – public support and funding attractiveness.

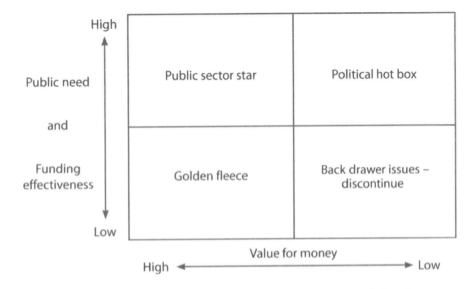

The four potential positions for services can lead to the following strategies for each service:

Position	Characteristics	Strategy
Public sector star	Attractive to the public and well-funded. Funds are used well and the service goals are achieved.	Continue at current funding levels.
Golden fleece	Very effective, but the public believe that it is over-funded.	Move funds to other services, aim to reduce the service or cut staff numbers.
Back drawer issues	Not effective and not desired by the public.	Remove this service.
Political hot box	Very popular but not very effective. Putting a drain on funding that could be used elsewhere.	Either aim to change the public's perceptions and change it into a back drawer issue, or try to improve effectiveness (for example, by providing extra resources) and turn it into a star. Lobby for more funding.

The major problem with the application of the public sector portfolio matrix is that its dimensions (the organisation's ability to serve effectively by providing value for money, and the public's need and support and the funding attractiveness) are all subjective, and largely dependent on the user's own perceptions as to what the body should be doing, and what the public sector body is good at.

Also, some public services may be mandated centrally. For example, the advertisement of jobs at a provided employment centre may be provided in many different languages. The difficulty of the task may lead to many inaccuracies and be expensive to achieve (and therefore struggle to provide value for money). It may not be desired by the public. This would make it a back drawer issue which maybe should be abandoned by the employment centre. But it may be that the provision of this service is part of a legal requirement for employment centres set out by the national government. It therefore could not be abandoned and must be continued.

The Ashridge portfolio display

The Ashridge portfolio display, or parenting matrix, developed by Campbell, Goold and Alexander, focuses on the benefits that corporate parents can bring to business units and whether they are likely to add or destroy value (as discussed earlier in this chapter).

The matrix considers two particular questions.

- How good is the match between perceived parenting opportunities and the parent's skills?

- How good is the match between the CSFs of the business units and the skills and resources that the parent can bring?

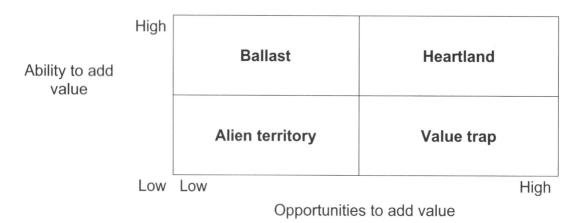

Explanation of the matrix

Heartland business units

- These are where there is a high degree of match and the parent company has the capabilities and experience to add value by providing the support required by the business unit.

- These businesses should be central to future strategy.

Ballast businesses

- These are those where the parent understands the business well but there are limited opportunities to offer help, sometimes because the business has been owned for a long time and has no further support needs.

- These businesses would do better if left alone or indeed divested.

Value trap businesses

- These are those where there appear to be many parenting opportunities but there is a poor fit with the critical success factors of the business.

- There appears to be good potential but in practice because of the lack of fit with the strategy there is a high possibility of destruction of value.

Alien businesses

- These are those where there is a complete mismatch.

- These should not remain part of the corporate portfolio.

Using the Ashridge portfolio display indicates which types of companies should be divested and why. Businesses that may be candidates for disinvestment are:

- alien businesses – the parent cannot do good to these organisations and they would achieve more in another group

- value trap businesses – despite potential, a lack of fit leads to a high possibility of a loss of value

- ballast businesses – may do better as the parent has little to offer.

The matrix can be expanded to introduce what are called 'edge of heartland' business units

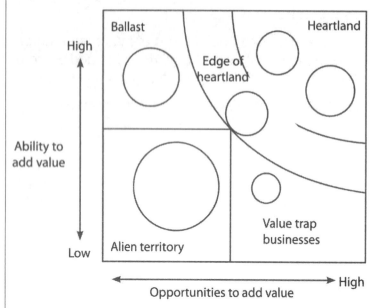

Edge of heartland business units

- These are those where there is a good fit in some areas where the parent can bring particular skills that add value to the business unit, but not in others, where the parent may destroy value.

- However, if the parent develops sufficient understanding of the business to avoid this, then the business may move into the heartland.

Test your understanding 4

Anudir started as a single restaurant and has developed into a large quoted fast food provider. Over the last ten years it has diversified as follows:

- trendy hotels

- commercial property development – a depressed market at present

- jeans manufacture.

The main skills of the parent holding company lie in identifying consumer trends regarding food and designing menus to match those trends.

Required:

Using the above information, label the different business units using the Ashridge portfolio display.

4 Chapter summary

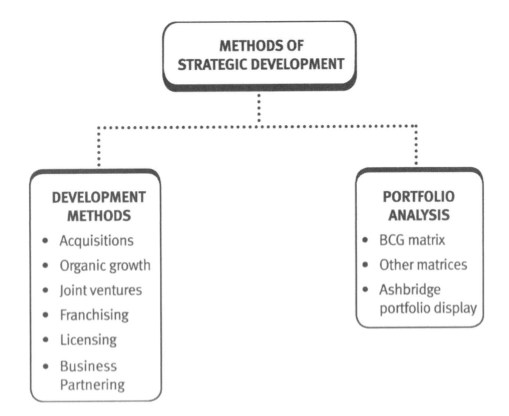

Test your understanding answers

Test your understanding 1

Suitability

- The hotel market is becoming increasingly more competitive, so it might make more sense for Blueberry to try to diversify its activities more.

- Furthermore, the acquisition does not address Blueberry's underlying problems of inconsistent customer service levels.

- On the other hand, the Villa d'Oesta already has a world class spa facility and would fit well into Blueberry's current strategy of moving more up-market.

- Also the goodwill attached to the Villa's reputation could enhance Blueberry's image, depending on branding decisions.

Feasibility

- Financing the acquisition could prove problematic:

- Debt finance: Historically, the board has chosen to keep Blueberry's financial gearing level relatively low. Blueberry's existing clientele of shareholders may thus resist any major increase in gearing.

- Equity finance: Given losses in two out of the last three years, Blueberry may struggle to raise the purchase price via a rights issue.

Acceptability

- Growth by acquisition is generally quicker than organic growth, thus satisfying institutional shareholders' desire to see growth in revenues and dividends.

- Further work is needed to assess whether the $50m asking price is acceptable.

- Buying another hotel should enable Blueberry to gain additional economies of scale with respect to insurance, staff costs such as pensions and purchasing economies on drinks. This should boost margins and profitability further.

- The new hotel would fit well into Blueberry's existing portfolio of hotels, for example, by having significant cash inflows throughout the year in contrast to Blueberry's highly seasonal business, thus reducing the overall level of risk.

Preliminary Recommendations

- The opportunity to acquire the Villa d'Oeste should be rejected on the grounds that financing the acquisition would be problematic at present.

- Blueberry should instead focus on improving facilities and quality in existing hotels before looking to expand through acquisition.

Test your understanding 2

1   A franchise arrangement would work well here. There is more than just manufacturing involved – there is the whole retail offering, and entering into franchise agreements would be a quick, effective way of expanding.

2   Unless the oil company feels that, because of its size, there is no need for joint research, development, marketing and lobbying, a strategic alliance of some sort could be useful. Research costs and findings could be shared with other oil companies. Together they could bring powerful pressure to bear on governments to, for example, allow more generous time scales for implementation of the new technology. Alternatively, the new energy technology could be developed within a joint venture organisation.

3   Almost certainly, this company would expand by licensing (refer to chapter 5; section 4) local brewing companies to make and distribute its product.

Test your understanding 3

Orange juice is a cash cow.

Pomegranate juice is a question mark, which the company wants to turn into a star.

Professional skill:

This answer would not be sufficient to score well in the examination. This paper is not about simply getting to the correct categorisation or answer. It is about evidencing the route taken to get to that answer through reasoned analysis. The best approach to take to a BCG question would be

- try to justify whether market growth is high or low

- try to justify why you think market share is high or low

- categorise the business according to the BCG terminology

- evaluate whether the suggested BCG strategy would be appropriate in this instance

---

Let's examine how an examination answer might look for orange juice:

The market for orange juice appears to be mature (low growth). It sells in huge quantities but these volumes do not appear to have changed for many years.

Fruity Drinks' market share is high. It sells in huge quantities and the marketing manager suggests that the company does very well in this market.

This would suggest that the product is a 'cash cow' in terms of the BCG terminology and should be exploited in order to support Fruity Drinks' other products. Fruity Drinks has long term contracts with a number of supermarket chains which should support this strategy, and Fruity Drinks' investment in advanced production and bottling suggests that it is unlikely to consider exiting the market altogether. The orange juice business unit should be used to support other products such as pomegranate juice.

Professional skill:

Compare this answer to the original 'answer'. This answer is more detailed, has shown a better understanding of the model, has used the scenario better and has a reasoned and justified opinion. This is what would be needed in order to score sufficient marks in this type of requirement in the exam.

Test your understanding 4

While in practice you would have more detail on which to base your findings – the model could be applied as:

- fast food outlets – heartland (or ballast as it is debatable whether further opportunities exist for value to be added)

- jeans – alien (possibly edge of heartland if you believe that skills can be transferred to identifying consumer trends in clothing as well)

- hotels – value trap. Head office may believe that it has the skills to add value on the food side but in reality CSFs are more concerned with marketing, staffing, cost control

- property development – alien.

As with using the BCG matrix, it will be important in the examination that your answer is not laid out as we see above. You will need to provide more relevance and depth. You should have a separate evaluation for each business unit that follows these steps:

- comment on the opportunities to add value to this business unit (therefore discuss the problems or issues being faced by this business unit)

- comment on the ability of the parent to add value to this business unit (this therefore means that you should be identifying and explaining the parent's abilities and how they relate to the problems identified)

- suggest how the business unit would be classified under the parenting matrix

- evaluate whether the suggested strategy from the parenting matrix would be appropriate in this scenario.

Governance general principles

Chapter learning objectives

Upon completion of this chapter you will be able to:

- discuss the nature of the principal-agent relationship in the context of governance

- analyse the issues connected with the separation of ownership and control over organisation activity

- discuss public sector, private sector, charitable status and non-governmental (NGO and quasi-NGOs) forms of organisation, including agency relationships, stakeholders' aims and objectives and performance criteria

- assess and evaluate the strategic objectives, leadership and governance arrangements specific to public sector organisations as contrasted with private sector

- explain democratic control, political influence and policy implementation in public sector organisations

- discuss obligations of the public sector organisations to meet the economy, effectiveness, efficiency (3 'E's) criteria and promote public value

PER

One of the PER performance objectives (PO4) is that you contribute to effective governance in your area. You evaluate, monitor and implement risk management procedures, complying with the spirit and the letter of policies, laws and regulations Working through this chapter should help you understand how to demonstrate that objective.

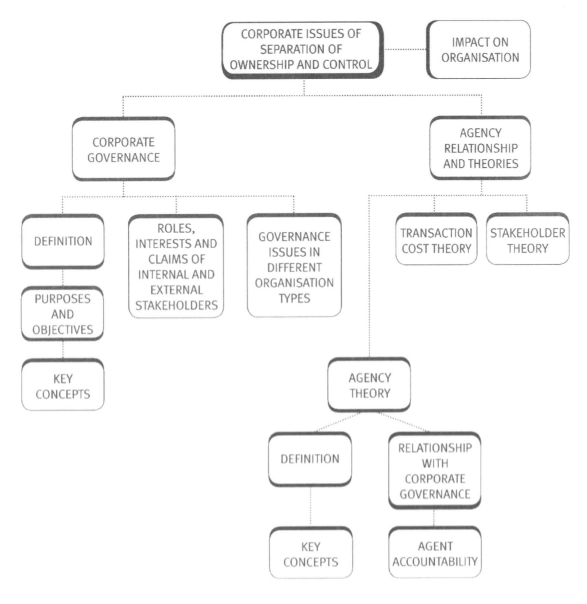

1 Company ownership and control

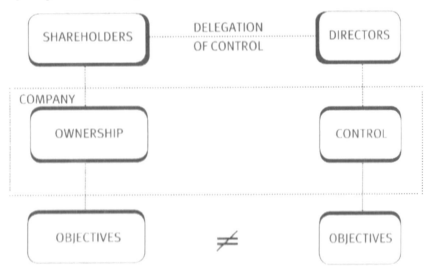

A 'joint stock company' is a company which has issued shares.

- Since the formation of joint stock companies in the 19th century, they have become the dominant form of business organisation within the UK.

- Companies that are quoted on a stock market such as the London Stock Exchange are often extremely complex and require a substantial investment in equity to fund them, i.e. they often have large numbers of shareholders.

- Shareholders delegate control to professional managers (the board of directors) to run the company on their behalf. The Board members act as agents (see later).

- Shareholders normally play a passive role in the day-to-day management of the company.

- Directors own less than 1% of the shares of most of the UK's 100 largest quoted companies and only four out of ten directors of listed companies own any shares in their business.

- Separation of ownership and control leads to a potential conflict of interests between directors and shareholders.

- This conflict is an example of the principal-agent (discussed later in this chapter).

2   What is 'corporate governance'?

The **Cadbury Report 1992** provides a useful definition:

- 'the system by which companies are directed and controlled'.

An expansion might include:

- 'in the interests of shareholders' highlighting the agency issue involved

- 'and in relation to those beyond the company boundaries' or

- 'and stakeholders' suggesting a much broader definition that brings in concerns over social responsibility.

To include these final elements is to recognise the need for organisations to be accountable to someone or something.

 Governance could therefore be described as:

- **'the system by which companies are directed and controlled in the interests of shareholders and other stakeholders.'**

Coverage of governance

Companies are directed and controlled from inside and outside the company. Good governance requires the following to be considered:

Direction from within:

- the nature and structure of those who set direction, the board of directors

- the need to monitor major forces through risk analysis

- the need to control operations: internal control.

Control from outside:

- the need to be knowledgeable about the regulatory framework that defines codes of best practice, compliance and legal statute

- the wider view of corporate position in the world through social responsibility and ethical decisions.

3 The business case for governance

Providing a business case for governance is important in order to enlist management support. Corporate governance is claimed to bring the following benefits:

- It is suggested that strengthening the control structure of a business increases accountability of management and maximises sustainability.

- Institutional investors believe that better financial performance is achieved through better management, and better managers pay attention to governance, hence the company is more attractive to such investors.

- The above points may cause the share price to rise – which can be referred to as the "governance dividend" (i.e. the benefit that shareholders receive from good corporate governance).

- Additionally, a socially responsible company may be more attractive to customers and investors hence revenues and share price may rise (a "social responsibility dividend").

The hard point to prove is how far this business case extends and what the returns actually are.

4   Purpose and objectives of corporate governance

Corporate governance has both purposes and objectives.

For the private sector:

- The basic purpose of corporate governance is to monitor those parties within a company which control the resources owned by investors.

- The primary objective of sound corporate governance is to contribute to improved corporate performance and accountability in creating long term shareholder value.

For the public and not-for-profit sectors:

Often objectives within these organisations are more complex and conflicting.

Organisations are often appraised according to the "value for money" (VFM) that they generate.

Value for money may be defined as performance of an activity to simultaneously achieve economy, efficiency and effectiveness.

This means maximising benefits for the lowest cost and has three constituent elements:

- Economy – a measure of inputs to achieve a certain service or level of service.

- Effectiveness – a measure of outputs, i.e. services/facilities.

- Efficiency – the optimum of economy and effectiveness, i.e. the measure of outputs over inputs. These concepts will be discussed in greater detail in section 6 of this chapter.

CORPORATE GOVERNANCE

PURPOSES

Primary:

Monitor those parties within a company who control the resources owned by investors.

Supporting:

- Ensure there is a suitable balance of power on the board of directors.
- Ensure executive directors are remunerated fairly.
- Make the board of directors responsible for monitoring and managing risk.
- Ensure the external auditors remain independent and free from the influence of the company.
- Address other issues, e.g. business ethics, corporate social responsibility (CSR), and protection of 'whistleblowers'.

OBJECTIVES

Primary:

Contribute to improved corporate performance and accountability in creating long-term shareholder value.

Supporting:

- Control the controllers by increasing the amount of reporting and disclosure to all stakeholders.
- Increase level of confidence and transparency in company activities for all investors (existing and potential) and thus promote growth.
- Ensure that the company is run in a legal and ethical manner.
- Build in control at the top that will 'cascade' down the organisation.

Test your understanding 1

Briefly describe the role of corporate governance.

 5   Key concepts

The foundation to governance is the action of the individual. These actions are guided by a person's moral stance.

Importance of concepts in governance

Importance in governance

An appropriate level of morality or ethical behaviour is important for a number of reasons:

- Codes provide the principle to behaviour; it is the individual's ethical stance that translates this into action in a given business situation.

- The existence of given levels of ethical behaviour improves vital public perception and support for the accountancy profession and actions of individuals within that profession.

- Such moral virtue operates as a guide to individual, personal behaviour as well as in a business context.

- The existence of such moral virtue provides trust in the agency relationship between the accountant and others such as auditors. This trust is an essential ingredient for successful relationships.

Characteristics which are important in the development of an appropriate moral stance include the following:

Fairness

- A sense of equality in dealing with internal stakeholders.

- A sense of even-handedness in dealing with external stakeholders.

- An ability to reach an equitable judgement in a given ethical situation.

Openness/transparency

- One of the underlying principles of corporate governance; it is one of the 'building blocks' that underpin a sound system of governance.

- In particular, transparency is required in the agency relationship. In terms of definition, transparency means openness (say, of discussions), clarity, lack of withholding of relevant information unless necessary.

- It has a default position of information provision rather than concealment.

Innovation

- Innovation occurs when a firm "transforms knowledge and ideas into new products, processes and systems for the benefit of the firm and its stakeholders".

- In the context of corporate governance, this covers innovation and experimentation in reporting, allowing the business to move away from rigid compliance, and towards the better communication of its individual value creation story for its providers of financial capital.

- Ultimately, innovation improves a firm's reporting performance to the benefit of investors and consumers.

- Much of the knowledge from which innovation stems is tacit and "local," meaning that such knowledge is unique to the company and the environment in which the knowledge arises.

- In addition, the capacity of a firm to integrate external knowledge is crucial for successful innovation.

Scepticism

- Scepticism (often referred to as professional scepticism) is an attitude which includes a questioning mind, being alert to conditions which may indicate possible misstatement due to error or fraud. This is to provide a critical assessment of evidence.

- For example, The UK Corporate Governance Code provisions advocate for non-executives to apply scepticism in order to challenge and scrutinise management effectively.

Independence

- Independence from personal influence of senior management for non-executive directors (NEDs).

- Independence of the board from operational involvement.

- Independence of directorships from overt personal motivation since the organisation should be run for the benefit of its owners.

- A quality possessed by individuals and refers to the avoidance of being unduly influenced by a vested interest.

- This freedom enables a more objective position to be taken on issues compared to those who consider vested interests or other loyalties.

Probity/honesty

- Honesty in financial/positional reporting.

- Perception of honesty of the finance team(s) from internal and external stakeholders.

- A foundation ethical stance in both principles- and rules-based systems.

Illustration 1 – Sibir Energy

In 2008 Russian oil giant Sibir Energy announced plans to purchase a number of properties from a major shareholder, a Russian billionaire. These properties included a Moscow Hotel and a suspended construction project originally planned to be the world's tallest building.

This move represented a major departure from Sibir Energy's usual operations and the legitimacy of the transactions was questioned. The company was also criticised for not considering the impact on the remaining minority shareholders.

The Sibir CEO's efforts to defend the transactions were in vain and he was suspended when it emerged that the billionaire shareholder owed Sibir Energy over $300m. The impact on the company's reputation has been disastrous. The accusations of 'scandal' led to stock exchange trading suspension in February 2009 and a fall in the share price of almost 80% since its peak in 2008.

Responsibility

- Willingness to accept liability for the outcome of governance decisions.

- Clarity in the definition of roles and responsibilities for action.

- Conscientious business and personal behaviour.

Accountability

- The obligation of an individual or organisation to account for its actions and activities.

- Accounting for business position as a result of acceptance of responsibility.

- Providing clarity in communication channels with internal and external stakeholders.

- Development and maintenance of risk management and control systems.

Reputation

- Developing and sustaining personal reputation through other moral virtues.

- Developing and sustaining the moral stance of the organisation.

- Developing and sustaining the moral stance of the accounting profession.

Illustration 2 – BP Chief Executive

> Lord Browne resigned from his position as CEO of oil giant BP in May 2007 due to media stories regarding his private life.
>
> His resignation was to save BP from embarrassment after a newspaper had won a court battle to print details of his private life. Lord Browne apologised for statements made in court regarding a four year relationship with Jeff Chevalier that he described as being 'untruthful' (he had actually lied, this relationship had existed).
>
> Due to this 'untruthfulness' Lord Browne gave up a formidable distinguished 41 year career with BP, and did the honourable thing by resigning as the damage to his reputation would have impacted adversely on BP.

Judgement

- The ability to reach and communicate meaningful conclusions.

- The ability to weigh up numerous issues and give each due consideration.

- The development of a balanced and evaluated approach to making business decisions and personal relationships covering intellectual and moral aspects.

- To make decisions in the best interests of the organisation.

Integrity

- A steadfast adherence to strict ethical standards despite any other pressures to act otherwise.

- Integrity describes the personal ethical position of the highest standards of professionalism and probity.

- It is an underlying and underpinning principle of corporate governance and it is required that all those representing shareholder interests in agency relationships both possess and exercise absolute integrity at all times.

Test your understanding 2 – Key concepts

Fred is a certified accountant. He runs his own accountancy practice from home, where he prepares personal taxation and small business accounts for about 75 clients. Fred believes that he provides a good service and his clients generally seem happy with the work Fred provides.

At work, Fred tends to give priority to his business friends that he plays golf with. Charges made to these clients tend to be lower than others – although Fred tends to guess how much each client should be charged as this is quicker than keeping detailed time-records.

Fred is also careful not to ask too many questions about client affairs when preparing personal and company taxation returns. His clients are grateful that Fred does not pry too far into their affairs, although the taxation authorities have found some irregularities in some tax returns submitted by Fred. Fortunately the client concerned has always accepted responsibility for the errors and Fred has kindly provided his services free of charge for the next year to assist the client with any financial penalties.

Required:

Discuss whether the moral stance taken by Fred is appropriate.

6 Operational areas affected by issues in corporate governance

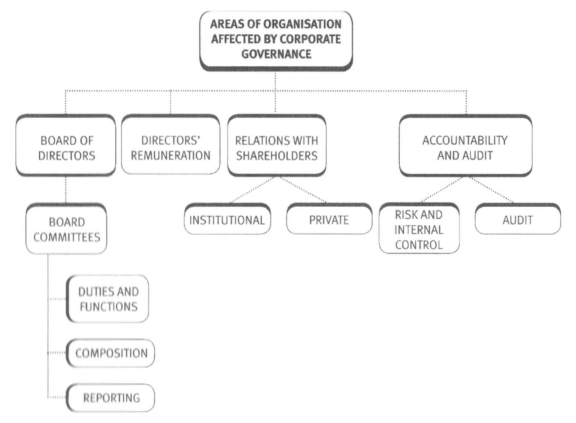

Further detail of the impact on these areas will be covered in later chapters.

Is governance relevant to all companies?

Issues in corporate governance relate to companies, and in particular listed companies whose shares are traded on major stock markets. However, similar issues might apply to smaller companies, and certainly to many large not-for-profit organisations.

	Large listed company	Private company	Not-for-profit organisation
Primary accountability	Shareholders and regulators	Shareholders	Fund providers, regulators, general public, members (where applicable)
Principal stakeholders	Shareholders	Shareholders	Donors, grant providers, regulators, general public, service users, members (if applicable)
Main methods of monitoring performance	Financial statements	Financial statements	Financial statements, other financial and non-financial measures
Governance board structure	Executive and NEDs. Appointment through formal process in line with governance requirements	Executive directors. Appointment may be the result of shareholding or other recruitment processes	Volunteer trustees, paid and unpaid management team. Appointments through recruitment, recommendation or word of mouth, or election process
Openness and transparency	In line with corporate governance requirements	Limited disclosure requirements	Limited requirements but large demand due to methods of funding

- Corporate governance is a matter of great importance for large public companies, where the separation of ownership from management is much wider than for small private companies.

- Public companies raise capital on the stock markets, and institutional investors hold vast portfolios of shares and other investments. Investors need to know that their money is reasonably safe.

- Should there be any doubts about the integrity or intentions of the individuals in charge of a public company, the value of the company's shares will be affected and the company will have difficulty raising any new capital should it wish to do so.

- The scope of corporate governance for private and not-for-profit organisations will be much reduced when compared with a listed company, especially as there are no legal or regulatory requirements to comply with.

- The ownership and control, organisational objectives, risks and therefore focus may be different from a listed company. However, many of the governance principles will still be applicable to other entities.

- The public and not-for-profit sectors have voluntary best practice guidelines for governance which, while appreciating the differences in organisation and objective, cover many of the same topics (composition of governing bodies, accountability, risk management, transparency, etc.) included within the UK Corporate Governance Code (2010).

- In not-for-profit organisations, a key governance focus will be to demonstrate to existing and potential fund providers that money is being spent in an appropriate manner, in line with the organisations' objectives.

7 Public Sector Governance

Public Sector Governance

A range of organisations exists in most economies with three types predominant.

- Private sector – exist to make a profit

- Charities – which are charitable or benevolent

- Public sector – delivering goods or services not provided by "for profit" entities

The latter are operated predominantly by the state (self-governing autonomous region), made up of four aspects:

- The government – an elected body

- The legislature – e.g. in the UK Houses of Parliament

- The judiciary – independently appointed

- The secretariat – separate administrative body to carry out state functions e.g. Education

In addition government organisations can exist at different levels. For example:

National government

Usually based in the capital city and is subdivided into central government departments e.g. in the UK the Ministry of Defence and is led by a Minister from the elected governing political party.

They are also supported by permanent government employees (in the UK known as the Civil Service) who are employed to provide advice to the Minister in charge and assist in the implementation of government policy.

Sub-national government

At this level, countries can be organised into regional local authorities e.g. in the UK local council authorities.

They are, in many countries, managed by elected representatives as with the national governments and supported by permanent officials similar to the Civil Servants noted above.

They take control of specific functions which are deemed to be best controlled by local people who will have knowledge of various demographic needs. As such the services they control e.g. Town Planning will report to the local authority on selected performance measures.

Supranational government

In this case National governments come together for a specific purpose e.g. the European Union in Brussels.

The purpose is to prevent disagreement between member states and foster a collective opinion on high level international issues.

Stakeholders and the Public Sector

The complexity of the stakeholder relationship and the claims that stakeholders have are more complicated in the public sector.

Of particular sensitivity in this context is the use of taxpayers' funds which can be perceived to be used for services which are of no benefit to the person paying the tax. This gives rise to the question of agent and principal within the public sector.

The problem of agency in the public sector

Those that manage a business (the agents) do not own that business but manage the business on behalf of those who do own it (the principals), hence the concept of agency. This is a key concept in the context of corporate governance.

In the public sector the principals are different and rather than being for example shareholders are often those that fund and/or use the activity.

Therefore whilst private and public companies have shareholders, public sector organisations carry out their important roles on behalf of those who fund the service, mainly taxpayers, and the users of the services e.g. patients in a hospital. Funders and service users are therefore sometimes the same people (i.e. taxpayers placing their children in state school) but often they are not, giving rise to disagreements on how much is spent and on what service provision – the fundamental nature of political debate is about how much state funding should be allocated.

Public sector organisations emphasise different types of objectives to the private sector. Whereas private companies tend to seek to optimise their competitive strategy and advantages, public sector organisations tend to be concerned with social purposes and delivering their services efficiently, effectively and with good value for money.

Their objectives can therefore be more complex to develop.

This is often depicted as the three Es:

- Economy – to deliver the service on time and within budget and to obtain the service at the lowest cost thus delivering value to the taxpayers, as well as those working in them and those using the service. This will achieve consistency with policy objectives.

- Effectiveness – to deliver the service the organisation was created to provide.

- Efficiency – to deliver the service with the best use of resources; an efficient organisation delivers more for a given level of resource input than an inefficient one.

Other forms of organisations

In addition to the private and public sector, there is also a "third sector".

This term is used to describe those organisations that are designed to deliver services or benefits that cannot be delivered by the other two categories.

- Non-governmental organisations NGO'S

These are task-oriented and driven by people with a common interest providing a variety of service and humanitarian functions, e.g. the Red Cross.

They are often privately funded, managed by executive and non-executive boards. In addition, they often have to answer to a board of trustees. This board is in place to ensure that the NGO operates in line with its stated purpose.

In this instance the agency relationship exists between the NGO and the donors.

- Quasi-autonomous non-governmental organisations – QuANGOs

They are organisations funded by taxpayers, but not controlled directly by central government e.g. The Forestry Commission, offering expertise and a degree of independence. QuANGOs are often criticised for not being accountable as their reporting lines are blurred.

They are predominantly funded by the taxpayer and hence should account for their actions. The problem exists as they report to many principals (part of the purpose of the QuANGO).

The agency relationship in this instance is therefore unclear.

Governance arrangements in the Public Sector

With no one single mechanism being appropriate to control and monitor the achievement of objectives, accountability is achieved, at least in part, by having a system of reporting and oversight.

This entails those in charge of the service delivery reporting to an external body of oversight which may be a board of governors or trustees.

The oversight body acts in the interest of the providers of finance, the taxpayer to ensure that the service is delivered on time and is for the benefit of the users. Membership may include executive and non-executive positions similar to the private sector.

The roles of the oversight bodies include:

- To ensure the service complies with government rules
- To ensure that performance targets are met
- To set and monitor performance against budgets
- To oversee senior appointments
- To monitor management performance
- To remove underperforming senior managers
- To report to higher authorities on the organisations being monitored.

Changing policy objectives

There is constant debate about the extent, operation and often the need for public sector organisations.

In part this discussion revolves around which political ideology you support but also the change to policy objectives mean that public sector organisations are also required to change over time. For example, there is currently a debate in the UK over the size and expense of the defence budget and therefore the structure of the Ministry of Defence.

This has raised the argument surrounding the process of privatisation i.e. allowing a previously publicly funded organisation to be provided by the private sector often by making it a publicly listed company and encouraging the people to buy shares in it. For example the privatisation of the Post Office in the UK (2013).

The debate continues as to the success of these ventures, arguments for and against ranging depending on your political bias.

Those in favour argue:

- More efficiency in delivery via profit driven performance measures

- Increased competition driving better value for money to the consumer

- Better quality management

- Improved governance.

Those against argue:

- Profit is not the motive for improved strategic services e.g. health

- Increased competition will lead to detrimental change

- Key services e.g. transport should always remain under state control to ensure effective delivery.

In a democracy, political parties argue over the nature of public policy and they do so from a particular set of underlying assumptions. Some of these underlying assumptions influence the way they argue for particular outcomes and the way in which they guide a government when they achieve political power. It tends to be the case (with exceptions) that left-leaning governments prefer a larger state sector, with more state spending and more public sector employment, while right-leaning governments prefer more to be achieved in the private sector and less by government.

In addition, changing policy objectives mean that some public sector organisations are required to change over time, both in size and in what they are asked to do. As governments change, some public sector organisations grow in size and become more important, and others become small and less important.

The debate is often intense and enduring. In the case of health services, for example, some believe that health should always be entirely within the public sector and entirely funded by the taxpayer. This means that, for the service user (the patient), everything is free at the point of use. Others strongly believe that this is a misuse of public funds and that people should pay for health services in other ways, such as through an insurance or subscription scheme. Likewise with university education: some believe it should be paid for by the state and others believe that students should pay. In each case, debates are complicated.

If there were easy and convincing answers, there would be less debate, but public opinion is split on most areas of public debate and this fuels political debate and, in turn, how public sector organisations are configured in line with particular political influences.

Strategic objectives and leadership in the public sector

While most private sector organisations are independent in that they are 'stand-alone' companies answerable to their shareholders, most public sector organisations are part of a larger public sector structure. A health authority, such as the NHS, cannot act alone and as it sees fit. It is funded by government and is tightly controlled in what it is asked to do and how it achieves its aims. Likewise, a school in the public sector will rarely have the freedom to do as it likes in terms of what and how it teaches, who it appoints and where it locates itself. In each case, the public sector organisation is helping to achieve and implement a set of higher government policy objectives.

This is not to say that individual public sector organisations do not have strategic objectives, however. Each one must work out how it will achieve what it is asked to do but the autonomy given to individual organisations varies.

The 'three Es' framework discussed earlier assists in understanding this:

Each public sector organisation must be strategically **effective** in that it must achieve the objectives established for it in carrying out government policy.

Because they are funded by public money, they must also be **efficient** and make the most of whatever resources they are provided with.

Finally, they must also be **economical** in that they must work within a specified budget and deliver desired outputs within that budget.

Accordingly, there is an emphasis on "value for money" (VFM) and service delivery. When public sector organisations are occasionally criticised in the media, it is usually because they have either overspent, underperformed, or both.

Governance and leadership arrangements

There is no single way in which public sector organisations are governed. Accountability is gained in part by having a system of reporting and oversight of one body over others. Because there is no market mechanism of monitoring performance (as there is with listed companies, for example), other ways must be found to ensure that organisations achieve the objectives and service delivery targets established for them.

In some cases, then, a head of service or a board of directors must report to an external body of oversight. The oversight body may be a board of governors, a council of reference, a board of trustees, an oversight board or similar. In each case, its role is to hold the management of the service to account for the delivery of the public service and to ensure that the organisation is run for the benefit of the service users. Because public sector organisations are not held to account by shareholders as with business companies, the oversight body is often put in place as a means of holding the management to account. In this respect, oversight bodies are acting in the interests of service funders (usually taxpayers) in making public sector organisations accountable.

Typical (and general) roles of oversight bodies include the following, although their roles do vary substantially depending on jurisdiction and government policy.

- Firstly, they are there to comply with government rules on whichever public sector governance applies. So a school may have a board of governors in order to comply with the local authority or education department rules on school governance. A hospital's management may, likewise report to a superordinate body possibly overseeing several other hospitals at the same time.

- Secondly, it is their role to ensure the organisation is well-run and meets the performance targets established for it by higher levels of government. It may receive internal or external audit reports to help achieve this or make visits and other interventions to ensure that the organisation is performing to expectation.

- Thirdly, the oversight body may be involved in budget negotiations and then in monitoring performance against budget and any number of other agreed financial measures in a similar way that a management accountant might in a conventional business.

- Fourthly, it is likely to be involved in making senior appointments to the public sector body and in monitoring the performance of management on an ongoing basis. In many cases, boards of governors in schools or universities, for example, have the power to remove a senior manager (perhaps a head teacher) if they believe he or she is underperforming and not delivering the quality of services required.

- Finally, they are sometimes required to report upwards, perhaps to local or central authorities, on the organisations they have oversight over.

In conclusion, there is an increasing move in some situations to run some public services along similar lines to private companies. This means they may have an executive board and also some non-executive membership on the board also.

Agency in not-for-profit organisations

In a not-for-profit organisation, such as a charity, there are no residual claims to be paid out and no owners expecting to earn a profit. Therefore, within these organisations, any agency relationship between owners and managers is clouded.

Furthermore, without residual claims or stock, there is no need for management to worry about the organisation being bought or sold in the marketplace. These conditions may suggest that managers in a not-for-profit organisation have increased opportunity to pursue self-interest.

In the place of these owners are the donors. They contribute to the organisation with the expectation that something good will result such as lives being saved, the environment cleaned up, or people educated. Although it is not financial, they anticipate a return from their investment and will invest elsewhere if their expectations are not met.

Often, the largest donors also become board members of the organisation. Although the function of a not-for-profit board is similar to for profits, there are some differences that are a result of the absence of residual claims. For example, in for profits, the threat of outside takeover provides the discipline to allow insiders to play a significant role on the board.

Without this threat and to prevent collusion or expropriation of funds, not-for-profit boards should be dominated by outsiders. Furthermore, not-for-profit board members are often substantial donors who serve without pay as this shows their interest in the well-being of the organisation.

The decision control role of not-for-profit boards is the same as for profits boards. In general, not-for-profit boards also have a special responsibility for generating and managing financial resources. They are often called on to personally contribute to the institution, lead campaigns to encourage others to contribute, and manage the financial resources held by the institution. Together, these two responsibilities, decision control and financial management, are among the most important duties of the boards of not-for-profit organisations.

(NB: see also chapter 23 section 2 which considers the financial objectives of NFP organisations)

8 Internal corporate governance stakeholders

Within an organisation there are a number of internal parties involved in corporate governance. These parties can be referred to as internal stakeholders.

Stakeholder theory will be covered in more detail in chapter 9. A useful definition of a stakeholder, for use at this point, is **'any person or group that can affect or be affected by the policies or activities of an organisation'**.

Each internal stakeholder has:

- an operational role within the company

- a role in the corporate governance of the company

- a number of interests in the company (referred to as the **stakeholder 'claim'**).

Stakeholder	Operational role	Corporate governance role	Main interests in company
Directors	Responsible for the actions of the corporation.	Control company in best interest of stakeholders.	• pay • performance-linked bonuses • share options • status • reputation • power.
Company secretary	Ensure compliance with company legislation and regulations and keep board members informed of their legal responsibilities.	Advise board on corporate governance matters.	
Sub-board management	Run business operations. Implement board policies.	• Identify and evaluate risks faced by company • Enforce controls • Monitor success • Report concerns	• pay • performance-linked bonuses • job stability • career progression • status • working conditions
Employees	Carry out orders of management.	• Comply with internal controls • Report breaches.	
Employee representatives, e.g. trade unions	Protect employee interests.	Highlight and take action against breaches in governance requirements, e.g. protection of whistle-blowers.	• power • status

Internal stakeholders

The board of directors

- Has the responsibility for giving direction to the company.

- Delegates most executive powers to the executive management, but reserves some decision-making powers to itself, such as decisions about raising finance, paying dividends and making major investments.

- Executive directors are individuals who combine their role as director with their position within the executive management of the company.

- Non-executive directors (NEDs) perform the functions of director only, without any executive responsibilities.

- Executive directors combine their stake in the company as a director with their stake as fully paid employees, and their interests are, therefore, likely to differ from those of the NEDs.

- More detail on directors will be found in chapter 11.

The company secretary

- Often responsible for advising the board on corporate governance matters and ensuring board procedures are followed.

- Duties vary with the size of the company, but are likely to include:
  - arranging meetings of the board
  - drafting and circulating minutes of board meetings
  - ensuring that board decisions are communicated to staff and outsiders
  - completing and signing of various returns
  - filing accounts with statutory authorities
  - maintaining statutory documents and registers required by the authorities.

- Company secretary may act as the general administrator and head office manager. This role may include a responsibility for maintaining accounting records, corresponding with legal advisers, tax authorities and trade associations.

- Does not have the same legal responsibilities as directors.

- Should always act in the interests of the company in any event of conflict or dispute with directors.

- Is responsible to the board and accountable through the chairman and Chief Executive Officer (CEO) for duties carried out.

- Has the same interests and claims in the company as other employees.

- Remuneration package should be settled by the board or remuneration committee.

Management

- Responsible for running business operations.

- Accountable to the board of directors (and more particularly to the CEO).

- Will take an interest in corporate governance decisions which may impact their current position and potential future positions (as main board directors, possibly).

- Individual managers, like executive directors, may want power, status and a high remuneration.

- As employees, they may see their stake in the company in terms of the need for a career and an income.

Employees

- Have a stake in their company because it provides them with a job and an income.

- Have expectations about what their company should do for them, e.g. security of employment, good pay and suitable working conditions.

- Some employee rights are protected by employment law, but the powers of employees are generally limited.

9 External corporate governance stakeholders

A company has many external stakeholders involved in corporate governance.

Each stakeholder has:

- A role to play in influencing the operation of the company

- Its own interests and claims in the company

A stakeholder claim is where a stakeholder wants something from an organisation. These claims can be concerned with the way a stakeholder may want to influence the activities of an organisation or by the way they are affected by the organisation.

There are:

- Direct claims – made by stakeholders directly with the organisation and unambiguous e.g. trade unions. Effectively they have their own voice.

- Indirect claims – where the stakeholder is "voiceless", e.g. an individual customer of a large retail organisation or the environment with the inevitable problem of interpretation.

External party	Main role	Interests and claims in company
Auditors	Independent review of company's reported financial position.	<ul><li>fees</li><li>reputation</li><li>quality of relationship</li><li>compliance with audit requirements.</li></ul>
Regulators	Implementing and monitoring regulations.	<ul><li>compliance with regulations</li><li>effectiveness of regulations.</li></ul>
Government	Implementing and maintaining laws with which all companies must comply.	<ul><li>compliance with laws</li><li>payment of taxes</li><li>level of employment</li><li>levels of imports/ exports.</li></ul>
Stock exchange	Implementing and maintaining rules and regulations for companies listed on the exchange.	<ul><li>compliance with rules and regulations</li><li>fees.</li></ul>
Small investors	Limited power with use of vote.	<ul><li>maximisation of shareholder value.</li></ul>
Institutional investors	Through considered use of their votes can (and should) beneficially influence corporate policy.	<ul><li>value of shares and dividend payments</li><li>security of funds invested</li><li>timeliness of information received from company</li><li>shareholder rights are observed.</li></ul>
Trade unions	Primary interest will be in the pay and working conditions of their members.	<ul><li>concerned by poor corporate governance</li><li>poor management of health and safety risks</li><li>industrial relations.</li></ul>

Institutional investors

Institutional investors and corporate governance

Pressure is being brought to bear on institutional investors to give more attention to corporate governance issues.

- Due to the size of their shareholdings, institutional investors can exert significant influence on corporate policy and take an active role in bringing under-performing companies to task.

- Guidelines issued by the Institutional Shareholders Committee in 2002 encourage institutional investors to develop a policy on corporate governance and to apply this policy when voting in company meetings.

- It is argued that just as directors have obligations to their shareholders, institutional investors have obligations to the many individuals (pension scheme holders, unit trust investors and so on) whose money they invest.

- The main kind of institutional investors are:

    - Pension funds

    - Insurance companies

    - Mutual funds

    - Sovereign funds

One of the largest institutional investors in the UK is Legal and General.

Stakeholder conflict

Stakeholder conflict arises when the needs of some stakeholder groups compromise the expectations of others. A business has to make choices which some stakeholders might not like.

For example, the cheapest supplier goods, which can help keep prices down for customers, must not come at the expense of ethical practice by suppliers or product safety. Whilst the end product may be cheaper, association with an unethical supplier or low quality product risks damaging our business reputation and financial loss.

10   What is agency theory?

 Agency theory is a group of concepts describing the nature of the agency relationship deriving from the separation between ownership and control.

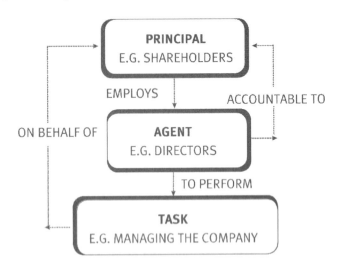

Agency theory and corporate governance

Agency theory can help to explain the actions of the various interest groups in the corporate governance debate.

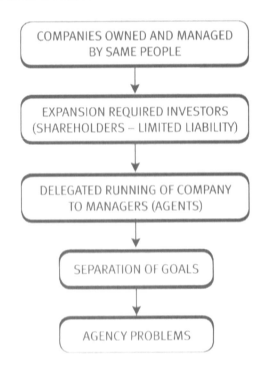

Agency theory and corporate governance

Examination of theories behind corporate governance provides a foundation for understanding the issue in greater depth and a link between an historical perspective and its application in modern governance standards.

- Historically, companies were owned and managed by the same people. For economies to grow it was necessary to find a larger number of investors to provide finance to assist in corporate expansion.

This led to the concept of limited liability and the development of stock markets to buy and sell shares.

- Limited liability – the concept that shareholders are legally responsible for the debts of the company only to the sum of the nominal value of their shares.

- Stock market – the "market" in which publicly held shares are issued and traded.

- Delegation of running the firm to the agent or managers.

- Separation of goals between wealth maximisation of shareholders and the personal objectives of managers. This separation is a key assumption of agency theory.

- Possible short-term perspective of managers rather than protecting long-term shareholder wealth.

- Divorce between ownership and control linked with differing objectives creates agency problems.

Short-term perspective

This relates to a tendency to foreshorten the time horizon applied to investment decisions or to raise the discount rate well above the firms' cost of capital.

- This can come from within through managers operating in their self interest.

- This can come from outside through large institutional investors churning shares to maximise return on investment (ROI) for their investment funds and individual fund manager bonuses.

11   Key concepts of agency theory

A number of key terms and concepts are essential to understanding agency theory.

- An **agent** is employed by a **principal** to carry out a task on their behalf.

- **Agency** refers to the relationship between a principal and their agent.

- **Agency costs** are incurred by principals in monitoring agency behaviour because of a lack of trust in the good faith of agents.

- By accepting to undertake a task on their behalf, an agent reputation becomes **accountable** to the principal by whom they are employed.

- Directors (agents) have a **fiduciary responsibility** to the shareholders (principal) of their organisation (usually described through company law as 'operating in the best interests of the shareholders').

- **Stakeholders** are any person or group that can affect or be affected by the policies or activities of an organisation.

- Agent **objectives** (such as a desire for high salary, large bonus and status for a director) will differ from the principal's objectives (wealth maximisation for shareholders).

- The most important agency costs are the external audit fee, attending meetings and reading both annual reports and analyst's reports.

 Examples of principal-agent relationships

Shareholders and directors

The separation of ownership and control in a business leads to a potential conflict of interests between directors and shareholders.

- The conflict of interests between principal (shareholder) and agent (director) gives rise to the 'principal-agent problem' which is the key area of corporate governance focus.

- The principals need to find ways of ensuring that their agents act in their ('the principals') interests.

- As a result of several high profile corporate collapses, caused by over-dominant or 'fat cat' directors, there has been a very active debate about the power of boards of directors, and how stakeholders (not just shareholders) can seek to ensure that directors do not abuse their powers.

- Various reports have been published, and legislation has been enacted, in the UK and the US, which seek to improve the control that stakeholders can exercise over the board of directors of the company.

Shareholders and auditors

The other principal-agent relationship dealt with by corporate governance guidelines is that of the company with its auditors.

- The audit is seen as a key component of corporate governance, providing an independent review of the financial position of the organisation.

- Auditors act as agents to principals (shareholders) when performing an audit and this relationship brings similar concerns with regard to trust and confidence as the director-shareholder relationship.

- Like directors, auditors will have their own interests and motives to consider.

- Auditor independence from the board of directors is of great importance to shareholders and is seen as a key factor in helping to deliver audit quality. However, an audit necessitates a close working relationship with the board of directors of a company.

- This close relationship has led (and continues to lead) shareholders to question the perceived and actual independence of auditors so tougher controls and standards have been introduced to protect them.

- Who audits the auditors?

Other countries

Different ownership models in other countries raise additional principal-agent relationships which need to be considered in the context of corporate governance.

For example:

- Institutional arrangements in German companies, typified by the two-tier board (see chapter 8), allow employees to have a formal say in the running of the company.

- In Japan, there is an emphasis on a consensual management style through negotiation between the interested parties.

- In the US, there is a much greater likelihood of debt holders/major creditors or chief executives of other companies being represented on the board.

The cost of agency relationships

Agency cost

Agency costs arise largely from principals monitoring the activities of agents, and may be viewed in monetary terms, resources consumed or time taken in monitoring. Costs are borne by the principal, but may be indirectly incurred as the agent spends time and resources on certain activities. Examples of costs include:

- incentive schemes and remuneration packages for directors
- costs of management providing annual report data such as committee activity and risk management analysis, and cost of principal reviewing this data
- the cost of meetings with financial analysts and principal shareholders
- the cost of accepting higher risks than shareholders would like in the way in which the company operates
- the cost of monitoring behaviour, such as by establishing management audit procedures.

Residual loss

This is an additional type of agency cost and relates to directors furnishing themselves with expensive cars and planes etc. These costs are above and beyond the remuneration package for the director, and are a direct loss to shareholders.

Agency problem resolution measures

- Meetings between the directors and key institutional investors.
- Voting rights at the Annual General Meeting (AGM) in support of, or against, resolutions.
- Proposing resolutions for vote by shareholders at AGMs.
- Accepting takeovers.
- Divestment of shares is the ultimate threat.

Need for corporate governance

- If the market mechanism and shareholder activities are not enough to monitor the company then some form of regulation is needed.
- There are a number of codes of conduct and recommendations issued by governments and stock exchanges. Although compliance is voluntary (in the sense it is not governed by law), the fear of damage to reputation arising from governance weaknesses and the threat of delisting from stock exchange renders it difficult not to comply.
- These practical elements make up the majority of the rest of governance issues discussed in subsequent chapters.

Examples of codes

Examples of codes of conduct include:

- The UK Corporate Governance Code (2016) for Corporate Governance adopted by the Financial Conduct Authority (FCA) in the UK.

- OECD code on ethics.

- ACCA codes.

- Specific regulation regarding director remuneration and city code on takeovers.

Agent accountability

Accountability relates to:

- the need to act in shareholders' interests

- the need to provide good information such as audited accounts and annual reports

- the need to operate within a defined legal structure.

With specific regard to directors:

- Directors are accountable to shareholders.

- Directors must prove that they are discharging their responsibilities in line with shareholder expectations in the form of financial results, a clean audit report and reported compliance with codes of corporate governance.

- If the shareholders do not like what they see, they ultimately (although not necessarily practically) have the power to remove the directors and replace them.

Other accountabilities that exist within a company:

- Managers to directors – the day-to-day operation of companies is usually delegated to sub-board level management by the directors. Senior managers are therefore accountable to the directors for their actions, which are usually demonstrated through the results of the company.

- Employees to managers – managers delegate the 'doing' of the company to their employees, holding them accountable for the success, or otherwise, of how their job is done.

- Management to creditors – suppliers hold the management of a company accountable for payment of invoices on a timely basis.

- Auditors to shareholders – the audit is viewed as an essential component of corporate governance, providing an independent review of the company's financial report. Shareholders hold the auditors accountable for ensuring their review is conducted on an independent, competent and adequate basis, so that they can rely on the outcome.

Test your understanding 3

For each of the following scenarios, decide which kind of principal- agent conflict exists.

Scenario	Conflict
The CEO of a frozen food distributor decides that the company should buy the car manufacturing company Ferrari, because he is a big fan of the car.	
An employee discovers that one of the key financial controls in his area is not operating as it should, and could potentially result in losses to the company. He has not said anything because he does not want to get into trouble.	
The financial director decides to gamble £1 million of company money, obtained from a bank loan, on a football match result.	

12 Stakeholder theory

The basis for stakeholder theory is that companies are so large and their impact on society so pervasive that they should discharge accountability to many more sectors of society than solely their shareholders.

As defined in an earlier section, stakeholders are not only are affected by the organisation but they also affect the organisation.

Stakeholder theory may be the necessary outcome of agency theory given that there is a business case in considering the needs of stakeholders through improved customer perception, employee motivation, supplier stability and shareholder conscience investment.

Agency theory is a narrow form of stakeholder theory.

Refer to chapter 9 for more detail on stakeholders and the technical articles "All about stakeholders – parts 1 and 2".

Test your understanding 4

Founded in 1983 as a long distance phone operator, Globe Line has relied heavily on acquisitions to fund its growth. In the last decade it has made over 60 acquisitions, extending its reach around the planet and diversifying into data and satellite communications, internet services and web hosting. Almost all acquisitions have been paid for using the company's shares.

This high fuelled 'growth through acquisition' strategy has had a number of outcomes. One is the significant management challenge of managing diversity across the world, straining manpower resources and systems. In particular, the internal audit department has been forced to focus on operational matters simply to keep up with the speed of change.

Shareholders have, on the whole, welcomed the dramatic rise in their stock price, buoyed up by the positive credit rating given by SDL, Globe Line's favoured investment bank, who have been heavily involved in most of the acquisitions, receiving large fees for their services. Recently, some shareholders have complained about the lack of clarity of annual reports provided by Globe Line and the difficulty in assessing the true worth of a company when results change dramatically period to period due to the accounting for acquisitions.

Ben Mervin is the visionary, charismatic CEO of Globe Line. Over the course of the last three years his personal earnings topped $77 million with a severance package in place that includes $1.5 million for life and lifetime use of the corporate jet. He is a dominant presence at board meetings with board members rarely challenging his views.

Recently, a whistle-blower has alleged financial impropriety within Globe Line and institutional shareholders have demanded meetings to discuss the issue. The Chairman of the audit committee (himself a frequent flyer on the corporate jet) has consulted with the CEO over the company's proposed response.

Required:

(a)   Discuss agency costs that might exist in relation to the fiduciary relationship between shareholders and the company, Globe Line, and consider conflict resolution measures.

Professional skills:
Illustrate analysis skills when considering the agency costs that might exist and evaluation skills when considering conflict resolution measures.

13 Chapter summary

Corporate issues of separation of ownership and control
- Shareholders are the owners of a company.
- Control usually delegated to directors.
- Large company may have many shareholders.
- Interests of shareholders and directors may conflict.
- Directors may not act in the best interests of the shareholders.

Impact on organisation
- Duties of directors and functions of the board
- Composition and balance of the board (and board committees)
- Reliability of financial reporting and external auditing
- Directors' remuneration and rewards
- Risk management systems and internal control
- Rights and responsibilities of shareholders.

Corporate governance
Largely concerned with governing the relationship between shareholders and directors.

Definition
'a system by which organisations are directed and controlled'

Purposes and objectives
- Monitor those who control the assets owned by investors.
- Contribute to improved corporate performance and accountability in creating long-term shareholder value.

KEY UNDERPINNING CONCEPTS

Roles, interests and claims of stakeholders

Internal stakeholders
- Directors
- Company secretary
- Managers
- Employees
- Employee representatives.

External stakeholders
- Auditors
- Regulators
- Shareholders
- Stock exchange
- Government.

Issues and scope of governance on public, private and NGO sectors
- Influenced by the size, ownership, model and objectives of organisation.
- Democratic control, political influence and policy implementation.

AGENCY RELATIONSHIPS AND THEORIES

See diagram on next page

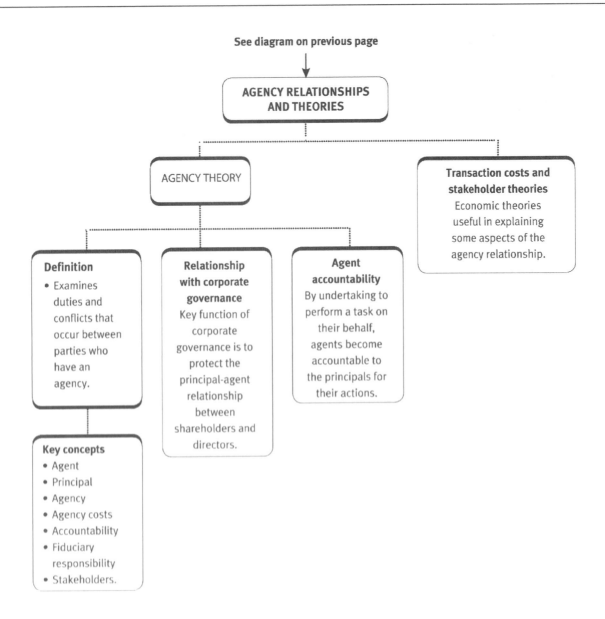

See diagram on previous page

AGENCY RELATIONSHIPS AND THEORIES

AGENCY THEORY

Transaction costs and stakeholder theories
Economic theories useful in explaining some aspects of the agency relationship.

Definition
- Examines duties and conflicts that occur between parties who have an agency.

Key concepts
- Agent
- Principal
- Agency
- Agency costs
- Accountability
- Fiduciary responsibility
- Stakeholders.

Relationship with corporate governance
Key function of corporate governance is to protect the principal-agent relationship between shareholders and directors.

Agent accountability
By undertaking to perform a task on their behalf, agents become accountable to the principals for their actions.

Test your understanding answers

Test your understanding 1

The role of corporate governance is to protect shareholder rights, enhance disclosure and transparency, facilitate effective functioning of the board and provide an efficient legal and regulatory enforcement framework.

Test your understanding 2

Overall, it can be argued that Fred is providing a professional service in accordance with the expectations of his clients.

However, the moral stance taken by Fred can be queried as follows.

- The guessing of the amounts to charge clients implies a lack of openness and transparency in invoicing and has the effect of being unfair. Friends may be charged less than other clients for the same amount of work. If other clients were aware of the situation, they would no doubt request similar treatment.

- The lack of questioning of clients about their affairs appears to be appreciated. However, this can be taken as a lack of probity on the part of Fred – without full disclosure of information Fred cannot prepare accurate taxation returns. It is likely that Fred realises this and that some errors will occur. However, Fred does not have to take responsibility for those errors; his clients do instead.

- While Fred does appear to be acting with integrity in the eyes of his clients, the lack of accuracy in the information provided to the taxation authorities eventually will affect his reputation, especially if more returns are found to be in error. In effect, Fred is not being honest with the authorities.

- Fred may wish to start ensuring that information provided to the taxation authorities is of an appropriate standard to retain his reputation and ensure that clients do trust the information he is preparing for them.

Test your understanding 3

Scenario	Conflict
The CEO of a frozen food distributor decides that the company should buy the car manufacturing company Ferrari, because he is a big fan of the shareholders.	**Shareholder – director** Director is acting in his own interests, not those of the car.
An employee discovers that one of the key financial controls in his area is not operating as it should, and could potentially result in losses to the company. He has not said anything because he does not want to get into trouble.	**Management – employee** Employee is acting in his own interests, not in those of the company.
	(**Shareholder – director** is also potential, as directors are responsible for ensuring risk and control are managed within the organisation on behalf of the shareholders.)
The financial director decides to gamble £1 million of company money, obtained from a bank loan, on a football match result.	**Bank – directors** It is the directors' responsibility to manage funds lent to it by the bank without taking excessive risks.
	Shareholders – directors It is the directors' responsibility to manage the company's assets in the best interests of the shareholders.

Test your understanding 4

(a) **Agency costs**

Agency costs exist due to the trust placed by shareholders on directors to operate in their best interests. These costs will rise when a lack of trust exists, although misplaced trust in a relationship will have hidden costs that may lead to poor management and even corporate failure.

Residual costs are a part of agency costs. These are costs that attach to the employment of high calibre directors (outside of salary) and the trappings associated with the running of a successful company. The corporate jet and possible proposed severance pay could be seen as residual costs of employment. Ensuring incentives exist to motivate directors to act in the best interests of shareholders is important. These incentives typically include large salaries such as the multi-million dollar remuneration of the CEO. Stock options will also be used to assist in tying remuneration to performance.

Agency costs also include costs associated with attempts to control or monitor the organisation. The most important of these will be the annual reports with financial statements detailing company operations. Shareholders have complained about the opaqueness of such reports and the costs of improving in this area will ultimately be borne by them.

Large organisations are required, usually as part of listing rules, to communicate effectively with major shareholders. Meetings arranged to discuss strategy, possibly involving the investment bank, and certainly involving the CEO, will take time and money to organise and deliver.

A hidden cost associated with the agency relationship, and one of particular significance here, relates to the increased risk taken on by shareholders due inevitably through relying on someone else to manage an individual's money, and specifically due to the acquisitive strategy employed by the company and the difficulty in gauging the financial performance and level of internal control within the corporation.

Conflict resolution

The market provides a simple mechanism for dealing with unresolved conflict, that of being able to divest shareholding back into the market place. This option is always available to shareholders if they consider the risks involved too great for the return they are receiving.

A less drastic measure might be to pursue increased communication and persuasion possibly via the largest shareholders in order to ensure the organisation understands shareholders' concerns and is willing to act upon their recommendations. The threat of a wide scale sale of shares should have an impact since this will affect directors' share options and the ability to continue its acquisitive strategy.

Since acquisition is a two-way street it might be possible for shareholders to persuade another company to bid to take over the organisation should the situation become desperate, although this seems unlikely in this scenario since, although the situation is dire, it does not appear to be terminal.

Shareholder activism may simply require interested parties to propose resolutions to be put to the vote at the next AGM. These might include a reluctance to reappoint directors who may have a conflict of interest in supporting the management or the owners of the company. Such a conflict may exist between the CEO and the Chairman of the audit committee.

Professional skills:

The analysis skills are demonstrated by linking the information in the scenario to the agency costs and the relationship between the shareholders and the company.

The evaluation skills are demonstrated by considering the pros and cons of each conflict resolution proposed. The aim is to consider options rather than come to one definitive solution.

Approaches to governance

Chapter learning objectives

Upon completion of this chapter you will be able to:

- compare rules- versus principles-based approaches to governance and when they may be appropriate

- discuss different models of organisational ownership that influence different governance regimes (family firms versus joint stock company-based models) and how they work in practice

- apply general principles of international corporate governance network (ICGN) codes to organisations' corporate governance

  (Note: reference to specific versions of the above documents is not included as they change periodically and only high level principles will be examined)

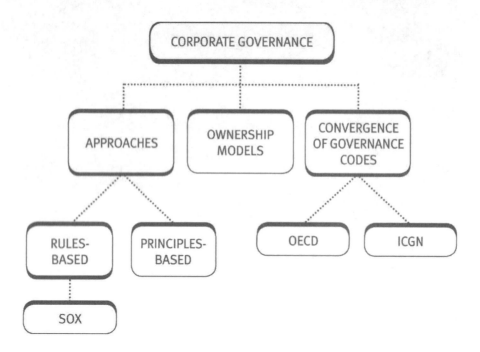

1 Rules- and principles-based approaches to corporate governance

There are different approaches to the communication, management and monitoring of codes.

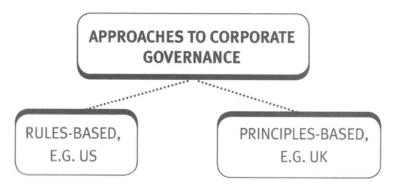

- A rules-based approach instils the code into law with appropriate penalties for transgression.

- A principles-based approach requires the company to adhere to the spirit rather than the letter of the code. The company must either comply with the code or explain why it has not through reports to the appropriate body and its shareholders.

The UK model is principles based and although it requires the company to adhere to the spirit of the code, and therefore adopt best practice, it is governed by the Stock Exchange Listing Rules.

The listing rules provide statutory authority (via the Financial Service and Markets Act 2000) and require public listed companies to state how they have complied or explain why they have not under the "comply or explain" clause noted above. This provides a basis for comparing Corporate Statements.

There is no such requirement for disclosure of compliance in private company accounts.

The US model is enshrined into law by virtue of Sarbanes – Oxley (SOX). It is, therefore, a rules-based approach.

Choice of governance regime

The decision as to which approach to use for a country can be governed by many factors:

- dominant ownership structure (bank, family or multiple shareholder)
- legal system and its power/ability
- government structure and policies
- state of the economy
- culture and history
- levels of capital inflow or investment coming into the country
- global economic and political climate.

Comply or explain

A principles-based code requires the company to state that it has complied with the requirements of the code or to explain why it could not do so in its annual report. This will leave shareholders to draw their own conclusions regarding the governance of the company.

UK Corporate Governance Code (2016) stated – "The "comply or explain" approach is the trademark of corporate governance in the UK. It has been in operation since the Code's beginnings and is the foundation of its flexibility. It is strongly supported by both companies and shareholders and has been widely admired and imitated internationally."

Illustration 1 – Marks & Spencer

On 10 March 2008, Marks & Spencer announced board and senior management changes.

The announcement stated that "Lord Burns will stand down as Chairman with effect from 1 June 2008" and that "Sir Stuart Rose is appointed Executive Chairman from the same date".

This action meant that Sir Stuart Rose would become CEO and chairman and, in allowing one individual to hold both positions, Marks & Spencer would not be in compliance with the UK Corporate Governance Code. Furthermore (and also in contravention of the code), the directors had not fully consulted major shareholders in advance of this announcement.

> In their corporate governance statement for the year ended 29 March 2008, Marks & Spencer stated that they had complied with all the provisions of the code with the exception of the two noted above and went on to explain the non-compliance. A letter was also written to the shareholders (dated 3 April 2008) explaining in full the reasons for the departure.

UK Corporate Governance Code (2018) retains the "comply or explain" approach and emphasis on high-quality reporting.

More specifically, companies will have to avoid a "tick-box" approach and use explanations as an opportunity to communicate with their shareholders and stakeholders.

It states – "At the heart of this Code is an updated set of Principles that emphasise the value of good corporate governance to long-term sustainable success. By applying the Principles, following the more detailed Provisions and using the associated guidance, companies can demonstrate throughout their reporting how the governance of the company contributes to its long-term sustainable success and achieves wider objectives.

Achieving this depends crucially on the way boards and companies apply the spirit of the Principles. The Code does not set out a rigid set of rules; instead it offers flexibility through the application of Principles and through 'comply or explain' Provisions and supporting guidance. It is the responsibility of boards to use this flexibility wisely and of investors and their advisors to assess differing company approaches thoughtfully."

Reporting on the Code

"The 2018 Code focuses on the application of the Principles. The Listing Rules require companies to make a statement of how they have applied the Principles, in a manner that would enable shareholders to evaluate how the Principles have been applied. The ability of investors to evaluate the approach to governance is important.

Reporting should cover the application of the Principles in the context of the particular circumstances of the company and how the board has set the company's purpose and strategy, met objectives and achieved outcomes through the decisions it has taken.

Arguments in favour of a rules-based approach (and against a principles-based approach)

Organisation's perspective:

- Clarity in terms of what the company must do – the rules are a legal requirement, clarity should exist and hence no interpretation is required.

- Standardisation for all companies – there is no choice as to complying or explaining and this creates a standardised and possibly fairer approach for all businesses.

- Binding requirements – the criminal nature makes it very clear that the rules must be complied with.

Wider stakeholder perspective:

- Standardisation across all companies – a level playing field is created.

- Sanction – the sanction is criminal and therefore a greater deterrent to transgression.

- Greater confidence in regulatory compliance.

Arguments against a rules-based approach (and in favour of a principles-based approach)

Organisation's perspective:

- Exploitation of loopholes – the exacting nature of the law lends itself to the seeking of loopholes.

- Underlying belief – the belief is that you must only play by the rules set. There is no suggestion that you should **want** to play by the rules (i.e. no 'buy-in' is required).

- Flexibility is lost – there is no choice in compliance to reflect the nature of the organisation, its size or stage of development.

- Checklist approach – this can arise as companies seek to comply with all aspects of the rules and start 'box-ticking'.

Wider stakeholder perspective:

- 'Regulation overload' – the volume of rules and amount of legislation may give rise to increasing costs for businesses and for the regulators.

- Legal costs – to enact new legislation to close loopholes.

- Limits – there is no room to improve, or go beyond the minimum level set.

- 'Box-ticking' rather than compliance – this does not lead to well governed organisations.

2 Sarbanes-Oxley (SOX)

In 2002, following a number of corporate governance scandals such as Enron and WorldCom, tough new corporate governance regulations were introduced in the US by SOX.

It is named after Senator Paul Sarbanes and Representative Michael Oxley, who were its main architects, and it set a number of non-negotiable rules and deadlines for compliance.

- SOX is a rules-based approach to governance.
- SOX is extremely detailed and carries the full force of the law.
- SOX includes requirements for the Securities and Exchange Commission (SEC) to issue certain rules on corporate governance.
- It is relevant to US companies, directors of subsidiaries of US-listed businesses and auditors who are working on US-listed businesses.

Illustration 2 – Enron

On 2 December 2001, Enron, one of the US' top 10 companies filed for chapter 11 bankruptcy protection. The size of the collapse sent shock waves around the world and 'Enronitus' spread through investors and boards of directors shaking confidence in the markets and continued global economic prosperity.

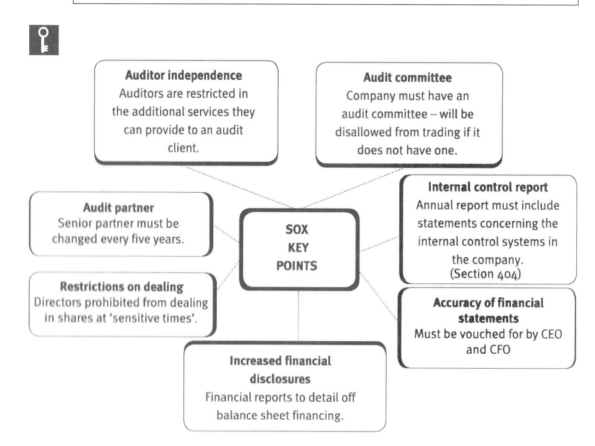

Auditor independence
Auditors are restricted in the additional services they can provide to an audit client.

Audit committee
Company must have an audit committee – will be disallowed from trading if it does not have one.

Audit partner
Senior partner must be changed every five years.

SOX KEY POINTS

Internal control report
Annual report must include statements concerning the internal control systems in the company. (Section 404)

Restrictions on dealing
Directors prohibited from dealing in shares at 'sensitive times'.

Accuracy of financial statements
Must be vouched for by CEO and CFO

Increased financial disclosures
Financial reports to detail off balance sheet financing.

Key effects of SOX:

- Personal liability of directors for mismanagement and criminal punishment
- Improved communication of material issues to shareholders
- Improved investor and public confidence in corporate US
- Improved internal control and external audit of companies
- Greater arm's length relationships between companies and audit firms
- Improved governance through audit committees.

Negative reactions to SOX

- Doubling of audit fee costs to organisations
- Onerous documentation and internal control costs
- Reduced flexibility and responsiveness of companies
- Reduced risk taking and competitiveness of organisations
- Limited impact on the ability to stop corporate abuse
- Legislation defines a legal minimum standard and little more.

Test your understanding 1

The ASD company is based in a jurisdiction which has strong principles of corporate governance. The directors realise that if the rules of governance are broken, then there are financial penalties on them personally. However, the rules that must be followed are clear and the directors follow those rules even though they may not agree with them.

Recently, one director has noted that if one of the reports required under corporate governance is simply placed into the postal system, then it is deemed to have been received by the shareholders. However, with a significant percentage of items being 'lost in the mail' this provides the company with a good excuse for non-receipt of the report – the director even went so far as to suggest privately that the report should not be produced.

Required:

(a) Briefly explain the principles- and rules-based approaches to corporate governance.

(b) Contrast the advantages and problems of the system of corporate governance in ASD company's jurisdiction with the alternative approach to governance.

Professional skills:

Illustrate evaluation skills when contrasting the advantages and problems of the governance system in ASD.

3 Divergent governance

The committees and codes of practice in the UK are implemented through the Financial Conduct Authority (FCA) and the Prudential Regulation Authority of the Bank of England. Adherence is a requirement of listing on the stock exchange.

Corporate governance also impacts on other types of organisational structure:

- non-governmental organisations (NGOs)
- smaller limited companies
- US companies (see earlier in this chapter – SOX)
- private or family companies (see later in this chapter)
- global organisations (see later in this chapter).

NGOs

Governance issues for NGOs are similar to those raised for public sector organisations since both are not-for-profit (NFP) structures (discussed in chapter 7).

In general, there is a need for increased commercialisation in operations, the need to run the charity as a business for the benefit of all. Reasons for the movement towards a more commercially run operation include:

- the need to be seen to run resources efficiently by stakeholders
- the need to get the most out of budgets, gifts and grants in service provision
- the increased use of directors drawn from the private sector to run NFPs
- increased awareness and skills among employees in relation to business management techniques.

The shift in terms of increased accountability and performance measure is not without its cost. The culture clash between serving a social need and running a business often leads to a dilution of resolve:

- Boards are councils or governing bodies.
- Managers are administrators or organisers.
- Boards struggle to find a method or function which is not at odds with their association's configuration and philosophy.

Key reasons for this are:

- dormant or silent patrons

- the anti-industry bias/culture

- the discretionary nature of the sector, using volunteers

- the ambiguity of mission and commercial imperative

- historical mode of operation/custom and precedence

- lack of commercial skills in senior management

- unwillingness of directors to move beyond their parental, devotional view.

Smaller limited companies

There is a duty on all organisations to operate within the law and, for those of any given size, to produce audited accounts. In governance terms, the agency problem does not tend to arise in private limited companies since shareholding is restricted and those with shares tend to have a direct involvement with the running of the firm.

Particular problems arise due to the limited size of such concerns:

- role and numbers of NEDs

- size of the board

- use of audit and nomination committees.

Despite this there is generally a perception that all companies should comply and, like all other companies, in order to foster the key need for improved communication, should either comply or explain.

4 Governance structures

A wider world view of governance requires consideration of the nature of ownership, power and control.

Illustration 3 – Share ownership analysis

La Porta 1999 analysed company structures in 49 countries and found that 24% of large companies have a wide share ownership compared to 35% being family controlled (Walmart, Barclays, Cadbury).

- Families tend to have control rights in excess of their cash flow rights in terms of preferential share voting rights.

- Controlling families tend to participate in the management of their firms.

- Other large shareholders are usually not there to monitor controlling shareholders.

Family structures v Joint Stock companies (refer to chapter 7, Section 1 for outline of Joint Stock Companies)

A family structure exists where a family has a controlling number of shares in a company. This has potential benefits and problems for the company, and the other shareholders involved.

Benefits that arise include:

- Fewer agency costs – since the family is directly involved in the company there are fewer agency costs.

- Ethics – it could be said that threats to reputation are threats to family honour and this increases the likely level of ethical behaviour.

- Fewer short-term decisions – the longevity of the company and the wealth already inherent in such families suggest long-term growth is a bigger issue.

Problems include:

- Gene pool – the gene pool of expertise in owner managers must be questionable over generations.

- Feuds – families fight, and this is an added element of cultural complexity in the business operation.

- Separation – families separate and this could be costly in terms of buying out shareholding and restructuring.

Insider-dominated structures (as opposed to outsider-dominated structures where the owners of firms tend not to have close relationships with those in senior managerial positions within the company)

This is an extension of the same idea. Insider-dominated structures are where the listed companies are dominated by a small group of shareholders. These:

- may be family owned

- may be banks, other companies or governments

- predominate in Japan and Germany.

The close relationship suggests benefits including:

- The agency problem is reduced i.e. easier to establish links between owners and managers

- Greater access and potentially lower cost of capital i.e. smaller base of shareholders

- Smaller base of shareholders willing to take a long term strategic view of investment

- Improved communication and influence over management policy and dialogue

Problems include:

- Lack of minority shareholder protection (unlike protection in law in outsider-dominated structures).

- Opaque operations and lack of transparency in reporting.

- Misuse of power i.e. reluctance to employ outsiders in influential positions and NEDs.

- The market does not decide or govern (shareholders cannot exit easily to express discontent).

- Tend to be reluctant until forced to develop formal governance structures.

- Reluctance of large independent shareholders to invest.

National differences

The insider/outsider model deals with the issue of national differences. These tend to lie in the nature of the legal system and the degree of recourse investors (minority investors) have.

Little recourse leads to insider dominated structures.

- Insider orientation: termed the French structure because of its origin.

- Outsider orientation: Anglo-American structure because of its origin.

The global diffusion of such governance standards tends to be initially led by Anglo-Saxon countries because of the agency problems and similarity between legal systems from the UK origin.

Chapter 7 described developments in corporate governance regulation in the UK. Similar developments have occurred in other countries. This section considers other international developments, in particular the development of corporate governance guidelines in the commonwealth and European Union.

Corporate governance and the European Union

In May 2003, the EU Commission presented a Communication entitled "Action Plan on Modernising Company Law and Enhancing Corporate Governance in the European Union". The aim of this report was to put forward recommendations designed to lead to greater harmonisation of the corporate governance framework for EU listed companies in all countries in the EU.

The recommendations in the report included measures such as:

- An EU directive requiring listed companies to publish an annual statement on corporate governance, including a 'comply or explain' regulation

- Another directive on collective board responsibilities for the disclosure of certain key financial and non-financial information.

On 5 April 2011, the EU Commission launched a public consultation on possible ways forward to improve existing corporate governance mechanisms. The objective of the Green Paper is to have a broad debate on the issues raised and allow all interested parties to see which areas the Commission has identified as relevant in the field of corporate governance.

However, new EU Directives or amendments to existing Directives will have to be incorporated into the national law of all the member states of the EU.

Corporate governance and the Commonwealth Countries

Concern for the need to establish good corporate governance practice has led to an initiative from the Commonwealth countries, which began with the first King report (South Africa) in 1994.

Many commonwealth countries have emerging economies and some such as South Africa have developing Stock Markets. Good corporate governance is seen as essential to the further development of national economies and the growth of the capital markets in those countries.

The work of the first King report lad to the setting up in 1998 of the Commonwealth Association for Corporate Governance (CACG). It produced a set of Corporate Governance guidelines in 1999.

The CACG guidelines put forward a list of fifteen principles of corporate governance. These are fairly similar to corporate governance guidelines of other organisations it is useful to view them from the 'emerging markets' viewpoint.

Corporate governance in Japan

Some new corporate governance provisions were introduced into the Japanese Commercial Code in 2003, including provisions for US-Style board committees. However not many Japanese listed companies have yet decided to adopt this new system.

5   International convergence

The competitiveness of nations is a preoccupation for all governments.

- Harmonisation and liberalisation of financial markets mean that foreign companies now find it easy to invest in any marketplace.

- This has led to a drive towards international standards in business practices to sit alongside the global shift in applying International Accounting Standards (IASs).

Two organisations have published corporate governance codes intended to apply to multiple national jurisdictions. These organisations are:

- the Organisation for Economic Cooperation and Development (OECD) and

- the International Corporate Governance Network (ICGN).

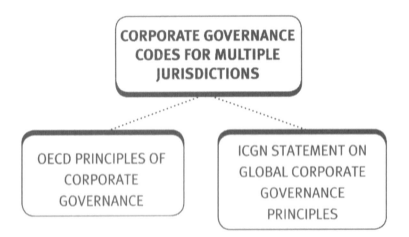

Organisation for Economic Cooperation and Development (OECD)

What is it?

- Established in 1961, the OECD is an international organisation composed of the industrialised market economy countries, as well as some developing countries, and provides a forum in which to establish and co-ordinate policies.

Objectives of the OECD principles

- The principles represent the first initiative by an intergovernmental organisation to develop the core elements of a good corporate governance regime.

- The principles are intended to assist OECD and non-OECD governments in their efforts to evaluate and improve the legal, institutional and regulatory framework for corporate governance in their countries, and to provide guidance and suggestions for stock exchanges, investors, corporations, and other parties that have a role in the process of developing good corporate governance.

- The principles focus on publicly-traded companies, both financial and non-financial. However, to the extent that they are deemed applicable, they might also be a useful tool for improving corporate governance in non-traded companies, e.g. privately-held and state-owned enterprises.

- The principles represent a common basis that OECD member countries consider essential for the development of good governance practices.

- The principles are intended to be concise, understandable and accessible to the international community.

- The principles are not intended to be a substitute for government, semi-government or private sector initiatives to develop more detailed 'best practice' in corporate governance.

The OECD principles were updated and republished in 2004.

Content of the OECD principles:

- ensuring the basis for an effective corporate governance framework

- the rights of shareholders and key ownership functions

- the equitable treatment of shareholders

- the role of stakeholders in corporate governance

- disclosure and transparency

- the responsibilities of the board.

International Corporate Governance Network (ICGN)

What is it?

- ICGN, founded in 1995 at the instigation of major institutional investors, represents investors, companies, financial intermediaries, academics and other parties interested in the development of global corporate governance practices.

Objectives of the ICGN principles

- The ICGN principles highlight corporate governance elements that ICGN-investing members take into account when making asset allocations and investment decisions.

- The ICGN principles mainly focus on the governance of corporations whose securities are traded in the market – but in many instances the principles may also be applicable to private or closely-held companies committed to good governance.

- The ICGN principles do, however, encourage jurisdictions to address certain broader corporate and regulatory policies in areas which are beyond the authority of a corporation.

- The ICGN principles are drafted to be compatible with other recognised codes of corporate governance, although in some circumstances, the ICGN principles may be more rigorous.

- The ICGN believes that improved governance should be the objective of all participants in the corporate governance process, including investors, boards of directors, corporate officers and other stakeholders as well as legislative bodies and regulators. Therefore, the ICGN intends to address these principles to all participants in the governance process.

Content of the ICGN principles:

- Corporate objective – shareholder returns

- Disclosure and transparency

- Audit

- Shareholders' ownership, responsibilities, voting rights and remedies

- Corporate boards

- Corporate remuneration policies

- Corporate citizenship, stakeholder relations and the ethical conduct of business

- Corporate governance implementation.

Limitations

- All codes are voluntary and are not legally enforceable unless enshrined in statute by individual countries.

- Local differences in company ownership models may mean parts of the codes are not applicable.

6   Chapter summary

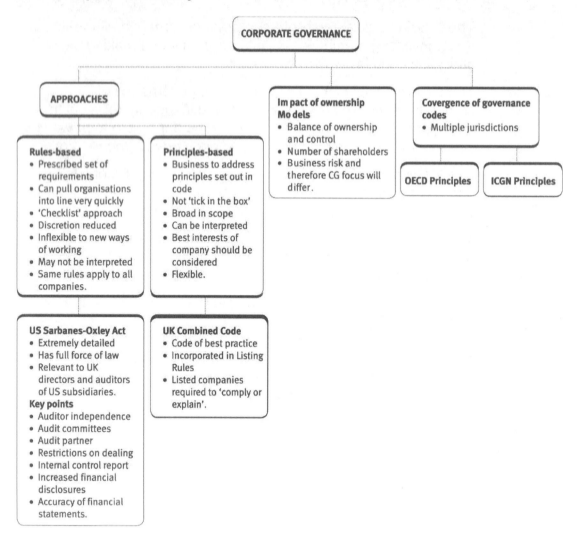

Test your understanding answers

Test your understanding 1

(a) **Rules- and principles-based approaches to corporate governance**

A rules-based approach to corporate governance instils the code into law with appropriate penalties for transgression. The code therefore has to be followed, and if it is not followed then the directors are normally liable to a fine, imprisonment or both.

A principle-based approach requires the company to adhere to the spirit rather than the letter of the code. The company must either comply with the code or explain why it has not through reports to the appropriate body and its shareholders. However, in many principles-based jurisdictions, the code has to be followed in order to obtain a listing on the relevant stock exchange. This means that the code is not quite 'voluntary'.

(b) **In the example, the ASD company is in a rules-based jurisdiction.**

Benefits of the rules-based approach

There is clarity in terms of what the company and directors must do to comply with the corporate government regulations. In this instance, clarity simply means that the requirements must be followed; there is no option to comply or explain why the requirements have not been followed as there is in a principles-based system.

Even though ASD is a medium-sized company, there is one set of rules to be followed. This has the effect of limiting uncertainty regarding the standard of corporate governance which can be a problem with a principles-based approach (which rules were actually complied with?).

There are criminal sanctions for non-compliance which means that there is a greater likelihood that the regulations will be followed. In a principles-based approach, although there may be the threat of de-listing, there is no penalty on the directors meaning that there can be less incentive to actually follow the code.

Problems with the rules-based approach

The fact that the regulations are statutory tends to lead to methods of avoiding the 'letter of the law' – that is loopholes will be found and exploited. A principles-based approach provides the guidelines which can then be applied to any situation, effectively avoiding this problem.

The rules are simply there; agreement with the rules is not required, only compliance. In principles-based systems, there is the underlying belief that the principles are accepted. In other words compliance is more likely simply because companies and directors want to follow them to show good corporate governance.

Companies and directors must follow the rules that have been set – there is no incentive to improve on the basic minimum standard, for example, in terms of providing additional disclosure. A principles-based system allows interpretation of the minimum standards and in effect encourages additional disclosure where necessary as this complies with the 'spirit' of the regulations.

Professional skills:

To demonstrate evaluation skills the student needs to use judgement when considering the issues facing ASD.

In this case the answer above does this by providing a comparison of each problem and advantage identified with the "rules-based" and "principles-based" approach, before recommending any solution.

Stakeholders and corporate social responsibility

Chapter learning objectives

Upon completion of this chapter you will be able to:

- discuss and critically assess the concept of stakeholder power and interest using the Mendelow model and apply this to strategy and governance

- evaluate the stakeholders' roles, claims and interests in an organisation and how they may conflict and be resolved

- explain social responsibility and viewing the organisation as a 'corporate citizen' in the context of governance

PER

One of the PER performance objectives (PO2) is that you manage stakeholder expectations and needs, developing and maintaining productive business relationships. You listen to and engage stakeholders effectively and communicate the right information to them when they need it. Working through this chapter should help you understand how to demonstrate that objective.

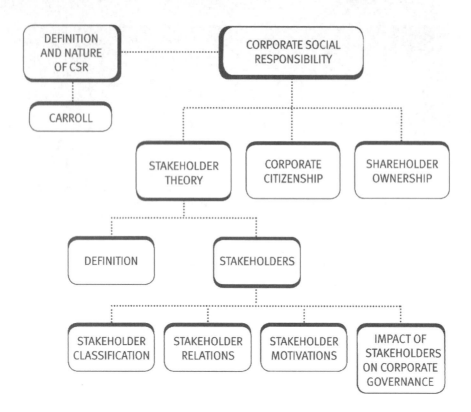

1 Corporate social responsibility (CSR)

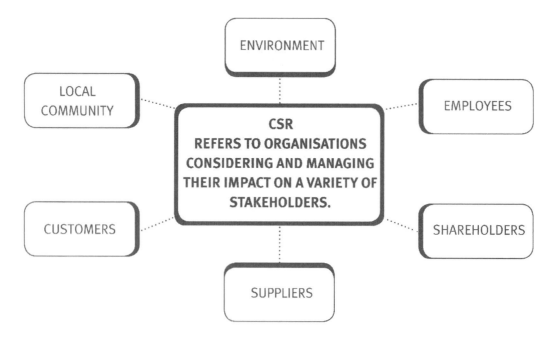

CSR is a concept with many definitions and practices. The way it is understood and implemented differs greatly for each company and country. Moreover, CSR is a very broad concept that addresses many and various topics such as human rights, corporate governance, health and safety, environmental effects, working conditions and contribution to economic development. Whatever the definition is, the purpose of CSR is to drive change towards sustainability.

A corporation:

- Is an artificial person in law. It has the same rights and responsibilities as human beings.

- Is notionally owned by shareholders but exists independently of them. The shareholder has a right to vote and be paid a dividend but the company owns its assets.

- Managers have a fiduciary duty to protect shareholder investment.

Milton Friedman argued that, in relation to this definition, a corporation has no responsibility outside of making profit for shareholders:

- Only human beings have moral responsibility for their actions.

- It is the managers' duty to act solely in the interest of shareholders:

  - this is a point of law. Any other action is shareholder betrayal.

- Social issues are the province of the state and not corporations.

The argument against this viewpoint needs to provide the organisation with an alternative view that leads to the same outcome of profit.

Enlightened self-interest

- Corporations perceived as ethically sound are rewarded with extra customers.

- Corporations which are ethically unsound are boycotted.

- Employees are more attracted to work for, and are more committed to, socially responsible companies.

- Voluntarily committing to social actions and programmes may forestall legislation and promote independence from government.

- Positive contribution to society may be a long-term investment in a safer, better educated and more equitable community creating a more stable context in which to do business.

 2   Stakeholders and their claims

As already stated in chapter 1 Freeman defines stakeholders as **'any person or group that can affect or be affected by the policies or activities of an organisation'.**

- The definition is important since it shows the directionality of stakeholder claims in as much as they can impact on the corporation as well as being the recipient of the actions of the firm.

The traditional model of capitalism provides us with:

- customers, suppliers, shareholders and employees.

The stakeholder model extends this to include:

- government, civil society and competitors.

Stakeholder claims

These are the demands that the stakeholder makes of an organisation. They essentially 'want something' from an organisation.

- The stakeholders may seek to influence the organisation to act in a certain way, or may want it to increase or decrease certain activities that affect them.

- **Direct** stakeholder claims are usually unambiguous, and are often made directly between the stakeholders and the organisation.

- Stakeholders typically making direct claims will include trade unions, employees, shareholders, customers and suppliers.

- **Indirect** claims are made by those stakeholders unable to express their claim directly to the organisation. They have no 'voice'.

- This lack of expression may arise from the stakeholder being powerless (an individual customer of a large organisation), not existing yet (future generations), having no voice (natural environment) or being remote from the organisation (producer groups in distant countries).

- The claim of an indirect stakeholder will need to be interpreted by someone else in order to be expressed.

 ## 3 Stakeholder classifications and relations

Classifications of stakeholders

There are a number of ways of classifying stakeholders according to criteria based on how stakeholders relate to organisational activities.

Internal and external stakeholders

This is the distinction between stakeholders inside the organisation and those outside.

- Internal: includes employees and management, and possibly trade unions.

- External: includes customers, competitors and suppliers.

Narrow and wide stakeholders

This is the extent to which the stakeholder group is affected by organisational activity.

- Narrow: those most affected or who are dependent on corporation output, such as shareholders, employees, management, customers and suppliers.

- Wide: those less affected or dependent on company output such as government, the wider community and non-dependent customers.

Primary and secondary stakeholders

This focuses on the opposing view in Freeman's definition, that stakeholders affect organisations as well as being affected by organisations.

- Primary: those that have a direct effect on the company and without whom it would be difficult to operate, such as the government,

- Secondary: those that have a limited direct influence on the organisation and without whom the company would survive, such as the community and management.

Active and passive stakeholders

This categorisation distinguishes between those that seek to participate in organisational activity and those that do not.

- Active: those that wish to participate, so includes management and employees, but may also include regulators, environmental pressure groups and suppliers.

- Passive: those that do not wish to participate and may include shareholders, local communities, government and customers.

Voluntary and involuntary stakeholders

This categorisation removes the element of choice associated with active and passive participation, sub dividing the active group into two elements.

- Voluntary: those stakeholders that choose to be involved in organisational decision making such as management, employees, environmental groups and active shareholders. These stakeholders can withdraw their stake holding in the short term.

- Involuntary: those stakeholders that do not choose to be involved in organisational decisions but become involved for a variety of reasons. This could include regulators, key customers, suppliers, government, natural environment and local communities. They cannot withdraw in the short to medium term.

Legitimate and illegitimate stakeholders

This is the extent to which the claim of the stakeholder is considered a valid claim. It can be a subjective classification with debate surrounding certain group's claims, and can lead into the concept of whether stakeholders are recognised by the organisation or not.

- Legitimate: those with, for example, an active economic relationship with an organisation, such as customers and suppliers.

- Illegitimate: those without such a link, such as terrorists, where there is no case for taking their views into account when making decisions.

Managing stakeholder relations

Stakeholder mapping: The Mendelow model

		Interest	
		Low	High
Power	Low	Minimal effort	Keep informed
	High	Keep satisfied	Key players

Stakeholder identification is necessary to gain an understanding of the sources of risks and disruption. It is important in terms of assessing the sources of influence over the objectives and outcomes for the business decisions or projects (such as identified in the Mendelow model).

In strategic analysis, stakeholder influence is assessed in terms of each stakeholder's power and interest, with higher power and higher interest combining to generate the highest influence.

It is necessary in order to identify areas of conflict and tension between stakeholders, especially relevant when it is likely that stakeholders of influence may be in disagreement over the outcomes of the decisions.

There is similarly a moral case for knowledge of how decisions affect stakeholders both internal and external to the organisation.

Examples of stakeholder conflict in business decisions may include the following:

- Closure of work places and the resultant loss of jobs due to economic conditions. This decision is likely to be supported by shareholders and providers of finance but opposed by employees and trade unions.

- Increase selling prices to improve profit margins. This decision is likely to be opposed by customers but supported by shareholders and management.

- Automation of work processes to reduce costs and improve productivity. This decision is likely to be supported by management, customers and shareholders but opposed by those employees affected.

- The addition of extra shifts to improve factory productivity. This decision is likely to be supported by management, customers and suppliers but opposed by the local community and environmental pressure groups.

Mendelow model

The matrix was designed to track interested parties and evaluate their viewpoint in the context of some change in business strategy.

Power relates to the amount of influence (or power) that the stakeholder group can have over the organisation. However, the fact that a group has power does not necessarily mean that their power will be used.

The **level of interest** indicates whether the stakeholder is actively interested in the performance of the organisation. The amount of influence the group has depends on their level of power.

Low interest – low power

These stakeholders typically include small shareholders and the general public. They have low interest in the organisation primarily due to lack of power to change strategy or influence corporate governance.

High interest – low power

These stakeholders would like to affect the strategy or influence corporate governance of the organisation but do not have the power to do this. Stakeholders include staff, customers and suppliers, particularly where the organisation provides a significant percentage of sales or purchases for those organisations. Environmental pressure groups would also be placed in this category as they will seek to influence company strategy, normally by attempting to persuade high power groups to take action.

Low interest – high power

These stakeholders normally have a low interest in the organisation, but they do have the ability to affect strategy and/or influence corporate governance should they choose to do so. Stakeholders in this group include the national government and in some situations institutional shareholders. The latter may well be happy to let the organisation operate as it wants to, but will exercise their power if they see their stake being threatened.

High interest – high power

These stakeholders have a high interest in the organisation and have the ability to affect strategy and/or influence corporate governance. Stakeholders include directors, major shareholders and trade unions.

Assessing stakeholder importance

Customers, shareholders and employees may be the most important stakeholders but continual assessment helps to focus in on those that require immediate action.

Three attributes may be assessed:

- Power: the perceived ability of the stakeholder to affect organisational action.

- Legitimacy: whether the company perceives the stakeholder action to be legitimate.

- Urgency: whether the stakeholder claim calls for immediate action.

Definitive stakeholders (possessing all three) require immediate action, the others are **latent** stakeholders.

Further stakeholder relationships

Beyond the specific nature of the action taken, there are different relationships between the company and its stakeholders. In general we consider these to be antagonistic but they do not necessarily need to be so.

- Challenge: relationship based on mutual opposition and conflict.

- Sparring partners: relationship based on healthy conflict.

- One-way support: relationship based on sponsorship and philanthropy from one party to the other.

- Mutual support: formal and informal two-way support.

- Endorsement: relationship based on paid public approval through a specific product or programme, e.g. ISO standards.

- Project dialogue: major regeneration and construction project dialogue.

- Strategy dialogue: relationship based on discussion over future regulation.

- Joint venture: mutual commitment to achieve a specific goal.

Organisational motivations regarding stakeholders

Donaldson and Preston draw a distinction between two motivations as to why organisations act in relation to the concerns of stakeholders.

The **instrumental** view of stakeholders:

- This relates to motivation stemming from the possible impact of stakeholder action on the objectives of the organisation.

- The organisation reacts to stakeholder input because it believes that not to do so would have an impact on its primary objectives (which may be profit, but could be other objectives for organisations such as charities).

- Such a view of stakeholders is therefore devoid of any moral obligation.

The **normative** view of stakeholders:

- This relates to motivation stemming from a moral consciousness that accepts a moral duty towards others in order to sustain social cohesion (the good of society).

- Such an altruistic viewpoint appreciates the need to act in a general sense of what is right rather than in a narrow interpretation of what is right for the company to achieve its profit targets.

4 Impact of stakeholders on corporate governance

A key area of impact is in relation to the increased need for, and existence of, social accounting. There are various forms of social accounting produced for inclusion in the Business Review as part of annual accounting reports.

- Ethical accounting: tends to focus on internal management systems or codes of practice at an individual level and how the company audits and complies with this.

- Environmental accounting: tends to focus exclusively on the organisation's impact on the natural environment.

- Social accounting: has a broader remit to incorporate employee conditions, health and safety, equal opportunities, human rights and charity work.

- Sustainability accounting: is a grand title that incorporates the triple bottom line of the first three with possible emphasis on environmentalism.

Effective social accounting

The following factors are key to ensuring effective social accounting:

- Inclusivity: suggests a two-way conversation with key stakeholders not just a one-way reporting process.

- Comparability: benchmarking previous periods or industry standards provides meaning to the extent of work being carried out.

- Completeness: suggests inclusion of negative as well as positive areas of organisational activity.

- Evolution and continuous improvement: commitment to learning from the past and changing practices.

- Management policies and systems: the development and consolidation of policies into real systems for evaluation and control.

- Disclosure: clear disclosure in reporting to meet stakeholders' needs.

- External verification: the perceived independence of verifiers where needed.

5 The organisation as a corporate citizen

Corporate citizenship

The key aspect about corporate citizenship is that it goes beyond compliance, obligations and that which is required by law.

It is the conferral of rights on stakeholders and the acceptance by the company of its responsibilities. The company therefore embraces responsibility for its actions and encourages a positive impact on the stakeholders with whom it interfaces. This is achieved via its activities for example by its interaction with the environment, consumers etc.

It is linked to the concept of corporate accountability.

- Corporate accountability refers to whether the organisation is in some way answerable for the consequences of its actions beyond its relationship with shareholders.

The demands for corporations to be more accountable and step up to their new role as valid members of society comes from two main sources: government failure and corporate power.

Government failure

One consequence of a modern society with an abundance of products and services is the failure of governments to deal with risks that accompany these rapid changes.

- Sometimes the risks are beyond the control of a single government.

- Sometimes electoral impact dampens political will.

- Sometimes they are part of the problem.

- Sometimes it is simply too difficult to change lifestyles.

- Sometimes sub-political activism such as Greenpeace impedes political will.

Corporate power

Corporations can shape lives in many ways:

- Liberalisation and deregulation of markets increase market power and restrict the ability of governments to intervene.

- Privatisation of many previous state monopolies places greater power in the corporate hand.

- Countries struggle with unemployment and yet the decision to locate and support societies is often not theirs but that of corporations.

- The pressure on low-wage economies to maintain low wages (and hence low costs to attract customers) is vast.

- Complex cross-border legal agreement is very difficult and so corporations are encouraged to self-regulate.

Scope of corporate citizenship

Corporate citizenship (CC) implies a role for corporations in the societies upon which they impact.

There are three views as to the scope and nature of CC.

- Limited view of CC: this is a philanthropic view. The scope is limited to charitable donations to the local community in which the organisation operates.

- Equivalent view: this is CC as being the equivalent to CSR. 'The extent to which business meets economic, legal, ethical and discretionary responsibilities.'

- Extended view: this is the most appropriate viewpoint since here citizenship (both individual and corporate) has rights and responsibilities. Rights include the right to freedom of speech and the right to own property. Responsibilities include the right to uphold civil liberties where governments may be failing in their duty.

Test your understanding 1

JV Limited manufactures cleaning chemicals at its factory in a small town in the Lake District. It employs 300 people, and is the largest employer within a 20-mile radius.

The factory is located on the side of a lake, at the end of a single track road.

Identify five social responsibilities of this company.

Test your understanding 2

The LKJ company is a distributor of electricity in a large country. In effect, LKJ purchases electricity from companies making electricity and then distributes this through a network of cables to companies and private individuals throughout the country. Electricity is generated from a variety of sources including burning coal and natural gas, nuclear power and a small amount from renewable resources such as wind and wave power.

LKJ's shares are owned by three other companies, large investors who take an active interest in the profitability of LKJ. There are three other electricity distribution companies in the country LKJ operates in.

The board of LKJ is currently considering the proposal to purchase electricity from another country. This source of supply is quoted as being cheaper from those within LKJ's home country, although the electricity is generated by burning coal. If this supply is taken, LKJ will stop purchasing electricity from an old nuclear power station and some of the expensive wind power plants. The Clean-Earth environmental group has learnt of the proposal and is currently participating in a media campaign in an attempt to block the change by giving LKJ bad publicity.

The board, managers and employees in LKJ appear indifferent, although changing the source of supply will provide a price advantage over LKJ's competitors, effectively guaranteeing their jobs for the next few years.

Required:

Identify the stakeholder groups who will be interested and/or affected by the decision of the LKJ company to change electricity suppliers, evaluating the impact of that decision on the group.

Discuss the actions the board can take with respect to each stakeholder group.

6 Chapter summary

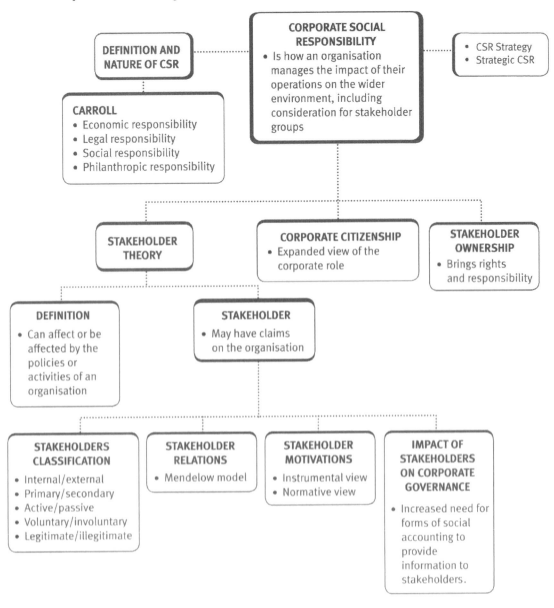

Test your understanding answers

Test your understanding 1

Many points can be included:

- not polluting the lake with waste chemicals

- making sure employees use adequate protection when working with the chemicals

- complying with legislation regarding the use of hazardous chemicals

- minimising the impact of traffic on local roads

- minimising the visual impact of the factory on the area.

Test your understanding 2

Large institutional investors

The main strategy of the board regarding a large institutional investor is communication with the need for change followed by participation in strategy determination. Most codes of corporate governance indicate the bi-lateral approach to be taken. The large investor is interested in the success of the organisation while at the same time having the ability to adversely affect the organisation if their shareholding is sold. The organisation must therefore keep the stakeholder informed regarding important strategic decisions. Similarly, there is a responsibility on the part of the stakeholder to take an interest in the activities of the organisation and to use their influence responsibly.

The three investors in LKJ are likely to be keen for the electricity to be purchased from the different country as this will increase the return on their investment.

Potential actions by the board

A dialogue should be established between the chairman and large shareholders, as a minimum by discussion at the annual general meeting. However, more frequent meetings throughout the year are also expected. The chairman needs to ensure that the expectations of return from LKJ are congruent with the investing companies.

Environmental pressure group (Clean Earth)

The pressure group will attempt to influence other groups with high power to change the strategy of the organisation. The board of LKJ therefore needs to communicate with the group with the aim of explaining and educating them in respect of the actions being taken by LKJ.

Currently Clean-Earth are attempting to influence the strategy of LKJ by the media campaign. The basis of this campaign is likely to be the fact that obtaining electricity from coal is more harmful to the environment than renewable sources and possibly nuclear generation. Explanation of the reason for change in terms of increased profit may not, however, be acceptable.

Potential actions by the board

The board must be prepared to learn from the pressure. Many pressure groups do have responsible and knowledgeable people within the group. Not to listen may mean that valuable advice and assistance is rejected on grounds of prejudice against this type of stakeholder. While it is likely that advice from the group will be biased towards renewable resources, they may have ideas regarding cost efficiency that LKJ can use.

Directors/managers/employees of LKJ

The directors of LKJ are stakeholders in the organisation. In terms of corporate governance, they have the responsibility to act in the best interests of the company and its shareholders. In this sense, there is no conflict in the decision to source electricity supplies from another country; LKJ profits are forecast to increase while there is job security for the directors. While the directors have high power and interest in LKJ, this power appears to be being used correctly.

Similarly, the actions of the directors appears to meet the requirements of the managers and employees of LKJ in that their jobs are protected.

Potential actions by the board

The environmental impact of board action with relation to alternative supply may be a cause for concern. If LKJ, and therefore the directors, are considered not to be acting ethically then customers may choose alternative suppliers. This action will mean that the profit forecasts are incorrect and the directors may need to consider alternative courses of action rather than change the source of supply as indicated.

Effective leadership

Chapter learning objectives

Upon completion of this chapter you will be able to:

- explain the role of effective leadership and identify the key leadership traits effective in the successful formulation and implementation of strategy and change management

- apply the concepts of entrepreneurship and 'intrapreneurship' to exploit strategic opportunities and to innovate successfully

- discuss the importance of leadership in defining and managing organisational culture

- advise on the style of leadership appropriate to manage strategic change

PER

One of the PER performance objectives (PO5) is that you manage yourself and your resources effectively and responsibly. You contribute to the leadership and management of your organisation – delivering what's needed by stakeholders and the business. Working through this chapter should help you understand how to demonstrate that objective.

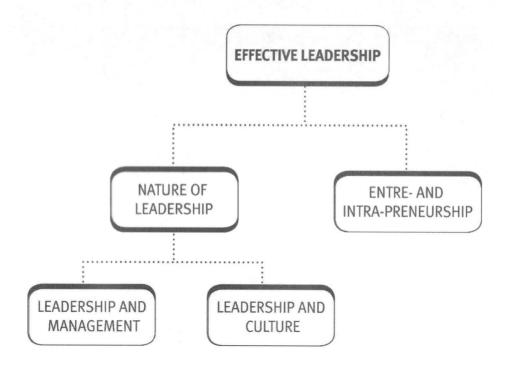

1 The nature and importance of leadership

The nature and importance of leadership

Buchanan and Huczynski define a leader as 'someone who exercises influence over other people'. Another definition is: Leadership is an interpersonal influence directed toward the achievement of a goal or goals. Three important parts of this definition are the terms interpersonal, influence, and goal:

- Interpersonal – means between persons. Thus, a leader has more than one person (group) to lead.

- Influence – is the power to affect others.

- Goal – is the end one strives to attain.

Basically, this traditional definition of leadership says that a leader influences more than one person towards a goal.

Leadership can be viewed from three standpoints:

- an attribute or a position, e.g. the managing director

- a characteristic of a person – a natural leader

- a category of behaviour.

Leadership is all about moving people and things on, getting them from A to B – improving performance, changing the way things are done, making a new product – and if the designated leader cannot communicate the why, how and when of moving from A to B then he or she will neither behave like a leader, nor succeed in the task.

As a function, leadership involves facilitating the achievement of group goals and has been defined in many ways from 'that which leaders do' to long, complex paragraphs including many elements. Fiedler, in one of his definitions, writes that a leader is 'the individual in the group given the task of directing and co-ordinating tasks – relevant group activities or who, in the absence of a designated leader, carries the primary responsibility for performing these functions in the group'.

From the definitions given (and there are lots more) you may still wonder what leadership is. Are leaders born or made? Can anyone be a leader, or only the favoured few? Is there a particular trick to it, or a particular style, something that, if we could learn it, would transform our lives? Are there models we should imitate, great men we can learn from? Do you have to be popular to be an effective leader? Can you be both well-liked and productive? The search for answers to questions like these has prompted a large number of studies and, unfortunately, none of these has produced a definitive solution to the leadership puzzle.

2 What makes an effective leader?

In Business and Technology (BT) you learnt how there are a wide range of different theories, models and research that seek to determine what the ideal leader or manager should be like.

Trait theories

Early studies focused on the qualities required by effective leaders. Lists were compiled of required leadership qualities including:

- physical traits, such as drive, energy, appearance and height
- personality traits, such as adaptability, enthusiasm and self-confidence; and
- social traits, such as co-operation, tact, courtesy and administrative ability.

Certain other writers selected other personal qualities which were thought to be desirable in leaders, who are 'born and not made'. Many great leaders were considered to have:

- above-average intelligence
- initiative – independence and inventiveness and the capacity to perceive a need for action
- motivation
- self-assurance and self-confidence
- the 'helicopter factor' – the ability to rise above the particulars of a situation and perceive it in relation to the surrounding context
- other 'essential' qualities included enthusiasm, sociability, integrity, courage, imagination, determination, energy, faith, even virility.

The problem with personality or trait theories is that there are always counter-examples that can be given, for instance, when one theorist suggested a good leader must be tall, a short yet effective leader was identified; when one theorist suggested a leader must be tactful and courteous, a rude yet effective leader was found. Clearly good leadership is more than simply possession of particular physical or psychological attributes.

Behavioural/style theories

The essence of leadership style theories is that a successful leader will exhibit a pattern of behaviour (i.e. 'style') in gaining the confidence of those they wish to lead. Style is a difficult factor to measure or define. The style of a manager is essentially how he or she operates, but it is a function of many different factors.

The research at Ashridge Management College distinguished four main management styles:

- Tells (autocratic) – the manager makes all the decisions and issues instructions which are to be obeyed without question.

- Sells (persuasive) – the manager still makes all the decisions, but believes that team members must be motivated to accept them in order to carry them out properly.

- Consults (participative) – the manager confers with the team and takes their views into account, although still retains the final say.

- Joins (democratic) – the leader and the team members make the decision together on the basis of consensus.

Ashridge discovered that most people preferred operating under the 'consults' style, though the most important thing was consistency – staff disliked it when managers changed between different styles.

Lewin worked with similar categories and concluded that in terms of productivity and satisfaction, it was the democratic style that was the most productive and satisfying. On the other hand, an autocratic authoritarian style was the least productive of all and carried with it lots of frustration and instances of aggression among group members.

Unfortunately, as with trait theories, it is possible to find counter examples.

For example, you could argue that Warren Buffett (an extremely successful and high profile investor) has a hands-off, laissez-faire management style that is highly successful because he focuses on hiring very capable people, and the autonomy of these executives is key to the success. On the other hand, Steve Jobs (Apple) was well known for his authoritarian approach and reluctance to delegate, so could be described as having an autocratic approach. Lewin's work indicated that this style was the least effective, but according to Forbes, Apple was the largest tech company in the world in 2017, and also the 9th largest company in the world.

Contingency/contextual theories

The difficulty with style theories, even when they attempt to reflect the multidimensional nature of leadership, is that they ignore the important influence of the context in which the leader is operating. The modern consensus is that there is no one best style of leadership that is equally effective for all circumstances.

One example studied in F1 is Adair's action-centred leadership approach. He argued that the leader needs to adapt to three competing needs:

- The needs of the group (communication, team building, motivation, discipline)

- The needs of individuals (coaching, counselling, motivating and developing)

- Task needs (setting objectives, planning tasks, allocating responsibilities and performance standards)

Such a balancing act is just as relevant to the CEO in the boardroom as it is to a supervisor on the shop floor.

A theory that is a mixture of both trait and contingency is the situational approach. The theory here is that leaders are products of particular situations, e.g. Hitler in Germany of the 1930s, Churchill in Britain of the early 1940s and Mao in China after 1946. A given set of factors exists in certain situations, e.g. economic depression, weak government, high unemployment and disenchantment with traditional politics. The theory suggests that a leader emerges who recognises the problems and has characteristics or traits that fit the needs of the situation.

Test your understanding 1

Before taking up her position as Head of the Finance department of QRS, T had enjoyed a career in the Army where she had attained the rank of major. The military style of command had suited T's personality. She is by nature an assertive kind of individual, so giving orders is something that comes naturally to her.

The start of her new post as Head of Finance has not been easy. She has found that her previous style of management has not been well received by her new staff. Her enthusiasm for improving the way things are done in the department is not matched by that of her staff. In fact, if anything, an air of resentment seems to exist in the department. More generally, T is finding it difficult to adjust to the whole way of operating in QRS. In her view, so much time seems to be spent in meetings and in consultation generally that she wonders how the organisation manages to compete in the market place as successfully as it does.

> **Required:**
>
> Using any appropriate theory of management style, write an email to T explaining why she is experiencing the difficulties described in her new post, and recommend the kind of management style that might be more appropriate.
>
> **(15 minutes)**

3 Leadership and management

A leader can be a manager, but a manager is not necessarily a leader. The leader of the work group may emerge informally as the choice of the group. If a manager is able to influence people to achieve the goals of the organisation, without using formal authority to do so, then the manager is demonstrating leadership.

Management is the process of setting and achieving the goals of the organisation through the functions of management: planning, organising, directing (or leading), and controlling. A manager is hired by the organisation and is given formal authority to direct the activity of others in fulfilling organisational goals. Thus, leading is a major part of a manager's job. Yet a manager must also plan, organise, and control.

Generally speaking, leadership deals with the interpersonal aspects of a manager's job, whereas planning, organising, and controlling deal with the administrative aspects. Leadership deals with change, inspiration, motivation, and influence. Management deals more with carrying out the organisation's goals and maintaining equilibrium.

The key point in differentiating between leadership and management is the idea that employees willingly follow leaders because they want to, not because they have to. Leaders may not possess the formal power to reward or sanction performance because leadership does not necessarily take place within the hierarchical structure of the organisation. However, employees give the leader power by complying with what he or she requests. On the other hand, managers may have to rely on formal authority to get employees to accomplish goals.

The skills of a leader

The basic aim of leaders is to succeed in completing the task set with the help of their group. An effective leader will need to inspire confidence and trust so that there is maximum co-operation from the group. In order to achieve this aim, leaders need certain skills, which include:

- An understanding of the precise requirements needed from the group.
- The ability to make decisions, sometimes under pressure.
- An understanding of human nature to appreciate the attitude of the group.
- Confidence both in the group and themselves.

- The ability to create a sense of direction. Leaders should have a clear idea of what they are trying to achieve with their group, department, business unit or organisation. This needs to be a vision which is appealing to the staff and well communicated to them, allowing staff, who do not share the vision, to leave the unit over time and bond together those that remain around a common purpose.

- The ability to think strategically. Innovation and vision take a long while to see through from inception through to fruition or failure. The leader must be interested in the long-term view of the group.

- Entrepreneurial abilities. Leaders should be able to identify opportunities and win the resources necessary to exploit them.

- The ability to lead from the front. Leaders must be able to inspire and motivate, to translate the vision into achievement.

- The possession of good communication skills. If leaders are to conceive a vision, develop it into a strategy, win scarce organisational resources and gain the support of their staff, then they will need to be a competent communicator.

The leader needs to use these skills to satisfy Adair's three principal requirements of leadership:

- Satisfy the task's needs. The leader ensures that the purpose – completion of the task – is fulfilled.

- Satisfy the group's needs. Until the task is completed, the group has to be held together; the leader must maintain team spirit and build morale.

- Satisfy the individual's needs. Each member of a group or team has individual needs and the leader should try to ascertain these needs and work towards satisfying them as far as is possible within the group's needs.

4 Leadership and culture

Bennis proposed that there were two types of leaders:

- Transactional leaders see the relationship with their followers in terms of a trade: they give followers the rewards they want in exchange for service, loyalty and compliance.

- Transformational leaders see their role as inspiring and motivating others to work at levels beyond mere compliance. Only transformational leadership is said to be able to change team/organisational cultures and move them in a new direction.

Transactional leaders tend to be more passive and transformational leaders more proactive. While a transactional leader would work within the confines of the organisational culture, the transactional leader would seek to change and improve the culture. Transformational leadership enhances the motivation, morale, and job performance of followers.

They act as a role model and inspire others to develop and innovate. They would advocate empowerment, encouraging followers to take greater ownership for their work.

Transformational leadership has become more important in recent years. The dynamic nature of the environment facing many organisations today means that there is a constant need to innovate and change. It is suggested that to cope with this type of environment, leaders need to have vision and creativity, be innovative and capable of inspiring others. The distinguishing feature of transformational leadership is the ability to bring about significant change.

NB The role of leadership and culture in managing change is discussed in further detail in chapter 24.

5 Entre and Intrapreneurship

Many large businesses were set up by entrepreneurs who had new ideas and were willing to take risks to convert those ideas into successful products. However, a growing trend within business is to encourage employees 'intrapreneurs' to come up with new ideas and take risks to grow the business.

Major brands such as Sony PlayStation and the Post-it Note were developed in a culture of intrapreneurship. Even the idea of the 'Like' button on Facebook was developed by a junior member of staff at the company.

Ways to encourage such intrapreneurship include the following:

- Set up a culture where employees are encouraged to explore new ideas, even if they are not related to their official roles. This works even better if employees are given time to do this.

- Managers should have open door policies making it easy for their staff to come and discuss new ideas.

- Removing administrative barriers and bureaucracy so that new ideas can be presented.

- Develop a culture where innovation is valued and failure is not the final word – calculated risk taking is essential to commercial success.

- Budget for resources to develop new ideas. Intrapreneurs should not be expected to finance development themselves.

- Give employees a degree of ownership of new ideas – for example, allowing them to present the concepts to senior management.

- Try to identify intrapreneurs and give them more time and resources to develop ideas further.

Differences between entrepreneurs and intrapreneurs

An entrepreneur is an individual that 'starts up' a business and is the owner. Whereas, an intrapreneur is an employee of the company and does not usually have any ownership.

However, some employees, likely the intrapreneurs among them, may hold shares in the company they work for in the form of shares. Ownership of a company gives the entrepreneur the ultimate control over what the business does. The entrepreneur is the risk-taker of the business.

The intrapreneur may take 'risks' within the corporation where he works. However, the final risk comes down to the responsibility of the business owner. There is no actual financial risk taken by the intrapreneur. In addition the difference between entrepreneurs and intrapreneurs is with regards to the "ultimate sacrifice". The entrepreneur will use his own money for his start-up business. They may use their own assets (like their own home) to secure loans to finance their small business start-up and therefore the ultimate sacrifice being made by an entrepreneur is one of potential financial loss. An intrapreneur will not usually be in a position to raise funds for the organisation. The intrapreneur is therefore not risking any of their own money in any organisation where they are involved.

Financial loss for the entrepreneur comes in two forms. Firstly, if the business makes a loss, and runs out of cash, the entrepreneur is the one who has to make up the difference. Secondly, where a company collapses and goes into liquidation, the entrepreneur could lose everything. This will depend on what monies are owned by the company, and what's personally secured by the entrepreneur.

Conversely, it is the entrepreneur who will reap the rewards of success. First, where the company makes a profit, the entrepreneur will be able to reward him or herself with profits in the way of dividends. Secondly, the final benefit to the entrepreneur is on the sale of the business. Where the organisation has done exceptionally well, the entrepreneur could be in for a significant gain from the sale proceeds.

It's possible that due to the nature of an intrapreneur, they may have arranged a 'profit share' for themselves. This will mean they receive a reward for their efforts. However, this will always only be a share of profits, compared to the entrepreneur, who is entitled to 100% of the balance of the profits. Also, the intrapreneur will not gain from the sale of the business in the same way. The exception to this is where they have an agreement in place with the business owner to take a share of the proceeds at the point of sale.

All intrapreneurs are dependent on entrepreneurs in the first place to start the business. Without entrepreneurs there would be no intrapreneurs to flourish. Good 'entrepreneur-leadership' will lead to having intrapreneurs within their businesses and entrepreneurs will encourage intrapreneurship.

However, there's always the worry that the intrapreneur will leave to set up in competition. The risk exists of losing a key employee who acts as an intrapreneur, making it extremely difficult to replace that individual. It is the entrepreneur's duty therefore to not only encourage intrapreneurship, but also to support and look after their intrapreneurs within the business. Being an entrepreneur carries with it a certain level of risk, whereas intrapreneurs can simply walk away when a business goes wrong.

A small business's survival can sometimes depend upon the entrepreneur's ability and willingness to raise funds for example from financial sources, like banks and other lenders. A loan will more than likely need personal security and personal guarantees.

Intrapreneurs never have to carry this level of risk. They are fully reliant on the entrepreneur to carry the burden of risk of things going wrong. In addition in the case of cash flow problems, it is the entrepreneur, and not the intrapreneur that will have to provide the funds.

Effectively the resources used by an entrepreneur are provided by him or herself. Entrepreneurs have to be extremely resourceful. Whilst intrapreneurs are resourceful, they are not required to provide the resources needed by the company. The resources needed by the intrapreneur are already provided to themselves by the company.

The resources we are referring to here are not just 'cash' and capital, as discussed above, but all the other resources needed to run a business. At no time is an intrapreneur expected to provide funds for the business. These resources are not necessarily physical resources either. There are personal resources required to succeed in business also which include educational resources, emotional resources and human resources.

An entrepreneur always also has the final say in what happens within a business. So although intrapreneurs do tend to have a high level of autonomy and creativity, they are under the ultimate control and guidance of the entrepreneur who owns the business. The exceptions to this rule are where a business is jointly owned and run, or whereby lenders are involved and have a certain amount of say over certain business decisions.

Intrapreneurs, by their very nature, are often extremely autonomous, and should be encouraged to be so. However, there will always be certain larger decisions where the intrapreneur will need to seek approval and clear boundaries must be set.

6 Chapter summary

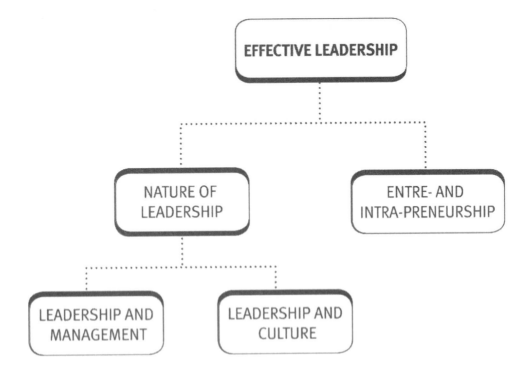

Test your understanding answers

Test your understanding 1

EMAIL

To: **T**

From: **Management accountant**

Date: **Today**

Subject: **Management style**

Management style is concerned with how a manager deals with subordinates. There are a number of different models but one that is commonly used is that of Lewin.

Using Lewin's conclusions, you could be described as adopting an autocratic style of management. This means that you are telling the subordinates what to do. This style of management probably comes naturally to you since it is the style adopted in the armed forces where subordinates are trained to not question their orders. Since you have spent a long time in this environment it is, understandably, the style you are used to.

The workers that you are supervising in the Finance department however may well be professionally qualified people used to carrying out tasks in their own way without a great deal of supervision.

With these kind of workers an autocratic style is unlikely to be successful, since the workers will resent the reduction in the amount of decision-making they are allowed. You may find it more useful to adopt a more democratic management style in which decisions are discussed with the employees rather than being imposed. This should lead to greater worker contentment with resulting gains in productivity and morale.

There will probably be a number of difficulties in changing your management style. You are used to doing things in 'the army way' (which you clearly did successfully having risen to the rank of major) and you are a naturally assertive person to whom an autocratic style of management is probably most comfortable.

Another factor that could cause problems is the potential for you to feel that you are 'losing face' by changing to suit your subordinates. You might question the effect this will have on your authority both now and in the future, for example, what happens if they dislike something else, will you be expected to adapt to them again?

Although there are many practical difficulties surrounding this change in style they are not insurmountable. You may have to gradually change your style over time, perhaps by getting key subordinates more involved now and gradually extending this.

An alternative solution would be to involve another senior manager from a different department to help mentor you. This would involve working with a mentor who could help you discuss practical ways in which your style can evolve.

The above measures are likely to be unsuccessful unless you recognise that it is in your interests as well as that of your sub-ordinates and the company to change your style.

I hope you have found the above helpful. Please do not hesitate to get in touch if you require any further information.

The board of directors

Chapter learning objectives

Upon completion of this chapter you will be able to:

- assess the duties and roles of directors and functions of the board (including setting a responsible 'tone at the top' and being accountable for the performance and impact of the organisation)

- evaluate the cases for, and against, unitary and two-tier board structures

- describe and assess the purposes, responsibilities and performance of Non-Executive Directors (NEDs)

- describe and assess the importance of induction, performance appraisal and the continuing professional development of directors on boards of directors

- explain the meaning of 'diversity' and critically evaluate issues of diversity on boards of directors

- assess the importance, roles, purposes and accountabilities of the main committees within the effective governance

- describe and assess the general principles of remunerating directors and how to modify directors' behaviour to align with stakeholder interests

- explain and analyse the regulatory, strategic and labour market issues associated with determining directors' remuneration

PER

One of the PER performance objectives (PO4) is that you contribute to effective governance in your area. You evaluate, monitor and implement risk management procedures, complying with the spirit and the letter of policies, laws and regulations. Working through this chapter should help you understand how to demonstrate that objective.

1 Board of directors – roles and responsibilities

In relation to corporate bodies:

- a director is an officer of the company charged by the board of directors with the conduct and management of its affairs

- the directors of the company collectively are referred to as a board of directors

- the shareholders appoint the chairman of the board and all other directors (upon recommendations from the nominations committee)

- directors, individually and collectively, as a board of directors, have a duty of corporate governance.

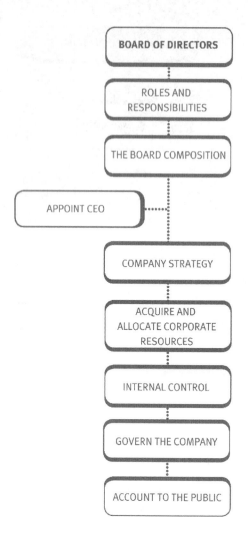

From the principles in the UK Corporate Governance Code (2016), the key roles and responsibilities of directors are to:

- provide entrepreneurial leadership of the company

- represent company view and account to the public

- decide on a formal schedule of matters to be reserved for board decision

- determine the company's mission and purpose (strategic aims)

- select and appoint the CEO, chairman and other board members

- set the company's values and standards

- ensure that the company's management is performing its job correctly

- establish appropriate internal controls that enable risk to be assessed and managed

- ensure that the necessary financial and human resources are in place for the company to meet its objectives

- ensure that its obligations to its shareholders and other stakeholders are understood and met

- meet regularly to discharge its duties effectively
- for listed companies:
  - appoint appropriate NEDs
  - establish remuneration committee
  - establish nominations committee
  - establish audit committee
- assess its own performance and report it annually to shareholders
- submit themselves for re-election at regular intervals. All directors in FTSE 350 companies should be put forward for re-election every year.

The UK Corporate Governance Code (2016) has been developed as a source of good practice. Although it is not global in its application it remains a useful guide for examination purposes.

Effective board

An effective board demonstrates the following capabilities:

- clear strategy aligned to capabilities
- vigorous implementation of strategy
- key performance drivers monitored
- sharp focus on the views of the City and other key stakeholders
- regular evaluation of board performance.

'Tone at the Top'

The term, originally created in the field of accounting, refers to how an organisation's leadership creates an environment or atmosphere in the workplace, for example via ethical (or unethical) working practices.

Management's "tone" has a trickle-down effect on employees. If top managers uphold ethics and integrity so will employees. But if senior management appears unconcerned with ethics and focuses solely on the bottom line, employees will perhaps be more prone to commit fraud and feel that ethical conduct isn't a priority.

In short, employees will follow the examples of their bosses.

Potential problems for boards

Sometimes achieving all of this in practice can be difficult due to 'barriers'.

- Most boards largely rely on management to report information to them (and may not have the time or the skills to understand the details of company business), thus allowing management to obscure problems and the true state of a company.

- A board that meets only occasionally may be unfamiliar with each other. This can make it difficult for board members to question management.

- CEOs often have forceful personalities, sometimes exercising too much influence over the rest of the board.

- The current CEO's performance is judged by the same directors who appointed him/her making it difficult for an unbiased evaluation.

2   What is diversity?

Diversity describes the range of visible and non-visible differences that exist between people.

Managing diversity harnesses these differences to create a productive environment in which everybody feels valued, where talents are fully utilised and in which organisational goals are met.

The concept of diversity encompasses acceptance and respect. It means understanding that each individual is unique, and recognising our individual differences. These can be along the dimensions of:

- race
- ethnicity
- gender
- sexual orientation
- socio-economic status
- age
- physical ability
- religious beliefs
- political beliefs or other ideologies.

Diversifying the board is said broadly to have the following benefits:

- More effective decision making.
- Better utilisation of the talent pool.
- Enhancement of corporate reputation and investor relations by establishing the company as a responsible corporate citizen.

Refer to technical article on ACCA website: **"Diversifying the Board – A step toward better governance"** – updated 14.01.2014

Women on the board

In the UK, in 2010, women made up only 12.5% of the members of the corporate boards of FTSE100 companies. This was up from 9.4% in 2004. But the rate of increase is too slow.

The business case for increasing the number of women on corporate boards is clear. Women are successful at university and in their early careers, but attrition rates increase as they progress through an organisation. When women are under-represented on corporate boards, companies are missing out, as they are unable to draw from the widest possible range of talent.

Evidence suggests that companies with a strong female representation at board and top management level perform better than those without and that gender-diverse boards have a positive impact on performance. It is clear that boards make better decisions where a range of voices, drawing on different life experiences, can be heard. That mix of voices must include women.

Diversity of Non-Executive Directors

The Higgs Review found that the majority of NEDs in UK companies are white, middle-aged males of British origin with previous plc director experience. In the survey of companies completed for the Higgs Review, non-British nationals accounted for only 7% of NED positions, while British citizens from ethnic minority backgrounds accounted for only 1% of such positions.

The survey also found that although about 30% of managers in the UK corporate sector are female, women hold only 6% of NED positions.

The striking homogeneity of board membership suggests that many UK companies are not searching broadly for talent, or at least have not done so in the past.

Aviva Chairman, Pehr Gyllenhammar, suggests useful guidelines for the selection of NEDs with the phrase **'No crooks, no cronies, no cowards.'**

Action for increasing board diversity

Lord Davies of Abersoch compiled a report in February 2011 commissioned by the Government on women on the board.

While there is still work to be done, progress since the report has been positive.

When Lord Davies and his steering group started this ambitious agenda in 2011 women made up just 12.5% of FTSE 100 boards; and just a few years later, we've seen that double – it is now at 26.1% on FTSE 100 boards and 19.6% on FTSE 250 boards.

There are more women on FTSE 350 boards than ever before, with representation of women more than doubling since 2011 – 550 women appointed to FTSE 350 boards since 2011.

We have also seen a dramatic reduction in the number of all-male boards. There were 152 in 2011. Today there are no all-male boards in the FTSE 100 and only 15 in the FTSE 250.

There remain 15 all-male boards in the FTSE 350 and progress has been far too slow in getting more women into Executive Director roles.

Board agenda items

A board agenda is likely to include the following:

Companies Act requirement

- Approval of interim and final financial statements.
- Approval of interim dividend and recommendation for final dividend.
- Approval of significant changes to accounting policies.
- Appointment or removal of key staff such as company secretary.
- Remuneration of auditors (where shareholders have delegated the power).
- Recommendation for the appointment or removal of auditors (where shareholders have delegated the power).

Stock exchange

- Approval of press releases concerning significant matters decided by the board.

Management

- Approval of group's commercial strategy.
- Approval of group's annual operating budget.
- Approval of group's annual capital expenditure plan.
- Changes relating to the group's capital structure.
- Terms and conditions/service agreements of directors.
- Major changes to the group's management and control structure.

3 Board structures

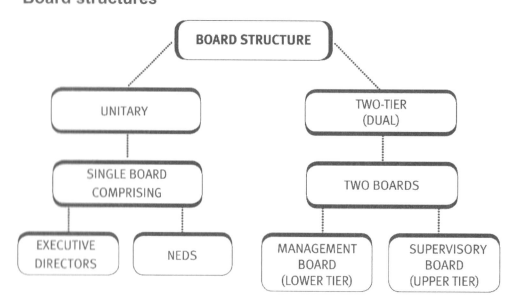

There are two kinds of board structure, unitary and two-tier (dual) boards.

Two-tier boards

These are predominantly associated with France and Germany. Using Germany as an example, there are two main reasons for their existence:

- Codetermination: the right for workers to be informed and involved in decisions that affects them. This is enshrined in the Codetermination Act (Germany) 1976.

- Relationships: banks have a much closer relationship with German companies than in the UK. They are frequently shareholders, and other shareholders often deposit their shares and the rights associated with them with their banks.

This creates a backdrop to creating structures where these parties are actively involved in company affairs, hence the two-tier structure.

Lower tier: management (operating) board:

- responsible for day-to-day running of the enterprise

- generally only includes executives

- the CEO co-ordinates activity.

Upper tier: supervisory (corporate) board:

- appoints, supervises and advises members of the management board

- strategic oversight of the organisation

- includes employee representatives, environmental groups and other stakeholders' management representatives (these NEDs are not considered to be 'independent NEDs')

- the chairman co-ordinates the work

- members are elected by shareholders at the annual general meeting (AGM)

- receives information and reports from the management board.

Advantages of a two-tier board

- Clear separation between those that manage the company and those that own it or must control it for the benefit of shareholders.

- Implicit shareholder involvement in most cases since these structures are used in countries where insider control is prevalent.

- Wider stakeholder involvement implicit through the use of worker representation.

- Independence of thought, discussion and decision since board meetings and operation are separate.

- Direct power over management through the right to appoint members of the management board.

Problems with a two-tier board

- Dilution of power, confusion over authority and hence a perceived lack of accountability. (NB Due to codetermination, there is a right for many different stakeholders to be involved in decisions which affect them.)

- Isolation of supervisory board through non-participation in management meetings.

- Agency problems between the boards where one will be acting on behalf of another e.g. the Management Board meetings excluding the Supervisory Board resulting in confusion over authority.

- Increased bureaucracy which may result in slower decisions being made.

- Lack of transparency over appointment of supervisory board members leading to inefficient monitoring and governance.

Advantages of a unitary board

Issues specific to the unitary board tend to relate to the role of NEDs.

- NED expertise: the implied involvement of NEDs in the running of the company rather than just supervising.

- NED empowerment: they are as responsible as the executives and this is better demonstrated by their active involvement at an early stage.

- Compromise: less extreme decisions developed prior to the need for supervisory approval.

- Responsibility: a cabinet decision-making unit with wide viewpoints suggests better decisions.

- Reduction of fraud, malpractice: this is due to wider involvement in the actual management of the company.

- Improved investor confidence: through all of the above.

4 Non-executive directors (NEDs)

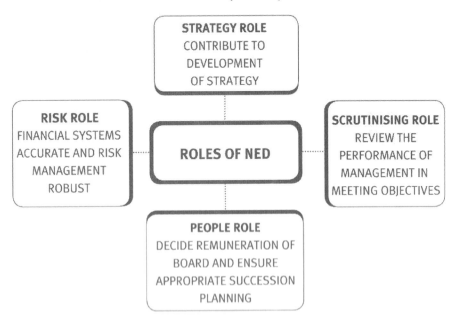

The key roles of NEDs

Strategy role: this recognises that NEDs have the right and responsibility to contribute to strategic success, challenging strategy and offering advice on direction.

Scrutinising role: NEDs are required to hold executive colleagues to account for decisions taken and results obtained.

Risk role: NEDs ensure the company has an adequate system of internal controls and systems of risk management in place.

People role: NEDs oversee a range of responsibilities with regard to the appointment and remuneration of executives and will be involved in contractual and disciplinary issues.

An effective NED

To be effective, a NED needs to:

- build a recognition by executives of their contribution in order to promote openness and trust

- be well-informed about the company and the external environment in which it operates

- have a strong command of issues relevant to the business

- insist on a comprehensive, formal and tailored induction, continually develop and refresh their knowledge and skills to ensure that their contribution to the board remains informed and relevant

- ensure that information is provided sufficiently in advance of meetings to enable thorough consideration of the issues facing the board

- insist that information is sufficient, accurate, clear and timely

- uphold the highest ethical standards of integrity and probity

- question intelligently, debate constructively, challenge rigorously and decide dispassionately

- promote the highest standards of corporate governance and seek compliance with the provisions of the Combined Code wherever possible.

 ## Independence

The Code states as a principle that the board should include a balance of NEDs and executives. This is to reduce an unfavourable balance of power towards executives.

The board should consist of half independent NEDs excluding the chair.

One NED should be the senior independent director who is directly available to shareholders if they have concerns which cannot or should not be dealt with through the appropriate channels of chairman, CEO or finance director.

The primary fiduciary duty that NEDs owe is to the company's shareholders. They must not allow themselves to be captured or unduly influenced by the vested interests of other members of the company such as executive directors, trade unions or middle management.

There are also concerns over the recruitment of NEDs and the challenge that this may bring to independence.

Recruiting those with previous industry involvement can result in a higher technical knowledge, a network of contacts and an awareness of what the strategic issues are within the industry. While these might be of some benefit to a NED's contribution, they can make the NED less independent as prior industry involvement might also reduce the NED's ability to be objective and uncontaminated by previously held views.

Accordingly, it is sometimes easier to demonstrate independence when NEDs are appointed from outside the industry.

In practice, many companies employ a mix of NEDs, and it is often this blend of talents and areas of expertise that makes a non-executive board effective.

Reasons for NED independence

- To provide a detached and objective view of board decisions.
- To provide expertise and communicate effectively.
- To provide shareholders with an independent voice on the board.
- To provide confidence in corporate governance.
- To reduce accusations of self-interest in the behaviour of executives.

Threats to independence

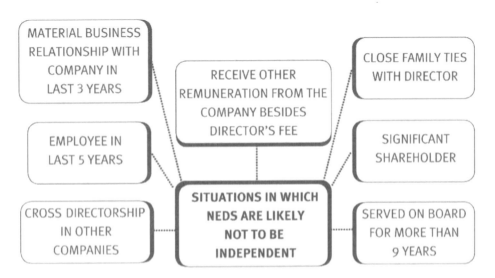

 Cross directorship

A cross directorship is said to exist when two (or more) directors sit on the boards of the other. In most cases, each director's 'second' board appointment is likely to be non-executive.

For example, director A is an executive director on the board of company X and also holds a non-executive position on the board of company Z. Director B is an executive on the board of company Z and also holds a non-executive position in company X.

Cross directorships could undermine the NED independence in that a director reviewing performance of a colleague who, in turn, may play a part in reviewing his or her own performance, is a clear conflict of interests. Neither director involved in the arrangement is impartial and so a temptation would exist to act in a manner other than for the benefit of the shareholders of the company on whose board they sit.

In practice, such arrangements may also involve some element of cross shareholdings which further compromises the independence of the directors involved.

It is for this reason the cross directorships and cross shareholding arrangements are explicitly forbidden by many corporate governance codes of best practice.

NEDs on the board

Advantages

* Monitoring: they offer a clear monitoring role, particularly on remuneration committees to dampen the excesses of executives.

* Expertise: to expand this resource available for management to use.

* Perception: institutional and watchdog perception is enhanced because of their presence.

* Communication: the implied improvement in communication between shareholders' interests and the company.

* Discipline: NEDs may have a positive influence on the success or otherwise of takeovers.

Disadvantages

* Unity: lack of trust and needless input can affect board operations.

* Quality: there may be a poor gene pool of NEDs willing to serve.

* Liability: the poor remuneration with the suggested (Higgs) removal of stock options from the package coupled with the equal liability in law for company operations might lead some to question whether they want the job or not.

 5   Chairman and CEO

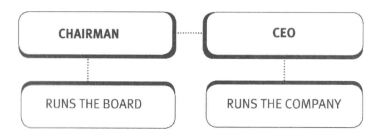

Responsibilities

It is vital for good corporate governance to separate the roles of chairman and CEO to avoid "unfettered powers".

The division of responsibilities between the chairman and CEO should be clearly established, set out in writing and agreed by the board.

The importance of the appointments of CEO and chairman are further underlined by the fact that the CEO frequently has most say over the appointment of executive directors to the board, while the chairman will frequently have a great deal of influence over the appointment of NEDs.

Chairman's responsibilities

The overall responsibility of the chairman is to:

- ensure that the board sets and implements the company's direction and strategy effectively, and

- act as the company's lead representative, explaining aims and policies to the shareholders.

Specific responsibilities of the chairman

The specific responsibilities of the chairman, inter alia, are to:

- provide leadership to the board, supplying vision and imagination, working closely with the CEO

- take a leading role in determining the composition and structure of the board which will involve regular assessment of the:

  - size of the board

  - balance between executive directors and NEDs

  - interaction, harmony and effectiveness of the directors

- set the board's agenda and plan board meetings

- chair all board meetings, directing debate toward consensus

- ensure the board receives appropriate, accurate, timely and clear information

- facilitate effective contribution from NEDs

- hold meetings with the NEDs, without the executive directors present

- chair the AGM and other shareholders' meetings, using these to provide effective dialogue with shareholders

- discuss governance and major strategy with the major shareholders

- ensure that the views of shareholders are communicated to the board as a whole.

 CEO's responsibilities

The overall responsibility of the CEO is to:

- take responsibility for the performance of the company, as determined by the board's strategy

- report to the chairman and/or board of directors.

Specific responsibilities of the CEO

The specific responsibilities of the CEO, inter alia, are to:

- develop and implement policies to execute the strategy established by the board

- assume full accountability to the board for all aspects of company operations, controls and performance

- manage financial and physical resources

- build and maintain an effective management team

- put adequate operational, financial, planning, risk and internal control systems in place

- closely monitor operations and financial results in accordance with plans and budgets

- interface between board and employees

- assist in selection and evaluation of board members

- represent the company to major suppliers, customers, professional associations, etc.

Splitting the role

The UK Corporate Governance Code (2010) is unequivocal with regard to the separation of the chairman and CEO roles:

'A clear division of responsibilities must exist at the head of the company. No individual should have unfettered power of decision.'

Chairmen should be independent in the same way that NEDs are designated as being independent. If not, reasons must be clearly disclosed to major shareholders.

The code states the chairman should, on appointment, meet the independence criteria set out in the provisions, but thereafter the test of independence is not appropriate to the chairman.

Reasons for splitting the role

- Representation: the chairman is clearly and solely a representative of shareholders with no conflict of interest having a role as a manager within the firm.

- Accountability: the existence of the separate chairman role provides a clear path of accountability for the CEO and the management team.

- Temptation: the removal of the joint role reduces the temptation to act more in self-interest rather than purely in the interest of shareholders.

Reasons against splitting the role

- Unity: the separation of the role creates two leaders rather than the unity provided by a single leader.

- Ability: both roles require an intricate knowledge of the company. It is far easier to have a single leader with this ability rather than search for two such individuals.

- Human nature: there will almost inevitably be conflict between two high-powered executive offices.

Test your understanding 1

Three years ago, the outgoing CEO/chairman of BrightCo decided to retire having served in the combined role for over ten years of a full 30 year BrightCo career. Succession was not an issue since Dan Bolowski had been operating as second in command for a number of years and had recently stepped firmly into "the old man's" shoes.

What followed was a roller coaster ride for investors, where the minor dips were more than compensated by the exhilarating rise in share price. Bolowski trebled the size of the company through his aggressive "slash and burn" acquisitive strategy, taking the company into uncharted markets around the globe where he bought, stripped and resold huge companies, reaping profits in the process.

The board of directors is rightfully pleased with its CEO's performance and the part it played in that success, seven out of ten board members being company executives. The remaining three were drafted in by the ex-CEO/chairman due to their key expertise in BrightCo's traditional markets. None have regular contact with shareholders. The board meets irregularly and (by its own admission) does not tend to do more than simply review current performance. Mr Bolowski has complete freedom to act and this is widely seen as the reason for the company's positive trading position.

Shareholders are also pleased with performance. However, some institutional investors have aired their concerns as to the sustainability of the current strategy, whether finances exist within BrightCo to support it and whether risks associated with unknown markets make the company overexposed and vulnerable.

At the last board meeting Mr Bolowski brushed aside any criticism stating that he was going to take the firm to new heights, a pronouncement met with loud applause from all those in attendance.

> **Required:**
>
> (a) With reference to the scenario, discuss changes to governance structure that you would recommend for this company.
>
> (b) Assuming the changes recommended in part (a) are carried out, describe the possible role of a new board of directors.
>
> **Professional skills:**
>
> Demonstrate communication skills when recommending changes to the governance structure for BrightCo and when describing the role of the new board of directors.

6 Directors' induction and CPD

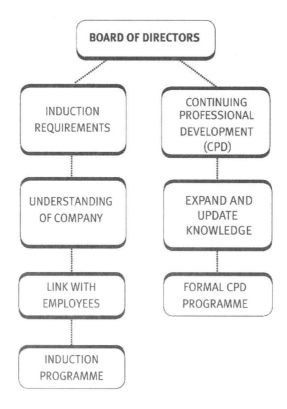

Induction

- Although aimed at NEDs, the principles of an induction programme will be the same for new executive directors coming to the company from another organisation.

- For an internally-promoted director, it will depend on the person's background as to which aspects of the programme must be undertaken.

- It is important, for effective participation in board strategy development, not only for the board to get to know the new NED, but also for the NED to build relationships with the existing board and employees below board level.

The induction process

Every company should develop its own formal induction programme and it should:

- be comprehensive

- be tailored to the needs of the company and individual directors

- contain selected written information plus presentations and activities such as meetings and site visits

- give new appointees a balanced and real-life overview of the company

- not overload the new director with too much information

- provide the new director with a list of all the induction information that is being made available to them so that they may call up items if required before these are otherwise provided.

The induction process should give the incoming director:

- an understanding of the nature of the company, its business and the markets in which it operates

- a link with the company's people

- an understanding of the company's main relationships (including meeting with the company's auditors).

Objectives of induction

- To communicate vision and culture.

- To communicate practical procedural duties.

- To reduce the time taken for an individual to become productive in their duties.

- To assimilate an individual as a welcome member of the board.

- To ensure retention of individuals for future periods.

Induction package

The company secretary is generally responsible for directors' induction. The Institute of Chartered Secretaries and Administrators (ICSA) induction package suggests the following items for immediate provision to the director.

Director's duties

- Brief outline of director's role and responsibilities under codes of best practice.

- Advice on share dealing and disclosure of price sensitive information.

- Company information on matters reserved for the board, delegated authority, policy for obtaining independent advice.

- Fire drill procedures.

Company strategies:

- Current strategies, plans and budgets/forecasts.

- Annual accounts, interims and KPIs.

- Company structures, subsidiaries and joint ventures.

- Treasury issues such as financing and dividend policy.

- Company brochures, mission statements.

Board operations:

- Memorandum and articles.

- Minutes of 4–6 previous meetings.

- Board composition/profiles of members.

- Details of committees, meeting procedures and schedule for future meetings.

A few months later:

- Company's history plus products and services brochures.

- Details of advisors and contacts (lawyers, auditors, banks).

- Details of major shareholders and shareholder relations policy.

- Copies of AGM circulars from three previous years.

- Copies of management accounts.

- Details of risk management procedures and disaster recovery plans.

- Policies: health and safety, whistleblower, environmental, ethics and charitable.

- Recent press releases, reports, articles, cuttings.

- Details of five largest customers and suppliers.

- Full details of the code of compliance and company policy in relation to it.

Continuing Professional Development (CPD)

The following offers guidance on directors' CPD requirements:

- To run an effective board, companies need to provide resources for developing and refreshing the knowledge and skills of their directors, including the NEDs.

- The chairman should address the developmental needs of the board as a whole with a view to enhancing its effectiveness as a team.

- The chairman should also lead in identifying the development needs of individual directors, with the company secretary playing a key role in facilitating provision.

- NEDs should be prepared to devote time to keeping their skills up to date.

Objectives of CPD

- To ensure directors have sufficient skills and ability to be effective in their role.

- To communicate challenges and changes within the business environment effectively to directors.

- To improve board effectiveness and, through this, corporate profitability.

- To support directors in their personal development.

- The overall purpose of these objectives is to provide benefits to the individual and the employing organisation.

7 Legal and regulatory framework governing the board of directors

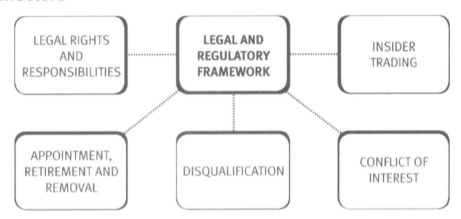

Legal rights and responsibilities

The legal duties of a director are a baseline for directorial action and a concern since breach can leave a director open to criminal prosecution and imprisonment (e.g. corporate manslaughter).

Objective

The law is there to protect the owners of the company. It exists because of the nature of a fiduciary relationship where one person acts on behalf of another. The law provides a framework for directors' actions in upholding the best principles in this owner/manager relationship.

Power

Directors do not have unlimited power.

- Articles of association: the articles of association provide a framework for how directors operate including the need to be re-elected on a 3 year rotation.

- Shareholder resolution: this curtails director action in a legal sense.

- Provisions of law: these could be health and safety or the duty of care.

- Board decisions: it is the board that makes decisions in the interests of shareholders, not individual directors, but rather a collective view.

Directors do however have unlimited liability in the sense that even though they may delegate actions to management below, in a legal sense they cannot delegate liability for the outcome.

Fiduciary duties

Being aware of the objective and the power vested in directors leads to consideration of the nature of the fiduciary relationship.

*   The duty to act in good faith: as long as directors' motives are honest and they genuinely believe they are acting in the best interests of the company they are normally safe from claims that they should have acted otherwise.

*   The duty of skill and care: this care is a specific fiduciary duty. The law requires a director to use reasonable skill and care in carrying out their tasks.

Penalties

Directors who breach duties may face civil action by the company. If the director is in breach:

*   any contract made by the director may be void

*   they may be personally liable for damages in compensation for negligence

*   they may be forced to restore company property at their own expense.

In the UK (for example purposes only) offences occur under the Companies Act 2006.

There are over 250 offences with penalties ranging from fines to imprisonment. Most are dealt with at contract magistrates' courts and relate to:

*   administrative and compliance issues such as those for filing accounts

*   restrictions and disclosure requirements such as insider trading and disclosure of share interests.

Conflict and disclosure of interests

The fiduciary duty of directors is to act in the best interests of shareholders, i.e. the directors may not put themselves in a position where their own personal interests conflict with the duties that they owe to the company as director.

A conflict of interest is a breach of this duty. A situation that has the potential to undermine the impartial nature of an individual's business dealing due to a clash of interest between the persons self-interest and public or professional interest.

A conflict of interest could be for directors of a company to also be involved with suppliers, buyers or competitors where clearly their independence would be threatened.

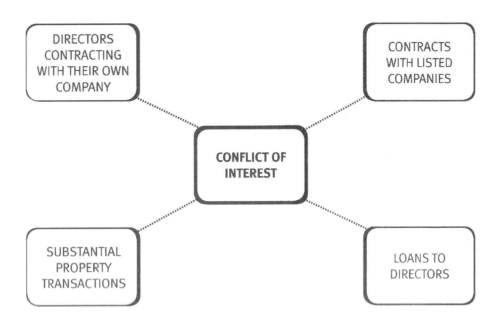

Area of conflict of interest

- Directors contracting with their own company: in general, directors cannot contract with their own company. However, the articles may specifically allow the director to have an interest as long as he discloses this interest to the board of directors.

- Substantial property transactions: the Companies Act in the UK (for example) requires any substantial asset sale above 10% of net worth to be approved by shareholders through ordinary resolution. Substantial property transactions – "The asset(s) in question need to be of "requisite value" to qualify as a substantial property transaction. If the asset is worth less than £5,000, it is not of requisite value and the transaction will not be a substantial property transaction. If the asset is worth more than £100,000 then it will always be a substantial property transaction. If the asset is worth between £5,000 and £100,000 then it will qualify as being of requisite value if it is worth more than 10% of the company's net assets (net worth) as stated in the company's most recent statutory accounts, or if no accounts have been prepared, 10% of the company's called up share capital."

- Contracts with listed companies: the Listing Rules of the London Stock Exchange (for example) stipulate that any substantial contract between the company and an interested party must be agreed by ordinary resolution before the transaction takes place.

- Loans to directors: generally, loans to directors are prohibited.

Disclosure

The Companies Act (CA 06) s 412 and 413 states that companies are required, in the form of notes in the annual accounts, to disclose any information concerning transactions involving the directors. This includes any transaction or arrangement that is a material interest.

Insider dealing/trading

Insider trading is the illegal purchase or sale of shares by someone (usually a director) who possesses inside information about a company's performance and prospects which, if publicly available, might affect the share price.

- Inside information is information which is not available to the market or general public and is supposed to remain confidential.

- These types of transactions in the company's own shares are considered to be fraudulent.

- The 'director insider', simply by accepting employment, has made a contract with the shareholders to put the shareholders' interests before their own, in matters related to the company.

- When the insider buys or sells based upon company-owned information, he is violating his contract with, and fiduciary duty to, the shareholders.

Test your understanding 2

Are these scenarios examples of insider trading?

Scenario 1

The chairman of Company ZZ knows (prior to any public announcement) that Company ZZ is to be taken over, and then buys shares in Company ZZ knowing that the share price will probably go up.

Scenario 2

While in a bar, an individual hears the CEO of Company ZZ at the next table telling the sales director that the company is to be taken over. That individual then buys the shares.

Performance evaluation of the board

Some of the questions that should be considered in a performance evaluation of the board include, inter alia:

- How well has the board performed against any performance objectives that have been set?

- What has been the board's contribution to the testing and development of strategy?

- What has been the board's contribution to ensuring robust and effective risk management?

- Is the composition of the board and its committees appropriate, with the right mix of knowledge and skills to maximise performance in the light of future strategy?

- Are relationships inside and outside the board working effectively?

- How has the board responded to any problems or crises that have emerged and could or should these have been foreseen?

- Are the matters specifically reserved for the board the right ones?

- How well does the board communicate with the management team, company employees and others?

- How effectively does it use mechanisms such as the AGM and the annual report?

- Is the board as a whole up to date with latest developments in the regulatory environment and the market?

- How effective are the board's committees? (Specific questions on the performance of each committee should be included such as, e.g. their role, their composition and their interaction with the board.)

The processes that help underpin the board's effectiveness should also be evaluated:

- Is appropriate, timely information of the right length and quality provided to the board and is management responsive to requests for clarification or amplification?

- Does the board provide helpful feedback to management on its requirements?

- Are sufficient board and committee meetings of appropriate length held to enable proper consideration of issues?

- Is time used effectively?

- Are board procedures conducive to effective performance and flexible enough to deal with all eventualities?

Performance evaluation: chairman and NEDs

Some specific issues relating to the chairman (which should be included as part of an evaluation of the board's performance) include:

- Is the chairman demonstrating effective leadership of the board?

- Are relationships and communications with shareholders well managed?

- Are relationships and communications within the board constructive?

- Are the processes for setting the agenda working?

- Do they enable board members to raise issues and concerns?

- Is the company secretary being used appropriately and to maximum value?

The chairman and other NEDs should consider the following issues and the individuals concerned should also be asked to assess themselves by answering the following questions:

- How well prepared and informed are they for board meetings and is their meeting attendance satisfactory?

- Do they demonstrate a willingness to devote time and effort to understanding the company and its business and a readiness to participate in events outside the boardroom, such as site visits?

- What has been the quality and value of their contributions at board meetings?

- What has been their contribution to development of strategy and to risk management?

- How successfully have they brought their knowledge and experience to bear in the consideration of strategy?

- How effectively have they probed to test information and assumptions?

- Where necessary, how resolute are they in maintaining their own views and resisting pressure from others?

- How effectively and proactively have they followed up their areas of concern?

- How effective and successful are their relationships with fellow board members, the company secretary and senior management?

- Does their performance and behaviour engender mutual trust and respect within the board?

- How actively and successfully do they refresh their knowledge and skills and are they up to date with:

  - the latest developments in areas such as corporate governance framework and financial reporting?

  - the industry and market conditions?

- How well do they communicate with fellow board members, senior management and others, e.g. shareholders?

- Are they able to present their views convincingly yet diplomatically and do they listen and take on board the views of others?

8 Board committees

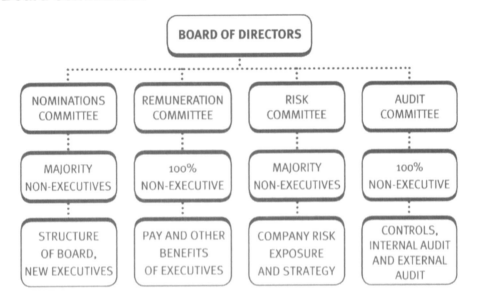

Importance of committees

Board sub-committees are a generally accepted part of board operations.

Positives that come out of the creation and use of such structures are:

- Reduces board workload and enables it to improve focus on other issues.

- Creates structures that can use inherent expertise to improve decisions in key areas.

- Communicates to shareholders that directors take these issues seriously.

- Increase in shareholder confidence.

- Communicates to stakeholders the importance of remuneration and risk.

- Satisfy requirements of the UK Corporate Governance Code (2010) (or other governance requirements).

🔑 9 Nominations committee

The need for a nominations committee is identified in many codes of best practice.

As an example, the UK Corporate Governance Code (2010) requires that **there should be a formal, rigorous and transparent procedure for the appointments of new directors to the board:**

Creation of a nominations committee.

- This should have a majority of NEDs, the chairman should chair except when considering his successor.
- Evaluation of candidate's skills, knowledge and expertise is vital.
- Chairman's other commitments should be noted in the annual report.
- NED terms and conditions available for inspection, other commitments stated.
- Executives should not be members of any other FTSE 100 company board.
- A separate section of the annual report should describe the work of the committee.

Responsibilities of nominations committee

The main responsibilities and duties of the nominations committee are to:

- Review regularly the structure, size and composition of the board and make recommendations to the board.
- Consider the balance between executives and NEDs on the board of directors.
- Ensure appropriate management of diversity to board composition.
- Provide an appropriate balance of power to reduce domination in executive selection by the CEO/chairman.
- Regularly evaluate the balance of skills, knowledge and experience of the board.
- Give full consideration to succession planning for directors.
- Prepare a description of the role and capabilities required for any particular board appointment including that of the chairman.
- Identify and nominate for the approval by the board candidates to fill board vacancies as and when they arise.
- Make recommendations to the board concerning the standing for reappointment of directors.
- Be seen to operate independently for the benefit of shareholders.

CEO/chairman succession

The search for a potential replacement CEO begins immediately after a new CEO is appointed:

- for the nomination committee to have access to senior managers to gauge performance

- to have some idea of a successor in case the new CEO dies or leaves

- to monitor senior managers and cultivate possible successors over time

- for a search firm ('head-hunters') to be retained for this and other directorship identification

- to think very carefully as to whether the company wants a visionary at

- the helm or someone who can execute strategy effectively

- the NED chairman should meet independence criteria at the time of appointment.

10 Development of corporate governance regarding directors' remuneration

The **Greenbury Report (1995)** contributed to the existing code with regards to directors' remuneration.

A committee was formed to investigate shareholder concerns over director's remuneration. The report focused on providing a means of establishing a balance between salary and performance in order to restore shareholder confidence.

 ## 11 Remuneration committee

The role of the remuneration committee

The role of the remuneration committee is to have an appropriate reward policy that **attracts, retains and motivates** directors to achieve the long-term interests of shareholders.

This definition creates a good balance between the opposing viewpoints of stakeholders.

Objectives of the committee

- The committee is, and is seen to be, independent with access to its own external advice or consultants.

- It has a clear policy on remuneration that is well understood and has the support of shareholders.

- Performance packages produced are aligned with long-term shareholder interests and have challenging targets.

- Reporting is clear, concise and gives the reader of the annual report a bird's-eye view of policy payments and the rationale behind them.

The whole area of executive pay is one where trust must be created or restored through good governance and this is exercised through the use of a remuneration committee.

Responsibilities of the remuneration committee

The overall responsibilities of the remuneration committee are to:

- Determine and regularly review the framework, broad policy and specific terms for the remuneration and terms and conditions of employment of the chairman of the board and of executive directors (including design of targets and any bonus scheme payments).

- Recommend and monitor the level and structure of the remuneration of senior managers.

- Establish pension provision policy for all board members.

- Set detailed remuneration for all executive directors and the chairman, including pension rights and any compensation payments.

- Ensure that the executive directors and key management are fairly rewarded for their individual contribution to the overall performance of the company.

- Demonstrate to shareholders that the remuneration of the executive directors and key management is set by individuals with no personal interest in the outcome of the decisions of the committee.

- Agree any compensation for loss of office of any executive director.

- Ensure that provisions regarding disclosure of remuneration, including pensions, as set out in the Directors' Remuneration Report Regulations 2002 and the Code, are fulfilled.

12   Directors' remuneration

Remuneration is defined as payment or compensation received for services or employment and includes base salary, any bonuses and any other economic benefits that an employee or executive receives during employment.

Behavioural impact on directors of remuneration components

Whatever remuneration package is determined, it is essential to ensure that the directors have a stake in doing a good job for the shareholder.

- Each element of a remuneration package should be designed to ensure that the director remains focused on the company and motivated to improve performance.

- A balance must be struck between offering a package:

  - that is too small and hence demotivating and leading to potential underachievement, and

  - that is too easily earned.

The company, following the work of the remuneration committee, should:

- Provide a package needed to **attract, retain and motivate** executive directors of the quality required, but avoid paying more than is necessary.

- Judge where to position the remuneration package relative to other companies and labour market conditions.

- Be aware of what comparable companies are paying and should take account of relative performance.

- Be sensitive to the wider scene, including pay and employment conditions elsewhere in the company (especially when determining annual salary increases).

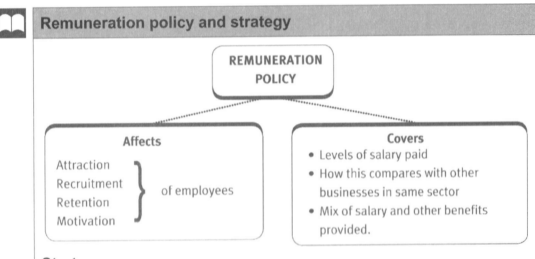

Remuneration policy and strategy

Strategy

A company's remuneration strategy may consider:

- offering more benefits in kind to compensate for lower basic salary

- non-cash motivators for all or some of the company employees, e.g. childcare vouchers, company car scheme, additional holiday

- availability of company resources, e.g. there may be insufficient cash available to pay an annual bonus, but share options might be an alternative

- encouraging long-term loyalty through share purchase schemes.

The need to develop a remuneration strategy that links reward to performance is the greatest challenge facing the remuneration committee. There is a critical need to ensure the board is:

- motivated to strive to increase performance

- adequately rewarded when performance improvements are achieved

- seen to be paid appropriately for their efforts and success

- not criticised for excessive pay

- retained through market-based pay levels.

> The remuneration strategy is therefore about creating a link to corporate strategy since corporate strategy is the process through which performance is improved.
>
> - the extent to which the remuneration strategy achieves this link or how close this link is, is a measure of the remuneration strategy's success.

Components of directors' remuneration package

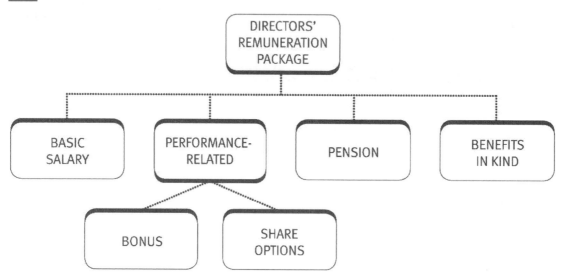

Basic salary

Companies set salary levels according to:

- the job itself
- the skills of the individual doing the job
- the individual's performance in the job
- the individual's overall contribution to company strategy
- market rates for that type of job.

The setting of base salary in relation to peer groups may give some indication of expectation of director performance since upper quartile salaries generally suggest the individual is being paid a premium for a premium effort over the future period.

Performance-related elements of remuneration

Defined as those elements of remuneration dependent on the achievement of some form of performance-measurement criteria.

- Performance-related element should form a significant part of the total remuneration package.

A short-term bonus may be paid to the director at the end of the accounting year. This could be based on any number of accounting measures.

Bases for short-term bonus

Short-term bonuses may be based on any of the following:

1 **Operating profits or pre-tax profits**

    – Percentage of bonus based on salary in relation to percentage yearly profit increase.

    – 2% of salary for each 1% increase in profit.

    – Fixed sum for achieving a given profit target.

2 **Earnings per share (EPS)**

    – This may exclude exceptional charges that affect earnings.

3 **Total shareholder return**

    – This includes both dividend and capital appreciation over time.

4 **Economic value added (EVA)**

    – This is the surplus calculated above a charge on all assets used using the weighted average cost of capital (WACC) as a threshold percentage minimum return before a bonus is achieved.

Executive stock options are the most common form of long-term market-orientated incentive scheme.

- Share options are contracts that allow the executive to buy shares at a fixed price or exercise price.

- If the stock rises above this price the executive can sell the shares at a profit.

Executives treat share options as part of their compensation and almost always exercise the option when it becomes available.

- Share options give the executive the incentive to manage the firm in such a way that share prices increase, therefore share options are believed to align the managers' goals with those of the shareholders.

- This alignment should, in theory, overcome the agency problem of the separation between ownership and control since the executive in effect becomes the owner.

- The actual shares or share option incentives should be:

    – approved by shareholders

    – preferably replace any existing schemes or at least form part of a well-considered overall plan, incorporating existing schemes

    – rewarding but should not be excessive.

- Payouts (or grant of options) should be:

  - subject to challenging performance criteria reflecting the company's objectives and performance relative to a group of comparator companies in some key variables such as total shareholder return

  - phased rather than awarded in one large block.

Share options

The company, following the work of the remuneration committee, should:

- consider whether the directors should be eligible for benefits under long-term incentive schemes

- weigh traditional share option schemes against other kinds of long-term incentive scheme

- ensure that executive share options are not offered at a discount

- ensure that shares granted or other forms of deferred remuneration should not vest, and options should not be exercisable, in under three years

- encourage directors to hold their shares for a further period after vesting or exercise, subject to the need to finance any costs of acquisition and associated tax liabilities.

Pension contributions

- In general, only basic salary should be pensionable.

- The remuneration committee should consider the pension consequences and associated costs to the company of basic salary increases and any other changes in pensionable remuneration, especially for directors close to retirement.

Benefits in kind

- Benefits in kind (also referred to as perks) are various non-wage compensations provided to directors and employees in addition to their normal wages or salaries.

- The remuneration committee should provide whatever other ancillary benefits would either be expected with the position of executive director or would increase their loyalty and motivation (examples of these would be a company car, health insurance, etc.).

Illustration 1 – Tesco CEO's remuneration packages

The following information is summarised from Tesco plc's 2017 Annual Report.

Element	Purpose	Calculation	£000
Basic salary	To attract and retain talented people	Determined by responsibilities, skills and experience Benchmarked against other large FTSE 100 retailers and international equivalents	1,563 (including benefits)

Short-term performance related pay

Cash bonus	Motivates year-on-year earnings growth and delivery of strategic business priorities	Based on specific objectives and EPS (earning per share) targets e.g. development of international and non-food businesses	2,300
Deferred share bonus	Generates focus on medium-term targets and, by incentivising share price and dividend growth, ensures alignment with shareholder interest	Based on total shareholder return targets	1,690

Long-term performance related pay

Performance share plans and share options	Assures a focus on long-term business success and shareholder returns	Based on a mix of ROCE (return on capital employed), EBIT (earnings before interest and tax) and EPS	1,205

Total £5,472,000

Other forms of compensation

The guaranteed bonus and 'golden hellos'

- The purpose of a bonus is to adjust pay on the basis of performance. To award a bonus regardless of any particular effort is to make the term meaningless.

- Although not common, guaranteed bonuses are sometimes used to retain CEOs in struggling organisations. The same is true for signing on (turning up) bonuses ('golden hellos'). For example, David Lewis CEO of Tesco was paid £3.2m as a "golden hello" by way of compensation for bonuses forfeited from his previous employer, Unilever.

Loyalty bonuses and retention payments

- As with guaranteed bonuses mentioned above, loyalty bonuses are also used to retain senior executives. For example, in May 2011 Citigroup awarded its chief executive, Vikram Pandit, a $16.7m (£10.3m) retention bonus.

- However, they have come under criticism for the following reasons:

    - The current preference in Western countries is for rotation of directors to ensure freshness and independence, rather than an emphasis on loyalty

    - Corporate governance codes recommend linking bonuses with performance

    - There have been many cases of directors leaving soon after receiving their loyalty bonus (e.g. easyJet boss Andy Harrison controversially banked a £1.2m retention bonus in 2009 and then left in 2010).

Loans

- Since corporate governance is a global issue there are many countries where loans to directors have not been outlawed as they have in the US under Sarbanes-Oxley (SOX).

- There is little justification in making loans to people who can get loans from any other commercial lending source, especially when these loans are often non-interest bearing and possibly even non-repayable.

Deferred payments and transaction bonuses

- In a down market no one wants to be top of the tree for bonuses. Stock options for future periods become a welcome alternative in these lean times, to be vested when the market recovers.

- Transaction bonuses may be given for successful conclusion to a business deal such as a takeover.

Retirement benefits

- All awards are ultimately given by the shareholders and should be viewed in relation to performance achieved by the director.

- A retirement benefit such as lifetime use of the company plane or a sizeable pension payout could be awarded.

Termination

- Awards may be made on termination of contract simply for services rendered over a number of years.

- Building protection into a contract at the time of employment in order to limit the likelihood of forced termination is one way of reducing the possibility of being asked to leave.

Test your understanding 3

Mr Smith, an executive director of Company XCX, is paid a salary of £100,000. In addition, he receives the use of a company car. He is reimbursed all his travel expenses to and from all the places he has to visit in the course of his work. If the company's share price rises above £5 he is entitled to 10,000 share options at a price of £1 each. He will also receive a bonus of 20% of his salary if company profit before tax rises above £2.5 million. His wife also receives a company car, paid for by the company. He has permanent health insurance paid for by the company and has death-in-service benefits as well.

All of this is contained within his service contract.

What elements in the above paragraph constitute the director's remuneration?

UK Corporate Governance Code (2010)

There is more written in the UK Corporate Governance Code (2010) about the issue of directors' remuneration than anything else. This is probably due to the fact that it is an area where:

- excess needs to be reined in

- it is too easy to be excessive

- excess is viewed very dimly by everyone except those benefitting from the excess.

In addition, Schedule A to the Code provides further guidance on performance-related pay.

- The committee must consider eligibility and upper limits to bonuses.

- The committee must consider eligibility and nature of long-term incentive schemes such as share option schemes.

- Long-term schemes should be approved by shareholders and should replace existing schemes where possible.

- Payouts under all schemes must relate to performance criteria.

- Payouts under share option schemes should be phased where possible.

- In general only basic salary should be pensionable.

- The committee must carefully consider pension costs and obligations.

Some of the issues that arise from this are:

- the importance of performance-related pay

- the conflict of interest that may arise in cross-determination of pay between directors

- the variety of pay and the impact of share option schemes.

13 Directors' remuneration: other issues

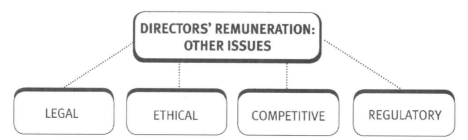

There are a number of other issues relating to directors' remuneration which a company should consider. These are:

- legal: what are the legal implications of the company/director relationship in terms of remuneration, especially when things go wrong?

- ethical: what ethical considerations should a company have in setting directors' remuneration?

- competitive: how does a company remain competitive and ensure that they attract good quality directors?

- regulatory: what are the regulatory requirements that a company should adhere to in relation to its directors' remuneration?

Other remuneration issues

Legal

A company (with the guidance of the remuneration committee) should:

- carefully consider what compensation commitments (including pension contributions and all other elements) their directors' terms of appointment would entail in the event of early termination

- aim to avoid rewarding poor performance.

Ethical

- The traditional view that ethics and business do not mix is now rarely accepted.

- Increasingly companies are demonstrating a sensitivity to combining ethical issues with commercial success.

- The commercial environment is progressively affected by the very ethical issues that companies are now dealing with.

- The 2006 Companies Act in the UK makes it a legal requirement for directors to act as 'good corporate citizens', in effect, that directors pay attention to the ethical effects of company decisions.

- Public reaction to high profile corporate failures where directors were receiving what was perceived as excessive remuneration in relation to their performance.

- Public perceptions of excessive pay rises in underperforming companies and privatised utilities.

- Recent changes to best practice disclosure requirements on board structure and executive pay have put pressure on companies to change their board policies to be seen to be in line with accepted best practice.

- The following recent developments have resulted in many leading companies incorporating business ethics into their management processes, directors' employment contracts and performance-related pay systems.

Competitive

It is vital that a company has a proficient, motivated board of directors working in the interests of its shareholders and that it can recruit and retain the individuals required for successful performance.

A balance must be struck with regards to the overall remuneration package.

If it is too small:

- unattractive for potential new appointees, hence a failure to recruit required calibre of individual

- demotivating for existing directors, hence potential underachievement.

If it is too big:

- too easily earned, hence shareholders not getting 'value for money' in terms of performance.

Regulatory

The UK Directors' Remuneration Report Regulations 2002 require that:

- directors submit a remuneration report to members at the annual general meeting (AGM) each year

- the report must provide full details of directors' remuneration

- the report is clear, transparent and understandable to shareholders

- where a company releases an executive director to serve as a NED elsewhere, the remuneration report should include a statement as to whether or not the director will retain such earnings and, if so, what the remuneration is.

There is an increasingly regulatory environment for companies to operate in and this in turn is placing greater demand on directors.

- Remuneration packages in general have risen in the wake of recent high profile corporate scandals and the passage of the Sarbanes-Oxley Act 2002 (SOX).

- This reflects:

  - the additional demands on directors

  - the additional responsibilities of directors

  - the potential liability of those individuals who agree to serve on boards of directors

  - heightened external scrutiny.

14 Non-executive directors' remuneration

To avoid the situation where the remuneration committee (consisting of NEDs) is solely responsible for determining the remuneration of the NEDs, the UK Corporate Governance Code (2016) states that the board and shareholders should determine the NED's remuneration within the limits set out in the company's constitution.

NED remuneration consists of a basic salary and non-executive directors may receive share awards.

Equity-based remuneration to non-executive directors should be fully vested on the grant date, but still subject to applicable holding periods.

Performance measures remuneration whilst advocated in executive remuneration packages is not generally supported for non-executive remuneration. Organisations such as the ICGN advocate that performance-based remuneration for non-executive directors has significant potential to conflict with their primary role as an independent representative of shareowners.

15 Chapter summary

UNITARY STRUCTURE
- a **unity board** structure is simply one board of directors accountable directly to the shareholders
- companies in countries like the US and the UK have unitary boards.

TWO-TIER STRUCTURE
- consists of a supervisory board and a management board.
- companies in France, Germany, Finland and the Netherlands are among those with two-tier board structures.

BOARD OF DIRECTORS

MEETINGS
- agenda balances long-and short-term issues
- supportive information
- regular and attendance expected
- chairman directs proceedings.

ROLES AND RESPONSIBILITIES
- act in good faith in the interests of the company as a whole
- display a certain amount of skill and exercise reasonable care.
- ensure company maintains full and accurate accounting records.
- produce, present and file proper annual accounts and directors' report.
- obey other laws.

LEGAL AND REGULATORY FRAMWORK
- appointment and retirement
- service contracts
- removal
- disqualification
- conflicts of interest
- insider dealing.

CHARACTERISTICS AND COMPOSITION
- balance of executive directors and NEDs
- not be dominated by a single powerful individual
- role of chair and the chief executive should be different people.

CHAIRMAN
- runs the board
- ensures that the board sets and implements the company's direction and strategy effectively
- acts as the company's lead representative.

INDUCTION PROGRAMME
gives incoming director:
- an understanding of the nature of the company, its business and the markets in which it operates
- a link with the company's people
- an understanding of the company's main relationships

CPD
Companies need to provide resources for developing and refreshing the knowledge and skills of their directors, including the NEDs.

PERFORMANCE EVALUATION
At least once a year, the performance of the board as a whole, its commitees and its members should be evaluated.

EXECUTIVE DIRECTORS
- members of a board of directors who are also senior managers of the company
- usually paid or remunerated as full time employees for their work.

NEDS
- members of the board of directors of a company who do not form part of the executive management team
- not full-time employees of the company or affiliated to it in any other way.

CHIEF EXECUTIVE
- takes responsibility for the perormance of the company, as determined by the board's strategy.
- reports to the chairman and/or board of directors.

INDEPENDENCE
- requires a certain detachment from the company.
- should be independent in judgement and have an enquiring mind.

Test your understanding answers

Test your understanding 1

(a) **Governance structure**

Changes to governance structure will emerge from failures manifest in current operations. Whilst BrightCo is an extremely successful company there is no assurance that this will continue. The concerns of institutional investors (assuming they are a substantial element within the overall shareholding of the firm) must be addressed since the company is their company and what they want is what the financial vehicle (company) must deliver.

Taking the governance issues as they are presented in the scenario, the first concerns the lack of separation between CEO and chairman. This is a contentious issue although the UK Corporate Governance Code (2010) is unequivocal in its recommendation that both functions should be performed by separate individuals. It is the role of the chairman to represent shareholders and the role of the CEO to run the company. It would appear that, at present, the CEO/chairman is more interested in the latter and ignoring shareholders wishes/needs/concerns.

The Code also recommends that the chairman role be independent in the sense that the individual chosen has no prior role within the company. This should lead to a greater likelihood of independence of thought and action outside of executive management influence. The succession of an "insider" into the role can potentially create a conflict in the actions of a joint role holder. This seems evident in the incumbents' pursuit of a strategy that may increase shareholders risk exposure beyond a level that is acceptable to them.

Perhaps the most important issue to address is the lack of adequate non-executive director membership on the board. Such individuals bring with them great expertise as well as operating in a monitoring capacity for shareholders. The UK Corporate Governance Code (2010) states that for UK companies the balance of non-executives to executives should be at least 50/50 with the chairman operating as a casting vote in favour of shareholder opinion should conflict arise. The current number of NEDs is inadequate to achieve this purpose.

In addition, current non-executives do not have regular contact with shareholders. The UK Corporate Governance Code (2010) calls for the creation of a senior independent role which provides a communication channel for shareholder contact should this be necessary. Recognition of this role could be part of the governance restructuring although the inclusion of more non executives is a necessary first step.

More subtle points mentioned in the scenario include the lack of appropriate skills on the board and, in particular, in relation to the non-executives. Recently, the nature of the company has changed dramatically and there is clearly a need for expertise in relation to its new business ventures in order to reduce the inherent risk and advise management accordingly. Induction and training were recommended in the Higgs report for NEDs and this should become part of governance operations at BrightCo.

Finally, the lack of regular board meetings is of some concern. Regular meetings of the board is the first provision of the UK Corporate Governance Code (2010), to ensure they are continually involved in strategic decision making and are well informed of the company's position. The scope and structure of such meetings will depend on the changing role of the board as discussed below.

(b) **Board Role**

There is no single or simple definition as to the nature of the role of the board of directors. The scenario does however give some indication of likely areas of concern in the monitoring function associated with board operation.

Fundamentally, the role of the board is to represent shareholder interests, offering a duty of care and loyalty to the owners of the organisation. This duty does not seem to fully exist at present, with allegiance seemingly towards the CEO/chairman rather than those outside of strategic management. The board must be clear as to its position in this critical area since it impacts on every aspect of their decision making detailed below.

The most obvious role of a board is to monitor performance, particularly financial performance, of the entity and to offer appropriate advice to executive management in order to improve in this area if possible. Current success may have dampened interest in the counselling element associated with this function as directors simply operate as bystanders applauding the CEO in his efforts. A more enquiring and critical stance should be adopted.

Advice regarding strategic direction is another key aspect, especially when the strategic direction of the firm is changing rapidly. This general function could embrace a variety of more detailed considerations such as the need to assess risks and the availability of finance to support future operations. These are specifically mentioned and are good examples of key strategic management concerns that the board should be involved in.

Since the company's strategy revolves around new markets and purchasing corporations the advice offered by the board in this area could be invaluable, especially with new, expert non-executive directors.

A key role of the board is to ensure the continued operation of the organisation. This will include the need to consider succession just as the succession issue arose three years ago in this scenario. If the new CEO was to become ill this would leave the company with a major void in strategic leadership that is bound to affect share price. Succession must be planned for in order to ensure contingency exists and to plan for long-term future retirements etc. The board is in a unique position to consider this issue since it is above all executive operations and vested interest.

Finally, the degree to which the board is merely a watchdog or an active participant in decision making must be considered as should the scope and formality of their operation (possible creation of committees). This is true of all boards and especially in this scenario since, at present, there is no useful purpose being served by this board of directors.

Professional skills:

Communication requires the student to demonstrate that they can inform the recipient of the facts objectively, unambiguously and in a clear and concise manner. Regurgitation of the information in the scenario is not enough. A good answer will require the student to interpret the facts, clarify them and present them in a persuasive manner.

Test your understanding 2

Scenario 1: Yes

Scenario 2: No

The individual that buys the shares is not guilty of insider trading unless there was some closer connection between him/her, Company ZZ or Company ZZ's directors.

Test your understanding 3

All of it apart from the expenses reimbursement.

Reporting to stakeholders

Chapter learning objectives

Upon completion of this chapter you will be able to:

- discuss the factors that determine organisational policies on reporting to stakeholders, including stakeholder power and interests

- assess the role and value of integrated reporting and evaluate the issues concerning accounting for sustainability

- advise on the guiding principles, the typical content elements and the six capitals of an integrated report, and discuss the usefulness of this information to stakeholders

- describe and assess the social and environmental impacts that economic activity can have (in terms of social and environmental 'footprints' and environmental reporting)

- describe the main features of internal management systems for underpinning environmental and sustainability accounting including EMAS and ISO 14000

- examine how the audit of integrated reports can provide adequate assurance of the relevance and reliability of organisation reports to stakeholders

PER

One of the PER performance objectives (PO2) is that you manage stakeholder expectations and needs, developing and maintaining productive business relationships. You listen to and engage stakeholders effectively and communicate the right information to them when they need it. Working through this chapter should help you understand how to demonstrate that objective.

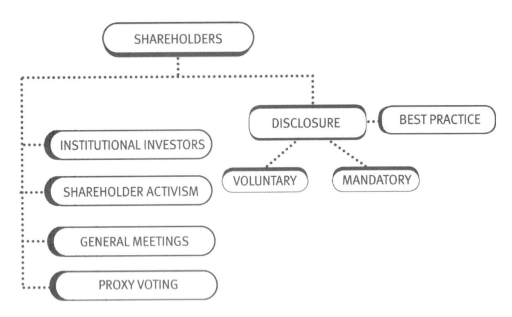

1 Development of corporate governance regarding shareholders and disclosure

The **Cadbury Report (1992)** first recognised the importance and role of the institutional shareholders. It was noted that there is a need for greater director dialogue and engagement with this group. From this dialogue would emerge a greater understanding of the need to appreciate and respond to the needs of shareholders and the other stakeholders who can affect or be affected by corporate decisions.

Also in the 2010 review of the **UK Corporate Governance Code** the Financial Reporting Council concluded that the impact of shareholders in monitoring the code could and should be enhanced by better interaction between the boards of listed companies and their shareholders.

The **UK Corporate Governance Code (2016)** recommends that there should be a dialogue with shareholders based on the mutual understanding of objectives.

The board as a whole has responsibility for ensuring that a satisfactory dialogue with shareholders takes place. The board should use general meetings to communicate with investors and to encourage their participation.

 ## 2 Institutional Investors

Institutional investors manage funds invested by individuals.

In the UK there are four types of institutional investor:

- pension funds
- life assurance companies
- unit trust
- investment trusts.

Importance of institutional investors

The key issue is the increasing dominance of this investor class and its potentially positive contribution to governance by concentrating power in a few hands.

Fund managers and other professionals working for the institutions have the skills and expertise to contribute towards the direction and management of a company.

Potential problems

In the separation between ownership and control there are a number of intermediaries, creating a complex web of agency relationships:

- investor
- pension fund trustee
- pension fund manager
- company.

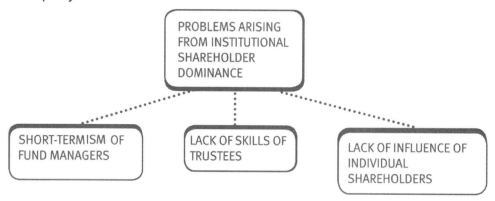

Institutional shareholder dominance

Problems that have arisen from institutional shareholder dominance involve:

- Fund managers: the short-termism of fund managers who, according to Keynes, are concerned 'not with what an investment is really worth to a man that buys it for keeps but with what the market will value it at under the influence of mass psychology three months or a year hence. Thus the professional concerns himself with beating the gun or anticipating impending change in the news or atmosphere'.

- Pension fund trustees: the trustee is often a lawyer or company secretary. 70% have no qualification in finance or investment and over 50% spend less than a day a year considering the issue. This woeful lack of interest and ambition does not suggest any interest in company operations beyond immediate short-term returns.

> In this model the distance between shareholder and company creates a governance vacuum:
>
> - Individual shareholders have no voice in how their investee companies operate since they do not directly own shares. Hence they do not have the right to attend the AGM and speak.
>
> - Pension funds need to examine their own governance structures as to how they invest and operate since they do have a voice and own shares in these companies.

Shareholder activism

The advent of the Cadbury report and the Code (UK example only) has seen a marked change in institutional investor relationships with organisations. This is from simply being a trader to one of responsible ownership, from a passive role to one of shareholder activism.

This activism can be in the form of:

- making positive use of voting rights

- engagement and dialogue with the directors of investee companies

- paying attention to board composition/governance of investee companies (evaluation of governance disclosure)

- presenting resolutions for voting on at the AGM (rarely used in UK)

- requesting an EGM and presenting resolutions.

Institutional shareholder intervention

Intervention by an institutional investor in a company whose stock it holds is considered to be a radical step. There are a number of conditions under which it would be appropriate for institutional investors to intervene:

- Strategy: this might be in terms of products sold, markets serviced, expansion pursued or any other aspect of strategic positioning.

- Operational performance: this might be in terms of divisions within the corporate structure that have persistently under-performed.

- Acquisitions and disposals: this might be in terms of executive decisions that have been inadequately challenged by NEDs.

- Remuneration policy: this might relate to a failure of the remuneration committee to curtail extreme or self-serving executive rewards.

- Internal controls: might relate to failure in health and safety, quality control, budgetary control or IT projects.

- Succession planning: this might relate to a failure to adequately balance board composition or recommendation of replacement executives without adequate consideration of the quality of the candidate.

- Social responsibility: this might relate to a failure to adequately protect or respond to instances of environmental contamination or other areas of public concern.

- Failure to comply with relevant codes: consistent and unexplained non-compliance in a principles-based country will be penalised by the market. In a rules-based country it would have been penalised as a matter of law.

Illustration 1 – Current need for institutional shareholder dialogue

According to the Organisation for Economic Cooperation and Development (OECD), the 2008 crash wiped a total of $5 trillion off the value of private pension funds in rich countries over the course of a single year.

Almost half of the total loss has been sustained by US investors although seismic shockwaves have affected all those whose wealth is intrinsically tied with the movements of the market.

The OECD calculates that UK pension funds declined by more than 15% ($300 billion) during 2008 and warns of far worse if the cost of falling property values were factored in. Among 28 countries covered in the study, Ireland's workers have been worse hit with their retirement fund falling by more than 30%.

In the light of these findings the OECD has called for a strengthening of governance regulation through bodies such as the Financial Services Authority, now Financial Conduct Authority, in order to ensure that institutional shareholders such as the large pension funds carry out adequate risk management of all portfolio organisations and do not simply rely on index tracking as a basis for investment decisions.

3   General meetings

A general meeting of an organisation is one which all shareholders or members are entitled to attend.

GENERAL MEETINGS

Annual General Meeting

- Must be held once every calendar year.
- Legally required.
- Separate resolutions for each issue.
- Not less than 21 days' notice required.
- First must be held no more than 18 months after date of incorporation, and thereafter no more than 15 months between meetings.
- All shareholders must be notified and entitled to attend.
- Annual accounts and appointment of auditors (if appropriate) approved at this meeting.

Extraordinary General Meeting

- No set timetable – held on an 'as required' basis.
- No legal obligation to have any.
- Separate resolutions for each issue.
- Not less than 14 days' notice required.
- All shareholders must be notified and entitled to attend.
- Agenda dictated by need for meeting.

Annual and extraordinary general meetings

AGM

- Held once a year by management to present the company to its shareholders.

- Various corporate actions may be presented and voted upon by shareholders or their proxies. These might include:

  - accepting the directors' report and statement of accounts for the year

  - reappointment of directors and auditors

  - approval of directors' and auditors' remuneration

  - approval of final dividends.

- The board should use the AGM to communicate with investors and to encourage their participation.

- Separate resolutions should be proposed on each substantially separate issue.

The UK Corporate Governance Code (2016) states that for listed companies:

- The chairman should arrange for the chairmen of the audit, remuneration and nomination committees to be available to answer questions at the AGM and for all directors to attend.

- The company should arrange for the notice of the AGM and related papers to be sent to shareholders at least 20 working days before the meeting.

- There must be a 'question and answer' session within the AGM to allow shareholders to respond to the presentation.

EGM

- These are irregularly held meetings arranged to approve special events such as acquisitions, takeovers, rights issues, etc.

- Separate resolutions should be proposed on each substantially separate issue.

- EGMs are usually called where an issue arises which requires the input of the entire membership and is too serious or urgent to wait until the next AGM.

- All general meetings, other than the AGM, are called EGMs. Notice for these meetings should be at least 14 days in advance.

4 Disclosure – general principles

Shareholders are the legal owners of a company and therefore entitled to sufficient information to enable them to make investment decisions.

- The AGM is seen as the most important, and perhaps only, opportunity for the directors to communicate with the shareholders of the company.

- As the only legally-required disclosure to shareholders, the annual report and accounts are often the only information shareholders receive from the company.

General principles of disclosure relate to the need to create and maintain communication channels with shareholders and other stakeholders. This disclosure becomes the mechanism through which governance is given transparency.

Principles of mandatory disclosure discuss the target for disclosure (particularly shareholders) and the mechanism for disclosure (annual report or meetings).

DIRECTORS UNDERSTANDING INTERESTS AND CONCERNS OF SHAREHOLDERS.

SHAREHOLDERS UNDERSTANDING WHAT THE COMPANY IS TRYING TO ACHIEVE.

MORE REGULAR AND CONSTRUCTIVE DIALOGUE BETWEEN COMPANY AND SHAREHOLDER.

=

INCREASED SHAREHOLDER INTEREST ENCOURAGING CHECKS ON MANAGERS OF COMPANY.

POTENTIAL BENEFITS FROM CLOSER INTEREST BY MAJOR SHAREHOLDERS IN COMPANY AFFAIRS.

5 Disclosure: best practice corporate governance requirements

The issue of governance and disclosure are closely intertwined. Disclosure is the means by which governance is communicated and possibly assured since it leads to stakeholder scrutiny and shareholder activism.

Codes such as the UK Corporate Governance Code (2016) provide best practice governance. Adherence can only be communicated through transparency of Code implementation, and in its detailed inclusion in the annual report.

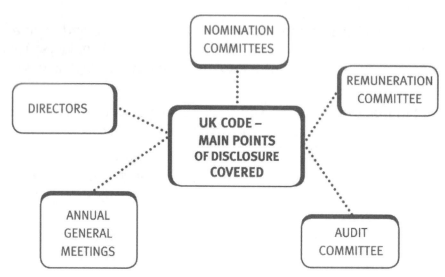

6 Mandatory versus voluntary disclosure

Organisations disclose a wide range of information, both mandatory and voluntary.

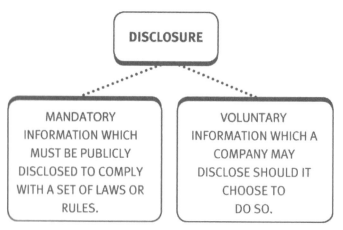

Test your understanding 1

Suggest examples of the following types of disclosure:

(a)   Mandatory disclosure

(b)   Voluntary disclosure

Annual report

The annual report becomes the tool for 'voluntary disclosure'. The report includes:

1 **Chairman and CEO statements regarding company position** – This is voluntary in the sense that it is a requirement of the Code but obviously to not include this would be unimaginable.

2 **Business review** (formerly OFR) – This detailed report is written in non-financial language in order to ensure information is accessible by a broad range of users, not just sophisticated analysts and accountants.

3 **The accounts** – Including statement of comprehensive income, statement of financial position and cash flow statements plus notes and compliance statements.

4 **Governance** – A section devoted to compliance with the Code including all provisions shown above.

5 **AOB (any other business)** – Shareholder information including notification of AGM, dividend history and shareholder taxation position.

6 **Stock exchange listing rules** are also a source of regulation over disclosure.

Operating and financial review – now Business Review

The OFR narrative was intended to be forward-looking rather than historical.

There were high hopes for the OFR when it became mandatory, but then it was almost immediately revoked as a mandatory requirement by government in the UK, and was replaced with the softer Business Review.

Stakeholders such as institutional investors and environmental lobbyists hoped the OFR would be a vehicle for:

*   risk disclosure

*   social and environmental reporting.

Expansion of disclosure beyond the annual report

Since disclosure refers to the whole array of different forms of information produced by the company it also includes:

*   press releases

*   management forecasts

*   analysts' presentations

*   the AGM

*   information on the corporate website such as stand-alone social and environmental reporting.

- in addition to financial information, organisations should disclose policies relating to business ethics, the environment and other public policy commitments, as this information can be important to investors and other stakeholders in better evaluating the relationships between companies and the communities in which they operate.

- information should be disclosed on key issues relevant to the organisation's market position and issues related to corporate citizenship.

- similarly organisations should disclose all important risk factors and its anticipated reaction. That may include risk specific to the industry or geographical areas in which the organisation operates, financial market risk, risk related to funding and risk related to environmental liabilities.

Improvements in disclosure result in better transparency, which is the most important aim of governance reform worldwide.

'The lifeblood of the markets is information and any barrier to the flow represents imperfection. The more transparent the activities of the company, the more accurately securities will be valued.' (Cadbury Report)

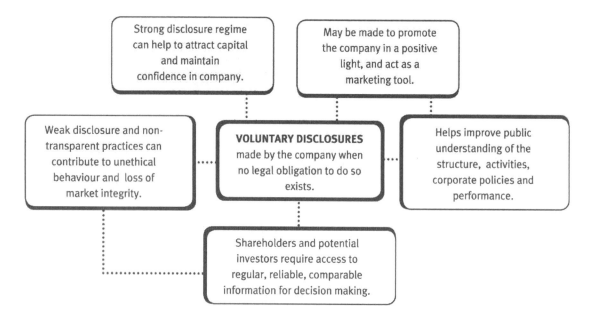

Motivations behind voluntary disclosure

Overall, in a principle-based reporting environment, the disclosure of voluntary information can enhance companies' accountability to investors, because voluntary disclosures are an effective way of redressing the information asymmetry that exists between management and investors.

In adding to mandatory content, voluntary disclosures give the following benefits:

- A fuller picture of the state of the company.

- More information helps investors decide whether the company matches investors' risk, strategic and ethical criteria, and expectations.

- Makes the annual report more forward looking (predictive) whereas the majority of the numerical content is backward facing on what has been.

- Helps transparency in communicating more fully thereby better meeting the agency accountability to investors, particularly shareholders. There is a considerable amount of qualitative information that cannot be conveyed using statutory numbers (such as strategy, ethical content, social reporting, etc.)

- Voluntary disclosure gives a more rounded and more complete view of the company, its activities, strategies, purposes and values.

- Voluntary disclosure enables the company to address specific shareholder concerns as they arise (such as responding to negative publicity).

In the USA the reporting regime under SOX offers little room for voluntary disclosures. The act itself contains various specific requirements, such as section 404:

- 'The commission shall prescribe rules requiring each annual report....to contain an internal control report which shall………' going on to detail very precisely all necessary disclosure.

The motivations for voluntary disclosure are thus as follows:

- **Accountability:** disclosure is the dominant philosophy of the modern system and the essential aspect of corporate accountability.

- **Information asymmetry:** attempts to deal with information asymmetry between managers and owners in terms of agency theory. The more this is reduced the less chance there is of moral hazard and adverse share selection problems.

- **Attracts investment:** institutional investors are attracted by increased disclosure and transparency. Greater disclosure reduces risk and with it the cost of capital to the company.

- **Compliance:** non-compliance threatens listing and fines through civil action in the courts. In the US non-compliance makes directors personally liable for criminal prosecution under SOX.

- **Alignment of objectives:** possibly 50% of directors' remuneration is in relation to published financial indicators.

- **Assurance:** the mass of disclosure gives the user assurance that the management are active and competent in terms of managing the operations of the organisation.

- **Stakeholders:** greater voluntary disclosure assists in discharging the multiple accountabilities of various stakeholder groups.

7 Sustainability

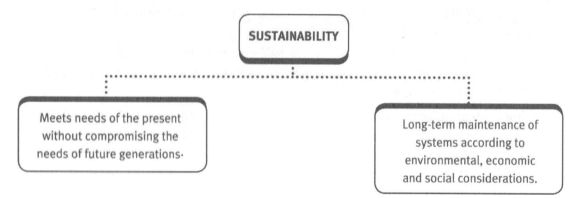

 Sustainable development is development that meets the needs of the present without compromising the ability of future generations to meet their own needs (World Commission on Environment and Development (WCED) 1987).

Sustainability can be thought of as an attempt to provide the best outcomes for the human and natural environments both now and into the indefinite future.

- It relates to the continuity of economic, social, institutional and environmental aspects of human society, as well as the non-human environment.

 Definitions of sustainability

The concept of sustainability has become important with growing awareness of the impact of organisations on the environment. It is linked to the concept of globalisation and large companies seeking to show that they wish to limit environmental damage. The production of corporate and social responsibility (CSR) reports by approximately 50% of global companies identifies commitment to this belief.

First definition

The first definition above focuses on sustainable development, which is the main focus of CSR reports. In other words, business activities should be sustainable. Companies including BP, Nokia, Shell and Volvo refer to this concept in their reports. Development is sustainable as long as future generations can also meet their requirements.

Sustainable development therefore refers to the concept of intergenerational equity, i.e. equality between one generation and another in terms of needs being satisfied. However, this definition is limited to environmental concerns. Recent thinking has also linked sustainability to economic and social concerns.

Second definition

This definition also incorporates economic and social concerns. To be precise, the definition includes the concept of the Triple Bottom Line (TBL) of **John Elkington**. TBL attempts to show the full cost of development and that businesses should have a triple goal set incorporating not only economic, but also social and environmental objectives.

Economic perspective

This perspective recognises that there are limits to economic growth (as outlined by Meadows in 1974 in the Report to the club of Rome – The limits to growth). Meadows recognised that the earth is a finite system and therefore economic development, based on this finite system, must also be limited.

Sustainability relates to the organisation in terms of planning for long-term growth, ensuring that the organisation will continue to be in existence for the foreseeable future.

Examples of unsustainable activities include:

- strategies for short-term gain (e.g. increase in share price)

- paying bribes or forming cartels (which are potentially unethical as well as unsustainable in terms of activities that can be continued indefinitely without adversely affecting markets)

- suspect accounting treatments and underpayment of taxes – being unsustainable in terms of the organisation not contributing to maintaining the countries' infrastructure (schools, roads, etc.).

Social perspective

This perspective recognises that organisations have an impact on communities and may in fact change their social make-up. The perspective is relatively new (1990s onwards) and results from recognition of the impact of businesses, with particular reference to the less-developed regions of the world.

Sustainability in this context relates to the concept of social justice. A UN report in 2001 (report on the world social situation) noted large and increasing differences between income and wealth with reference to richer and poorer nations.

- Examples of situations where social justice appears to be required include:

    - rich consuming countries and poorer manufacturing countries, and

    - urban 'rich' and rural 'poor'

Environmental perspective

This perspective recognises that organisations have an impact on the environment and that lack of concern means deterioration and eventual loss of some resources. The perspective was the first to be recognised, being linked initially to forestry management.

Sustainability in this context relates to the effective management of environmental resources so that they continue to be available for future generations. Human activities use environmental resources, so sustainability implies limiting use or replacing those resources in the medium- to long-term.

Examples of situations where the environmental perspective is seen as critical include:

- the use of non-renewable resources including oil, gas and coal

- long-term damage to the environment from carbon dioxide and chlorofluorocarbons (CFCs)

- whether future generations can actually enjoy the same standard of living, given the finite nature of many resources.

Significance of sustainability

- Sustainability affects every level of organisation, from the local neighbourhood to the entire planet.

- It is the long-term maintenance of systems according to environmental, economic and social considerations.

- Sustainability can be measured empirically (using quotients) or subjectively.

Illustration 2 – Rio Tinto

Rio Tinto is one of the world's largest mining corporations with operations spanning the globe. Its products include aluminium, copper and iron ore. One example of the size of its operations relates to iron ore extraction in Guinea which is forecast to exceed 600 million tonnes of iron ore per year in the near future.

To combat criticism relating to the depletion of non-renewable resources and the inevitable environmental and social impact its operations incur, the company has fought hard to improve its position regarding sustainable development.

In 2007 Rio Tinto was listed on the FTSE4Good and Dow Jones Sustainability index, achieving platinum rating on the Business in the Community's Corporate Responsibility, Environment and Community indexes.

Its environmental goals include a 10% reduction in freshwater usage and a 4% reduction in greenhouse gas emissions within a five year period and the need to ensure all sites achieve ISO14001 certification within 2 years of acquisition or commissioning.

Brundtland Commission

Another view on sustainability was provided by the 1983 World Commission on Environmental and Development (WCED) also known as the **Brundtland** Commission after its chairman Harlem Brundtland. The Brundtland Commission report 'Our Common Future' was published in 1987. The main emphasis of the report was the phrase:

'Sustainable development is development that meets the needs of the present without compromising the ability of future generations to meet their needs.'

The report provides detailed guidelines on four areas:

1   Provide environmental strategies for achieving sustainable development to the year 2000 and beyond.

2   Recommend ways in which concern for the environment can be translated into co-operation on environmental issues.

3   Consider ways in which the environmental community can deal more effectively with environmental concerns.

4   Provide methods of protecting and enhancing the environment in the long term.

The full report is available on the internet although this summary is sufficient for examination purposes.

Sustainability Audit

A sustainability audit is an in depth examination of an organisation's entire environmental management system and associated arrangements.

The audit aims to underpin the environmental sustainability performance of an organisation by examining its policies, processes and practices in relation to social, economic and environmental performance and recommending improvements.

It goes beyond the requirements of traditional environmental management systems such as ISO 14001 and assists the organisation in demonstrating its environmental credentials to customers, supply chain and other stakeholders.

More and more businesses are producing information on their social, economic and environmental performance (sustainability information) to respond to user needs and to meet regulatory requirements.

Organisations choose to get assurance on their sustainability information in order to:

*   challenge and confirm views expressed in the annual report as part of the narrative disclosure

*   complement internal processes, such as internal audit or stakeholder engagement, which are designed to improve business sustainability and enhance the trust of external stakeholders

*   enhance the credibility of information with those who use it to make economic and other decisions.

Users of sustainability information

Such assurance might be internal for management use or external, published together with management's sustainability report, for other stakeholders.

These include:

- the board of directors
- shareholders and investors
- trading partners (e.g. suppliers and customers)
- regulators
- other stakeholders (e.g. non-government organisations)
- members of the public

Benefits of producing sustainability information

- users read business sustainability information and the associated assurance report when making a major decision about business transactions e.g. whether to buy products, to supply goods, or to invest in a business.

- knowing how sustainability information will be used will help determine whether the scope of reports produced matches what users want.

- it will also determine if the criteria used to evaluate the information are suitable and available to users of your report.

- additionally, it may result in the organisation being more resource efficient and achieving cost efficiencies.

There are many ways to enhance the credibility of sustainability information. For example, internal auditors can monitor and check information or selected internal and external stakeholders could be asked to give feedback on the contents and scope of sustainability reports produced.

Getting an assurance report from an independent professional accountant is one of the most powerful ways to add credibility strategically, but clearly has cost implications.

8   Effects of economic activity

There are a number of different environmental and social effects which should be considered when examining economic activity.

- Economic activity is only sustainable where its impact on society and the environment is also sustainable.

 Environmental footprint

In the same way that humans and animals leave physical footprints that show where they have been, so organisations leave evidence of their operations in the environment. They operate at a net cost to the environment.

The environmental footprint is an attempt to evaluate the size of a company's impact on the environment in three respects:

- The company's resource consumption.
- Any harm to the environment brought about by pollution emissions.
- A measurement of the resource consumption and pollution emissions in terms of harm to the environment in either qualitative, quantitative or replacement terms.

Where resource use exceeds provision, then the activity can be termed unsustainable.

 Measuring impact of economic activity

Economic activity has social and environmental effects. In general terms, that activity is only sustainable where the long-term impact on the environment and effect on society is sustainable. If the impacts are not sustainable, then the economic activity itself is unsustainable.

In terms of organisations, the effect of their social and environmental activities, i.e. their social and environmental footprints, must be sustainable. Lack of sustainability implies that the organisation is also not sustainable.

There are two methods of measuring sustainability; the quotients approach and the subjective approach.

Quotients approach	Subjective approach
Measures sustainability in terms of the amount of a resource available compared with the actual use of that resource.	Measures intentions of organisations to achieve certain goals or objectives.
Similar in concept to the triple bottom line (TBL) method of accounting (see later in this chapter) as it provides a quantifiable method of checking social and environmental footprints.	However, lack of quantification means that 'progress' can be made towards the intention, although it will be difficult to determine how much progress has been made or whether that progress is sustainable.
For example, water usage can be compared with the amount of fresh water being generated. If usage > generation then the activity is not sustainable.	For example, the Millennium Development Goals of the United Nations have statements such as 'ensure environmental stability'.
Progress towards sustainability can be measured by comparing water usage over a period of time – the activity becoming sustainable where usage is less than production.	'Progress' can be made towards this in terms of reducing carbon emissions. However, the exact reduction will be unclear while reduction may have other negative impacts (e.g. increase resource use in other areas).

Illustration 3 – Environmental footprint

The environmental footprint

An economic activity may require 15 million gallons of water. If the organisation's share of available fresh water is less than this, then the activity can be termed unsustainable. Using the quotients approach, this can be shown as follows:

USE OF ENVIRONMENTAL RESOURCE

....

PRODUCTION OF ENVIRONMENTAL RESOURCE

=   RESULTS > 1 UNSUSTAINABLE

WATER USE = 15 MILLION GALLONS

....

WATER PRODUCTION = 10 MILLION GALLONS

=   1.5, e.g. UNSUSTAINABLE

However, the environmental footprint extends to more than just water use, e.g. the production of laundry detergent has various environmental impacts:

Activity	Environmental footprint – and how to decrease it
Production of detergent.	Use of chemicals within the product: • improving the chemical formula to decrease the amount of chemicals used • manufacturing the product in fewer locations to obtain manufacturing economies and reduce emissions.
Transportation from manufacturing plant to consumer.	Energy consumed moving the product: • manufacturing the product in fewer locations but using better logistical networks to distribute the product.
Packaging for the product.	Type and amount of material used in packaging: • using cardboard rather than plastic focuses packaging on renewable resources • decreasing the weight of packaging lessens resource use and transportation costs.

Test your understanding 2

Suggest ways in which an airline could seek to limit its environmental footprint.

Social footprint

The social footprint evaluates sustainability in three areas of capital:

- Human Capital, consisting of personal health, knowledge, skills, experience, and other resources (including human rights and ethical entitlements) that individuals have and use to take effective action.

- Social Capital, consisting of networks of people and the mutually-held knowledge and skills they have and use in order to take effective action.

- Constructed Capital, consisting of material things, such as tools, technologies, roads, utilities, infrastructures, etc., that people produce and use in order to take effective action.

Organisations need to ensure that their economic activities are sustainable in each of these three areas.

Social footprint

The social footprint evaluates sustainability in three areas termed 'Anthro capital'.

Anthro capital		
Social	**Human**	**Constructed**
Social networks and mutually-held knowledge for collectives to take effective action.	Personal health, knowledge, skills, experience and other resources (including human rights and ethical entitlements) required for individuals to take.	Physical infrastructures in society such as roads, utilities, etc. that people build.

Organisations need to ensure that their economic activities are sustainable in each of these three areas. The effect of the social footprint can be positive or negative. For example, regarding social capital, the government will set taxation rates, with those taxes being used to provide various services. Where the amount raised is less than the amount required for the provision of social capital, then the activities of society as a whole are unsustainable. The government will need to raise taxes meaning that companies will pay more tax.

Sustainability is achieved where the social capital needs of society are being met. It can be argued that economic activity itself is unsustainable if education is insufficient to meet the needs of society.

Sustainability can be shown using the quotients approach as follows:

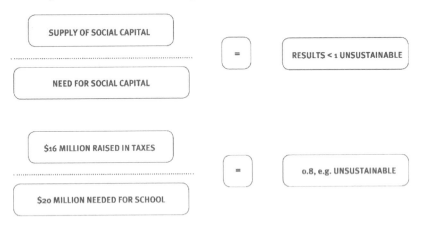

The importance of the social footprint is that more capital can be generated if required. E.g. people can decide to improve their knowledge. The aim of economic activity may therefore be to generate sufficient social capital, or have a large enough social footprint, to ensure sustainability.

Note: This is a relatively new area of research so watch out for relevant articles in the press, etc. as part of your studies.

Accounting for sustainability

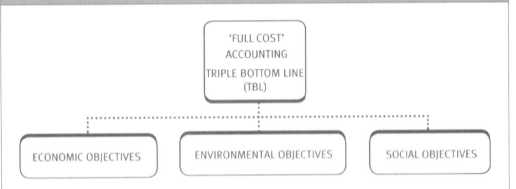

Two methods which attempt to account for sustainability are 'full cost' and 'triple bottom line' accounting.

Full cost accounting

- Full cost accounting means calculating the total cost of company activities, including environmental, economic and social costs.

- It attempts to include all the costs of an action, decision or manufacture of a product into a costing system, and as such will include many non-financial costs of certain actions.

- Full Cost Accounting (FCA) is about internalising all environmental costs onto the P&L, i.e. making external costs visible and chargeable as an expense.

Full Cost Accounting (FCA)

Full Cost Accounting (FCA) attempts to include all the costs of an action, decision or manufacture of a product into a costing system. Most budgets and financial accounts are based on actual costs incurred. FCA includes the additional (and in many situations non-financial) costs of those actions. The aim is to internalise all costs, including those which are incurred outside of the company.

Taking car manufacture as an example:

- An initial outlay on a factory will be included within one year's budget. However, that factory will incur costs in every year it is used and therefore those costs must be shown as being incurred over the life of the factory.

- The location of the factory may incur costs even though no cash outlay is involved. For example, the time lost from traffic queues as workers attempt to reach the factory, or the additional cost of pollution from cars in those queues are costs, even though the company has no financial outlay for them.

- The cars being manufactured will have a finite life, however the company has no obligation to dispose of the used product at the end of that life. FCA would include the disposal cost and associated environmental damage. Some car manufacturers have recognised this cost and now advertise their cars as being recyclable, even if the company does not actually carry out that recycling (yet).

  FCA is therefore the normal 'costs' in terms of running a company with the additional costs to recognise the additional external costs.

Triple Bottom Line (TBL) accounting

- TBL accounting means expanding the traditional company reporting framework to take into account environmental and social performance in addition to financial (economic) performance.

- The concept is also explained using the triple 'P' headings of **'People, Planet and Profit'**.

TBL

TBL attempts to show the full cost of development, and that businesses should have a triple goal set incorporating not only economic, but also social and environmental objectives. This is commonly shortened to the triple 'P' headings.

People

People expands the concept of stakeholder interests from simply shareholders (as in financial reporting) to other groups including employees and the community where the company carries out its business. Actions of the company are therefore considered in light of the different groups, not simply from the point of view of shareholders.

For example, a TBL business would attempt to pay its workers fair wages, maintain a safe working environment and not use child labour, although these practices will decrease the amount of profit available for shareholders.

Similarly, the company would promote its surrounding community, e.g. by providing educational opportunities or a safe community to live in (as in the Bournville estate established by Cadbury the chocolate maker in England).

Planet

Planet refers to the environmental practices of the company to determine whether they are sustainable or not. The TBL company attempts to reduce the 'ecological footprint' by managing resource consumption and energy usage. The company therefore attempts to limit environmental damage. For example, production processes will be efficient in terms of resource use and environmentally damaging outputs such as toxic waste eliminated. The company believes it is inappropriate to produce toxic waste as the environmental cost of disposal is normally borne by the government and society as a whole.

The drive for environmental stability also means that TBL companies will not be involved in resource depletion. For example, fish stocks are maintained at sustainable levels and timber use is balanced by replanting to retain the resource into the future.

Profit

Is the 'normal' bottom line measured in most businesses? As noted above, a non-TBL company will seek to maximise this measure to improve shareholder return. A TBL company on the other hand will balance the profit objective with the other two elements of the TBL.

> **TBL and business ethics**
>
> TBL implies that businesses must consider the full cost of their impact on the environment. However, that cost may also be seen in terms of the potential to contribute to sustainability.
>
> **Ethical practice may therefore simply relate to businesses limiting environmental, economic and social damage according to their actual ability in those areas. Accounting techniques are important for measuring success, but sustainability also implies desire for action which provides the ethical approach to the issues.**

9 Management systems

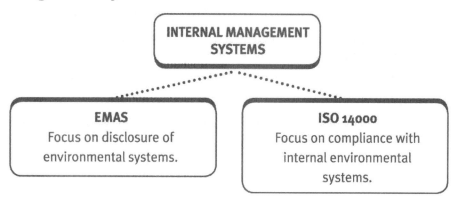

Environmental accounting relates to the need to establish and maintain systems for assessing the organisation's impact on the environment.

EMAS and ISO 14000 are both systems that support the establishment and maintenance of environmental accounting systems.

Many companies refer to the standards in their CSR reports.

Eco-Management and Audit Scheme (EMAS)

- EMAS is the Eco-Management and Audit Scheme. It is a voluntary initiative designed to improve companies' environmental performance.

- EMAS requires participating organisations to regularly produce a public environmental statement that reports on their environmental performance.

- Accuracy and reliability is independently checked by an environmental verifier to give credibility and recognition to that information.

- EMAS requires participating organisations to implement an environmental management system (EMS).

- There are four key elements of the scheme:
    - Legal requirement
    - Dialogue/reporting
    - Improved environmental performance
    - Employee involvement.

ISO 14000

- ISO 14000 is a series of standards dealing with environmental management and a supporting audit programme.

- The ISO formulates the specifications for an EMS.

- EMAS compliance is based on ISO 14000 recognition – although many organisations comply with both standards.

- ISO 14000 focuses on internal systems although it also provides assurance to stakeholders of good environmental management.

- To gain accreditation an organisation must meet a number of requirements regarding its environmental management.

 EMAS and ISO 14000

EMAS	ISO 14000
What is it?	
EMAS is the Eco-Management and Audit Scheme. It is a voluntary initiative designed to improve companies' environmental performance. It was established by the EU in 1993.	ISO 14000 is a 'series' of standards dealing with environmental management and a supporting audit programme. It was developed to support the UN initiative on 'sustainable development' in the 1992 Conference on Environment and Development.
What does it do (in overview)	
Its aim is to recognise and reward those organisations that go beyond minimum legal compliance and continuously improve their environmental performance. EMAS requires participating organisations to regularly produce a public environmental statement that reports on their environmental performance. Publication of environmental information is voluntary, although the accuracy and reliability is independently checked by an environmental verifier to give credibility and recognition to that information.	The ISO formulates the specifications for an Environmental Management System (EMS), guidance for its use and the standard against which it can be audited and certified. In this context, environmental management relates to what the organisation does to: - minimise harmful effects on the environment caused by its activities, and to - achieve continual improvement of its environmental performance.

What must the organisation do to comply?	
EMAS requires participating organisations to implement an EMS. The EMS must meet the requirements of the International Standard BS EN ISO 14001. Many organisations progress from ISO 14001 to EMAS and maintain certification/registration to both. In other words ISO 14000 is a prerequisite to applying for EMAS.	To gain accreditation, an organisation must: • implement, maintain and improve an EMS • assure itself of its conformance with its own stated environmental policy (those policy commitments of course must be made) • demonstrate conformance • ensure compliance with environmental laws and regulations • seek certification of its EMS by an external third party organisation • make a self-determination of conformance.
Key elements of the standard	
Legal requirement – organisations must show that they understand and can implement all relevant environmental legislation. Dialogue/reporting – information needs of stakeholders must be recognised and the company must provide environmental information to meet those needs. Improved environmental performance – companies are required to improve their environmental performance over time, e.g. using fewer raw materials, consuming less energy and producing less waste. Employee involvement – employees are involved from all levels of the organisation – this assists in team building as well as helping to ensure success of environmental initiatives.	Identify elements of the business that impact on the environment. Produce objectives for improvement and a management system to achieve them, with regular reviews for continued improvement. Applicable to any type of business – the standard is generic because the requirements for an effective EMS are the same for any business.

Benefits of compliance with either standard

- Reduced cost of waste management.

- Savings in consumption of energy and materials.

- Lower distribution costs.

- Improved corporate image among regulators, customers and the public.

- Framework for continuous improvement of the companies' environmental performance.

10 Social and environmental audit

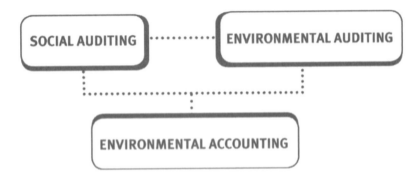

Social auditing

- A process that enables an organisation to assess and demonstrate its social, economic, and environmental benefits and limitations.

- Also measures the extent to which an organisation achieves the shared values and objectives set out in its mission statement.

- Provides the process for environmental auditing.

Elements of a social audit

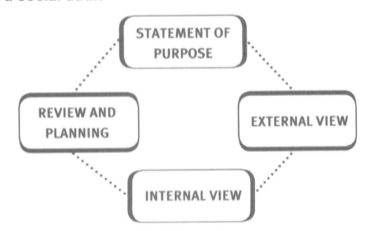

Social audit

The social audit – overview

- Statement of purpose.

- Review results of last year's purpose and plans.

- Establish this year's purpose and plans.

External view

Obtain the view of external stakeholders to form a view of the organisation's position within the wider context.

Internal view

Obtain views of the board of directors, staff and volunteers to assess satisfactory ways of working and reward. This helps to ensure that organisational management and systems can achieve the stated purpose and plans.

Review and planning

The social audit team manages the social audit and measures performance ready for input into next year's social audit.

Detail on social audit

The concept of social audit is to provide additional information on a company's activities over and above the financial accounts. In this sense it has links with TBL and FCA. The main difference in a social audit is the active involvement of external stakeholders, and in many situations the publication of a social audit by those external stakeholders. For example, one company, Social Audit Ltd, provides social audits on companies, sometimes without the active participation of the companies.

Typical sections of a social audit report include:

- an overview of the company including salient features of the financial accounts

- the company's stance regarding employees such as how pay and benefits are negotiated, provision of job security and policies on discrimination in the areas of sex, race and disabilities

- overview of products with negative environmental impacts

- the environmental impact of the company itself in terms of pollution, emissions, recycling, etc. and health and safety policies

- the social impact of the company in terms of community support

- response, if any, from the company.

In effect, the social audit is evaluating the organisation's footprint (social, environmental, etc.) within a given accounting period from the external perspective.

Environmental auditing

- Aims to assess the impact of the organisation on the environment.

- Normally involves the implementation of appropriate environmental standards such as ISO 14001 and EMAS.

- Provides the raw data for environmental accounting.

- An environmental audit typically contains three elements:

    - agreed metrics (what should be measured and how)

    - performance measured against those metrics

    - reporting on the levels of compliance or variance.

 Refer to the article SBL in ACCA study support resources "**Environmental Auditing**"

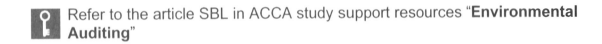
Environmental audit

The environmental audit – overview

An environmental audit leads into an environmental action plan.

The audit is based on the implementation of the appropriate environmental standards, e.g. ISO 14001 or EMAS, which were explained in the previous section.

The main areas to cover within the environment audit normally include:

- waste management and waste minimisation

- emissions to air

- ground and groundwater protection

- surface water management

- energy and utility consumption

- environmental emergencies

- protection of environmentally sensitive areas

- product/service stewardship

- management of contractors control of visitors

- local issues.

Environmental accounting

- This is the development of an environmental accounting system to support the integration of environmental performance measures.

- It builds on social and environmental auditing by providing empirical evidence of the achievement of social and environmental objectives.

- Without social and environmental auditing, environmental accounting would not be possible.

The aims of environmental accounting are:

- to use the metrics produced from an environmental audit and incorporate these into an environmental report, and

- to integrate environmental performance measures into core financial processes to generate cost savings and reduce environmental impact through improved management of resources.

Environmental accounting

Environmental accounting – overview

Definition: 'to develop an environmental accounting system to support the integration of environmental performance measures into our core financial processes, and to track internal environmentally significant expenditure' (Environmental Policy Statement 12 July 2000) issued by the UK Environment Agency.

Benefits of environmental accounting

Cost savings

To utilise resources efficiently and effectively, and in doing so generate cost savings.

Environmental improvements

To support the delivery of the environmental audit which will benefit the company and the environment – see above for a list of those areas involved with environmental audit.

Corporate governance

To assist in the management of environmental risks and operational costs including the publication of environmental accounting disclosures in corporate documents such as the annual and CSR reports.

Examples of measuring impact on environment

Examples of the areas discussed above include:

Environmental accounting	Social footprints	Environmental footprints
• Monitoring water usage. • Monitoring energy usage (including use of renewable and non-renewable energy). • Ensuring inventory is derived from renewable resources where possible. • Measuring waste emissions and the company's carbon footprint (amount of CO_2 generated).	• Obtaining supplies from sustainable sources and companies following appropriate social and environmental practices. • Enhancing social capital e.g. business/ community relationships to provide on-the-job training to assist some social groups 'return to work' (e.g. Jamie Oliver restaurants and Ben and Jerry's 'PartnerShops'. • Allowing employees paid time off to provide community services.	• Reduction in waste, e.g. CO_2 emissions. • Promotion of sustainable activities, e.g. metrics to ensure that dairy farming is sustainable.

Mass balance

Environmental accounting can also be explained in terms of the 'mass balance'. This system shows what inputs (that is materials) have been converted into finished goods as well as emissions and recyclable waste products. In effect, the mass balance shows the inputs to a production process in weight terms compared to the outputs produced. The aim is to minimise inputs and non-recyclable outputs.

11   Social and Environmental Reporting

Except in some highly regulated situations (such as water), the production of a social and environmental report is voluntary. The problem, and the subject of most debate is what should be the typical contents of such a report and how do we measure it.

Frameworks do exist, such as the data-gathering tools for the Global Reporting Initiative (GRI), AccountAbility (AA1000) and the ISO 14000 collection of standards, but essentially there is no underpinning compulsion to any of it.

Looking at the two elements separately:

Environmental reporting

Godfrey, Hodgson and Holmes (2003) have defined environmental reporting as the 'disclosure of information on environment related issues and performance by an entity'.

It typically contains details of environmental performance in areas such as:

- measures of emissions (e.g. pollution, waste and greenhouse gases)
- consumption (e.g. of energy, water and non-renewable mineral deposits).

The information is published in either the annual report and/or as a self-standing report.

Social reporting

Owen and Scherer (1993) explain that there is a significant concept underlying corporate social responsibility; this is that corporations should be concerned about society at large.

Social reporting is generally context specific, and typical contents will vary with industry, however the following issues should be included in a company's considerations:

- human rights issues
- work place, occupational health and safety
- training and employee issues
- fair pay for employees and suppliers
- fair business practices
- minority and equity issues
- marketplace and consumer issues
- community involvement
- indigenous peoples
- social development
- charitable, political donations and sports sponsorship.

Usefulness of this information to stakeholders

Social and environmental reporting is becoming increasingly important, as many investors and other stakeholders want to know about the organisation's social and environmental footprint in addition to its economic performance.

Reasons why the additional information is useful

- by reporting on social and environmental issues companies will become more aware of the potential risk, and less likely to suffer unforeseen liabilities due to reputational damage

- the ethical performance of a business is a factor in some investors' decision to invest

- employees may use ethical performance as a criterion in their choice of potential employer

- some consumers will not buy goods or services from unethical companies

- voluntary disclosure of social and environmental issues may pre-empt potential regulatory intervention

- more social and environmental reporting will provide an impetus for internal development and a higher level of Corporate Governance

- the benefits of brand strengthening, will have a positive impact on share price

- finally, shareholders as owners of the company simply have a right to as much information as possible.

However the additional cost of such reporting, and the ambiguous nature of the measures must also be considered.

Refer to the article SBL in ACCA study support resources on **"Environmental Accounting and Reporting"**.

12 Integrated Reporting

What is Integrated Reporting?

Integrated Reporting demonstrates the linkages between an organisation's strategy, governance and financial performance and the social, environmental and economic context within which it operates.

By reinforcing these connections, Integrated Reporting can help business to take more sustainable decisions and enable investors and other stakeholders to understand how an organisation is really performing. An Integrated Report should be a single report which is the organisation's primary report – in most jurisdictions the Annual Report or equivalent.

Central to Integrated Reporting is the challenge facing organisations to create and sustain value in the short, medium and longer term. Each element of an Integrated Report should provide insights into an organisation's current and future performance.

By addressing the material issues for an organisation, an integrated report should demonstrate in a clear and concise manner an organisation's ability to create and sustain value in the short, medium and longer term.

Integrated reporting is a process founded on integrated thinking that results in a periodic integrated report by an organisation about value creation over time and related communications regarding aspects of value creation.

An integrated report is a concise communication about how an organisation's strategy, governance, performance and prospects, in the context of its external environment, lead to the creation of value in the short, medium and long term.

Integrated reporting is needed by business and investors. Businesses need a reporting environment that is conducive to understanding and articulating their strategy, which helps to drive performance internally and attract financial capital for investment. Investors need to understand how the strategy being pursued creates value over time.

Traditional definition of capital

1   Financial assets or the financial value of assets, such as cash.

2   The factories, machinery and equipment owned by a business and used in production.

"Capital" however can have several different meanings. Its specific definition depends on the context in which it is used. In general, it refers to financial resources available for use, therefore companies and societies with more capital are better off than those with less capital.

Financial capital

Financial capital plays an important role in our economy, enabling the other types of capital to be owned and traded. However, unlike the other types, it has no real value itself but is representative of natural, human, social or manufactured capital, e.g. shares, bonds or banknotes.

Alternative definitions of capital

It is now recognised that there are five other types of sustainable capital from where we derive the goods and services we need to improve the quality of our lives. These are:

Manufactured capital

This form of capital can be described as comprising of material goods, or fixed assets which contribute to the production process rather than being the output itself – e.g. tools, machines and buildings.

Intellectual capital

This form of capital can be described as the value of a company or organisation's employee knowledge, business training and any proprietary information that may provide the company with a competitive advantage. Intellectual capital is considered an asset, and can broadly be defined as the collection of all informational resources a company has at its disposal that can be used to drive profits, gain new customers, create new products, or otherwise improve the business.

(NB: Some of the subsets of intellectual capital include human capital, information capital, brand awareness and instructional capital.)

Human capital

This can be described as consisting of people's health, knowledge, skills and motivation. All these things are needed for productive work. Enhancing human capital through education and training is central to a flourishing economy.

Social capital

This can be described as being concerned with the institutions that help us maintain and develop human capital in partnership with others; e.g. families, communities, businesses, trade unions, schools, and voluntary organisations.

Natural capital

This can be described as any stock or flow of energy and material within the environment that produces goods and services. Natural capital is the value that nature provides for us, the natural assets that society has and is therefore not only the basis of production but of life itself. It includes resources of renewable and non-renewable materials e.g. land, water, energy and those factors that absorb, neutralise or recycle wastes and processes, e.g. climate regulation, climate change, CO_2 emissions.

The concept of integrated reporting (<IR>)

Integrated Reporting (<IR>) is seen by the International Integrated Reporting Council (IIRC) as the basis for a fundamental change in the way in which entities are managed and reported to stakeholders.

A stated aim of <IR> is to support integrated thinking and decision making. Integrated thinking is described in the <IR> Framework as "the active consideration by an organisation of the relationships between its various operating and functional units and the capitals that the organisation uses or affects".

Purpose and objectives of integrated reporting

The <IR> Framework sets out the purpose of an integrated report as follows:

"The primary purpose of an integrated report is to explain to providers of financial capital how an entity creates value over time. An integrated report benefits all stakeholders interested in an entity's ability to create value over time, including employees, customers, suppliers, business partners, local communities, legislators, regulators, and policymakers."

The objectives for integrated reporting include:

- To improve the quality of information available to providers of financial capital to enable a more efficient and productive allocation of capital.

- To provide a more cohesive and efficient approach to corporate reporting that draws on different reporting strands and communicates the full range of factors that materially affect the ability of an organisation to create value over time.

- To enhance accountability and stewardship for the broad base of capitals (financial, manufactured, intellectual, human, social and relationship, and natural) and promote understanding of their interdependencies.

- To support integrated thinking, decision making and actions that focus on the creation of value over the short, medium and long term.

Value creation for the organisation and for others

An organisation's activities, its interactions and relationships, its outputs and the outcomes for the various capitals it uses and affects influence its ability to continue to draw on these capitals in a continuous cycle.

The capitals

The capitals are the resources and the relationships used and affected by the organisation, which are identified in the <IR> Framework as financial, manufactured, intellectual, human, social and relationship, and natural capital. However, these categories of capital are not required to be adopted in preparing an entity's integrated report, and an integrated report may not cover all capitals – the focus is on capitals that are relevant to the entity.

The value creation process

At the core of the value creation process is an entity's business model, which draws on various capitals and inputs, and by using the entity's business activities, creates outputs (products, services, byproducts, waste) and outcomes (internal and external consequences for the capitals).

The value creation process is depicted below, and is explained briefly in the following paragraphs:

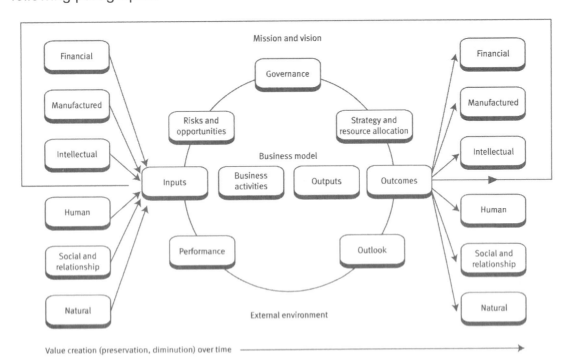

The external environment, including economic conditions, technological change, societal issues and environmental challenges, sets the context within which the organisation operates.

The mission and vision encompass the whole organisation, identifying its purpose and intention in clear, concise terms.

Those charged with governance are responsible for creating an appropriate oversight structure to support the ability of the organisation to create value.

At the core of the organisation is its business model, which draws on various capitals as inputs and, through its business activities, converts them to outputs (products, services, byproducts and waste).

The organisation's activities and its outputs lead to outcomes in terms of effects on the capitals. The capacity of the business model to adapt to changes (e.g. in the availability, quality and affordability of inputs) can affect the organisation's longer term viability.

Business activities include the planning, design and manufacture of products or the deployment of specialised skills and knowledge in the provision of services. Encouraging a culture of innovation is often a key business activity in terms of generating new products and services that anticipate customer demand, introducing efficiencies and better use of technology, substituting inputs to minimise adverse social or environmental effects, and finding alternative uses for outputs.

Outcomes are the internal and external consequences (positive and negative) for the capitals as a result of an organisation's business activities and outputs.

Continuous monitoring and analysis of the external environment in the context of the organisation's mission and vision identifies **risks and opportunities** relevant to the organisation, its strategy and its business model.

The organisation's **strategy** identifies how it intends to mitigate or manage risks and maximise opportunities. It sets out strategic objectives and strategies to achieve them, which are implemented through **resource allocation** plans.

The organisation needs information about its **performance**, which involves setting up measurement and monitoring systems to provide information for decision making.

The value creation process is not static; regular review of each component and its interactions with other components, and a focus on the organisation's **outlook**, lead to revision and refinement to improve all the components.

How to prepare an integrated report

Introduction

An integrated report should be a designated, identifiable communication.

A communication claiming to be an integrated report and referencing the <IR> Framework should apply all the key requirements (identified using bold type below), unless the unavailability of reliable data, specific legal prohibitions or competitive harm results in an inability to disclose information that is material (in the case of unavailability of reliable data or specific legal prohibitions, other information is provided).

The integrated report should include a statement from those charged with governance that it meets particular requirements (e.g. acknowledgement of responsibility, opinion on whether the integrated report is presented in accordance with the <IR> Framework) – and if one is not included, disclosures about their role and steps taken to include a statement in future reports (a statement should be included no later than an entity's third integrated report referencing the <IR> Framework).

The <IR> Framework sets out several guiding principles and content elements that have to be considered when preparing an integrated report.

Guiding principles – these underpin the preparation of an integrated report, informing the content of the report and how information is presented.

Content elements – the key categories of information required to be included in an integrated report under the Framework, presented as a series of questions rather than a prescriptive list of disclosures.

Guiding principles

The following seven guiding principles should underpin the preparation and presentation of an integrated report:

Strategic focus and future orientation

An integrated report should provide insight into the organisation's strategy, and how it relates to the organisation's ability to create value in the short, medium and long term and to its use of and effects on the capitals. For example, highlighting significant risks, opportunities and dependencies flowing from the organisation's market position and business model, and giving the management's view of how the organisation balances short, medium and long term interests.

Connectivity of information

An integrated report should show a holistic picture of the combination, inter-relatedness and dependencies between the factors that affect the organisation's ability to create value over time.

The more that integrated thinking is embedded into an organisation's activities, the more naturally will the connectivity of information flow into management reporting, analysis and decision making, and subsequently into the integrated report.

Stakeholder relationships

An integrated report should provide insight into the nature and quality of the organisation's relationships with its key stakeholders. This reflects the importance of relationships with key stakeholders because value is not created by or within an organisation alone, but is created through relationships with others. However, it does not mean that an integrated report should attempt to satisfy the information needs of all stakeholders. An integrated report enhances transparency and accountability, which are essential in building trust and resilience, by disclosing how key stakeholders' legitimate needs and interests are understood, taken into account and responded to.

Materiality

An integrated report should disclose information about matters that substantively affect the organisation's ability to create value over the short, medium and long term. The materiality determination process for the purpose of preparing and presenting an integrated report involves:

- Identifying relevant matters based on their ability to affect value creation.

- Evaluating the importance of relevant matters in terms of their known or potential effect on value creation.

- Prioritising the matters based on their relative importance.

- Determining the information to disclose about material matters.

This process applies to both positive and negative matters, including risks and opportunities and favourable and unfavourable performance or prospects. It also applies to both financial and other information. Such matters may have direct implications for the organisation itself or may affect the capitals owned by or available to others.

Conciseness

An integrated report should be concise. It should give sufficient context to understand the organisation's strategy, governance and prospects without being burdened by less relevant information.

Reliability and completeness

An integrated report should include all material matters, both positive and negative, in a balanced way and without material error.

Consistency and comparability

The information in an integrated report should be presented:

- On a basis that is consistent over time.

- In a way that enables comparison with other organisations to the extent it is material to the organisation's own ability to create value over time.

Audit of integrated reports (IR)

Independent assurance of non-financial reports has always proved to be challenging. Unlike financial reports, sustainability reports, for example, are rarely (if ever) mandated by listing authorities and the raw materials that underpin the reports are often less quantifiable and more qualitative in nature. Even those organisations that do issue sustainability reports do not always (or have not always been able to) commission independent assurance services that engender the same level of credibility and trust as do auditors' reports on the financial statements.

The same has held true for the new generation of integrated reports, which are now increasingly common – especially in the listed company sector – and in some areas are a listing requirement on an 'if not, why not' basis, for instance in South Africa. The increased attention to, and the potential wider adoption of, <IR> makes it important that a generally acceptable form of independent assurance is developed.

Key issues in this context are:

- organisations use a range of mechanisms to enhance credibility and trust, of which assurance is only one

- the internal systems needed for are far less mature than systems for 'financial' information

- the concept of integrated reporting is relatively new and is still evolving; likewise the assurance of an integrated report is evolving

- innovation and experimentation are necessary, although existing assurance principles and methodologies should not be prematurely rejected

- the total costs and benefits of assurance are difficult to assess, but it is likely that assurance will become more cost effective as time goes by

- assurance practitioners will need to develop a comprehensive understanding of how value is created (for the organisation and for others) across the full range of the resources employed by the entity and its relations with its stakeholders.

A recent survey carried in South Africa (where <IR> was made compulsory in 2010) by the ACCA has indicated the following concerns of ten practitioners interviewed:

- The range of skills of a traditional audit team was raised by several auditors as a limitation which would frustrate efforts to assure an entire integrated report

- Fear of potential issues relating to auditors' liability was also given as a reason why auditors might be unable, or unwilling, to provide assurance on the whole integrated report

- Cost was also seen as a major impediment to making the entire integrated report the subject of an assurance engagement

- Suitable criteria for expressing an opinion on the integrated report have not been developed

- Another reason given by a Big Four associate director for not providing assurance across the whole report was that some of the clients' record keeping was inadequate. Linked to this weakness, the quality of the clients' controls and the control environment were raised as a further impediment to assuring each part of the integrated report.

  Interconnected with this were the capacity and skills of a client's staff and the availability of resources to ensure that the controls covered all the relevant operations and the process necessary to provide audit evidence in support of the disclosures made in the integrated reports.

Although the situation is still clearly evolving, current recommendations are:

- In the short-term, a solution is to develop a set of guidelines which recommend those parts of the integrated report that should be the subject of an assurance engagement and offer a basis for describing how assurance is provided over the material components of the integrated report. This may be done by the auditor and/or those charged with governance.

- In the longer term, it may be possible to define an alternative assurance model which does not express an opinion on the extent to which the integrated report complies with the IIRC framework but instead provides something similar to a panel review by suitably qualified experts.

- However, a risk exists that this new form of assurance will fail to command the same respect as the audit of financial statements and will simply expand or perpetuate the audit expectation gap. Equally relevant is the possibility that this new type of assurance report will be substituted for stakeholder engagement and activism.

- As a result, before proceeding with radical changes to existing assurance models, companies should be given the time to refine their integrated reports and engage with stakeholders to determine the extent to which external assurance is actually required.

Test your understanding 3

TRE plc is a listed high street retailer that sells a range of goods such as food, drink, clothing, electrical goods, CDs, DVDs and garden equipment.

At a recent board meeting the topic of Integrated Reporting or <IR> was raised with very mixed views in the discussion.

- The Marketing Director argued that <IR> was simply a mixture of the sustainability report and the financial report into a single communication intended mainly for investors. As such it had very little new to offer and was just another compliance requirement.

- The Finance Director replied that, in his view, <IR> would give a greater emphasis on the different types of 'capital' within the firm and would enable a more effective assessment of organisational performance.

Required:

Explain FOUR objectives of integrated reporting and how the use of integrated reporting could enable a more effective assessment of organisational performance.

13 Chapter summary

SHAREHOLDERS
- Company owners entitled to information from the directors

INSTITUTIONAL INVESTORS
- Manage funds invested by individuals
- Create complex ownership and control issues

SHAREHOLDER ACTIVISM
- Use of voting rights
- Dialogue with directors
- Evaluating governance disclosure
- Resolutions for voting at AGM

GENERAL MEETINGS
- Meetings which all shareholders are entitled to attend and vote
- AGM and EGM

PROXY VOTING
- Means of allowing shareholders to register vote when absent

DISCLOSURE
Usually via
- Annual reports
- General meetings

BEST PRACTICE
- Guidance provided by governance codes

VOLUNTARY
- Company decides what to report

MANDATORY
- Required by law or other rules

Test your understanding answers

Test your understanding 1

(a) **Mandatory disclosure examples:**

- statement of comprehensive income (income or profit and loss statement)

- statement of financial position (balance sheet)

- statement of cash flow

- statement of changes in equity

- operating segmental information

- auditors' report

- corporate governance disclosure such as remuneration report and some items in the directors' report (e.g. summary of operating position)

- in the UK, the business review is compulsory

- Risk information on capital cover – Basel 11.

NB – The IIRC's stated objective was to develop an internationally accepted integrated reporting framework to enable organisations to provide concise communications of how they create value over time.

(b) **Voluntary disclosure examples:**

- risk information

- operating review

- social and environmental information

- chief executive's review.

Test your understanding 2

- Discuss more efficient engine design with manufacturers.

- Provide information to customers on the environmental impact of air travel.

- Limit the amount of baggage customers are allowed to carry – and impose surcharges for amounts over this limit.

Test your understanding 3

In its simplest form, integrated reporting can be understood as the merging of the sustainability report and the financial report into a single 'narrative', as described by the Marketing Director.

However, the International Integrated Reporting Council (IIRC) does not use the word 'sustainability' in its definition of the concept.

According to the IIRC's 'International <IR> Framework,' an integrated report is 'a concise communication about how an organization's strategy, governance, performance and prospects, in the context of its external environment, lead to the creation of value over the short, medium and long term'.

The key emphasis of this definition is the idea of sustainable **value creation**, which makes the report and the processes underpinning it far more valuable than simply a compliance or reporting exercise.

Furthermore, this framework is intended as **guidance** for all businesses producing integrated reports, rather than compliance with a set of rules.

The objectives for integrated reporting include:

- To improve the quality of information available to providers of financial capital to enable a more efficient and productive allocation of capital

- To provide a more cohesive and efficient approach to corporate reporting that draws on different reporting strands and communicates the full range of factors that materially affect the ability of an organisation to create value over time

- To enhance accountability and stewardship for the broad base of capitals (financial, manufactured, intellectual, human, social and relationship, and natural) and promote understanding of their interdependencies

- To support integrated thinking, decision making and actions that focus on the creation of value over the short, medium and long term.

The use of <IR> can enable a more effective assessment of organisational performance as follows:

- Traditionally, organisational performance has been assessed by calculating financial ratios based on the information in the financial statements, and by monitoring trends over time.

- However, integrated reporting requires the organisation to prepare a broader range of information than in the traditional financial statements.

- This information will cover financial aspects of the organisation's performance, but also non-financial aspects.

- Hence the assessment of organisational performance based on information contained in the integrated report will be much broader in scope that a traditional assessment of organisational performance, so should help stakeholders to better understand all aspects of the organisation's performance.

- Also, because of the integrated report's focus on value creation, stakeholders should be able to better assess whether the organisation is achieving its primary objective of maximising shareholder wealth.

Management internal control systems and reporting

Chapter learning objectives

Upon completion of this chapter you will be able to:

- evaluate the key components or features of effective internal control systems such as included under the COSO framework

- assess whether information flows to management are adequate for the purposes of the management of internal control and risk

- evaluate the effectiveness and potential weaknesses of internal control systems

- discuss and advise on the importance of sound internal control and compliance with legal and regulatory requirements and the consequences to an organisation of poor control and non-compliance

- recommend new internal control systems or changes to the components of existing systems to help prevent fraud, error, waste or harmful environmental impacts

- justify the need for reports on internal controls to shareholders

- discuss the typical contents of a report on internal control and audit including environmental and sustainability audit

- assess how internal controls underpin and provide information for reliable financial and sustainability reporting

PER

One of the PER performance objectives (PO12) is that you apply different management accounting techniques in different business contexts to effectively manage and use resources. Working through this chapter should help you understand how to demonstrate that objective.

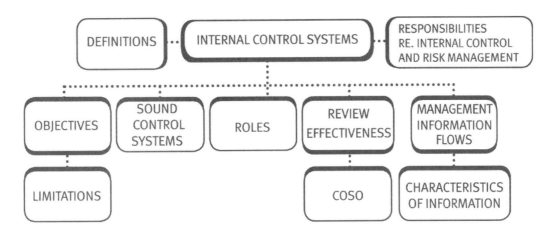

1 Development of corporate governance regarding accountability, audit and controls

Cadbury Report (1992)

The audit and accountability section of the Cadbury Report recognised the importance of corporate transparency and ensuring good communication and disclosure with shareholders and stakeholders.

The report confirmed that directors should establish a sound system of internal control and review this system on a regular basis.

Illustration 1 – Barings Bank

Barings Bank was founded in 1762. Despite surviving the Napoleonic Wars and two World Wars, Barings was brought down in 1995 due to unauthorised trading by its head derivatives trader in Singapore, Nick Leeson.

At the time of the massive trading loss, Leeson was supposed to be arbitraging, seeking to profit from differences in the prices of Nikkei 225 futures contracts listed on the Osaka Securities Exchange in Japan and the Singapore International Monetary Exchange.

Under Barings Futures Singapore's management structure Leeson acted as both the floor manager for Barings' trading on the Singapore International Monetary Exchange, and head of settlement operations. In effect, he was able to operate with no supervision from London (lack of segregation of duties).

Leeson traded to cover losses that he claims started when one of his colleagues bought contracts when she should have sold them, costing Barings £20,000. Using the hidden 'five-eights' account, by 23 February 1995, Leeson's activities had generated losses totalling £827 million (US$1.4 billion), twice the bank's available trading capital.

ING, a Dutch bank, purchased Barings Bank in 1995 for the nominal sum of £1 and assumed all of Barings' liabilities.

Turnbull Report (1999)

The Turnbull report states the need for directors to review their systems of internal control and report these to shareholders.

- Turnbull represented an attempt to formalise an explicit framework for establishing internal control in organisations.

- This framework can be used to help establish systems of internal control without being overly prescriptive. It provides guidance as to how to develop and maintain internal control systems and thus reduce risk.

- Work done by the Committee of Sponsoring Organisations (COSO) in 1992 was referred to within this report.

Illustration 2 – Société Générale

In January 2008 Société Générale lost approximately €4.9 billion closing out positions on futures contracts over three days of trading during a period in which the market was experiencing a large drop in equity prices.

The bank claimed that Jérôme Kerviel, a trader with the company, "had taken massive fraudulent directional positions in 2007 and 2008 far beyond his limited authority".

Société Générale characterises Kerviel as a rogue trader and claims Kerviel worked these trades alone, and without its authorisation. Kerviel, in turn, told investigators that such practices are widespread and that getting a profit makes the hierarchy turn a blind eye.

2 Internal control and risk management in corporate governance

- Internal control and risk management are fundamental components of good corporate governance.

- Good corporate governance means that the board must identify and manage all risks for a company.

- In terms of risk management, internal control systems span finance, operations, compliance and other areas, i.e. all the activities of the company.

Risk management

The UK Corporate Governance Code recommends that 'The board should maintain sound risk management and internal control systems'.

The Cadbury Report noted that risk management should be systematic and also embedded in company procedures. Furthermore there should be a culture of risk awareness.

The report's initial definition of risk management was **'the process by which executive management, under board supervision, identifies the risk arising from business and establishes the priorities for control and particular objectives'**.

While Cadbury recognised the need for internal control systems for risk management, detailed advice on the application of those controls was provided by the Committee of Sponsoring Organisations (COSO) and the Turnbull Report.

Internal controls and COSO

COSO was formed in 1985 to sponsor the national commission on fraudulent reporting. The 'sponsoring organisations' included the American Accounting Association and the American Institute of Certified Public Accountants. COSO now produces guidance on the implementation of internal control systems in large and small companies.

In COSO, internal control is seen to apply to three aspects of the business:

1   Effectiveness and efficiency of operations – that is the basic business objectives including performance goals and safeguarding resources.

2   Reliability of financial reporting – including the preparation of any published financial information.

3   Compliance with applicable laws and regulations to which the company is subject.

The elements of an effective control system recommended by COSO in 1992 are covered later in this chapter.

Internal controls and Turnbull

The Turnbull committee was established after the publication of the 1998 Combined Code in the UK to provide advice to listed companies on how to implement the internal control principles of the code.

The overriding requirement of their report was that the directors should:

(a)   implement a sound system of internal controls, and

(b)   that this system should be checked on a regular basis.

Turnbull Report requirements

The Turnbull Report requires:

(a) That internal controls should be established using a risk-based approach. Specifically a company should:

- Establish business objectives.

- Identify the associated key risks.

- Decide upon the controls to address the risks.

- Set up a system to implement the required controls, including regular feedback.

(b) That the system should be reviewed on a regular basis. The UK Corporate Governance Code (2010) contains the statement that:

'The directors should, at least annually, conduct a review of the effectiveness of the group's system of internal control and should report to shareholders that they have done so. The review should cover all controls, including financial, operational and compliance controls and risk management.'

 3 Internal control definitions

- **Controls** attempt to ensure that risks, those factors which stop the achievement of company objectives, are minimised.

- An **internal control system** comprises the whole network of systems established in an organisation to provide reasonable assurance that organisational objectives will be achieved.

- **Internal management control** refers to the procedures and policies in place to ensure that company objectives are achieved.

- The control procedures and policies provide the detailed controls implemented within the company.

4 Objectives of internal control systems

A popular misconception is that the internal control system is implemented simply to stop fraud and error. As the points below show, this is not the case.

A lack of internal control implies that directors have not met their obligations under corporate governance. It specifically means that the risk management strategy of the company will be defective.

The main objectives of an internal control system are summarised in the Auditing Practices Board (APB) and the COSO guidelines (detail provided below and in expandable text).

Objectives of an internal control system

An internal control system is to ensure, as far as practicable:

- the orderly and efficient conduct of its business, including adherence to internal policies
- the safeguarding of assets of the business
- the prevention and detection of fraud and error
- the accuracy and completeness of the accounting records, and
- the timely preparation of financial information.

Benefits of an internal control system are therefore:

- Effectiveness and efficiency of operations.
- Reliability of financial reporting.
- Compliance with applicable laws and regulations.

These may further give rise to improved investor confidence.

Effective financial controls, including the maintenance of proper accounting records, are an important element of internal control. They help ensure that the company is not unnecessarily exposed to avoidable financial risks and that financial information used within the business and for publication is reliable. They also contribute to the safeguarding of assets, including the prevention and detection of fraud.

A sound system of internal control therefore provides reasonable, but not absolute, assurance that a company will not be hindered in achieving its business objectives, or in the orderly and legitimate conduct of its business, by circumstances which may reasonably be foreseen. A system of internal control cannot, however, provide protection with certainty against a company failing to meet its business objectives or all material errors, losses, fraud, or breaches of laws or regulations.

Objectives of internal control

The objectives of an internal control system follow on from the need for internal control in risk management and corporate governance.

The actual objectives of internal control systems are mentioned in many different publications and reports. Two of those are given below.

APB objectives

The APB in the UK provides guidance to auditors with specific reference to the implementation of International Standards on Auditing. A definition of internal controls from the APB is:

The internal control system ... includes all the policies and procedures (internal records) adopted by the directors and management of an entity to succeed in their objective of ensuring, as far as practicable:

Definition	Commentary
the orderly and efficient conduct of its business, including adherence to internal policies	There will be systems in place to ensure that all transactions are recorded (so the business is conducted in an orderly manner) through to following policies such as provision of good customer service.
the safeguarding of assets	Assets in this case include buildings, cars, cash, etc. (e.g. those things that can be touched) through to other assets including the intellectual property of the company (e.g. those things which cannot be touched but are still an asset of the business).
the prevention and detection of fraud and error	This will include fraud and error at the operational level through to the strategic level (e.g. off balance sheet finance or the adoption of incorrect or suspect accounting policies (think of Enron)).
the accuracy and completeness of the accounting records; and	Again, ensuring that all transactions are recorded – so liabilities are not 'hidden' and assets are not overstated.
the timely preparation of financial information.	Reporting deadlines in many jurisdictions are quite strict (60 days in the US for some reports) hence the need to ensure information is available to produce those reports in a timely fashion.

The main point to note here, as in the previous section, is that the internal control system encompasses the whole business, not simply the financial records.

COSO objectives

COSO defines internal control as 'a process, effected by the entity's board of directors, management and other personnel, designed to provide reasonable assurance regarding the achievement of objectives', in three particular areas:

1   Effectiveness and efficiency of operations.

2   Reliability of financial reporting.

3   Compliance with applicable laws and regulations.

> This definition contains a number of key concepts which again illustrate the pervasiveness of internal control systems in a company.
>
> - Internal control is a process, rather than a structure. It is a continuing series of activities, planned, implemented and monitored by the board of directors and management at all levels within an organisation.
>
> - Internal control provides only reasonable assurance, not absolute assurance, with regard to achievement of the organisation's objectives.
>
> - The objectives of internal control relate to assurance not only about reliable financial reporting and compliance, but also with regard to the effectiveness and efficiency of operations.
>
> - Internal control is therefore also concerned with the achievement of performance objectives, such as profitability.
>
> - It is also useful to think of internal control as a system for the management and control of certain risks, to restrict the likelihood of adverse events or results.

Limitations of internal control systems

There are several possible causes of internal control failure.

The UK Turnbull report (in paragraph 22) gives examples of causes of failure but this list is not exhaustive.

- Poor judgement in decision-making. Internal control failures can sometimes arise from individual decisions being made based on inadequate information provision or by inexperienced staff.

- Human error can cause failures although a well-designed internal control environment can help control this to a certain extent.

- Control processes being deliberately circumvented by employees and others. It is very difficult to completely prevent deliberate circumvention, especially if an employee has a particular reason (in his or her opinion) to do so, such as the belief that higher bonuses will be earned.

- Management overriding controls, presumably in the belief that the controls put in place are inconvenient or inappropriate and should not apply to them.

- The occurrence of unforeseeable circumstances is the final cause referred to in the Turnbull Report. Control systems are designed to cope with a given range of variables and when an event happens outside that range, the system may be unable to cope.

5   Sound control systems

- It is not sufficient to simply have an internal control system since a system can be ineffective and fail to support the organisation and serve the aim of corporate governance.

- The Turnbull guidance described three features of a sound internal control system.

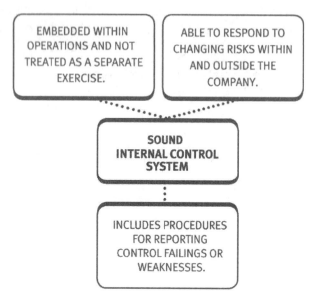

 Turnbull's sound systems

Principle 1 of the **Turnbull Report**: Establish and maintain a sound system of internal control.

Elements of internal control include:

1   Facilitate the effective and efficient operation of the company enabling it to respond **to any significant risks** which stand in the way of the company achieving its objectives. The risks could be business, compliance, operational or financial.

2   Ensure the quality of both internal (management) and external reporting.

3   Ensure compliance with laws and regulations and with the company's internal policies regarding the running of the business.

In terms of risk management, the internal control system is more than simply checking that, e.g. 'all goods despatched have been invoiced'. The Turnbull guidance described three features of a **sound internal control system**:

- Firstly, the principles of internal control should be embedded within the organisation's structures, procedures and culture. Internal control should not be seen as a stand-alone set of activities and by embedding it into the fabric of the organisation's infrastructure, awareness of internal control issues becomes everybody's business and this contributes to effectiveness.

> - Secondly, internal control systems should be capable of responding quickly to evolving risks to the business arising from factors within the company and to changes in the business environment. The speed of reaction is an important feature of almost all control systems. Any change in the risk profile or environment of the organisation will necessitate a change in the system and a failure or slowness to respond may increase the vulnerability to internal or external trauma.
>
> - Thirdly, sound internal control systems include procedures for reporting immediately to appropriate levels of management any significant control failings or weaknesses that are identified, together with details of corrective action being undertaken. Information flows to relevant levels of management capable and empowered to act on the information are essential in internal control systems. Any failure, frustration, distortion or obfuscation of information flows can compromise the system. For this reason, formal and relatively rigorous information channels are often instituted in organisations seeking to maximise the effectiveness of their internal control systems.

6   Roles in risk management and internal control

- Responsibility for internal control is not simply an executive management role.

- All employees have some responsibility for monitoring and maintaining internal controls.

- Roles in monitoring range from the CEO setting the 'tone' for internal control compliance, to the external auditor, reporting on the effectiveness of the system.

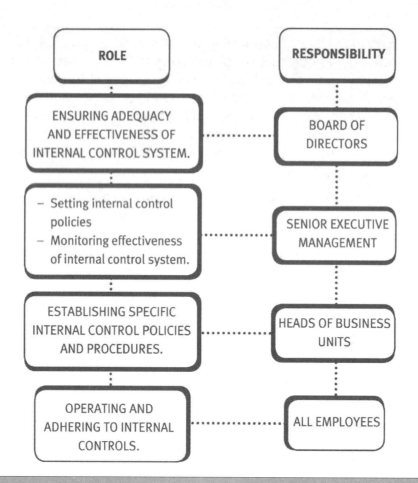

Turnbull Report roles

The Turnbull Report addresses the responsibilities of directors and management in relation to risk and control.

Directors

Directors should:

- Set appropriate internal control policies.

- Seek regular assurance that the system is functioning.

- Review the effectiveness of internal control.

- Provide disclosures on internal controls in annual reports and accounts.

Directors should review internal controls under the five headings identified by COSO in 1992 (see later in this chapter).

- Control environment

- Risk assessment

- Information systems

- Control procedures

- Monitoring.

Management

Management should:

- Implement board policies.

- Identify and evaluate the risks faced by the company.

The Turnbull Report also suggests that internal audit makes a significant and valuable contribution to a company.

 Roles in risk management

While the syllabus heading does state 'executive' roles in risk management, the COSO guidelines also note that **'everyone in an organisation has responsibility for internal control'**, hence the slightly wider explanation provided here.

The guidance below is an expanded version of the COSO recommendations.

Position	Responsibilities regarding internal control
Chief executive officer (CEO)	The CEO is ultimately responsible for the internal control system and therefore must assume ownership of that system. The CEO sets the 'tone' for internal controls – that is the company environment that indicates internal controls are important and that all staff (directors downwards) must act with integrity and in an ethical manner. The CEO sets this tone by their actions and the way in which senior managers are treated. In turn, senior managers are expected to cascade this tone to lower management levels. The CEO will monitor all staff, but in particular the financial officers as they have more power to adversely affect the company (e.g. by fraud).
Board of directors	Sets corporate government policies and procedures for the company. Has knowledge of the company's activities, and ensures they commit sufficient time to fulfil their board responsibilities. Ensures that the internal control system is adequate and effective for the company. Receives and reviews regular reports from senior management and takes action on any actual or perceived weakness in the internal control system. Provides the resources to implement and monitor the internal control systems.
Risk committee	Identifies risks affecting the company. Recommends risk strategy to the board.

Senior management	Responsible to the board of directors. Set and monitor the effectiveness of many internal controls in the company. Provide reports on a timely basis on their implementation and review of the internal control system in the company. Responsible for carrying out their activities with honesty and integrity – as they are in a position to override many internal controls should they choose to do so.
Internal auditors	Evaluate the effectiveness of internal control systems. Contribute to the ongoing effectiveness of those systems by reporting on systems and recommending improvements where necessary.
Heads of business units	Establish and monitor specific internal controls for their business unit.
Employees	Act with integrity and work within the internal control systems as directed. Communicate non-compliance with control systems, or weaknesses in control systems, to senior management.
Third parties	Provide useful information to management on internal control weaknesses (e.g. from external auditors) and general information on implementing internal controls, e.g. from legislators, regulators and specialist third parties (such as COSO).

SOX section 404 responsibilities

SOX sets out responsibilities regarding risk management. However, in direct contrast to other corporate governance systems, remember that these responsibilities are statutory rather than guidance. The comments below relate specifically to the s404 requirements of SOX, i.e. the audit and reporting of internal control systems within a company. More detail on this topic will follow in the audit and compliance chapter.

There are two main areas of responsibility. Management is likely to delegate the authority to obtain information on internal controls to the audit committee and/or internal audit department. Obviously, the responsibility for management's report cannot be delegated. In SOX terms, management refers to the board, with specific emphasis on the CEO and CFO – these individuals have to attest that the control system has been reviewed.

Role	Responsibility
Management	Learn about the system of internal control in place. Evaluate both the design and effectiveness of that system. Prepare a written assessment, at the year end, on the effectiveness of internal control which must be included in the company's annual return.
Independent auditor	Expresses an opinion on management's assessment of the effectiveness of internal controls in the company. Verifies that management's assessment is correct by independent testing of the control system. Expresses an opinion on the financial statements of the company.

7 Review effectiveness of internal control system

In respect of reviewing the internal control system, the Turnbull Report (principle 2) stated:

- the review is a normal responsibility of management

- the review itself, however, will be delegated to the audit committee (the board does not have the time nor the expertise to carry out the review)

- the board must provide information on the internal control system and review in the annual accounts

- the review should be carried out at least annually.

The COSO framework identifies five main elements of a control system against which the review should take place.

These range from the board setting the overall philosophy of the company in terms of applying internal controls to the detail of the control activities.

Elements of an effective internal control system

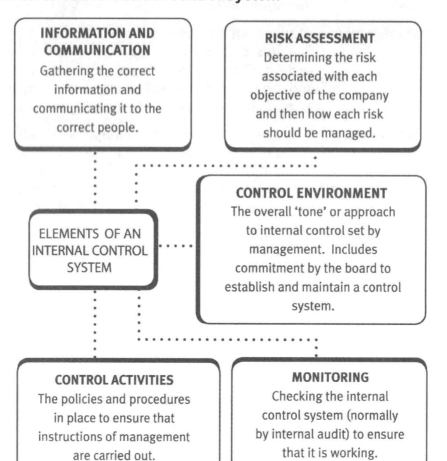

Elements of an effective internal control system

COSO identify five elements of an effective control system.

1   **Control environment**

This is sometimes referred to as the 'tone at the top' of the organisation. It describes the ethics and culture of the organisation, which provide a framework within which other aspects of internal control operate. The control environment is set by the tone of management, its philosophy and management style, the way in which authority is delegated, the way in which staff are organised and developed, and the commitment of the board of directors.

The control environment has been defined by the Institute of Internal Auditors as: 'The attitude and actions of the board and management regarding the significance of control within the organisation. The control environment provides the discipline and structure for the achievement of the primary objectives of the system of internal control.'

The control environment includes the following elements:

- Management's philosophy and operating style.

- Organisational structure.

- Assignment of authority and responsibility.

- Human resource policies and practices.

- Competence of personnel.

2 Risk assessment

There is a connection between the objectives of an organisation and the risks to which it is exposed. In order to make an assessment of risks, objectives for the organisation must be established. Having established the objectives, the risks involved in achieving those objectives should be identified and assessed, and this assessment should form the basis for deciding how the risks should be managed.

The risk assessment should be conducted for each business within the organisation, and should consider, for example:

- **internal factors**, such as the complexity of the organisation, organisational changes, staff turnover levels, and the quality of staff

- **external factors**, such as changes in the industry and economic conditions, technological changes, and so on.

The risk assessment process should also distinguish between:

- **risks that are controllable**: management should decide whether to accept the risk, or to take measures to control or reduce the risk

- **risks that are not controllable**: management should decide whether to accept the risk, or whether to withdraw partially or entirely from the business activity, so as to avoid the risk.

3 Control activities

These are policies and procedures that ensure that the decisions and instructions of management are carried out. Control activities occur at all levels within an organisation, and include authorisations, verifications, reconciliations, approvals, segregation of duties, performance reviews and asset security measures. These control activities are commonly referred to as internal controls.

Examples of control activities are provided on the following page.

4   Information and communication

An organisation must gather information and communicate it to the right people so that they can carry out their responsibilities. Managers need both internal and external information to make informed business decisions and to report externally. The quality of information systems is a key factor in this aspect of internal control.

Additional detail on information systems is provided later in this chapter.

5   Monitoring

It is critical that the internal control system is reviewed and monitored frequently.

It is the role of management to implement board policies on risk and control; part of these duties is to monitor the internal control system, identify deficiencies and report these findings to senior management and the board of directors.

The board may delegate some of its duties in this context to the Audit Committee/Risk Committee with the former having a review of Internal Financial Controls as part of its role.

Control activities

Within the control system, there are control activities. These are the detailed internal controls which are embedded within the operations of the company.

There have been various attempts at defining control activities – the list referred to most often is from the APC (the Auditing Practices Committee – now the APB). The APC provided a list of eight internal controls, as shown below. The controls are placed into three groups to show how they work together. However, they are normally listed in a different order to make them memorable, as the detailed explanation below shows.

Internal control	Explanation
Group 1 Organisational, Segregation of duties	Set the structure of the company providing responsibility for different areas of the company (organisational) as well as ensuring tasks are split between various people to minimise the risk of fraud and collusion (segregation of duties).

Group 2 Physical, Authorisation and approval, Arithmetic and accounting	Detailed controls embedded into the operational systems ensuring assets are safeguarded (physical), transactions are legitimate to the company (authorisation and approval) and the accounting records are correct (arithmetical and accounting).
Group 3 Personnel, Supervision, Management	Controls over the human resources of the company including selection of appropriate staff (personnel), ensuring those staff are working correctly (supervision) and management are checking the whole control environment (management) normally using internal audit.

The APC list of internal controls can be remembered as:

S Segregation of duties

P Physical

A Authorisation and approval

M Management

S Supervision

O Organisation

A Arithmetic and accounting

P Personnel

which provides a useful mnemonic but does not necessarily explain the original grouping. Note that at SBL you will be expected to move away from the detail of controls and take a high level view of the control activities, akin to that of a board of directors.

The controls are explained below in more detail.

Segregation of duties

Most transactions can be broken down into three separate duties: the **authorisation** or initiation of the transaction, the **handling of the asset** that is the subject of the transaction, and the **recording** of the transaction. This reduces the risk of fraud and may also reduce the risk of error.

For example, in the system for purchases and purchase accounting, the same individual should not have responsibility for:

- making a purchase

- making the payment, and recording the purchase and the payment in the accounts.

If one individual did have responsibility for more than one of these activities, there would be potential for fraud. The individual could record fictitious purchases (e.g. the purchase of goods ordered for personal use) and pay for transactions that had not occurred.

Segregation of duties can also make it easier to spot unintentional mistakes, and should not be seen simply as a control against fraud.

At board of director level, corporate governance codes state that the duties of the chairman of the board and the CEO should be segregated, to prevent one individual from acquiring a dominant position on the board.

Although segregating duties provides protection against fraud by one individual, it is not effective against collusion to commit fraud by two or more individuals.

Physical controls

Physical controls are measures and procedures to protect physical assets against theft or unauthorised access and use. They include:

- using a safe to hold cash and valuable documents
- using secure entry systems to buildings or areas of a building
- dual custody of valuable assets, so that two people are needed to obtain access to certain assets
- periodic inventory checks
- hiring security guards and using closed circuit TV cameras.

Authorisation and approval

Authorisation and approval controls are established to ensure that a transaction does not proceed unless an authorised individual has given specific approval, possibly in writing. For **spending transactions**, an organisation might establish **authorisation limits**, whereby an individual manager is authorised to approve certain types of transaction up to a certain maximum value.

Management control

Controls are exercised by management on the basis of information they receive.

Top level reviews. The board of directors or senior management might call for a performance report on the progress of the organisation towards its goals. For example, senior management might review a report on the progress of the organisation toward achieving its budget targets. Questions should be asked by senior management, prompting responses at lower management levels. In this way, top level reviews are a control activity.

Activity controls. At departmental or divisional level, management should receive reports that review performance or highlight exceptions. Functional reviews should be more frequent than top-level reviews, on a daily, weekly or monthly basis. As with top-level reviews, questions should be asked by management that initiate control activity. An example of control by management is the provision of regular performance reports, such as variance reports, comparing actual results with a target or budget.

Supervision

Supervision is oversight of the work of other individuals, by someone in a position of responsibility. Supervisory controls help to ensure that individuals do the tasks they are required to and perform them properly.

Organisation

Organisation controls refer to the controls provided by the organisation's structure, such as:

- the separation of an organisation's activities and operations into departments or responsibility centres, with a clear division of responsibilities
- delegating authority within the organisation
- establishing reporting lines within the organisation
- co-ordinating the activities of different departments or groups, e.g. by setting up committees or project teams.

Arithmetic and accounting

Controls are provided by:

- recording transactions properly in the accounting system
- being able to trace each individual transaction through the accounting records
- checking arithmetical calculations, such as double-checking the figures in an invoice before sending it to a customer (sales invoice) or approving it for payment (purchase invoice) to make sure that they are correct.

Personnel controls

Controls should be applied to the selection and training of employees, to make sure that: suitable individuals are appointed to positions within the organisation; individuals have the appropriate personal qualities, experience and qualifications where required; individuals are given **suitable induction and training**, to ensure that they carry out their tasks efficiently and effectively.

Staff should also be given **training** in the purpose of controls and the need to apply them. Specific training about controls should help to increase employee awareness and understanding of the risks of failing to apply them properly.

8 Information flows for management

To enable management to identify and manage risks and monitor internal controls within an organisation, they need adequate information flows from within the business.

- There should be effective channels of communication within the organisation, so that all managers receive timely information that is relevant to the performance of their tasks and duties.

- Information should be provided regularly to management so that they can monitor performance with respect to efficiency, effectiveness in achieving targets, economy and quality.

- Managers need both internal and external information to make informed business decisions and to report externally.

- The actual information provided to management varies depending on the different levels of management.

- Different information systems are available to provide the required information.

Management levels

Before considering the roles of management in internal control and risk management, the different levels of management must be revised.

The information requirements of managers will vary depending on their specific role with regard to internal control and risk. Within an organisation, management are normally divided into three different levels: strategic, tactical and operational. These three levels of management, as described by **Anthony**, can be illustrated by the following diagram:

In general terms, each level of management will be involved in specific activities but internal control is the responsibility of all employees as part of their accountability for achieving objectives:

Level	Activity
Strategic	Involved with monitoring and controlling the organisation as a whole, making decisions on areas such as opening of new shops and factories or investment in new product lines.
Tactical	Responsible for implementing the decisions of strategic managers and ensuring that the different divisions or departments within the organisation are operating correctly.
Operational	Controlling the day-to-day operations of the organisation, reporting queries or problems back to tactical management for decisions as necessary.

The two key activities of management are therefore:

Planning	Planning refers to setting the strategic direction of the company. This involves a significant degree of risk as strategic decision makers are effectively determining what the company will do in the context of a risky external environment.
Control	Control refers to monitoring the activities of the company – with the internal control systems checking that those activities are being carried out correctly. While control strategy is set by strategic management, the implementation and monitoring is a more junior activity.

The mix of the planning/risk and monitoring/internal control activities is sometimes shown in diagrammatic form as follows:

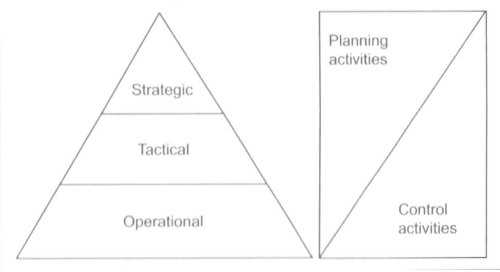

Internal control and risk management activities

Management and internal control/risk

The activities of the three management levels regarding internal control and risk are:

Management level	Management of internal control	Management of risk
Strategic	Strategic managers tend to be focused on planning – detailed control is a lower management function. However, strategic management are normally charged with ensuring that the internal control system is effective. They will therefore be responsible for ensuring that the importance of internal control is recognised in the organisation and providing the necessary resources to establish and monitor this system.	Risk management is a responsibility of strategic management. Strategic decisions such as deciding which products to manufacture or which areas to trade in will be taken here – with those decisions impacting on the amount of risk faced by the company. Information will be needed on the potential outcomes of different decisions so the amount of risk can be adequately assessed. Strategic managers will be advised by the risk committee.
Tactical	Managers will have responsibility for implementing strategic management's decisions – in this case the actual internal control systems within the company. Similarly, where control weaknesses are identified, tactical managers will need to remedy those weaknesses and where necessary inform strategic management of material weaknesses.	Managers will be responsible for implementing strategic management's decisions. They will also be reporting identified risks to strategic management, either from environmental monitoring or from use of decision making tools such as the decision support system (DSS). The latter may identify risks from falling sales for example, which will need strategic management action.

		Tactical managers will be collecting information on operational risk from lower level managers and recommending control activities to mitigate those risks.
Operational	Operational managers will be responsible for the operation of specific detailed internal controls, e.g. controls to ensure that stock is not stolen from company premises.	Operational managers will have little or no influence over the risk appetite of the company. They are, though, in a position to identify risks at the operational level and therefore report these to tactical management.

To carry out these activities, each management level will need specific information from specific information systems.

 Information systems for management control

The information systems providing that information must therefore vary so that appropriate information is provided to each level of management and focused on their specific objectives regarding internal control and risk. The diagram below reiterates the management levels and indicates the general type of information system that will be provided for that management level.

Types of information system

- **Executive Information System** (EIS): a computer-based system for total business modelling. It monitors reality and facilitates actions that improve business results.

- **Management Information System** (MIS): a system to convert data from internal and external sources into information, and to communicate that information in an appropriate form to managers at all levels and in all areas of the business to enable them to make timely and effective decisions.

- **Decision Support System** (DSS): a computer-based system which enables managers to confront ill-structured problems by direct interaction with data and problem-solving programs.

- **Transaction Processing System** (TPS): a system that routinely captures, processes, stores and outputs low level transaction data.

Management hierarchy

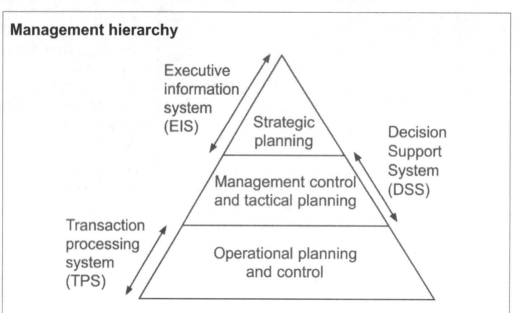

All systems provide information appropriate to each management level – see the next section for examples of how that information changes at the different levels.

Management level	System
Strategic (board of directors)	Information needs at the strategic level are considerably more difficult to predict than at the other levels of management. This usually leads to a greater reliance on informal and ad hoc information systems providing summary information focused on the specific risk areas relevant to that company. EISs should provide this range of information.
Tactical (divisional management)	Tactical information is also largely fed from transaction processing systems, although it may also come from external sources. DSSs will project current trends into the future while the MIS will concentrate on exception reporting on current information.
Operational (junior management /team leaders)	Operational decisions are programmable and require specific and detailed information. Many of the decisions taken are able to be programmed into the computer. Most of the information used for operational decisions comes from the simplest form of information system, TPSs. The outputs from these systems are simple reports and sorted lists of transactions.

9   Information characteristics and quality

The information received by management needs to be of a certain standard to be useful in internal control and risk management and monitoring.

There should be an adequate, integrated information system, supplying internal financial, operational and compliance data and relevant external data.

The information should meet the criteria of 'good' information:

- **A**ccurate

- **C**omplete

- **C**ost-beneficial

- **U**ser-targeted

- **R**elevant

- **A**uthoritative

- **T**imely

- **E**asy to use

The characteristics of that information will change depending on the management level using that information.

The table below shows the characteristics of information and how its quality varies depending on what is made available.

Characteristic	Strategic	→	Operational
Time period	Forecast	→	Historical
Timeliness	Delayed	→	Immediately available
Objectivity	Subjective	→	Objective
Quantifiability	Qualitative	→	Quantitative
Accuracy	Approximate	→	Accurate
Certainty	Uncertain	→	Certain
Completeness	Partial	→	Complete
Breadth	Broad	→	Specific
Detail	Little detail	→	Highly detailed

 Information characteristics

Strategic and operational information – characteristics

Given that management activities regarding internal control and risk management are different, the characteristics of information provided by the different management information systems will also differ. Characteristics of information for these management decision areas can be summarised as shown below:

Information characteristic	Strategic	Operational
Time period	Information can be both historical (enabling management to learn from what has happened in the past) and forecast.	Operational information must be actual historical information.
Timeliness	Generally speaking, the timeliness of information is not crucial as decisions are taken over a series of weeks or months. Significant changes, such as the acquisition of a competitor, will normally be reported quickly to senior management.	Information must be immediately available.

Objectivity	Strategic decision making will require a mixture of objective and subjective information. Building long-term plans needs future information, which incorporates subjective forecasts of what is likely to happen.	The highly structured and programmable decisions made at the operational level need information that is both objective and quantifiable. The comparatively junior level at which decisions are made requires strict guidelines to be set and disqualifies subjective data as a basis for this level of decision.
Quantifiability	Strategic decision making needs both qualitative and quantitative information, although attempts will often be made to quantify apparently qualitative data. This enables such data to be incorporated into the kind of mathematical models often used in the building of strategic plans.	
Accuracy	There is no demand for information to be completely accurate, it will often be rounded to the nearest thousand.	Information must be accurate to the nearest £ or $ – as it relates to low level or detailed decision making.
Certainty	By its very nature, future information is subject to uncertainty. Strategic planners must be capable of adjusting to the limitations of the data.	Information will have little or no uncertainty as it relates to historical recording of actual events, e.g. individual sales.
Completeness	Strategic planners will often need to work with only partial information, using assumptions and extrapolations to try to build as complete a picture as possible.	The sort of decisions to be made at this level are highly predictable, which enables the information needed to be specified and an appropriate information system built. This will ensure that a complete set of information is available when it is needed.

Breadth	A wide variety of data is needed for strategic planning. It must cover the whole gamut of the organisation's operations and can come in various forms.	Information will be focused on the specific decisions being made – any other data is irrelevant and potentially distracting.
Detail	It is unnecessary to have a great deal of detail when building a strategic plan, and detail is likely to be distracting and confusing. Aggregated and summarised data is most commonly used by senior management.	Information will be detailed to enable the manager to make decisions about individual items, e.g. the number of items to order.

Tactical information – characteristics

Just as tactical decision making forms a link between strategic and operational management, the information it requires has some of the characteristics of each.

Forecast and historical data are both required, although historical data is not needed as immediately as it is for operational decisions. Information is largely objective and quantitative but the greater experience of middle managers making tactical decisions makes this less important than for operational information.

For each of the other information qualities – accuracy, certainty, completeness, breadth and detail – tactical information occupies the midpoint between strategic and operational information.

Test your understanding 1

Why is it important for the board to have accurate information for the management of internal controls?

10 Fraud risk management strategy

In common with any other type of risk, a risk management strategy needs to be developed for fraud. This strategy should include three key elements:

- Fraud prevention.
- Fraud detection.
- Fraud response.

Together, these should result in a fourth element – risk deterrence.

For example, fraud detection acts as a deterrent by sending a message to likely fraudsters that the organisation is actively fighting fraud and that procedures are in place to identify any illegal activity that has occurred. Similarly, the possibility of being caught will often persuade a potential perpetrator not to commit a fraud.

As well as addressing the legal aspects of fraud, this process operates within the wider context of the organisation's risk management strategy, corporate governance and ethical culture.

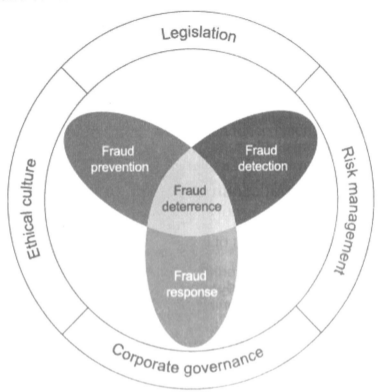

Fraud prevention

The aim of preventative controls is to reduce opportunity and remove temptation from potential offenders. Prevention techniques include the introduction of policies, procedures and controls, and activities such as training and fraud awareness to stop fraud from occurring.

Some specific examples of fraud prevention include:

- An anti-fraud culture
- Risk awareness
- Whistleblowing
- Sound internal control systems.

A **fraud policy statement**, effective recruitment policies and good internal controls can minimise the risk of fraud.

Fraud detection

A common misbelief is that external auditors find fraud. This is actually rarely the case – in fact their letters of engagement typically state that it is not their responsibility to look for fraud. Most frauds are discovered accidentally, or as a result of information received (whistleblowing).

Some methods of discovering fraud are:

- Performing regular checks, e.g. stocktaking and cash counts.

- Warning signals or fraud risk indicators (see previous section). For example:

    - Failures in internal control procedures

    - Lack of information provided to auditors

    - Unusual behaviour by individual staff members

    - Accounting difficulties.

- Whistleblowers

Fraud response

- The fraud response plan sets out the arrangements for dealing with suspected cases of fraud, theft or corruption.

- It provides procedures for evidence-gathering that will enable decision-making and that will subsequently be admissible in any legal action.

- The fraud response plan also has a deterrent value and can help to restrict damage and minimise losses to the organisation.

The organisation's response to fraud may include:

- Internal disciplinary action, in accordance with personnel policies.

- Civil litigation for the recovery of loss.

- Criminal prosecution through the police.

Within the response plan responsibilities should be allocated to:

- Managers, who should take responsibility for detecting fraud in their area.

- Finance Director, who has overall responsibility for the organisational response to fraud including the investigation. This role may be delegated to a fraud officer or internal security officer.

- Personnel (Human Resources Department), who will have responsibility for disciplinary procedures and issues of employment law and practice.

- Audit committee, which should review the details of all frauds and receive reports of any significant events.

- Internal auditors, who will most likely have the task of investigating the fraud.

- External auditors, to obtain expertise.

- Legal advisors, in relation to internal disciplinary, civil or criminal responses.

- Public relations, if the fraud is so significantly large that it will come to public attention.

- Police, where it is policy to prosecute all those suspected of fraud.

- Insurers, where there is likely to be a claim.

Test your understanding 2

Scenario

A large college has several sites and employs hundreds of teaching staff.

Trigger

The college has recently discovered a serious fraud involving false billings for part-time teaching.

The fraud involved two members of staff. M is a clerk in the payroll office who is responsible for processing payments to part-time teaching staff. P is the head of the Business Studies department at the N campus. Part-time lecturers are required to complete a monthly claim form which lists the classes taught and the total hours claimed. These forms must be signed by their head of department, who sends all signed forms to M. M checks that the class codes on the claim forms are valid, that hours have been budgeted for those classes and inputs the information into the college's payroll package.

The college has a separate personnel department that is responsible for maintaining all personnel files. Additions to the payroll must be made by a supervisor in the personnel office. The payroll package is programmed to reject any claims for payment to employees whose personnel files are not present in the system.

M had gained access to the personnel department supervisor's office by asking the college security officer for the loan of a pass key because he had forgotten the key to his own office. M knew that the office would be unoccupied that day because the supervisor was attending a wedding. M logged onto the supervisor's computer terminal by guessing her password, which turned out to be the registration number of the supervisor's car. M then added a fictitious part-time employee, who was allocated to the N campus Business Studies department.

P then began making claims on behalf of the fictitious staff member and submitting them to M. M signed off the forms and input them as normal. The claims resulted in a steady series of payments to a bank account that had been opened by P. The proceeds of the fraud were shared equally between M and P.

The fraud was only discovered when the college wrote to every member of staff with a formal invitation to the college's centenary celebration. The letter addressed to the fictitious lecturer was returned as undeliverable and the personnel department became suspicious when they tried to contact this person in order to update his contact details. By then M and P had been claiming for non-existent teaching for three years.

The government department responsible for funding the college conducted an investigation and concluded that the college's management had relied excessively on the application controls programmed into administrative software and had paid too little attention to the human resources aspects of the system.

Task

Write a memorandum to the board evaluating the difficulties associated with preventing and/or detecting this fraud.   **(20 minutes)**

11   Chapter summary

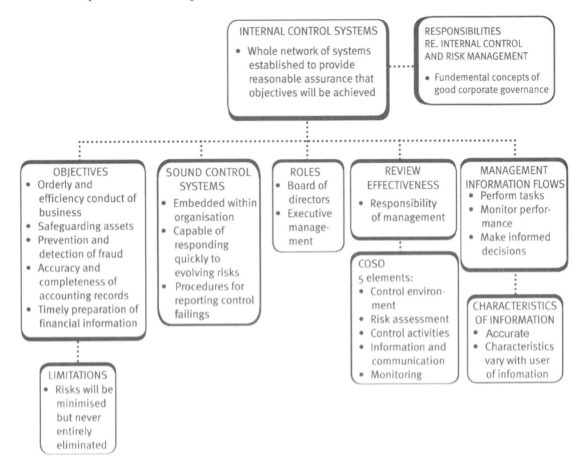

INTERNAL CONTROL SYSTEMS
- Whole network of systems established to provide reasonable assurance that objectives will be achieved

RESPONSIBILITIES RE. INTERNAL CONTROL AND RISK MANAGEMENT
- Fundemental concepts of good corporate governance

OBJECTIVES
- Orderly and efficiency conduct of business
- Safeguarding assets
- Prevention and detection of fraud
- Accuracy and completeness of accounting records
- Timely preparation of financial information

SOUND CONTROL SYSTEMS
- Embedded within organisation
- Capable of responding quickly to evolving risks
- Procedures for reporting control failings

ROLES
- Board of directors
- Executive management

REVIEW EFFECTIVENESS
- Responsibility of management

MANAGEMENT INFORMATION FLOWS
- Perform tasks
- Monitor performance
- Make informed decisions

LIMITATIONS
- Risks will be minimised but never entirely eliminated

COSO
5 elements:
- Control environment
- Risk assessment
- Control activities
- Information and communication
- Monitoring

CHARACTERISTICS OF INFORMATION
- Accurate
- Characteristics vary with user of infomation

Test your understanding answers

Test your understanding 1

The board has to meet its corporate governance responsibility to ensure that an effective internal control system exists within the organisation. In order to do this directors will require accurate reports from auditors and managers within the company regarding the current controls and any weaknesses identified.

Good information will enable the board to confirm that the monitoring activities, undertaken by auditors and critical to the internal control system, are being carried out in an effective and efficient manner.

Information regarding the costs and benefits of internal controls will enable the board to ensure that resources are not wasted on ineffective, or unnecessary controls.

Accurate information regarding the risks facing the organisation will enable the board to be aware of any critical issues that may arise in the near future, and hence take action accordingly to mitigate any problems.

The board can only provide the appropriate direction to the management of the company if it is fully aware of all the facts relating to any given situation. If the facts are distorted, the direction provided may be inappropriate.

Test your understanding 2

Memorandum

To: The Board

From: A.N. Accountant

Date: Today

Subject: Fraud mitigation

This fraud would have been extremely difficult to prevent and/or to detect.

The fraud involved collusion between two members of staff. Segregation of duties is one of the most powerful means of preventing fraud, but it can be defeated by fraudulent collusion. It would be virtually impossible to make a system effective without relying on segregation of duties.

The fact that one of the perpetrators was a senior member of staff made it more difficult to prevent. The head of an academic department in a college would be regarded as a trusted member of staff, who would not normally be expected to steal from the college.

Systems are often designed in the expectation that senior members of staff will not betray such trust.

The system was further defeated by the falsification of a record on the personnel department. There was a sound control in place that was only defeated because of a combination of human error and blatant falsification. It would be almost impossible to design any system so that it was foolproof in preventing all mistakes and in preventing fraudulent falsification.

Once the fictitious entry had been made in the personnel files the fraud would be difficult to detect because it would add only a very small amount to the overall payroll. A college would have a large number of lecturers and there would be a substantial turnover in staff.

The only people who could be expected to detect this fraud were implicated in it.

Audit and compliance

Chapter learning objectives

Upon completion of this chapter you will be able to:

- examine the need for an internal audit function in the light of regulatory and organisational requirements

- justify the importance of auditor independence in all client-auditor situations (including internal audit) and the role of internal audit in compliance

- justify the importance of having an effective internal audit committee overseeing the internal audit function

- assess the appropriate responses to auditors' recommendations

PER

One of the PER performance objectives (PO20) is that you complete an audit, preparing the formal documentation and reporting any control deficiencies to management. You report back to managers in a formal audit report. Working through this chapter should help you understand how to demonstrate that objective.

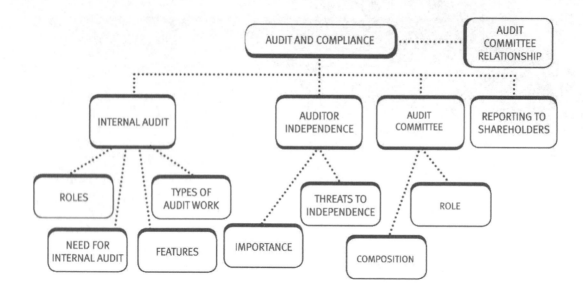

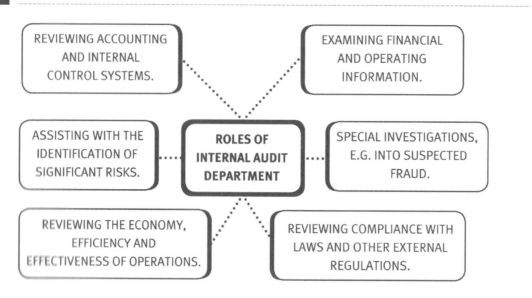

1   Function and importance of internal audit

- Internal audit is a management control. The department reviews the effectiveness of other controls within a company.

- It is part of the control systems of a company, with the aim of ensuring that other controls are working correctly.

- In some regimes, it is a statutory requirement to have internal audit. In others, codes of corporate governance strongly suggest that an internal audit department is necessary.

- The work of internal audit is varied – from reviewing financial controls through to checking compliance with legislation.

- The department is normally under the control of a chief internal auditor who reports to the audit committee.

Roles of internal audit

Roles of internal audit department

Work area	Comment
Reviewing accounting and internal control systems (financial audit)	This is the traditional view of internal audit. The internal auditor checks the financial controls in the company, possibly assisting or sharing work with the external auditor. The internal auditor would comment on whether appropriate controls exist as well as whether they are working correctly. In this work, the internal auditor does not manage risk, but simply reports on controls.
Assisting with the identification of significant risks	In this function, the internal auditor does start to work on risks. The auditor may be asked to investigate areas of risk management, with specific reference on how the company identifies, assesses and controls significant risks from both internal and external sources.
Reviewing the economy, efficiency and effectiveness of operations (operational audit)	This is also called a value for money (VFM) audit. The auditor checks whether a particular activity is cost effective (economical), uses the minimum inputs for a given output (efficient) and meets its stated objectives (effective).
Examining financial and operating information	Internal auditors ensure that reporting of financial information is made on a timely basis and that the information in the reports is factually accurate.
Special investigations	Investigations into other areas of the company's business, e.g. checking the cost estimates for a new factory.
Reviewing compliance with laws and other external regulations	This objective is particularly relevant regarding SOX where the internal auditor will be carrying out detailed work to ensure that internal control systems and financial reports meet stock exchange requirements.

Types of audit work

The internal audit department will carry out many different types of audit, as highlighted by the department's varied roles. The detail of these has been covered in Paper F8 (Audit and Assurance).

Examples of audit types are:

- financial audit

- operational audit

- project audit

- value for money audit

- social and environmental audit

- management audit.

Test your understanding 1 – Features of internal audit

Using your existing knowledge, and common sense, suggest some practical features of a good internal audit department, structuring your answer in the areas of:

- Organisational status.

- Scope of function.

- Technical competence.

- Due professional care.

Organisational structure of internal audit

- The basic structure is a chief internal auditor, responsible to the audit committee with an internal audit team reporting to that person.

- In large organisations the internal audit function will be a separate department.

- In a small company it might be the responsibility of individuals to perform specific tasks even though there will not be a full-time position.

- Some companies outsource their internal audit function, often to one of the large accountancy firms (but note the independence requirements of SOX in this respect).

2 Factors affecting the need for internal audit

There are a number of factors that affect the need for internal audit.

- The scale, diversity and complexity of the company's activities.
- The number of employees.
- Cost/benefit considerations.
- Changes in the organisational structures, reporting processes or underlying information systems.
- Changes in key risks (could be internal or external in nature).
- Problems with existing internal control systems.
- An increased number of unexplained or unacceptable events.

Factors affecting the need for internal audit

Why is internal audit important?

Because:

- in some situations it is required by statute (SOX)
- in some situations it is required by codes of good practice (codes of corporate governance)
- it provides an independence check on the control systems in a company (see below for more detail)
- it is a management control.
- it reassures investors and regulators
- it helps ensure the effectiveness and efficiency of operations
- it underpins investor confidence.

What factors affect the need for internal audit?

Apart from the obvious comment that companies which are listed are required to have an internal audit department, other factors will affect the decision to have an internal audit in non-listed companies.

Factor	Comment
The scale, diversity and complexity of the company's activities	The larger, the more diverse and the more complex a range of activities is, the more there is to monitor (and the more opportunity there is for certain things to go wrong).
The number of employees	As a proxy for size, the number of employees signifies that larger organisations are more likely to need internal audit to underpin investor confidence than smaller concerns.

Cost/benefit considerations	Management must be certain of the benefits that will result from establishing internal audit and they must be seen to outweigh the costs of the audit.
Changes in the organisational structures, reporting processes or underlying information systems	Any internal (or external) modification is capable of changing the complexity of operations and, accordingly, the risk.
Changes in key risks could be internal or external in nature	The introduction of a new product, entering a new market, a change in any of the PEST/PESTEL factors or changes in the industry might trigger the need for internal audit.
Problems with existing internal control systems	Any problems with existing systems signify the need for a tightening of systems and increased monitoring.
An increased number of unexplained or unacceptable events	System failures or similar events are a clear demonstration of internal control weakness.

The Turnbull Report notes 'in the absence of an internal audit function, management needs to apply other monitoring processes in order to assure itself and the board that the system of internal control is functioning as intended. In these circumstances, the board will need to assess whether such procedures provide sufficient and objective assurance'.

3 Auditor independence

- Internal audit is an independent objective assurance activity.

- To ensure that the activity is carried out objectively, the internal auditor must have his/her independence protected.

- Independence is assured in part by having an appropriate structure within which internal auditors work.

- Independence is also assured in part by the internal auditor following acceptable ethical and work standards.

Risks if auditors are not independent

4 Potential ethical threats

*   Auditor independence will be compromised where ethical threats are faced.

*   A threat to independence is anything that means that the opinion of an auditor could be doubted.

*   Threats can be real or perceived.

*   The conceptual framework in the ACCA code of ethics provides examples of generic threats that affect auditors, which can be viewed as affecting both external and internal auditors.

*   The code of ethics also provides examples of other threats that (normally) affect external auditors.

Ethical threats: ACCA conceptual framework

The following categories of threats are included in the ethical codes of the UK professional accountancy bodies. They can be applied to both external auditors and internal audit engagements.

Self-interest threat

Occurs when the audit firm or a member of the audit team could benefit from a financial interest in, or other self-interest conflict with, an audit client.

For example, in an external audit context:

- direct financial interest or material indirect financial interest in an audit client

- loan or guarantee to or from an audit client or any of its directors or officers

- undue dependence on total fees from an audit client

- concern about the possibility of losing the engagement

- having a close business relationship with an audit client

- potential employment with an audit client, and

- contingent fees relating to audit engagements.

In an internal audit context:

- the auditor's bonus is linked to the performance of the business area under review, for example, as part of overall business unit performance in meeting targets for 'clean' audit reports.

Self-review threat

Occurs when the audit firm, or an individual audit team member, is put in a position of reviewing subject matter for which the firm or individual was previously responsible, and which is significant in the context of the audit engagement.

For example, in an external audit context:

- member of the audit team being, or having recently been, a director, officer or other employee of the audit client in a position to exert direct and significant influence over the subject matter of the audit engagement

- performing services for an audit client that directly affect the subject matter of the current, or a subsequent, audit engagement and

- preparing original data used to generate financial statements or preparing other records that are the subject matter of the audit engagement.

In an internal audit context:

- where someone has recently transferred within the company into an audit role, and is found to be auditing their old department.

Advocacy threat

Occurs when the audit firm, or a member of the audit team, promotes, or may be perceived to promote, an audit client's position or opinion.

For example:

- dealing in, or being a promoter of, shares or other securities in an audit client, and

- acting as an advocate on behalf of an audit client in litigation or in resolving disputes with third parties.

Familiarity threat

Occurs when, by virtue of a close relationship with an audit client, its directors, officers or employees, an audit firm or a member of the audit team becomes too sympathetic to the client's interests.

For example, in an external audit context:

- a member of the audit team having a close family member who, as a director, officer or other employee of the audit client, is in a position to exert direct and significant influence over the subject matter of the audit engagement

- a former partner of the firm being a director, officer or other employee of the audit client, is in a position to exert direct and significant influence over the subject matter of the audit engagement

- long association of a senior member of the audit team with the audit client and

- acceptance of gifts or hospitality, unless the value is clearly insignificant, from the audit client, its directors, officers or employees.

In an internal audit context:

- where auditors have worked within a company for many years and have long-standing relationships with employees and management across a number of departments.

Intimidation threat

Occurs when a member of the audit team may be deterred from acting objectively and exercising professional scepticism by threats, actual or perceived, from the directors, officers or employees of an audit client.

For example, in an external audit context:

- threat of replacement over a disagreement regarding the application of an accounting principle

- pressure to reduce inappropriately the extent of work performed in order to reduce fees and

- dominant personality in a senior position at the audit client, controlling dealings with the auditor.

In an internal audit context:

- where the promotion prospects, pay rises or other rewards of the auditor can be influenced by the manager of a department being audited. The auditor may be put under pressure to provide a clean audit report in return for a favourable appraisal.

External auditor ethical threat examples

External auditors have many specific threats to their independence at audit clients, which are summarised below.

Threats to independence	Explanation/recommendation
Financial interests in a client. For example: - Auditor owns shares in a client company. - Audit firm's pension scheme owns shares in the audit client.	Auditor may disregard adverse events at the client or not qualify the audit report (when a qualification is required) due to the potential adverse effect on the share price of the client. Auditors/audit firms do not hold shares in client companies.
Loans and guarantees For example: - Auditor loans money to a client company. - Auditor receives a loan from a client company (other than in the ordinary course of business – e.g. a bank loan).	Auditor may not qualify an audit report in case the client goes out of business and is unable to repay the loan. Auditors do not make or accept loans/guarantees from audit clients.

Close business relationships For example: • Audit partner is director of a company with director of client company. • Audit firm enters into joint venture with audit client.	Auditor may not qualify audit report of client for fear of adverse effect on other business relationships. Auditors do not have close business relationships with audit clients/staff.
Family and personal relationships For example: • Director's spouse is director of client company. • Member of audit team is living with a member of the client's staff.	Independence is lost as the auditor has a conflict between maintaining professional standards and potentially upsetting or ending the personal relationship. Members of the audit team in family or personal relationship with client are removed from that team.
Employment with assurance clients For example: • Member of assurance team accepts senior position at client company.	Ex-audit team member may be able to exert significant influence over the auditor due to existing close personal/business relationships. Key members of audit team cannot accept senior appointment at client until 2 years have lapsed from involvement in the audit.
Size of fees For example: • Audit firm has a significant amount of fees derived from one client.	The auditor will not want to upset the client (e.g. qualify the audit report) in case the client moves to a different audit firm causing significant loss of fee income. Audit firms earn no more than 10% of their fees from one listed company, or 15% from other companies.
Gifts and hospitality For example: • Auditor is provided with a free holiday by the client.	Provision of gifts impairs independence – a familiarity threat is created. Audit firms have guidelines for staff on the level of gifts that can be accepted. E.g. a meal is probably acceptable but a holiday is not.

Test your understanding 2

Which of the following are independence issues?

1   Working as an audit junior on the statutory audit of a major bank with whom you have your mortgage.

2   Taking on a large new client whose fees will make up 90% of your total revenue.

3   Taking on a large new client whose fees will make up 10% of your total revenue.

4   Working as an audit partner and accepting a gold Rolex as a 'gift'.

5   Performing an internal audit review of controls that you put in place in your previous role.

6   Working as an external auditor at a company where you have a close personal relationship with a person who has a junior role in the marketing department.

7   Taking on the audit for a company with which your firm has recently been involved in a share issue.

Ethical conflicts of interest

Situations could occasionally arise in which an auditor, especially an internal auditor, might be asked to behave (or might be tempted to behave) in a way that conflicts with ethical standards and guidelines.

Conflicts of interest could relate to unimportant matters, but they might also involve fraud or some other illegal activity. The threat is more severe for internal auditors as the company they are reporting on is also their employer. Threats can therefore be carried out in ways that will not affect external auditors such as lack of salary increase through to termination of employment.

Examples of such ethical conflicts of interest are as follows:

Threat	Example
There could be pressure from an overbearing supervisor, manager or director, adversely affecting the auditor's integrity.	The auditor is asked not to report adverse findings. The threat could be made more personal, e.g. by indicating that the auditor's employment will be terminated if disclosure is made.

An auditor might mislead his or her employer as to the amount of experience or expertise he or she has, when in reality the expert advice of someone else should be sought.	The auditor wants to retain his or her position within the internal audit department or gain respect because of the apparent experience that they have.
An auditor might be asked to act contrary to a technical or professional standard. Divided loyalty between the auditor's superior and the required professional standards of conduct could arise.	An auditor is told to ignore the incorrect application of an accounting standard or the incorrect reporting of directors' remuneration.

Resolution of ethical conflicts of interest

Conflict resolution is explained in more detail in the ethical decision making chapter.

Protection of independence

- The internal auditors should be independent of executive management and should not have any involvement in the activities or systems that they audit.

- The head of internal audit should report directly to a senior director or the audit committee. In addition, the head of internal audit should have direct access to the chairman of the board of directors, and to the audit committee, and should be accountable to the audit committee.

- The audit committee should approve the appointment and termination of appointment of the head of internal audit.

Summary of independence

In summary, independence requires:

- **Independence of mind**: the state of mind that permits the provision of an opinion without being affected by influences that compromise professional judgement, allowing an individual to act with integrity, and exercise objectivity and professional scepticism.

- **Independence in appearance**: the avoidance of facts and circumstances that are so significant that a reasonable and informed third party, having knowledge of all relevant information, including safeguards applied, would reasonably conclude a firm's, or a member of the assurance team's, integrity, objectivity or professional scepticism had been compromised.

Further measures to protect independence

The independence of internal audit is enhanced by following accepted standards of internal audit work. Internal auditors can follow the same standards as external auditors. However, there are also International Standards for Internal Audit issued by the Internal Auditing Standards Board (IASB) of the Institute of Internal Auditors.

- **Attribute standards** deal with the characteristics of organisations and the parties performing internal auditing activities.

- **Performance standards** describe the nature of internal auditing activities and provide quality criteria for evaluating internal auditing services.

Attribute standards for internal audit

Objective of standard	Explanation
Independence	The internal audit activity should be independent, and the head of internal audit should report to a level within the organisation that allows the internal audit activity to fulfil its responsibilities. It should be free from interference when deciding on the scope of its assurance work, when carrying out the work and when communicating its opinions.
Objectivity	Internal auditors should be objective in carrying out their work. They should have an impartial attitude, and should avoid any conflicts of interest. For example, an internal auditor should not provide assurance services for an operation for which he or she has had management responsibility within the previous year.
Professional care	Internal auditors should exercise due professional care and should have the competence to perform their tasks. They should have some knowledge of the key IT risks and controls, and computer-assisted audit techniques.

Performance standards for internal audit

Area of work	Explanation
Managing internal audit	• The head of internal audit should manage the internal audit activity to ensure that it adds value to the organisation.
	• The head of internal audit should establish risk-based plans to decide the priorities for internal audit work, consistent with the organisation's objectives.
	• The internal audit plan should be reviewed at least annually.
	• The head of internal audit should submit the plan of work to senior management and the board for approval.
	Independence is maintained by the internal auditor/audit committee being able to decide the scope of internal audit work without being influenced by the board/senior management.
Risk management	• The internal audit department should identify and evaluate significant risk exposures and contribute to the improvement of risk management and control systems. It should evaluate risk exposures relating to governance, operations and information systems, and the reliability and integrity of financial and operating information, the effectiveness and efficiency of operations, safeguarding of assets, compliance with laws, regulations and contracts.
	Independence is maintained by the internal auditor being given access to information on all these areas and being able to report freely on any errors or omissions found.
Control	• The internal audit department should help to maintain the organisation's control system by evaluating the effectiveness and efficiency of controls, and by promoting continuous improvement.
	Independence is again maintained by ensuring full provision of information and independent reporting lines (via the audit committee).

Governance	• The internal audit department should assess the corporate governance process and make recommendations where appropriate for improvements in achieving the objectives of corporate governance. Independence is maintained by the internal auditor being able to report breaches of corporate governance code without fear of dismissal (as happened in the US prior to SOX).
Internal audit work	• Internal auditors should identify, analyse, evaluate and record sufficient information to achieve the objectives of the engagement. • The information identified should be reliable, relevant and useful with regard to the objectives of the engagement. • The auditors' conclusions should be based on suitable analysis and evaluation. • Information to support the conclusions of the auditors should be recorded. Independence is maintained by the internal auditor being able to show that normal standards of internal audit work have been followed; there has been no pressure to 'cut corners' either from senior management or because the internal auditor decided to carry out the work to a lower standard.
Communicating results	• Internal auditors should communicate the results of their engagement, including conclusions, recommendations and action plans. • The results should be communicated to the appropriate persons. Independence is maintained by the internal auditor being able to communicate to a committee or person separate from the board who also has the power to take appropriate action on the internal auditors' reports.

5 Audit committee

The audit committee is a committee of the board of directors consisting entirely of independent non-executive directors (NEDs) (at least three in larger companies), of whom at least one has had recent and relevant financial experience.

The audit committee's key function is to provide evidence of increased accountability to shareholders.

It is critical that the audit committee be independent, comprised of non-executive directors and have written terms of reference.

Roles of the audit committee

- The key roles of the audit committee are 'oversight', 'assessment' and 'review' of other functions and systems in the company.

- Most of the board objectives relating to internal controls will be delegated to the audit committee.

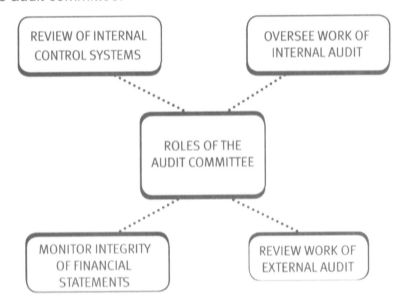

 Smith guidance

The Smith Guidance on audit committees states that:

'While all directors have a duty to act in the interests of the company the audit committee has a particular role, acting independently from the executive, to ensure that the interests of shareholders are properly protected in relation to financial reporting and internal control.'

Factors affecting the role of the audit committee

The role of the audit committee was considered in the UK Corporate Governance Code (2010) and Sarbanes-Oxley (SOX).

How effective the audit committee is in checking compliance and internal controls depends primarily on how it is constituted and the power vested in that committee. The following factors are relevant:

- The board should decide how much responsibility it wishes to delegate to the audit committee. The tasks of the committee will differ according to the size, complexity and risk profile of the company.

- The committee should meet as often as its responsibilities require, and it is recommended that there should be, at the very least, three meetings each year, to coincide with key dates in the audit cycle – for example, when the annual audit plans are available for review, when the interim statement is near completion and when the preliminary announcement/full annual report are near completion.

- The audit committee should meet at least once a year with the external and internal auditors, without management present, to discuss audit-related matters.

- Formal meetings of the audit committee are at the heart of its work. However, they will rarely be sufficient. The audit committee chairman in particular will probably wish to meet informally with other key people, such as the board chairman, CEO, finance director, senior audit partner and head of internal audit.

- Any disagreement between audit committee members that cannot be resolved within the committee should be referred to the main board for a resolution.

- The audit committee should review both its terms of reference and its effectiveness annually, and recommend any necessary changes to the board. The board should also review the effectiveness of the audit committee annually.

- To do its work properly, the audit committee must be kept properly informed by the executive management. Management is under an obligation to keep the audit committee properly informed and should take the initiative in providing information, instead of waiting to be asked.

The role of the committee becomes less important where the points made above are not dealt with correctly. For example, if the committee is denied access to executive management, then the committee will be less effective.

Audit committee and compliance

One of the primary activities of the audit committee, particularly under SOX, is to check compliance with external reporting regulations. The audit committee normally has a responsibility to ensure that the external reporting obligations of the company are met.

The audit committee should review the significant financial reporting issues and judgements in connection with the preparation of the company's financial statements. Management is responsible for preparing the financial statements and the auditors are responsible for preparing the audit plan and carrying out the audit.

However, the oversight function can sometimes lead to more detailed analysis. For example, if the audit committee is not satisfied with the explanations of the auditors and management about a particular financial reporting decision, then there may be no alternative but to grapple with the detail and perhaps seek independent advice.

The audit committee needs to satisfy itself that the financial statements prepared by management and approved by the auditors are acceptable. It should consider:

- the significant accounting policies that have been used, and whether these are appropriate

- any significant estimates or judgements that have been made, and whether these are reasonable

- the method used to account for any significant or unusual transactions, where alternative accounting treatments are possible

- the clarity and completeness of the disclosures in the financial statements.

The committee should listen to the views of the auditors on these matters. If it is not satisfied with any aspect of the proposed financial reporting, it should inform the board.

The committee should also review the financial-related information that accompanies the financial statements, such as the information in the business review and the corporate governance statements relating to audit and risk management.

6 The audit committee and internal control

The board is responsible for the total process of risk management, which includes ensuring that the system of internal control is adequate and effective.

The board delegates this internal control responsibility to the audit committee.

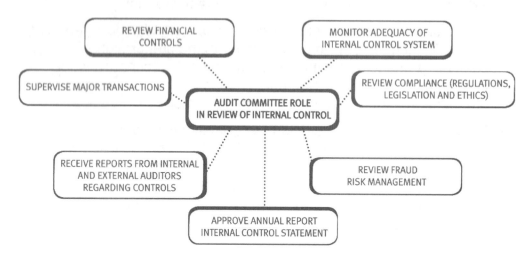

Audit committee and internal control

In relation to internal controls, the audit committee should:

- review the company's internal **financial controls**

- monitor the **adequacy of the internal control systems**, with a specific focus on:
    - control environment
    - management attitude
    - management controls

- review **compliance** with regulations, legislation and ethical practices (such as environmental policies and codes of conduct), and ensure that systems are in place to support such compliant behaviour

- review the company's **fraud risk management** policy, ensuring that awareness is promoted and reporting and investigation mechanisms exist

- give its approval to the **statements in the annual report** relating to internal control and risk management

- receive reports on the conclusions of any **tests** carried out on the controls by the internal or external auditors, and consider the recommendations that are made

- where necessary, the committee may be required to **supervise major transactions** for appropriateness and validity.

7 The audit committee and internal audit

As part of their obligation to ensure adequate and effective internal controls, the audit committee is responsible for overseeing the work of the internal audit function.

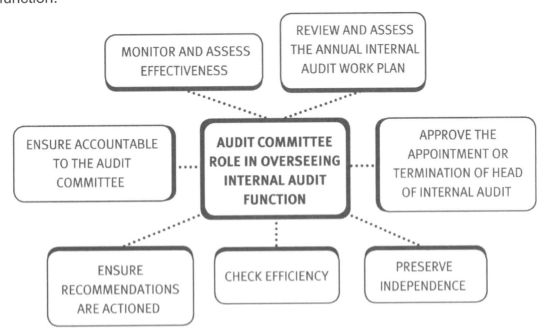

Audit committee and internal audit

The audit committee should:

- monitor and assess the role and effectiveness of the internal audit function within the company's overall risk management system

- check the efficiency of internal audit by, for example, comparing actual costs and output against a target

- approve the appointment, or termination of appointment, of the head of internal audit

- ensure that the internal audit function has direct access to the board chairman and is accountable to the audit committee

- review and assess the annual internal audit work plan

- receive periodic reports about the work of the internal audit function

- review and monitor the response of management to internal audit findings

- ensure that recommendations made by internal audit are actioned

- help preserve the independence of the internal audit function from pressure or interference.

The Smith Guidance on Audit Committees recommends that the committee meets with internal auditors at least once a year, without management present, to discuss audit-related matters.

If the company does not have an internal audit function:

- the committee should consider annually whether there is a need for an internal audit function and make a recommendation to the board, and

- the reasons for the absence of an internal audit function should be explained in the relevant section of the annual report.

Review of internal audit

The audit committee, and the external auditor where they are relying on the internal audit department, will need to ensure that the internal audit department is working effectively. Such a review will normally involve four key areas, as outlined below:

Area	Explanation
Organisational status	The internal auditor needs to be objective and independent. This means that internal audit can report to senior management (or the audit committee) so that their reports are considered and the internal auditor is not in fear of being reprimanded in any way for presenting adverse reports. Any constraints on internal audit, such as areas of the control system that they cannot look at, is a restriction on their work, and may imply management are attempting to hide discrepancies. Finally, the internal auditor is allowed to communicate directly with the external auditor. Any limitation in this respect again implies management have something to 'hide'.
Scope of function	As already noted, the external auditor should be allowed unlimited access to the books, records and control system in the company. Any report and recommendations made by internal audit should be acted on, or management should state why the report has not been actioned. Any review on effectiveness of the department would therefore ensure that their reports were heard and actioned.

Technical competence	Internal audit work should be carried out by persons who have had appropriate technical training. To check this, recruitment standards and the provision of training to internal audit staff will be checked. Any lack of training implies that the internal auditor will not be able to carry out their duties to the necessary standard.
Due professional care	The work of the internal audit department should be properly planned, supervised, reviewed and documented. Lack of documentation, etc. could imply that work has not been carried out or that it was carried out to a lower standard than required. Any review would therefore ensure that adequate working papers were produced and work programmes reflected the audit work that had to be carried out.

8   The audit committee and external auditors

The audit committee is responsible for oversight of the company's relations with its external auditors. The audit committee should:

- have the primary responsibility for making a recommendation to the board on the appointment, re-appointment or removal of the external auditors

- 'oversee' the selection process when new auditors are being considered

- approve (though not necessarily negotiate) the terms of engagement of the external auditors and the remuneration for their audit services

- have annual procedures for ensuring the independence and objectivity of the external auditors

- review the scope of the audit with the auditor, and satisfy itself that this is sufficient

- make sure that appropriate plans are in place for the audit at the start of each annual audit

- carry out a post-completion audit review.

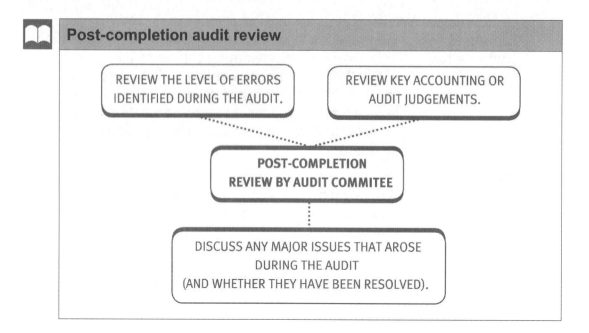

Post-completion audit review

REVIEW THE LEVEL OF ERRORS IDENTIFIED DURING THE AUDIT.

REVIEW KEY ACCOUNTING OR AUDIT JUDGEMENTS.

POST-COMPLETION REVIEW BY AUDIT COMMITEE

DISCUSS ANY MAJOR ISSUES THAT AROSE DURING THE AUDIT (AND WHETHER THEY HAVE BEEN RESOLVED).

Independence of external auditors

The audit committee should have annual procedures for ensuring the independence and objectivity of the external auditors.

The Smith Guidance suggests that the audit committee should:

- seek reassurance that the auditors and their staff have no family, financial, employment, investment or business relationship with the company (other than in the normal course of business)

- obtain each year from the audit firm information about its policies and processes for:

  1   maintaining its independence, and

  2   monitoring compliance with relevant professional requirements, such as rules regarding the rotation of audit partners and staff.

- agree with the board and then monitor the company's policy on employing former employees of the external auditor. It should monitor how many former employees of the external auditor now hold senior positions in the company, and if appropriate consider whether, in view of the situation, there may be some impairment (or appearance of impairment) of the auditors' independence with regard to the audit.

- develop and recommend to the board the company's policy on the provision of non-audit services by the external auditors. The provision of non-audit services must not impair the independence or objectivity of the auditors.

The audit committee should establish a policy that specifies the types of work:

- from which the external auditors are excluded

- for which the external auditors can be engaged without referral to the audit committee

- for which a case-by-case decision is necessary. In these cases, a general pre-approval might be given for certain classes of work, and if the external auditor is engaged to provide any such services, this should then be ratified at the next audit committee meeting.

The policy may also set fee limits generally or for particular classes of non-audit work.

A guiding set of principles is that the external auditor should not be engaged for non-audit work if, as a result:

- the external auditor audits work done by themselves

- the external auditor makes management decisions for the company

- a mutuality of interest is created, or

- the external auditor is put in the role of advocate for the company.

Test your understanding 3

ECG is the world's second largest arms exporter. It serves over 20 nations, fulfilling defence system contracts worth billions of dollars. These dealings require consent from its home government to ensure national security is maintained and that governmental embargos on sales to unfriendly countries are not breached.

ECG is currently serving the needs of a particular regime whose human rights record and hostile posturing may lead to such a ban on trade. ECG has already sold war planes and missile guidance systems to this country but is yet to receive payment.

ECG's audit committee and external auditors have an unusually difficult task performing their duties due to the unique nature of the company and the need to maintain high levels of security and confidentiality over much of the organisation's business. Because of this there is no line of communication to the committee other than through the CFO.

The committee and the external auditors work closely together, indeed one former audit partner now sits on the audit committee and is pleased that the firm has decided to retain his old company's services for the 15th year in succession. The committee is content to accept the audit firm's recommendation on the accounting treatment of all contracts due to their complexity and need for "hidden costs" to be removed. These include large payments to provide hospitality to 'would be' clients.

There is also a high degree of informality between external auditors and internal auditors due to the complexity of large non-audit contracts served by the audit firm. These are so large the external auditor appears to discount its audit costs as a way of ensuring these services are retained. National security is always an issue and audits are time-pressured due to limited staff resource allocation, so the external audit firm is guided by internal auditors in terms of its proposed risk assessment and work plan. This seems appropriate since many ex-audit firm staff now work for the company and so understand audit issues from both viewpoints.

The audit committee will make no recommendations for change this year, especially since the internal audit manager assured them there were no real problems during their annual hourly meeting.

Required:

(a) Describe the role of the audit committee and discuss potential problems in its operation.

(b) Consider the threats to auditor independence and propose actions to deal with them.

Professional skills:

Illustrate communication, analysis and evaluation skills when preparing your response.

9 Reporting on internal controls to shareholders

The UK Corporate Governance Code states that a company's board of directors should maintain a sound system of internal control to safeguard shareholders' investment and the company's assets.

- Shareholders, as owners of the company, are entitled to know whether the internal control system is sufficient to safeguard their investment.

- To provide shareholders with the assurance they require, the board should, at least annually, conduct a review of the effectiveness of the group's system of internal controls and report to shareholders that they have done so.

- The review should cover all material controls, including financial, operational and compliance controls and risk management systems.

- This review should be conducted against COSO's elements of an effective internal control system, as discussed in the previous chapter.

- The annual report should also inform members of the work of the audit committee.

- The chair of the audit committee should be available at the AGM to answer queries from shareholders regarding their work.

- Additional reporting requirements apply under SOX.

Test your understanding 4

Suggest two reasons why a company may choose to report on internal controls to its shareholders.

Audit committee reporting

The section in the annual report on the work of the audit committee should include:

- a summary of the role of the audit committee

- the names and qualifications of the audit committee members during the period

- the number of audit committee meetings held during the year

- a report on the way the audit committee has discharged its responsibilities

- if the external auditors provide non-audit services, an explanation of how auditor objectivity and independence are safeguarded.

Internal audit reporting

Once an internal control audit (or any other kind of audit) has been completed, the final stage of the assignment is the audit report.

- The audit report does not have a prescribed format, however it would be expected to feature a number of different parts.

- How much depth the report goes into will depend on the nature of the engagement.

Report section	Reason	Example
Objectives of audit work	Set the scene for report audience by describing purpose of review.	For a payroll audit 'check whether: • wages are paid to the correct individuals • deductions from gross pay are properly calculated'.

Summary of process undertaken by auditor	Describes how the evidence to support the opinion and recommendations was gathered.	'Recalculation of deductions was performed for a sample of 50 monthly and 50 weekly wages payments.'
Audit opinion (if required)	Summary of whether the control reviewed is working or not.	'In our opinion, the control is working as intended.'
Recommendations	Highlight areas of control weakness and suggest course of remedial action.	'We recommend that new employees are only added to the payroll system on receipt of an appropriately authorised Form (1a).'

Internal audit recommendations

When making recommendations auditors must always ensure that the recommendations:

- are practical and cost effective, and

- will reduce risk to a tolerable level.

The internal auditor should have a process of post-implementation review to ensure that recommendations have been actioned by management.

10   Chapter summary

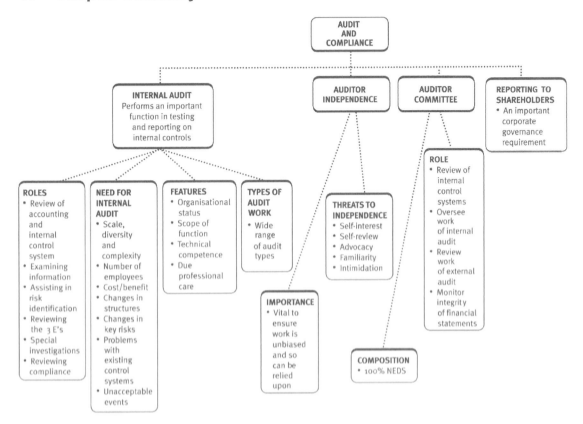

Test your understanding answers

Test your understanding 1 – Features of internal audit

Organisational status – Direct access to the highest level of management.

- Free of operating responsibility.

- Few constraints (e.g. reporting to external auditor).

Internal audit is a key reviewing and monitoring activity that is undertaken by management. In large organisations the internal audit function will be a separate department, whereas in a small company it might be the responsibility of individuals to perform specific tasks even though there will not be a full-time position.

When establishing the internal audit function it is important that it is structured and operated in an appropriate way.

Scope of function – Nature/extent of assignments.

- Evidence of recommendations being actioned.

The internal audit department will typically have the following scope and objectives as prescribed by the management of the business. Do not treat this as a comprehensive list of all the areas that the internal auditor considers, as management may prescribe different functions to meet the needs of their company.

- Review of the accounting and internal control system.

- Detailed testing of transactions and balances.

- Review of the economy, efficiency and effectiveness of operations (value for money and best practice audits).

- Review of the implementation of corporate policies.

- Special investigations.

- Assisting in carrying out external audit procedures.

Technical competence – Technical training/proficiency.

- Recruitment policy.

- Professional qualifications.

Due professional care – Evidence of planning, supervision, review and documentation.

- Existence of audit manuals and WPs. It would be expected that:

  - There is a formal plan of all audit work that is reviewed by the head of the audit and the board/audit committee.

  - The audit plans should be reviewed at least annually.

Each engagement should be conducted appropriately:

- Planning should be performed.

- Objectives should be set for the engagement.

- The work should be documented, reviewed, and supervised.

- The results should be communicated to management.

- Recommendations for action should be made.

The progress of the audit should be monitored by the head of the internal audit, and if recommendations that the head feels are appropriate are not acted on, the matters should be brought to the attention of the board.

Test your understanding 2

1   No – not a material financial interest, unlikely that you could influence the outcome of the audit.

2   Yes – self-interest threat – pressure to keep this client may reduce levels of objectivity.

3   No – less pressure to keep important client. Losing them would not be the end of the world.

4   Yes – familiarity threat – difficult to tackle formidable issues and maintain independence if you feel beholden to a client.

5   Yes – self-review threat – difficult to independently review something you were responsible for.

6   No – they are not in a position to 'exert direct and significant influence over the subject matter of the audit engagement', therefore no familiarity threat.

7   Yes – advocacy threat – it would be difficult to maintain independence in the face of any 'bad news' arising during the audit.

Test your understanding 3

(a)   **Audit committee**

The role of the audit committee can be viewed with reference to the UK Corporate Governance Code (2010) where explicit mention is made of its operation and need for independence. ECG has major problems in relation to these issues which are dealt with in context of each code provision relating to the audit the committee.

Monitor the integrity of financial statements and announcements

Emphasis is placed on the need to monitor as opposed to being directly involved in the preparation of financial statements, preparation being the responsibility of the CFO. Integrity is the central point, to ensure the records give a truthful reflection of company operations and adhere to appropriate GAAP or compliance requirements.

There must be some concern over the accounting treatment of contracts and hidden costs. Accepting the recommendation of the external auditor is not sufficient as a monitoring tool. Independent advice should be sought since the board as a whole is legally liable for errors and omissions in this area. The lack of control in this area can lead to a culture of secrecy that increases the risk of fraudulent activity.

Review financial and internal controls

The evaluation of the existence and worth of internal controls will have a direct bearing on the quality of financial reporting. Internal controls may be evaluated using the COSO framework that include consideration of the effectiveness of the control environment as well as control activities. The control environment is not supported by the inherent culture of secrecy and the presumed lack of communication across the organisation.

A specific failure is in relation to the direct exclusion of a whistleblower clause whereby concerns over internal control can be reported directly to the committee. The CFO's insistence of the need to exclude this on security grounds should be very carefully considered with regard to the cost of such a measure in terms of a loss of internal control within the company.

Review the effectiveness of the internal audit function

The UK Corporate Governance Code (2010) makes a number of recommendations in this area, highlighting its importance in committee operation. These include the need for direct accountability of the internal auditor to the committee and the need to review annual work plans and management's responsiveness to internal audit findings and recommendations.

The hour long meeting carried out on an annual basis would seem insufficient to consider these issues in depth unless the audit committee carries out a number of functions independent of the audit manager's involvement. In particular no mention is made of the need to assess the effectiveness of internal audit as a tool of internal control.

In a general sense there is an impression of a lack of concern over this critical issue raising the risk profile of this organisation. The internal auditor does not mention anything concerning the huge risks involved in potential misstatement of accounting results and the risk of exposure to non-payment of contracts due to the company's involvement with the country under investigation by the government. This risk may leave the company with substantial debts that remain unpaid and this in turn can affect shareholder wealth and risk. These are certainly issues that should be reported to the board.

External auditor engagement

The role of the committee is to review and recommend external auditor engagement for the company. This includes an assessment of the qualification, expertise, resources, effectiveness and independence of the external auditor.

There appear to be failings in relation to most of these roles in this scenario. The issue of independence will be discussed below in more detail. The existence of an ex-employee on the audit committee may seem inappropriate and does little to support the need for independence in committee operation for the benefit of shareholders.

Implement policy regarding external auditor non audit services.

The audit committee should consider whether, taken as a whole with regard to the views of the external auditor, management and the internal audit function, these relationships impair the auditor's judgement and independence.

It is very likely that in this case the existence of large contracts for non-audit services do impair the judgement and integrity of the audit firm. In particular, the appearance of discounting audit costs because of these contracts is completely inappropriate since this threatens the integrity of the audit and the subsequent information upon which shareholders rely.

The lack of independence is the most serious issue raised and must be dealt with as a matter of urgency by the committee. The ex-employee should resign his position as non-executive director and a formal review of the role and responsibilities of the committee should take place as soon as possible.

(b) **Independence**

Auditor independence is important in maintaining the agency relationship between the shareholders and their company. The auditors work independently of the organisation in order to provide shareholders with information as to the financial position and level of control that exists within the company.

This independence is initially threatened due to the company selecting, recommending and paying the fees of the auditor. The existence of an audit committee filled with non-executive directors who take over these responsibilities is an attempt to create separation between the company and the auditors and so improve the level of independence that exists.

The fact that the ex-audit firm director sits on the audit committee does not necessarily impact on independence if it is assumed the non-executive directors operate independently of the board.

However, the risk is that the audit committee is not truly independent, being employed by the company, and so in this sense it creates a problem. The audit firm non-executive should resign for this reason.

All audit firms must work closely with their customers. This outside/inside relationship creates the independence dilemma and it is a thin line between working with rather than for a client. The existence of large numbers of ex-employees within ECG does not assist in maintaining an air of independence and the audit committee should consider both its recruitment policy and replacing the audit firm with another for this reason.

The length of contract seems very high and beyond any recommendation likely to be made by governing bodies. Long relationships inevitably threaten the perception of independence if not independence itself and this should be understood by the audit committee and acted upon.

Specific threats are mentioned in relation to the undue influence the internal audit function has over external audit risk identification and audit focus. This is entirely inappropriate. A key aspect to the role of the external auditor must be independence in action, organising their own work without influence from the client. The lack of professionalism suggests a need for the external audit firm to re-evaluate its working procedures and the audit committee to consider the need for change in engagement.

Other concerns relate to the volume of non-audit work and its impact on audit integrity and the lack of sufficient manpower devoted to the audit. These were mentioned above.

Professional skills:

It is important when writing the response to this question to describe the role of the audit committee and the problems in its operation concisely and unambiguously, using the facts presented in the scenario. This will earn the communication marks.

The analysis marks will be earned by noting the threats to auditor independence and justifying why they are threats. The evaluation marks will result by exercising judgement and developing appropriate actions to deal with those threats.

Test your understanding 4

Some answers might include:

- Companies that are more open with their disclosures regarding internal controls may benefit from increased shareholder satisfaction as they know their assets are being well looked after.

- By reporting on their internal controls, a company opens itself to additional scrutiny by shareholders (and other interested parties) which may improve corporate governance.

- The knowledge that their work will be reported on externally may help regulate the work of the audit committee.

- By making the chair of the audit committee available for questions at the AGM, the company demonstrates that it has nothing to hide, therefore increasing shareholder confidence.

Identification, assessment and measurement of risk

Chapter learning objectives

Upon completion of this chapter you will be able to:

- discuss the relationship between organisational strategy and risk management strategy

- apply a framework for risk management and establishing risk management systems using an enterprise risk management (ERM) approach

- identify and evaluate the key risks including environment and climate related risks and their impact on organisations and projects

- distinguish between strategic and operational risks

- assess attitudes towards risk and risk appetite and how this can affect risk policy

- discuss the dynamic nature of risk and the ways in which risk varies in relation to the size, structure and development of an organisation

- assess the severity and probability of risk events

- explain and evaluate the concepts of related and correlated risk factors

PER

One of the PER performance objectives (PO4) is that you contribute to effective governance in your area. You evaluate, monitor and implement risk management procedures, complying with the spirit and the letter of policies, laws and regulations. Working through this chapter should help you understand how to demonstrate that objective.

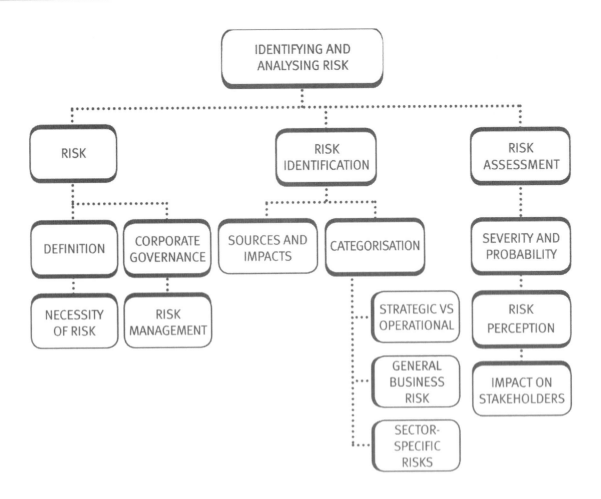

1 Risk and corporate governance

- The issue of corporate governance and how to manage risk has become an important area of concern across the world.

- Reviews, such as the UK Turnbull Committee, have identified risk management as key to effective internal control.

- In turn, following good corporate governance procedures (including having sound internal control systems) will decrease the impact of many risks on an organisation.

- Risk analysis is best carried out in the context of the OECD principles of good corporate governance.

- An overriding risk is that an organisation fails to meet the appropriate corporate governance regulations.

OECD principles of good corporate governance	
Principle	**In the context of risk**
Rights of shareholders Shareholders' rights are protected and facilitated.	Company does not allow shareholders their rights e.g. does not provide necessary communications to, or allow comments in, general meetings.
Equitable treatment of shareholders & stakeholders All shareholders (including those with small shareholdings or those in foreign countries) and stakeholders are treated the same.	Under an acquisition all shareholders may not be offered the same price for their holding. Companies may ignore stakeholders or treat some stakeholder groups incorrectly (e.g. attempt to make employees redundant without appropriate consultation).
Disclosure and transparency Timely and adequate disclosure should be made of all material matters (e.g. financial situation of the company).	Directors do not provide appropriate reports or financial statements and do not disclose the true situation of the company (as in situations such as Enron). This heading implies that internal control systems will also be adequate to detect fraud and other irregularities.
Responsibility of the board The board should be effective and provide strategic guidance for the company.	The board either does not control the company adequately (leading to losses) or attempts to run the company for its benefit rather than for the benefit of other stakeholders.

2 Necessity of risk and risk management

A risk can be defined as an unrealised future loss arising from a present action or inaction.

- Risks are the opportunities and dangers associated with uncertain future events.

- Risks can have an adverse ('downside exposure') or favourable impact ('upside potential') on the organisation's objectives.

Why incur risk?

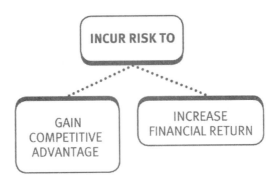

- To generate higher returns a business may have to take more risk in order to be competitive.

- Conversely, not accepting risk tends to make a business less dynamic, and implies a 'follow the leader' strategy.

- Incurring risk also implies that the returns from different activities will be higher – 'benefit' being the return for accepting risk.

- Benefits can be financial – decreased costs, or intangible – better quality information.

- In both cases, these will lead to the business being able to gain competitive advantage.

Benefits of taking risks

Consider the following grid in terms of the risks a business can incur and the benefits from undertaking different activities.

		Activity risk	
		Low	High
Ability to gain competitive advantage	Low	2 Routine	4 Avoid
	High	1 Identify and develop	3 Examine carefully

Focusing on low-risk activities can easily result in a low ability to obtain competitive advantage – although where there is low risk there is also only a limited amount of competitive advantage to be obtained. For example, a mobile telephone operator may produce its phones in a wide range of colours. There is little or no risk of the technology failing, but the move may provide limited competitive advantage where customers are attracted to a particular colour of phone.

Some low-risk activities, however, will provide higher competitive advantage. When these can be identified, then the activity should be undertaken because of the higher reward. For example, the mobile phone operator may find a way of easily amending mobile phones to make them safer regarding the electrical emissions generated. Given that customers are concerned about this element of mobile phone use, there is significant potential to obtain competitive advantage. However, these opportunities are few and far between.

High-risk activities can similarly generate low or high competitive advantage. Activities with low competitive advantage will generally be avoided. There remains the risk that the activity will not work, and that the small amount of competitive advantage that would be generated is not worth that risk.

Other high-risk activities may generate significant amounts of competitive advantage. These activities are worth investigating because of the high returns that can be generated. For example, a new type of mobile phone providing, say, GPS features for use while travelling, may provide significant competitive advantage for the company; the risk of investing in the phone is worthwhile in terms of the benefit that could be achieved.

The point is, therefore, that if a business does not take some risk, it will normally be limited to activities providing little or no competitive advantage, which will limit its ability to grow and provide returns to its shareholders.

Why manage risk?

Management needs to manage and monitor risk on an ongoing basis for a number of reasons:

- To identify new risks that may affect the company so an appropriate risk management strategy can be determined.

- To identify changes to existing or known risks so amendments to the risk management strategy can be made. For example, where there is an increased likelihood of occurrence of a known risk, strategy may be amended from ignoring the risk to possibly insuring against it.

- To ensure that the best use is made of opportunities.

- Risk management is a key part of Corporate Governance. It is required by the Combined Code and codes of other jurisdictions.

Managing the upside of risk

Historically, the focus of risk management has been on preventing loss. However, recently, organisations are viewing risk management in a different way, so that:

- risks are seen as opportunities to be seized (as discussed above)

- organisations are accepting some uncertainty in order to benefit from higher rewards associated with higher risk

- risk management is being used to identify risks associated with new opportunities to increase the probability of positive outcomes and to maximise returns

- effective risk management is being seen as a way of enhancing shareholder value by improving performance.

3 Risk management

- Risk management is therefore the process of reducing the possibility of adverse consequences either by reducing the likelihood of an event or its impact, or taking advantage of the upside risk.

- Management are responsible for establishing a risk management system in an organisation.

- The process of establishing a risk management system is summarised in the following diagram:

Risk management process

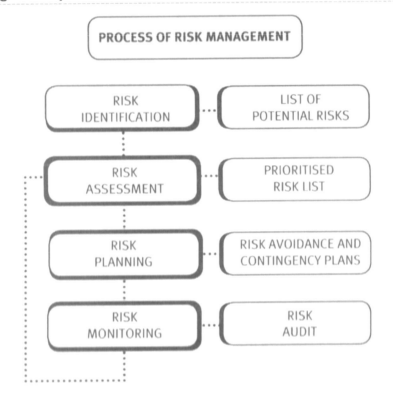

The process of risk management	
Element	**Explanation**
Risk identification	Risks are identified by key stakeholders. Risks must obviously be identified before they can be managed.
Risk assessment	Risks are evaluated according to the likelihood of occurrence and impact on the organisation. This assessment provides a prioritised risk list identifying those risks that need the most urgent attention.
Risk planning	Planning involves establishing appropriate risk management policies. Policies include ceasing risky activities through to obtaining insurance against unfavourable events. Contingency planning involves establishing procedures to recover from adverse events, should they occur.
Risk monitoring	Risks are monitored on an ongoing basis. Where risks change or new risks are identified then those risks are added to the risk assessment for appropriate categorisation and action.

Enterprise Risk Management (ERM)

- Risk management has transformed from a 'department focused' approach to a holistic, co-ordinated and integrated process which manages risk throughout the organisation.

- Drivers for this transformation include globalisation, the increased complexity of doing business, regulatory compliance/corporate governance developments, and greater accountability for the board and senior management to increase shareholder value.

- These drivers mean that an organisation and its board must have a thorough understanding of the key risks affecting the organisation and what is being done to manage them. ERM offers a framework to provide this understanding.

- ERM is a COSO initiative and depicts the ERM model in the form of a cube. COSO intended the cube to illustrate the links between objectives that are shown on the top and the eight components shown on the front, which represent what is needed to achieve the objectives. The third dimension represents the organisation's units and portrays the model's ability to focus on parts of the organisation as well as the whole.

Enterprise risk management

Enterprise Risk Management (ERM) can be defined as the:

> 'process effected by an entity's board of directors, management and other personnel, applied in strategy setting and across the enterprise, designed to identify potential events that may affect the entity, and manage risk to be within its risk appetite, to provide reasonable assurance regarding the achievement of entity objectives.'

Enterprise Risk Management – Integrated Framework, the Committee of Sponsoring Organisations, COSO, 2004.

Principles of ERM

The key principles of ERM include:

- consideration of risk management in the context of business strategy

- risk management is everyone's responsibility, with the tone set from the top

- the creation of a risk aware culture

- a comprehensive and holistic approach to risk management

- consideration of a broad range of risks (strategic, financial, operational and compliance)

- a focused risk management strategy, led by the board (embedding risk within an organisation's culture)

The COSO ERM framework reflects the relationships between:

- The four objectives of a business (strategic, operations, reporting and compliance) which reflect the responsibility of different executives across the entity and address different needs.

- The four organisational levels (subsidiary, business unit, division and entity) which emphasise the importance of managing risks across the enterprise as a whole.

- The eight components that must function effectively for risk management to be successful.

COSO ERM framework matrix

The COSO ERM framework is represented as a three dimensional matrix in the form of a cube which reflects the relationships between objectives, components and different organisational levels.

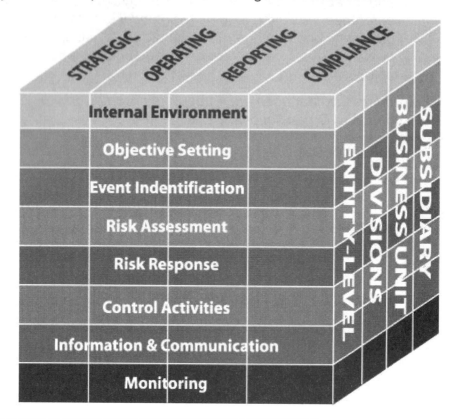

Components of the ERM framework

The eight components are closely aligned to the risk management process addressed above, and also reflect elements from the COSO view of an effective internal control system (discussed in chapter 13):

*   **Internal environment:** This is the tone of the organisation, including the risk management philosophy and risk appetite (see more in the next chapter).

*   **Objective setting:** Objectives should be aligned with the organisation's mission and need to be consistent with the organisation's defined risk appetite.

*   **Event identification:** These are internal and external events (both positive and negative) which impact upon the achievement of an entity's objectives and must be identified.

*   **Risk assessment:** Risks are analysed to consider their likelihood and impact as a basis for determining how they should be managed.

- **Risk response:** Management selects risk response(s) to avoid, accept, reduce or share risk. The intention is to develop a set of actions to align risks with the entity's risk tolerances and risk appetite.

- **Control activities:** Policies and procedures help ensure the risk responses are effectively carried out.

- **Information and communication:** The relevant information is identified, captured and communicated in a form and timeframe that enables people to carry out their responsibilities.

- **Monitoring:** The entire ERM process is monitored and modifications made as necessary.

Benefits of effective ERM include:

- enhanced decision-making by integrating risks

- the resultant improvement in investor confidence, and hence shareholder value

- focus of management attention on the most significant risks

- a common language of risk management which is understood throughout the organisation

- reduced cost of finance through effective management of risk.

Test your understanding 1 – Holistic approach to risk

A national chain of fast food retailers has suffered a large increase in counterfeit $20 and $50 bank notes being received in its stores from customers in the capital city's region. This has led to a significant impact on profitability in this region that has threatened its ability to meet financial targets.

The finance team decided to manage this financial risk by imposing a series of new profit protection controls that were implemented immediately by all stores across the country. These measures were:

- All bank notes to be tested for authenticity by counterfeit note detector pen.

- All $20 bank notes to be tested for authenticity using a UV (ultra-violet) light detector as well as the detector pen.

- $50 notes will no longer be accepted by any stores.

- Any counterfeit notes taken by an individual working on a till would be recovered by the business from that person's next wage payment.

> - Any suspected counterfeit notes will be confiscated by the store supervisor and handed over to the police. The customer will be issued with a receipt and advised that they must contact the police directly to take the matter further.
>
> - Any store employees who do not follow these procedures will face disciplinary action which may include dismissal from the company.
>
> **Required:**
>
> Evaluate the impact of these procedures on the business. Your answer should consider the impact on the customers, employees and the company.

4 Risk identification: Strategic and operational risks

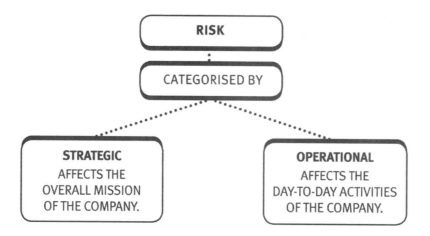

Strategic risks:

- are risks arising from the possible consequences of strategic decisions taken by the organisation

- also arise from the way that an organisation is strategically positioned within its environment

- should be identified and assessed at senior management and board or director level

- PESTEL and SWOT techniques can be used to help identify these risks.

Operational risks:

- refer to potential losses that might arise in business operations

- include risks of fraud or employee malfeasance, poor quality production or lack of inputs for production

- can be managed by internal control systems.

Strategic and operational risks

Strategic risks:

- are risks arising from the possible consequences of strategic decisions taken by the organisation. For example, one company might pursue a strategy of growth by acquisitions, whilst another might seek slower, organic growth. Growth by acquisition is likely to be much more high-risk than organic growth, although the potential returns might also be much higher.

- strategic risks will also arise from the way that an organisation is strategically positioned within its environment. A company may decide to expand into higher or lower risk areas perhaps by manufacturing new products or simply enhancing older products.

- strategic risks should be identified and assessed at senior management and board or director level.

Operational risks:

- refer to potential losses that might arise in business operations.

- can be defined broadly as 'the risk of losses resulting from inadequate or failed internal processes, people and systems, or external events' (Basel Committee on Banking Supervision).

- include risks of fraud or employee malfeasance as well as risks from production (such as poor quality) or lack of production (not having inputs available at the correct time).

- can be managed by internal control systems.

Test your understanding 2

Identify examples of strategic and operational risks which might face a telecommunications company.

5 Risk identification: Business risks

Business risk refers to the classic risks of the world of business such as uncertainty about demand for product (Product risk.)

The risks businesses face will vary greatly between companies and derive from a number of different sources, including those shown below.

In the exam you may be required to identify risks, or types or risk, facing a business. The risks listed below are not exhaustive but illustrate many of the typical risks that affect a business.

- **Market risks.** Risks which derive from the sector in which the business is operating, and from its customers.

- **Product risk.** The risk that customers will not buy new products (or services) provided by the organisation, or that the sales demand for current products and services will decline unexpectedly.

- **Commodity price risk.** Businesses might be exposed to risks from unexpected increases (or falls) in the price of a key commodity.

- **Product reputation risk.** Some companies rely heavily on brand image and product reputation, and an adverse event could put its reputation (and so future sales) at risk.

- **Credit risk.** Credit risk is the possibility of losses due to non-payment, or late payment, by customers.

- **Currency risk.** Currency risk, or foreign exchange risk, arises from the possibility of movements in foreign exchange rates, and the value of one currency in relation to another.

- **Interest rate risk.** Interest rate risk is the risk of unexpected gains or losses arising as a consequence of a rise or fall in interest rates.

- **Political risk.** Political risk depends to a large extent on the political stability in the countries in which an organisation operates and the attitudes of governments towards protectionism.

- **Legal,** or **litigation risk** arises from the possibility of legal action being taken against an organisation.

- **Regulatory risk** arises from the possibility that regulations will affect the way an organisation has to operate.

- **Compliance risk** is the risk of losses, possibly fines, resulting from non-compliance with laws or regulations.

- **Technology risk** arises from the possibility that technological change will occur.

- **Economic risk** refers to the risks facing organisations from changes in economic conditions, such as economic growth or recession, government spending policy and taxation policy, unemployment levels and international trading conditions.

- **Environmental risk** refers to the risks that a business faces due to the environmental effects of its operations, such as pollution resulting from business activity or restrictions on the supply of natural resources to the business due to environmental factors.

- **Climate risk** refers to the risks emanating from climate change. These risks can be event-driven (acute), such as increased severity of extreme weather events (e.g. cyclones, droughts, floods and fires). They can also relate to longer-term shifts (chronic) in precipitation and temperature, and increased variability in weather patterns (e.g. sea level rise).

- **Health and safety risks.** Many companies engage in potentially hazardous activities, such as coal mining, that can give rise to injury or the loss of life.

- **Business probity risk** is related to the governance and ethics of the organisation.

- **Derivatives risk** refers to risks due to the use of financial instruments.

- **Entrepreneurial risk.** This is the necessary risk associated with any new business venture or opportunity.

- **Financial risk.** This is a major cause of business risk, and can be further defined as:

  - **Gearing risk.** Gearing risk for non-bank companies is the risk arising from exposures to high financial gearing and large amounts of borrowing.

  - **Liquidity risk** relates to the possibility of a company's cash inflows not being sufficient to meet its cash outflows.

Business risks

Market risks. Risks which derive from the sector in which the business is operating, and from its customers. These risks can apply to:

- resource (not being able to obtain the required inputs)

- production (risks in poor manufacturing, etc.)

- capital markets (not being able to obtain necessary finance)

- liquidity (the risk of having insufficient cash for the day-to-day running of the business).

Product risk. The risk that customers will not buy new products (or services) provided by the organisation or that the sales demand for current products and services will decline unexpectedly. A new product launched onto the market might fail to achieve the expected volume of sales, or the take-up might be much slower than expected. For example, the demand for 3G mobile communications services grew much slower than expected by the mobile telephone service providers, due partly to the sluggish development of suitable mobile phone handsets of its credit rating.

Commodity price risk. Businesses might be exposed to risks from unexpected increases (or falls) in the price of a key commodity. Businesses providing commodities, such as oil companies and commodity farmers, are directly affected by price changes. Equally, companies that rely on the use of commodities could be exposed to risks from price changes. For example, airlines are exposed to the risk of increases in fuel prices, particularly when market demand for flights is weak, and so increases in ticket prices for flights are not possible.

Product reputation risk. Some companies rely heavily on brand image and product reputation, and an adverse event could put its reputation (and so future sales) at risk. Risk to a product's reputation could arise from adverse public attitudes to a product or from negative publicity: this has been evident in Europe with widespread hostility to genetically-modified (GM) foods.

Credit risk. Credit risk is the possibility of losses due to non-payment, or late payment, by customers. The exposure of a company to credit risks depends on factors such as:

- the total volume of credit sales

- the organisation's credit policy

- credit terms offered (credit limits for individual customers and the time allowed to pay)

- the credit risk 'quality' of customers: some types of customer are a greater credit risk than others

- credit vetting and assessment procedures.

Liquidity risk relates to the possibility of a company's cash inflows not being sufficient to meet its cash outflows. This may arise from poor credit control or cash management, and may show itself in late payment to suppliers, or even in downgrading of its credit rating.

Currency risk or foreign exchange risk, arises from the possibility of movements in foreign exchange rates, and the value of one currency in relation to another.

Interest rate risk is the risk of unexpected gains or losses arising as a consequence of a rise or fall in interest rates. Exposures to interest rate risk arise from borrowing and investing.

Gearing risk for non-bank companies is the risk arising from exposures to high financial gearing and large amounts of borrowing.

Political risk depends to a large extent on the political stability in the countries in which an organisation operates and the attitudes of governments towards protectionism. A change of government can sometimes result in dramatic changes for businesses. In an extreme case an incoming government might nationalise all foreign businesses operating in the country. Even in countries with a stable political system, political change can be significant, e.g. an incoming government might be elected on a platform of higher or lower taxation.

Legal, or **litigation risk**, arises from the possibility of legal action being taken against an organisation. For many organisations, this risk can be high. For example, hospitals and hospital workers might be exposed to risks of legal action for negligence. Tobacco companies have been exposed to legal action for compensation from cancer victims. Companies manufacturing or providing food and drink are also aware of litigation risk from customers claiming that a product has damaged their health.

Regulatory risk arises from the possibility that regulations will affect the way an organisation has to operate. Regulations might apply to businesses generally (e.g. competition laws and anti-monopoly regulations) or to specific industries.

Compliance risk is the risk of losses, possibly fines, resulting from non-compliance with laws or regulations. Measures to ensure compliance with rules and regulations should be an integral part of an organisation's internal control system.

Technology risk arises from the possibility that technological change will occur. Like many other categories of risk, technology risk is a two-way risk, and technological change creates both threats and opportunities for organisations.

Economic risk refers to the risks facing organisations from changes in economic conditions, such as economic growth or recession, government spending policy and taxation policy, unemployment levels and international trading conditions.

Environmental risk relates to the environmental effects of operations. These effects may include pollution resulting from business activity, such as oil spillages (and hence the risk of being held liable for such pollution, along with punitive action) or restrictions on the supply of natural resources to the business due to environmental factors (e.g. global warming). The risk may even extend to changes in regulations relating to environmental issues or public opinion on environmental impacts of businesses.

Climate related risk emanating from climate change can be event-driven (acute), such as increased severity of extreme weather events (e.g., cyclones, droughts, floods and fires). It can also relate to longer-term shifts (chronic) in precipitation and temperature, and increased variability in weather patterns (e.g. sea level rise). Climate-related risks can also be associated with the transition to a lower-carbon global economy, the most common of which relates to policy and legal actions, technology changes, market responses and reputational considerations.

Health and Safety risk. Many companies engage in potentially hazardous activities that can give rise to injury or the loss of life of those working in a particular environment such as:

- an oil rig

- a factory

- a farm.

Health and safety risks are an inherent part of these industries and so the risk management task cannot be to avoid the risks completely. To reduce the risk to an acceptable level will involve incurring the costs of risk mitigation:

- Installing protective shielding

- Issuing safety equipment like hats and protective glasses etc.

Business probity risk is related to the governance and ethics of the organisation. It can arise from unethical behaviour by one or more participants in a particular process. It is often discussed in the context of procurement, where issues such as failing to treat information as confidential, lack of trust in business dealings and time spent in resolution of disputes may arise.

Derivatives risk refers to the risks due to the use of financial instruments. There is a risk of significant losses (or gains) from trading speculatively in derivatives such as futures or options. The risk can be many times larger than the margins paid to enter these markets.

Entrepreneurial risk is the necessary risk associated with any new business venture or opportunity. It is most clearly seen in entrepreneurial business activity, hence its name. In 'Ansoff' terms, entrepreneurial risk is expressed in terms of the unknowns of the market/customer reception of a new venture or of product uncertainties, for example product design, construction, etc. There is also entrepreneurial risk in uncertainties concerning the competences and skills of the entrepreneurs themselves.

The list of risks given above is fairly comprehensive.

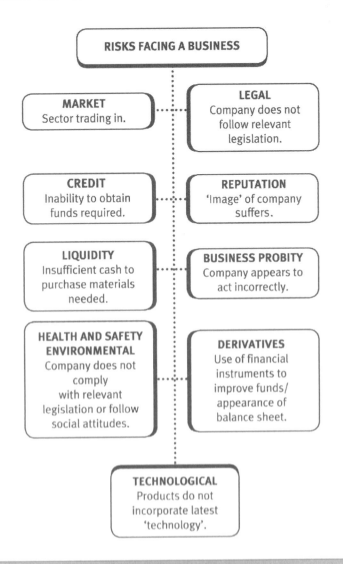

Sources and impacts of business risks

Examples of some different risks and possible impacts:

Risk	Sources	Impact
Market	• Failure to provide goods customers require. • Market sector overall declines.	• Company ceases to trade.
Credit	• Company's credit rating is down-rated by a recognised organisation (e.g. Standard and Poor). • There are going concern problems so suppliers are paid late.	• Company may not obtain materials needed for production.

Liquidity	• Customers are not paying quickly enough. • There is poor credit rating (as above). • There is poor cash management.	• Company may not obtain materials needed for production or not pay for other inputs such as labour. • Company may have to borrow at a high rate for short-term funding to cover liquidity problems. • Company cannot meet its commitments which may lead to company failure.
Technological	• There is lack of investment in research and development (R&D). • Competitors achieve technological advantage.	• Products appear to be out of date. • There is loss of market share.
Legal	• There is a breach of regulations, e.g. Companies Act. • Company is sued by third party for breach of contract.	• Adverse publicity. • Fines and penalties payable by company and/or officers.
Health, safety and environmental	• Breach of relevant legislation. • Company trading in sector with adverse reputation (e.g. testing on animals).	• Adverse publicity. Fine payable by company. • Legal damages payable (accidents at work).
Climate	• Climate changes affecting business continuity.	• Company ceases to trade.

Reputation	• Production of poor quality products. • Product recalls/ adverse publicity against company.	• Loss of market share. • In the extreme – company closure.
Business probity	• Directors/officers receive high bonuses when company is making losses. • Company trading in sector with adverse reputation (e.g. arms trade with 'enemy' countries).	• Adverse publicity. • Possible boycott of company products.
Derivatives	• Losses made on forward exchange contracts. • Financial statements do not adequately disclose company's transactions/assets/ liabilities.	• Financial loss to company. • Adverse publicity. • Possible closure of business if losses are large.

 Use of risk categories

To make the risk management process understandable and manageable, it is recommended that organisations use no more than 20-30 risk categories for identifying their risks. Risk categories should not overlap.

Two examples of risk categorisation by major companies are given here.

Snecma, the avionics group, identifies its risks under five different headings:

• Financial

• Human

• Image (corporate reputation, product reputation)

• Customers and partners

• Technical and production.

The commercial banking and insurance group, **Lloyds TSB**, uses 11 risk categories:

- Strategic
- Credit
- Market
- Insurance indemnity
- Operational
- Governance
- People and organisation
- Products and services
- Customer treatment
- Financial soundness
- Legal, regulatory and change management.

The bank does not have a separate risk category for reputation risks, because it considers that its reputation can be affected by all the other categories of risk.

Test your understanding 3

The ZXC company manufactures aircraft. The company is based in Europe and currently produces a range of four different aircraft. ZXC's aircraft are reliable with low maintenance costs, giving ZXC a good reputation, both to airlines who purchase from ZXC and to airlines' customers who fly in the aircraft.

ZXC is currently developing the 'next generation' of passenger aircraft, with the selling name of the ZXLiner. New developments in ZXLiner include the following.

- Two decks along the entire aircraft (not just part as in the Boeing 747 series) enabling faster loading and unloading of passengers from both decks at the same time. However, this will mean that airport gates must be improved to facilitate dual loading at considerable expense.

- 20% decrease in fuel requirements and falls in noise and pollution levels.

- Use of new alloys to decrease maintenance costs, increase safety and specifically the use of Zitnim (a new lightweight conducting alloy) rather than standard wiring to enable the 'fly-by-wire' features of the aircraft. Zitnim only has one supplier worldwide.

> Many component suppliers are based in Europe although ZXC does obtain about 25% of the sub-contracted components from companies in the USA. At present, the US$ exchange rate is relatively weak.
>
> ZXC also maintains a significant R&D department working on the ZXLiner and other new products such as alternative environmentally friendly fuel for aircraft. At present, the relatively weak US$ is in ZXC's favour and so this risk is currently negligible.
>
> Although the ZXLiner is yet to fly or be granted airworthiness certificates, ZXC does have orders for 25 aircraft from the HTS company. However, on current testing schedules the ZXLiner will be delivered late.
>
> ZXC currently has about €4 billion of loans from various banks and last year made a loss of €2.3 billion. ZXC's chief executive has also just resigned taking a leaving bonus of around two years' salary.
>
> **Required:**
>
> Identify and explain the sources of business risk that could affect ZXC.
>
> For each of those risks evaluate the impact of the risk on ZXC and where necessary, discuss how that risk can be mitigated by ZXC.

6 Risk identification: Categories and risk relationships

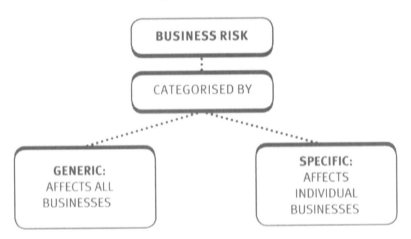

There are four stages in any risk audit (internal or external): identify, assess, review, and report. Together, these comprise an audit or review of the risk management of an organisation.

Identification

New risks emerge and old ones disappear.

Identification is therefore particularly important for those organisations existing in turbulent environments.

Assessment

Once identified, the next task is to assess the risk. Each identified risk needs to be measured against two variables: the probability (or likelihood) of the risk being realised; and the impact or hazard (what would happen if the risk was realised).

These two intersecting continua can be used to create a probability/impact grid on to which individual risks can be plotted. It is important to realise that it may not be possible to gain enough information about a risk to gain an accurate picture of its impact and/or probability.

The auditor will then review the organisation's responses to each identified and assessed risk.

Review

At the review stage, the auditor analyses the controls that the organisation has in the event of the risk materialising. Review can represent a substantial task, as the response to each assessed risk is a part of the review and there may be many risks to consider.

Report

A report on the review is produced and submitted to the principal which, in most cases, is the board of the organisation that commissioned the audit. Management will probably want to know about the extent of the key risks (those with high probability, high impact, and especially both high impact and high probability), the quality of existing assessment and the effectiveness of controls currently in place. Clearly, any ineffective controls will be a key component of the report and they would be the subject of urgent management attention.

 Generic or specific

Business risks can be either generic that is the risk affects all businesses, or specific to individual business sectors.

- Examples of generic risks include changes in the interest rate, non-compliance with company law, or poor use of derivative instruments.

- Generic risks can also affect different businesses in different ways, a company with substantial borrowing will be affected more by an increase in interest rates than a company with little or no borrowings.

- Similarly, a company manufacturing computers will be more at risk from the possibility of changes in legislation affecting VDUs than a company providing legal services.

The concept of related risk factors

To understand risk there is a need to appreciate certain risks are related to each other. This relationship can be either positively or negatively correlated.

Related risks are risks that vary because of the presence of another risk or where two risks have a common cause. This means when one risk increases, it has an effect on another risk and it is said that the two are related. Risk correlation is a particular example of related risk.

Positively correlated risks are positively related in that one will fall with the reduction of the other, and increase with the rise of the other.

Negatively correlated risks are negatively related in that one rises as the other falls.

The Deepwater Horizon oil spill in 2010 clearly had a huge environmental impact but also severely affected BP's reputation. This relationship would be described as a positive correlation. As one risk increases, so does the other.

A negative correlation would see the risks moving in opposite directions. For example, as BP spends more money to limit the risk of environmental damage, the company would also be depleting its cash reserves substantially and thus increasing its financial risk.

```
                    ┌─────────────────────────────────┐
                    │   CORRELATION BETWEEN RISK       │
                    └─────────────────────────────────┘
                         /                      \
        ┌──────────────────────────┐   ┌──────────────────────────┐
        │ POSITIVE CORRELATION     │   │ NEGATIVE CORRELATION     │
        │ Both risks move in the   │   │ Each risk moves in an    │
        │ same direction           │   │ opposite direction.      │
        │ For example:             │   │ For example:             │
        │ As the Environmental risk│   │ As more money is spent   │
        │ increases so does the    │   │ on reducing the          │
        │ Reputational risk        │   │ Environmental damage,    │
        │                          │   │ therefore reducing the   │
        │                          │   │ risk. There is an        │
        │                          │   │ increase in the          │
        │                          │   │ financial risk facing    │
        │                          │   │ the company              │
        └──────────────────────────┘   └──────────────────────────┘
```

Examples of sector-specific risks

Sector-specific risks vary depending on the industry sector. Good sources of identifying these risks are the business pages of quality newspapers or their associated websites. Reading these pages a few times a week will keep you up to date with events in the business world and the reasons for them.

Here are four sectors and a summary of the risks affecting each (some comments being drawn from newspaper reports to show how knowledge does help here):

Banks	Nuclear	Tobacco	Mining
Reputation – high profits and overcharging customers.	Reputation – safety risk (perhaps not as bad since 'three mile island' and 'Chernobyl').	Reputation – increased awareness of the risk of ill health from smoking and passive smoking.	Reputation – poor working conditions and prolonged ill health resulting from working in mines.
Reputation – trust in security of funds and availability for withdrawal on demand by customers.	Political – risk that new power stations will not be built as this will be a political not a technological decision.	Political – fall in sales following increased taxes.	Political – demand for some products (e.g. coal) dependent on political decisions (building new power stations).
Fraud – illegal use of customer credit cards – decreased somewhat following 'chip and pin' introduction.	Compliance/credit – cost of decommissioning old power stations.	Regulatory – decreased sales resulting from smoking being banned in public places.	Environmental – reduced sales of coal based on increased social awareness of the environmental damage caused by fossil fuels.

Technology – linked to the above – forged credit cards extracting cash from ATMs.			

The overall point is that the risk profile is different for each sector – even though the risk areas can remain the same (reputation risk has been used for each of the areas above).

Current 'real-life' events will show how risks facing businesses are constantly evolving. The credit crunch impact on the banking sector is a prime example of this.

Test your understanding 4

Identify FIVE examples of sector-specific risks that might affect a university.

7   The impact on stakeholders

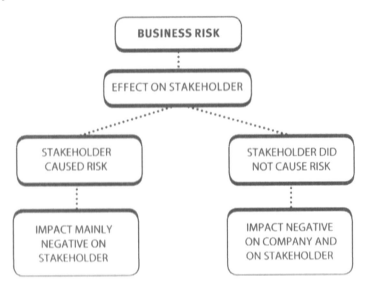

Business risks initially affect the company subject to those risks. However there will be a 'knock-on' effect of those risks on stakeholders:

*   The amount of the effect will depend on how close the stakeholder is to the company.

*   In many situations, the actual impact is to affect the company again; the stakeholders will mitigate the risk by distancing themselves from the company.

*   Impact on stakeholders is likely to be more severe where they actually cause the business risk in the first place.

Impact on stakeholders

A summary of different stakeholders and the impact of business risks on them is provided below:

Stakeholder	Impact of business risk
Shareholders	Potential loss of value of investment in company (fall in share price) and loss of income (decreased dividends).
Directors	Loss of income (assuming that remuneration is linked in some way with company performance). Also potential for poor reputation if any business risks are identified as resulting from actions of a specific director.
Managers	Likely to mean that the department they are in charge of falls behind budget in some way. Quite likely therefore that managers become demotivated, especially if business risk was not their fault. Possible fall in remuneration if part of salary is performance related.
Employees	Similar impact to managers – may see any fall in output and/or remuneration as 'not their fault' and become demotivated as a result.
Customers	The impact is likely to depend on the nature of the risk. However, risks such as poor product reputation will have an impact on customers in that the company's product will not be purchased. The overall impact is therefore mainly negative on the company in terms of lost sales.
Suppliers	If business risk results from poor quality of supplies, then the impact of the risk is loss of supply to that particular company. Loss of supply may also occur where the risk is not the fault of the supplier, e.g. the purchasing company manufactures fewer items, decreasing the amount of inputs purchased.
Government	The main impact is likely to be less revenue raised (either in terms of sales taxes and/or corporation taxes). It is probable that the company will make less profit, resulting in a fall in tax revenue.

Banks	At the extreme, any loans and interest due to the bank are not repaid because the company is no longer trading. Impact may be less severe, in terms of the company's profitability or ability to repay loans, which will enable the bank to limit its risk. In other words, the risk assessment of the company increases, limiting the amount of money the bank is willing to lend.
Trade unions	Loss of jobs will impact on their membership, affecting status and power, as well as subscription income.
Communities	If the local community is the provider of the majority of the workforce, it will be affected by any job losses. However, if the organisation has not operated in harmony with the local community it may benefit from any downturn in business.

8 Assessing risks

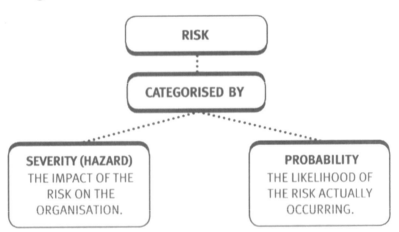

A common qualitative way of assessing the significance of risk is to produce a 'risk map':

- The map identifies whether a risk will have a significant impact on the organisation and links that into the likelihood of the risk occurring.

- The approach can provide a framework for prioritising risks in the business.

- Risks with a significant impact and a high likelihood of occurrence need more urgent attention than risks with a low impact and low likelihood of occurrence.

- The significance and impact of each risk will vary depending on the organisation:

  - e.g. an increase in the price of oil will be significant for an airline company but will have almost no impact on a financial services company offering investment advice over the internet.

- The severity of a risk can also be discussed in terms of 'hazard'. The higher the hazard or impact of the risk, the more severe it is.

- Risks can be plotted on a diagram, as shown.

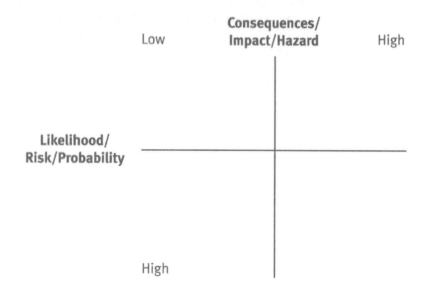

This diagram will be revisited in the next chapter when we consider risk management strategies.

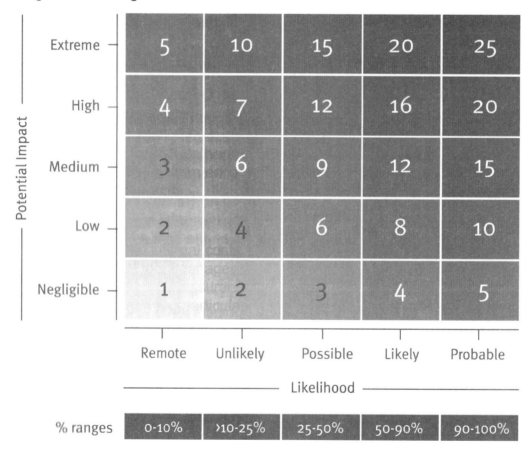

A risk heat map is a tool used to present the results of a risk assessment process visually and in a meaningful and concise way.

Whether conducted as part of a broad-based enterprise risk management process or more narrowly focused internal control process, risk assessment is a critical step in risk management. It involves evaluating the likelihood and potential impact of identified risks.

Heat maps are a way of representing the resulting qualitative and quantitative evaluations of the probability of risk occurrence and the impact on the organisation in the event that a particular risk is experienced.

The development of an effective heat map has several critical elements – a common understanding of the risk appetite of the company, the level of impact that would be material to the company, and a common language for assigning probabilities and potential impacts.

The 5x5 heat map diagram below provides an illustration of how organisations can map probability ranges to common qualitative characterisations of risk event likelihood, and a ranking scheme for potential impacts. They can also rank impacts on the basis of what is material in financial terms, or in relation to the achievement of strategic objectives. In this example, risks are prioritised using a simple multiplication formula.

Organisations generally map risks on a heat map using a 'residual risk' basis that considers the extent to which risks are mitigated or reduced by internal controls or other risk response strategies.

The risk management strategies that will be adopted depend on how risk is assessed on this map. They will be:

- Transfer

- Accept

- Reduce

- Avoid

Illustration of risk mapping

Bogle Freight is a freight-forwarding business. It sends containers of freight from Heathrow to airports around the world. It specialises in consolidating the freight of different shippers into a single container, to obtain the benefit of lower freight charges for large shipments. The prices that Bogle charges its clients cover a share of the airline flight costs and insurance, and provide a margin to cover its running costs and allow for profit.

To make a satisfactory profit, Bogle needs to fill its containers to at least 75%, and at the moment is achieving an average 'fill' of 78%.

International trade and commerce have been growing in the past year, although at a slow rate.

Bogle's management is aware that airline flight costs are likely to rise next year due to higher fuel costs, and because several major airlines that have been suffering large losses will be hoping to increase their prices.

Required:

Prepare a 2 × 2 risk map, with one risk identified in each quadrant of the map. Explain your reasons for assessing the probability and impact of the risk as high or low in each case.

Solution

The suggested solution below uses the information provided, but also considers how the business of an international freightforwarder might be affected by risk factors. Your solution might identify different risks.

		Impact/consequences	
		Low	**High**
Probability/ likelihood	**High**	Higher airline flight costs.	Insufficient freight to fill containers.
	Low	A major airline will go out of business.	Downturn in international trade.

Explanations

1   High probability, high impact risk. The business will be affected if the average 'fill' for containers falls from its current level of 78%. Profits will be unsatisfactory if the 'fill' is less than 75%, suggesting that there could be a high risk of falling and inadequate profitability due to failure to win enough business.

2   Low probability, high impact risk. A downturn in international trade will affect the volume of freight and so would reduce Bogle's income. Since international trade has been growing, the likelihood of a downturn would seem to be low.

3   High probability, low impact risk. It seems inevitable that airlines will charge higher prices, but Bogle can pass on these costs to its own customers, therefore the impact of this risk is low.

4   Low probability, low impact risk. The collapse of a major airline is possible due to high losses, but is perhaps unlikely. If an airline did go out of business, international freight should not be affected, because businesses would switch to other airlines.

Test your understanding 5

Suggest a risk that could be included in each quadrant of a risk map for an accountancy tuition company.

Dynamic nature of risk assessment

- Risks change over time.

- The environments that companies operate within (both internal and external) vary with respect to the degree of change that is faced.

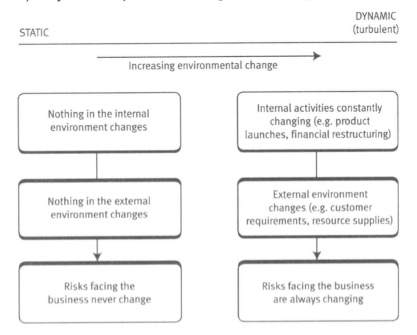

- In a dynamic environment these changing risks will lead to the assessment of probability and impact in the risk map constantly altering.

 Examples of changing risk assessments

As the assessments of probability or impact of a risk change so does the position of a risk on a risk map.

Taking the following two risks to an oil company as examples:

Risk X: This is the risk of a major leak at one of the offshore oil platforms operated by this company. It has been classified as high impact, due to the fact that it would require a substantial expenditure to repair and rectify the environmental damage, and as high likelihood based on the complexity of the deep-sea oil drilling operations and the large number of platforms operated. At this stage the risk would be shown at X1 in the risk map below.

There is a subsequent change in the regulations of this industry placing restrictions on the establishment of new deep-sea oil platforms. The company will therefore have fewer platforms in operation (several are due to close soon, and new ones cannot be opened) and hence the probability of such a leak occurring is now reduced. The risk has therefore moved to position X2 on the risk map.

Risk Y: This is the risk of the company being unable to recruit permanent members of staff to work on the offshore platforms. The risk is classified as low impact, since contract staff can be utilised instead of permanent employees, but high probability due to the company offering below market-average salaries – shown at position Y1.

An internal policy decision is made to improve the salary package for offshore operatives, which has the effect of moving this risk to position Y2 – low impact and now low probability.

In the situations of both risks X and Y the strategies implemented to mitigate these risks will need to be amended following the revised risk assessments.

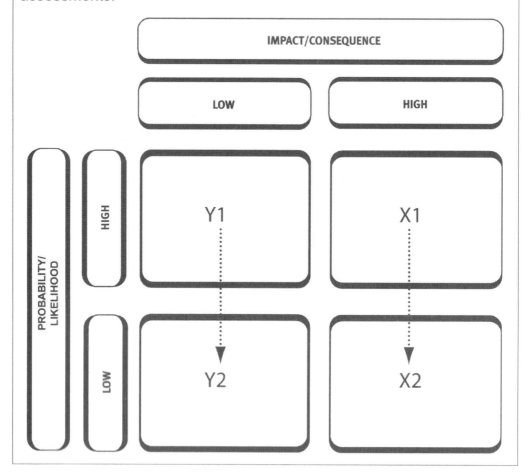

As a result of risks changing, a company must adapt its risk management accordingly.

- Organisations in dynamic environments must invest more in risk management processes to keep abreast of changes.

- Organisations in dynamic environments may need to have more rigorous (and costly) risk response strategies in place to be able to adapt to the changes.

9 Risk perception

A further complication to risk assessment is the quality of information available upon which to assess the risks.

Subjective risk perception has obvious limitations, including:

- it may affect the suitability of selected risk mitigation techniques

- it may impact resource decisions.

Examples of objective and subjective risk assessment

Objective measurement	Subjective measurement
Impact: number of homes affected if a local power distribution plant ceases to operate. (The number of homes served by that plant is known since it covers a precise geographical area.)	**Impact:** the amount of revenue lost by businesses if websites are "down" due to loss of power. (This would depend on the amount of revenue that flows through the website, and it is hard to determine exactly how much would have been earned in the specific period of a power outage.)
Likelihood: drawing an ace of spades out of a normal pack of cards. (1 in 52 chance.)	**Likelihood:** the FTSE100 rises by 50 points in the next week. This could be affected by so many variables that it would be impossible to quantify.

Tools and techniques for quantifying risks

A number of tools can be used to quantify the impact of risks on the organisation, some of which are described below. These will have been covered in your earlier studies, in papers F5 and F9.

- **Scenario planning:** in which different possible views of the future are developed, usually through a process of discussion within the organisation.

- **Sensitivity analysis:** in which the values of different factors which could affect an outcome are changed to assess how sensitive the outcome is to changes in those variables.

- **Decision trees:** often used in the management of projects to demonstrate the uncertainties at each stage and evaluate the expected value for the project based on the likelihood and cash flow of each possible outcome.

- **Computer simulations:** such as the Monte Carlo simulation which uses probability distributions and can be run repeatedly to identify many possible scenarios and outcomes for a project.

- **Software packages:** designed to assist in the risk identification and analysis processes.

- **Analysis of existing data:** concerning the impact of risks in the past.

Illustration 1 – Northern Rock and risk management

The share price of Northern Rock plummeted by over 90% during the credit crunch crisis of 2007/2008. In the end it became the first UK bank to experience a run by its customers since 1866. State nationalisation followed shortly afterwards.

The reasons relate to the lack of risk management in its lending policy and its almost total reliance on other bank lending to fund its growth. In addition, the bank used investment products so complex that its own staff didn't fully understand them, which meant that it was unable to adequately evaluate its own risk exposure or that of its customers.

In line with all major banks Northern Rock spends millions of dollars employing qualified individuals to assess its risks through risk management software, and yet despite all of this its shareholders were faced with receiving 5 pence per share in compensation after nationalisation (against a share price at the time of the company's flotation in 2000 of around £5.00).

10 Risk registers

The risk register is a very important and practical risk management tool that all companies should have these days. It takes several days, if not weeks, to produce, and needs to be reviewed and updated regularly – mainly annually (in conjunction with corporate governance guidelines).

The risk register is often laid out in the form of a tabular document with various headings:

(1) The risk title – stating what the risk might be.

(2) The likelihood of the risk – possibly measured numerically if a scale has been set e.g. 1 is unlikely, 5 is highly likely.

(3) The impact of the risk should it arise. Again this might be graded from, say, 1 (low impact) to 5 (high impact).

(4) The risk owners name will be given – usually a manager or director.

(5) The date the risk was identified will be detailed.

(6) The date the risk was last considered will be given.

(7) Mitigation actions should be listed i.e. what the company has done so far to reduce the risk. This might include training, insurance, further controls added to the system, etc.

(8) An overall risk rating might be given e.g. 1–10, so that management can immediately see which risks are the ones they should be concentrating on.

(9) Further actions to be taken in the future will be listed (if any).

(10) The 'action lead' name will be detailed i.e. who is responsible for making sure that these future actions are implemented.

(11) A due date will be stated – by when the action has to be implemented.

(12) A risk level target might be given i.e. a score lower than that given in step 8 above. This might mean that by implementing a control, the risk rating is expected to lower from, say, 8 to, say, 2 (the target risk level).

For example, using the steps detailed above, one row of a tabulated risk register might show:

(1) Loss of personal data i.e. unsecure use of mobile devices could result in personal identifiable information being lost, stolen or unauthorised access gained.

(2) Likelihood = 3

(3) Impact = 5

(4) Risk owner = Mike Smith (IT manager)

(5) 1.1.12

(6) 2.2.14

(7) Staff receive training every 2 years which highlights the risks. All laptops are encrypted. Regular audits are undertaken. Any incidents are reported to the Audit Committee.

(8) Overall risk rating = 7

(9) Encryption technology to be implemented which meets industry standard.

(10) Mike Smith

(11) 31.7.14

(12) Risk level target = 3

11 Chapter summary

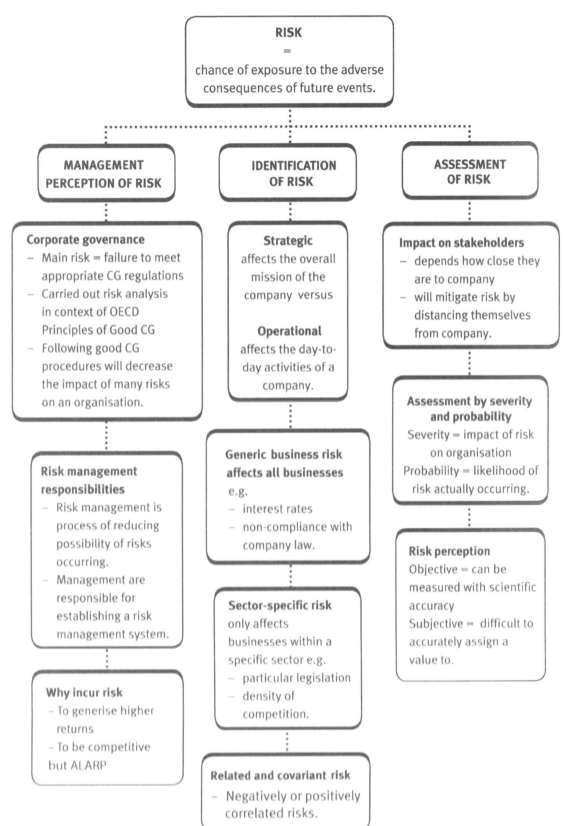

RISK
=
chance of exposure to the adverse consequences of future events.

MANAGEMENT PERCEPTION OF RISK

IDENTIFICATION OF RISK

ASSESSMENT OF RISK

Corporate governance
- Main risk = failure to meet appropriate CG regulations
- Carried out risk analysis in context of OECD Principles of Good CG
- Following good CG procedures will decrease the impact of many risks on an organisation.

Risk management responsibilities
- Risk management is process of reducing possibility of risks occurring.
- Management are responsible for establishing a risk management system.

Why incur risk
- To generise higher returns
- To be competitive but ALARP

Strategic
affects the overall mission of the company versus

Operational
affects the day-to-day activities of a company.

Generic business risk affects all businesses
e.g.
- interest rates
- non-compliance with company law.

Sector-specific risk
only affects businesses within a specific sector e.g.
- particular legislation
- density of competition.

Related and covariant risk
- Negatively or positively correlated risks.

Impact on stakeholders
- depends how close they are to company
- will mitigate risk by distancing themselves from company.

Assessment by severity and probability
Severity = impact of risk on organisation
Probability = likelihood of risk actually occurring.

Risk perception
Objective = can be measured with scientific accuracy
Subjective = difficult to accurately assign a value to.

Test your understanding answers

Test your understanding 1 – Holistic approach to risk

By imposing changes without considering the impact on other business departments the disadvantages of the new procedures are likely to outweigh the advantages gained.

Advantages

- It is likely that the number of counterfeit bank notes taken by the stores throughout the country will decrease. This should increase the profitability of each transaction.

- The finance team is likely to hit any KPIs relating to counterfeit notes being taken in the company stores.

- Goodwill is likely to be generated between the police and the company.

- A positive impact on customer goodwill may be achieved as customers like the way the company is taking a stand against crime.

Disadvantages

- The speed of service to customers is likely to be adversely affected. The increased time to serve each customer is likely to reduce a core KPI for a 'fast food' business.

- Goodwill with customers is likely to be adversely affected due to the reduction in speed of service.

- Company employees who work at the till are more likely to be put in difficult confrontational situations with customers if they follow the company policy to confiscate possible counterfeit notes.

- In addition the employees are likely to be significantly demotivated as any breach of the new procedures may be subject to disciplinary action, up to and including dismissal from the company.

- The Human Resources team may face a significantly increased workload due to employees not applying the procedures and/or facing subsequent disciplinary action.

- The operations of the stores may be adversely affected since staff facing disciplinary action are likely to be suspended from duty increasing the risk of staff shortages.

- Recruitment, in a business sector that has a traditionally high staff turnover rate, may be negatively impacted as potential new staff may join competitors that don't have such rigid procedures in place.

Test your understanding 2

Strategic risks

- Failure of strategic partner.

- Competitors make more technological advances.

- Major corporate customer decides to discontinue contract.

- Competitor launches a price war for broadband supply.

Operational risks

- Poor service quality.

- Service outages.

- Network fraud.

- Inaccurate billing.

- Unauthorised system changes.

Test your understanding 3

Product/market risk

This is the risk that customers will not buy new products (or services) provided by the organisation, or that the sales demand for current products and services will decline unexpectedly.

For ZXC, there is the risk that demand for the new aircraft will be less than expected, either due to customers purchasing the rival airplane or because airports will not be adapted to take the new ZXLiner.

Commodity price risk

Businesses might be exposed to risks from unexpected increases (or falls) in the price of a key commodity.

Part of the control systems of the ZXLiner rely on the availability of the new lightweight conducting alloy Zitnim. As there is only one supplier of this alloy, there is the danger of the monopolist increasing the price or even denying supply. Increase in price would increase the overall cost of the (already expensive) ZXLiner, while denial of supply would further delay delivery of the aircraft. ZXC needs to maintain good relations with their key suppliers to mitigate this risk.

Product reputation risk

Some companies rely heavily on brand image and product reputation, and an adverse event could put its reputation (and so future sales) at risk.

While the reputation of ZXC appears good at present, reputation will suffer if the ZXLiner is delayed significantly or it does not perform well in test flights (which have still to be arranged). Airline customers, and also their customers (travellers) are unlikely to feel comfortable flying in an aircraft that is inherently unstable. ZXC must continue to invest in R&D and good quality control systems to mitigate the effects of this risk.

Credit risk

Credit risk is the possibility of losses due to non-payment by debtors or the company not being able to pay its creditors, which will adversely affect the company's credit rating.

Given that the ZXLiner has not been sold at present, there are no debtors.

However, ZXC is heavily dependent on bank finance at present – any denial of funds will adversely affect ZXC's ability to continue to trade. Credit risk is therefore significant at present.

Currency risk

Currency risk, or foreign exchange risk, arises from the possibility of movements in foreign exchange rates, and the value of one currency in relation to another.

ZXC is currently based in Europe although it obtains a significant number of parts from the USA. If the €/$ exchange rate became worse, then the cost of imported goods for ZXC (and all other companies) would increase. At present, the relatively weak US$ is in ZXC's favour and so this risk is currently negligible.

Interest rate risk

Interest rate risk is the risk of unexpected gains or losses arising as a consequence of a rise or fall in interest rates. Exposures to interest rate risk arise from borrowing and investing.

As ZXC does have significant bank loans, then the company is very exposed to this risk. As interest rates are expected to rise in the future then ZXC would be advised to consider methods of hedging against this risk.

Gearing risk

Gearing risk for non-bank companies is the risk arising from exposures to high financial gearing and large amounts of borrowing.

Again, ZXC has significant amounts of bank loans. This increases the amount of interest that must be repaid each year. In the short term ZXC cannot affect this risk as the bank loans are a necessary part of its operations.

Political risk

Political risk depends to a large extent on the political stability in the countries in which an organisation operates, the political institutions within that country and the government's attitude towards protectionism.

As ZXC operates in a politically stable country this risk is negligible.

Legal risk or litigation risk

The risk arises from the possibility of legal action being taken against an organisation.

At present this risk does not appear to be a threat for ZXC. However, if the ZXLiner is delayed any further there is a risk for breach of contract for late delivery to the HTS company. There is little ZXC can do to guard against this risk, apart from keep HTS appraised of the delays involved with the ZXLiner.

Regulatory risk

This is the possibility that regulations will affect the way an organisation has to operate.

In terms of aircraft, regulation generally affects noise and pollution levels. As the ZXLiner is designed to have lower noise and pollution levels than existing aircraft then this risk does not appear to be a threat to ZXC.

Technology risk

Technology risk arises from the possibility that technological change will occur or that new technology will not work.

Given that ZXC is effectively producing a new product (the ZXLiner) that has not actually been tested yet, there is some technology risk. At worse, the ZXLiner may not fly at all or not obtain the necessary flying certificates. ZXC appears to be guarding against this risk by not decreasing its investment in product development.

Economic risk

This risk refers to the risks facing organisations from changes in economic conditions, such as economic growth or recession, government spending policy and taxation policy, unemployment levels and international trading conditions.

Demand for air travel is forecast to increase for the foreseeable future, so in that sense there is a demand for aircraft which ZXC will benefit from. The risk of product failure is more significant than economic risk.

Environmental risk

This risk arises from changes to the environment over which an organisation has no direct control, such as global warming, to those for which the organisation might be responsible, such as oil spillages and other pollution.

ZXC is subject to this risk – and there is significant debate concerning the impact of air travel on global warming. At the extreme, there is a threat that air travel could be banned, or made very expensive by international taxation agreements, although this appears unlikely at present. ZXC needs to continue to monitor this risk, and continue research into alternative fuels etc. in an attempt to mitigate the risk.

Business probity

This is the risk that a company does not follow rules of good corporate governance or show appropriate ethical awareness.

In ZXC, the departure of the chief executive with a bonus of more than two years' salary appears to act against business probity – why should the chief executive obtain a bonus when ZXC is making a loss and workers may be made redundant? However, the impact of this risk on ZXC is unclear. It is unlikely to affect sales as customers are more interested in the ZXLiner than the departure of the chief executive. There is more of an association risk in terms of business probity not being followed in other areas such as perceived cost cutting in research and development affecting the quality of the product. Again, ZXC is guarding against this risk.

However, the board of ZXC should ensure that the remuneration committee reviews directors' service contracts to ensure risk in this area does not occur in the future.

Test your understanding 4

- An inability to attract good-quality staff as academic salaries fall below those in business.

- A major private university is established that is attractive to typical applicants to this university.

- Research income threatened by poor financial position of donors to major projects.

- Admissions policy of university is portrayed by media as discriminatory.

- Government policy for funding further education is diverted in favour of other types of institution.

Test your understanding 5

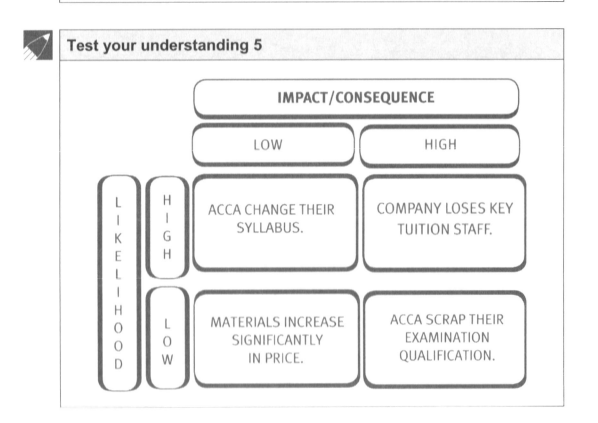

Managing, monitoring and mitigating risk

Chapter learning objectives

Upon completion of this chapter you will be able to:

- explain and assess the role of a risk manager

- evaluate a risk register and use heat maps when identifying or monitoring risk

- evaluate the concept of embedding risk in an organisation's culture and values

- explain and analyse the concepts of diversifying risk and when this would be appropriate

- advise on risk management strategies, including the use of the TARA model

- explain and assess the benefits of incurring or accepting some risk as part of competitively managing an organisation referring to the 'as low as reasonably practicable' (ALARP) principle

- apply the concept of assurance mapping to modern risk management using the 'four lines of defence'

PER

One of the PER performance objectives (PO4) is that you contribute to effective governance in your area. You evaluate, monitor and implement risk management procedures, complying with the spirit and the letter of policies, laws and regulations. Working through this chapter should help you understand how to demonstrate that objective.

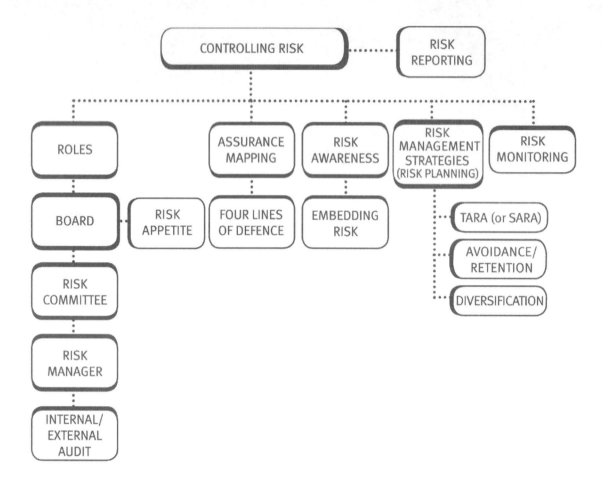

1 The role of the board

The board of an organisation plays an important role in risk management.

- It considers risk at the strategic level and defines the organisation's appetite and approach to risk.

- The board is responsible for driving the risk management process and ensuring that managers responsible for implementing risk management have adequate resources.

- The board is responsible for ensuring that risk management supports the strategic objectives of the organisation.

- The board will determine the level of risk which the organisation can accept in order to meet its strategic objectives.

- The board ensures that the risk management strategy is communicated to the rest of the organisation and integrated with all the other activities.

- The board reviews risks, and identifies and monitors progress of the risk management plans.

- The board will determine which risks will be accepted, which cannot be managed, or which it is not cost-effective to manage, i.e. residual risk.

- The board will generally delegate these activities to a risk committee, as discussed later in this chapter.

A framework for board consideration of risk is shown below

Board consideration of risk

- The business strategy explains what products and services an organisation will sell in which particular markets.

- The risk appetite identifies the amount of risk the board/organisation is willing to accept to fulfil the business strategy.

- For some business strategies, there will be a higher risk appetite (e.g. entry into a new market) and for others a lower appetite (e.g. ensuring ongoing product quality).

- The approach to risk is then summarised in the risk strategy. The strategy shows how risk will be managed within the business by reducing the likelihood of occurrence or minimising the impact, e.g. by taking out insurance or by diversification.

- Residual risk is risk that cannot be managed, or which it is not cost-effective to manage.

 Risk appetite

Risk appetite is a measure of the general attitude to accepting risk.

It can be determined by:

- **risk capacity** – the amount of risk that the organisation can bear, and

- **risk attitude** – the overall character of the board, in terms of the board being risk averse or risk seeking.

```
                        RISK APPETITE


  RISK AVERSE                    RISK SEEKING
  Seeking to avoid risks and     Actively seek risk, in the
  withdraw from risky            belief that higher the risk
  situations.                    equals the higher the returns.
```

How risk appetite affects risk policy

Risk appetite has an important influence on the risk strategies an organisation has in place.

Risk-averse organisation

For example a charity or public sector organisation will be characteristically risk averse – the organisation would seek to avoid risky situations.

- Therefore the risk management system the organisation develops may be less sophisticated and less costly.

Risk-seeking organisation

Conversely an organisation actively seeking additional risk, financial derivative traders for example, should:

- See risk management as of strategic importance.

- Invest in a comprehensive risk management system.

Risk appetite factors

The factors or business strategies, which could affect the risk appetite of the board of a company include:

Nature of product being manufactured	A high risk of product failure in certain products (e.g. aircraft) must be avoided due to the serious consequences of such an event. This will, out of necessity, limit the risk appetite of the board with regard to these specific products. For other products the risk of failure will be less (e.g. a fizzy drink having small changes from the normal ingredients – customers may not even notice the difference). Additionally if a business is taking significant risks with part of its product range it may be limited in the risk it can take with other products.

The need to increase sales	The strategic need to move into a new market will result in the business accepting a higher degree of risk than trying to increase sales or market share in an existing market. At that stage the business will appear to have a higher risk appetite.
The background of the board	Some board members may accept increased risk personally and this may be reflected in the way they manage the company.
Amount of change in the market	Operating in a market place with significant change (e.g. mobile telephones) will mean that the board has to accept a higher degree of risk. For example, new models of phone have to be available quickly.
Reputation of the company	If the company has a good reputation then the board will accept less risk – as they will not want to lose that good reputation.

Risk appetite and organisational factors

Risk appetite can be seen on a continuum from risk averse to risk seeking.

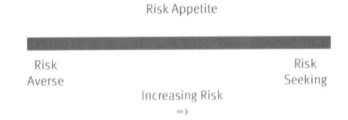

- There is no easy correlation between the risk appetite of an organisation and its size, structure and development.

- In general terms:

  - a small, young company may have a higher risk appetite as it takes risks in order to get its product into the market.

  - a larger, older company may appear to be more risk averse as it seeks to protect its current market position.

Risk attitude factors

Size	Structure	Development
Size normally relates to the overall size of an organisation in terms of turnover, market share or value on the balance sheet.	Structure normally relates to the internal structure of an organisation in terms of functional or divisional format.	Development normally relates to the stage of development of an organisation, possibly in terms of the product life cycle.

Small size	Functional structure	Product life cycle
Small size normally indicates higher risk for the organisation.	A functional structure normally indicates that risk is managed at board level.	The initial stages of the product life cycle are more risky.
A small organisation will have a smaller product range meaning it is more likely to be adversely affected by a fall in sales of one product. This would suggest a risk-averse stance due to the necessity to tighten controls to protect limited product range.	Consider a company selling the same product in many countries (e.g. Dell computers). The board will consider the risk of selling computers and the related risk of selling in different jurisdictions.	Initial investment may not result in a viable product, while the launch of a new product does not mean it will actually be accepted into the market. However, organisations will take high risk here because new products are required to replace older products.
However, small size may also be indicative of a young company attempting to sell its first products. In this case, more risk will be accepted in order to get the product 'launched'.	Depending on the attitude of the board, the company will accept more or less risk, e.g. expansion into related fields such as printer sales, or expansion into new jurisdictions.	Products at the end of the life cycle are declining in sales. The organisation will limit risk by stopping investment in the product and finally withdrawing it from the marketplace.

Large size	Divisional structure
Large size normally indicates lower risk for the organisation.	A divisionalised structure indicates that risk is managed by having a diversified portfolio of companies.
A larger company will have a wider product range meaning it is less dependent on any one product; a fall in sales of one product does not necessarily place the organisation at risk.	Risk appetite will be determined by the current portfolio of companies in terms of their overall risk for the organisation.
However, large size may also be indicative of the organisation having many employees, good brand names, etc. The organisation will therefore be keen to minimise reputation risk, attempting to protect its own, and its stakeholders' interests.	A portfolio with limited risk may indicate that more risky investments can be made. Similarly, a higher-risk portfolio indicates that lower-risk investments will be attractive.

The overall point here is that general trends can be established. However, there is no definitive link between size, structure and development and the level of risk within an organisation.

2 Risk committee

- Though corporate governance codes do not specifically require a risk committee to be established, many companies will set up a separate risk committee or establish the audit committee as a 'risk and audit committee'.

- The risk committee is sometimes referred to as a **risk management committee**.

- Where no risk committee is formed, the audit committee will usually perform similar duties.

Roles of the risk committee

Composition of risk committee

The committee will include both executive and non-executive directors, with the majority being NEDs.

Executive directors are involved as they are responsible for the day-to-day operations and therefore have a more detailed understanding of the associated risks.

Roles of the risk committee

In broad terms, the risk (management) committee within an organisation has the following main aims:

- Raising risk awareness and ensuring appropriate risk management within the organisation.

- Establishing policies for risk management.

- Ensuring that adequate and efficient processes are in place to identify, report and monitor risks.

- Updating the company's risk profile, reporting to the board and making recommendations on the risk appetite of the company.

Supporting these objectives of the risk (management) committee, there are many secondary objectives. These objectives may also be contained in the terms of reference of the risk (management) committee.

- Advising the board on the risk profile and appetite of the company and as part of this process overseeing the risk assurance process within the company.

- Acting on behalf of the board, to ensure that appropriate mechanisms are in place with respect to risk identification, risk assessment, risk assurance and overall risk management.

- Continual review of the company's risk management policy including making recommendations for amendment of that policy to the board.

- Ensuring that there is appropriate communication of risks, policies and controls within the company to employees at all management levels.

- Ensuring that there are adequate training arrangements in place so that management at all levels are aware of their responsibilities for risk management.

- Where necessary, obtaining appropriate external advice to ensure that risk management processes are up to date and appropriate to the circumstances of the company.

- Ensuring that best practices in risk management are used by the company, including obtaining and implementing external advice where necessary.

Responsibilities of the risk committee

Detailed tasks of the risk committee are to:

- Assess risk management procedures (for the identification, measurement and control of key risk exposures) in accordance with changes in the operating environment.

- Emphasise and demonstrate the benefits of a risk-based approach to internal control.

- If appropriate, consider risk audit reports on key business areas to assess the level of business risk exposure.

- Assess risks of any new ventures and other strategic initiatives.

- If appropriate, review credit risk, interest rate risk, liquidity risk and operational risk exposures with regard to full board risk appetite.

- Consider whether public disclosure of information regarding internal control and risk management policies and key risk exposures is in accordance with the statutory requirement and financial reporting standards.

- Make recommendations to the full board on all significant matters relating to risk strategy and policies.

Some of these tasks may be directed toward the audit committee, especially the areas of internal control where there already is an internal audit function.

3 Role of the risk manager

- The risk manager is a member of the risk management committee, reporting directly to that committee and the board.

- The role focuses primarily on implementation of risk management policies.

- The manager is supported and monitored by the risk management committee.

- The role is more operational than strategic.

- Policy is set by the board and the risk management committee and implemented by the risk manager.

Risk manager activities

Typical activities carried out by a risk manager include:

- Provision of overall leadership for risk management team.

- Identification and evaluation of the risks affecting an organisation from that organisation's business, operations and policies.

- implementation of risk mitigation strategies including appropriate internal controls to manage identified risks.

- Seeking opportunities to improve risk management methodologies and practices within the organisation.

- Monitoring the status of risk mitigation strategies and internal audits, and ensuring that all recommendations are acted upon.

- Developing, implementing and managing risk management programmes and initiatives including establishment of risk management awareness programmes within the organisation.

- Maintaining good working relationships with the board and the risk management committee.

- Ensuring compliance with any laws and regulations affecting the business.

- Implementing a set of risk indicators and reports, including losses, incidents, key risk exposures and early warning indicators.

- Liaising with insurance companies, particularly with regards to claims, conditions and cover available.

- Depending on specific laws of the jurisdiction in which the organisation is based, working with the external auditors to provide assurance and assistance in their work in appraising risks and controls within the organisation.

- Again, depending on the jurisdiction, producing reports on risk management, including any statutory reports (e.g. Sarbanes-Oxley (SOX) reports in the US).

4 Risk awareness

As previously discussed, one of the roles of the risk committee is to raise risk awareness within the organisation.

In general terms, a lack of risk awareness means that an organisation has an inappropriate risk management strategy.

- Risks affecting the organisation may not have been identified meaning there will be a lack of control over that risk.

- Risks may occur and the control over that risk is not active due to lack of monitoring and awareness.

- Continued monitoring within the organisation is therefore required to ensure that risk management strategies are updated as necessary.

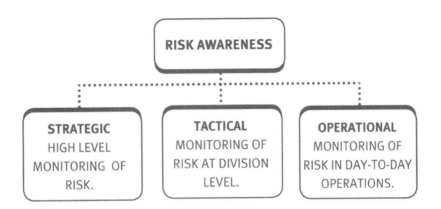

 Levels of risk awareness

Strategic level	There is a need for continued monitoring of risks affecting the organisation as a whole. For example, threats such as new competitors and new technologies must be identified on a timely basis and the risk management strategy updated to reflect these changes. At best, lack of monitoring will result in the organisation starting to fall behind competitors in terms of functionality or design of products. At worst, lack of monitoring may threaten the ongoing existence of the organisation.
Tactical level	Monitoring is required for risks that affect tactical managers. Risks in this category may affect individual divisions or units of the organisation, or individual departments depending on how the organisation is structured.
	For a divisional structure, lack of monitoring may affect continuity of supply or availability of distribution channels. e.g. not recognising that a supplier is in liquidation will result in a delay in obtaining alternative sources of material.
	For a functional structure, lack of monitoring may affect continuity of process completion.
	The resignation of key staff may result in key processes not being completed, e.g. customers not invoiced for goods delivered. Staff motivation should be monitored to give early warning of staff leaving.

Operational level	Monitoring is required for risks at the operational level, i.e. the day-to-day running of the organisation. Lack of monitoring is unlikely to be a specific threat to the organisation initially, but continued errors or risks will add to reputation risk over time. For example, lack of specific items to sell because sales patterns have not been monitored will result in customers choosing alternatives, or moving to other suppliers in the short term. However, continued lack of key goods will increase customer dissatisfaction, potentially resulting in significant and ongoing decreases in sales.

Sources of information on risk

The risk committee will obtain information about risks, and weaknesses in controls, from a variety of sources including:

- reports from departmental managers
- whistleblowers
- reports on key project and new business areas
- results of internal audit reviews (possibly from the audit committee)
- customer feedback
- performance monitoring systems (internal and external factors)
- directors' own observations.

5 Embedding risk

- The aim of embedding risk management is to ensure that it is 'part of the way we do business' (to misquote Handy).
- It can be considered at two levels:
    - embedding risk in systems
    - embedding risk in culture.

Embedding risk in systems

- Embedding risk in systems applies to the concept of ensuring that risk management is included within the control systems of an organisation.
- In this context, a control system helps ensure that other systems (e.g. the accounting system) are working correctly.
- Risk management is not seen as a separate system.
- In many jurisdictions, this is a statutory requirement (e.g. US) while in others it is a code of best practice (e.g. UK).
- To be successful, embedding risk management needs approval and support from the board.

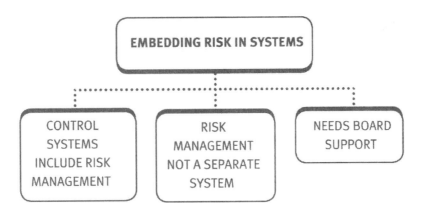

The **process of embedding risk management** within an organisation's systems and procedures can be outlined as follows:

1   Identify the controls that are already operating within the organisation.

2   Monitor those controls to ensure that they work.

3   Improve and refine the controls as required.

4   Document evidence of monitoring and control operation (using performance metrics or independent assessment such as internal or external audit).

Success of embedding risk in systems

Embedding risk management is unlikely to be successful within an organisation unless it is:

- supported by the board and communicated to all managers and employees within the organisation

- supported by experts in risk management

- incorporated into the whole organisation, i.e. not part of a separate department seen as 'responsible' for risk

- linked to strategic and operational objectives supported by existing processes such as strategy reviews, planning and budgeting, e.g. again not seen as an entirely separate process

- supported by existing committees, e.g. audit committee and board meetings rather than simply the remit of one 'risk management' committee

- given sufficient time by management to provide reports to the board.

Embedding risk in culture

- As noted above, risk management needs to be embedded into policies and procedures in an organisation.

- However, the policy may still fail unless all workers in a company (board to employees) accept the need for risk management.

- Embedding risk into culture and values therefore implies that risk management is 'normal' for the organisation.

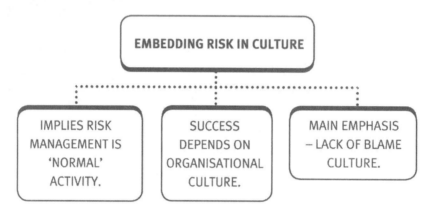

Methods of embedding risk management in the culture and values of an organisation include:

- aligning individual goals with those of the organisation

- including risk management responsibilities within job descriptions

- establishing reward systems which recognise that risks have to be taken in practice (e.g. not having a 'blame' culture)

- establishing metrics and performance indicators that can monitor risks and provide an early warning if it is seen that risks will actually occur and affect the organisation

- informing all staff in an organisation of the need for risk management, and publishing success stories to show how embedding risk management in the culture has benefited both organisation and staff.

 Success of embedding risk in culture

Various cultural factors that affect the extent to which risk management can be embedded into the culture and values of an organisation include:

- whether the culture is open (to new ideas, procedures and change) or closed

- the overall commitment to risk management policies at all levels in the organisation

- the attitude to internal controls, e.g. are they viewed as constraints within the organisation or to provide benefits in terms of lowering risk?

- governance, e.g. the need to include risk management in the organisation to meet the needs and expectations of external stakeholders

- whether risk management is a normal part of the organisation's culture, e.g. whether it is taken for granted or not.

 ## 6 Risk management: TARA (or SARA)

- The risk management process was described in the previous chapter. We will now move on to the third step of the process: risk planning and formulating the risk management strategies.

- Strategies for managing risks can be explained as TARA (or SARA): **T**ransference (or **S**haring), **A**voidance, **R**eduction or **A**cceptance.

 Risk management using TARA

Transference. In some circumstances, risk can be transferred wholly or in part to a third party, so that if an adverse event occurs, the third party suffers all or most of the loss. A common example of risk transfer is insurance. Businesses arrange a wide range of insurance policies for protection against possible losses. This strategy is also sometimes referred to as sharing.

Risk sharing. An organisation might transfer its exposures to strategic risk by sharing the risk with a joint venture partner or franchisees.

Avoidance. An organisation might choose to avoid a risk altogether. However, since risks are unavoidable in business ventures, they can be avoided only by not investing (or withdrawing from the business area completely). The same applies to not-for-profit organisations: risk is unavoidable in the activities they undertake.

Reduction/mitigation. A third strategy is to reduce the risk, either by limiting exposure in a particular area or attempting to decrease the adverse effects should that risk actually crystallise.

Other examples of risk reduction:

Risk minimisation. This is where controls are implemented that may not prevent the risk occurring but will reduce its impact if it were to arise.

Risk pooling. When risks are pooled, the risks from many different transactions of items are pooled together. Each individual transaction or item has its potential upside and its downside. For example, each transaction might make a loss or a profit in isolation but by treating them all as part of the same pool, the risks tend to cancel each other out, and are lower for the pool as a whole than for each item individually.

An example of risk reduction through pooling is evident in the investment strategies of investors in equities and bonds. An investment in shares of one company could be very risky, but by pooling shares of many different companies into a single portfolio, risks can be reduced (and the risk of the portfolio as a whole can be limited to the unavoidable risks of investing in the stock market).

Reducing Financial Risk – Hedging techniques

Risks in a situation are hedged by establishing an opposite position, so that if the situation results in a loss, the position created as a hedge will provide an offsetting gain. Hedging is used often to manage exposures to financial risks, frequently using derivatives such as futures, swaps and options.

With hedging, however, it often happens that if the situation for which the hedge has been created shows a gain, there will be an offsetting loss on the hedge position.

In other words, with hedging, the hedge neutralises or reduces the risk, but:

- restricts or prevents the possibility of gains from the 'upside risk'

- as well as restricting or preventing losses from the 'downside risk'.

Neutralising price risk with a forward contract

In some situations, it is possible to neutralise or eliminate the risk from an unfavourable movement in a price by fixing the price in advance.

For example, in negotiating a long-term contract with a contractor, the customer might try to negotiate a fixed price contract, to eliminate price risk (uncertainty about what the eventual price will be and the risk that it might be much higher than expected). The contractor, on the other hand, will try to negotiate reasonable price increases in the contract. The end result could be a contract with a fixed price as a basis but with agreed price variation clauses.

Fixed price contracts for future transactions are commonly used for the purchase or sale of one currency in exchange for another (forward exchange contracts).

Acceptance. The final strategy is to simply accept that the risk may occur and decide to deal with the consequences in that particular situation. The strategy is appropriate normally where the adverse effect is minimal. For example, there is nearly always a risk of rain but, unless the business activity cannot take place when it rains, then the risk of rain occurring is not normally insured against.

Risk mapping and risk management strategies

Risk maps can provide a useful framework to determine an appropriate risk management strategy.

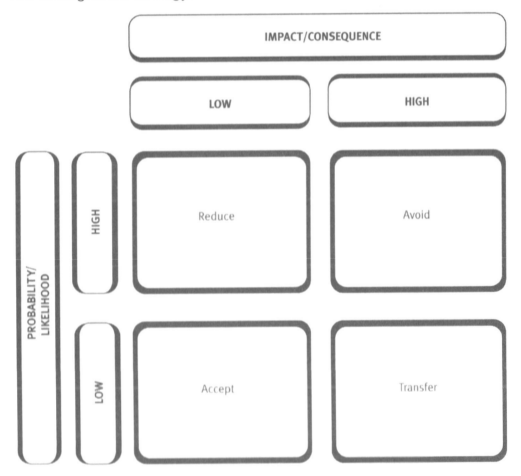

Test your understanding 1

The TGB Company runs sporting events such as tennis tournaments and downhill skiing events in various countries. The company has been fairly successful in the past in running events that attract a significant number of customers, and in the last 10 years TGB has always made a profit.

The board of TGB is now considering a number of sporting events for the next financial year.

- A repeat of this year's successful two-week long outdoor tennis tournament at a time of year when there is a 10% probability of rain on any given day. If it rains, customers are allowed access to the tournament on the following day. However, if there is rain on two consecutive days, tickets for those days are declared void and cannot be used.

- A new proposal to hold curling championships in 25 different countries in one year. (Curling is a sport played on ice where football sized stones are slid across the ice with the aim of stopping them as close as possible to a target on the ice.) Organisation of the championships will mean TGB either has to hire additional staff or run fewer sporting events in other sports. Demand for the curling championships is high in colder countries, but unclear in warmer countries where the sport has never been played.

- A new proposal to hold motor bike racing on the streets of a major European city. The city would effectively be closed to other traffic for a week with races taking place on normal public roads. There is a probability of 95% that at least one rider will be killed during the week and an 85% probability of serious injury to more than 10 spectators and the result of a crash. TGB's insurers have indicated that they would not be prepared to insure this event. However, TGB's financial accountant indicates that the event would be highly profitable.

- A repeat of a successful skiing championship in the Alps. The championship has been run for the last 25 years and is always well attended. However, analysts indicate that due to global warming there is a remote possibility that the Alps will not receive sufficient snow and the championship will not be able to go ahead. The board considers this risk to be so remote that it is not worth worrying about.

Required:

(a) Using the risk management model of TARA, explain the elements of the model and discuss how the TGB Company should manage risks for each of its proposed sporting events.

(b) Compare and contrast the roles of the risk manager and the risk committee.

7 Further risk management strategies

The "As Low As Reasonably Practicable" Principle (ALARP)

As we cannot eliminate risk altogether the ALARP principle simply states that residual risk should be as low as reasonably practicable. Taking into consideration the costly nature of risk reduction:

- The ALARP principle expresses a point at which the cost of additional risk reduction would be grossly disproportionate to the benefits achieved.

- The ALARP principle is usually applied to safety critical, high integrity systems where health and safety risks cannot be eliminated e.g. Oil rigs.

- An extreme example to clarify the point:

  - A company spending a million pounds to prevent a member of staff suffering from a bruised knee is grossly disproportionate.

  - A company spending a million pounds to prevent a major explosion capable of killing 150 people is proportionate.

Risk avoidance and retention

- **Risk avoidance:** the risk strategy by which the organisation literally avoids a risk by not undertaking the activity that gives rise to the risk in the first place.

- **Risk retention:** risk strategy by which an organisation retains that particular risk within the organisation.

  - This is a similar concept to risk acceptance.

Avoidance and retention strategies

- Risk avoidance and risk retention strategies relate, in part, to the risk appetite of the organisation, and then the potential likelihood of each risk, and the impact/consequence of that risk as discussed in the last chapter.

- A risk avoidance strategy is likely to be followed where an organisation has a low risk appetite. The strategy will involve avoiding those activities that will incur risk, e.g. activities that have a higher probability of failure; or where alternative risk strategies such as transference cannot be used:

  - a new project with a very low likelihood of success will not be started

  - an organisation may amend its portfolio of companies (where the organisation is a holding company) if it considers one particular area to be too risky.

- A risk retention strategy will be followed where the risk is deemed to be minimal or where other risk strategies such as transference are simply too expensive:

  - an organisation may 'self-insure' against minor damage to its vehicles because taking out comprehensive insurance to cover all damage would be too expensive

  - the organisation may decide not to insure against significant movements in interest rates as this risk is minimal but smaller movements in interest rates will be insured against.

Diversifying/spreading risk

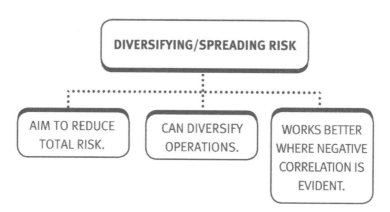

DIVERSIFYING/SPREADING RISK

AIM TO REDUCE TOTAL RISK.

CAN DIVERSIFY OPERATIONS.

WORKS BETTER WHERE NEGATIVE CORRELATION IS EVIDENT.

- Risk can be reduced by diversifying into operations in different areas, such as into Industry X and Industry Y, or into Country P and Country Q.

- Poor performance in one area will be offset by good performance in another area, so diversification will reduce total risk.

- Diversification is based on the idea of 'spreading the risk'; the total risk should be reduced as the portfolio of diversified businesses gets larger.

- From your F9 studies you will remember that diversification works best where returns from different businesses are negatively correlated (i.e. a change in the business environment causes returns to move in opposite directions). It will, however, still work to a degree as long as the correlation is less than +1.0.

- Example of poor diversification – swimming costumes and ice cream – both reliant on sunny weather for sales.

- Spreading risk relates to portfolio management where an investor, or company, spreads product and market risks.

Diversification

Risk can be diversified in terms of market/product management.

- **Market/product management** attempts to spread risk according to the **portfolio** of companies held within a group based more on links within the supply chain.

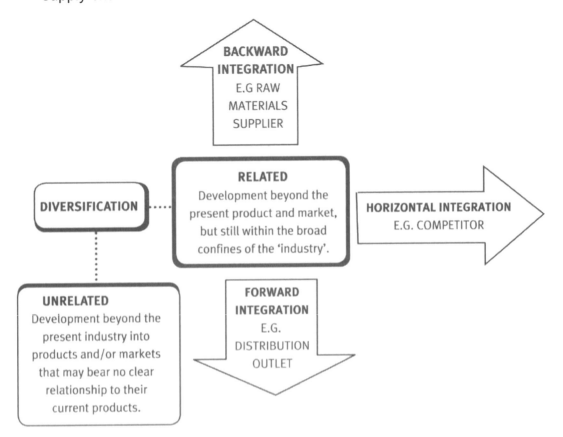

Related risks are risks that vary because of the presence of another risk or where two risks have a common cause. This means when one risk increases, it has an effect on another risk and it is said that the two are related.

Risk correlation is a particular example of related risk (refer to previous discussion on risk correlation for further detail).

Spreading risk by portfolio management

Within an organisation, risk can be spread by expanding the portfolio of companies held. The portfolio can be expanded by integration – linking with other companies in the supply chain, or diversification into other areas.

This is development beyond the present product and market, but still within the broad confines of the 'industry'.

- **Backward integration** refers to development concerned with the inputs into the organisation, e.g. raw materials, machinery and labour.

- **Forward integration** refers to development into activities that are concerned with the organisation's outputs such as distribution, transport, servicing and repairs.

- **Horizontal integration** refers to development into activities that compete with, or directly complement, an organisation's present activities. An example of this is a travel agent selling other related products such as travel insurance and currency exchange services.

Unrelated diversification

This is development beyond the present industry into products and/or markets that may bear no clear relationship to their present portfolio. Where appropriate an organisation may want to enter into a completely different market to spread its risk.

Problems with diversification:

- If diversification reduces risk, why are there relatively few conglomerate industrial and commercial groups with a broad spread of business in their portfolio?

- Many businesses compete by specialising, and they compete successfully in those areas where they excel.

- Therefore, it is difficult for companies to excel in a wide range of diversified businesses. There is a possible risk that by diversifying too much, an organisation might become much more difficult to manage. Risks could therefore increase with diversification, due to loss of efficiency and problems of management.

- Many organisations diversify their operations, both in order to grow and to reduce risks, but they do so into related areas, such as similar industries (e.g. banking and insurance, film and television production, and so on) or the same industry but in different parts of the world.

- Relatively little advantage accrues to the shareholders from diversification. There is nothing to prevent investors from diversifying for themselves by holding a portfolio of stocks and shares from different industries and in different parts of the world.

Test your understanding 2

Briefly consider whether it is always a good business strategy for a listed company to diversify to reduce risk.

Risk strategy and Ansoff's matrix

The strategy of an organisation will be affected by risk in the following ways.

- If the risk capacity has been reached, then the organisation will tend to seek low-risk activities. However, if the risk capacity is high then risky projects may be undertaken.

- Overall, the organisation's strategy is likely to have a portfolio of projects, some incurring more risk than others, so that the overall risk appetite is met from that portfolio. A high-risk appetite will indicate that the organisation will normally seek a higher number of higher-risk/return activities. However, a low-risk appetite indicates that a higher number of low-risk/lower-return activities will be preferred.

- Finally, a risk strategy of primarily self-insurance may limit the organisation's strategy regarding undertaking risky projects. Self-insurance implies risk minimisation as an overall strategy.

- Similarly, a risk strategy of risk transference may imply an overall strategy that incorporates a higher level of risk. However, risk will then be limited by the amount of insurance premiums charged to transfer the risk. Where premiums become too high, the organisation will seek less risky projects.

Ansoff's product/market matrix provides a summary of strategic options for an organisation when looking to expand. The matrix is shown below.

	Existing product	**New product**
Existing market	Internal efficiency and market penetration (1)	Product development (2)
New market	Market development (3)	Diversification (4)

In summary, the matrix illustrates that an organisation can expand using existing or new products into existing or new markets. The level of risk associated with each strategy is:

Option 1 – low risk as the product and the market are known – the risk here is attempting to sell a product in the marketplace when demand is falling (e.g. video players).

Option 2 – higher risk – although the market is known there is a risk that customers will not like the enhanced or new product (e.g. a mobile telephone that can double as an MP3 player).

Option 3 – again higher risk – the product is known but the marketplace is not. The main risks relate to poor sales strategy or poor market research indicating that customers want the product when they do not (e.g. Asda retreating from Germany).

Option 4 – highest risk option – both the market and the product are new combining the risks from Options 2 and 3. While the risk is highest here, so are potential returns if the new product can be successfully sold in the new market.

Test your understanding 3

Azure Ltd was incorporated in Sepiana on 1 April 20X4. In May, the company exercised an exclusive right granted by the government of Pewta to provide twice-weekly direct flights between Lyme, the capital of Pewta, and Darke, the capital of Sepiana.

The introduction of this service has been well advertised as 'efficient and timely' in national newspapers. The journey time between Sepiana and Pewta is expected to be significantly reduced, so encouraging tourism and business development opportunities in Sepiana.

Azure operates a refurbished 35-year-old aircraft which is leased from an international airline and registered with the Pewtan Aviation Administration (the PAA). The PAA requires that engines be overhauled every two years. Engine overhauls are expected to put the aircraft out of commission for several weeks.

The aircraft is configured to carry 15 First Class, 50 Business Class and 76 Economy Class passengers. The aircraft has a generous hold capacity for Sepiana's numerous horticultural growers (e.g. of cocoa, tea and fruit) and general cargo.

The six-hour journey offers an in-flight movie, a meal, hot and cold drinks and tax-free shopping. All meals are prepared in Lyme under a contract with an airport catering company. Passengers are invited to complete a 'satisfaction' questionnaire which is included with the in-flight entertainment and shopping guide. Responses received show that passengers are generally least satisfied with the quality of the food – especially on the Darke to Lyme flight.

Azure employs ten full-time cabin crew attendants who are trained in air-stewardship, including passenger safety in the event of accident and illness. Flight personnel (the captain and co-pilots) are provided under a contract with the international airline from which the aircraft is leased. At the end of each flight the captain completes a timesheet detailing the crew and actual flight time.

Ticket sales are made by Azure and travel agents in Sepiana and Pewta. On a number of occasions Economy seating has been over-booked. Customers who have been affected by this have been accommodated in Business Class as there is much less demand for this, and even less for First Class. Ticket prices for each class depend on many factors, for example, whether the tickets are refundable/non-refundable, exchangeable/non-exchangeable, single or return, mid-week or weekend, and the time of booking.

Azure's insurance cover includes passenger liability, freight/baggage and compensation insurance. Premiums for passenger liability insurance are determined on the basis of passenger miles flown.

Required:

Identify and explain the risks facing Azure Ltd. Describe how these risks could be managed and maintained at an acceptable level by Azure Ltd. [No specific risk management model is required.]

 8   Risk auditing

- Risk audit is a systematic way of understanding the risks that an organisation faces.

- Unlike financial auditing, risk audit is not a mandatory requirement for all organisations but, in some highly regulated industries, a form of ongoing risk assessment and audit is compulsory in most governance jurisdictions.

- Some organisations employ internal specialists to carry out risk auditing, others utilise external consultants to perform the work.

 Internal or external risk auditors?

The case for Internal Audit:

- The actual management of risk is a responsibility of management and is therefore an internal function. Thus many companies prefer to keep their assessment 'in-house'.

- Internal audit teams have the advantage of familiarity with the organisation's culture, systems, procedures and policies. Given their familiarity with the nature of the business and how things are supposed to work, internal audit should be able to perform a highly specific and focused risk assessment. It can be argued that an external team would take a long time to develop the same understanding and could never, in practice, maintain the same knowledge of a company's nuances as it evolves as an internal team.

- Internal teams are flexible in terms of the way they are deployed. As they are controlled by management they can be directed to perform a variety of engagements that can be changed at a moment's notice. All engagements with external teams are subject to the restrictions of engagement letters, availability of resources and the fees they charge.

- Internal audit should produce work that is written and structured according to the expectations and norms of the organisation and is therefore relevant for the intended use. External teams could be criticised for pitching their reports at too high a technical level for the intended audience or perhaps in an area the audience was not specifically concerned with.

The case for External Audit:

- External teams should comply with IFAC's (and ACCA's) code of ethics. They should therefore be more objective than an internal team, who will suffer from over-familiarity with the company. It is likely that external auditors will have no link to anybody inside the organisation being audited and so there will be fewer prior friendships and personal relationships to consider.

- The fact that these threats are avoided or reduced will create a higher degree of confidence for investors and, where applicable, regulators.

- Any external auditor brings a fresh pair of eyes to the task, identifying issues that internal auditors may have overlooked because of familiarity. When internal employees audit a system or department, they may be so familiar with the organisation's routines, procedures, culture and norms that a key risk might be overlooked or wrongly assessed.

- Best practice and current developments can be introduced if external consultants are aware of these. Given that consultants typically promote themselves on the currency of their skills, it is often more likely that their knowledge will be more up to date than that of internal staff, whose skills may be geared specifically to their organisation's needs and expectations.

Purpose of risk auditing

- Risk auditing assists the overall risk monitoring activity (last step in the risk management process) by providing an independent view of risks and controls in an organisation.

- As with any audit situation, a fresh pair of eyes may identify errors or omissions in the original risk monitoring process.

- In many situations, audit work is obligatory (e.g. SOX requirements).

- Following review, internal and external audit can make recommendations to amend the risk management system or controls as necessary.

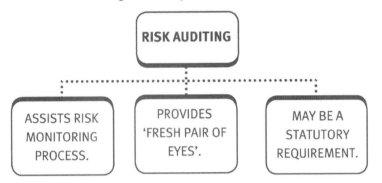

Stages of a risk audit

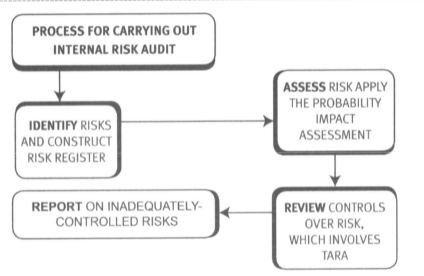

Process of a risk audit

The process of internal and external audit in monitoring risks will include:

1   Identifying the risks that exist within an organisation.

2   Assessing those risks in terms of likelihood of occurrence and impact on the organisation should the risk actually occur.

3   Reviewing the controls that are in place to prevent and/or detect the risk and assessing if they are appropriate.

4   Informing the board (or risk management committee where one exists) about risks which are outside acceptable levels or where controls over specific risks are ineffective.

9 Process of external reporting of internal controls and risk

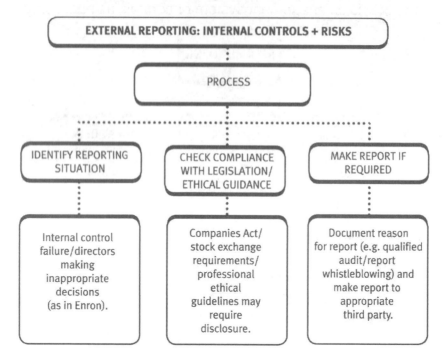

Analysis of internal control and risk may also be required for external reporting.

- The provision of information regarding internal controls is important to safeguard shareholders' interests and companies' assets.

- Reporting may be voluntary or required by statute (e.g. specified in the USA by section 404, Sarbanes-Oxley).

- In the extreme, third parties will be required to report where the company is either unaware of reporting situations or declines to report voluntarily.

- Some reporting systems are geared towards internal reporting (e.g. audit committees) but external reporting may also be required.

- The process of reporting implies some form of decision making prior to an external report being made.

- The process will normally imply compliance with the relevant statutory or ethical guidance appropriate to the entity and the person making the external report.

SOX reporting

In the US system, external reporting is regular and follows a set pattern. Sarbanes-Oxley reporting applies to companies listed on a US stock exchange such as the NASDAQ or NYSE.

Reporting is split between the directors and the auditors as shown below:

Directors	Auditors
Identify key business activities and the risk associated with them.	Identify and document internal controls in the company.
Identify controls over each risk.	Test those controls.
Test those controls.	Report on material control deficiencies in the auditor's report.
Report control deficiencies in the company's annual returns (form 10K, etc.).	Review the directors' report on internal controls.
Repeat the above for each financial year.	Report on the accuracy of that report – add separate qualification to audit report if the directors' report on internal controls is deficient.
Keep auditors informed of the results of controls testing.	
Fines incurred for incorrect or misleading reports.	Fines incurred for incorrect reports and/or destroying audit documentation.

See chapter 13 for further detail of **SOX section 404**, which has proved to be a significant burden on smaller companies.

UK external reporting

In the UK, the reporting system is based on the concept of comply (with the corporate governance regulations) or explain (the non-compliance). While regulations apply to listed companies, corporate governance is still a code, rather than statutory, so it is more difficult to enforce.

Directors	Auditors
Recognise overall responsibility for maintaining control systems in company.	Identify and document internal controls in the company.
Appoint internal auditors and internal audit committee to review and maintain control systems.	Test those controls.
Controls tested by internal auditors on a regular basis and recommendations for improvements made to the board.	Report on material control deficiencies in the audit report.
Control systems improved.	
Repeat the above for each financial year.	
Keep auditors informed of the results of controls testing (by statute auditors must be provided with all the information they require for the purposes of their audit).	
Where Combined Code has not been followed, possibility that company will be delisted from the stock exchange.	Fines incurred for incorrect reports (in Companies Act 2006 – implemented in 2006 and 2007).

Reporting sources will focus on different elements of risk management, as discussed below:

Reporting source	Internal control	Risk
Annual accounts	Disclosure required by corporate governance regulations for listed companies. Overview of internal control systems and how directors maintain those systems.	Summary of how the board have addressed some risks, such as environmental risk, in the corporate and social responsibility report (CSR).
Auditors	Any material deficiencies in the internal control systems will be reported in the audit report as a qualified audit report.	Risks will only be reported if they result in a material error in the financial statements.
Audit committee	As part of internal reporting, the audit committee will report control weaknesses to the board. External reporting will only take place where the board do not follow the advice of the audit committee and the situation is serious. External reporting in this situation is similar to 'whistleblowing'.	Again the focus of reporting is internal rather than external.

10 Assurance mapping and risk management

We have already recognised the benefits of identifying and managing strategic and operational risks, within the parameters of the organisation's risk appetite. In the case of smaller organisations, this may be as simple as investing owner/manager time in assessing the impact and likelihood of occurrence and instigating corrective action if necessary.

Larger organisations (as we have seen in chapter 15) may need to implement Enterprise Risk Management systems in their risk assessment processes to manage and mitigate identified risks to match their culture and risk appetite.

A key question remains however despite organisations having sound risk management practices i.e. "How do we get assurance regarding the effectiveness of our risk management processes?

Assurance is an objective examination of evidence for the purpose of providing an independent assessment on governance, risk management and control processes for the organisation.

Assurance can come from a variety of sources, with the number and complexity of these sources changing as the organisation grows. This is particularly the case given the consistency of technological change affecting many industry sectors. This variety provides an often overwhelming source of information regarding assurance over a wide range of different risks and issues leading management to believe that risks are controlled effectively when that may not be the case.

The key reasons for this are:

- assurances are frequently un-coordinated, resulting in insufficient or inferior information

- some of the assurances provided may not be relevant leading to inappropriate reliance on the processes we adopt.

As technological change facilitates better monitoring of risks and the development of controls, there is a greater necessity to ensure that the assurance provided must also reflect this change. In that context, assurance maps are designed to help businesses overcome these weaknesses and add value to the process.

What is an assurance map?

An assurance map is a structured means of identifying and mapping the main sources and types of assurance in an organisation across the four lines of defence (see later for detailed explanation), and coordinating them to best effect. While good risk management practices will help an organisation to identify and focus on major risks, good governance requires effective management and mitigation of those risks.

An effective and efficient framework is therefore needed to give sufficient, continuous and reliable evidence of assurance on organisational stewardship, the management of major risks to organisational success and the delivery of improved, cost effective products and services. This is where the assurance map can play a significant role.

An assurance map shows:

- key elements over which assurance is required. This will change depending on the type and size of organisation

- the 'four lines of defence'. The details of who provides what can vary for each organisation

- any gaps where assurance is limited or not provided at all

Example of an assurance map:

	1st Line		2nd Line				3rd Line	4th Line	
	Control Framework	Management Review	Control Self Assessment	Risk and Compliance review	Group Legal	Board Review	Internal Audit	External Audits	other Third Party
Financial Reporting									
Financial Controls									
Legal									
IT									
Treasury									
Tax, Pension and insurance									
Human Resources									
Fraud									
Health & Safety									

KEY

High Assurance	Medium Assurance	Low Assurance	No assurance - but should be assurance in this area	Not Applicable

Further useful information can be added to enhance the assurance map depending on the circumstances facing the organisation e.g. the quality of assurance provider.

The **benefits** of assurance mapping:

- provides a basis on which to communicate with stakeholders and begin quality conversations.

- because there are benefits for each of the groups (or the four lines of defence) that may make use of the map. Together they should enable the board to make more reliable and robust reports to its stakeholders about the organisation's state of internal control.

- without an assurance map it is unlikely that the audit and risk committee will have access to a sufficiently well-structured analysis or assurance to enable them to evidence, safely, their satisfaction with the state of internal control.

- the assurance map will enable the members of the audit/risk committee to focus on those specific areas that remain a concern.

- senior management will have evidence to support its assertions as to the state of internal control in any public reports and as communicated to the external auditors and shareholders.

- the assurance-related work of the individuals operating within the four lines of defence can be best directed to avoid overlaps.

- enhanced communication as the benefits of assurance maps for stakeholders will be set out in any presentation designed to promote the concept to senior management.

The 'four lines of defence' model and benefits provided

By defining the sources of assurance in four broad categories (see risk assurance map above), the model helps users to understand how each contributes to the overall level of assurance provided and how best they can be integrated and mutually supportive.

First line: the way risks are managed and controlled day-to-day.

Benefit: Assurance comes directly from those responsible for delivering specific objectives or processes. It may lack independence but its value is that it comes from those who know the business, culture and day-to-day challenges.

Second line: the way the organisation oversees the control framework so that it operates effectively.

Benefit: The assurance provided is separate from those responsible for delivery, but not independent of the management chain, such as risk and compliance functions.

Third line: objective and independent assurance, e.g. internal audit

Benefit: Provides reasonable (not absolute) assurance of the overall effectiveness of governance, risk management and controls. The level and depth of assurance provided will depend on the size and focus of the internal audit function and management's appetite for internal audit assurance.

Fourth line: assurance from external independent bodies such as the external auditors and other external bodies.

Benefit: External bodies may not have the existing familiarity with the organisation that an internal audit function has, but they can bring a new and valuable perspective. In addition, their outsider status is clearly visible to third parties, so that they can not only be independent but be seen to be independent.

Each line of defence has a purpose and can provide robust assurance. There is no one line which provides better quality assurance than any of the others. A range of assurance activities from across all lines of defence will provide comprehensive coverage and add value to the overall assurance picture.

11   Chapter summary

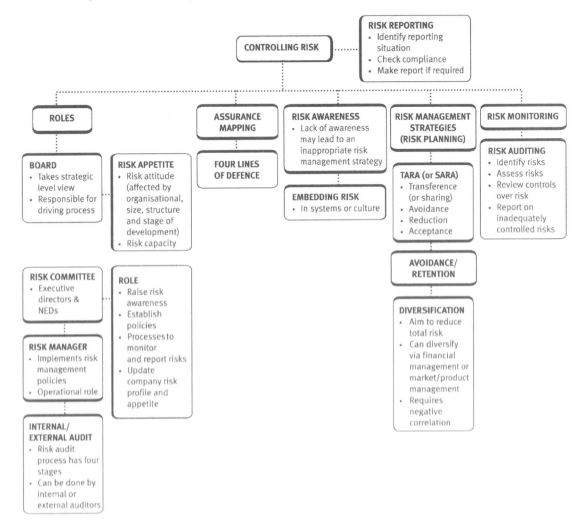

Test your understanding answers

Test your understanding 1

(a) **TARA model**

The TARA model of risk management assists decision makers in choosing the appropriate risk management option for different events and circumstances. There are four options, as explained below.

Transference

In this option, risk is transferred wholly or in part to a third party, so that if an adverse event occurs, the third party suffers all or most of the loss. A common example of risk transfer is insurance. All businesses arrange a wide range of insurance policies for protection against possible losses.

There is a risk that part or all of the outdoor tennis tournament is rained off (a 10% probability of rain suggests on average that one day's play each year will be lost because of rain). While TGB can accept the risk of 1 day being lost to rain and hopefully build contingencies into their time budgets for this, the risk of losing any more days must be guarded against. TGB is likely to take out insurance against this possibility. Insurance will be for loss of profit and possibly to repay customers for their tickets where more than two days' consecutive play is lost.

Avoidance

Another strategy for an organisation is to avoid a risk altogether. However, since many risks are unavoidable in business ventures, they can be avoided only by not investing (or withdrawing from the business area completely).

In terms of business probity, running a sporting event where it is almost certain that deaths and injury will occur does not appear to be acceptable. TGB may incur adverse publicity as a result of any accidents partly as the board knew these were likely to occur. Even if the event occurred, TGB will not be able to obtain insurance. Any claims for negligence, for example, would directly impact on TGB. Even though the event appears profitable, the best course of action appears to be not to run the event.

Reduction/mitigation

Another option is to reduce the risk, either by limiting exposure in a particular area or attempting to decrease the adverse effects should that risk actually occur.

For the curling championships, the best option for TGB appears to be to limit the risk in this area. Holding the championships in all 25 countries appears risky as demand is not known, and will involve TGB in additional costs. One option, therefore, is to hold the championships this year only in the colder countries where demand is higher.

Depending on the success this year, the feasibility of extending the championships in the following year can be assessed.

Acceptance

Finally, an organisation can simply accept that the risk may occur and decide to deal with the consequences in that particular situation. The strategy is appropriate normally where the adverse effect is minimal.

The skiing championships are threatened by global warming but the board considers the threat to be remote. While the loss of the championships could presumably be insured against, the premium is unclear and the likelihood of lack of snow, at least at present, is remote. The board's decision to do nothing is therefore correct. However, the situation should be monitored in the future and the need for insurance reviewed again as necessary.

(b) **Risk manager and risk committee**

Overview

The risk manager is a member of the risk committee. The manager reports to that committee as well as the board of directors. The risk committee will normally include board members as well as senior management. Where there is no risk committee then the audit committee will normally take on this role.

Risk awareness

The risk committee is responsible for raising risk awareness in a company and ensuring that there is appropriate risk management.

The risk manager is responsible for implementing any policies of risk awareness and reporting deficiencies in risk management to the board.

Monitoring risks

The risk committee will ensure that there are adequate and efficient processes in place in the company to identify, report and monitor risks. In this sense, the committee will be identifying risks and ensuring that the risks are dealt with effectively.

The risk manager will also be identifying risks and reporting those to the risk committee. The monitoring undertaken by the manager will be at a lower level to that of the committee. The manager is likely to be liaising with internal auditors to monitor the detailed implementation and review of risk mitigation strategies and internal audits of those strategies.

Company risk profile

The risk committee will be responsible for updating the company's risk profile as well as reporting to the board and making recommendations regarding the risk appetite of the company.

The risk manager will be advising the committee on the risk profile and risk appetite.

Operational/strategic

The risk committee has a strategic role in a company. They monitor the whole risk management process and make recommendations to the risk manager.

The risk manager implements the recommendations from the risk committee. In this sense the role is more operational than strategic as the manager is responsible for the detailed internal controls necessary to manage identified risks.

Risk management policy

The company's overall risk management policy is set by the board with the assistance of the risk committee.

The risk manager is then responsible for implementing that policy.

Best practice in risk management

The risk committee will ensure that the best practices in risk management are followed within the company. This means that changes to risk management strategies will be recommended where necessary.

The risk manager will provide reports to the committee on risk management practices obtained from detailed research. The manager will also monitor the external environment for new legislation and again inform the committee of this, recommending action where necessary.

Test your understanding 2

Arguments for and against diversification.

For:

- Reduces risks and enables company to give more predictable return to investors.

- Attracts investors who want low-risk investments.

Against:

- Management may not understand all the businesses that the company operates in – increases the risk.

- It is not necessary to diversify for investors – they can diversify themselves by investing in a number of different companies. A listed company is likely to have many institutional shareholders who will generally be fully diversified in their own investments.

- New business areas can attract risks, e.g. going into a new country may increase the risk of not understanding a company culture.

Test your understanding 3

Risk: Rights to operate

All terms and conditions of the rights to operate, which provide assurance that Azure is a going concern for the time-being, must be met. For example, twice-weekly flights may be a 'guaranteed' minimum.

Terms and conditions attached to the rights may threaten Azure's operational existence if, for example, there are any circumstances under which the rights could be withdrawn. For example, if the standard of service falls below a minimum specified level.

Management:

- Accept at the present level (as one that has to be borne) but, bear in mind (e.g. when making strategic decisions) the impact that management's actions could have on any renewal of the rights.

- Relevant terms and conditions should be communicated to all staff so they are clear about the importance of their areas of responsibility.

Risk: Competition

Although at the moment there appears to be none (as the rights are exclusive), any competition in the future could reduce profitability (e.g. if the rights were to become non-exclusive or an indirect service between Sepiana and Lyme should be established).

Management:

- Monitor the progress of applications for flights to destinations which could provide transit to Lyme.

- Reduce the risk by increasing the reliability and reputation of Azure's service, improving comfort, etc. (e.g. by increasing leg-room and air-conditioned lounges).

Risk: Age of aircraft

The age of the aircraft (35 years) is likely to have a bearing on fuel consumption and other costs (e.g. repairs and maintenance).

Management:

- Azure should manage its cash flows and borrowing capability (e.g. bank loan facility) to carry out ongoing operating repairs as and when needed.

Risk: Engine overhaul

If the lease is a finance lease it is likely that Azure will have to bear the costs of the overhaul – which may have a detrimental effect on cash flows.

The service would need to be suspended while the engine is being overhauled unless an alternative is planned for.

Management:

- As above, Azure should budget its financial resources to meet the costs of the overhaul, the timing of which can be planned for.

- The lease agreement with the airline should provide that an equivalent aircraft be available.

Risk: Leased asset

Azure operates with just one leased asset which may be withdrawn from service:

- in the interests of passenger safety (e.g. in the event of mechanical failure)

- for major overhaul

- if Azure defaults on the lease payments.

Management:

- Azure should enter into a contractual arrangement (e.g. may be included within the terms of an operating lease) for a replacement aircraft in the event that the aircraft be grounded.

- Azure should carry adequate insurance cover for remedying and/or providing compensation to customers for significant disruptions to the scheduled service.

Risk: Fuel prices

Increases in fuel prices (a major operational cost) will reduce profitability.

Management:

- Fuel surcharges should be included in the flights' price structure so that significant increases can be passed on to the customers.

- Hedging against the effect of energy price (and exchange rate) risks through forward contracts.

Risk: Weather

Weather conditions may delay or cancel flights. Actual and potential customers may choose not to plan trips if the flight schedule is so unreliable that they expect to face disruptions and uncertain journey times.

Management:

- Manage the impact of the risk/modify the business activity. For example, as any form of travel may be hazardous if weather conditions are so bad as to disrupt the flight schedule, there should be air-conditioned facilities in which travellers can relax before their journey.

Risk: Horticultural cargo

Certain produce may be prohibited from import (e.g. due to the risk of spread of disease). Azure may face fines for carrying banned produce.

Growers may seek to hold Azure liable for:

- produce which perishes (e.g. if successive flights are cancelled);

- impounded goods.

Management:

- Contracts with growers should clearly state items of produce that cannot be carried.

- Azure's operational controls should include verification checks on produce carried.

- Azure should have adequate insurance cover against claims for damaged/lost cargo.

Risk: Economy

With significantly less demand for Business Class than for Economy (which gets over-booked) and even less for First Class, the service is operating at well below capacity (economy is only 54% of seating capacity).

Azure may not be recouping fixed operating costs in the long run, making the service uneconomical.

Management:

- Keep demand for the classes of tickets under review and respond to the excess of supply over demand for Economy seating (and demand shortfall for First and Business Class seats). For example:

  - charge higher prices for economy on peak flights;

  - offer larger discounts for advance bookings on First and Business Class seats;

  - introduce a loyalty scheme for frequent users which offers 'preferred customer' seat upgrades.

Risk: Service levels

Azure's schedule is described as 'efficient and timely'. If the level of service delivered does not meet expectations it is unlikely that a regular customer base will be established.

Management:

- Azure should benchmark the timeliness of its service, against a comparable airline service operating under similar weather conditions.

Risk: On-board services

Passengers are expressing dissatisfaction with meals provided, especially on the 'return' flight from Darke. The food prepared in Lyme may be stale or contaminated by the time it is served.

Passengers may be deterred from using this flight if they are subject to the risk of illness.

Management:

Azure should consider:

- changing caterer in Lyme

- a contract with a caterer in Darke

- expert advice (e.g. of a chef) on preserving the quality of meals for long-haul flights.

Risk: Passenger safety

Penalties for non-compliance with safety regulations (e.g. maintenance checks on life jackets, etc.) may be incurred if inspection logs are not kept.

Azure may face lawsuits for personal injury or illness (e.g. deep vein thrombosis 'DVT').

Management:

- Staff training should be on-going with regular safety drill procedures (e.g. in evacuation procedures and the use of life-rafts).

- Safety procedures must be demonstrated before take-off on every flight and passengers referred to safety information, including how to reduce the risk of DVT, provided with each seat.

Risk: Air stewards/Cabin crew safety

Azure will have difficulty recruiting and maintaining the services of appropriately qualified cabin crew if it does not have sufficient regard for their health and safety.

Management:

Flight personnel rotas should ensure, for example, that:

- pilots take 'ground leave' between flights;

- there is adequate 'cover' when crew are sick or taking leave.

Risk: Emergency

A serious accident (e.g. fire), collision or breakdown may threaten operations in both the short and longer-term.

Management:

Accept at the present level, but taking all practicable safety checks now implemented in the airline industry to ensure that Azure is not exposed to preventable risks. For example:

- x-ray screening of checked-in baggage;

- security screening of cabin baggage and passengers, etc.

Risk: Flight personnel

Azure may not be able to service the flight in the event of non-supply of flight personnel by the international airline (e.g. due to strike action).

Management:

- The agreement with the airline should indemnify Azure for all costs and losses incurred if flights are cancelled due to non-availability of flight personnel.

Risk: Flight tickets

Tickets are sold by more than one party (Azure and travel agents) and at more than one location. Also, pricing is complex, with a range of tariffs depending on many factors. This increases the risk that:

- revenue may be lost if passengers are under-charged or ticket sales unrecorded; and

- flights may be over-booked, with consequent loss of customer goodwill.

The configuration of the aircraft does not currently meet the demand profile of passengers and under the terms of an operating lease may not be changeable.

Management:

- Strict controls must be exercised over:
    - unused tickets
    - ticket pricing
    - real-time reservations; and
    - ticket refund and exchange transactions.

- Commence negotiations with the international airline for an amendment to the current lease terms allowing flexibility in the seating arrangements.

Tutorial note: Candidates are not expected to have specific knowledge of the airline industry. However, marks will be awarded for relevant comments, for example, concerning quotas for landing/take-off slots and IATA's levy. The preceding answer is not exhaustive. For example, that the aircraft is flying for only 24 hours a week is a risk as this is a low capacity at which to operate for the recovery of overheads.

Professionalism, ethical codes and the public interest

Chapter learning objectives

Upon completion of this chapter you will be able to:

- critically evaluate the concept of responsible leadership and the creation of public value in the public interest

- assess management behaviour against the codes of ethics relevant to accounting professionals including the IESBA (IFAC) or professional body codes

- analyse the reasons for and resolve conflicts of interest and ethical conflicts in organisation

- assess the nature and impacts of different ethical threats and recommend appropriate safeguards to prevent or mitigate such threats

- recommend best practice for reducing and combating fraud, bribery and corruption to create greater public confidence and trust in organisations

PER

One of the PER performance objectives (PO 1) mean you should always act in the wider public interest. You need to take into account all relevant information and use professional judgement, your personal values and scepticism to evaluate data and make decisions. You should identify right from wrong and escalate anything of concern. You also need to make sure that your skills; knowledge and behaviour are up-to-date and allow you to be effective in your role. Working through this chapter should help you understand how to demonstrate that objective.

1 'Profession' versus 'professionalism'

 The terms profession and professionalism can be explained as follows:

- **Profession:** a body of theory and knowledge which is used to support the public interest.

- **Professionalism:** taking action to support the public interest.

Profession

A profession is distinguished by certain essential and defining characteristics:

Characteristic	Applicability to accounting profession
Body of theory and skills	• technical skills (such as auditing or accounting standards) • acquired by training and education • an examination system which ensures accountants obtain the knowledge required to act responsibly within their profession • maintained by continuing professional development (CPD).
Adherence to common code of values and conduct	• established by administrating body • maintains an objective outlook • ethical standards applicable to all members (such as ACCA's code of ethics, discussed in section 6 of this chapter).
Acceptance of a duty to society as a whole	• professions can be trusted to act in the public interest • in return members are granted a qualification and usage of a title (such as ACCA).

Professionalism

- Members are seen to be acting professionally, or literally having professionalism.

- Professionalism may also be interpreted more as a state of mind, while the profession provides the rules that members of that profession must follow.

- Professional behaviour imposes an obligation on members to comply with relevant laws and regulations and avoid any action that may bring discredit to the profession.

- Professional behaviour will mean complying with the ethical standards laid down by the professional body.

The accounting profession

- Over time, the profession appears to be taking more of a proactive, than a reactive, approach.

A reactive approach

Taking responsibility for any negative consequences of accounting practice and, where appropriate, amending those practices to remove those consequences.

Illustration 1 – A reactive approach

- Accounting practice failed to identify the risk that the Special Purpose Entities established by Enron to 'hide' its debts may not have actually been incorporated into Enron's main accounts.

- This may have contributed to the eventual downfall of Enron and the loss of pensions due to many Enron staff.

- The practice was removed by the requirement from the accounting profession to include this off balance sheet financing in the main accounts of companies.

- In this sense the accounting profession was reacting to a situation.

A proactive approach

Seeking out and positively contributing to the public interest.

Illustration 2 – A proactive approach

- The accounting profession recognises that guidance on how to carry out an environmental audit, or to accumulate appropriate metrics to include within an environmental audit, is not available.

- Guidance is provided 'in the public interest' as a benefit to society, rather than waiting until society as a whole requests the guidance.

2 The public interest

- The distinguishing mark of a profession is the acceptance of a responsibility to the public.

- The accountancy profession's public includes:

    - clients

    - credit providers

    - governments

    - employees

    - employers

    - investors.

What is 'the public interest'?

The public interest can be defined as that which supports the good of society as a whole (as opposed to what serves the interests of individual members of society or of specific sectional interest groups).

- For an accountant, acting in the public interest is acting for the collective well-being of the community of people and institutions that it serves.

- Public interest concerns the overall welfare of society as well as the sectional interest of the shareholders in a particular company. It is generally assumed, for example, that all professional actions, whether by medical, legal or accounting professionals, should be for the greater good rather than for sectional interest.

- Accounting has a large potential impact and so the public interest 'test' is important. In auditing and assurance, for example, the working of capital markets – and hence the value of tax revenues, pensions and investment – rests upon accountants' behaviour.

- In management accounting and financial management, the stability of business organisations – and hence the security of jobs and the supply of important products – also depends on the professional behaviour of accountants.

 Defining 'public interest'

There is much debate over a definition of the term 'public interest'. However, the public interest is normally seen to refer to the 'common wellbeing' or 'general welfare.'

An action is usually thought to be in the public interest where it benefits society in some way. It is unclear though how many members of society must benefit before the action can be declared to be in the public interest. Some people would argue an action has to benefit every single member of society in order to be truly in the public interest. At the other extreme, any action can be in the public interest as long as it benefits some of the population and harms none.

There is a potential clash between the public interest and the interests of society as a whole. In other words, what is good for society may not necessarily be good for individuals, and vice versa.

Public interest versus human rights

Acting in the public interest may seriously affect the idea of human rights, i.e. the degree to which members of society are allowed to act on their own. One view is that individuals should be free to act, as long as those actions do not harm other individuals.

The public interest and human rights will clash where:

- the action of an individual adversely harms other members of society, and

- actions of the state adversely affect some or all members of society.

For example, the action of an individual in injuring another member of society clearly affects the rights of the injured person. The state may legislate against injury, and remove rights from individuals involved in injuring others, e.g. imprison them. While this may be against the human rights of the person carrying out the injury, the overall public interest is served because society is a safer place.

Public interest and companies

The concept of public interest may affect the working of an organisation in a number of ways:

- The actions of a majority of the shareholders may adversely affect the minority shareholders. Protection of minority rights, in the public interest, may be required where the minority are denied certain rights such as access to dividends or decision-making processes.

- The actions of the organisation itself may be harmful to society, e.g. from excessive pollution or poor treatment of the labour force. The government may then decide, in the public interest, to limit the actions of that organisation for the greater good of society as a whole.

Public interest and legal cases

In law, public interest is a defence to certain lawsuits (e.g. some libel actions in the UK) and an exemption from certain laws or regulations (e.g. freedom of information laws in the UK).

Accountants and the public interest

- Accountants do not generally act against the public interest.

- The ethical code applicable to most accountants confirms that such action is not normally appropriate.

An area of particular relevance to accountants will be that of disclosure of information:

- The concept of acting in the public interest tends to apply to providing information that society as a whole should be aware of.

- In many cases 'public interest' disclosure is used to establish that disclosure is needed although there is no law to confirm this action.

- This can affect companies where they are acting against the public interest as disclosure may well be expected.

Disclose or not?

The accountant will need to evaluate each situation on its merits and then justify the outcome taken:

- In some situations lack of disclosure may be against the public interest.

- In other situations, disclosing information may be against the public interest, and such information should be kept confidential to avoid harm to society.

Acting in the public interest

The public interest can be defined as that which supports the good of society as a whole (as opposed to what serves the interests of individual members of society or of specific sectional interest groups). Acting against the public interest therefore means acting against the good of society as a whole, or alternatively serving the interests of individual members of society or interest groups rather than society as a whole.

Acting in the public interest can also be applied to the provision of information about accounting or the actions of organisations or other institutions. Acting against the public interest therefore implies that information is not being made available by accountants to the public when that information should be made available. Similarly, there may be situations when disclosure would not be in the public interest, i.e. information should be kept confidential to avoid harm to society.

Public interest disclosure of information is expected within the ethical guidance provided by most accountancy bodies. Taking action against the public interest is not therefore something that accountants contemplate lightly.

Test your understanding 1

Provide examples of situations where:

- Disclosure of information could be seen as acting in the public interest.

- Lack of disclosure of the information could be seen as acting in the public interest.

Responsible leadership

The dynamic and complex nature of the business world, a variety of lifestyles and beliefs about what is right or wrong, as well as differing legal regulations make the task of leading organisations in both the private and public sector responsibly in a global economy difficult, complex, and uncertain.

Challenges such as global warming, rising inequality, global migration, and poverty, put not only pressure on governments and international organisations, but also on business firms to contribute to a sustainable future for stakeholders and the planet. As a consequence, those in leadership positions find themselves increasingly facing demands to assume responsibility, not only toward shareholders but also toward wider stakeholder groups such as society and the environment.

Stakeholders, including NGOs now desire transparency of business conduct as well as socially and ecologically responsible decisions from business leaders. The notion of responsibility and responsible leadership is clearly an important one for a firm operating in the 21st century, but unlike other more traditional aspects of business, responsibility raises many questions for which the answers are not always simple.

One reason for this is that the concept of responsibility is difficult to define. While responsibility can and should permeate through the whole entity and should underpin and influence every business action, it runs the risk of being perceived as something that is difficult to grasp and less concrete than other aspects of doing business. As a result of this and because of the far-reaching nature of responsibility and responsible leadership, business leaders often find themselves faced with an initial and key challenge: how to define what responsible leadership really is.

In a very basic sense, responsible leadership can be defined as the management of a business entity's interactions with society aimed at addressing the entity's various stakeholder concerns and contributing to the multiple bottom lines of economic, social, and environmental performance.

The leader is thereby the one who enables and moderates interactions with the various stakeholders of the company.

Research amongst managers facing these challenges revealed common themes. These themes also reflect what academics consider responsible leadership to be in today's globalised business environment.

Recent research has identified the following attributes for leaders that are important to demonstrate responsible leadership.

- **The ability to make informed ethical judgments;** about existing norms and rules, especially when overseeing global business operations, where leaders face a diversity of rules and regulations, have to engage with various cultural norms and operate in contexts where there might be insufficient legal guidance. Here responsible leaders should be able to critically question norms of business conduct they deem wrong.

- **Displaying moral courage and aspiring to positive change;** responsibility within a company should mean helping to remedy injustice internally and externally. The aim is therefore not only to do the best for the firm but also to aspire to be a general force for good that generates positive change.

- **A business leader requires a forward-looking rather than a backward-looking responsibility orientation;** rather than basing responsibility on the retroactive logic of holding accountable those who have already performed an unethical act, forward-looking business leaders make proactive efforts to prevent such accidents and scandals.

- **Engaging in long-term thinking and in perspective-taking;** anticipating the consequences of their decisions, orientating their thinking to the long-term and considering the potentially negative impact carrying out their business can have on people, society, and the planet

- **Communicating effectively with stakeholders;** while total transparency is perhaps not possible, responsible leaders should try to foster healthy relations with those who can affect or be affected by their business decisions (stakeholders). Responsibility brings with it the recognition of wider stakeholder groups such as employees, unions, local communities, NGOs, professional bodies, and the like. Establishing channels of communication with all these stakeholders is a first step that must then be followed by a clear and coordinated plan that allows these channels to inform each group of the firm's progress and, at the same time, enables the firm to incorporate the responses of stakeholders into its decision making processes

- **Participating in collective problem-solving;** there is usually not a single person or entity who is responsible for creating the unethical, irresponsible, or unsustainable conditions in global business. Responsible leadership offers the possibility of uncovering mutually beneficial solutions for all stakeholders engaged in the problem-solving process.

Benefits of Responsible Leadership

- A firm's sense of collective strength can be enhanced as can its image and reputation. The business leaders of today must accept that what may have previously been viewed by many as a fad is now a necessary and desirable change in business culture.

- Responsible leadership can contribute to solving pressing problems of our time, like the problem of how to integrate foreign workers into the workforce in countries where the tolerance for other cultures and other ways of living is diminishing.

- It might also be a relevant counterbalance in what appears to be an age of emerging populism. In such an environment, where discussions are no longer based on facts and reason but on sentiments, responsible leaders are required who can steer these discussions toward a more rational exchange of ideas.

- The values that members of the organisation want to endorse, must be considered alongside those of the members of the community in which the organisation is doing business, in order to work to solve problems collectively.

3 Accountants' role and influence

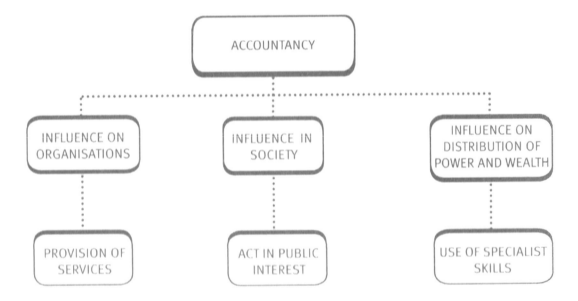

Influence on organisations

- The influence of the accountancy profession on organisations is potentially very significant.

- This is largely due to the range of services that accountants can provide, including:

    - financial accounting

    - audit

    - management accounting

    - taxation advice

    - consultancy.

Limitations on influence

The influence of accountants is limited regarding ethical and other areas by the following factors:

- the extent of organisational reporting, particularly with regards to organisations in financial difficulties

- conflicts of interest in selling additional services

- long-term relationship with clients

- overall size of accountancy firms

- focus on growth and profit.

Limitations on influence on organisations

Accountants provide various services to organisations, audit being one of the most significant.

- Provision of services can result in various ethical challenges for the accountant.

- While the profession may be seen as influential in terms of setting standards for audit and regulating its members, there are still difficulties in actually providing those services.

Auditing organisations in difficulties

One role of auditors is to check whether an organisation is preparing accounts that show a true and fair view.

- If that organisation is in financial difficulties, then the auditor needs to ensure that the accounts do not show too favourable a picture of that organisation.

- Reporting adversely on the accounts may have the effect of pushing the organisation into insolvency.

- Conversely, keeping quiet about difficulties may have the effect of auditors being adversely criticised should the organisation go into insolvency in any event.

- Other clients may lose confidence and ultimately change auditors if the auditor reports adversely on a company.

- Deciding on the appropriate report can be difficult and in effect involves a judgement between the public interest of society to be informed about the organisation and allowing the organisation time to resolve its difficulties.

Selling of additional services

Audit firms obtain a significant amount of knowledge about their clients as well as attracting staff with specialist skills in finance, systems, consultancy, etc.

- It is logical that accountancy firms provide additional services to the client over and above the audit, as the firm is in an excellent position to provide those services.

- Providing additional services may undermine the position of independence of the auditor – with the accountancy firm becoming too dependent on the organisation in terms of fees from other sources (for example Arthur Andersen and Enron).

- In terms of society as a whole it is cost-beneficial for the auditor to provide additional services, but the lack of independence implies that those services should be provided by another firm.

Relationships with clients

Accountancy firms provide relatively personal and confidential services to their accounting and audit clients.

- The firm and the organisation may favour longer-term relationships as this limits the costs in terms of information transfer, and the number of people privy to that confidential information.

- Long-term relationships may cause the auditing firm to be too familiar with the organisation, and therefore lose independence in terms of making adverse audit reports on their clients.

- Public interest is therefore not served by the longer-term arrangement.

- Many countries do limit the length of time an audit partner can provide services to a specific client (e.g. five years in the US and seven years in the UK) to mitigate this risk.

Size of accountancy firms

Provision of audit services by large firms can be argued to be in the public interest because a larger firm gains economies of scale.

- Costs are reduced in terms of staff training and the implementation and standardisation of auditing procedures.

- Large firms can affect individuals adversely in terms of loss of personal service and responsibility for tasks carried out.

- The actual quality of service may fall due to this distancing effect of bureaucracy.

- Conversely, it can be argued that large firms are essential because it is only these firms that can effectively audit multinational companies.

Competition

The 'big 4' auditing firms are competitive, which could imply cutting costs in an attempt to increase market share.

- This would not be in the public interest as it can be argued that the standard of audits will fall. However, it is not in the interests of audit firms themselves to provide poor quality audits. The possibility of legal action for negligence serves to limit cost cutting.

Influence in society

Accountancy can be seen as a profession involved with accountability.

- It is seen, at least by accountants, as being able to act in the public interest.

- Although the profession has the skills and knowledge to assist in the development of new initiatives, it may not be trusted fully due to past failings.

- Barriers exist with the accountancy profession that lead to accountants avoiding change and maintaining the status quo.

- But, the accountancy profession does have the knowledge to become involved in new initiatives.

  - an example of new public interest work is CSR reporting.

Accountancy and society

Accountancy can be seen as a profession involved with accountability. The accountant's role in society is largely one of working for and defending the public interest. However, this does not automatically mean that accountants will be seeking new methods of fulfilling this role. The profession of accountancy has various 'barriers' which imply accountants are more comfortable with existing, rather than applying new, structures.

Why accountants tend to enjoy the 'status quo'

Reasons why accountants may not become involved in new initiatives include:

- The nature of accounting itself – accountants tend to be rule followers rather than makers. Accountancy education is geared towards explaining and implementing rules of accountancy and not necessarily querying or finding fault with those rules.

- Accountants tend to be very busy people and therefore have little time to be involved in newer areas/do not need additional tasks to fill an already hectic social and professional life.

- Many accountants are employed by organisations, meaning that their freedom of action is constrained by the expectations of their employing organisation. In other words, where activities are not value-added in terms of what the organisation expects, then accountants may well be discouraged from undertaking those activities.

- Accountants enjoy a reputation of being impartial. Being involved in a new initiative may break that impartiality.

- A minority of accountants are also responsible for many of the excesses and inappropriate acts of many organisations (take Enron as a basic example). Overall, this may imply a lack of trust of accountancy as a profession and specifically a lack of ability of accountants to develop new/ethical standards.

Why accountants may become involved in change

However, it is appropriate for accountants to be involved in new initiatives for the following reasons:

- Many new initiatives involve or require the design and management of information systems and the collection and verification of data by those systems. These are some of the key skills of accountants.

- In many situations, the accountant does not have to be an expert in any specific field. Accountancy training per se equips the accountant with a range of generic skills which can be applied to any situation. As long as system design/reporting requirements are understood, then accountants will be able to apply that training to the specific area in question.

- Any new initiative is likely to have some financial impact, whether that be in pure accounting terms or regarding value for money or investment appraisal. Accountants obviously have the relevant skills in these areas.

- New initiatives are also business opportunities for accountants. Money remains a strong motivator meaning that if the opportunity is profitable, then accountants will want to be involved.

Other reasons for involvement of accountants in new initiatives include:

- Accountancy normally purports to be a profession with a commitment to the public interest. Any developments in accountability are in the public interest and will therefore involve accountants.

- Where existing or previous accounting systems have developed errors (e.g. off balance sheet financing) then accountants will have the skill and knowledge to understand those errors and develop revised systems to overcome them.

Illustration 3 – An unusual approach to tax advice

A major tax consultancy has been seen to be adopting a surprising approach to the tax advice and assistance it provides for its clients.

Traditionally it would be expected that the purpose of utilising the services of a tax specialist would be to enable an organisation to fully exploit the tax allowances permitted to it, and to seek any 'loopholes' that may enable it to reduce its final tax bill.

The consultancy in question has recently started to propose an alternative view: a major organisation making significant profits can afford to pay taxes to the government of the country. Those taxes can be used to benefit the wider society.

Hence, rather than spending money on consultancy fees to find tax loopholes the organisation would be better advised to adopt a more socially responsible stance and, potentially, pay a little more tax than necessary for the good of society.

Influence on power and wealth distribution

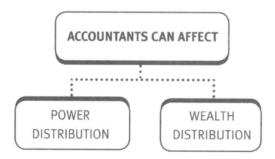

- Accountants have specialist skills and knowledge which can be used in the public interest.

- Society may have the objective of obtaining a more equal distribution of power and wealth.

- Given their abilities, accountants can probably advise on how that power and wealth can be distributed.

Distribution of power and wealth

Accountants may be able to influence the distribution of power and wealth in society in the following ways:

- Ensuring that organisations comply with legislation regarding payment and disclosure of directors' emoluments. If emoluments are fully disclosed then directors may be less inclined to pay large incentives or bonuses as the public may react unfavourably to them and their organisation.

- Advising the government on different tax regimes that may appear to be more equitable than others (e.g. a 'negative' income tax providing tax rebates to those on lower salaries).

- Advising on the contents of Companies Acts, e.g. in the UK where a new Act contains provisions for the protection of creditors and employees.

- Whistleblowing on the illegal actions of company officials.

This list is obviously incomplete!

Accounting (rather than accountants) in its basic form (i.e. the reporting of numbers) tends to serve the interests of capital and therefore capitalism. A set of accounts provides information to shareholders on the performance of their company. Accounts are therefore an indication of how 'rich' the shareholders or capitalists are.

Accountants (and primarily auditors) therefore serve capitalists because they simply check that accounts follow the appropriate rules. A criticism of accountants can be that they simply follow the rules and rarely check the relevance or appropriateness of those rules.

Accountants working within business can support capitalism in numerous ways. For example, the finance director providing advice on how to increase profit margins or the internal auditor putting in place controls to ensure cost efficiencies.

4   Corporate Code of Ethics

Corporate ethics relates to the application of ethical values to business behaviour.

- It encompasses many areas ranging from board strategies to how companies negotiate with their suppliers.

- It goes beyond legal requirements and is to some extent therefore discretionary.

- Many companies provide details of their ethical approach in a corporate and social responsibility (CSR) report.

- Key areas included in a code of corporate ethics:

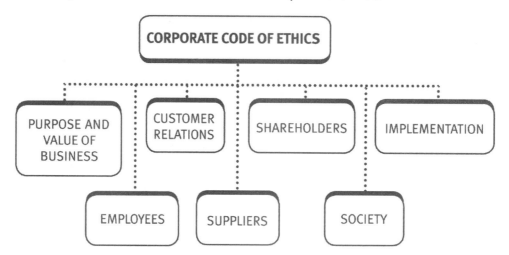

Areas covered by Corporate Ethics

Key area	Explanation
The purpose and values of the business	This provides the reason for the organisation's existence. Key areas in the purpose or mission statement of the company will include: the products or services to be provided, the financial objectives of the company, and the role of the business in society as seen by the company itself.
Employees	There must be information on how the business relates to its employees. Employees have rights and they must not be seen simply as a means of producing goods/services. The company will therefore have policies on: • working conditions • recruitment • development and training • rewards • health, safety and security • equal opportunities • retirement • redundancy • discrimination • use of company assets by employees, and • any other areas required by statute or thought appropriate by the company.
Customer relations	The company has a responsibility to produce quality goods/services for customers at a reasonable price (taking into account the fact that the company needs to make some profit). Customer faith in the company and its products must be established and built up over time. Key areas for the company to invest in include: • product quality • fair pricing • after sales service.

Shareholders or other providers of money	Shareholders are investors in the company – they therefore expect an appropriate and proper return on the money they have invested. The company therefore must commit to: <ul><li>providing a proper return on shareholder investment</li><li>providing timely and accurate information to shareholders on the company's historical achievements and future prospects.</li></ul> Shareholders will normally be involved to a greater or lesser extent with the decision making in the company under the principles of good corporate governance.
Suppliers	Suppliers provide goods and services for a company. They will usually attempt to provide those goods and services to an appropriate quality in a timely fashion. The company will therefore normally: <ul><li>attempt to settle invoices promptly</li><li>co-operate with suppliers to maintain and improve the quality of inputs</li><li>not use or accept bribery or excess hospitality as a means of securing contracts with suppliers</li><li>attempt to select suppliers based on some ethical criteria such as support of 'fair trade' principles or not using child labour in manufacture.</li></ul>
Society or the wider community	The company is located within society, which implies some social and corporate responsibility to that society. Many companies produce a CSR report as a means of communicating this relationship to third parties. Explained in the CSR report will be features of the company's activities including: <ul><li>how it complies with the law</li><li>obligations to protect, preserve and improve the environment</li><li>involvement in local affairs, including specific staff involvement</li><li>policy on donations to educational and charitable institutions</li></ul>

Implementation	The process by which the code is finally issued and then used. Implementation will also include some form of review function so the code is revisited on an annual basis and updated as necessary.

5 Corporate and professional codes

Purpose of corporate and professional codes

The presence of a code may assist in resolving an ethical dilemma.

Benefits of a code	Drawbacks of a code
• Provides framework for conflict resolution.	• Is a code only – therefore may not fit the precise ethical issue.
• Provides guidelines for similar ethical disputes and methods of resolution.	• As a code, it can be interpreted in different ways – two different conflicting actions may appear to be ethically correct to two different people.
• Provides the 'boundaries' across which it is ethically incorrect to pass.	• Punishment for breaching the code may either be unclear or ineffective.

NB Although the code has many drawbacks, the benefit of a principles-based approach is to adopt the spirit of the code in line with the general principles.

Therefore even though not every outcome is or can be covered, the general principles are.

Effectiveness of corporate and professional codes

The effectiveness of the code will be limited due to factors such as:

- the code can be imposed without communication to explain what it is trying to achieved; this will only lead to resentment, particularly amongst employees
- some codes are written, launched and then forgotten as it is now 'in place'. Unless there are reminders that the code is there, then it will not be effective in promoting ethical decision making
- codes that are implemented, and then breached by senior management without apparent penalty are not going to be followed by more junior staff.

To be effective, the code must have:

- participation from all groups as the code is formed (to encourage 'buy-in')
- disciplinary actions for breach of the code
- publicity of breaches and actions taken, as this is effective in promoting others to follow the code
- communication and support from top-down to ensure that the code is embedded into company culture.

6   Professional code of ethics

Content

Professional codes of ethics are issued by most professional bodies; the ACCA code was revised and reissued in 2006.

- The main reason for professional codes of ethics is to ensure that members/students observe proper standards of professional conduct (as discussed in section 1 of this chapter).

- Members and students will therefore refrain from misconduct and not make any serious departure from the ethical code.

- If the standards are not observed, then disciplinary action may be taken.

- Maintenance of a professional code of ethics helps the accountancy profession to act in the public interest by providing appropriate regulation of members.

Content of a professional code of ethics

The following are usually included:

Introduction	Provides the background to the code, stating who it affects, how the code is enforced and outlines disciplinary proceedings.
Fundamental principles	The key principles that must be followed by all members/students of the Association. The principles may be stated in summary format.
Conceptual framework	Explains how the principles are actually applied, recognising that the principles cannot cover all situations and so the 'spirit' of the principles must be complied with.
Detailed application	Examples of how the principles are applied in specific situations.

Principles

Behind a professional code of ethics, there are underpinning principles, the main ones being:

- integrity
- objectivity
- professional competence
- confidentiality, and
- professional behaviour.

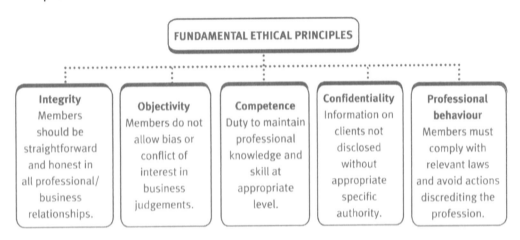

Fundamental ethical principles are obligations (or responsibilities) placed on members of a professional institute.

- Principles apply to all members, whether or not they are in practice.
- The conceptual framework provides guidance on how the principles are applied.
- The framework also helps identify threats to compliance with the principles and then applies safeguards to eliminate or reduce those threats to acceptable levels.
- Five fundamental principles (taken from the ACCA code of conduct) are shown above.

Fundamental ethical principles

Integrity

Integrity implies fair dealing and truthfulness.

Members are also required not to be associated with any form of communication or report where the information is considered to be:

- materially false or to contain misleading statements

- provided recklessly

- incomplete such that the report or communication becomes misleading by this omission.

Objectivity

Accountants need to ensure that their business/professional judgement is not compromised because of bias or conflict of interest.

However, there are many situations where objectivity can be compromised, so a full list cannot be provided. Accountants are warned to always ensure that their objectivity is intact in any business/professional relationship.

Professional competence and due care

There are two main considerations under this heading:

1   Accountants are required to have the necessary professional knowledge and skill to carry out work for clients.

2   Accountants must follow applicable technical and professional standards when providing professional services.

Appropriate levels of professional competence must first be attained and then maintained. Maintenance implies keeping up to date with business and professional developments, and in many institutes completion of an annual return confirming that continued professional development (CPD) requirements have been met.

Where provision of a professional service has inherent limitations (e.g. reliance on client information) then the client must be made aware of this.

Confidentiality

The principle of confidentiality implies two key considerations for accountants:

1   Information obtained in a business relationship is not disclosed outside the firm unless there is a proper and specific authority or unless there is a professional right or duty to disclose.

2   Confidential information acquired during the provision of professional services is not used to personal advantage.

The need to maintain confidentiality is normally extended to cover the accountants' social environment, information about prospective clients and employers, and where business relationships have terminated. Basically there must always be a reason for disclosure before confidential information is provided to a third party.

The main reasons for disclosure are when it is:

1   permitted by law and authorised by the client

2   required by law, e.g. during legal proceedings or disclosing information regarding infringements of law

3   there is professional duty or right to disclose (when not barred by law), e.g. provision of information to the professional institute or compliance with ethical requirements.

Ethical considerations on disclosure

The accountant needs to consider the extent to which third parties may be adversely affected by any disclosure.

The amount of uncertainty inherent in the situation may affect the extent of disclosure – more uncertainty may mean disclosure is limited or not made at all.

The accountant needs to ensure that disclosure is made to the correct person or persons.

Professional behaviour

Accountants must comply with all relevant laws and regulations.

There is also a test whereby actions suggested by a third party which would bring discredit to the profession should also be avoided.

An accountant is required to treat all people contacted in a professional capacity with courtesy and consideration. Similarly, any marketing activities should not bring the profession into disrepute.

Test your understanding 2

Explain why each of the following actions appears to be in conflict with fundamental ethical principles.

1   An advertisement for a firm of accountants states that their audit services are cheaper and more comprehensive than a rival firm.

2   An accountant prepares a set of accounts prior to undertaking the audit of those accounts.

3   A director discusses an impending share issue with colleagues at a golf club dinner.

4   The finance director attempts to complete the company's taxation computation following the acquisition of some foreign subsidiaries.

5   A financial accountant confirms that a report on his company is correct, even though the report omits to mention some important liabilities.

7 Conflicts of interest and ethical threats

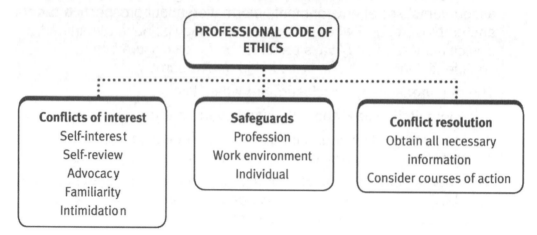

Conflicts of interest and their resolution are explained in the conceptual framework to the code of ethics.

- A framework is needed because it is impossible to define every situation where threats to fundamental principles may occur or the mitigating action required.

- Different assignments may also create different threats and mitigating actions – again it is not possible to detail all the assignments an accountant undertakes.

- The framework helps to identify threats – using the fundamental principles as guidance.

- This approach is preferable to following a set of rules – which may not be applicable (see later in this chapter).

- Once a material threat has been identified, mitigating activities will be performed to ensure that compliance with fundamental principles is not compromised.

- Where conflicts arise in the application of fundamental principles, the code of ethics provides guidance on how to resolve the conflict.

Conflicts of interest

The potential threats which may lead to conflicts of interest and lack of independence were discussed in detail in the audit and compliance chapter. These are:

- self-interest
- self-review
- advocacy
- familiarity
- intimidation.

A threat to independence is any matter, real or perceived, that implies the accountant is not providing an independent view or report in a specific situation.

- An accountant needs to be independent so others can place reliance on his/her work.

- Lack of independence implies bias, meaning less reliance would be placed.

Threats to independence	
Threat to independence	**Possible effect on ethical behaviour**
Financial interests – an accountant holds shares in a client company.	Conflict between wanting a dividend from the shareholding and reporting the financial results of the company correctly. May want to hide liabilities or overstate assets to improve dividends. **(Self-interest threat)**
Financial interests – an auditor holds shares in a client company.	Conflict between wanting a dividend from the shareholding and providing an honest audit report on the entity. May want to hide errors found in the financial statements to avoid qualifying the audit report and potentially decreasing the dividend payment. **(Self-interest threat)**
Close family member has an interest in the assurance client.	**Self-interest threat.** May decide not to qualify the audit report to ensure that the financial interests of the family member are not compromised. May also be an **intimidation threat** – if an employee, the assurance client may threaten to sack the family member if a qualified audit report is produced.
The assurance partner plays golf on a regular basis with the chairman of the board of the assurance client.	**Familiarity threat.** There may be a conflict between potential qualification of the company financial statements and losing the friendship/golf with the chairman.
Fee due from a client is old and the assurance firm is concerned about payment of that fee.	**Intimidation threat.** The client may threaten to default on the payment unless more work is carried out by the assurance firm. The assurance firm may also be seen to be supporting the client financially, implying that any report will be biased because the firm wants the 'loan' to be repaid.

A company offers an assurance partner an expensive car at a considerable discount.	Potential conflict because the partner may want the car, but also recognises the ethical threat of appearing to be bribed by the client. The partner may accept the car and not report this. **(Self-interest threat)**
A close family member is a director of a client company.	Potential conflict because an assurance partner would not want to qualify the audit report and create bad feeling between the partner and the director. The audit report may therefore not be qualified when it should be. **(Familiarity threat)**
An assurance partner serves as an officer on the board of an assurance client.	**Self-interest and self-review threats.** The partner would have a conflict between producing information for audit and then reporting on that information. The partner may either miss errors or even decide to ignore errors identified to avoid having to admit to mistakes being made.

8   Conceptual framework and safeguards

A conceptual framework can be explained as follows:

- It provides an initial set of assumptions, values and definitions which are agreed upon and shared by all those subject to the framework.

- It is stated in relatively general terms so it is easy to understand and communicate.

- It recognises that ethical issues may have no 'correct' answer and therefore provides the generalised guidelines and principles to apply to any situation.

Safeguards

Safeguards seek to reduce or eliminate threats. They fall into three categories created by the:

- **Profession**

  These include:

  - education and training including CPD requirements

  - setting of corporate governance regulations and professional standards

  - monitoring of professional work including disciplinary proceedings.

- **Work environment**

  There are many examples which include:

  - internal control systems

  - review procedures

  - disciplinary procedures

  - organisational codes of ethics

  - separate review and reporting for key engagements.

- **Individual**

  These include:

  - complying with professional standards

  - maintaining records of contentious issues

  - mentoring

  - contacting professional bodies with queries.

Ethical threats and safeguards

- An ethical threat is a situation where a person or corporation is tempted not to follow their code of ethics.

- An ethical safeguard provides guidance or a course of action which attempts to remove the ethical threat.

- Ethical threats apply to accountants – whether in practice or business.

- The safeguards to those threats vary depending on the specific threat.

- The professional accountant must always be aware that fundamental principles may be compromised and therefore look for methods of mitigating each threat as it is identified.

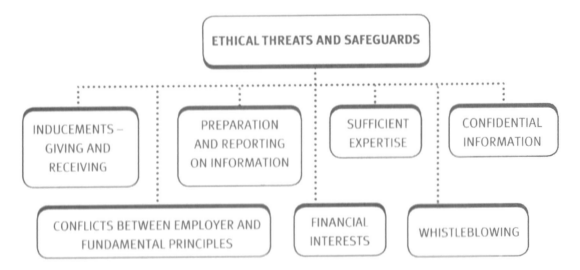

Ethical threats and safeguards

Ethical threat	Safeguard
Conflict between requirements of the employer and the fundamental principles. For example, acting contrary to laws or regulations or against professional or technical standards. (**Intimidation** threat)	• Obtaining advice from the employer, professional organisation or professional advisor. • The employer providing a formal dispute resolution process. • Legal advice.
Preparation and reporting on information Accountants need to prepare/report on information fairly, objectively and honestly. However, the accountant may be pressurised to provide misleading information. (**Intimidation** threat)	• Consultation with superiors in the employing company. • Consultation with those charged with governance. • Consultation with the relevant professional body.
Having sufficient expertise Accountants need to be honest in stating their level of expertise – and not mislead employers by implying they have more expertise than they actually possess. Threats that may result in lack of expertise include time pressure to carry out duties, being provided with inadequate information or having insufficient experience.	• Obtaining additional advice/training. • Negotiating more time for duties. • Obtaining assistance from someone with relevant expertise.
Financial interests Situations where an accountant or close family member has financial interests in the employing company. Examples include the accountant being paid a bonus based on the financial statement results which they are preparing, or holding share options in the company. (**Self-interest** threat)	• Remuneration being determined by other members of management. • Disclosure of relevant interests to those charged with governance. • Consultation with superiors or relevant professional body.

Inducements – receiving offers Refers to incentives being offered to encourage unethical behaviour. Inducements may include gifts, hospitality, preferential treatment or inappropriate appeals to loyalty. Objectivity and/or confidentiality may be threatened by such inducements. (**Self-interest** threat)	• Do not accept the inducement! • Inform relevant third parties such as senior management and professional association (normally after taking legal advice).
Inducements – giving offers Refers to accountants being pressurised to provide inducements to junior members of staff to influence a decision or obtain confidential information. (**Intimidation** threat)	• Do not offer the inducement! If necessary, follow the conflict resolution process outlined in the next section.
Confidential information Accountants should keep information about their employing company confidential unless there is a right or obligation to disclose, or they have received authorisation from the client. However, the accountant may be under pressure to disclose this information as a result of compliance with legal processes such as anti-money laundering/terrorism – in this situation there is a conflict between confidentiality and the need for disclosure.	• Disclose information in compliance with relevant statutory requirements, e.g. money laundering regulations.
Whistleblowing Situations where the accountant needs to consider disclosing information, where ethical rules have been broken by the client.	Follow the disclosure provisions of the employer, e.g. report to those responsible for governance. Otherwise disclosure should be based on assessment of: legal obligations, whether members of the public will be adversely affected, gravity of the matter, likelihood of repetition, reliability of the information, reasons why employer does not want to disclose.

9 Ethical dilemmas and conflict resolution

Rules- and principles-based approaches

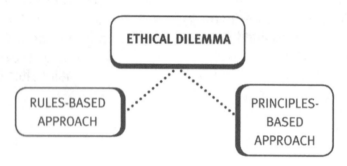

- Most professional institutes use a principles-based approach to resolving ethical dilemmas.

- Use of a rules-based approach is normally inappropriate as rules cannot cover every eventuality.

Rules and principles-based approaches	
Rules-based approach	**Principles-based approach**
1 Establish ethical rules that members must follow.	1 Establish fundamental ethical principles that members must follow.
2 Ensure members are aware of the rules.	2 Ensure members are aware of the principles.
3 Ensure members comply with those rules.	3 Require members to identify and address threats to compliance with the principles and make an appropriate response to mitigate each threat.

Rules-based approach

Benefits:

- Easy to check compliance as based on fact.

- Easy to amend rule set as required.

Disadvantages:

- The list of rules may not be complete.

- There is no room for individual decision making.

Principles-based approach

Benefits:

- Recognises that every threat cannot simply be 'listed'.

- Allows for subjective judgement, so the member can apply the principles in accordance with their specific situation and nature of the threat.

Disadvantages:

- In some situations it may be difficult to confirm that the compliance action was appropriate as two people may make different and valid decisions based on the same threat and circumstances.

These points can be related back to rules- and principles-based approaches to corporate governance, discussed in chapter 7.

 Ethical conflict resolution

Ethical conflicts can be resolved as follows:

1   Gather all relevant facts.

2   Establish ethical issues involved.

3   Refer to relevant fundamental principles.

4   Follow established internal procedures.

5   Investigate alternative courses of action.

6   Consult with appropriate persons within the firm.

7   Obtain advice from professional institute.

8   If the matter is still unresolved, consider withdrawing from the engagement team/assignment/role.

More will be seen in the following chapter on ethical decision making.

Ethical conflict resolution

```
                    ETHICAL CONFLICT
                      RESOLUTION

                          OBTAIN

  RELEVANT FACTS   ETHICAL ISSUES    RELEVANT      ESTABLISHED    ALTERNATIVE
                     INVOLVED       FUNDAMENTAL      INTERNAL      COURSES OF
                                    PRINCIPLES     PROCEDURES       ACTION

    CONSIDER                                                  CONSIDER CONSULTING
  CONSEQUENCES OF EACH   DECIDE COURSE OF ACTION              WITH THOSE CHARGED
  COURSE OF ACTION                                           WITH GOVERNANCE

                                                              CONSULT WITH
                        MATTER REMAINS UNRESOLVED          APPROPRIATE PERSONS IN
                                                                  FIRM

  OBTAIN ADVICE FROM
  PROFESSIONAL INSTITUTE    MATTER STILL UNRESOLVED

                                                          CONSIDER WITHDRAWING
                          MATTER STILL UNRESOLVED         FROM ENGAGEMENT TEAM/
                                                             ASSIGNMENT
```

Note that the diagram provides only one method of thinking through an ethical situation. Examination questions are more likely to ask for the factors that may be taken into consideration when making a decision, rather than following a global system. The diagram reminds you that there are many areas to take into account in ethical decision-making, but that the structure of making that decision may not always be this clear.

Test your understanding 3

Explain your response to the following ethical threats.

A   Your employer asks you to suggest to a junior manager that they will receive a large bonus for working overtime on a project to hide liabilities from the financial statements.

B   In selecting employees for a new division, you are advised to unfairly discriminate against one section of the workforce.

C   You have been asked to prepare the management accounts for a subsidiary located in South America in accordance with specific requirements of that jurisdiction. In response to your comment that you do not understand the accounting requirements of that jurisdiction, your supervisor states 'no problem, no one will notice a few thousand dollars' error anyway'.

10   Corruption and Bribery

Introduction

Corruption is now recognised to be one of the world's greatest challenges.

For example, KPMG surveyed FTSE 100 companies in August 2009 and found that two thirds said it was not possible to do business in some countries without being involved in bribery and corruption, yet only 35 percent had stopped doing business there.

The World Bank has stated that "bribery has become a $1 trillion industry".

What is corruption?

Corruption is behaviour in relation to persons entrusted with responsibilities in the public or private sector which violates their duties and is aimed at obtaining undue advantages of any kind for themselves or for others.

The main forms of corruption, embezzlement, fraud and extortion.

Examples include but are not limited to

- Bribery, including excessive 'hospitality'

  Note: firms are allowed to provide hospitality, promotional or other business expenditure. For example, to provide tickets to sporting events, take clients to dinner, offer gifts to clients as a reflection of good relations, or pay for reasonable travel expenses in order to demonstrate goods or services to clients, if that is reasonable and proportionate for your business.

  However where hospitality is really a cover for bribing someone, the authorities would look at such things as the level of hospitality offered, the way in which it was provided and the level of influence the person receiving it had on the business decision in question.

- Facilitation payments

  Facilitation payments are additional payments to induce officials to perform routine functions they are otherwise obligated to perform. For example, additional payments to customs officials so they prioritise processing the import of your goods.

  The distinction between facilitation and bribery is not always clear. Some countries (e.g. the United Kingdom and Germany) criminalise facilitation payments abroad. Other countries, such as the United States, do not prohibit such payments abroad and have no upper limit for them, although only very low amounts of money would be regarded as facilitation payments rather than outright bribes.

  Note: you can pay for legally required administrative fees or fast-track services. These are not facilitation payments.

- Buying votes

- Illicit payments to political parties

- Misappropriation of public funds.

Why corruption is wrong – the ethical argument

Corruption is inherently wrong:

- It is a misuse of power and position and has a disproportionate impact on the poor and disadvantaged.

- It undermines the integrity of all involved and damages the fabric of the organizations to which they belong.

The reality that laws making corrupt practices criminal may not always be enforced is no justification for accepting corrupt practices. To fight corruption in all its forms is simply the right thing to do.

Why corruption is wrong – the business argument

There are many reasons why it is in any company's business interest to ensure that it does not engage in corrupt practices:

- **Legal risks**

  Regardless of what form a corrupt transaction may take, there are obvious legal risks involved. Not only are most forms of corruption illegal where it occurs, but also it is increasingly becoming illegal in a company's home country to engage in corrupt practices in another country.

- **Reputational risks**

  Based on the experience of recent years, companies whose policies and practices fail to meet high ethical standards, or that take a relaxed attitude to compliance with laws, are exposed to serious reputational risks. The argument that although what they may have done may have been against the law or international standards, it was simply the way business was done in a particular country is not an acceptable excuse. Nor is it good enough to claim that other companies and competitors have engaged in similar practices.

- **Financial costs**

  There is now clear evidence that in many countries corruption adds upwards of 10 per cent to the cost of doing business and that corruption adds as much as 25 per cent to the cost of public procurement. This undermines business performance and diverts public resources from legitimate sustainable development.

- **Pressure to repeat-offend**

  There is growing evidence that a company is less likely to be under pressure to pay bribes if it has not done so in the past. Once a bribe is paid, repeat demands are possible and the amounts demanded are likely to rise. Zero tolerance is the only practical solution.

- **Blackmail**

  By engaging in corrupt practices, company managers expose themselves to blackmail. Consequently the security of staff, plant and other assets are put at risk.

- **Impact on staff**

  If a company engages in or tolerates corrupt practice, it will soon be widely known, both internally and externally. Unethical behaviour erodes staff loyalty to the company and it can be difficult for staff to see why high standards should be applied within a company when it does not apply in the company's external relations. Internal trust and confidence is then eroded.

- **Impact on development**

  It is now clear that corruption has played a major part in undermining the world's social, economic and environmental development. Resources have been diverted to improper use and the quality of services and materials used for development seriously compromised.

  Business has a vested interest in social stability and in the economic growth of local communities. It has therefore suffered, albeit indirectly, from the impact of lost opportunities to extend markets and supply chains.

Relevant legislation

It is becoming increasingly illegal in a company's home country to engage in corrupt practices in another country.

- **The US Foreign and Corrupt Practices Act (1977)**

    The principle that it is illegal to bribe **foreign** officials was first established in the US Foreign and Corrupt Practices Act of 1977. This Act gives the Federal authorities power to prosecute companies who have almost any kind of US footprint, not just US firms.

- **The UN Convention against Corruption (2003)**

    Since then, this principle has gained legal standing within the whole of the OECD and in a number of other countries. It is a principle that was universally recognized in 2003, through the adoption of the UN Convention against Corruption.

- **The UK Bribery Act (2010)**

    More recently the UK Bribery Act 2010, which applies to all UK businesses, overseas businesses with some presence in the UK and UK registered businesses operating overseas, details four offences:

    - Offering, promising or giving a bribe.

    - Requesting, agreeing to receive or accepting a bribe.

    - Bribing a foreign public official.

    - A corporate offence of failing to prevent bribery.

    A commercial organisation is now liable for the activities of **associated third parties**. It will be guilty of an offence when one of them bribes another person with the intention of obtaining or retaining business, or a business, advantage for the organisation.

    Corporate ignorance of individual wrong-doing will provide no protection against prosecution.

    However, it is a defence if you can show that you had **adequate procedures** in place to prevent bribery.

Assessing risk exposure

Relevant factors to consider include:

- The particular country in which you want,

- The sector in which you are dealing,

- The value and duration of your project

- The kind of business you want to do

- The people you engage to do your business.

Evaluating anti-bribery and corruption (AB&C) procedures

As stated above, the UK Bribery Act means that many firms will now have to ensure that they have **adequate** procedures and controls to prevent bribery and corruption. Even for firms outside the jurisdiction of the UK Act, good corporate governance practices would suggest that firms should have adequate control procedures to reduce the risks associated with bribery and corruption.

The UK Act sets out six principles to help a business decide if they need to introduce changes.

1   **Proportionality**

Any action your business takes to introduce procedures only needs to be in proportion to the risks your business faces.

2   **Top-level commitment**

The Ministry of Justice (MoJ) advises that your business will need to show that it has been active in ensuring that staff and key business contacts understand that you do not tolerate bribery.

3   **Risk assessment**

This shows you have considered the possible risks you face as a company, especially if you are entering into new business arrangements.

4   **Communication**

Communicating your policies and procedures to staff and others who will perform services for you.

5   **Due Diligence**

Knowing who you are dealing with can help protect business – so it's advised that you do a few checks and ask a few questions before engaging others to represent you in business.

6   **Monitoring and review**

You may want to keep an eye on any anti-bribery steps you take so that they keep pace with any changes in the risks your business faces.

Examples of AB&C measures and procedures

Measures include

- improved reporting
- screening of staff and associates
- accounting policies e.g., high-level approval for certain categories of payments
- depth of audit
- clear and transparent procurement regulations
- controls on the setting of prices and discounts, and
- guidelines for handling major bids.

Other practical steps one can take to assess and mitigate risks include the following:

- Use simple internet searches to find out about the levels of corruption or bribery in the particular country you propose to do business in.

- Consult diplomatic posts for advice.

- Consult business representative bodies here and in the relevant country for up to date local knowledge.

- UK firms can use the Government-sponsored Business Anti-Corruption Portal aimed at small and medium sized businesses involved in overseas trade.

Barriers to implementing AB&C policies

A number of obstacles can be thrown up, or unwittingly created, when implementing AB&C policies:

- **Competitive advantage**

  The most obvious is the belief that new policies are a tedious and unnecessary chore, together with the fear that unscrupulous competitors will break any rule to win.

- **Managerial apathy**

  Chief executives and finance directors may argue that they deal with risks every day and do not need new systems to spot bribery and corruption.

- **Off-the-shelf solutions**

  Many firms implement policy and off-the-shelf procedures before (or in place of) assessing their own unique circumstances.

  For example, some companies operating in France have set up whistleblowing hotlines without realising that French law makes them potentially illegal.

- **Corporate structures**

  Decentralised organisations may have more complex issues to address, as do firms with far flung offices.

  For example, many firms with distant operations tend to focus on the needs of the centre, rather than the local operations, making it more difficult to ensure that your sales team in, say, China, is following policy. A silo mentality can also get in the way because people tend to compartmentalise risk – financial, operational etc. – rather than considering cross-cutting dangers.

- **"Shadow" hierarchies**

  The real dynamics of internal control are sometimes different from what appears on an organisational chart. Individual employees can wield power well beyond their formal spheres of responsibility. Shadow power networks not only facilitate bribery, they may have arisen in order to conceal it.

- **Excessive pressure to hit targets**

  Internal controls can become marginalised in a culture of immediate results.

- **Cultures of secrecy**

  Excessive sensitivity about disclosure can prevent one part of a business from learning about incidents that have occurred elsewhere. Secrecy always works to the advantage of the corrupt employee or associated party.

- **Heterogeneous cultures**

  Problems can occur where any staff do not share the values of the organisation. Such situations can arise from mergers and acquisitions, rapid expansion, poor training of new staff or from inadequate supervision of overseas offices.

The UN Global Compact

The UN Global Compact is a strategic policy initiative for businesses that are committed to aligning their operations and strategies with ten universally accepted principles in the areas of human rights, labour, environment and anti-corruption. By doing so, business, as a primary driver of globalization, can help ensure that markets, commerce, technology and finance advance in ways that benefit economies and societies everywhere.

On 24 June 2004, during the UN Global Compact Leaders Summit it was announced that the UN Global Compact henceforth includes a tenth principle against corruption:

Principle 10: "Businesses should work against corruption in all its forms, including extortion and bribery."

The UK Bribery Act 2010

Introduction

- When did it apply from?

  The UK Bribery Act 2010 became law on 1 July 2011.

- What is the purpose of the Act?

  Fighting business corruption by modernising the law on bribery and corruption.

- Who does it apply to?

  The act applies to all UK businesses, overseas businesses with some presence in the UK and UK registered businesses operating overseas.

Criminal liability

The legislation makes paying or receiving a bribe, bribing a foreign official and failing to prevent bribery at corporate level criminal offences.

Examples:

- If a senior person, like an MD, commits a bribery offence.

- If someone, like an employee or agent, pays a bribe in order to win business for the company, to retain it or to gain a business advantage.

The Act is unusual in that a business can be guilty of an offence if a rogue employee or associate commits an offence even if the management are not aware of or did not condone the unlawful behaviour. Because of this KPMG have described the Act as "one of the most draconian pieces of anti-bribery and corruption (AB&C) legislation in the world".

Defence

However, it is a defence to show that you had adequate procedures in place to prevent bribery. The Act thus forces firms to look at bribery and corruption as key business risks that need effective corporate governance and control systems to mitigate.

Potential punishments

The Act provides for unlimited fines.

An indication of the potential damage can be gleaned from the £2.25 million plus costs paid by Balfour Beatty in a civil action brought by the SFO (under older legislation) in 2008. This was despite prosecutors acknowledging there had been no financial benefit to any individual employee – and that the offence had taken place up to ten years before.

Test your understanding 4

A medium sized company ('A') has acquired a new customer in a foreign country ('B') where it operates through its agent company ('C').

Its bribery risk assessment has identified facilitation payments as a significant problem in securing reliable importation into B and transport to its new customer's manufacturing locations. These sometimes take the form of 'inspection fees' required before B's import inspectors will issue a certificate of inspection and thereby facilitate the clearance of goods.

Required:

Outline some action A could take with respect to these facilitation payments.

Test your understanding 5

A company ('L') exports a range of seed products to growers around the globe. Its representative travels to a foreign country ('M') to discuss with a local farming co-operative the possible supply of a new strain of wheat that is resistant to a disease which recently swept the region. In the meeting, the head of the co-operative tells L's representative about the problems which the relative unavailability of antiretroviral drugs cause locally in the face of a high HIV infection rate.

In a subsequent meeting with an official of M to discuss the approval of L's new wheat strain for import, the official suggests that L could pay for the necessary antiretroviral drugs and that this will be a very positive factor in the Government's consideration of the licence to import the new seed strain. In a further meeting, the same official states that L should donate money to a certain charity suggested by the official which, the official assures, will then take the necessary steps to purchase and distribute the drugs.

L identifies this as raising potential bribery risks.

Required:

Recommend steps L could take in this situation.

11 Ethical decision making

- Ethical decision making models are used in ethics education to provide a framework for ethical decision making.

- The main reference in this section is to the International Accounting Education Standards Board (IAESB) where a framework for ethical decision making is developed (known as the Ethics Education Framework (EEF)) and then applied using two models.

IAESB ethics framework

The IAESB Ethics Education Framework (EEF) shown above is designed to provide a structure for the development of ethical education. It recognises that ethics education is actually a lifelong process and will continue through the career of an accountant or any other professional. The framework establishes a four-stage learning continuum which professionals will generally move through during their careers.

This framework can then be applied to ethical decision-making using the two models.

	Stage	Explanation
1	Ethical knowledge	Education focuses on communicating fundamental ethical knowledge about professional values, ethics and attitudes. The aim is to develop ethical intelligence by obtaining knowledge of the different ethical concepts and theories relating to the accountant's work. This stage explains the fundamental theories and principles of ethics. Having obtained knowledge of these theories, the accountant will understand the ethical framework within which they operate.
2	Ethical sensitivity	This stage applies the basic ethical principles from stage 1 to the actual work of the accountant in the functional areas being worked on, e.g. auditing, taxation, consultancy, etc. The aim of this stage is to ensure that accountants can recognise ethical threats. The stage is developed by providing case studies and other learning aids to show how and where ethical threats can arise. In other words the accountant is sensitised to ethical issues, i.e. the areas where ethical threats appear can be identified.
3	Ethical judgement	This stage teaches the accountant how to integrate and apply ethical knowledge and sensitivity from stages 1 and 2 to form reasoned and hopefully well-informed decisions. This stage therefore aims at assisting accountants in deciding ethical priorities and being able to apply a well-founded process for making ethical decisions. It is taught by applying ethical decision- making models to ethical dilemmas, showing how ethical judgement is being applied.

4	Ethical behaviour	This stage is primarily concerned with explaining how an accountant should act ethically in all situations (i.e. not just the workplace but other situations where the profession of accountancy must be upheld).
		This stage therefore explains that ethical behaviour is more than believing in ethical principles; it also involves acting on those principles. In terms of lifelong education, the accountant must therefore continue to be aware of ethical theory, ethical threats and continually seek to judge actions in the light of expected ethical behaviour. Teaching is primarily through case studies.

12 Ethical behaviour

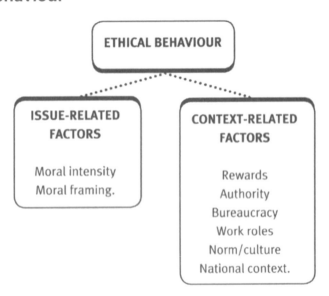

Accountants are normally expected to behave ethically. However, that behaviour also depends on:

- the nature of the ethical issue – issue-related factors, and

- the context in which the issue takes place – context-related factors.

Issue-related factors

- How important the decision is to the decision maker.

- The higher the intensity, the more likely it is that the decision maker will make an ethical rather than an unethical decision.

Moral Intensity/Moral Stance

The factors affecting moral intensity are shown below.

CONCENTRATION OF EFFECT

Whether effects of action are concentrated on a few people or affect many people a little.

E.g. concentration on a few increases intensity.

PROXIMITY

The nearness the decision maker feels to people affected by the decision.

E.g. being 'nearer' increases intensity.

TEMPORAL IMMEDIACY

How soon the consequences of any effect are likely to occur.

E.g. long time delay lowers intensity.

FACTORS AFFECTING MORAL INTENSITY/MORAL STANCE

MAGNITUDE OF CONSEQUENCE

Sum of the harms or benefits impacted by the problem or action.

E.g. financial loss caused by faulty advice.

SOCIAL CONSENSUS

Degree to which people agree over the ethics of a problem or action.

E.g. act deemed unethical by others.

PROBABILITY OF EFFECT

The likelihood that harms (or benefits) will actually happen.

E.g. higher probability = higher intensity.

Actions with higher intensity are noted for each factor.

Moral framing

This refers to the language in which moral issues are discussed in the workplace – a problem or dilemma can be made to appear inoffensive if described (or 'framed') in a certain way.

This may lead to people in different organisations perceiving the moral intensity differently.

- Where morals are discussed openly then decision making is likely to be more ethical.

- Use of moral words (e.g. integrity, honesty, lying and stealing) will normally provide a framework where decision making is ethical.

- However, many businesses use 'moral muteness' which means that morals are rarely discussed so ethical decision making may suffer.

Test your understanding 6

Explain the moral intensity of the following situations.

1   Your advice to a client regarding tax planning was incorrect, causing the client to lose several thousand dollars.

2   You read a newspaper report regarding poor working conditions in a remote country which indicates those conditions may cause cancer for 10% of the workers.

3   You falsify an expenses claim to include lunch for your spouse/partner because this is the normal behaviour for your work group.

Context-related factors

These factors relate to how a particular issue would be viewed within a certain context.

For example:

- If certain behaviours are seen to be rewarded, encouraged, or demanded by superiors despite being ethically dubious, decision making may be affected.

- If everyone in a workplace does something in a certain way, an individual is more likely to conform: this can result in both higher and lower standards of ethical behaviour.

Key contextual factors are:

- system of reward
- authority
- bureaucracy
- work roles
- organisational group norms and culture
- national and cultural context.

Contextual factors

Managers tend to reframe moral decisions into organisational or practical issues for one of three reasons:

1   **harmony** – belief that moral talk would promote confrontation and recrimination

2   **efficiency** – belief that moral talk could cloud issues making-decision making more time consuming

3   **image of power and effectiveness** – managers believe that their image will suffer if they are seen to be idealistic, i.e. making decisions for ethical reasons.

However, where the approach to moral dilemmas tends to the 'principles-based' then reframing moral decisions is inappropriate. There are no rules to follow, therefore ethics must be discussed and actions justified based on sound ethical judgement.

Factor	Effect on ethical decision making
Systems of reward	Where rewards are based on achievement (e.g. number of sales made) then ethical decision-making may be affected. Unethical decision making may also increase where unethical behaviour is unpunished or even supported by the organisation.
Authority	Junior managers tend to follow instructions from senior managers. Where senior managers make unethical decisions these are likely to be followed by juniors. Senior management may also promote a climate where unethical decision-making is accepted.
Bureaucracy	Bureaucracies tend to make employees follow rules rather than think about the ethics of decisions being made. More bureaucracy may therefore mean a lower level of ethical decision-making – although this depends on authority – see above.
Work roles	Managers tend to follow the 'work role' expected – hence an ethical role such as an accountant will normally find managers behaving ethically – because that is expected. In other roles where ethics are believed to be compromised regularly, managers will usually also behave less ethically.

Organisational group norms and culture	Managers tend to share the norms of the group they are in, so what may be described as unethical behaviour overall may be 'ethical' for the group.
	E.g. A group may decide that copying work-related software at home is 'ethical' and therefore all members of the group participate in this behaviour.
National and cultural context	Different countries or cultures will have different ethics. Whether a decision is ethically correct or not may therefore depend on the specific culture.

13 Chapter summary

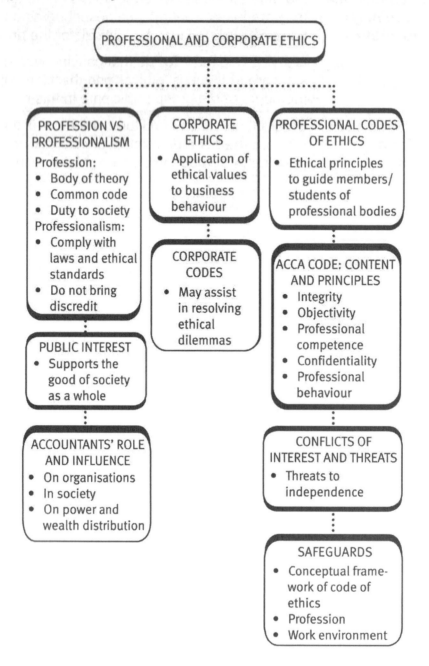

Test your understanding answers

 Test your understanding 1

(a) **Disclosure in the public interest:**

- Where a lack of disclosure would lead to lack of enforcement of appropriate laws.

    - This would mean a criminal could continue a crime such as money-laundering in breach of money-laundering regulations.

- Where a lack of disclosure would decrease accountability or limit decision making of the public.

    - Not providing information on illegal actions of companies (e.g. Enron) allows actions to continue to the long-term detriment of stakeholders.

- Where a lack of disclosure would impair the health and safety of the public.

    - Not disclosing information on potential contamination of land by an organisation.

    - Non-disclosure of this information would not be in the public interest as health and safety could be compromised.

(b) **Lack of disclosure in the public interest:**

- Where disclosure would adversely affect the economic interests of the jurisdiction in which the accountant is working.

    - Disclosing price sensitive information on a company's share price or details of interest rate movements before they had been authorised could harm businesses in the jurisdiction or the jurisdiction as a whole.

    - Disclosure would be inappropriate because the public interest would be harmed.

Test your understanding 2

1   Potential conflict with professional behaviour – audit services observe the same standards, therefore implying that a rival has lower standards suggests that a firm is not complying with professional standards.

2   The accountant is likely to lose objectivity because errors in the accounts made during preparation may not be identified when those accounts are reviewed.

3   As the information is likely to be confidential, discussing it in a public place is inappropriate.

4   The accountant needs to ensure that knowledge of the foreign country's taxation regime is understood prior to completing the return, otherwise there is the possibility that the appropriate professional skill will not be available.

5   There is an issue of integrity. The accountant should not allow the report to be released because it is known that the report is incorrect.

Test your understanding 3

Threat A

*   Do not offer the inducement!

*   If necessary, follow the conflict resolution process of the employer.

*   Consider the impact of the financial statements being misrepresented.

Threat B

*   Obtaining advice from the employer, professional organisation or professional advisor.

*   The employer providing a formal dispute resolution process.

*   Legal advice.

Threat C

*   Obtaining additional advice/training.

*   Negotiating more time for duties.

*   Obtaining assistance from someone with relevant expertise.

Test your understanding 4

Given that facilitation payments are normally viewed as examples of bribery and corruption, A should consider the following:

- Communication of its policy of non-payment of facilitation payments to C and its staff.

- Seeking advice on the law of B relating to certificates of inspection and fees for these to differentiate between properly payable fees and disguised requests for facilitation payments.

- Building realistic timescales into the planning of the project so that shipping, importation and delivery schedules allow where feasible for resisting and testing demands for facilitation payments.

- Requesting that C trains its staff about resisting demands for facilitation payments and the relevant local law and provisions of relevant legislation such as the UK Bribery Act 2010.

- Proposing or including as part of any contractual arrangement certain procedures for C and its staff, which may include one or more of the following, if appropriate:

    - questioning of legitimacy of demands

    - requesting receipts and identification details of the official making the demand

    - requests to consult with superior officials

    - trying to avoid paying 'inspection fees' (if not properly due) in cash and directly to an official

    - informing those demanding payments that compliance with the demand may mean that A (and possibly C) will commit an offence under A's domestic law

    - informing those demanding payments that it will be necessary for C to inform A's country's embassy of the demand.

- Maintaining close liaison with C so as to keep abreast of any local developments that may provide solutions and encouraging C to develop its own strategies based on local knowledge.

- Use of any diplomatic channels or participation in locally active nongovernmental organisations, so as to apply pressure on the authorities of B to take action to stop demands for facilitation payments.

Test your understanding 5

L could consider any or a combination of the following:

- Making reasonable efforts to conduct due diligence, including consultation with staff members and any business partners it has in country M in order to satisfy itself that the suggested arrangement is legitimate and in conformity with any relevant laws and codes applying to the foreign public official responsible for approving the product.

  It could do this by obtaining information on:

- M's local law on community benefits as part of Government procurement and, if no particular local law, the official status and legitimacy of the suggested arrangement.

- The particular charity in question including its legal status, its reputation in M, and whether it has conducted similar projects, and any connections the charity might have with the foreign official in question, if possible.

- Adopting an internal communication plan designed to ensure that any relationships with charitable organisations are conducted in a transparent and open manner and do not raise any expectation of the award of a contract or licence.

- Adopting company-wide policies and procedures about the selection of charitable projects or initiatives which are informed by appropriate risk assessments.

- Training and support for staff in implementing the relevant policies and procedures of communication which allow issues to be reported and compliance to be monitored.

- If charitable donations made in country M are routinely channelled through government officials or to others at the official's request, a red flag should be raised and L may seek to monitor the way its contributions are ultimately applied, or investigate alternative methods of donation such as official 'off-set' or 'community gain' arrangements with the government of M.

- Evaluation of its policies relating to charitable donations as part of its next periodic review of its anti-bribery procedures.

Test your understanding 6

1   While the magnitude of loss is not high overall, it does affect only one person to whom you are quite close – the moral intensity is likely to be high.

2   Given that the situation is neither proximate (some distance away) nor immediate (the effect of the action will not be felt for some years), the moral intensity will be low.

3   As the act is deemed 'ethical' then the intensity is likely to be low. The fact that you are unlikely to be caught (low probability of effect) confirms this assessment.

Organising for success: structure and processes

Chapter learning objectives

Upon completion of this chapter you will be able to:

- advise on how organisation structure and internal relationships can be re-organised to deliver a selected strategy

- advise on the implications of collaborative working and partnering, such as franchising, organisation process outsourcing, shared services and global business services

- evaluate the effectiveness of current organisational processes

- establish and appropriate scope and focus for organisation process change using Harmon's process-strategy matrix

- assess and advise on possible redesign options for improving the current processes of an organisation

- assess the feasibility of possible redesign options

- recommend an organisation process redesign methodology for an organisation

One of the PER performance objectives (PO 13) is that you plan business activities and control performance, making recommendations for improvement. Working through this chapter should help you understand how to demonstrate that objective.

PER

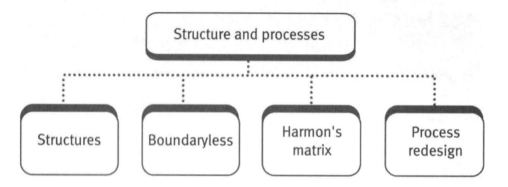

1 Factors affecting organisational structure

The links between strategy and structure

The influences that have a bearing on organisational structure and design include:

- strategic objectives
- nature of the environment
- diversity
- future strategy
- technology
- people.

Explanation of these influences

- The organisation's strategic objectives – if co-ordination between specific parts of the organisation is of key importance then the structure should facilitate relationships between them.

- The nature of the environment in which the organisation is operating, now and in the future – generally, product-based structures are more flexible and are more suitable in a dynamic or complex environment where organisations have to be adaptable.

- The diversity of the organisation – the needs of a multinational are different from those of a small company.

- The future strategy – for example, if a company may be making acquisitions in the future, then adopting a divisional structure now will make the acquired companies easier to assimilate.

- The technology available – IT has a significant impact on the structure, management and functioning of the organisation because of the effect it has on patterns of work, the formation and structure of groups, the nature of supervision and managerial roles. New technology has resulted in fewer management levels because it allows employees at clerical/operator level to take on a wider range of functions.

- The people within the organisation and their managerial skills.

One of the key influences on organisational structure is the size and growth of the organisation. As an organisation grows its organisational structure must change in order to support this growth. The typical changes required are:

- more specialisation (and specialists)

- more decentralisation

- more levels of authority

- more bureaucracy.

Explanation of these changes

When an organisation is small then staff may not be specialists. For example, in a very small sole trader business the sole trader might even prepare its own financial statements. But as it grows it is likely to have staff that are more focused on these types of specialist tasks and it might, say, employ an accountant to prepare the financial statements. Further growth will require more accountants etc. The same specialisation will occur across most business functions. So, for example, marketing experts will be employed in the marketing function, training experts employed in the training function etc.

These experts will need to be empowered in order to maximise their efficiency and effectiveness. As, for example, a specialist accountant is employed, he/she should be empowered to make decisions on areas such as how to finance the business, how to invest surplus funds, the most appropriate accounting policies etc. This will require a level of decentralisation where power is passed away from central decision makers to these specialist functions.

As the organisation continues to grow there will need to be a division of labour and an increase in the levels of authority. It may be, for example, that large organisations with a dedicated financing function might have an overall finance director who is then supported by a financial accountant and a management accountant. The management accountant might then have a team of specialists responsible for individual tasks such as budgeting, treasury management, payroll etc. Each of these specialists may in turn have staff reporting to them so that, say, the payroll manager might have a payroll clerk, a payroll processor, a payroll supervisor etc. Each new layer or level will have a narrower focus and area of specialisation and more levels will be required as the organisation grows.

Unfortunately, these changes are likely to require much more bureaucracy within the organisation. When a business is very small, such as a sole trader, all decisions can be made quickly and easily by the key decision maker. However, as the organisation grows decisions will need to be passed through the levels of authority. This will require forms and authorities that are likely to slow the decision making process down. There will also be a greater need for planning, target setting, staff appraisals and performance analysis which will all add to the bureaucracy that increases as organisations become bigger.

2   Organisational structures

Different structural types were studied in detail in paper F1. The key emphasis at this level is matching structure with strategy.

Here is a revision of the structural types suggested by Henry Mintzberg with some ideas of which type of strategy and environment may be best suited to each type:

Mintzberg's configurations

	Environment	Internal factors	Key building block	Key co-ordinating mechanism
Simple structure	Simple/ dynamic	Small Young Simple tasks	Strategic apex	Direct supervision
Machine bureaucracy	Simple/static	Large Old Regulated tasks	Techno-structure	Standardisation of work
Professional bureaucracy	Complex/ static	Professional control Simple systems	Operating core	Standardisation of skills
Divisionalised	Simple/static Diverse	Very large Old Divisible tasks	Middle line	Standardisation of outputs
Adhocracy	Complex/ dynamic	Young Complex tasks	Operating core Support staff	Mutual adjustment

Explanation

Building blocks and co-ordinating mechanisms

Mintzberg argues that the organisation structure exists to co-ordinate the activities of different individuals and work processes and that the nature of co-ordination changes with the increasing size of an organisation. He suggests that there are six main types of structure with configurations based on the following building blocks

- strategic apex – higher levels of management

- technostructure – provides technical input that is not part of the core activities

- operating core – members involved in producing goods and services

- middle line – middle and lower-level management

- support staff – support that is not part of the operating core

- ideology – beliefs and values.

Organisational structures

The importance and relative size of these building blocks will vary with organisations and the configuration chosen to support the organisation's strategies will depend on the mix of building block and co-ordinating mechanism. Mintzberg discusses six possible configurations, related to the environment, the type of work and the complexity of tasks facing the organisation. These are outlined below.

- Simple structure. The strategic apex, possibly consisting of a single owner-manager in a small business, exercises direct control over the operating core, and other functions are pared down to a minimum. There is little or no middle line, and technostructure and support staff are also absent. Co-ordination is achieved by direct supervision, so that this structure is flexible, and suited to dynamic environments.

- Machine bureaucracy, which arises from the power of the technostructure. The emphasis is on regulation: bureaucratic processes govern all activities within the organisation. This means that speedy reaction to change is impracticable, and this arrangement is best suited to simple, static environments.

- Professional bureaucracy, which arises from the predominance of the operating core. This type of structure commonly arises in organisations where many members of staff have a high degree of professional qualification (for example the medical staff in a hospital or the analysts and programmers in a software developer).

- Divisionalised form, which is characterised by a powerful middle line in which a large class of middle managers each takes charge of a more or less autonomous division. Depending on the extent of their autonomy, managers will be able to restrict interference from the strategic apex to a minimum.

- The 'adhocracy', a complex and disorderly structure in which procedures and processes are not formalised and core activities are carried out by project teams. This structure is suited to a complex and dynamic environment. There are two types of adhocracy:

    - operating adhocracy – innovates and solves problems directly on behalf of its clients. Admin work and operating work are blended together (consultancy firm, advertising agency)

> – administrative adhocracy – undertakes projects to serve itself, so it has its own operating core (research department, hi-tech companies).

Matching structure to strategy

Using Ansoff's matrix to explain different growth phases, the following gives some idea as to which strategy might be most appropriate at each stage of growth:

Growth strategy	Suitable organisational structure	Rationale
Market penetration	Simple	There are not too many decisions to be taken and little specialisation is required in the early stages.
Market or product development	Bureaucratic	More specialisation and decentralisation is required. A greater reliance can be placed on staff. The strategic apex can focus on the bigger picture.
Diversification (in stable markets)	Divisional	Each division can have its own focus and be appraised separately. Some functions can be centralised for specialisation or economies of scale.
Diversification in unpredictable markets	Adhocracy	Each customer or market can get a bespoke product or service. Functions or services can be easily added or removed to projects in order for the organisation to be extremely flexible.

Test your understanding 1

Yellow is a well-known national chain of physiotherapists. It provides high quality, paid-for treatment aimed at restoring movement and function to individuals affected by injury, illness or disability.

Yellow is currently organised in a functional, bureaucratic manner. Each individual store has a store manager who reports to a regional manager who in turn reports to the retail director. Other functions operate in similar ways. For example, the HR director has regional HR managers who report into him and some of the larger stores have dedicated HR staff who report to the HR managers.

Yellow is now considering a diversification into the training of physiotherapists. This is seen as a high growth area and Yellow believes that it has the expertise to become a large player in this market as well as cutting its own costs of recruitment and training of physiotherapists.

The managing director of Yellow wants the new training business to be created as a separate division and for Yellow to move to a divisional structure. However, she is concerned that functional directors and managers may believe that such a change will diminish their power and the value of their position.

Required:

Briefly consider the benefits of Yellow from moving to a divisional structure.

Professional skill:

Illustrate commercial acumen that shows an insight into the work-related issues for staff in making this change.

Multinational and global structures

The critical issue in deciding global structure is the extent to which local independence or responsiveness should take precedence over global co-ordination.

- The different types of multinational structure are shown in the diagram.

Local independence and responsiveness

	Low	High
Low (Global co-ordination)	International divisions	International subsidiaries
High	Global products companies	Transnational corporations

International divisions

- Here the home-based structure may be retained at first, whether functional or divisional, but the overseas interests are managed through a special international division.

- The international divisions will draw on the products of the home company and gain advantage from this technology transfer.

- The disadvantage is a lack of local tailoring of products or technology.

- Such structures tend to work best where there is a wide geographical spread but quite closely related products.

International subsidiaries

- Are geographically based and operate independently by country.

- In these companies virtually all the management functions are nationally based, allowing for higher degrees of local responsiveness.

- The control of the parent company is likely to be dependent on some form of planning and reporting system and perhaps an ultimate veto over national strategies, but the extent of global co-ordination is likely to be low.

- The main problem lies in failing to achieve synergy between business units.

Global product companies

- Represent a move away from the international divisional or subsidiary structure to an integrated structure.

- Here the multinational is split into product divisions, which are then managed on an international basis.

- The logic of such an approach is that it should promote cost efficiency (particularly of production) on an international basis, and should provide enhanced transfer of resources (particularly technology) between geographical regions.

- The international development of many Japanese companies in electronics and car manufacture has been managed in this way.

- Research has shown that the theoretical benefits of the global product structure are not always realised. Although cost efficiency is improved, it does not appear that technology transfer is necessarily enhanced. Also, while the structure is well suited to promoting defensive or consolidation strategies, it does not seem to meet the expected benefits of better strategic planning and is not suited to the promotion of aggressive or expansionist strategies.

KAPLAN PUBLISHING

Transnational corporations

- Are matrix-like structures that attempt to combine the local responsiveness of the international subsidiary with the advantages of co-ordination found in global product companies.

- A major strength is in transferring knowledge across borders.

- The key lies in creating an integrated network of interdependent resources and capabilities.

Potential problems for transnational corporations

- Managers must be able and willing to work hard to simultaneously improve their specific focus (e.g. region, product, function) as well as looking at the global picture.

- The same control problems as found in matrices.

Combining structures via acquisition

Care should be taken when combining structures or imposing structures on new business units, as conflicts might arise between the different building blocks. For example, if a business with a machine bureaucracy (and therefore lots of rules, standardisation and controls) were to acquire an adhocracy (where the balance between the blocks is more even, and there is flexibility in the application of rules and controls), there may be difficulties both in achieving business objectives and in motivating staff.

3   Boundaryless organisations

Organisations are working together, often as a network, more than ever before. Organisations often find themselves working more collaboratively with suppliers and customers as well as relying more heavily on the outsourcing of many business activities.

 Boundaries created in traditional structures

Traditional structures are often seen as being bureaucratic and slow to react to change. The move to more collaborative structures (often referred to as boundaryless organisations) is a move towards welcoming and thriving on change. Traditional structures have clearly defined roles for those involved in the organisation as well as controls on their authority. These place barriers (or boundaries) on both employees and the organisation itself in terms of working together, making changes and working with those outside the organisation such as suppliers and customers.

The aim of a boundaryless organisation is to remove barriers to growth and change and ensure that employees, the organisation, customers and suppliers can collaborate, share ideas and identify the best way forward for the organisation. Typical boundaries found in organisations are:

- Vertical boundaries
- Horizontal boundaries
- External boundaries.

More details

- Vertical boundaries: these are the levels of authority that exist within an organisation and the pathway through which decision making takes places. The more levels of authority that exist then the slower and more bureaucratic decision making becomes. It also limits communication and interaction between employees at different levels within the organisation. This could, for example, limit the ability to share ideas within the organisation. A boundaryless organisation will aim to have fewer levels of authority, more communication and interaction between all employees, and create a more collaborative decision making process. It often means that rank and role become much less important within the organisation. There is often a less formal management style, a greater desire to transform and improve staff, and a move towards a culture that embraces change more readily so that the organisation is better prepared for change (these ideas are explored further in later chapters).

- Horizontal boundaries: these are the boundaries that exist between functions in an organisation. Functions may follow their own goals rather than organisational goals and it may be that there is poor communication between employees who work within each function. The communication may be driven by bureaucracy and controls such as the budgeting system. In turn these may create cultural and knowledge boundaries – there may be different working methods in each function and it may well be that there is less sharing of knowledge that could create better performance in each function. For example, the sales function may understand well what types of components that customers would like to see in a finished product, but if this knowledge is not shared with the purchasing or production team then the organisation will underperform. To overcome these boundaries, boundaryless organisations will often have cross-functional teams, encourage staff to make secondments between departments, have more regular and quicker communications (e.g. by using more digital communications) as well as having better controls in place to ensure improved goal congruence. Areas such as knowledge management and redesigned job roles, explored elsewhere in the syllabus, can play a part in overcoming these boundaries.

- External boundaries: these are boundaries that exist between the organisation and the outside world, including customers and suppliers. These boundaries can affect the two-way communications that are vital for an organisation's success. For example, it may well be that customers are not informed of what the organisation is planning or what new developments are taking place. Likewise, it may also mean that the organisation is not gathering information from customers that will require the organisation to change if it is to be successful. Similar problems can accrue if communications with suppliers are poor. Boundaryless organisations aim to collaborate with their customers and suppliers. For example, communications with customers can be improved through user contributions (reviews, expertise, feedback) and crowdsourcing (for example, asking motorists to phone in with reports of traffic hold ups). Information is provided through internet forums and regular electronic communications. Supplier collaboration is improved through systems such as e-procurement (explored later in the syllabus), strategic alliances and outsourcing.

There are three main types of boundaryless organisation:

- The hollow structure – where non-core activities are outsourced

- The modular structure – where some parts of product production are outsourced

- The virtual structure – where the organisation is made up of a collaboration of other organisational parts.

Details in the types of structure

- Hollow structure: hollow organisations focus on their core competencies and outsource all other activities. Typically, processes such as human relations, information technology and event management are outsourced to a specialist provider. This leaves the company free to focus on what it considers to be its core value-adding activities. Critical to the success of this structure is the ability of the organisations to identify which core processes are critical to its mission, create a current or future competitive advantage and drive growth. It will also be important to align the suppliers' incentives and the company's strategic goals. The choice of supplier will be vital to the structure's success. As some processes become commoditised, these decisions become easier to take.

- Modular structure: modular organisations divide their product into manageable chunks and then order different parts from internal and external providers which the organisation then assembles into an overall finished product. For example, a cellular phone company might design the product and build the chip, the software and the built-in apps themselves, but then outsource the production of the glass, the chassis, the gyroscope etc. This can lead to a faster and improved production process as well as using market forces to drive down the production cost of each module of the product. It can also force internal production functions to become more efficient. Ultimately, it may well be that internal production can in turn produce elements to be sold externally. Samsung, for example, have made screens for other companies such as Apple and Sony.

- Virtual structure: virtual organisations rely heavily on information technology to link people, assets and ideas to form an (often temporary) organisation. Links are formed with external partners (which may be whole organisations, a part of an organisation or simply a team of experts) where each partner brings their own domain of expertise. This expertise is combined together to achieve common goals. A virtual organisation appears as a single entity from outside to its customers, but it is in fact a network of different organisational nodes created to respond to an exceptional, and often temporary, market opportunity. Over time, the parts (or members) of the virtual organisation might change. Once the market opportunity evaporates or is fully exploited, the virtual organisation either disbands or is absorbed into the larger organisation.

  This is a way of responding quickly to the market without having to develop new areas of expertise or new production capacity, say. It makes use of valuable expertise that may exist outside the organisation.

  As well as suffering from similar problems seen in other strategic alliances such as joint ventures (for example, in terms of the giving away of core knowledge or in the ability to find a common goal and agreement), virtual organisations require intensive communication to avoid duplicating effort. This is why information technology plays such an important role in these organisations.

Illustration 1 – A boundaryless organisation

Example of a successful network – Amazon

Amazon is now one of the best known online retailers. Amazon operates its website but relies on external book publishers and other suppliers, book warehouses, couriers and credit card companies to deliver the rest of the customer experience. These partners are also expected to provide Amazon with information on, for example, stock availability, delivery times, promotional material, etc. The customer feels that they are dealing with one organisation, not many. In addition, the Amazon Marketplace allows other organisations and individuals to sell their goods through the Amazon website, and its Associates system provides a means for others to earn referral fees by directing customers from their own website to Amazon products.

Test your understanding 2

What are likely to be the key advantages and disadvantages of a boundaryless organisation?

Outsourcing, business partnerships and the use of shared services can play a vital role in the success of a boundaryless organisation.

Outsourcing, business partnering and shared services

Outsourcing

Outsourcing plays a key role in the boundaryless organisation. It can typically have the following advantages and disadvantages:

Advantages

- The main perceived benefit of outsourcing is reduced cost. Using external services can be much cheaper than employing in-house IT staff and not using them fully or efficiently.

- It is used to overcome skills shortages. For example, the IT function of the organisation may not have all the resources necessary to carry out the full range of activities required, or the requirements of the organisation might not justify an in-house IT department, particularly in the areas of systems development. Facilities management specialists will have a larger pool of technical staff than the organisation.

- Outsourcing can bring flexibility. Using external providers allows an organisation to be flexible in its choice of services and it can buy in services as and when it needs them.

- It is argued that outsourcing allows organisations to focus on their core skills and activities where they have a clear competitive advantage, and sub-contract non-core activities. Outsourcing frees up management time, and allows management to concentrate on those areas of the business that are most critical. However, defining core activities can be problematic. Different definitions include the following activities:

  - activities critical to the performance of the organisation

  - activities that create current potential for profits and returns (or non-financial benefits, in the case of public sector organisations)

  - activities that will drive the future growth, innovation or rejuvenation of the organisation.

- Outsourcing is not without risks as there is no direct management control over the organisation providing the services.

Disadvantages

- Dependency on supplier for the quality of service provision. When a company cedes control to a single supplier, it becomes dependent on the quality of the supplier's skills, management, technology and service know-how.

- A risk of loss of confidentiality, particularly if the external supplier performs similar services for rival companies.

- Difficulties in agreeing and enforcing contract terms.

- The length of contract (the risk of being 'locked in').

- Lost in-house expertise and knowledge.

- A loss of competitive advantage (if the function being outsourced is a core competence, they must not be outsourced).

- Outsourcing might be seen by management as a way of off-loading problems onto someone else, rather than as a way of managing them constructively.

The notion of working 'in partnership', which is encouraged by vendors, is problematic. Firstly, it should be remembered that client organisations and vendors are usually both commercial organisations with separate statements of profit or loss and balance sheets, and different goals and objectives. While each organisation may wish for an effective and successful partnership, problems arise when the outsourcing company fails to realise the expectations of the client. A common example is the situation whereby the vendor imposes additional fees for work that was not in the original contract.

The client organisation should have a management team with responsibility for the oversight of the contract, to ensure that service levels are met and that any problems are resolved. Outsourcing can be a risky option, and it is essential that the risks should be properly controlled. Equally, the internal controls should be as effective with outsourcing as they would be if the function operated in-house.

Off-shoring is the outsourcing of a business process to another country. For example, Apple offshores the assembly of the iPhone to China because, even with transport delays, production is still quicker than having the unit assembled in the US. Off-shoring is another form of outsourcing. It is made easier when the destination country has the same language and skill base as the domestic country. But many organisations are reversing the trend (moving to in-shoring) as political and social pressure is building to protect domestic jobs.

Business partnerships

Business partnerships can take many forms, from loose informal agreements, partnerships and formal joint ventures to contracting out services to outside suppliers within a boundaryless organisation.

- Business partnerships are co-operative business activities, formed by two or more separate organisations for strategic purposes.

- Ownership, operational responsibilities, financial risks and rewards are allocated to each member, while preserving their separate identity and autonomy.

- Business partnerships can be long-term collaborations bringing together the strengths of two or more organisations to achieve strategic goals. For example, IBM formed links with Ricoh for distribution of low-end computers. This allowed them to move into the Japanese market quickly, inexpensively and with a relatively high prospect for success.

- Business partnerships can also help result in improved access to information and technology.

- Some organisations form business partnerships to retain some of the innovation and flexibility that is characteristic of small companies. They are balancing bureaucracy and entrepreneurship by forming closer working relationships with other organisations.

- Business partnerships may be used to extend an organisation's reach without increasing its size.

- Other business partnerships are motivated by the benefits associated with a global strategy, especially where the organisation lacks a key success factor for some market. This may be distribution, a brand name, a selling organisation, technology, R&D or manufacturing capability. To remedy this deficiency internally would often require excessive time and money.

Shared services

A shared service refers to the centralisation of a service (or services) that has previously been carried out remotely at each business unit. Common examples happen in areas of IT and accounting, but more recently organisations have created shared services for functions such as marketing, process redesign, property management and even content management (which simplifies the storage and security of company information).

Unlike systems such as outsourcing, shared services will still be carried out within the organisation and will not require the use of a third party external organisation. But the provision of the service will typically be moved to one location with fewer staff and a consolidated IT system.

Shared services go beyond a simple 'back officing' of common services. The shared service is typically treated as a separate and discrete business unit and its services are charged to other business units at arm's length prices. It will have its own targets to achieve and will be expected to produce continuous improvements.

Advantages

- There should be economies of scale on cost.

- The service can be benchmarked against external service providers.

- Efficiency can be improved (for example, a single IT system can be used and reduce the need for multiple systems that may have difficulty in communicating with each other).

- All talent and expertise in the service can be gathered in one place so that knowledge management within the organisation is improved.

- Shared services can also help remove organisational boundaries between business units. For example, there may be significant boundaries between one business unit that is a manufacturing company and another that is, say, another business unit that provides consultancy services. But these boundaries can be reduced and removed if the business units are sharing services such as marketing, management information systems, email systems, training etc.

Disadvantages

- There is likely to be initial resistance to change, especially as the move will often lead to redundancies across business units. But also because local business managers will lose control of a service that they may consider vital to their success.

- Creating appropriate targets for the service can be time consuming and difficult.

- There may be issues in determining the price that should be charged to business units for the use of the service.

The POPIT model (covered later in the syllabus) will play a key role in moving to a shared service system. Processes will have to change, there will be new consolidated technology required, the organisation will have to be re-organised and there will be a fundamental shift in the way that people work and manage.

Test your understanding 3

How important do you feel IT is to developing a virtual organisation?

4 Business process improvements

Introduction

As well as considering the structure of the organisation as a whole, strategists might also consider the role and management of individual processes within the organisation. A change to an individual business process might lead to a competitive advantage or remove existing competitive disadvantages by either reducing costs or differentiating the business.

For example, if a bank can reduce its mortgage approval period from 10 days to 1 day, then this could allow the mortgage activity to stand out from rivals. In order to achieve this change the bank will have to redesign the approval process (for example, by changing job roles, using more efficient IT systems etc.).

These improvements can come in many ways – some might be outsourced to more efficient business partners whilst others might be redesigned from scratch. What follows are techniques for examining both of these issues:

- firstly, we consider which processes should be outsourced and which should be redesigned (using Harmon's matrix), and

- secondly, we consider how an individual process might be redesigned.

The importance of business processes

Processes should contribute to the overall strategy of an organisation and the individual process goals should align with the strategic goals. For example, if the overall goal of the organisation is to become a quality leader in its respective market, process goals such as 'shortest execution time' may lead to counter-productive behaviour by process participants who receive incentives for finishing work fast – even if it does not meet the highest quality standards.

Alternatively, the investigation and potential re-design of the way processes take place within an organisation supports the lenses that Johnson, Scholes and Whittington termed, respectively, experience and ideas. An investigation of current processes might suggest that process goals and measures may not be aligned with strategy.

This may be because the processes have diverged from their original specification or it may be because the strategy is not operationally feasible and the people undertaking the processes to implement it know this. Consequently, processes are often modified by employees and managers to make them workable and eventually, strategy is modified to accept this.

The re-design of processes may lead to incremental changes or it may lead to a significant strategic shift. Opportunities discovered while focusing on specific processes may have very significant repercussions for strategy.

Harmon's process-strategy matrix

According to Paul Harmon a process-strategy matrix is a matrix formed by an estimate of:

- the **strategic importance** of a process on the horizontal axis

- the process **complexity** and dynamics on the vertical axis.

This matrix can be used to determine how to manage individual processes.

Strategic importance

Complexity		Low	High
	High	Outsource	Undertake process improvement
	Low	Minimum effort	Automate

Further explanation on Harmon's matrix

Assuming that 'low' is positioned at the bottom left corner:

- Processes that lie at the upper-right are complex, dynamic and of high strategic importance. These are usually the processes that provide the organisation with its competitive advantage and should be nurtured accordingly. These processes should get constant attention and are the ones that should be considered for redesign – any improvements are likely to bring large benefits to the organisation.

- Processes that fall in the lower-left are of little complexity, do not change very often and do not have much strategic importance. They should be given the minimum resources necessary for efficient functioning.

- Processes in the top left of the matrix are very complex but are not core activities of the organisation (and are not likely to be valued by customers). Spending time and effort on these processes will distract from core processes and bring very little benefit. These are the processes which should be outsourced.

- Processes in the bottom right of the matrix are valued by customers but they are likely to be stable and easily copied by rivals due to a lack of complexity. These processes should be automated in order to either improve efficiency and/or reduce costs.

Illustration 2 – The role of process and change initiatives

Applying Harmon's process-strategy matrix to a children's bicycle manufacturer – Wheelies Co. The company manufactures bicycles which are then sold on to retailers for sale in their retail outlets. The management at Wheelies have identified the processes that need to be done.

- New product design.

- Negotiating partnership deals with other organisations.

- Online purchasing.

- Stock control.

- Credit card approval.

- Bicycle assembly.

- Delivery – international.

- Funds investment.

Now they need to place them on the matrix by deciding how important and how complex the processes are:

		Strategic importance	
		Low	High
Process complexity	High	Delivery – international Funds investment	Negotiating partnership deals New product designs
	Low	Stock control Credit card approval	Bicycle assembly Online purchasing

- New product designs and negotiating partnership deals are really important and complex – these are the likely candidates for analysing and redesigning.

- Bicycle assembly is not quite as important – the company should attempt to automate this as much as possible in order to speed up assembly time and reduce costs.

- Online purchasing is important but routine – bespoke software could be used to ensure that this process is automated in a way that best suits the company's needs. Wheelies could perhaps look at linking the process to the IT systems of key customers in order to offer e-procurement opportunities (e-procurement is explored in detail in the next chapter).

- Stock control and credit approval both lack importance. They are likely to be routine and well understood – these processes can be left alone at present and no process improvements are likely to be needed in these areas.

- International delivery is complex but does not add much value, and funds investment is important but no one in the company has any expertise in that field – outsourcing these processes is a popular solution.

Advantages and disadvantages of outsourcing an individual business process

Harmon suggests how each process should be managed. However, the model should not be followed blindly by organisations and each action should be fully evaluated. For example, although outsourcing is suggested for activities which are complex but of low strategic importance, outsourcing has its own advantages and disadvantages which should be considered before a decision is made.

Claimed advantages of business process outsourcing (BPO) include:

- Cost savings (currently the main decision making factor).
- Improved customer care.
- Allows management to focus on core activities.

Problems of BPO include:

- As more processes become commoditised, it is more difficult for organisations to differentiate themselves from rivals.

- Problems finding a single supplier for complex processes, resulting in fragmentation.

- Firms are unwilling to outsource whole processes due to the strategic significance or security implications of certain elements.

- Inflexible contracts and other problems managing suppliers.

- Problems measuring performance.

- Data security.

Note: The "usual" pros/cons of outsourcing discussed earlier in the chapter – cost, quality, control, risk – still apply here.

The commoditisation of business processes

As more processes become 'commoditised', there is a greater use of outsourcing by organisations. Commoditisation is the evolutionary process that reduces all products and services to their lowest common denominator. Commoditisation tends to happen when

- there is **comparability** between the firm's processes and the competences of outside suppliers

- there is **standardisation** of processes making it easy to assess whether the process will be improved by outsourcing and to find appropriate outsource agents, and

- the costs of outsourcing these services can be lower than the cost of providing them internally.

For example, when running, say, a music concert a venue may have previously arranged its own security and ticket checks. However, this process is now widespread at events such as political rallies, sports events, festivals etc., so that the process itself has become very standardised and has moved towards commoditisation. It is therefore very common now for music venues to outsource security and ticket checks as the venue will know that the outsource agency is likely to have the experience and economies of scale to provide the activity in a cheaper and better way than the music venue would be able to so itself.

Test your understanding 4

Assess which of the following processes is most suitable for outsourcing.

- Environmental reporting.

- Processing online customers' credit card purchases.

- Customer queries and complaints.

5 Improving the processes of an organisation

Process redesign, often called Business Process Re-engineering or Redesign (BPR), Business Process Management (BPM) or Business Process Improvement (BPI) takes a 'clean sheet' approach to the process, which is usually either broken, or so slow that it is no longer competitive in delivering the company's value to its customers.

Typical problems and solutions

The key stages in a process redesign are to firstly identify problems in the process before then coming up with some relevant solutions. There are some typical issues to look out for:

Typical causes of problems in processes

- activities are unnecessary
- activities are in the wrong order
- activities are in the wrong swim lane
- activities are missing
- activities take too long.

Typical solutions in processes

- removing swim lanes
- removing unnecessary activities
- combining job roles
- combining activities
- reducing handovers between swim lanes
- changing the order of activities
- outsourcing activities.

NB – "swim lanes" visually distinguish job sharing and responsibilities for sub-processes of a business process. Swim lanes may be arranged either horizontally or vertically.

Evaluating effectiveness of a business process

In an exam you may be asked to:

- evaluate the effectiveness of an existing process, and
- make suggestions for its redesign.

Evaluating the effectiveness of an existing process

You may be given a diagram to analyse for this part of the question.

Diagrams are particularly useful to see who is responsible for what and it is also easy to start identifying potential inefficiencies and potential areas of improvement.

- Are there any gaps or steps missing?
- Is there duplication?
- Are there overlaps, where several people or teams perform the same task or activity?
- Are there activities that add no value?

Process redesign solutions

Once the potential areas for improvement have been identified, the next step is to decide how to address the issues and make changes.

- Diagrams can also be used at this stage to map out the proposed process changes. In an exam, however, you will not be asked to create such diagrams.

- As with any proposed changes in the organisation, the pros and cons need to be analysed, and any changes that follow must be carefully planned.

Solutions

As seen earlier, solutions can include ideas such as removing activities, automating activities, combining activities etc.

In a similar manner to strategy evaluation (suitability, feasibility, acceptability), these redesign options need to be evaluated. Options are likely to have varying degrees of feasibility due to such factors as money, culture, effect of change, etc.

Project management

There are very strong links between process redesign and project management (covered in detail elsewhere in this study text). A process redesign is a type of project and many of the areas covered in project management such as developing the business case for the redesign, controlling the process when it is out of control and reviewing the success or failure of the redesign effort.

Test your understanding 5

Going back to our bicycle manufacturer – Wheelies Co.

Performing step 2 of the redesign process on one of the manufacturing processes shows the following existing process:

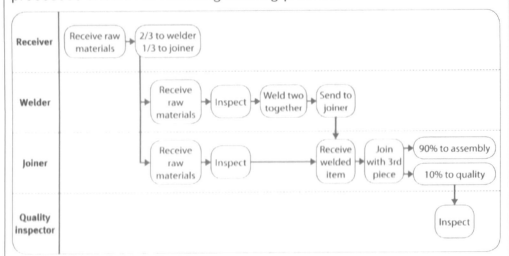

Each area of responsibility is given its own swim lane. A swim lane visually distinguishes job sharing and responsibilities for sub-processes of a business process.

This particular process starts with three pieces of metal, two of which are welded together and then joined with the third. You should be able to see from the diagram how the metal moves across swim lanes towards the final output.

Required:

Explain the problems in this process and how these might be resolved.

6 Chapter summary

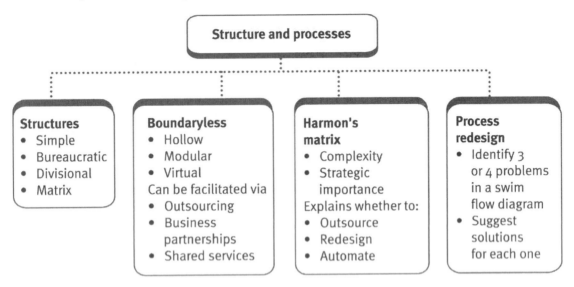

Structure and processes

Structures
- Simple
- Bureaucratic
- Divisional
- Matrix

Boundaryless
- Hollow
- Modular
- Virtual

Can be facilitated via
- Outsourcing
- Business partnerships
- Shared services

Harmon's matrix
- Complexity
- Strategic importance

Explains whether to:
- Outsource
- Redesign
- Automate

Process redesign
- Identify 3 or 4 problems in a swim flow diagram
- Suggest solutions for each one

Test your understanding answers

Test your understanding 1

Moving to a divisional structure will allow each division to have a better focus on its own market where competences, resources and the environment are likely to be very different. For example, the HR function in the current business is likely to focus on sales training, health and safety training, store manager development etc. But in the new training division, HR may be focused on very different elements such as training for lecturers and administrators in running physiotherapy courses. Having separate divisions will allow better focus on the needs of each division.

As a new strategy for Yellow, the organisation will want to evaluate its immediate and long-term success or failure. This would be difficult to do if the activity was incorporated into existing functions where it would be more difficult to separate out the attributable costs and revenues. This would be much easier in a divisional structure where the division would have its own discrete costs and revenues so that the financial results would be much more easy to evaluate. The same issue would apply to other, possibly non-financial criteria such as market share, customer satisfaction, etc.

The marketing of each business unit is likely to be very different, not least because of the different target markets. The retail units will be targeting individual consumers who may have suffered an injury or may even target doctors for business referrals. Issues such as promotion and service will be key elements of the marketing mix. The training divisions may be more focused on graduate recruitment where marketing of career paths and salaries may be more important.

Staff in the current functional structure appear to be concerned about the value of their role if a divisional structure is adopted. However, existing role and power is unlikely to change – store managers will still report to regional managers who will in turn continue to report to the retail director. There may be an added level of authority above this in the form of a divisional manager, but this should be no different to reporting to the existing board. In fact, it may be that this extra level of authority creates a greater career path for staff – an extra level of promotion/responsibility for them to aim at. This might actually provide greater motivation going forward for those staff who want to achieve greater levels of career progression. This can be promoted to staff as one of the rationales for the change in the business structure.

Professional skill:

It is the final paragraph which covers the necessary professional skill. The answer is showing a clear understanding of work-related and organisational issues. It also explains a solution to the managing director's (and staff) concerns. This is strong commercial acumen.

Test your understanding 2

The key advantages of a boundaryless organisation are:

- Increased flexibility and ability to cope with change.
- Removes geographical barriers to productivity.
- Collaboration can bring specialisation and comparative and absolute advantages.
- More efficient communication between functions.

The key problems are:

- The organisation is only as strong as the weakest collaborator.
- Employee management and goal congruence can become more complex and difficult.
- Some boundary-spanning activities are still required (e.g. marketing).

Test your understanding 3

The idea of the virtual organisation emphasises:

- the decentralisation of control
- the creation of more flexible patterns of working
- a greater empowerment of the workforce
- the displacement of hierarchy by team working
- the development of a greater sense of collective responsibility
- the creation of more collaborative relationships among co-workers.

A key element in supporting the transformation is IT.

- This is mainly through the systems that facilitate co-ordination and communication, decision-making and the sharing of knowledge, skills and resources.

- Information systems can reduce the number of levels in an organisation by providing managers with information to manage and control larger numbers of workers spread over greater distances and by giving lower-level employees more decision-making authority. It is no longer necessary for these employees to work standard hours every day, nor work in an office or even the same country as their manager.

- With the emergence of global networks, team members can collaborate closely even from distant locations. Information technology permits tight co-ordination of geographically dispersed workers across time zones and cultures.

- Different companies can join together to provide goods and services.

Test your understanding 4

Environmental reporting is likely to be complex and require great specialisation and depth of knowledge so would be difficult to outsource (except to an environmental reporting specialist?)

Processing credit card purchases is high-volume and repetitive so would appear to be ideal for outsourcing. However, issues of confidentiality and data security would need to be met first.

Dealing with customer queries requires detailed product knowledge, which might be lacking. Also there is a high risk of damaging the firm's reputation and goodwill if complaints are not handled sensitively. Many firms who used off-shore call centres to manage customer queries and complaints in the 1990s have since brought these services back in-house.

Test your understanding 5

Some problems can be identified in this process:

- Firstly, inspection is in the wrong 'swim lane', happening at the wrong place.

- Secondly, the inspection is happening after the materials are received by the welder and joiner.

Solutions to these problems could be:

- The inspection should happen in the quality inspector swim lane.

- The quality inspector should inspect materials before they are issued to the welder and joiner.

However, more advanced redesign options may go even further. Common solutions in redesign methods are to combine job roles and responsibilities, for example. It may be possible in this process to combine all three job roles into one job role. One employee could be trained to perform the welding, joining and inspecting of the parts.

The receiving might also be made part of their role. In this way:

- staff costs are reduced

- the process becomes more efficient

- there are less handovers between swim lanes – reducing time taken and the likelihood of errors.

E-business

Chapter learning objectives

Upon completion of this chapter you will be able to:

- assess the organisation's approach to delivering e-business

- assess and advise on the potential application of information technology to support e-business

- discuss from a strategic perspective the continuing need for effective information systems control within an organisation

- assess and advise on the adequacy of information technology and systems security controls for an organisation

- evaluate and recommend ways to promote cyber security

- evaluate, and if necessary, recommend improvements or changes to controls over the safeguard of information technology assets to ensure the organisation's ability to meet business objectives

PER

Two of the PER performance objectives (PO3) and (PO13) are that you contribute to the wider business strategy of your organisation through your personal and team objectives. You identify innovative ways to improve organisational performance and plan business activities and control performance, making recommendations for improvement. Working through this chapter should help you understand how to demonstrate these objectives.

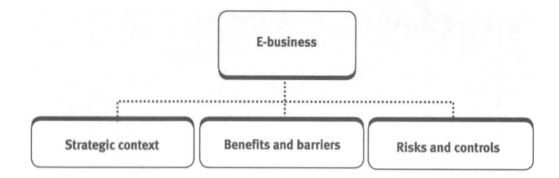

1 Information technology – the strategic context

Business strategy and information strategy

This section looks at information technology (IT) strategy in the context of the strategic planning tools met in earlier chapters.

IT is likely to permeate all elements of the strategic planning process. For example:

- as part of **strategic analysis** it can help provide strengths and strategic capabilities for a business or help it reduce the impact of threats coming, for example, from its competitive forces.

Illustration 1 – Information technology – the strategic context

MP3 sound compression, the internet and fast broadband connections have forced companies like Sony and EMI to reassess their music retailing strategies. Technology is a threat to these companies.

IT and Porter's five forces

Management could use Porter's 5 Forces model to determine which of the forces poses a threat to the future success of the organisation. By ranking these threats in terms of intensity and immediacy, the most critical can then be considered in terms of how information technology or systems can be used to gain advantage or avoid disadvantage.

Threat of entry – new entrants into a market will bring extra capacity and intensify competition. The strength of the threat from new entrants will depend upon the strength of the barriers to entry and the likely response of existing competition to a new entrant. IT can have two possible roles to counteract the threat.

- **Defensively,** by creating barriers that new entrants to the market find difficult to overcome. IT can increase economies of scale by using computer-controlled production methods, requiring a similar investment in the technology of new entrants. Another defensive move is to colonise the distribution channels by tying customers and suppliers into the supply chain or the distribution chain. The harder the service is to emulate, the higher the barrier is for new entrants.

- **Offensively**, by breaking down the barriers to entry. An example is the use of telephone banking, which reduces the need to establish a branch network. Automated teller machines (ATMs) created new distribution channels enabling 'bank branches' to be set up in airports, out-of-town supermarkets and other areas where there are many potential customers. These machines provided not only expansion of the total market, but also a low-cost method of overcoming the barriers to entry in the areas where the cost of entry was high and space was at a premium.

Intensity of competitive rivalry – this is rivalry between firms making similar products, or offering the same services, and selling them in the same market. The most intense rivalry is where the business is more mature and the growth has slowed down.

IT can be used to compete. Cost leadership can be exploited by IT, for example, where IT is used to support just-in-time (JIT) systems. Alternatively, IT can be used as a collaborative venture, changing the basis of competition by setting up new communications networks and forming alliances with complementary organisations for the purpose of information sharing. When Thomson Holidays introduced its online reservation system into travel agents' offices, it changed the basis of competition, allowing customers to ask about holiday availability and special deals and book a holiday in one visit to the travel agent.

Threat of substitute products – this threat applies both between industries (e.g. rail travel with bus travel and private car) and within an industry (e.g. long-life milk as substitute for delivered fresh milk). In many cases IS themselves are the substitute product. Word-processing packages are a substitute for typewriters.

IT-based products can be used to imitate existing goods as in electronic keyboards and organs. In the case of computer games, IT has formed the basis of a new leisure industry.

Computer-aided design and computer-assisted manufacture (CAD/CAM) have helped competitors to bring innovative products to the market more quickly than in the past.

Interactive information systems add value by providing an extra service to an existing product. An example of this is provided by ICI's 'Counsellor', an expert system that advises farmers on disease control. It analyses data input by the farmer on areas such as crop varieties grown, soil type and previous history of disease and recommends fungicides or other suitable ICI products to solve the farmer's problems.

The threat from substitutes can be minimised by ensuring that an organisation develops a product before its rivals and then protects that product for a number of years by means of patents. This approach is widely used in the pharmaceutical and biotech industries where specialist software is now widely used in the drug discovery process, enabling drugs to be developed that target specific human and animal diseases.

Bargaining power of customers – the bargaining power of customers can be affected by using IT to create switching costs and 'lock' the buyer into products and services. The switching costs may be in both cash terms and operational inconvenience terms. For example, PCs run under Microsoft operating systems are not very efficient when using non-Microsoft application software.

Another form of locking customers in is to develop customer information systems that inform the organisation about the customer's behaviour, purchases and characteristics. This information enables the organisation to target customers in terms of direct marketing and other forms of incentive such as loyalty schemes, where methods of rewarding customer loyalty by giving them 'preferred customer' status are used. If a clothing retailer is launching a new collection it can offer its loyal customers a private viewing. Some airlines have deals such as frequent flyers and air miles as incentives.

The IT techniques at play here include 'data warehousing' – the collection and storage of large volumes of customer information on spending and purchasing patterns, social group, family make-up, etc. This then allows for 'data mining' – the extraction of relevant data from the warehouse as the source for target marketing drives. It was reported recently that Tesco, the UK's largest supermarket group, was mining its customer data to identify customers over the age of 60 who regularly purchased children's clothes, food and toys – possibly leading to a marketing push aimed at grandparents.

Bargaining power of suppliers – the bargaining power of suppliers, and hence their ability to charge higher prices, will be influenced by:

- the degree to which switching costs apply and substitutes are available

- the presence of one or two dominant suppliers controlling prices

- the products offered having a uniqueness of brand, technical performance or design not available elsewhere.

Reducing the suppliers' power to control the supply can erode this power. Where an organisation is dependent on components of a certain standard in a certain time, IT can provide a purchases database that enables easy scanning of prices from a number of suppliers. Suppliers' data can be shared so that the supplier and the organisation both benefit from performance improvements. The Ford Motor Company set up CAD links with its suppliers with the intention of reducing the costs of design specification and change. Both the time taken and the error rate were reduced because specifications did not have to be re-keyed into the suppliers' manufacturing tools.

KAPLAN PUBLISHING

Link to strategic analysis

Porter suggested three ways in which IT in general can affect the competitive environment and an organisation's ability to compete. Though these points apply to IT in general, they are particularly important when considering e-business.

- New businesses might become possible. For example, auction sites and photo-album sites.

- The industry structure can be changed. For example, in the music business it can be argued that the large CD publishers have less power because music can be self-published on the internet.

- IT can provide an organisation with competitive advantage by providing new ways of operating. For example, airlines save money by encouraging internet bookings.

- this in turn could lead to new **strategic choices**, and IT can, for example, support new competitive strategies.

How IT can play a role in generic strategies

Porter identified three generic strategies for dealing with the competitive forces. The two basic strategies are overall cost leadership and differentiation. The third strategy – a focus strategy – concentrates on a particular segment of a product line or geographical market – a niche. If it is known which strategy an organisation is currently using to promote their products and/or services, it should be possible to define a role for IS to enhance that strategy.

- **Overall cost leadership** is about competing by offering products or services at low cost and value for money. The emphasis is on cost reduction. For example, driving down inventory levels, with the assistance of IT for supply chain planning and scheduling, can reduce costs. Sales forecasting software that can be fed into manufacturing resources planning applications can be used in shop floor planning and scheduling applications to increase efficiency.

- **Differentiation** is about showing that your product or service is different from those of your competitors through, e.g. brand image, customer service or design. A way of differentiating may be to make the ordering process as easy and flexible as possible. This can be done by providing online information services to identify the most appropriate product or service, followed up by a simple online ordering process. Where the differentiation is by customisation, CAD (computer-aided design) can reduce costs effectively.

- **Focus** concentrates on a niche market, e.g. a particular buyer group, market, geographic area, segment or product line. The opportunities for IS/IT include providing access to customer information, trends and competitors so as to maximise competitive thrust and exclude competitors.

- finally, IT can play a role in putting **strategy into action**. For example, we have already seen in the previous chapter how IT can play a vital role in process redesign efforts.

Test your understanding 1

Foxtrot is a commercial property realtor (agent) who sells commercial properties on behalf of other businesses. Five years ago it experienced its fifth consecutive year of declining sales.

Analysis showed that one of the key reasons for this was the growth of rivals offering internet based alternative services. These services allowed prospective customers to choose a property that was for sale and view floor plans, planning authority permissions, internal videos and pictures etc. before having to visit the actual site. This was different to Foxtrot's business model which required prospective buyers to visit Foxtrot's office and the site that was for sale. At the other end of the market, Foxtrot lacked the economies of scale and cost efficiencies to provide a no-frills service that had been successfully employed by some companies in the market.

Foxtrot took the decision that it needed to react to this changed environment. The company decided to do this by differentiating its service and focusing on executive properties. It aimed to introduce services that were not available from rivals. It aimed to have a website which allowed prospective buyers to not only do the things that they could do on rivals' sites, but also to use elements of Computer Aided Design (CAD) to redesign interiors, try out different layouts and colour schemes and even add or remove virtual walls, doorways and non-supporting pillars.

In order to make this possible a significant investment was made in a new software system and a new e-business website. This investment allowed the business to differentiate itself from rivals. It turned out to be a very worthwhile investment for the business and over the last five years growth has returned and Foxtrot is in a position near the top of the market.

The company has now decided to move into the non-commercial market. It believes that the software that it has available to users on its website will help it stand out from other rivals selling or renting property to non-commercial customers.

Required:

Analyse the relationship between information technology and strategic planning using the context of Foxtrot to illustrate your analysis.

2 E-Business

The meaning and use of e-business

 E-business has been defined as the transformation of key business processes through the use of internet technologies.

E-commerce is a subset of e-business. The most generic description of e-commerce is trading on the internet, buying and selling products and services online.

Categories of e-business

The categories of e-business functions are shown below:

	Exchange initiated by:	
	Business	**Consumer**
Business **Delivery by**	B2B Business models, e.g. VerticalNet	B2C Business models, e.g. Amazon.com
 Consumer	C2B Business models, e.g. Priceline.com	C2C Business models, e.g. eBay.com

- B2B (business to business). For example, a supermarket IS system automatically placing orders into suppliers' IS systems.

- B2C (business to consumer). Selling over the internet – books, flights, music, etc.

- C2B (consumer to business). Some internet sites display a selection of suppliers' offerings from which the user can choose. A model that largely depends on the internet.

- C2C (consumer to consumer). Auction sites, such as ebay, putting consumers in touch with each other. Amazon does the same by offering second-hand books. This model largely depends on the internet.

- 'Buy side' e-commerce focuses on transactions between a purchasing organisation and its suppliers.

- 'Sell side' e-commerce focuses on transactions between a purchasing organisation and its customers.

The stages of e-business

The stages of e-business can be described as:

Stage		Characteristics
1	Web presence	Static or dynamic web-pages but no transactions are carried out. Would show information about the organisation, products, contact details, FAQs (Frequently Asked Questions). Faster updates are possible than with paper-based information and could be cheaper than paper-based catalogues.
2	E-commerce	Buying and selling transactions using e-commerce. Might cut out middlemen, but there is probably no fundamental change in the nature of the business.
3	Integrated e-commerce	For example, information can be gathered about each customer's buying habits. This can allow the organisation to target customers very precisely and to begin to predict demand.
4	E-business	E-business is now fundamental to the business strategy and may well determine the business strategy.

This model helps businesses to understand where they are in the process of e-business, and this will help them to decide where to go next with further development.

Illustration 2 – E-business

In the book-selling industry, small, independent second-hand or antiquarian booksellers might simply place themselves at stage 1 of the e-business cycle. They may simply use an internet site to explain the services they provide, the types of book they sell, their location etc. They are unlikely to use the site to actually buy or sell books (though they may do so as they get larger and therefore move onto stage 2 in the cycle).

Large national retailers, such as Barnes and Noble, WH Smith, Empik, Page One etc., have moved on to stage 2. They replicate offline sales via internet sites where customers can buy books at the same price as they can in stores and have these books delivered straight to their homes.

It is predicted that over the next few years some of these businesses might then move to stage 3 in the cycle. They will offer additional online content to supplement their offline or e-commerce sales. So there might be author interviews, deleted chapters, previews of new books etc. to provide a much rounder product and service. They also hope to capture more information about their customers so they can use this in e-marketing and Customer Relationship Management (both of these are explored in detail in the next chapter).

A business such as Amazon is at stage 4 of the cycle. The use of internet, e-commerce, e-marketing etc. are fundamental to how it operates and are the sole focus of its strategic plans for book selling.

Benefits of e-business

Most companies employ e-business to achieve the following:

- Cost reduction – e.g. lower overheads, cheaper procurement
- Increased revenue – e.g. online sales, better CRM
- Better information for control – e.g. monitoring website sales
- Increased visibility
- Enhanced customer service – e.g. via extranets
- Improved marketing – e.g. emailing customers with special offers
- Market penetration – e.g. even small suppliers can gain a global presence via the internet
- The combination of the above should be to enhance the company's competitive advantage.

Barriers to e-business

Barriers to e-business can be seen in both the organisation itself and in its suppliers and customers. They include:

- technophobia
- security concerns
- set-up costs
- running costs
- limited opportunities to exploit e-business
- limited IT resources in house
- customers not likely to be interested in e-business.

 Explanation of the barriers to e-business

- Technophobia. Senior managers are distrustful and sceptical about the alleged benefits of e-business.

- Security concerns about hackers and electronic fraud.

- Set-up costs. Simple, static pages are cheap to set up, but dynamic pages, linking to e-commerce systems and databases, with impressive design values are expensive to set up.

- Running costs. As well as renting space on a web-server, maintenance of websites is very important as most users are very unforgiving about out-of-date sites. Updating, say with special offers, is also needed to encourage return visits, perhaps linked to email campaigns.

- Limited opportunities to exploit e-business. Some businesses (such as selling books) are more suitable for e-business than others (such as selling carpets).

- Limited IT resources in house (e.g. a lack of staff skills creating staff resistance) so recruitment is needed or all development and maintenance has to be sub-contracted.

- Customers not likely to be interested in e-business (e.g. firms targeting retired pensioners).

E-business hardware

E-business infrastructure is the combination of hardware, software and content used to deliver e-business to both employees and customers. The quality of the hardware will have a direct link to the quality of the e-business offered. The hardware decisions that an organisation will face include areas such as:

- computers

- networks

- servers

- back-up.

Alongside these decisions the organisation will also have to consider:

- the degree of outsourcing: the location and management of the hardware in terms of whether the hardware is located and managed internally or whether it is outsourced to third parties, and

- the degree of flexibility: whether the system will be able to cope as technology improves and employee and customer needs change.

 More details on the hardware in an IT system

Some of the key elements of the hardware used in e-business are examined below.

Computers

There are three key elements of a computer that determine its speed and capability:

- the speed of the central processing unit (CPU),

- the amount of random access memory (RAM), and

- the ability of the graphics processing unit (GPU).

The CPU is the brains of the computer. The faster the CPU the quicker the computer can perform tasks and exchange signals with the RAM.

The more RAM that the computer has then the more tasks it can complete at once. This may be important, for example, if employees need to have more than one software application open at once such as a customer enquiry portal and an inventory portal.

The GPU is designed to rapidly manipulate and alter memory to accelerate the creation of images. The better the GPU then the quicker that the outcome of tasks can be displayed visually, for example.

Networks

In e-business, computers cannot stand alone. They need to be connected together so that users can share data and more easily and quickly communicate with each other. For internal, employee-only communication then a local area network (LAN) might suffice. This is where the computers are physically linked via wiring to each other. However, this will restrict access to those who are physically wired into the system and will make it very difficult to connect users over large distances.

Therefore, it is more common to use a wide area network (WAN) using internets, intranets and extranets that are connected through infrastructure provided by internet service providers (ISPs). These WANs allow very fast communication and transfer of data over large distances.

Servers

Servers are used to manage network traffic, share data in applications and store data (if necessary). The more CPU speed and RAM that the server has the greater number of users who can access the network at once and the quicker the network will work.

Because servers are providing and storing data for many users and applications they will need lots of RAM and physical storage space. They are typically the most powerful computer in the system. Many organisations will use what is known as a client-server model – this means that some data processing is performed locally (on the users computer, or client), but the most demanding tasks are handled by the more powerful server.

Back-up

The server holds a lot of vital information that is accessed and created by users. It will therefore be vital that this data is backed up regularly (and later in the chapter we consider how the data can be made physically secure and access to the data can be limited to the correct users).

Data will be stored on a hard disk and a typical server will have 5 hard disks working together in what is known as a RAID system. 2 disks hold and share the data with users and these 2 disks are then copied (or mirrored) regularly to 2 back-up disks. A fifth disk is ready to step into action if one of the other disks fail.

When users download data to their own client hard disk it can be used and changed. But it will only be backed up when it is copied back to the server so that the RAID system can mirror it. It is therefore better to store as much data as possible on the server than on local hard drives.

Intranets and extranets

Intranets are internal internets. They exist inside the organisation only, using website and browser technology to display information.

Commonly they contain:

- information about customers
- information about products
- information about competitors
- news/updates
- procedure manuals.

However, there's no reason why accounting information cannot be delivered over intranets.

Extranets are intranets that are connected to external intranets.

For example, a supplier could give customers access to their order processing system so that orders can be placed and tracked. It is when these types of external connection are made that e-business can begin to produce spectacular results.

Other requirements needed to deliver an e-business strategy

Connection to the internet will not, of itself, deliver e-business. Suitable hardware, software and business processes have to be in place. Here are some examples of how e-business could affect various business areas.

Business area	Where e-business could impact	Strategic aim
Research and development	<ul><li>Internet used for research purposes</li><li>Access to research databases</li><li>Access to patent databases</li></ul>	To be a leader in innovation. To develop unique, differentiated products

Design	Computer-aided design	Fast production of new designs and products. CAD will make designs cheaper (cost leading) and faster (differentiation)
Manufacturing/ service provision	Computer-aided manufacturing Just-in-time inventories	Flexible, low cost, but tailored to customers' requirements
Communication with customers	Website and email	
Inbound logistics	Organisation of the supply chain	Low cost, low inventory balances, flexible manufacturing
The buy side e-commerce transactions	Automating the purchases cycle	Low cost as less human intervention
Outbound logistics	Organisation of the distribution chain	Low cost, low inventory balances, fast delivery to customers
The sell side e-commerce transactions	Automating the sales cycle	Low cost as less human intervention. Greater accuracy

Risks and benefits of internet and intranet use

Many organisations have intranet systems or use the internet directly. Using an intranet or the internet has obvious advantages, but also creates substantial risks.

The advantages of intranets and the internet

- Employees have ready access to vast sources of external data that would not otherwise be available. Using external information can help to improve the quality of decision making.

- Organisations can advertise their goods and services on a website, and provide other information that helps to promote their image.

- Organisations can use the internet to purchase goods or supplies, saving time and money. For example, the internet is used regularly by businesses to purchase standard items such as stationery, and to reserve hotel rooms and purchase travel tickets.

- The internet/intranet provides a means of operating an email system. Communication by email is fast and should remove the requirement for excessive quantities of paper. Using emails might also reduce the non-productive time spent by employees on the telephone.

- Intranets create the opportunity for more flexible organisation of work. For example, employees who are away from the office can access the organisation's IT systems and files through the internet. Similarly, employees can work from their home but have full access to the organisation's systems.

The disadvantages of intranets and the internet

There are disadvantages with using intranets and the internet.

- Email systems can become inefficient if too many messages are sent and users have to look through large amounts of 'junk mail' to find messages of value.

- Emails can be disruptive, especially if a prompt appears on an individual's computer screen whenever a new message is received.

- Senders of emails often expect an immediate reply to their messages, and a delay in responding can create bad feelings and ill-will.

- Employees might waste too much time looking for information on the internet, when the value of the information is not worth the time spent looking for it.

- Without suitable controls, employees might spend large amounts of time on the internet or exchanging emails for their personal benefit, rather than on carrying out their work responsibilities.

The greatest problem with using intranets and the internet, however, is the vulnerability of the organisation's IT systems to:

- unauthorised access by hackers, including industrial spies

- the import of viruses in attachments to email messages and other malicious software.

Test your understanding 2

RBT manufactures tractors, harvesting machinery and similar farm equipment. It operates from one integrated office and factory near the capital of the country in which it is based. Due to restricted demand and the cost of manufacture of individual items, all equipment is manufactured to specific orders from clients. No inventories of finished goods are maintained although inventories of spare parts are available for sale.

The farm equipment is sold to farm owners by one of 20 sales representatives. The general procedure for making a sale is for the representative to visit the farm owner to discuss the owner's requirements. Basic price and model specification information is obtained from printed manuals that the representative carries. The representative then telephones the RBT office and confirms with production staff that the order can be made, checks the price and receives an estimated delivery date. An order confirmation is written out and the representative moves on to the next appointment. The farmer pays for the equipment on receipt.

As the country in which RBT operates is large, representatives cannot often visit RBT's office, so their price and model specification manuals may be out of date. The board of RBT is considering the introduction of a new information system. Each representative will be given a portable PC. Information on such things as products and prices will be kept on an intranet and downloaded by telephone line when needed by the representative. Access to production managers and sales representatives will also be made via the intranet. The voice telephone system will be discontinued and email is thought to be unnecessary.

Required:

(a) Evaluate the proposed use of the intranet within the RBT Company showing whether it would provide an appropriate communication channel for the sales representatives. Suggest ways in which any problems you have identified with the new systems may be resolved.

(b) Identify and evaluate any information systems that can be used to provide clients with information on the progress of their orders with RBT while they are being manufactured.

Making websites interactive

One of the most effective things you can do with your website is to give users power over it. Give them choices, tools and features that encourage them to interact with the site and provide them with a sense of control over it.

- Search – Provide users with the ability to search your website for words, phrases and/or provide them with key topics from which to choose. Consider in what format the results are to be presented.

- Online forms – How many, number of fields in each, what needs to be verified before the user submits the form – e.g. have they completed the field for email address?

- 'Members only' section to the site – Is there a section that can only be accessed via a user name and password? Where are the user names and passwords to be stored? How will you handle people who forget their password?

- Interactive questionnaires/surveys/polls – How many, how long, how will they be presented? What will you do with the information provided by the users?

- Animations – How can you (should you) use Flash or other programming devices to bring life into your site and illustrate products and services?

- Subscription email lists – What can users subscribe to by way of email lists, such as e-newsletters?

- Links to other sites – How many and what tools are to be employed during maintenance to check automatically on the veracity of the link?

- Downloadable files – PDFs, images, audio files – how many, in what format, with what restrictions?

- Contact Us – What contact details should be on the site – e.g. email, telephone, street address?

- Site map – What is the site map of the website to look like? Just text as links or is a diagram preferred?

- Text-only version of the site – Will you need a text-only version of the website for customers who are visually impaired or with a slow/expensive connection?

- Multilingual requirements – How many languages? How much of the site is to be multilingual? At what point are users to nominate which language they want to view the site in – e.g. home page, a splash page?

- Provision for printing and bookmarking (i.e. allowing users to store the website address in their browser's memory or 'favourites' section) – Are users to be able to bookmark specific pages or is the home page sufficient? Do you want any special print function other than the default function supplied by the browser?

3 Information Technology risks

Computer systems have unique risk and control issues that need to be addressed by business. As with any risk factor the company needs to make an assessment of the risks and decide on the appropriate level of control to reduce the risks to an acceptable level.

Risks to a computer system

A risk to a computer system could be anything that prevents the managers getting the information they need from the system at the time that they need it.

 Risks to information processing facilities may arise from:

- Dissatisfied employees might deliberately modify or destroy information in the system.

- A hacker or industrial spy might break into the system.

- Viruses or malicious software could be introduced.

- Accidental mistakes could be made on input to the system.

- Inadequate security of the hardware or data.

- Faults in the hardware system.

Such risks result in the loss of information (or the loss of its integrity or confidentiality), business disruption and a loss of time and money.

Further detail on risks

Information security

Risks to information security can be categorised as follows:

Risks	Description
Risk of hardware theft	This risk might seem fairly obvious, but the theft of computer hardware is common.
Physical damage to hardware and computer media (disks, etc.)	Physical damage can be caused by: • malicious damage • poor operating conditions causing damage to equipment and files • natural disasters, such as fire and flooding.
Damage to data	Data can be damaged by hackers attacking the system, viruses, program faults in the software and faults in the hardware or data storage media. Software, particularly purpose-written software, can become corrupted. Programs might be altered by a hacker or computer fraudster. Alternatively, a new version of a program might be written and introduced, but contain a serious error that results in the corruption or loss of data on file.
Operational mistakes	Unintentional mistakes can cause damage to data or loss of data; for example, using the wrong version of a computer program, or the wrong version of a data file, or deleting data that is still of value.
Fraud and industrial espionage	This can lead to the loss of confidentiality of sensitive information, or the criminal creation of false data and false transactions, or the manipulation of data for personal gain.

Data protection legislation

Some countries give individuals the right to seek compensation against an organisation that holds personal data about them, if they suffer loss through the improper use of that data. In the UK, for example, rights are given to 'data subjects' by the Data Protection Act. There could be a risk that an organisation will improperly use or communicate personal data about individuals, in breach of the legislation.

Erroneous input

Many information systems, especially those based on transaction processing systems and with large volumes of input transactions, are vulnerable to mistakes in the input data.

- Some input items might be overlooked and omitted. Other transactions might be entered twice.

- There might be errors in the input data, particularly where the data is input by humans rather than by electronic data transfer. For example, in a system relying on input via keyboard and mouse, data accuracy depends on the ability of the operator to input the data without making a mistake.

Where input errors are high, the integrity of the data and information becomes doubtful.

Hacking

Hacking is the gaining of unauthorised access to a computer system. It might be a deliberate attempt to gain access to an organisation's systems and files, to obtain information or to alter data (perhaps fraudulently).

Once hackers have gained access to the system, there are several damaging options available to them. For example, they may:

- gain access to the file that holds all the user ID codes, passwords and authorisations

- discover the method used for generating/authorising passwords

- interfere with the access control system, to provide the hacker with open access to the system

- obtain information which is of potential use to a competitor organisation

- obtain, enter or alter data for a fraudulent purpose

- cause data corruption by the introduction of unauthorised computer programs and processing on to the system (computer viruses)

- alter or delete files.

Viruses

A virus is a piece of software that seeks to infest a computer system, hiding and automatically spreading to other systems if given the opportunity. Most computer viruses have three functions – avoiding detection, reproducing themselves and causing damage. Viruses might be introduced into a computer system directly, or by disk or email attachment.

> Viruses include:
>
> - trojans – whilst carrying on one program, secretly carry on another
> - worms – these replicate themselves within the systems
> - trap doors – undocumented entry points to systems allowing normal controls to be by-passed
> - logic bombs – triggered on the occurrence of a certain event
> - time bombs – which are triggered on a certain date.

4 Controls in an information systems environment

To combat the types of risks discussed above companies will put in place control procedures.

The rationale for strong information system controls

From a strategic perspective, effective information system controls are vital for a business. The realisation of IT risks can have a number of consequences for a business such as:

- Incorrect decisions based on incorrect information. If, say, standard cost systems are recording standard costs incorrectly then strategic decisions on areas such as pricing may in turn be incorrect.

- Poor performance measurement and appraisal. For example, if sales totals have been input incorrectly then this will impact on the appraisal of sales targets for staff and may, in turn, impact on bonus and reward payments. Knock-on effects on motivation levels could have serious consequences for the business.

- Unhappy customers and suppliers. If customers are receiving incorrect information, such as totals on sales invoices or payments then they can lose trust in the business. This may mean that they take their business elsewhere.

- Reputational damage may arise from deliberate hacks and viruses that corrupt, steal or destroy data in the system. Potential customers may not believe that their data is safe and may not want the business to hold their data. A loss of a sense of security can drive customers elsewhere – especially if the business is transacting online.

- Correcting problems and creating adequate new controls can lead to significant business disruption. This can result in a loss of business as well as significant costs in solving the problems.

- Hackers or malicious employees may gain access to crucial business information. This may be very valuable to competitors or may prematurely disclose business plans. It may even be that the information is of a negative nature such as problems with proposed new developments that could adversely impact on the business' share price and ability to raise finance, for example.

- Protection of data is highly regulated. Failure to do so may result in fines being imposed upon and restrictions being placed on the business.

Examples of information system controls

Controls can be classed as belonging to one of four categories:

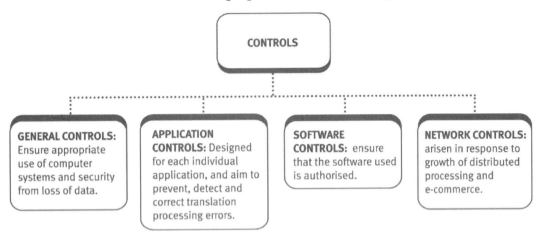

GENERAL CONTROLS: Ensure appropriate use of computer systems and security from loss of data.

APPLICATION CONTROLS: Designed for each individual application, and aim to prevent, detect and correct translation processing errors.

SOFTWARE CONTROLS: ensure that the software used is authorised.

NETWORK CONTROLS: arisen in response to growth of distributed processing and e-commerce.

Alternative control classification

There are a number of different ways in which controls can be classified in an IT environment.

An alternative to the classification described above is:

- **Security controls:** controls designed to ensure the prevention of unauthorised access, modification or destruction of stored data.

- **Integrity controls:** controls to ensure that the data are accurate, consistent and free from accidental corruption.

- **Contingency controls:** in the event that security or integrity controls fail there must be a back-up facility and a contingency plan to restore business operations as quickly as possible.

General controls

Personnel controls

Recruitment, training and supervision needs to be in place to ensure the competency of those responsible for programming and data entry.

 Logical access controls

Security over access is often based on a logical access system. This is illustrated by the following diagram:

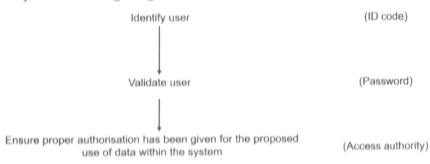

Identify user (ID code)

Validate user (Password)

Ensure proper authorisation has been given for the proposed use of data within the system (Access authority)

Passwords and user names are a way of identifying who is authorised to access the system, and granting access to the system, or to specific programs or files, only if an authorised password is entered. There may be several levels of password, with particularly sensitive applications protected by multiple passwords.

 Problems with passwords

Password systems can only be effective if users use them conscientiously. There are several inherent problems with a password system:

- Authorised users may divulge their password to a colleague.

- Many passwords may have associations with the user so that a hacker can discover them by experimentation.

- Passwords are often written down close to the computer (e.g. pinned to the notice board inside the office) and so easily discovered.

To protect passwords and user numbers against discovery, a number of precautions should be adopted:

- Users should be required to change their passwords regularly.

- Passwords should be memorable but not obviously related to a user's private life.

- Users should be encouraged never to write down their passwords.

- There should be strict controls over passwords – they should never be 'lent' or written down where they can be easily seen.

- There should be automatic sentinel or watchdog programs to identify when a password has been keyed incorrectly.

Access logging

The system will produce regular reports including a system access report and various pre-determined exception reports. The effectiveness of these reports is determined by:

- The frequency of report production.

- The follow up of detected breaches in security.

Audit trail

An audit trail consists of a record or series of records that allows the processing of a transaction or an amendment by a computer or clerical system to be identified accurately, as well as verifying the authenticity of the transaction or amendment, including the identity of the individuals who initiated and authorised it.

Audit trails are also used to record customer activity in e-commerce on a company's website. The audit trail records the customer's initial access to the website, and then each subsequent activity (purchasing and payment, confirmation of order and delivery of the product). The audit trail can be used to deal with any subsequent enquiry or complaint from the customer. In some cases, 'audit trails' can be used to track down hackers into a system. A hacker might sometimes unknowingly leave a trail of where he came from, for example through records in the activity log of the hacker's internet service provider.

Facility controls

 Physical access

There are various basic categories of controlling access to sensitive areas. These include:

- security guards in buildings
- working areas to which access is through a locked door or a door with an ID card entry system or entry system requiring the user to enter a personal identification code (PIN number)
- using safes and lockable filing cabinets
- closed circuit TV used to monitor what is happening in a particular part of a building – this may be backed up by security video cameras
- doors automatically locked in the event of a security alarm.

Additionally, procedural controls to protect files and output include:

- disks should not be left lying around on desks and working surfaces
- computer printout and disks should be shredded or otherwise destroyed before being thrown away.

Location of IT facilities

It is imperative that the location of the system is considered, and hence all equipment is located so as to protect against:

- Fire

- Flood

- Smoke

- Food

- Drinks

- Power failure

- Environment

- Business continuity.

Business continuity planning (**disaster recovery planning**) takes place in order to recover information systems from business critical events after they have happened. It involves:

- Making a risk assessment

- Developing a contingency plan to address those risks.

More on disaster recovery plans

An unexpected disaster can put an entire computer system out of action. For large organisations, a disaster might involve damage from a terrorist attack. There could also be threats from fire and flood damage. A disaster might simply be a software or hardware breakdown within a system.

Disaster recovery planning involves assessing what disasters might occur that would pose a serious threat to the organisation, and trying to ensure that alternative arrangements are available in the event that a disaster occurs.

In the case of a computer system for a clearing bank, this would mean having an entire back-up computer system in place that could be brought into operation if a disaster puts the main system out of action.

Not all organisations have extensive disaster recovery plans. Certainly, however, back-up copies of major data files should be kept, so that in the event that the main files are destroyed, the data can be re-created with the back-up files.

System back-ups

All files containing important information should be backed up on a regular basis. Backing up provides protection against the loss or corruption of data due to:

- faults in the hardware (e.g. hard disk)

- the accidental deletion of a file by a computer operator

- damage to a data file by a hacker.

A back-up is simply a copy of the file. If the original file is lost or becomes corrupt, the back-up can be substituted in its place, and the master file can be re-created.

There will be some loss of data if the input to the system since the most recent back-up copy of the file was made.

- However, if back-ups are made regularly, the loss of data should be limited. If there are paper records of input transactions since the most recent back-up copy was made, the file can be brought up to date by re-inputting the data.

- Some systems provide back-up copies of both master files and transaction data files, and copies of these files can be used to re-create an up-to-date master file if the original master file is lost or corrupted.

Back-up copies might be stored on the same physical computer file as the original file, but this is risky, since damage to the physical file will result in the loss of the back-up as well as the main file.

Back-up files might be created by copying them on to a disk or tape. Where security is important, any such back-up copies should be held in a secure place, such as a safe.

To counter the risk of damage to a file due to a fire or similar disaster at the premises where the IT system is located, a back-up copy might be taken off-site and held somewhere else.

Application controls

These are controls to ensure that data are correctly input, processed and maintained, and only distributed to authorised personnel.

Application controls are specific to each application, but these can include controls such as spell checks and format checks that ensure that inputted data is accurate and complete.

The accounting system may have additional controls such as credit limits for customers which cannot be altered.

Software controls

Software control prevents making or installing unauthorised copies of software. Illegal software is more likely to fail, comes without warranties or support, can place systems at risk of viruses and the use of illegal software can result in significant financial penalties.

Software can be controlled by:

- Buying only from reputable dealers.

- Ensuring that the original disks come with the software.

- Ensuring that licences are received for all software.

- Retaining all original disks and documentation.

Network controls

Risks on networks

The increase in popularity of the LAN (local area network) has brought concerns in relation to system security. An LAN allows for many more breaches of security than does a single computer.

The main areas of concern are:

- Tapping into cables

- Unauthorised log in

- Computer viruses

- File copying

- File server security.

Controls

Controls must exist to prevent unauthorised access to data transmitted over networks and to secure the integrity of data.

Methods include:

- Firewalls

- Flow

- Data encryption

- Virus protection.

More on network controls

Firewalls: A firewall will consist of a combination of hardware and software located between the company's intranet (private network) and the public network (internet). A set of control procedures will be established to allow public access to some parts of the organisation's computer system (outside the firewall) whilst restricting access to other parts (inside the firewall).

Flow: This regulates movement of data from one file to another. Channels are specified along which information is allowed to flow, i.e. confidential/non-confidential, and these are linked by authority levels.

Data encryption: Encryption is a technique of disguising information to preserve its confidentiality. It is disguised during processing/storage. In essence it is a method of scrambling the data in a message or file so that it is unintelligible unless it is unscrambled (or decrypted).

Virus protection: It is extremely difficult to protect systems against the introduction of computer viruses. Preventative steps may include:

- control on the use of external software (e.g. checked for viruses before using new software)

- using anti-virus software, regularly updated, to detect and deal with viruses

- educating employees to be watchful for viruses being imported as attachment files to email messages.

Test your understanding 3

Robson has over 200 other hotels around the world. It is now considering investing in the building of a new hotel in an area that is attracting very wealthy people. The hotel is to be 'state of the art', and Robson's management is hoping that it will be the first 7-star hotel in the area. It is expected that the richest people in the world will want to holiday here and the hotel will, therefore, command a premium price.

Robson hotel rooms can be booked online but only through an agent or intermediary travel website. Robson has heavily invested in IT security and typical processes in place at each hotel are listed below:

- A security policy to allocate responsibility for the information and systems in the hotel.

- A management structure with roles defined and documented, covering authorisation of purchases of software and hardware, and systems to prevent unauthorised access to data. In particular, some staff have access to clients' details and credit card information and this is protected by employing reputable staff, investing in comprehensive training and by having supervision at all times.

- An asset register of all hardware and software owned by the hotel.

- Systems in place and monitored to minimise risks from error, fraud, theft or hacking. All staff are fully trained to be able to use the systems, reducing the number of errors that might occur.

- Controls to restrict access and provide physical security against fire and theft of reception and hotel computer equipment. This includes passwords, locks on doors, security cameras and fire extinguishers.

- All systems are developed in accordance with standards, tested and documented.

- Change control systems are in place to control all development and maintenance work thereafter.

- A continuity/disaster-recovery plan to cover all information systems, including backup, offsite fireproof storage of data and alternative hardware, software and building site requirements for recovery.

- Adequate insurance.

The new hotel will have suites rather than standard rooms meaning that there will be a living and dining area as well as a number of rooms attached to each suite. Each suite will follow an individual theme such as suites themed on a famous movie or international location. Each suite will be unique and prospective visitors will be able to choose their desired suite through their agent or intermediary website.

Suites may often be used for business reasons as well as for pleasure and therefore each suite will have open access to the internet via superfast wired connections. This goes beyond the service provided in existing hotels where visitors often have to share a slow and simple wifi connection that has web filtering software that restricts downloads and access to certain types of internet sites.

Required:

Explain the IT risks that the new hotel might bring to Robson and recommend controls to overcome these risks.

Professional skill:
Illustrate analysis skills in considering each risk.

5 Chapter summary

```
                    ┌─────────────────────┐
                    │     E-business      │
                    └─────────────────────┘
```

Strategic context
- Can create strengths
- Improves the value chain
- Can create new strategic options
- Can aid strategy implementation

Benefits and barriers
- Market penetration
- Cost reduction
- Facilitates e-marketing

But:
- Expensive set up
- Requires new skills

Risks and controls

Risks
- Viruses
- Security
- Cyber attacks

Controls
- General
- Software
- Network

Test your understanding answers

Test your understanding 1

The choice and use of information technology can be seen as part of the implementation stage of strategic planning. Johnson, Scholes and Whittington suggest that strategic planning has three elements:

- strategic analysis – this involves an analysis of the organisation's environment and assessing the organisation's fit to that environment

- strategic choice – this involves designing corporate and business level strategies to take account of the organisation's environment and improving the organisation's position in that environment

- strategy into action (or implementation) – this involves facilitating strategic choices through making changes to business processes, staffing, marketing, etc.

Johnson, Scholes and Whittington suggest that the three elements are inter-related. In that manner, strategy into action will be affected by strategic analysis and choice.

For example, Foxtrot analysed their environment and spotted both weaknesses and threats. This in turn affected its strategic choice. It chose to move to a new position on the strategy clock and compete in a new way. This strategic analysis and choice in turn affected its IT strategy – a new system was needed and it had to provide services that were not available elsewhere in the market in order to differentiate the company's service. The choice to differentiate meant that bespoke systems would have been needed with the ability to incorporate elements of online CAD.

So part of the relationship between IT and strategic planning can be seen here: IT decisions are clearly impacted by strategic analysis and strategic choices.

But because these elements are inter-related, Johnson, Scholes and Whittington suggested that the strategic planning process can effectively begin at any stage.

For example, it would appear that the new strategic direction is being driven by the IT investment. The investment in the new software appears to have not only given the company strengths in terms of a competitive advantage over existing rivals, but it also appears to have provided an opportunity to move into the non-commercial market. This strategic analysis has in turn impacted on the strategic choice to develop this new market and the IT system in place is likely to support a focused differentiation in this new market development.

In this way, we can see that IT strategies can impact on strategic plans. Overall, therefore, IT strategies and strategic planning are closely related. We have seen how strategic planning can impact on IT strategies, but also how IT strategies can impact on the strategic plans of an organisation.

Test your understanding 2

Key answer tips

The requirement "evaluate" is a high level verb requiring you to look at the value of something. It is often helpful to consider advantages and disadvantages of an idea when tackling this requirement. Your answers to both parts (a) and (b) of this question need to utilise information from the scenario to score high marks. Points that do not relate to RBT will not be rewarded, particularly if they are inappropriate suggestions for this type of organisation.

(a) **Intranet**

An intranet is an internal company information system where a wide variety of internal information can be posted for access by staff members. Internal information often includes company news, telephone directories, standard forms, copies of rules and procedures, and so on. In this case of the system under consideration by RBT, the intranet would hold up-to-date information on products and prices, so that sales representatives can download this information to their laptops from a customer's premises and other remote locations.

Advantages

The proposed new system has the following advantages over the old system:

– More regularly updated information

An intranet site is very easy and cheap to update, and product and price information can be kept fully up-to-date by head office. The downloaded product information will therefore be much more up-to-date than the old printed materials, and a better customer service can be provided. All the latest products would be made available to customers and customers would always be given the correct prices.

– Reduced costs of producing price lists/brochures.

Regular price lists and brochures will no longer be required, and the production and printing costs of paper-based products should be reduced.

Disadvantages

The intranet site has the following disadvantages compared with the old system:

– Slower communication with the production department.

Since the telephone system will be discontinued, the sales people will not have access to production staff to resolve any queries or difficulties with customers. This would be a serious weakness in the system. Good communications between sales and production staff must be maintained.

Solutions

Possible solutions to this problem include:

(i)   Email system

Email might provide an efficient way for sales representatives to communicate directly with the production staff, although controls would need to be in place to ensure that the production staff responds promptly to email queries they receive.

(ii)   Maintain telephone access

Voice telephone access offers immediate communication. A sales person can get in contact with a member of the production staff and get an immediate reply. Maintaining telephone access for certain queries would be a useful way of ensuring very quick communication where needed.

(iii) Access to production scheduling system

Allowing salespeople access to the production scheduling system over the intranet would allow them to estimate a delivery date themselves thus reducing the need for direct contact between production and sales.

–   Less personal communication with production department

The intranet is a very impersonal way to communicate with people. It does not allow for two-way conversation, whereas personal contact may be required to resolve difficult issues.

Solution

Both email and a voice telephone system are more personal forms of communication than the intranet. The voice telephone system in particular allows a two-way conversation to take place so that more difficult issues can easily be resolved.

–   Rejection of new technology

The sales people may dislike the new technology that they are required to use. At present they do not use IT significantly in their work, and so new skills may be required. Many new systems also have 'teething problems' on implementation, which may also make users dislike the new system.

Solutions

(i) Training

Training will be required so people know how the system works and can get the best use from it.

(ii) Consultation

Consulting users early in the development process is an excellent way of getting user buy-in to the new system. It will also ensure the system is practical from a day-to-day usage point of view.

(iii) Testing

Testing systems well prior to implementation will help avoid the teething problems which may be encountered, particularly if the end users are involved since they know better than anyone else the way the system will be used in practice.

– Up-front costs

The proposed new system will require significant up-front costs both in terms of developing the new system and training staff. Given the relatively small number of sales representatives (just 20) the investment may not be financially justified.

Solution

A cost-benefit analysis can be undertaken to ascertain whether the costs of the investment are justified.

(b) **Information systems – order progress**

Manufacturing system – order tracking

As part of the manufacturing process, progress on orders will need to be recorded. The information recorded will include work done, work still to do and the expected completion date. This information might already exist within the current system or it may need to be input into a database which can be accessed by clients.

EDI or extranet

Using electronic data interchange the customer would be able to log on to RBT's systems to directly access the production data.

An extranet is an extension of an intranet. External parties are allowed to log into the intranet site and use it to access sections of the intranet. The intranet site would need to be connected to the manufacturing system/database so that up-to-date information is available.

Advantages

1   Clients could access information themselves. This could save staff time and resources in RBT, since there will be fewer customer queries to deal with.

2   An extranet would be relatively easy to provide if the manufacturing system is already linked to the intranet for the benefit of the salespeople.

3   Other information could also be provided to customers (such as past order information, account balances and so on).

Disadvantages

1   There would be a loss of personal contact with customers. The salesperson would not have as many opportunities to make contact with customers in order to build an ongoing relationship. As a consequence, they might identify fewer sales opportunities or find it harder to make a sale because they are less trusted by the customer.

2   External parties would be accessing internal systems. There is a danger that hackers will get into parts of the system that are confidential, and a risk that important information is stolen or damaged. It could also increase the possibility of viruses being brought in which could damage internal systems.

Internet

Alternatively the RBT could put tracking information on a database which is connected to the company's website. Clients would then be able to access their information through this site.

Advantages

1   Labour cost savings, as described for an extranet.

2   Customers will be familiar with the internet and so find it easier to use than an extranet or internal system accessed via EDI. It also means they will not have to dial in directly to the company's internal network, saving them time and effort.

3   There is less opportunity for hackers or viruses to enter the internal systems using a website on the internet, since they are not directly accessing internal systems.

4   Other information could also be provided to customers on the internet site.

Disadvantage

The company may not currently have an internet site. This could be a significant extra expense, in terms of designing, creating and maintaining the site.

Test your understanding 3

The new hotel will differ from a technology perspective to the existing hotels and it is these differences that will open up new risks and require new technology controls. The existing controls should be fully implemented and then supplemented with new controls.

The first risk from the new hotel is that system access controls will need to be in place. It will be important that only visitors to each suite can access the internet in that suite, to ensure that visitors can't access the internet in other suites, and ensure that non-visitors cannot access visitor systems. Robson should have secure passwords for each suite that are changed regularly. These passwords should only be provided to the relevant visitor (s) and the system should have authentication software to ensure that a valid password is used in each suite.

Agents will be able to choose a suite prior to actual check-in at the hotel. There is a risk that the room may not actually be available. It will therefore be important to have application controls which match up agent requirements with room availability. This will highlight for the agent when there is conflict and the required suite is not available. It may also be possible to have the system indicate alternative suites that are available on the dates requested.

There is an added risk here that the system may indicate that a suite is unavailable but it is actually free on the dates requested. Robson should run regular tests to check for this problem. The test could attempt to book a suite that Robson knows is empty or full and ensure that the system returns the correct result.

This will be a preventative control that will avoid problems and embarrassment when a visitor arrives for a suite that is double booked. In existing hotels these visitors could be moved to an alternative room, but this will be a bigger problem when a visitor wants to stay in a particular themed suite.

Visitors will have unrestricted access to the internet in their suites. There is a risk that they will inadvertently download viruses, for example. A strong investment in firewalls and virus protection will be required for every suite and device that is accessed by visitors.

It may be prudent to provide visitors with advice and warning material in suites to help them understand the risks of internet usage and to help them improve their own practices. If, for example, a user was to fall prey to a phishing attack whilst using the hotel's internet they may feel that the hotel is at fault and it would therefore be best for the hotel to at least reduce the chance of such events occurring.

There may also be a problem with visitors accessing inappropriate content. For example, open access to the internet may allow children to visit sites that are not age appropriate and which they are not allowed to access at home. Robson should employ a web filtering service to its servers (this means that certain sites such as gambling and pornography, for example, cannot be accessed). The web filtering could be removed on a visit by visit basis at the visitors written consent/request so that visitors who do want to access the internet openly can do so but the risks are made known to them and the hotel is not policing the content.

Professional skill:

You may have identified other risks and controls that could be used here. The key to exam success will be to ensure that you **analyse** these in sufficient depth. You need to explain what the risk is, what the impact might be, the controls that should be put in place to overcome these risks and why these controls will remove or reduce the risk for the business. You do not need to have the same answer as the examiner (in terms of which risks are assessed), but you do need to exhibit the requisite analytical skills.

Using IT successfully

Chapter learning objectives

Upon completion of this chapter you will be able to:

- explore different methods of acquiring and managing suppliers and customers through exploring e-business technologies

- discuss how information technology and data analysis can effectively be used to inform and implement organisation strategy

- describe big data and discuss the opportunities and threats big data represents to organisations

- identify and analyse relevant data for strategic decisions about new product developments, marketing and pricing

- identify and assess the potential impact of disruptive technologies such as Fintech, including cryptocurrencies

- discuss from a strategic perspective the need to explore opportunities for adopting new technologies such as cloud, mobile and smart technology within an organisation

- discuss key benefits and risks of cloud, mobile and smart technology

- assess and advise on using the cloud as an alternative to owned hardware and software technology to support organisation information system needs

- explain the potential benefits of using artificial intelligence (AI), robotics and other forms of machine learning to support strategic decisions and the pursuit of corporate objectives as a strategic tool

- assess the risk, control and ethical implications of using (AI), robotics and other forms of machine learning

PER

Two of the PER performance objectives (PO3) and (PO13) are that you contribute to the wider business strategy of your organisation through your personal and team objectives. You identify innovative ways to improve organisational performance and plan business activities and control performance, making recommendations for improvement. Working through this chapter should help you understand how to demonstrate these objectives.

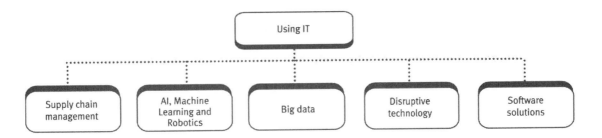

1 Introduction

As seen in the previous chapter, IT is becoming a strategic weapon which many organisations are using to improve their competitive position. This can come in many forms. For example, using IT can improve efficiency and reduce costs in order to compete better, or it can help an organisation react more quickly to a changing environment, it can create new areas of opportunity etc. This chapter explores some of the ways that IT is aiding businesses to be more strategically successful.

2 Supply chain management (SCM)

Many businesses prosper or fail depending on the success of their relationship with their suppliers and with those who they supply. Businesses that rely on other businesses to this extent are in what is called a supply chain – each supplying each other right up to the final link in the chain, the consumer. The internet can help make this relationship work more effectively and efficiently.

About supply chains

 A supply chain encompasses all activities and information flows necessary for the transformation of goods from the origin of the raw material to when the product is finally consumed or discarded.

 More details

This typically involves distribution of the product from the supplier to the manufacturer to the wholesaler to the retailer and to the final consumer, otherwise known as nodes in the supply chain.

It is helpful to make a distinction between upstream and downstream supply chain management. For an internet retailer, for example, upstream SCM would involve transactions between the firm and its suppliers (equivalent to buy-side e-commerce) and downstream, customers (equivalent to sell-side e-commerce).

The transformation of product from node to node includes activities such as:

- production planning

- purchasing

- materials management

- distribution

- customer service

- forecasting.

While each firm can be competitive through improvements to its internal practices, ultimately the ability to do business effectively depends on the efficient functioning of the entire supply chain.

Illustration 1 – Supply chain management (SCM)

In the supply chain shown, ABC Manufacturing Ltd must be responsive to its customers. Direct supplier 1 and Direct supplier 2 must be responsive to ABC Manufacturing Ltd, and Indirect supplier 1 must be responsive to Direct supplier 2.

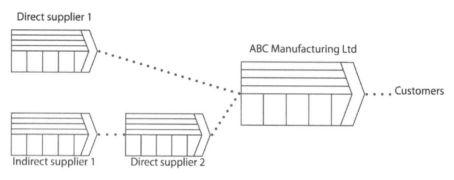

Obviously, if e-business capability is present in all members of the supply chain, management of the chain becomes more feasible: selling, delivering, ordering, designing and manufacturing can all be linked electronically permitting:

- cost savings

- time savings

- faster innovation

- better marketing

- better quality.

Managing the chain

Active management of supply chain activities aims to maximise customer value and achieve a sustainable competitive advantage. It represents a conscious effort by the supply chain firms to develop and run supply chains in the most effective and efficient ways possible. Supply chain activities cover everything from product development, sourcing, production, and logistics, as well as the information systems needed to coordinate these activities. Managing the chain primarily therefore concentrates on the management and progression of the following three items:

- materials/inventory
- information
- funds.

Inventory control

Amongst other things, this will include a consideration of:

- number, location and size of warehouses and distribution centres
- production scheduling (including life cycle management to ensure that new products can be successfully integrated into the chain)
- a transportation strategy (in terms of routes, timing etc.)

Information management

The key elements of information required for successful supply chain management include:

- potential levels of end-user and customer demand
- daily production and distribution plans
- resource availability and utilisation.

Fund management

For the system to work it needs to be sufficiently liquid at all nodes to ensure that bottlenecks are avoided and supply can be sustained. There also needs to be a strong relationship of trust between each party in the chain.

Importance of Information Technology

IT plays an obvious role in providing, storing, managing and interrogating the information management part of supply chain management. However, IT can also provide aid for all of the areas that require consideration through systems such as e-procurement and customer relationship management (covered in the next chapter), and there will also be links to other areas of the syllabus such as BPR, project management, organisational structure etc.

Illustration 2 – Supply chain management (SCM)

For example, a wholesaler's inability to adequately maintain inventory control or respond to sudden changes in demand for inventory may mean that a retailer cannot meet final consumer demand. Conversely, poor sales data from retailers may result in inadequate forecasting of manufacturing requirements.

Push and pull supply chain models

One key element in supply chain management is choosing between having a 'push' or a 'pull' model.

Push vs pull

Push model

- Products are built, distributed, and ready for the customer demand.

- Product design is led by the manufacturer.

- Product quality is often determined by raw material suppliers and component manufacturers.

- There is little product personalisation to customers.

- Low set-up costs and economies of scale are possible.

- Inventories are built up waiting for customers to demand them (a push system is sometimes referred to as a Make to Stock (MTS system)).

Pull model

- Planning for a product starts when the customer places the order and creates firm demand.

- Product design is often customer led (a pull system is sometimes referred to as a Make to Order (MTO system)).

- Personalisation of the product by the customer is possible.

- Inventory levels are minimised (systems such as JIT and TQM can be used).

- Lead times can be much higher.

- Set-up costs are higher and economies of scale are not always possible.

The pull business model is less product-centric and more directly focused on the individual consumer – a more marketing-oriented approach.

- In the pull model, customers use electronic connections to pull whatever they need out of the system.

- Electronic supply chain connectivity gives end customers the opportunity to give direction to suppliers, for example, about the precise specifications of the products they want.

- Ultimately, customers have a direct voice in the functioning of the supply chain.

Driven by e-commerce's capabilities to empower clients, many companies are moving from the traditional 'push' business model, where manufacturers, suppliers, distributors and marketers have most of the power, to a customer-driven 'pull' model. E-commerce creates a much more efficient supply chain that benefits both customers and manufacturers. Companies can better serve customer needs, carry fewer inventories, and send products to market more quickly.

Today, many companies have introduced elements of the pull model so that their systems use a combination of push and pull. Nike iD is a good example of this.

 Illustration 3 – Adding pull systems to a supply chain

The running shoe industry has traditionally used a push model for the supply chain. Products were built to a standardised form and consumers had to wait to find out what would be available in stores this year.

However Nike took a decision to allow customers to create their own designs for shoes and have them made to order. This product was known as Nike iD. It initially allowed consumers to create bespoke designs on the Nike website, but from 2009 this was extended so that consumers could even use an iPhone app to do this.

Nike iD allows customers to (amongst other things):

- choose colour schemes (customers can choose from a predetermined list or even take a picture with their mobile phone of the colour they want and Nike will make a shoe of that colour)

- choose the firmness of the sole

- choose lace colours

- add personal names to the running shoe.

Delivery is promised in less than 4 weeks.

The system will not be a full pull system however. Nike has continued to build inventory of the common components for the shoes (such as laces, rubber, insoles, logos etc.). These inventories are built up in order to achieve economies of scale and to keep the cost of personalised Nike iD products as low as possible.

There is therefore a combination of push and pull elements within the system.

Test your understanding 1

What factors should a company consider when choosing between a push and pull supply chain model?

Revisiting the value chain

Porter's value chain revisited

The theory behind the value chain is that, somewhere within the organisation, it carries out activities that customers value, are willing to pay for, and that result in profits being made. The activities could be skill and knowhow related, organisational or manufacturing.

The traditional value chain has been criticised because it:

- is designed primarily to describe manufacturing businesses

- does not emphasise the importance of the customer enough. It is product led rather than market led.

Deise proposed an alternative value chain that places more emphasis on the customer:

Market research	New product development	Market products	Purchase materials	Produce products	Manage selling, delivery, etc.

In terms of this model, e-business enables companies to:

- carry out continuous market research as products are ordered and sold

- use the results of continuous monitoring to order goods, design new products and design special offers

- gain greater flexibility and speed of response, provided that other members of the up-stream supply chain (suppliers) also embrace e-business.

Note the last point carefully: the whole supply chain must be flexible and efficient if any one member of it is to benefit from better market information. There's no point one company knowing what its customers want if its suppliers and distributors cannot respond adequately.

3 Upstream SCM

The key activity of upstream SCM is e-procurement.

What is e-procurement?

The term 'procurement' covers all the activities needed to obtain items from a supplier: the whole purchases cycle.

Electronic Procurement (also known as e-procurement) is the business-to-business purchase and sale of supplies and services over the internet. It is a way of using the internet to make it easier, faster, and less expensive for businesses to purchase the goods and services they require. While e-procurement is a general term that covers a wide assortment of techniques, its overall goal is to streamline the purchasing process in order to reduce costs, increase speed and allow managers to focus on other strategic matters. An important part of many B2B sites, e-procurement is also sometimes referred to by other terms, such as supplier exchange.

The purchases cycle

- Identifying when items are needed, how many are needed and gaining authority to acquire them.
- Finding suitable suppliers.
- Choosing which supplier to order from.
- Agreeing the price or perhaps a range of prices depending on volumes.
- Ordering the goods with the chosen supplier(s).
- Receiving goods into the organisation.
- Checking the goods are as ordered and handling queries.
- Recording the goods in inventory or the non-current asset register as appropriate.
- Storing of goods.
- Receiving, checking and processing the supplier's invoice.
- Paying the supplier according to cash flow/cash discount priorities.

E-procurement is the term used to describe the electronic methods used in every stage of the procurement process, from identification of requirement through to payment. It can be broken down into the stages of e-sourcing, e-purchasing and e-payment.

E-sourcing covers electronic methods for finding new suppliers and establishing contracts.

Not only can e-sourcing save administrative time and money, it can enable companies to discover new suppliers and to source more easily from other countries.

Issuing electronic invitations to tender and requests for quotations reduces:

- administration overheads
- potentially costly errors, as the re-keying of information is minimised
- the time to respond.

E-purchasing covers product selection and ordering.

Buying and selling online streamlines procurement and reduces overheads through spending less on administration time and cutting down on bureaucracy. E-purchasing transfers effort from a central ordering department to those who need the products. Features of an e-purchasing system include:

- electronic catalogues for core/standard items
- recurring requisitions/shopping lists for regularly purchased items. The standard shopping lists form the basis of regular orders and the lists can have items added or deleted for each specific order
- electronic purchase orders despatched automatically through an extranet to suppliers
- detailed management information reporting capabilities.

Improvements in customer service can result from being able to place and track orders at any time of day. An e-catalogue is an electronic version of a supplier's paper catalogue including product name, description, an illustration, balance in hand and so on. User expectations have increased dramatically in recent years as a result of their personal experiences of shopping on the internet. Well-designed websites and web interfaces are essential to offer good functionality so as to maintain user satisfaction.

E-payment includes tools such as electronic invoicing and electronic funds transfers. Again, e-payment can make the payment processes more efficient for both the purchaser and supplier, reducing costs and errors that can occur as a result of information being transferred manually from and into their respective accounting systems. These efficiency savings can result in cost reductions to be shared by both parties.

Illustration 4 – E-procurement

ITAB Interiors is a company which specialises in shop refits. When a new tenant takes over a shop lease it will usually refit the shop with new fixtures and fittings, etc. in order to meet its own particular needs. ITAB's clients include HSBC, Warehouse, Benetton and Bellway and it has many projects in operation at one time.

On each project, purchasing of required materials and fittings typically occurred in a manual manner with the following being typical stages in the process:

- Identify or anticipate material needs.

- Evaluate potential suppliers.

- Select suppliers and confirm price.

- Submit a purchase order form to management for approval.

- On receiving approval, place the order.

Evaluating and selecting suppliers could, at times, take several days as could the confirmation of management approval. This made the process time-consuming and expensive.

ITAB's switch to e-procurement involved the following:

- Having pre-approved suppliers for the most commonly purchased parts.

- Having an electronic system that could link inventory requests to the appropriate supplier.

- In the event that no existing supplier for the part was available, the system could perform a search of a number of suppliers and provide a range of prices and delivery estimates.

It means that the purchasing process can now take minutes instead of days. Requirements can be entered into the system and, usually, the system does the rest of the work. On the rare occasion when a non-approved supplier is necessary, manager approval can take place electronically and is now much more efficient than in the past.

Many organisations have expanded e-procurement beyond production-related procurement (which is directly related to the core activities of the organisation) into non-production procurement (which looks at ancillary services such as meeting administrative and distribution needs). For example, Kaplan have an e-procurement system that staff use for obtaining rail travel tickets for journeys to clients and meetings.

Benefits	Risks
• savings in labour and procurement costs	• become over reliant on the technology
• better inventory control	• there may be staff resistance
• better control over suppliers (may even be able to influence their design and production)	• cost savings may fail to materialise
• reduction in errors	• prices may become out of date or uncompetitive

Benefits and risks of e-procurement

The benefits of e-procurement

The more of the procurement process that can be automated, the better as there will be considerable financial benefits.

- Labour costs will be greatly reduced.

- Inventory holding costs will be reduced. Not only should overstocking be less likely, but if orders are cheap to place and process, they can be placed much more frequently, so average inventories can be lower.

- Production and sales should be higher as there will be fewer stock-outs because of more accurate monitoring of demand and greater ordering accuracy.

Other benefits include the following:

- The firm may benefit from a much wider choice of suppliers rather than relying on local ones

- Greater financial transparency and accountability

- Greater control over inventories

- Quicker ordering, making it easier to operate lean or JiT manufacturing systems

- Fewer errors in terms of ordering unnecessary items, mispricing items, overpaying for items, using an incorrect supplier etc.

- There are also considerable benefits to the suppliers concerned, such as reduced ordering costs, reduced paperwork and improved cash flow, that should strengthen the relationship between the firm and its suppliers

- Staff time is freed up to focus on other operational and managerial duties.

Potential risks of e-procurement

There are some risks associated with e-procurement. These are:

- Technology risks. There is a risk that the system (whether software or hardware) will not function correctly. There are risks that it might not interface properly with the organisation's system. There are very high risks that it will not communicate properly with a wide range of supplier systems. There are also increased risks over issues such as data security.

- Organisational risks. Staff might be reluctant to accept the new procurement methods and may become concerned over possible redundancies.

- No cost savings realised. As with all IS/IT projects, it is very difficult to predict all the benefits that can arise. Tangible benefits (such as might arise if fewer staff have to be employed) are relatively easy to forecast. However, intangible benefits (such as better customer service giving rise to an improved reputation) are very difficult to estimate with any accuracy.

- The buying company can become entrenched with existing, approved suppliers and there may be disincentives to find alternative, cheaper sources of supplies.

Illustration 5 – The growth of e-procurement

In April 2012, Amazon announced the launch of Amazon Supply:

"a new website dedicated to offering a broad selection of parts and supplies to business, industrial, scientific and commercial customers at competitive prices."

This is a move away from its typical B2C model to a B2B model. The hope is that businesses may find it more attractive to implement an e-procurement strategy if they can link systems to a business as large and valued as Amazon.

Amazon Supply "offers more than 500,000 items from leading brands" across a range of categories, including: lab & scientific, test, measure & inspect, occupational health & safety, janitorial & sanitation, office, fleet & vehicle maintenance, power & hand tools, cutting tools, abrasives & finishing, materials handling, materials (e.g. metals), hydraulics pneumatics & plumbing, fasteners and power transmission.

As Amazon adds basic buying controls, workflow, compliance and analytics capability that are commonly featured in e-procurement technologies and allow procurement to be automated (and therefore cheaper and more efficient), it is likely to become a vital part of the value chain of many businesses in the future.

Test your understanding 2

XL Travel is a tour operator based in the country's capital. It runs weekly trips to the seaside resort of Black Rock (around 140 km away) for four day visits (typically Friday to Monday).

The tours are very popular – especially with people aged over 65 (who make up over 90% of XL's customers). The company has traded profitably for many years on the back of premium pricing. But recently profits have started to fall, coinciding with a minority of complaints from regular users. Some users feel that the quality of the trips has fallen and is not up to previous high standards. Other users feel that, whilst XL itself has invested (with plush new offices, better marketing, more staff, easier booking systems etc.), this investment has gone into the wrong areas.

XL has built up a large cash surplus for further investment. One of the ways that it is considering using this cash is to invest and improve its supply chain.

Required:

(a) What are likely to be the elements of XL's upstream supply chain?

(b) What areas could XL aim to change?

(c) How might IT play a role in facilitating this change?

Restructuring the supply chain

In an earlier chapter we looked at strategic choices of outsourcing, vertical integration and strategic alliances, where the key issues of cost, quality and control were highlighted.

These are still relevant for online businesses as much as for conventional 'bricks and mortar' organisations. All organisations must decide between:

- vertical integration – manufacturing in-house

- virtual integration – the majority of supply chain activities are undertaken by third parties

- virtual disintegration (disaggregation) – in between these two extremes.

However, internet technology allows more efficient and cheaper communications within the chosen structure and may make virtual integration preferable to vertical integration.

4 Downstream SCM

Downstream supply change management is about managing relationships with both customers and consumers, as well as any other intermediaries along the way.

Examples of downstream supply chain management actions are:

- providing displays for retailers
- creating a website for end users
- creating user forums on websites
- determining which retailers and distributors to use
- use of different logistical methods/providers
- changes to finished goods inventory policies
- setting recommended retail prices
- giving retail exclusivity rights
- forward integration.

Advantages	Disadvantages
• can tie in customers/increase switching costs	• can be expensive to implement
• can improve customer loyalty and retention	• as a differentiation strategy it is easily copied
• can increase market visibility	• it relies on suppliers' willingness to adapt to customer needs (often needs corresponding upstream management)
• provides better information on customer needs, tastes etc.	• the organisation might become reactive rather than proactive to customer needs
• product failure rates can be reduced	• forward integration can increase business risk and exit barriers
• can facilitate pull supply chain management	• must ensure that forum/website users are representative of all users
• more regular and better communication with customers (e.g. can provide software/ product updates etc.)	• requires skills and experience for the benefits to be fully realised
• gives users a voice	• there is a risk of loss of focus on core competences and activities

Dealing with intermediaries

A typical downstream for a manufacturer might involve selling to distributors, who then sell on to retailers, who in turn sell on to end users. Distributors and retailers are therefore intermediaries between the manufacturer and the consumer of the product. One element of supply chain management is to manage intermediaries.

- E-commerce can lead to **disintermediation**. In this process intermediate organisations (middlemen) can be taken out of the supply chain.

- The process of **reintermediation** is also found, i.e. new intermediaries are introduced to the value chain, or at least to some aspects of it.

- **Countermediation** is where established firms create their own new intermediaries to compete with established intermediaries.

Examples

An example of disintermediation is evidenced in the travel industry, where travel agents have been cut out of many transactions as the public can book directly with hotels, airlines and rail companies.

The travel industry also gives an example of reintermediation. Companies like lastminute.com and expedia.com are like new travel agents, presenting a wide choice of products and services.

An example of countermediation is Opodo.com, set up by a collaboration of European airlines to encourage customers to book flights directly with them rather than using cost-comparison intermediaries such as lastminute.com.

Test your understanding 3

Following on from TYU 2, would you recommend downstream supply chain management for XL Travel?

Professional skill:

Illustrate commercial acumen in exercising judgement on whether downstream supply chain management would be useful for XL Travel.

5 Using Big Data to inform and implement business strategy

The ability of organisations to extract valuable information from Big Data is becoming a strategic capability. Like any capability, it requires investment in technologies, processes and governance.

Laney suggested that Big Data has the following characteristics, known as the 3V's:

- Volume – there is lots of it

- Velocity – it is generated very quickly

- Variety – it can take many varied forms.

What is Big Data?

Traditionally, organisations collected data that was mainly of a transactional nature. They stored data in a database that recorded details such as customer and supplier transaction history, identifying information and they may occasionally have asked customers the question 'How did you hear about us?' This data was used primarily to keep track of operations or forecast needs.

But more recently, both the sources and volume of data collected have exploded. Much of the information will be non-transactional such as collecting data from social networks (who likes your Facebook page? who follows you on Twitter? Who else do they follow on Twitter? What videos do they like on YouTube?), examining reviews that people leave about your products (on either your own site or on someone else's site, exploring internet forums to discover what people are discussing and what they want to see, examining where people are, what they are doing, where they are checking in, what they are buying elsewhere etc. Most of this data is out there. These sources of data have created modern-day treasure troves that can be mined to glean insights into products, services and customers. While this is conceptually possible, it requires the implementation of new processes, technology and governance mechanisms that are collectively being referred to as Big Data.

Characteristics of Big Data

The 3Vs are commonly used to describe Big Data:

Volume

Big Data is characterised by its sheer volume. IBM believe that we create over 2.5 quintillion bytes of data every day. If the average PC can hold 100 gigabytes of data on its hard drive, there is enough Big Data created every day to completely fill 25 million PCs. per day. For example, there are over 5 billion Facebook status likes per day. Facebook has to store this data on servers, and businesses would like to use and interpret these links to find patterns.

So there is already a large volume of Big Data out there and it's only going to get bigger. The University of London's (UCL) Big Data Institute believes that Big Data will double in size every two years. On top of that, UCL believes that currently less than 0.5% of the data that exists is ever analysed.

But this volume of Big Data causes problems for businesses. In order to perform meaningful analysis of this volume of data organisations will require new skill sets, large investments and a deliberate focus on Big Data. It is also likely that organisations will have to collaborate and share databases on Big Data. For example, the World Health Organisation has used mobile phone data held by service providers in Kenya to match human travel patterns to the spread of malaria (which it holds on its own database).

Velocity

The problem is worsened by the speed at which Big Data is created. The UK magazine, Baseline, reports that there are over 570 new websites created every minute. It also reports the commonly held belief that 90% of the world's data that is in existence has been created in the last two years.

Big Data is created quickly and moves around quickly. There are 300 hours of new content uploaded and shared to YouTube every minute, for example. For businesses wishing to exploit Big Data, they will have to obtain the information quickly, analyse it quickly and exploit it quickly. If, for example, there is a road crash or traffic build up on a particular major road, providers of satellite navigation systems for roads will want to get that information as quickly as possible (by, for example, measuring the average road speed for vehicles on a particular road), assess whether the cause is a temporary one, and then suggest an alternative route for road users. The more quickly that this can be done then the better the navigation system, and users of the system will be much more satisfied with its use.

Software systems will play a significant role in dealing with the volume and velocity of Big Data. New systems such as in-memory analytics mean that the analysis can happen in real time without the need to even store the data onto disks on computer servers.

Variety

Big Data is also characterised by its variety. Consider the data that might exist and be stored about yourself, for example. You might have banking transactions, you might be following particular organisations on Twitter, you may have recorded your interests on LinkedIn, you might have a store card or loyalty card that has recorded your past transactions, you might have saved photographs in the cloud, you might have given a thumbs up to a music video on YouTube etc. The types and sources of Big Data are many fold.

These types are often subdivided into two categories:

- Structured data

  Structured data resides in a fixed field within a record or file (such as a database or spreadsheet). Your banking transactions, your contact list or your past store purchases are therefore likely to be stored as structured data. This type of data is easier to access and analyse, as long as the model is well designed (for example, past store purchases on a store card may be less useful if the file does not record quantity, timing and value).

- Unstructured data

  The vast majority of Big Data is unstructured. It does not have set fields or sizes and includes data such as your personal interests, your photographs and videos, your likes and dislikes etc. Organisations need to find ways to make the most use of this type of data. For example, an organisation might attempt to monitor and react to user actions so that if, say, you upload lots of holiday photographs then you could be presented with holiday promotions on your next visit to a website. Or an organisation might ask employees to record their skills and interests in a central database in order to best use these to exploit opportunities in future projects.

Big data is unlocking the ability of businesses to understand and act on what are typically their biggest environmental impacts – the ones outside their control. Organisations that previously had limited information on consumers now have many opportunities to collect and leverage data.

Using Big Data strategically

There are many ways that Big Data can be used strategically, based on common data analysis techniques.

Predictive modelling can predict user behaviour based on their previous business transactions and preferences. This can facilitate new product or new market development.

Cluster analysis can be used to segment customers into groups based on similar attributes. Once these groups are discovered, managers can perform targeted actions such as customising marketing messages and cross-selling to each unique group. Another popular use case is to predict what group of users may "drop out". Armed with this information, managers can proactively devise strategies to retain this user segment and lower the churn rate.

Social analytics often involves metrics such as the number of video views and the number of followers or community members. This can allow content to be updated, removed or promoted depending on changes in these metrics.

Engagement measures the level of activity and interaction among platform members, such as the frequency of user-generated content. For example, Foursquare has begun to provide 'rewards' (such as a free coffee) to those users who check in and have the greatest number of connections (number of Twitter followers, for example). This can spread brand awareness and possibly cut marketing costs so that they are better aimed at the most influential users.

Reach measures the extent to which content is disseminated to other users across social platforms. Reach can be measured with variables such as the number of retweets on Twitter and shared likes on Facebook. Products or marketing campaigns with a poor reach can be changed or removed from the business portfolio.

Decision scientists explore Big Data as a way to conduct "field research" and to test hypotheses. Big Data is therefore used prior to strategy implementation and will influence strategic choice.

There is now a general consensus that data is a most valuable asset that, when farmed in the right way, will deliver organisations increased opportunities and insights to provide a stronger competitive advantage in existing markets, and to find and develop new products and markets.

Real world examples

Financial services

Morgan Stanley uses Hadoop to analyse investments and claims to see better results in doing portfolio analysis compared to when using traditional databases and traditional grid computing due to the scale and complexity of data involved. This allows the company to identify and understand the most appropriate investments for clients.

Supply Chain, Logistics, and Industrial Engineering

UPS uses telematics to improve performance. Delivery vehicles are equipped with sensors which monitor data on speed, direction, braking performance, drive train performance and other mechanical aspects of the vehicle. This information is then used to optimise maintenance schedules and improve efficiency of delivery routes saving time, money and reducing wastage.

Data from the vehicles is combined with customer data, GPS information and data concerning the normal behaviour of delivery drivers. Using this data to optimise vehicle performance and routes has resulted in several significant improvements:

- Over 15 million minutes of idling time were eliminated in one year. This saved 103,000 gallons of fuel.

- During the same year 1.7 million miles of driving was eliminated, saving 183,000 gallons of fuel.

Retail

It is widely reported that Walmart tracks data on over 60% of adults in the US. Data gathered includes online and instore purchasing pattern, Twitter interactions and trends, weather reports and major events. This data, according to the company, ensures a highly personalised customer experience. Walmart detractors criticise the company's data collection as a breach of human rights and believe the company uses the data to make judgements and conclusions on personal information such as sexual orientation, political view and even intelligence levels.

Entertainment

Time Warner is using big data to track which types of media customers are watching and when. This can help to manage bandwidth and therefore optimise customer experience. The company also uses sophisticated systems to integrate public data such as voter registration and property records with local viewing figures. This enables targeted advertising campaigns by Time Warner's advertising clients.

Netflix has 44 million users worldwide who watch 2 billion hours of programmes a month. The company uses information gathered from analysis of viewing habits to inform decisions on which shows to invest in. Analysing past viewing figures and understanding viewer populations and the shows they are likely to watch allows the analysts to predict likely viewing figures before a show has even aired. This can help to determine if the show is a viable investment.

Test your understanding 4

MC is a mobile (cellular) phone network provider, offering mobile phones and services on a range of different tariffs to customers. The company enjoyed financial success until three years ago but increasing competitive pressure has led to a recent decline in sales. There has also been an increase in the level of complaints regarding the customer service provided and the company's churn rate (number of customers leaving the company within a given time frame) is at an all-time high.

Discuss how an understanding of Big Data can drive the strategic direction of MC.

6 Disruptive technology

Disruptive technology relates to instances where technology is used to fundamentally change and 'disrupt' the existing business model in an industry.

An example of a disruptor

An example of a disruptor is the passenger service Uber which created a business model using technology which avoided the need for licensed drivers, a vehicle fleet, local booking services etc. Instead, customers use their internet connected device to hail a ride and all payments are handled by a smartphone app.

Uber has disrupted the existing business model for traditional passenger services. Uber was set up in San Francisco in the United States and its initial key competitor was the Yellow Cab Co-operative, but whilst Uber has grown to a business worth over $60bn, the Yellow Cab Co-operative has since filed for bankruptcy.

The key reason for the growth of new disruptive businesses is from technology. Not only from the technology that they employ in order to cut costs and improve efficiency, but also in the access that consumers now have to technology in the modern on-demand economy. For example, many disruptive businesses rely on smartphone applications or have internet-only based transactions.

The two largest growth sectors for disruptive technology are in health services and financial services. Financial technology (commonly known as Fintech) is, for example, completely disrupting the traditional banking sector – long seen as a highly technical, highly regulated industry dominated by giant banks.

Fintech businesses exist which can provide investment advice, offer banking services, transfer money internationally, provide mortgages and loans, exchange currency etc. These are typically big earners for traditional financial institutions. Goldman Sachs estimates that upstarts could steal up to $4.7 trillion in annual revenue, and $470 billion in profit, from established financial services companies.

Fintech examples

Zopa is a peer-to-peer (or person-to-person) loan company. What this means is that Zopa has technology which allows a person who wants to borrow money to be matched with a person who wants to lend money. This completely removes the role of traditional banks from the transaction. Lenders receive higher returns than they would from depositing in a bank but it is still cheaper for borrowers to borrow directly from lenders rather than pay bank margins. Zopa has a low margin fee for setting up the transaction. Zopa has no physical branches and therefore avoids many of the overheads and operating costs of traditional lenders.

The loans are unsecured but credit scores are available to lenders so that they can match lending rates to different credit scores. Lenders can also sell their loan if they want to cash in early (for a 1% fee).

Some borrowers and lenders who use peer-to-peer markets suggest that they do this for ethical reasons. They argue that traditional banks often have unethical practices and a peer-to-peer system avoids giving big banks more profits.

New entrants into the market such as Funding Circle are now offering a similar service for business customers with larger loans and longer periods.

Another example of a Fintech is a company called Betterment. Betterment aims to become a financial portfolio management platform – taking business away from the typically person-to-person financial advisers. Users can use a smartphone app to get investment advice and manage their investment portfolio.

Here is an extract from Betterment's mobile app description:

Why we're here

Betterment is an online financial advisor with one purpose: to help you make the most of your money. We're taking investment strategies that have worked for decades and using technology to make them more efficient. Our goal: to increase your long-term returns.

What we do for you

We make tailored recommendations, from how much to invest to how much risk to take on in your portfolio. Then, we invest your money in a globally diversified portfolio of low-cost ETFs and help lower taxes in ways many traditional investment services can't match.

Seek higher returns:

- Automated portfolio management
- Globally diversified portfolio of ETFs
- Tax efficient investing features, like tax loss harvesting and asset location.

Get a better investing experience:

- Sync your external investments
- Customer support 7 days per week
- Access to CFP® professionals and licensed financial experts.

Invest and save with transparency:

- Low-cost, straightforward pricing plans
- Low fund fees
- No trading or rebalancing fees.

The advantages that Fintechs have are:

- better use of data – providing better understanding of their customer and giving customers a wider choice

- a frictionless customer experience using elements such as smartphone apps to provide a broad and efficient range of services

- more personalisation of products/services to individual customers

- the lack of a physical presence (with associated overheads and operating costs)

- access to cheap capital to fund growth – much like when internet based businesses first came to prominence in the 1990s, investors want to get in on the growth potential that Fintechs offer. This gives Fintechs a wide scope for raising cheap finance in order to fund their future expansion.

Test your understanding 5

What potential defences might be employed by traditional financial services businesses to defend themselves against Fintech?

Further examples of disruptive technology

Cryptocurrencies

These aim to be a digital form of money, meeting the attributes of a store of value, unit of account and medium of exchange. That is not to say that all cryptocurrencies irrefutably meet these criteria, but their main purpose is to achieve this status.

Hundreds of cryptocurrencies now exist, originating with bitcoin, each providing different attributes – "zcash", for example, offers privacy guarantees.

Blockchain

Blockchain is a distributed database existing on multiple computers at the same time. It is constantly growing as new sets of recordings, or 'blocks', are added to it. Each block contains a timestamp and a link to the previous block, so they actually form a chain.

The database is not managed by any particular body; instead, everyone in the network gets a copy of the whole database. Old blocks are preserved forever and new blocks are added to the ledger irreversibly, making it virtually impossible to manipulate by faking documents, transactions and other information.

All blocks are encrypted in a special way, so everyone can have access to all the information but only a user who owns a special cryptographic key is able to add a new record to a particular chain. As long as you remain the only person who knows the key, no one can manipulate your transactions. In addition, cryptography is used to guarantee synchronisation of copies of the blockchain on each computer (or node) in the network.

> **For example**, think of blockchain as a digital medical record. Every record is a block which has a label stating the date and time when the record was entered. The medical history is extremely important for diagnosis and treatment purposes, so neither the doctor nor the patient should be able to modify the records already made. Nevertheless, the doctor owns a private key that allows him to make new records, and the patient owns a public key that allows him to access the records anytime. This method makes the data both accessible and secure. So, blockchain is by definition independent, transparent, and secure. The advantages of such a distributed ledger are obvious: being cost and risk reduction, data security, and/or transactions transparency; companies from most industries can benefit from this new technology.
>
> We are all pretty much used to sharing information through a decentralised interactive platform – the internet, but when it comes to sending money or other valuables we usually have to use the same old services provided by centralised financial institutions (i.e. banks). There are methods of making payments via the internet (the most obvious example is PayPal), but they usually require integration with a bank account or credit card; otherwise they cannot really be used. Blockchain technology offers an attractive opportunity to get rid of this "extra link". It's perfectly designed to take on all three most important roles of the traditional financial services: registration of transactions, identity verification and contracting.
>
> The financial services industry is the world's largest market in terms of capitalisation. If some part of those services will switch to using blockchain, this will certainly disrupt the industry, but at the same time it will significantly improve the efficiency of those services.
>
> As transactions are completed directly between the parties with no intermediary and in digital form, settling a deal can be faster than ever.
>
> The benefits noted below of perfect transparency, traceability and security provide further reasons to understand its potential. Moreover, blockchain can be used not only for sending digital money but as well for tracking physical goods in a supply chain, helping companies to monitor their suppliers in real time.

7   Cloud and mobile computing

Cloud and mobile computing is computing based on the internet. It avoids the needs for software, applications, servers and services stored on physical computers. Instead it stores these with cloud service providers who store these things on the internet and grant access to authorised users.

Benefits of cloud and mobile computing

- Sharing data

- On-demand self-service

- Flexibility

- Collaboration

- More competitive

- Easier scaling

- Reduced maintenance

- Back-ups

- Disaster recovery

- Better security.

More details

Store and share data – cloud services can often store more data than traditional, local physical drives and the data can be shared more easily (regardless of physical location).

On-demand self-service – customers and users can gain access to technology on demand. For example, every time you download an app from iTunes or the Play store you are downloading it from a cloud service where it is stored.

Better workforce flexibility – employees no longer need to be 'plugged into' work networks or facilities to access the data they need.

The cloud facilitates better workforce collaboration – documents, plans etc. can be worked on concurrently by many numbers of staff all at the same time.

Smaller firms can get access to technology and services that, without significant financial investment, may otherwise only be available to the largest organisations. This can allow small organisations to compete better with larger rivals.

Cloud services provide high levels of flexibility in terms of size, number of authorised users etc. – this means that the service can grow as the business grows and allows businesses to scale up much more easily.

There is no longer need for regular maintenance and (security or software) updates of IT services – the cloud provider will take care of this.

It can be used to back up data – this adds an extra layer of security and removes the need for physical devices to store backed-up data.

This means that it can also aid disaster recovery – using cloud technology makes this faster and cheaper.

The cloud can increase security of data – in the past if an employee lost, say, a laptop with sensitive data stored on it then this would be a high risk security event for the organisation.

Risks of cloud and mobile computing

- Reliance on the service provider
- Regulatory risks
- Unauthorised access of business and customer data.

More details

As with any outsourcing decision, relying on the cloud service provider means that any failings at the service provider could be more problematic without back-up plans for bringing services back in-house. There is not only issues with the trust and security required with the service provider, but also it needs to be considered whether the provider's services are suitable for the required tasks, whether the technology is advanced enough to give adequate competitiveness, whether the service provider will continue as a going concern, whether the service provider can ensure continuity in the light of external events such as system failures, whether initial prices will be maintained etc.

Data security is often highly regulated in terms of what can be stored, who can access it, how long it can be stored for, how it can be used etc. Organisations will be reliant on cloud service providers for this compliance. This may become a problem if the service provider is in a different jurisdiction with different regulations and rules.

Unauthorised access of business and customer data can come in two forms. Firstly, the cloud service provider is more likely to be a target of hacking than the individual small businesses that use it. If the service provider is targeted all users suffer even if they were not individual targets themselves. Secondly, providing business and customer data to an outsourced service provider means that the data can be accessed by that service provider's staff. It will also be important that the service provider does not share this data with unauthorised users such as other users of the service provider's services.

SMART technology

The word "SMART" refers to "self-monitoring, analysis, and reporting technology".

It is a technology that uses artificial intelligence, machine learning, and big data analysis (further discussed in section 9) to provide cognitive awareness to objects that were in the past considered inanimate. For example:

Internet of Things (IoT) devices

A network of devices that make use of sensors, chips, software, online connectivity, analytics, and applications to bring static physical objects to life. These devices create substantial value, and they are futuristic, scalable, and automated.

Some prominent examples include smart cities, smart homes, and smart factories.

Smart Connected Devices

Controlled via a remote and connected via the internet or Bluetooth, smart connected devices can offer a customised experience but have to be handled given that they don't adapt to the extent IoT devices do.

Smart security cameras, smart bulbs, and smartphones are some examples of smart connected devices.

Smart Devices

With limited automation, no need for internet connectivity, and programmable nature, smart devices, such as smart coffeemakers, provide certain personalised services at a particular time.

Examples of the benefits and risks of SMART technology

Benefits	Risks
• Convenience – provides the ability to do many tasks simultaneously with minimal effort.	• Privacy intrusion – for example, having house appliances and devices so connected gives service providers a great chance to collect vital information about you.
• Sustainability – smart technology can play a pivotal role in helping conserve energy, regulating and automating the use of energy, for example by switching off or adjusting lights, heating, and cooling appliances when they are not in use, or when the required conditions have been achieved.	• Cyber-attacks – aimed at extorting money from unsuspecting users, interrupting the normal operation of connected appliances, accessing, altering or destroying sensitive information and personal data, and interfering with normal business operations and processes.
• Security – it offers more reliable security than traditional, manually operated security systems. In addition, smart digital smoke, gas, water and sewerage leakage can not only be detected, but also the technology enables real-time preventive action.	• Power outages and technology failure – research has proven that security systems that are run through the internet are the most vulnerable during power outages. This is because power loss usually leads to internet outage as well.
• Efficiency – makes use of data to understand how improvements can be made. It tracks and analyses data to deliver better information to improve results in the future.	• Identity theft – cybercriminals have the potential to hack devices, steal sensitive information such as bank accounts, social security numbers, and passwords. They may use this information to carry out other malicious activities elsewhere.
• Saves money and time – energy bills can be reduced by using smart technological devices such as a smart thermostat, smart lighting, for example as they can optimise the use of energy and in turn, use less of it to do more. Smart technology automates repetitive chores and eliminates lost or wasted time.	

8 Software solutions

A key element in making IT a success is choosing the correct software. There are a number of areas to consider when buying new software:

- establishing what we need the software to do
- deciding between generic and bespoke solutions
- choosing a supplier of our chosen solution
- implementing the software solution.

Establishing business information needs

Various methods are available for establishing business information needs, including the following:

Technique	Suitability
• Interviewing	• Standard technique for most scenarios.
• Written questions	• Where people are not available for interview.
• Questionnaires	• Where the user population is too large to interview. • Generally unsuitable due to superficial nature of questions and lack of interaction.
• Observation	• Particularly useful if carried out before interviewing.
• Document analysis of existing processes	• Good source of design and analysis material.
• Workshops	• Useful for resolving conflicts and for new processes where high uncertainty exists.
• Protocol analysis – a mixture of interview and observation	• Ensures all aspects of the process are considered and none 'taken for granted' by users.
• Prototyping	• Where requirements are unclear. • Helps users reassess their desired functionality.

Using generic software solutions

There are various ways to produce a software solution.

- Purchase a standard ('generic') software package and:
    - use this without any modification
    - make suitable amendments to customise this for the organisation's specific requirements
    - add company specific modules as necessary.
- Pay for a bespoke system to be developed using existing hardware.

The advantages and disadvantages of generic solutions are as follows:

Advantages	Disadvantages
• They are generally cheaper to buy than bespoke solutions are to develop.	• They do not fit precisely the needs of the organisation – the users may need to compromise what they want with what is available.
• They are likely to be available almost immediately.	• The organisation is dependent upon an outside supplier for the maintenance of the software; many software suppliers are larger than most of their customers, and are therefore difficult to influence.
• Any system bugs should have been discovered by the vendors before sale.	
• Good packages are likely to come with good training programs and excellent documentation and on-screen help facilities.	
• New updated versions of the software are likely to be available on a regular basis.	• Different packages used by the organisation may have incompatible data structures.
• The experience of a great number of users with similar needs to those in the organisation has been incorporated into the design of the package.	• Using the same packages as rival organisations removes the opportunity of using IS for competitive advantage.
• Different packages will be available for different operating systems or data structures.	

Application packages can be altered and tailored to a buyer's requirements, but amendments to an existing package have to be paid for, and so add to the purchase cost of the software. In addition, an altered package may not accept the standard updates provided by the supplier.

Choosing software and a supplier

Choosing software

When evaluating software the following factors should be assessed as a minimum:

- whether the software will match the expected organisational and user **requirements**

- the level of **flexibility** in adapting the software as these requirements change

- the **competencies** of the organisation in using and exploiting the software

- the availability of **future** updates and ongoing support and maintenance

- the **compatibility** with existing hardware and software

- the provision of **training**, user manuals and/or online help

- the interface design and **user-friendliness** (referred to as the non-functional requirements)

- the **cost** of the software and the ease of implementation/transfer

- security and **controls** over access to the software.

Choosing a supplier

Before tying the organisation into a particular supplier, the procurement manager should consider the following (as a minimum) for each prospective supplier:

- long-term **viability** (this could include obtaining records of financial performance and position)

- length of **time in business**

- **references** from previous customers

- **ethical** standards (this might include an assessment of the directors and any potential links to our own organisation)

- availability of **demonstrations**

- the ability to provide guarantees and **warranties** for non-compliance, later delivery, failure to meet functional and non-functional requirements etc.

- security and **controls**

- **copyright** (for bespoke solutions)

- **user base** (for generic solutions)

- **maintenance** and after-sales support.

Implementation

Implementing software solutions involves three key elements:

- data migration – transferring data from the old system to the new
- training – training staff on the new system
- changeover – introducing the new system to the business operations.

Data migration

It is vital to consider the stages that will be addressed during the migration process. Some of the stages include:

- Planning
- Data mapping
- Manual input
- Testing the solution
- Implementing the solution.

Stages in data migration

It is vital to consider the stages that will be addressed during the migration process. Some of the stages include:

- **Planning** – the organisation may need to create a Steering Committee that has representatives from a number of areas of the organisation including payroll, personnel, etc.; they may be from various levels, e.g. operational, tactical and strategic.

- **Data mapping** – this is the stage when the data is moved from one system into the field heading and file structures of the new system. An evaluation will need to take place of the structures within the new system and the existing computer system to ensure that the allocation for field headings is consistent.

- **Manual input** – there may be a requirement to enter some of the data manually from the old format to the new. This will require the organisation to consider the method of manual input as there are many issues with this type of transfer such as the type of input method, e.g. keyboard or scanner. The use of a keyboard, for example, greatly increases the chances of transposition errors that will reduce the quality of the input made.

- **Testing the solution** – there will need to be a period of testing after the conversion process to ensure that all of the data is accurate and that the system is running properly. A test environment will have to be created by the team to ensure that all the outputs from the tests made are accurate; this may include test plans and scripts for the conversion software.

- **Implementing the solution** – once the file conversion has been tested and accepted it can be run on the live data. Procedures will have to be specified to test that records are accurately converted.

Training

Training and a strategy for training are crucial. In order for this to be successful and resources not to be wasted it is vital that there is clarity about a number of issues. These are:

- Who needs to be trained and why.

- Whether training takes place on or off the job.

- Who will provide the training.

- If training should occur in a short period or be ongoing.

- What the line management involvement will be.

Methods of training

The chosen approach will depend on organisational structure, company policy and ethos. However, it is important that the approach is clear to the users.

The nature of training that users will require will vary dependent upon:

- User backgrounds.

- Purposes of the system.

- Features of the system.

- The kind of user interfaces – menus, graphics, speech, etc.

Methods of training

A number of alternative training methods are available to the organisation, but the most important factor to consider is that the type of training used is matched to the level of experience of the user. For example, it would not help an inexperienced user to be presented with a manual; to ensure success the user would need to receive first-hand information, probably in the form of a taught course. This will also help to improve the acceptance of the new system by the users.

- **External courses** – users go to the providers' premises to enable them to obtain the knowledge and the skills to use the new information system.

- **Internal courses** – the organisation runs a course in-house relating to the use of the information system. The course can be conducted by the internal training or IS department or an external provider may come into the company to run the course.

- **Computer-based training** – as an alternative the staff may be trained using a software tutorial that is often supplied with the original software purchase. The tutorial can be quickly installed onto the PC.

Changeover techniques

- Parallel running.

- Direct changeover.

- Phased.

Changeover techniques

- **Parallel running**

  This is when the new and the old system run side by side for a period of time, e.g. several weeks, until the analyst is satisfied with the operations of the new information system. It is known as the high-cost low-risk approach.

- **Direct changeover**

  This approach is when the old system finishes, and the new system takes over immediately, so requires that there is a high level of confidence in the effectiveness of the new system. For example, the old finishes at 8.59.59 seconds and the new starts at 9.00.00 seconds. It is known as the high-risk low-cost approach.

- **Phased**

  This is when the new information system can be introduced part by part or stage by stage. This may be useful if the organisation is implementing an information system in a number of departments, as it will help to limit the impacts of the new system. It must be remembered that the phase can be either direct or parallel in each of the stages.

Test your understanding 6

You are responsible for implementing a payroll system for weekly paid employees, using a bought-in package on a stand-alone microcomputer system. There are 3,000 records (one for each employee) in the current manual system. Each record is held on a card. The information about each employee comprises personal details (personnel number, name, date of birth, grade, section, rate of pay, allowances, deductions from pay, etc.), held in the top section of the card. In the body of the card are held a series of line entries, one for each week of the year. As each week is worked the details are entered in the appropriate line: gross pay; tax and national insurance, by reference to the relevant tables; and net pay.

(a) Describe a procedure for transferring data from the manual to the computer to create the master file prior to going live on the new system.

(b) Specify the checks and controls to be incorporated into the process to ensure that the computerised master file is accurate, complete, up to date and suitable for running the live system.

9 Artificial Intelligence (AI)

 Definition

Artificial Intelligence is an area of computer science that emphasises the creation of intelligent machines that work and react like human beings.

A common definition from Kaplan and Haenlein describes AI as a **"system's ability to correctly interpret external data, to learn from such data, and to use those learnings to achieve specific goals and tasks through flexible adaptation"**. This is often considered in the context of human-type robotics (for example health care practices, such as surgery, rehabilitation, therapy, patient companionship) but reaches much further than this, and is set to transform the way we live and work.

Some of the more advanced activities and skills artificial intelligence can now master, and therefore present huge opportunity for developers and companies alike, include:

- Voice recognition

- Planning

- Learning

- Problem solving.

 Illustration 6 – Artificial intelligence

Companies such as Apple and Amazon have developed and marketed voice recognition systems, either to be built into an existing product (such as Apple with its Siri system) or developed new products whose main function is voice recognition (such as Amazon and Alexa).

A further simple example is that of Facebook, and its process of recommending new friends for users to connect with.

There are many, more complex examples of Artificial Intelligence, but a common factor to both the simple and the more involved is **machine learning**.

Machine learning

Machine learning is a subset of AI where effectively AI computer code is built to mimic how the human brain works. It essentially uses probability based on past experiences through data, events and connections between events. The computer then applies this learning to a given situation to give a fact driven plausible outcome. If the conclusion the computer reaches turns out to be incorrect this will act to add more experience and enhance its understanding further, so in future the same mistake will not be repeated.

Most recent advances in AI have been achieved by applying machine learning to very large data sets. Machine learning algorithms detect patterns and learn how to make predictions and recommendations by processing data and experiences, rather than by explicit programming instruction. The algorithms themselves then adapt to new data and experiences to improve their function over time.

There are three major types of machine learning:

- Supervised learning
- Unsupervised learning
- Reinforcement learning.

Supervised learning

In this instance an algorithm uses training data and feedback from humans to learn the relationships of given inputs to given outputs. For example, if the objective is to predict future house prices, the inputs might be "time of year" and "interest rates".

This sort of approach can be used when the user knows how to classify the input data and the type of behaviour that they want to predict, but the algorithm is needed to calculate it on new data.

There are three steps to how supervised learning works:

1. A human labels every element of the input data (e.g. "time of year", "interest rates" etc.) and defines the output variable (e.g. "house prices").

2. The algorithm is trained on the data to find the connection between the input variables and the output.

3. Once training is complete – typically when the algorithm is sufficiently accurate in providing output data from input – then the algorithm is applied to new data.

Unsupervised learning

With unsupervised learning, an algorithm interrogates input data without being given any explicit output variable. For example, the input data might be "customer demographic data" and the algorithm is then used to explore and identify patterns.

This can be used when there is no known classification of the data, and the user wants the algorithm to find patterns and classify the data for them.

The three steps for using unsupervised learning are:

1. The algorithm receives unlabelled data; for example, a set of data describing customer journeys on a website.

2. The algorithm then infers some sort of structure on the data.

3. The algorithm identifies groups of data that exhibit similar behaviour; for example, clusters of customers of similar age that exhibit similar buying patterns, such as choice of destination, length of trip, amounts spent etc.

Reinforcement learning

This is when an algorithm learns to perform a task by trying to maximise the rewards it receives for the actions it takes. For example, in managing an investment fund, the rewards would be gains in value of the fund based on which investments it has decided to put capital into.

Reinforcement learning can be used when there isn't a lot of training data available, the ideal end state cannot be clearly defined, or the only way to learn about the environment is to interact with it.

The three steps for reinforcement learning are:

1   The algorithm takes an action on the environment; for example, it makes a trade in a financial portfolio.

2   It receives a reward if the action taken brings the machine a step closer to its objective. For example, it makes a return on the investment chosen.

3   The algorithm optimises for the best series of actions by correcting itself over time. For example, if it makes losses, or could have made better returns through investing elsewhere, it will do better at the next time of investing.

Rewards for reinforcement learning will depend on the application to which the AI is put.

For example, a courier company that decides to adopt AI in this way might see reductions in fuel consumption, or an increase in the number of deliveries made to customers on time, as a gain.

Reinforcement learning has famously been used in training computers how to play games.

Illustration 7 – AlphaGo

In May 2017, reinforcement learning helped the AI system AlphaGo to defeat the world champion Ke Jie in the ancient Chinese board game of Go.

A particular advantage of reinforcement learning compared to supervised and unsupervised learning is that it is not based on the limitations that can result from human labelling. Even experienced operators can introduce natural and social bias into labels, which will limit the learning process for the machine.

In a recent development, the AI system AlphaGo Zero defeated its predecessor AlphaGo at the board game Go, even though it had not been "trained" to play by human beings; instead, it learnt to play Go from scratch, rather than training on Go games played by and with human beings.

Illustration 8 – 'intelligent' vehicles

Jaguar Land Rover has introduced self-learning vehicles into its range of vehicles. The system within the vehicle integrates with different passengers' mobile phones, and learns to recognise their individual behaviours and preferences. It can then apply such understanding to adapt issues such as comfort controls within the vehicle, and the entertainment choices that are offered.

For example, the car can link up with the fitness and activity tracker worn by the driver to detect a visit to the gym, and start the air conditioning to create a cooler interior as the driver returns to the vehicle once the gym session is over.

Test your understanding 7

RTY company sells a wide range of products via its website. Management believe that in order to maximise sales the company needs to understand the way customers navigate around its website and the interaction between customer purchasing patterns and a range of other factors such as competitor behaviour, economic indicators, and local weather conditions.

RTY plans to use an Artificial Intelligence Application to interrogate the data. First staff will label the relevant input data and then an algorithm will be used to find the relevant connections.

Which ONE of the following forms of machine learning is RTY planning to adopt?

A   Supervised learning

B   Unsupervised learning

C   Reinforcement learning

D   Feature learning

Artificial Intelligence and finance

Although artificial intelligence techniques such as machine learning are not new, and the pace of change is fast, widespread adoption in business and accounting is still in relatively early stages.

Increasingly, we are seeing systems that are producing outputs that far exceed the accuracy and consistency of those produced by humans. In the short to medium term, AI brings many opportunities for finance professionals to improve their efficiency, provide more insight and deliver more value to businesses. In the longer term, AI brings opportunities for much more radical change, as systems increasingly carry out decision-making tasks currently performed by humans.

AI, no doubt, will contribute to substantial improvements across all areas of accounting, equipping those in finance with powerful new capabilities, as well as leading to the automation of many tasks and decisions.

Examples include:

- using machine learning to code accounting entries and improve on the accuracy of rules-based approaches, enabling greater automation of processes

- improving fraud detection through more sophisticated, machine learning models of 'normal' activities and better prediction of fraudulent activities

- using machine learning-based predictive models to forecast revenues

- improving access to, and analysis of, unstructured data, such as contracts and emails.

Despite the opportunities that AI brings, it must be remembered that it does not replicate human intelligence. The strengths and limits of this different form of intelligence must be recognised, and we need to build an understanding of the best ways for humans and computers to work together.

Internet of things

 The internet of things (IoT) describes the network of smart devices with inbuilt software and connectivity to the internet allowing them to constantly monitor and exchange data.

What devices are connected to the internet of things? Essentially anything with an on off switch can become a 'smart' device and be connected over the internet. This allows them to talk to us, applications and each other, which is at the core of their functionality.

Common devices currently connected as part of the internet of things include:

- **Smart meters** (contain in-home display screens that show how much energy is used in real-time) and **home control thermostat devices** (allow control of heating, electricity and hot water).

- **Doorbells and security:** these talk to your smart device. A live connection is established if the doorbell is pressed or the motion sensors activated, allowing immediate interaction.

- **Wearable tech** such as smart watches and fitness trackers capture and record an array of data to monitor and record your fitness.

- **Home appliances** such as smart lights, fridges, washing machines, ovens etc... the connectivity built in allows remote access and control of these devices, for instance turnings your lights on if you're out at night can be done using a smart phone.

- **Cars:** the computer systems used to control cars are increasingly sophisticated. They track and monitor thousands of parameters on every journey. This capability is central in the continued pursuit of autonomous vehicles.

- **Transport and infrastructure:** smart motorways are a common feature in many countries with traffic sensors monitoring the flow and build-up of traffic and responding to provide extra lanes or activate temporary speed limits.

- **Manufacturing equipment and plant:** monitoring of business assets facilitates efficient utilisation, it allows continual live feedback to track performance and flag maintenance requirements earlier.

The growth in the **internet of things** often termed '**smart technology**' is fuelled by improvements in broadband connectivity and the development of 4G communication networks. As governments look to roll out the next generation 5G networks connectivity will be improved further.

Coupled with the fact the people and businesses are increasingly comfortable with the idea and operation of this **smart technology**, it is anticipated that the **internet of things** will continue grow, becoming increasingly central to how we live and work as new and innovative applications for the technology emerge all the time.

Illustration 9 – Farming

Connected devices are becoming increasingly prevalent in the world of farming. It is an industry that is particularly vulnerable to adversity, through climate and weather effects, disease and pests. Therefore the ability to monitor data on climatic conditions and the health of animals allows farmers to be forewarned of potential problems at an earlier stage. This allows farmers to take preventative action to fix problems or switch to alternative strategies, resulting in increased yields and importantly saving costs, wastage and loss.

A company called Allflex use smart sensors, built into collars which are worn by each animal in the herd. These sensors monitor temperature, health, breathing, activity and nutrition of individual animals and the herd overall. Early warning signs can alert the farmer to potential problems and early preventative action can be taken such as veterinary care or isolating an animal showing markers of infection.

Test your understanding 8

X Co has created a brand of electronic toothbrushes that can sync with a mobile phone to let the user know the appropriate length of time they should be spending brushing their teeth.

This is an example of what?

A   Big data

B   Internet of things

C   3D printing

D   Mobile technologies

Mobile technologies

 Code-division multiple access (CDMA) is the technology that underpins mobile technology. It has developed rapidly over the last decade and increased the capability of mobile technology.

Developments in mobile technology have seen mobile phones progress from basic call and message devices in the late 1980s and 1990s to the **smart phones** and **tablets** we see today. These devices are more like computers than telephones and this is reflected in the prices of the latest models.

The rapid development in the capability of mobile technology has emerged at the same time as huge advances in internet technology and together the two technologies have been perfect partners.

All aspects of modern life are impacted by mobile technology, with major industries being completely transformed or new ones emerging, including:

- **Newspapers** – Physical sales of newspapers are in terminal decline. News is now consumed via mobile devices and is live rather than being a record of yesterday's news. Newspaper companies have attempted to evolve to maintain a presence in this mobile online world.

- **Advertising** – Closely linked with newspapers and other media, advertising is being transformed. Large scale mass advertising is in decline with a growth in smarter, targeted adverts.

- **Music** – CDs were replaced by MP3s which were seen as the future but have in turn have been replaced by music streaming services like **Spotify**.

- **Banking** – Increasingly people bank via mobile apps, designed for ease and convenience, the traditional high street branch continues to decline.

- **Socialising** – Social media has transformed how people socialise and communicate with friends using smartphones to post and tag and photograph their every move.

- **TV/Film** – Video streaming services such as **Netflix** and **Amazon Prime** as well as OnDemand TV and video sites like **YouTube** are designed for mobile internet technology and are transforming how we watch TV and films.

However it is important to recognise that AI has many risks associated with its use and application.

Elon Musk (Tesla and SpaceX founder) said at a conference in 2022 – "I am really quite close... to the cutting edge in AI, and it scares the hell out of me it's capable of vastly more than almost anyone knows, and the rate of improvement is exponential."

The late Professor Stephen Hawking also commented – "Unless we learn how to prepare for, and avoid, the potential risks," he explained, "AI could be the worst event in the history of our civilization."

Potential risks of AI

- **Automation-spurred job loss** – job automation is generally viewed as the most immediate concern. It's no longer a matter of if AI will replace certain types of jobs but when and to what degree. In many industries, particularly but not exclusively those whose workers perform predictable and repetitive tasks, disruption is well underway. According to a 2019 Brookings Institution study, 36 million people work in jobs with "high exposure" to automation, meaning that before long at least 70 percent of their tasks ranging from retail sales and market analysis to hospitality and warehouse labour will be done using AI.

- **Privacy violations** – malicious use of AI could threaten digital security (e.g. through criminals training machines to hack or socially engineer victims at human or superhuman levels of performance), physical security (e.g. non-state actors weaponising consumer drones), and political security (e.g. through privacy-eliminating surveillance, profiling, and repression, or through automated and targeted disinformation campaigns).

- **'Deepfakes'** – created by manipulating voices and likenesses. Using machine learning, a subset of AI that's involved in natural language processing, an audio clip of any given politician could be manipulated to make it seem as if that person voiced racist or sexist views when in fact they uttered nothing of the sort. If the clip's quality is high enough so as to fool the general public and avoid detection, it could completely derail a political campaign and career.

- **Socioeconomic inequality** – Widening socioeconomic inequality sparked by AI-driven job loss is another cause for concern. Along with education, work has long been a driver of social mobility. However, when it's a certain kind of work, the predictable, repetitive kind that's prone to AI takeover, research has shown that those who find themselves without work are much less able to obtain alternative work or seek retraining compared to those in higher-level positions who have more money and resources.

- **Weapons automatisation** – not everyone agrees that AI is more dangerous than nuclear weapons, but what if AI decides to launch these weapons or, biological weapons without human intervention? Alternatively, what if an enemy manipulates data to return AI-guided missiles from where they came? Both are possibilities and both would be disastrous.

- **Market volatility** – algorithmic trading occurs when a computer, unencumbered by the instincts or emotions that could cloud a human's judgement, executes trades based off of pre-programmed instructions. These computers can make extremely high-volume, high-frequency and high-value trades that can lead to big losses and extreme market volatility.

Mitigating the risks of AI

One way to prevent or at least temper the most malicious AI from wreaking havoc is some sort of regulation. Elon Musk suggested:

"It needs to be a public body that has insight and then oversight to confirm that everyone is developing AI safely. This is extremely important."

His comments were in regards to the regulation of AI implementation, he said, but not of the research itself which needs to be less regulated in his opinion.

Any country that lags in AI development is at a distinct disadvantage militarily, socially and economically. The solution, is therefore selective application:

10 Ethics of technology usage

10.1 Legal considerations of technology use

Technology – as discussed above, data is a central aspect of the technology developments driving the 4th industrial revolution.

The amount of personal data available to and used by organisations means that the privacy, sensitivity and security of this data are very significant considerations in modern business.

A business must ensure it is compliant with all legislation but there are also considerations from an ethical and social responsibility point of view in terms of what is right and wrong in the eyes of the public.

Data protection – General Data Protection Regulation (GDPR) was introduced throughout the EU in 2018. It is legislation which details the following principles about data:

- Used fairly, lawfully and transparently
- Used for specified, explicit purposes
- Used in a way that is adequate, relevant and limited to only what is necessary
- Accurate and, where required, kept up to date
- Kept for no longer than is necessary
- Handled in a way that ensures appropriate security. Including protection against unlawful or unauthorised processing, access, loss, destruction or damage.

Data controllers within organisations have to ensure adequate safeguards and controls to implement these data principles.

Background to GDPR

This new legislation was designed to overhaul the previous data protection act from 1995. This was written at a time when the internet was in its infancy, smartphones didn't exist and some of the largest and most influential companies in the world such as Facebook, Google and Amazon were barely even conceived.

The way data is used in 2018 and beyond required new laws that were fit for purpose and designed with the modern landscape in mind and are therefore able to safeguard the privacy and rights of individuals today.

Illustration 10 – Facebook and Cambridge Analytica scandal

Facebook received a £500,000 fine for its role in the Cambridge Analytica scandal. The fine was the maximum available under the data protection legislation in place at the time (prior to the introduction of GDPR legislation).

Facebook was found to have breached data protection legislation by allowing third party app developers access to users' data without sufficiently clear and informed consent. They also failed to make suitable checks on apps and developers using the platform.

What was the Cambridge Analytica scandal?

A third party app designed as a personality quiz collected the data of 87 million Facebook users without their knowledge or explicit consent. This data was then sold on to third parties, one of whom was Cambridge Analytica.

They then used this data to profile voters in the US election based on personality and psychology before targeting advertising which took advantage of this information.

Around 1 million UK users' data was obtained in the scandal.

Test your understanding 9

GDPR legislation in the EU attempts to ensure that organisations follow the principles about data.

Which TWO of the following are contained in those principles?

A   Data is kept up to date

B   Data is kept for longer than is necessary

C   Data is used for implicit purposes

D   Data is protected against unlawful access

E   Data should always be in hard copy format

10.2 Ethical and social considerations of technology use

Ethics was introduced in chapter 17. Let's begin by recapping what is meant by ethics:

 Ethics is a system of moral principles that affects how people and organisations make decisions. It involves acting in a way deemed acceptable by society.

Ethical and social considerations – Compliance with legislation such as the **GDPR** laws noted above is something that all companies should achieve. However, the question of whether this is sufficient opens up ethical considerations as to what companies should do and how they should act.

When considering the way in which an organisation handles technology and data, **ethical and social considerations are important** for the following reasons:

- A company that handles technology and data in an ethical way will give investors confidence

- Customer confidence in data security is vital in the digital age and is an important element of brand confidence

- Consumers feel safer dealing with companies that are proactive and responsible in their use of data

- Employees are attracted to companies that exhibit a strong ethical stance when it comes to how they use technology and data

- Ethical handling of technology and data helps ensure long-term sustainability of an organisation through stakeholder confidence and trust

- It demonstrates a proactive awareness of the risks associated with data and technology

 Illustration 11 – Microsoft AI ethical principles

Microsoft is one of a number of high profile technology companies to lay down a voluntary set of ethical principles surrounding its use of **artificial intelligence** (AI). AI is an area of technology that presents some of the most challenging ethical questions.

Microsoft's AI principles:

Fairness – AI systems should treat all people fairly

Reliability & safety – AI systems should perform reliably and safely

Privacy & security – AI systems should be secure and respect privacy

Inclusiveness – AI systems should empower everyone and engage people

Transparency – AI systems should be understandable

Accountability – AI systems should have algorithmic accountability

10.3 Corporate digital responsibility

Corporate digital responsibility or **CDR** is a relatively new concept which extends the idea and ethos of **corporate social responsibility (CSR)** to the digital world.

It is a voluntary commitment by organisations to go beyond mere compliance with legislation, when it comes to how they handle technology and data. It considers the broader ethical values of organisations driving forward the advancement of technology to do so in a manner that is fundamentally leading toward a positive future.

CDR involves a commitment to protecting both customers and employees and ensuring that new technologies and data are used both productively and wisely.

The development of a **CDR strategy** is increasingly common in modern business and would include the following **5 key areas**:

- **Digital stewardship**, using data in a responsible and secure way that is in line with customers' and employees' expectations of what is reasonable

- **Customer expectations** around data use and the need for transparency are increasing. The ability to opt in and be rewarded for sharing data empowers the consumer

- **Giving back** means that companies can share data in a benevolent way to help society. For example, a bank with knowledge of financial information could help to inform a customer's choices to improve their financial management, even if it meant a loss of overdraft or credit card fees. Additionally, a pharmaceutical company sharing clinical trial data with university researchers for no gain

- **Data value** is becoming increasingly apparent to customers as well as businesses, so the need to reward and incentivise customers to give more data will become the norm

- **Digital inclusion** is about ensuring all members of society have the skills, tools and ability to access the online digital world, and are not left behind through lack of education or opportunity. Businesses need to be proactive to help and support users and reduce barriers and obstacles.

Test your understanding 10

X Co is a traffic data management company, involved in town planning and transport logistics. They heavily invest in software to look at real time data on the impact of cycle lanes, new roads, types of cars etc. on traffic times in city centres. This wealth of knowledge has been built up for years, and recently X Co has looked at the possibility of sharing this information with hospitals and the emergency services, free of charge. This is to help the emergency services get to incidents quicker.

What is this project a specific example of?

A   Corporate digital responsibility

B   Corporate social responsibility

C   Lobbying

D   Artificial intelligence

11 Chapter summary

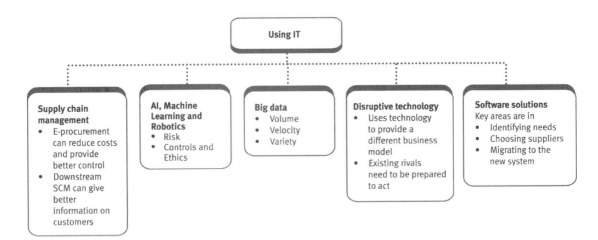

Using IT

Supply chain management
- E-procurement can reduce costs and provide better control
- Downstream SCM can give better information on customers

AI, Machine Learning and Robotics
- Risk
- Controls and Ethics

Big data
- Volume
- Velocity
- Variety

Disruptive technology
- Uses technology to provide a different business model
- Existing rivals need to be prepared to act

Software solutions
Key areas are in
- Identifying needs
- Choosing suppliers
- Migrating to the new system

Test your understanding answers

Test your understanding 1

The factors to consider are:

- Variability and knowledge of demand. A pull system will require knowledge of what customers want and when they want it. Alternatively, it will rely on customers being willing to wait for production. For example, luxury yacht supply chains typically use a pull system because buyers are willing to wait for up to two months for delivery of the product.

- The competitive strategy pursued. Low cost and no-frills companies will often follow a push supply chain as this can provide economies of scale. A differentiator might follow a pull system as product personalisation might be a way to differentiate a product.

- Inventory costs. Inventory costs and risks are higher in a pull system, so companies that have high inventory costs (such as luxury cars) may prefer a pull system.

- Manufacturing set up costs. Set ups are more frequent in a pull system so that if set up costs are high a pull system may be too expensive to operate successfully.

- Rivals' systems. If rivals are all using one model then a competitive advantage might be achieved by using an alternative model. For example, the detergent industry typically uses a push system. But some companies have found a focused differentiation model by allowing users to suggest ingredients and smells for soaps and detergents before they are then made to order. This allows these companies to charge a premium price for these services.

- IT systems. Strong IT systems will be necessary to support a pull model. The growth in e-commerce has been a major reason for the recent high growth in the creation of pull supply chain systems. E-procurement plays a vital role in pull systems.

Test your understanding 2

(a) The key elements of XL's upstream supply chain is likely to include:

- travel providers (such as bus, train or airline companies)
- accommodation providers
- local food producers and suppliers (some of these will actually be the suppliers to the accommodation providers)
- attractions, activity and excursion providers.

But it could be widened further to include:

- laundry providers

- waste disposal companies

- energy and water suppliers

- sports events

- entertainment venues

- local infrastructure providers.

However, any initial step in supply chain management is likely to focus on the management of the first group of key elements.

(b) There is an opinion amongst a minority of customers that the quality of the service has deteriorated due to a lack of investment. One element of supply chain management is to ensure that the chain contains the correct value system to support the firm's competitive advantage. XL should therefore consider whether it is using the correct travel companies, accommodation providers, attractions etc.

If existing suppliers are deemed to be appropriate then XL should look to introduce a move towards elements of a 'pull' system. XL should communicate with a selection of customers (not just those who are complaining) to determine what they would like from their tour, what their expectations are, how things could be improved etc.

This will allow XL to have a better idea of what is needed from suppliers. It will allow XL to complete thorough inspections of suppliers and also to provide suppliers with information on potential changes that might be required. So focusing on the key elements of XL's supply chain, the following gives some ideas of the areas that XL could look to improve, change, redesign or remove:

- accommodation

  - location

  - ease of access

  - furniture used

  - bedding used

  - staffing

  - facilities

- travel providers

  - capacity

  - safety measures

  - check-in facilities

  - age of transport

  - in journey refreshments, facilities and entertainment (where appropriate)

  - luggage capacity, security and safety

- food suppliers
  - ingredients used
  - range of menus
  - facilities
  - capacity
  - waiting times
  - service
- attractions etc.
  - availability
  - ease of access
  - waiting times
  - safety record
  - facilities
  - range of products.

Supply chain management will require a consideration and possible investment in all of these areas and many more.

(c) Information Technology can play a very important role in supply chain management. Firstly it can gather information. Initially, in a pull system, this should be customer focused. So, for example, Customer Relationship Management (CRM – see next chapter) software can be used to determine customer needs, buying patterns, likes/dislikes etc.

The next set of information can be on elements of the upstream supply chain. For example, in part (b) some suggestions were given on what needs to be considered for each of the four key elements of XL's upstream supply chain, XL can obtain information on current performance using software to record and interrogate the data.

IT can also be used to provide and share data. Customer feedback and suggestions can be provided to suppliers. Also, suppliers can more easily access information on the potential number, age, requirements etc. of potential visitors. For example, the software might flag in advance that one of the visitors has a physical disability so that suppliers can prepare for this.

The IT system might also be able to cope with and alleviate potential 'bottlenecks' in the system. If, for example, a particular accommodation supplier doesn't have the capacity to cope with the number of visitors who are arriving on a particular date, the system should allow for alternative accommodation for the excess to be found quickly and easily.

The system could even be expanded for advance planning of elements of the system such as meals and entertainment. Customers could perhaps pre-book tickets for events or particular items on the menus of food providers.

Overall, the system is likely to provide benefits for all parties in the chain. XL can retain its competitive advantage, customers can receive a better and more personalised service, and suppliers will get better information for planning.

Test your understanding 3

Benefits to XL Travel from introducing downstream management include the following:

- e-marketing might be more easily used to give more up-to-date and personalised information to customers

- updates to schedules, events etc. might be more easily communicated to customers

- customers might feel more obliged to rebook with XL Travel if IT systems improve the convenience of making a booking.

However, for XL, downstream supply chain management may not be attractive for a number of reasons. Firstly, it already deals directly with its customers so there would be no 'dis-intermediation' benefits.

Also, given the age of its typical customer base, there may be little take-up of e-marketing and online booking systems. This is an age group that are typically low users of technology and the cost of investment in these downstream systems is unlikely to be recovered by the benefits highlighted above.

In fact, moving away from its existing personal levels of service might actually further alienate its client base and be seen as a further example of investment happening in the wrong areas.

Overall, XL Travel should focus on upstream supply chain management and avoid downstream management until a time when customers are ready for it and demanding it.

Professional skill:

The last two sentences of this answer show good judgement. The big picture, longer-term issues are explained along with a clear recommendation on how XL Travel should proceed. Judgement, where (in this case) longer-term and bigger picture issues are weighed against short-term elements, is a key skill in illustrating commercial acumen.

Test your understanding 4

Big Data management involves using sophisticated systems to gather, store and analyse large volumes of data in a variety of structured and unstructured formats. Companies are collecting increasing volumes of data through everyday transactions and marketing activity. If managed effectively this can lead to many business benefits although there are risks involved.

A company like MC will already collect a relatively large amount of data regarding its customers, their transactions and call history. It is likely that a significant proportion of its customers are also fairly digitally engaged and therefore data can be gathered regarding preferences and complaints from social media networks. This will be particularly useful to MC as it has seen an increase in complaints and has a high churn rate, so engaging with customers will be highly beneficial.

Recent competitive pressure has led to a decline in sales and so MC needs to consider the strategic direction which is most appropriate for it to improve performance.

Analysing the large amount of data available to them will inform decisions on areas such as:

- The type of handsets currently most in demand and therefore the prices required when bundling with tariffs.

- Main areas of complaint and therefore the areas of weakness which need to be resolved.

- Which types of communication are most popular (e.g. data, call minutes, text messages) to ensure the tariffs have the right combinations.

- Usage statistics for pay as you go customers to drive the most appropriate offers and marketing activity.

- Most popular competitor offerings with reasons.

Test your understanding 5

Traditional financial services providers need to meet the threat from Fintech head on. There are a number of defences that they are employing to fight back against this emerging threat such as:

- Improving their own services in order to, for example, promote a more personal service that differentiates from the impersonal Fintech products.

- Offering more flexible products that are tailored to individual needs.

- Offering additional services not available via Fintech (such as the ability to use a physical location for cashing services).

- Seeking out legislative help – the financial services industry is heavily regulated but many Fintech businesses fall outside the scope of current legislation. Traditional banks want to have more and tougher legislation of Fintechs, arguing that this will level the playing field for everyone.

- Relying on technophobia and hoping that a few bad actors in the Fintech market will destroy consumer confidence and bring consumers back to the relative safety of traditional lenders (though there is no evidence yet that this will happen).

- Better environmental analysis so that Fintech opportunities and threats are recognised and acted upon much earlier.

- Launching their own Fintech divisions or acquiring growing Fintech businesses.

Test your understanding 6

(a) File conversion takes place during the last stages of systems development. When the new system is in place, then all data has to be transferred onto it. This process can take a considerable time when converting from a manual to a computerised system.

The way in which files are converted depends, to some extent, upon their size and complexity. In this case, there are 3,000 records for input onto a stand-alone microcomputer.

Assuming that there is only one input device, presumably a keyboard, the following sequence of events is likely to occur.

– The changeover will be thoroughly planned and a suitable time identified. In the scenario given, it would not be feasible to run any sort of parallel system and as the package being used is a bought-in package, then it will have been tried and tested and will be free from 'bugs'.

- Once a time has been chosen, it is necessary to ensure that all the data held within the present system is accurate and up to date. Dead records should be removed from the system.

- The records will be in continuous use, therefore they will have to be entered in batches. Alternatively, all the cards could be photocopied and then entered onto the system.

- Initially, only the static data will be entered on the computer. This includes such data as name, address, personnel record number, etc. A record will be created for each employee containing all his or her personal static data.

- Once the static data has been entered, then it will be a relatively easier task to enter the up-to-date variable information. This method avoids data becoming out of date before the system is in operation.

- Once all the data has been transferred to the computer, tests will be carried out using test data to ensure that the system is working correctly.

- Hard copies of all records would be printed out in order for employees to verify their record and also in order to comply with the terms of relevant Data Protection legislation.

- Amendments will be necessary from time to time, as in the case of changes in tax tables and national insurance rates. However, there should be standard programs within the package to facilitate amendment.

(b) Controls that would be incorporated into the process to ensure that the computerised master file is accurate, complete, up to date and suitable for running the live system would include the following:

- The controls used to check the completeness and accuracy of the existing manual system.

- The controls over the total number of records and the values imposed on certain key fields. Data entry should be controlled by use of a batch register to ensure that all records have been entered.

- Data should be validated by input programs to check correctness of input.

- Strict control should be exercised over any rejected records.

- Notes and records should be kept of any changes to the manual system prior to conversion.

- A check should be made by record once the data has been entered and this should be compared with the manual records.

- A full test run should be initiated in order to check the system's and operator's accuracy.

Test your understanding 7

The correct answer is A

RTY is using supervised learning where the machine is given data classifications and then applies them to the data. Unsupervised learning is used where no clear classifications can be identified in advance and the algorithms are used to explore the data and find the intrinsic patterns. Reinforcement learning is where the algorithm has a result to achieve (like maximising returns) and then interacts with the environment to learn the best way to achieve it. Feature learning is a technique used in machine learning which allows the system to discover what is needed to identify features or classifications from raw data.

Test your understanding 8

The correct answer is **B**

Internet of things allows everyday objects to be connected to the internet and interact with us. Big data gets generated from products like this. There is no mention that this is done via 3-D printing (though toothbrushes could be!). Mobile technologies involve using them for the transactions, which is not the case here.

Test your understanding 9

The correct answer is **A and D**

GDPR wants data to be kept up to date and protected. It also requires data to only be kept for as long as necessary and that it is used for explicit, specified purposes. Data can be stored in a variety of formats.

Test your understanding 10

The correct answer is **A**

Corporate digital responsibility (CDR) goes beyond legislation when handling technology and data. Corporate social responsibility looks at maximising positive impacts on society and minimising negative, and may incorporate CDR. Lobbying tries to influence the policies of government officials. Artificial intelligence is the creation of intelligent machines that work and react like humans.

Chapter

21

E-marketing

Chapter learning objectives

Upon completion of this chapter you will be able to:

- analyse customers and markets including market segmentation

- advise on how the 7Ps, including price-based strategies, differentiation and lock-in can help an organisation sustain its competitive advantage

- explore the characteristics of the media of e-marketing using the 6 'I's of Interactivity, Intelligence, Individualisation, Integration, Industry structure and Independence of location

- assess the importance of online branding in e-marketing and compare it to traditional branding

- explore different methods of acquiring and managing suppliers and customers through exploiting e-business technologies

PER

Two of the PER performance objectives (PO3) and (PO13) are that you contribute to the wider business strategy of your organisation through your personal and team objectives. You identify innovative ways to improve organisational performance and plan business activities and control performance, making recommendations for improvement. Working through this chapter should help you understand how to demonstrate these objectives.

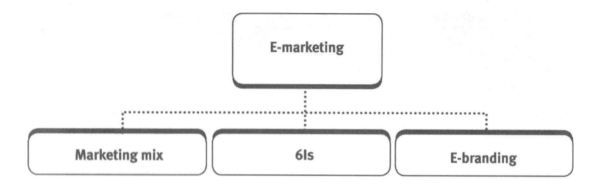

1 Stages in the marketing process

There are a number of techniques for marketing a product, but they generally follow a number of distinct stages:

1 **Market analysis** – used to identify gaps and opportunities in a business' environment (as explored in chapter 3).

2 **Customer analysis** – examining customers so that potential customers can be divided into segments with similar purchasing characteristics.

3 **Market research** – determining characteristics of each segment such as size, potential, level of competition, unmet needs etc.

4 **Targeting** – deciding which segments to target (again, chapter 3 techniques such as PESTEL, 5 forces and forecasting would be used here).

5 **Marketing mix strategies** – developing a unique marketing mix for each segment in order to exploit it properly.

Marketing mix strategies are an important element of downstream supply chain management (explored in the previous chapter). This chapter focuses primarily on this element of marketing, though you should have an awareness of all 5 stages.

Market and customer analysis

Market analysis

Market analysis helps identify the appropriate marketing strategy. This analysis will include the following:

- appraisal and understanding of the present situation – this would include an analysis for each product showing its stage in the product life cycle, strength of competition, market segmentation, anticipated threats and opportunities, customer profile

- definition of objectives of profit, turnover, product image, market share and market position by segment

- evaluation of the marketing strategies available to meet these objectives, e.g. pricing policy, distribution policy, product differentiation, advertising plans, sales promotions, etc.

- definition of control methods to check progress against objectives and provide early warning, thereby enabling the marketing strategies to be adjusted.

There are two purposes of the analysis:

- to identify gaps in the market where consumer needs are not being satisfied

- to look for opportunities that the organisation can benefit from, in terms of sales or development of new products or services.

Customer analysis

There are three sets of strategic questions that are used to analyse customers – segmentation, motivation and unmet needs.

Segmentation – sets of strategic questions include the following.

- Who are the biggest, most profitable existing customers and who are the most attractive potential customers?

- Do the customers fall into any logical groups on the basis of characteristics, needs or motivations?

- Can the market be segmented into groups requiring a unique business strategy?

Traditional segmentation focuses on identifying customer groups based on a number of variables that include:

- geographic variables, such as region of the world or country, country size, or climate

- demographic variables, such as age, gender, sexual orientation, family size, income, occupation, education, socioeconomic status, religion, nationality/race, and others

- psychographic variables, such as personality, life-style, values and attitudes

- behavioural variables, such as benefit sought (quality, low price, convenience), product usage rates, brand loyalty, product end use, readiness-to-buy stage, decision-making unit, and others.

Value-based segmentation looks at groups of customers in terms of the revenue they generate and the costs of establishing and maintaining relationships with them.

For example, a food manufacturer will approach supermarket chains very differently to the small independent retailer, probably offering better prices, delivery terms, using different sales techniques and delivering direct to the supermarket chain. They might also supply own-label products to the large chain but they are unlikely to be able to offer the same terms to the corner shop. The benefit of segmentation to the company adopting this policy is that it enables them to get close to their intended customer and really find out what that customer wants (and is willing to pay for). This should make the customer happier with the product offered and, hence, lead to repeat sales and endorsements.

Motivation – concerns the customers' selection and use of their favourite brands, the elements of the product or service that they value most, the customers' objectives and the changes that are occurring in customer motivation.

Unmet needs – considers why some customers are dissatisfied and some are changing brands or suppliers. The analysis looks at the needs not being met that the customer is aware of.

Customer lifecycle segmentation model

This is another method for segmenting customers – as visitors use online services they pass through seven stages:

1   First-time visitor

2   Return visitor

3   Newly registered visitor

4   Registered visitor

5   Have made one or more purchases

6   Have purchased before but now inactive

7   Have purchased before and are still active and e-responsive.

Illustration 1 – Customers and markets

The market for package holidays can be split up into a variety of different sub-markets – the family market, the elderly market, the young singles market, the activity holiday market, the budget holiday market, etc.

Because it would be virtually impossible to provide one single product that would satisfy all people in all markets, an organisation can tailor its marketing approach with a specific product and go for:

• undifferentiated marketing – one product and one market with no attempt to segment the market. For example, a provider might offer trips to a holiday location such as Florida that can cater to all market segments due to the ability to personalise the experience with trips, parks, activities, etc., once the visitor has arrived.

> - differentiated marketing – the market is segmented with products being developed to appeal to the needs of buyers in the different segments. For example, a holiday company could offer a range of different locations such as activity holidays, family holidays, city breaks etc. which would appeal to different market segments.
>
> - niche or target marketing – specialising in one or two of the identified markets only. Some package holidays may only be sold to one particular market segment, such as 18 to 30 clubs.

 ## 2 Marketing mix strategies

The marketing mix is the set of controllable variables that the firm can use to influence the buyers' responses (Kotler). The variables are commonly grouped into four classes that McCarthy refers to as 'the four Ps' – product, price, promotion and place (or distribution).

 The original 4Ps model

- Price – pricing strategies include price skimming, when a premium price is charged because the product has a technological advantage or brand loyalty that outweighs a price difference and market penetration, a deliberately low price to dominate the market and block competition entry.

- Promotion – the promotion mix consists of four elements: advertising, sales promotion, public relations and personal selling.

- Place – the design of a channel of distribution will be influenced by the type of product, the abilities of the intermediaries and the expectations of the consumer.

- Product – the product needs to be augmented if it is to stand out from rivals' products. This can be done by changing its brand name, its aesthetics, its quality, its packaging, or by widening the product mix or increasing/improving the services that the product comes with.

Product	Price	Promotion	Place
• Brand name • Packaging • Features • Options • Quality • Warranty • Service • Style appeal	• Level • Discounts • Allowances • Payment terms • Delivery options	• Sales promotion • Personal selling • Publicity • Advertising	• Distribution channels • Distribution coverage • Outlet locations • Sales territories • Inventory levels • Inventory locations

Test your understanding 1

Suggest how the marketing mix might differ for a consumer product in the first two stages of the product's life cycle.

E-marketing: the 7Ps

E-marketing is marketing carried out using electronic technology.

Opportunities for e-marketing can be examined using the traditional 4Ps of:

- product
- price
- promotion and
- place,

plus an additional 3Ps:

- people/participants (for example, having adequately trained staff and support services)
- process (for example, payment and delivery processes) and
- physical evidence (for example, website layout and navigation).

The additional 3Ps are particularly relevant to the marketing of services.

Test your understanding 2

Hartley's Books is a firm that specialises in selling antiquarian books. Antiquarian books are usually in excess of 50 years old and often out of print, and collectors pay a premium price for books which are likely to increase in value over time, such as first editions signed by the author.

Hartley's has six stores spread across the country. James Hartley, the grandson of the original founder, has recently taken over the role of Managing Director of the company. He is concerned with the downturn in sales that has been experienced in the recent tough economic climate and he believes that the stores need to be better marketed if they are to take advantage of the likely upturn in the economy that he believes is 'just around the corner'.

One of the areas where he is considering investing is in launching an e-commerce website to run alongside the existing business.

Required:

Consider how Hartley's Books could be marketed, paying particular attention to the e-commerce aspect of James's plans.

Professional skill:

Illustrate analysis skills in considering the wider context of e-commerce.

The effects of electronic methods on marketing

Here are examples of the effects of electronic methods on marketing:

Product	• Retailers often offer a wider range of products through online websites compared with traditional catalogues.
	• Customisation. e.g. holidays no longer have to be for the precise seven days a tour company dictates.
	• Many companies use the internet to vary the extended product. e.g. online assistance.
Price	• Prices can be lower because of e-business techniques automating processing.
	• From customers' perspectives, prices are easy to compare on the internet (greater transparency) so there is more pressure on retailers to be competitive.
	• Prices can be changed to reflect demand e.g. car rental firms in the USA will continually monitor demand and rivals' prices and change their prices accordingly. This is known as "dynamic pricing".
	• New pricing approaches become feasible, such as auctions.

	Here are examples of the effects of electronic methods on marketing:
Promotion	• Using banner adverts or pop-ups in websites. • Sending personalised emails (possibly based on past shopping history). • Promoting social media distribution and viral campaigns.
Place	• Delivery over the internet (e.g. music, software, video). • Availability on a wider range of devices and in a wider geographic scope.
People/ participants	• Service businesses usually have high person-to-person contact. It is important that these contacts are conducted well as there is often no quality control step that can intervene between employee and customer. • A simple example of the use of electronics is to provide employees with an on-screen script for dealing with queries. Depending on customers' answers, the script branches to different options.
Processes	• Again, in a service business, a customer is often exposed to more business processes. For example, a lot of information has to be provided if a customer is buying online insurance. The process has to be made high quality and easy to use. • Many people become frustrated with e-commerce sites because a small error is only reported at the end of the process, and then the customer has to start from the beginning again.
Physical evidence	• Is the website well designed? Does it look good? • The website frequently gives potential customers their first impressions of the organisation.

3 E-marketing: the 6Is

The 6Is of marketing is a summary of the differences between the new media and traditional media. By considering each of these aspects of the new media, marketing managers can develop plans to accommodate the characteristics of the new media.

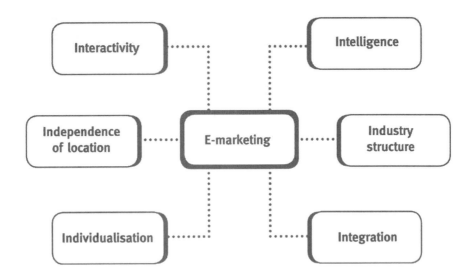

Explanation of the 6Is		
Interactivity	•	Traditional media are mainly 'push' media – the marketing message is broadcast from company to customer – with limited interaction.
	•	On the internet it is usually a customer who seeks information on a web – it is a 'pull' mechanism.
Intelligence	•	The internet can be used as a low-cost method of collecting marketing information about customer perceptions of products and services.
	•	The website also records information every time a user clicks on a link. Log file analysers will identify the type of promotions or products customers are responding to and how patterns vary over time.
Individualisation	•	Communications can be tailored to the individual, unlike traditional media where the same message is broadcast to everyone.
	•	Personalisation is an important aspect of CRM and mass customisation, e.g. every customer who visits a particular site is profiled so that when they next visit information relevant to their product interest will be displayed.

Integration	• The internet can be used as an integrated communications tool, e.g. it enables customers to respond to offers and promotions publicised in other media. • It can have a direct response or call back facility built in. • It can be used to support the buying decision, even if the purchase does not go through the internet – with web-specific phone numbers on websites.
Industry structure	• The relationship between a company and its channel partners can be dramatically altered by the opportunities available on the internet. For example, disintermediation and reintermediation.
Independence of location	• Electronic media gives the possibility of communicating globally – giving opportunities of selling into markets that may not have been previously accessible.

Test your understanding 3

McClair's is a local hairdressing salon. It offers services exclusively for females. McClair's customers tend to be very fashion conscious and will attend McClair's at least once per fortnight for treatment.

McClair's is a well-known brand in the area and its sole large site is located in the main street of the city's most fashionable district and clients will travel up to 5 kilometres to visit the store. Prices are set at a premium level and services are consistently rated as excellent. McClair's promotes itself by advertising in the city's fashion magazines and supplements as well as having high quality shop frontage which appeals to passing trade. Adverts feature pictures of models with fashionable hair and provide information on McClair's location and opening times.

Clients are encouraged to book an appointment well in advance as stylists at the salon are often operating at full capacity and can be in high demand for popular appointment times. Stylists are regularly asked for advice on areas such as current trends, how to look after hair to ensure vitality, and recommended hair products.

Clients will often want to be served by a particular stylist therefore McClair's keeps a manual booking system (going forward for 1 month in advance) which attempts to match appointments to available stylists.

McClair's is considering expanding its capacity by purchasing recently vacated premises adjacent to its current site. It aims to support this expansion with the launch of a new website accompanied with social media pages on popular social media networks in order to increase the business' visibility. It is however unsure whether the new website is actually necessary and whether it will gain any extra benefits beyond its usual marketing efforts.

Required:

Evaluate how the principles of interactivity and independence of location could be exploited through the launch of the new website.

4 E-branding

A brand is a name, symbol, term, mark or design that enables customers to identify and distinguish the products of one supplier from those offered by competitors.

E-branding has become more and more important as companies decide to offer their services and products online. Website design, corporate branding, e-commerce and search engine optimisation are critical components in building a company's e-branding.

E-branding strategies

Organisations have a number of choices about how to handle e-branding.

- Carry out exactly the same branding on the website as in other places. The organisation has to be careful to ensure that the website style, quality and commercial offers are consistent with the existing brand.

- Offer a slightly amended product or service, still connected to the original brand. The slight differentiation is often signalled by putting the word 'online' after the original brand name. For example 'Timesonline.co.uk'. This site describes itself as 'The best of The Times and The Sunday Times in real time'. So the products are slightly different from the paper-based products, so are differentiated but still strongly linked. The 'online' description also promises interactivity and might suggest a free service.

- Form a partnership with an existing brand.

- Create an entirely new brand, perhaps to emphasise a more modern, flexible approach. This has been common with financial institutions such as HBOS and IF. HBOS runs a conventional banking operation and IF is its direct finance operations that makes high use of the internet.

Illustration

Aspirin's land-based brand positioning statement was 'Aspirin – provides instant pain relief'. This does not hold true for a meaningful web presence, you can't get instant pain relief on the web. So the management utilised their new e-branding creative strategies to develop a website for Aspirin that made sense to a consumer in the disintermediated world of brands on the web. The result was 'Aspirin – your self-help brand', which offered visitors meaningful health-oriented intelligence and self-help, over the web.

Comparison to traditional marketing

E-branding, like traditional branding, aims to create a specific brand image, but to create it and manage it by using the tools and opportunities offered by the internet. It has the same objectives as traditional branding in terms of creating awareness, creating a distinction from rivals and developing loyalty from customers.

But both forms are different in many aspects. E-branding differs from traditional branding in that:

- The information needs to be delivered in a more efficient manner
- It requires a more visual identity
- It needs to be easier to find
- It can be more interactive
- It can more easily evolve.

 More details

With traditional branding, the brand is developed through the customer experience. This can entail many things. For example, for a retailer focused on a differentiation strategy, it might entail how a customer is welcomed to the store, how goods are displayed, the facilities available, the service received etc. E-branding needs to replicate this same experience but it is difficult to do this online. Therefore an e-brand needs to project this same differentiation but it cannot use elements such as the in-store experience and it needs to project the strategy very quickly and efficiently. Elements of the marketing mix such as people and processes can play a key role here.

This can rely on having a more 'visual' identity. Traditional brands are often intangible and difficult to visualise – they may be more about a feeling or an emotion. However, e-brands rely on what a user can see on their screen. The e-brand therefore needs to be more appealing and project the necessary competitive strategy. This can be done via the physical layout of a website or communication portal. A differentiator's e-brand needs to be supported by a professional website with high quality images. Emails need to be professional in tone. The brand image needs to be prominent and consideration needs to be given to its visual design. Social media needs to have a high quality message etc.

E-brands will be located via systems such as internet search engines, social media adverts, banner ads etc. Care needs to be given to placement and uniqueness. Elements such as the domain name will become important. Avoiding similarities to other names will be much more difficult due to the independence of location brought about by e-marketing. For example, a local retailer called Barbara's Beauty Salon can easily see how other local rivals are projecting themselves to consumers and try to differentiate themselves from local rivals. In e-branding this will be much more difficult – a Google search for Barbara's Beauty Salon throws up nearly 100,000 businesses spread across the world.

But e-brands can be more interactive. They have the ability to provide greater information. Users can more easily pick the messages and information they receive. Consumers can interact better with e-brands. So that when e-branding is successful it can bring large benefits to organisations.

Also, evolving and changing an e-brand can be easier than traditional brands. Websites can be quickly transformed, colour schemes are cheaper to change, the message can be quickly adapted etc. It is much more difficult and slower when attempting to do this with traditional branding.

5 Customer relationship management (CRM)

E-business can play an important role in the management of customers. It can help acquire customers and manage them to ensure loyalty and repeat business. This process is often referred to as customer relationship management (CRM).

Research

Research into e-businesses suggests the following:

- It is 20 – 30% more expensive to acquire new online customers than for traditional businesses.

- Retaining an extra 5% of customers can boost online company profits by between 25 and 95%.

CRM can aid an organisation in achieving the following:

1   Customer **acquisition** – convincing the potential customers within the segment to become actual customers

2   Customer **retention** – better understanding customer needs in order to ensure that repeat custom

3   Customer **extension** (or 'customer development') – increasing the range of products bought by the customer.

Customer acquisition

Methods of acquiring customers can be split between traditional offline techniques (e.g. advertising, direct mail, sponsorship, etc.) and rapidly-evolving online techniques:

Search engine marketing

- Search engine optimisation – improving the position of a company in search engine listings for key terms or phrases. For example, increasing the number of inbound links to a page through 'link building' can improve the ranking with Google.

- Pay per click (PPC) – an advert is displayed by search engines as a 'sponsored link' when particular phrases are entered. The advertiser typically pays a fee to the search engine each time the advert is clicked.

- Trusted feed – database-driven sites such as travel, shopping and auctions are very difficult to optimise for search engines and consequently haven't enjoyed much visibility in the free listings. Trusted Feed works by allowing a 'trusted' third party, usually a search engine marketing company, to 'feed' a website's entire online inventory directly into the search engine's own database, bypassing the usual submission process.

Online PR

- Media alerting services – using online media and journalists for press releases.

- Portal representation – portals are websites that act as gateways to information and services. They typically contain search engines and directories.

- Businesses blogs (effectively online journals) can be used to showcase the expertise of its employees.

- Community C2C portals (effectively the e-equivalent of a village notice board) – e.g. an oil company could set up a discussion forum on its website to facilitate discussion on issues including pollution.

Online partnerships

- Link-building – reciprocal links can be created by having quality content and linking to other sites with quality content. The objective is that they will then link to your site.

- Affiliate marketing – a commission-based arrangement where an e-retailer pays sites that link to it for sales. For example, hundreds of thousands of sites direct customers to Amazon to buy the books or CDs that they have mentioned on their pages.

- Sponsorship – web surfers are more likely to trust the integrity of a firm sponsoring a website than those who use straight ads.

- Co-branding – a lower cost form of sponsorship where products are labelled with two brand names. For example, as well as including details about their cars, the website Subaru.com also includes immediate co-branded insurance quotes with Liberty Mutual Insurance and pages devoted to outdoor lifestyles developed with LL Bean.

- Aggregators – these are comparison sites allowing customers to compare different product features and prices. For example, moneysupermarket.com allows analysis of financial services products. Clearly a mortgage lender would want their products included in such comparisons.

Interactive adverts

- Banners – banners are simply advertisements on websites with a click through facility so customers can surf to the advertiser's website.

- Rich-media – many web users have become immune to conventional banner ads so firms have tried increasingly to make their ads more noticeable through the use of animation, larger formats, overlays, etc. For example, an animated ad for Barclays banking services will appear on some business start-up sites.

- Some ads are more interactive and will change depending on user mouse movements, for example generating a slide show.

Opt-in email

It is estimated that 80% of all emails are spam or viruses. Despite this email marketing can still deliver good response rates. One survey found only 10% of emails were not delivered (e.g. due to spam filters), 30% were opened and 8% resulted in 'clickthroughs'. Options for email include the following:

- Cold, rented lists – here the retailer buys an email list from a provider such as Experian.

- Co-branded email – for example, your bank sends you an email advertising a mobile phone.

- 3rd party newsletters – the retailer advertises itself in a 3rd party's newsletter.

- House list emails – lists built up in-house from previous customers, for example.

Viral marketing

- Viral marketing is where email is used to transmit a promotional message from one person to another.

- Ideally the viral ad should be a clever idea, a game or a shocking idea that is compulsive viewing so people send it to their friends.

Evaluating online customer behaviour

Recency, frequency, monetary value analysis (RFM) is the main model used to classify online buyer behaviour.

Recency

- The time since a customer completed an action – e.g. purchase, site visit, email response.

- Considered to be a good indicator of potential repeat purchases.

- Allows 'vulnerable' customers to be specifically targeted.

Frequency

- The number of times an action is completed in a specified time period – e.g. five log-ins per week.

- A related concept is latency – the average time between actions – e.g. the average time between first and second purchases.

- Together these allow the firm to put in place triggers that alert them to behaviour outside the norm. For example, a customer may be taking longer than normal between first and second purchases. This could indicate that they are currently considering a purchase prompting the firm to email or phone them with relevant offers.

Monetary value

- The monetary value of purchases can be measured in many different ways such as average order value, total annual purchases, etc.

- High monetary value is usually a good indicator of customer loyalty and higher future potential purchases. Such customers could be deliberately excluded from special promotions.

RFM is also known as FRAC:

- Frequency

- Recency

- Amount = monetary value

- Category = types of product purchased – not in RFM.

Customer retention

Customer retention has two goals:

- to keep customers
- to keep customers using the online channel.

Customer satisfaction

Key to retention is understanding and delivering the drivers of customer satisfaction as satisfaction drives loyalty and loyalty drives profitability.

The 'SERVQUAL' approach to service quality developed by **Parasuraman et al** focuses on the following factors.

Tangibles

- The 'tangibles' heading considers the appearance of physical facilities, equipment, personnel and communications.
- For online quality the key issue is the appearance and appeal of websites – customers will revisit websites that they find appealing.
- This can include factors such as structural and graphic design, quality of content, ease of use, speed to upload and frequency of update.

Reliability

- Reliability is the ability to provide a promised service dependably and accurately and is usually the most important of the different aspects being discussed here.
- For online service quality, reliability is mainly concerned with how easy it is to connect to the website.
- If websites are inaccessible some of the time and/or emails are bounced back, then customers will lose confidence in the retailer.

Responsiveness

- Responsiveness looks at the willingness of a firm to help customers and provide prompt service.
- In the context of e-business, excessive delays can cause customers to 'bail-out' of websites and/or transactions and go elsewhere.
- This could relate to how long it takes for emails to be answered or even how long it takes for information to be downloaded to a user's browser.

Assurance

- Assurance is the knowledge and courtesy of employees and their ability to inspire trust and confidence.
- For an online retailer, assurance looks at two issues – the quality of responses and the privacy/security of customer information.

- Quality of response includes competence, credibility and courtesy and could involve looking at whether replies to emails are automatic or personalised and whether questions have been answered satisfactorily.

Empathy

- Empathy considers the caring, individualised attention a firm gives its customers.

- Most people would assume that empathy can only occur through personal human contact but it can be achieved to some degree through personalising websites and email.

- Key here is whether customers feel understood. For example, being recommended products that they would never dream of buying can erode empathy.

There are three stages to applying the SERVQUAL framework.

1   Understanding customer expectations through research.

2   Setting and communicating the service promise.

3   Delivering the service promise to ensure that a service quality gap does not exist.

Techniques for retaining customers

Given the above consideration of service quality, firms use the following techniques to try to retain customers.

- Personalisation – delivering individualised content through web-pages or email. For example, portals such as Yahoo! enable users to configure their home pages to give them the information they are most interested in.

- Mass customisation – delivering customised content to groups of users through web-pages or email. For example, Amazon may recommend a particular book based on what other customers in a particular segment have been buying.

- Extranets – for example, Dell Computers uses an extranet to provide additional services to its 'Dell Premier' customers.

- Opt-in email – asking customers whether they wish to receive further offers.

- Online communities – firms can set up communities where customers create the content. These could be focused on purpose (e.g. Autotrader is for people buying/selling cars), positions (e.g. the teenage chat site Doobedo), interest (e.g. Football365) or profession. Despite the potential for criticism of a company's products on a community, firms will understand where service quality can be improved, gain a better understanding of customer needs and be in a position to answer criticism.

Customer extension

Customer extension has the objective of increasing the lifetime value of a customer and typically involves the following:

- 'Re-sell' similar products to previous sales.

- 'Cross sell' closely related products.

- 'Up sell' more expensive products.

- For example, having bought a book from Amazon you could be contacted with offers of other books, DVDs or DVD players.

- Reactivate customers who have not bought anything for some time.

Key to these are propensity modelling and the 'sense, respond, adjust' model.

Propensity modelling

Propensity modelling involves evaluating customer behaviour and then making recommendations to them for future products. For example, if you have bought products from Amazon, then each time you log on there will be a recommendation of other products you may be interested in.

This can involve the following:

- Creating automatic product relationships – e.g. through monitoring which products are typically bought together.

- Using trigger words or phrases – e.g. 'customers who bought ...also bought...'.

- Offering related products at checkout – e.g. batteries for electronic goods.

'Sense, respond, adjust'

- Sense – monitor customer activities to classify them according to value, growth, responsiveness and defection risk. RFM analysis, discussed above, would also be relevant here.

- Respond with timely, relevant communications to encourage desired behaviours.

- Adjust – monitor responses and continue with additional communications.

Illustration 2 – E-marketing

The Amazon website provides the following facilities, all of which can be linked to marketing and customer service, and that help Amazon to acquire customers, retain customers and increase income from them.

- Home delivery of products (using place and independence of location to acquire customers).

- Customers can write reviews and read other people's reviews of products (using promotion and interactivity to retain customers).

- Based on previous buying habits, other products are recommended (using intelligence and individualisation to extend customer purchases).

- 'Customers who bought this product also bought these products...' (using intelligence and promotion to extend customer purchases).

- Order tracking (using integration to retain customers).

- Prices of new and used items are displayed. Prices of new items are usually lower than conventional shops (using price to acquire customers).

- Very smart-looking interface (using physical evidence to acquire and retain customers).

- Search facilities (using interactivity and processes to acquire customers).

- Emails if orders are delayed (using processes and individualisation to retain customers).

- Allowing a 'wish list facility (using processes and individualisation to retain customers).

6 Chapter summary

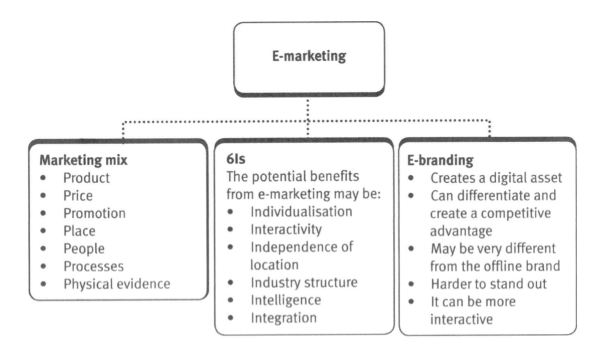

Marketing mix
- Product
- Price
- Promotion
- Place
- People
- Processes
- Physical evidence

6Is
The potential benefits from e-marketing may be:
- Individualisation
- Interactivity
- Independence of location
- Industry structure
- Intelligence
- Integration

E-branding
- Creates a digital asset
- Can differentiate and create a competitive advantage
- May be very different from the offline brand
- Harder to stand out
- It can be more interactive

Test your understanding answers

Test your understanding 1

In the introduction phase.			
Product	**Place**	**Price**	**Promotion**
• Build product awareness • Where applicable, obtain protection for intellectual property rights (patents, etc.) • Establish the brand and the quality to be associated with the brand	• Develop the market and distribution channels	• Possibly choose a market penetration pricing strategy, or a 'price skimming' (high price) market strategy	• Promotions should be aimed at innovators and early adopters in the customer population: develop product awareness

In the growth phase.			
Product	**Place**	**Price**	**Promotion**
• Build the brand • Maintain product quality, but add additional features to create product differentiation	• Add distribution channels	• Keep prices unchanged: sales growth is rising therefore there is no need yet to change pricing strategy	• Promotion should aim now at a broader audience of potential customers

Test your understanding 2

The best way to consider how the company could be marketed is to examine the elements of the **marketing mix**:

Price

Hartley's Books is likely to use an element of perceived value pricing. There is unlikely to be a 'going rate' for such books and other strategies such as penetration or skimming are unlikely to be appropriate due to the uniqueness of the product.

Books should be valued and priced based on likely demand, uniqueness/rarity and the current economic climate. This may mean that book prices change over time – for example, they may go down as the economic climate deteriorates, but they might increase as they become older and rarer. Due to the likely low level of competition, there should be no need for discounting on the website and delivery charges could be added to the normal price that would be charged in shops.

But pricing is unlikely to be a key element of the marketing mix.

Place

It would appear that Hartley's Books has already determined the method in which books will be sold. They will have a physical presence through their six stores as well as an e-commerce website for internet sales.

Other aspects that they could consider would be some elements of integrated e-commerce. Perhaps if a book is purchased in a store extra content such as author biographies, links to author websites etc. could be available online. There might also be a 'reserve and collect' facility on the website so that a book could be reserved online and then collected in the store in order to speed up the delivery process and reduce the threats that might arise from the transport of some books.

Promotion

Techniques such as television and radio advertising, or sales promotion techniques are unlikely to be of much use to Hartley's Books due to the small size of the target market and the unlikelihood of regular purchases. There may be specialist journals or magazines in which the company could advertise but a more important avenue that may be open to the company is likely to be trade shows and exhibitions.

There may be regular events for antiquarian book collectors or even specialist author events. Hartley's Books could aim to have a physical presence at such events displaying a range of suitable books and could even aim to provide sponsorship and branding of such events. This would provide them with direct access to potential customers as well as increasing awareness of the company and more 'hits' on its website.

The lack of common promotional avenues is likely to reinforce the value of the internet venture. Hartley's Books should look to have banner adverts on author websites that link back to its own website and could even attempt to provide sponsorship in forum groups that are used by its target market. They should seek to have a high appearance rate on popular search engines and perhaps seek endorsements from authors (or their site managers) on the author's own site.

Product

The company's 'product' will be the service it provides, the shops in which sales are made and the range of books that it sells. These are the areas that it should look to differentiate from rivals.

It could improve service by offering reading or viewing facilities within its shops and by having knowledgeable staff who are experienced in understanding and meeting customer needs. Shops should reflect the nature of the product being sold and could, for example, have antique furniture such as reading chairs and indexing so that customers can find what they are looking for. The range of books should be as wide as possible in order to attract as many buyers as possible, and Hartley's Books could perhaps seek to offer certificates of authenticity in order to provide reassurance to buyers.

Processes

There will need to be clear security on the website for payments and if the 'reserve and collect' facility is offered it should be clear and simple to use. Due to the nature of the product the key process may be transportation and delivery as some books might be delicate and fragile. This process should be made as safe and reassuring as possible and customers could be given the option of choosing or arranging their own courier as an alternative. Worldwide delivery could be offered and as many different payment methods as possible should be allowed in order to maximise potential sales. Regular customers should be given the ability to store their details for personal use and perhaps software could be used to recommend further purchases based on past buying behaviour.

People

The nature of the product undoubtedly will mean that buyers are likely to have questions when they find a book that they are interested in. It will therefore be vital that the internet site is supported by knowledgeable service staff who can answer questions on the book in question. Given the likely low numbers of sales (particularly in the early days of the site) these calls could be directed to shop floor staff, perhaps with one member of staff at each store allocated each day to answer such calls. These staff may have to work more flexible times in order to meet the times of highest demand on the internet site during the day.

This may mean that more staff need to be recruited into stores. Also, as the internet site grows, some staff could be dedicated full time to such queries.

This facility needs to be supported with email support as some customers may be shopping at times when stores are closed. But most buyers may be happy to wait for a call back facility as speed of delivery is unlikely to be a critical success factor in the industry.

Physical evidence

The website should be easy to navigate and well presented. One of the key elements will be to have a search facility so that buyers can find particular books that they may be interested in. There should also be a 'request' option where, if Hartley's Book does not have a copy of a particular book, a potential buyer can express an interest and be kept informed if Hartley's Books manages to source a copy.

Another aspect that may be offered could be a buying facility. Hartley's Books will not have suppliers like other bookshops. They will rely on sourcing books from individuals and estates. The internet might provide an excellent opportunity to source rare books which can be sold on at a profit through either shops or the website.

Professional skill:

The key to achieving the analysis skills is to use a recognised model to provide structure (here the 7Ps is used), ensure full coverage of the model, make the answer as relevant to the scenario as possible (rather than simply having a shopping list of areas to consider) and to ensure that there is a focus on e-commerce. Each issue needs to be 'analysed' – this means that it isn't good enough to simply identify an issue, it needs to be explained and the benefits of the change communicated and justified.

Test your understanding 3

Interactivity

The new website should allow clients to interact with it rather than simply providing static information on elements such as opening times, location etc. A key advantage that McClair's could derive would be providing the facility for clients to book appointments online. Availability of stylists could be listed and clients could book an appointment of their choosing. This will make bookings simpler and encourage clients to revisit the website. This will open further benefits to McClair's in terms of its ability to highlight promotions or business innovations.

Further interactivity could come in the form of help and advice sections on the website. Articles and blogs on latest fashions and hair care products could be made available on the website. Clients could choose articles that they are interested in. This has the advantage of providing an element of differentiation to McClair's website as well as potentially freeing up some stylist time in the store. It may even drive sales of particular types of treatments offered by McClair's.

Independence of location

Independence of location concerns the geographical location of the company. Having a website increases the potential geographical reach of a company. For many companies this gives opportunities to sell into international markets which had previously been inaccessible to them.

This facet of the new media is unlikely to be appropriate to McClair's. Most clients live within 5 kilometres of the store. Hair treatments are typically undertaken on a local level and clients are unlikely to travel from beyond the city simply because McClair's has an attractive website.

There will be little advantage gained by McClair's from having a wider geographical spread of customers with access to its website. The new expanded capacity is the same location as at present and unless or until McClair's expands its locations into new geographical areas this will not be an important aspect of the new website.

Project management

Chapter learning objectives

Upon completion of this chapter you will be able to:

- determine the distinguishing features of projects and the constraints they operate in

- discuss the implications of the triple constraint of scope, time and cost

- prepare a business case document and project initiation document

- analyse, assess and classify the costs and benefits of a project investment

- assess the importance of developing a project plan and its key elements

- establish the role and responsibilities of the project manager and the project sponsor

- monitor and control project risks, issues, slippage and changes

- discuss the benefits of a post-implementation and a post-project review

PER

One of the PER performance objectives (PO5) is that you manage yourself and your resources effectively and responsibly. You contribute to the leadership and management of your organisation – delivering what's needed by stakeholders and the business. Working through this chapter should help you understand how to demonstrate that objective.

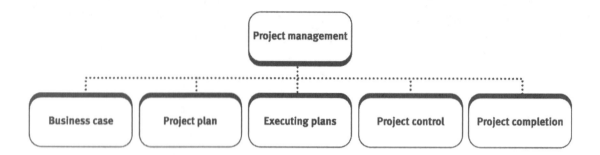

1 Project features

 A project can be defined simply as an activity, which has a start, middle and end, and consumes resources. It will:

- have a specific objective
- have a defined start and end date (timescale)
- consume resources (people, equipment and finance)
- be unique (a one-time-only configuration of these elements)
- have cost constraints that must be clearly defined and understood to ensure the project remains viable
- require organisation.

2 Stages in the project life cycle

Every project is different, but each will include at least the following five stages:

- initiation
- planning
- execution
- control
- completion.

This chapter explores these stages in more detail.

3 Project initiation – building the business case

Project management has become a formal process in most organisations. If an organisation were to apply for a loan from a bank the bank would demand a business plan to justify the loan and explain how it would be repaid. This is what boards of directors are now demanding from project managers – if a project manager wants to implement a new project the project needs to be supported by a strong business case provided in a business case document.

Reasons for building a business case:

- to obtain funding for the project

- to compete with other projects for resources

- to improve planning

- to improve project management.

The need for a business case

Not every project that managers propose can be undertaken. There may be constraints on resources which mean that, for example, there is not enough finance to fund every project, or it may simply be that in some projects the benefits do not outweigh the costs.

Therefore, a business case should be put together for any proposed project. The aim of this is to achieve approval for the project and to obtain adequate resources to achieve its goals.

Contents of a business case

Organisations who have performed many projects will often have developed their own method of presenting a business case. However, they are likely to have the following key elements in common:

- an assessment of the current **strategic position**

- the **constraints** that are likely to exist for any project

- the **risks** that might arise for the project and how these will be managed

- an assessment of the **benefits and costs** of performing the project and how these will be managed.

These key elements are now explored in more detail.

The formal business case document

It is very unlikely that in an exam a student would be asked to create the formal business case document. Instead you are likely to be asked to focus on providing some of the key elements.

However, the formal document put together for management typically pulls the key elements together into the following sections:

1   **Introduction**

    This sets the scene and explains the rationale behind why the project has been considered.

2   **Executive summary**

This is the most important part of the document as it is likely that this will be the part that is read in most detail by the senior management team. It will include the key considerations that have been made, the options considered, the rationale behind the recommendation and a summary of the key numbers (e.g. the output from a financial project appraisal).

3   **Description of current situation**

This will be a strategic and operational assessment of the business. It will include a SWOT analysis and aim to identify the problems that the business is facing and the opportunities available to solve those problems.

4   **Options considered**

This will have an assessment of each option that has been considered and provide reasons for the rejection of options that have not been recommended.

5   **Analysis of costs and benefits**

This will have the key elements for the project assessment. The detail will be provided in the appendices. This section will provide quantifiable benefits and costs but will also make some attempt to quantify intangible benefits and costs such as the impact on customer satisfaction and staff morale. The output from any project appraisal techniques will also be provided.

6   **Impact assessment**

This will examine the impact on elements of the cultural web (studied in a later chapter) such as the organisation culture, the management style, staff roles and routines etc.

7   **Risk assessment**

This section will aim to identify the risks to successful project performance and suggest how each risk should be managed. It may also contain some contingency planning to give guidance on different possible directions for the project in the face of these risks arising (though this is often left until the detailed planning stage).

8   **Recommendations**

This will contain the justification for the suggested path that the project has pursued. It will pull a lot of the other sections of the business case together.

9   **Appendices**

This will lay out the detailed costs and benefits and schedules for areas such as project appraisal.

Strategic analysis

The aim of the strategic analysis in the business case document will be to identify and justify the strategic reasons and drivers for the project. This will often be linked to changes in the external environment such as a new threat or major new opportunity.

The use of a SWOT analysis may be helpful to the project manager in communicating the organisation's current strategic position and the justification of the changes proposed to this position through the implementation of the project.

 Further explanation on the use of SWOT analysis

SWOT analysis was discussed in earlier chapters as a tool for strategic position analysis. A SWOT analysis can also be used in building the business case for a project as well as being used as part of a periodic report to the project sponsor to summarise progress and raise issues.

The internal appraisal should identify:

- strengths – the organisation's strengths that the project may be able to exploit

- weaknesses – organisational weaknesses that may impact on the project.

The external appraisal should identify:

- opportunities – events or changes outside the project that can be exploited to the advantage of the project

- threats – events or changes outside the project that should be defended against.

The four parts of the SWOT analysis are shown in the diagram below.

Strengths	Weaknesses
• The things that are going well (or have gone well) in the projects	• The things that are going badly (or have gone badly) in the projects
• The skills that are prized	• The skills that are lacking
• Major successes	• Major failures
• Parts of the project that are well received by the users or were completed early	• Parts of the project that are poorly received by the users or were completed late

Opportunities	Threats
• Events or changes outside the project (elsewhere in the organisation or its business environment) that can be exploited to the advantage of the project	• Events or changes outside the project (elsewhere in the organisation or its business environment) that should be defended against
• Things likely to go well in the future	• Things likely to go badly in the future

Project constraints

There are three key project constraints:

- cost
- time
- scope.

More details

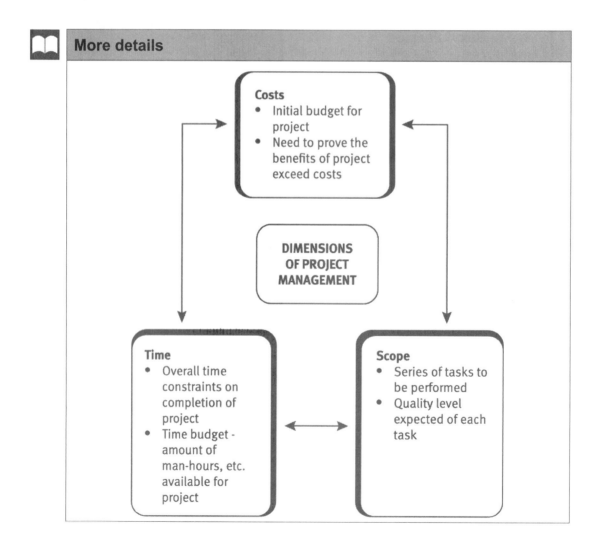

The key elements that a manager must understand are:

- The three constraints are linked together – for example, if a manager wants to increase the scope of the project then he/she is likely to have to increase both the amount of money spent on the project and the time taken to complete it.

- In building the business case, the manager should focus on the constraint that is likely to be most important to the key decision makers (or stakeholders). For example, if key decision makers are concerned primarily with the cost of projects, the project manager should ensure that the proposed project falls within this constraint.

- In project control, it will be important to understand the ranking of the constraints and to ensure that the key constraint is changed as little as possible.

Illustration 1 – Project features and constraints

It is important for project managers to determine which of the constraints (time, costs or scope/performance) is the most important and which is the least important in order to focus resources in the most effective way. Additionally, when there are problems, managers should use the least important constraint (weak constraint) to aid in the solution. The most important of the constraints, the driver, should be the last to be compromised.

If scope is the key constraint, then when the project is out of control it is best to spend more time or increase the budget rather than sacrifice quality or features. On the other hand, if scope is the weak constraint, managers might consider scaling back on features or quality to meet either time or cost constraints.

The key driver may change during a project. That is part of the dynamics of project management. However, managers have to know the initial order of the constraints before they begin the project planning step.

Risk analysis

 Risk is explored in more detail elsewhere in this text. For projects, a risk is anything that will have a negative impact on any one or all of the primary project constraints – time, scope and cost.

You should be aware that risk analysis has three key elements:

- identifying risks

- assessing risks

- managing risks.

Identifying risks

All projects include some risk associated with the following:

- Cost over-runs
- Missed deadlines
- Poor quality
- Disappointed customers
- Business disruption.

Risks can result in four types of consequences:

- benefits are delayed or reduced
- timeframes are extended
- outlays are advanced or increased
- output quality (fitness for purpose) is reduced.

Assessing risks

Risks can be analysed and evaluated according to:

- the likelihood that they will occur, and
- the impact that they could have on the project.

Managing risks

This in turn can lead to plans on how each risk should be managed:

<table>
<tr><td colspan="2" rowspan="2"></td><td colspan="2" align="center">Likelihood</td></tr>
<tr><td align="center">Low</td><td align="center">High</td></tr>
<tr><td rowspan="4">Impact</td></tr>
<tr><td align="center">Low</td><td align="center">Accept</td><td align="center">Reduce</td></tr>
<tr><td></td><td></td><td></td></tr>
<tr><td align="center">High</td><td align="center">Transfer</td><td align="center">Avoid</td></tr>
</table>

Reducing risk can involve the use of techniques such as internal controls. Transferring risk means moving it to another body, such as an insurance company. Risks that are high in both likelihood and impact need to be avoided in the business case, otherwise management are less likely to approve the project. The project manager might need to create contingency plans for avoiding these risks or delay the project until the likelihood is resolved.

Examples of risk management

The potential risks involved in undertaking a project can be presented in a tabular format as set out below:

Risk	Odds	Impact	Management approach – mitigating actions	Warning signs
Inability to recruit suitably qualified staff	Low	Med.	Ensure remuneration is appropriate to skill level.	Low numbers and poorly qualified applicants.
Retention of staff	Med.	Med.	Motivation via contractual terms, good job design, good working environment and personal development. Consider retention clauses in contract for key staff.	Low morale. High turnover.
Necessary premises not available	Med.	High	Accommodation available to project is currently limited. There could be implications for future of project if additional functionality is required and appropriate accommodation is not available to support it.	Delay to work plans caused by lack of facilities.
Failure to get all parties to share same understanding of purpose	Low	High	Definition of stakeholder needs and clear plan with well-defined deliverables. Use of sound project management methodology.	Differing views on forward plan. Confused messages in draft publications.

Test your understanding 1

A leisure company has just approved a large-scale investment project for the development of a new sports centre and grounds in a major city. The forecast NPV is approximately $6m, assuming five years' steady growth in business and constant returns in perpetuity thereafter.
A number of specific risks have been identified:

1   A potential lawsuit may be brought for death or injury of a member of the public using the equipment. No such event has ever occurred in the company's other centres.

2   The loss of several weeks' revenue from pool closure for repairs following the appearance of cracks in the infrastructure. This has occurred in several of the other centres in the past few years.

3   Income fraud as a result of high levels of cash receipts.

4   Loss of playing field revenue from schools and colleges because of poor weather.

Required:

Suggest how these risks could best be managed.

Professional skill:
Illustrate evaluation skills in assessing each risk.

Project benefits

There can be a wide variety of benefits from new projects such as:

*   strategic benefits
*   productivity gains
*   management benefits
*   operational benefits
*   functional and support benefits
*   intangible benefits
*   emergent benefits.

More details on project benefits

Strategic benefits

A new project might be a way to gain a competitive advantage as already seen with areas such as business process redesign and supply chain management.

Productivity gains

A project may make operations more efficient or remove non value adding activities from the value chain in order to increase overall productivity of the business. This may be tied-in to a strategic benefit such as cost leadership.

Management benefits

A project may make the organisation more flexible and reactive to its environment. It might give more up-to-date information to managers so that they can make more agile decisions. These benefits often arise from projects which involve organisational redesign or investments in new IS/IT systems.

Operational benefits

These involve benefits seen in areas such as resources and assets. The project may lead to better management and utilisation of these areas – for example, it may simplify job roles or reduce staff turnover.

Functional and support benefits

Other areas of the value chain may also see benefits such as HRM, marketing, service etc.

Intangible benefits

These can only be measured subjectively. A benefit of a project might be to improve staff morale or customer satisfaction. These benefits should be included in the business case, and many organisations try to put some value on them regardless of how subjective that value might be.

Emergent benefits

Often referred to as secondary or unexpected benefits these benefits might not be expected at the outset of a project but they 'emerge' over time. For example, we've seen how a change to a divisional structure for a business might lead to greater focus and responsibility accounting, but it might also provide opportunities for further diversification that was not envisaged as part of the original change project. The benefits might only emerge as the organisation becomes more comfortable with its new structure. Benefits management (discussed later) aims to manage for these benefits as well as for planned benefits.

The scale of benefits

In order to make a business case on the basis of these benefits, the scale of the benefits should be assessed. The benefits can often be classified along the following scale:

1   Observable

2   Measurable

3   Quantifiable

4   Financial

In order to convince management of the business case for the project, the aim should be to have each benefit as high up the scale as possible (where level 4 is higher than level 1). However, this then brings in the scope for the project manager to upscale or overstate the project benefits in order to get project approval.

The scale of benefits

1   **Observable**

Intangible benefits (such as improvements in staff morale) often fall into this category. Individuals or groups in the organisation with a level of expertise in this area will often use agreed criteria to determine whether or not this benefit has been realised.

Despite the fact that the benefits aren't measurable, they should still be included in the business case as they will be important to many stakeholders. It will also be important that they form part of the benefits management process (covered later).

2   **Measurable**

A measure may exist for this type of benefit, but it may not be possible to estimate by how much performance will improve when the changes are completed. This means that the business can often tell where it is at the moment but cannot specify where it will be post project.

Many strategic benefits fall into this category – for example, a project to improve product quality is likely to lead to an increase in market share, but it may not be possible to quantify by how much the increase in market share will be. However, a timescale should be set for when the measure will be tested to show the benefits of this particular project (rather than being the result of other factors such as competitor actions).

If it is deemed too difficult or expensive to measure the increase in performance, then the benefit should be relegated to an observable benefit.

3 Quantifiable

These benefits should be forecastable in terms of the benefit that should result from the changes. This means that their impact can be estimated before the project commences (unlike measureable benefits where the impact can only be assessed after the project has been completed). Often, productivity gains and operational benefits will fall into this category. For example, it may be possible to estimate that new machines will be able to produce 20% more units per hour.

4 Financial

These benefits can be given a financial value – either in terms of a cost reduction or a revenue increase. The aim should be to have as many benefits as possible in this category so that a financial appraisal of the project is possible.

Test your understanding 2

In seeking to gain approval for a new project a manager has put together the following financial assessment in her business case document:

Net financial benefit from new project:

	$000
Extra revenue from increased market share	140
Savings from increased staff motivation	50
Savings from one staff redundancy	15
Extra revenue from 20% reduction in customer response times	60
Total project costs	(75)
	———
Net benefit	$190
	———

Required:

Consider the types of benefit included in this analysis and whether the manager's appraisal of the financial impact on the project is accurate.

Professional skill:
Illustrate scepticism skills relating to information presented by the manager.

Project costs

In order to properly assess a project the potential benefits need to be measured against the potential costs. Typical project costs might be:

- capital investment costs
- development costs
- centrally allocated costs/infrastructure costs
- external consultancy costs
- resource costs
- quality costs
- flexibility costs
- disruption costs.

Further details on project costs

- capital investment costs* – this would include the costs of IT hardware and software, project specific assets etc.

- development costs* – historic development costs may be easier to ascertain than future development costs which arise as the project is better understood and modifications are required. But an estimate of such costs should still be made.

- centrally allocated costs/infrastructure costs* – these would be costs for the use of premises and central services (such as accounting or personnel services) and may also include an allocation of charges such as depreciation. However, again, only those costs that are incurred exclusively for the project should be included as a project cost.

- external consultancy costs – these might be incurred in project design, quality management, procuring software etc.

- resource costs – these can include the ongoing staff and material costs. In the project appraisal it is normal to include only **incremental** costs here, so if staff, for example, are transferred from elsewhere in the business no cost might actually be attributed to the project.

- quality costs – this can include the cost of training staff, monitoring performance, reworks etc.

- flexibility costs – project management teams need to be as flexible as possible and there may be costs associated with achieving this. These could be costs involved in facilitating flexible working (such as providing IT equipment in staff homes) or in flexible production or servicing (such as lower batch sizes or depackaged services).

- disruption costs – an attempt should be made to quantify these (often) intangible costs from elements such as a loss of productivity during project changeover or from resource reallocations.

* these costs may be deemed to be capital costs and therefore charged to the statement of financial position (balance sheet) rather than the statement of profit or loss. From an accounting perspective, the cost would then be spread (through either depreciation or amortisation) over a number of accounting periods. This can give different results for project appraisal depending on the method of appraisal used (for example, the ARR method will use the accounting treatment whereas the NPV method will follow the timing of the cash flows and ignore the accounting treatment).

Costs are often more tangible than benefits so the important element will be to identify all costs, attempt to quantify them and determine when they will occur.

4 The project plan

Alongside the business case, the project team will also need a detailed plan for resources, timings, interim targets etc. This will be the project plan.

Importance of a project plan

A project plan aims to ensure that the project objectives are achieved within the constraints of quality, cost and time. Planning is essential as it helps to:

- communicate what has to be done, when and by whom

- encourage forward thinking

- provide the measures of success for the project

- make clear the commitment of time, resources (people and equipment), and money required for the project

- determine if targets are achievable

- identify the activities the resources need to undertake.

The plan is likely to be recorded as an element of a Project Initiation Document (PID). This is not a one-off, pre-project document like the business case document. It will contain the business case document and project plans, but it is also likely to be constantly revised and updated throughout the project life to reflect key changes and project completion phases.

Project Initiation Document (PID)

The PID is a formal, detailed document which contains planning information extracted from other sources such as:

- business case
- the dissemination plan
- the risk assessments
- Gantt charts, etc.

It contains all the information necessary for the execution of the project.

It is more operational than a business case document and its focus is very different. The business case is aimed at gaining project approval whereas the PID is aimed at ensuring that an approved project is successfully completed.

It will give guidance to the project team on what is expected from the project, when it is expected, and what level of performance is expected. It will have detailed plans (such as Gantt charts), control plans for when risks arise, responsibilities for tasks etc.

The PID is likely to be constantly revised and updated throughout the project life to reflect key changes and project completion phases. However, this can be a problem in a project as often the PID is updated and changed but it moves further away from the original business case and objectives. Benefits management becomes even more important when this occurs.

Typical contents might include:

- a purpose statement (project drivers)
- project and investment objectives
- a scope statement
- project deliverables (part of the product breakdown structure, explained later)
- cost and time estimates
- benefit and change owners
- chain of command
- team responsibilities
- project gateways, performance measures and results (updated regularly).

Contents of a project plan

For a large project the contents of the plan will be made up of several parts:

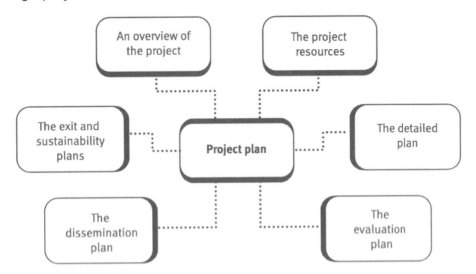

Details on the contents of a project plan

To provide an **overview of the project** the project plan will include the following:

- Background to the project – a summary of the background to the project (and how it builds on previous work) and the need for it (and why it is important).

- Aim and objectives – a list of the broad aim or purpose of the project, and the specific objectives you intend to achieve.

- Overall approach – a description of the overall approach you will take to achieve the objectives outlined above, including:

    - strategy and/or methodology and how the work will be structured

    - important issues to be addressed, e.g. interoperability

    - scope and boundaries of the work, including any issues that will not be covered

    - link to critical success factors.

- Project outputs – a list of the tangible deliverables (including reports) your project will create, and the less tangible knowledge and experience you hope to build and share.

- Project outcomes – a list of the outcomes you envisage and what change they will stimulate or enable.

- Stakeholder analysis using Mendelow's power-interest matrix – a list of the key stakeholder groups and individuals that will be interested in your project outcomes, will be affected by them, or whose support/approval is essential, both within your organisation and in the community, and assess their importance (low/medium/high).

- Risk analysis – a list of the factors that could pose a risk to the project's success and an assessment of their likelihood and severity, and how you will prevent them from happening (or manage them if they occur). Cover the types of risks listed and any others that apply.

- Standards – a list of the standards the project will use.

- Intellectual property rights – an indication of who will own the intellectual property created by the project and a list of any owned by third parties that will be incorporated into project outputs, when/how you will obtain permission to use them, and any implications for project outputs after the project ends.

The **project resources** part of the plan will contain details of the project partners and project management with a brief description of the project management framework, including:

- organisation

- reporting relationships

- decision process

- the role of any local management committee.

The **detailed part of the plan** will outline:

- the project deliverables and reports

- when they are due

- the phasing of the work and any dependencies.

It may also contain a Gantt chart, diagram, or flowchart to illustrate the phasing budget. It may alternatively include a product breakdown structure (covered later).

The **evaluation plan** will indicate how you will evaluate the quality of the project outputs and the success of the project. It will list the factors you plan to evaluate, questions the evaluation will answer, methods you will use, and how success will be measured.

The **dissemination plan** will explain how the project will share outcomes and learning with stakeholders. It will list the important dissemination activities planned throughout the project – indicating:

- purpose
- target audience
- timing
- key message.

The **exit and sustainability plans** should explain what will happen to project outputs at the end of the project (including knowledge and learning). They will focus on the work needed to ensure they are taken up by the owners and any work needed for project closedown, e.g. preservation, maintenance, documentation.

The sustainability plan will list any project outputs that may have potential to live on after the project ends, why, how they might be taken forward, and any issues involved in making them sustainable in the long term.

5 Project execution

Executing consists of the processes used to complete the work defined in the project management plan to accomplish the project's requirements. The execution process involves co-ordinating people and resources, as well as integrating and performing the activities of the project in accordance with the project management plan. The deliverables are produced as outputs from the processes performed as defined in the project management plan.

Managing and leading projects

Projects require people with different skills to work together in a coordinated way. The project team consists of individuals brought together purely for undertaking a specific project. Teams will cut across functional boundaries, giving rise to 'matrix' organisations. The size of the team and the period of their existence will be determined by the nature of the project.

Matrix structures

Projects are often inter-disciplinary and cross organisational reporting lines. The project team is likely to be made up of members drawn from a variety of different functions or divisions: each individual then has a dual role, as he or she maintains functional/divisional responsibilities as well as membership of the project team.

Test your understanding 3

Consider what advantages and disadvantages a matrix structure might bring to project teams.

Team members

A team member is selected to join the core team because of their specialist knowledge or expertise. They are usually drawn from a functional department and therefore have a further responsibility in representing that department. Some of the roles taken on by team members in organisations include:

- Specialist or technical expert – brings specialist knowledge and advice to the team.

- Representative – as part of the core team, the member represents their 'home' department and as part of the project team communicates the project team's views and decisions when back in their 'home' department.

- Monitor – will monitor their progress against the plan appropriately and regularly.

- Change manager – as changes are identified, will ensure that the full implications have been assessed before the changes are agreed and implemented.

- Problem solver – will be faced with many problems during any project and will be required to solve them by drawing on the resources of the project team and their 'home' department and through the use of problem-solving techniques.

Assembling team members

There are two methods for assembling team members:

- the first approach is to use specialist project staff who are seconded to the project and removed from their existing roles. This may be backed up by external consultants who fill in any skills gaps. This approach is likely to lead to an efficient project which is completed quickly. However, there may be a lack of buy-in from line managers and staff who may resent a lack of involvement in the key project decisions.

- the second approach is to 'add on' the project to existing duties for operational staff. In this way staff would complete the project alongside their existing duties. This may mean that the project takes longer to complete but it should benefit from decision makers being closer to the decision point and from improved staff buy-in.

Project sponsor

The project sponsor or project facilitator will normally be a senior member of the management team.

- They are often chosen as the person with the most to gain from the success of the project and the most to lose from the failure of it.

- Their job is to direct the project, and allow the project manager to manage the project.

Typical roles of a project sponsor

The roles taken on by project sponsors in organisations include:

- gatekeeper – choosing the right projects for the business means ensuring that only projects that support the business strategy are started and that they are of sufficiently high priority and have clear terms of reference

- sponsor and monitor – steering the project by requesting regular meetings with the project leader and giving advice and guidance

- supporter and coach – provides practical support for the project leader, especially if they are taking on a project that is larger or more significant than they have handled before

- decision-maker – if decisions are required that are outside the scope of the project then the project sponsor will make the decision on behalf of the organisation

- champion or advocate – involves informal communication with other senior managers to ensure that they continue to have an objective view of the importance of their project in relation to other projects within the business

- problem solver – when the team faces problems that it is unable to solve or does not have the skills or experience to solve

- resource negotiator – a project's success will depend on the availability of the right resources at the right time. In cross-functional projects the sponsor may provide assistance in negotiating resources around the company.

The project manager

The project manager is the person appointed by the organisation to lead the team, and manage it on a day-to-day basis. Primarily the project manager's responsibility is to deliver the project and to ensure that effectiveness and efficiency are achieved across the entire project.

Typical roles of a project manager

Some of the roles taken on by project managers in organisations include:

- Team leader – will spend time building the team, motivating individuals and ensuring that the project has a clear purpose and that every core team member understands that purpose.

- Planner and co-ordinator – will ensure that the team creates a realistic plan and will often consolidate the individual team members' plans into a full project plan. They will then co-ordinate the activities of the team to meet that plan and deal with changes in a systematic way.

- Task manager – involves clarifying the goals of the project and ensuring that every action is moving the project towards those goals.

- Communicator and relationship manager – will take the lead in proactively communicating the project in an appropriate way to all the stakeholders and manage the relationship with key stakeholders to ensure their needs are being met.

- Problem solver – will be faced with many problems during any project and will be required to solve them through team problem-solving techniques.

- Monitor and change manager – will put controls in place to ensure the project progresses against the plan and is monitored appropriately and regularly.

- Budget manager – will involve setting up the budget and then monitoring its use to ensure the best use of resources.

- Meeting manager – most project teams only meet as a team during project meetings so it is very important that each meeting is well managed.

While there are clearly overlaps, there are some important differences between a project manager and a 'normal' line manager:

- line managers are usually specialists whereas project managers are often generalists

- line managers operate close to the technical tasks in their departments, whereas project managers may have to oversee work in many different areas

- line managers exercise direct supervisory authority, whereas project managers facilitate rather than supervise team members.

Problems faced by project managers

Typical problems faced by a project manager will include:

- managing staff who are assigned to the project part-time and have responsibilities in their 'home' departments

- managing the relationship with the departmental managers who have staff on the project team

- managing the size of the team given variable resource requirements throughout the project life cycle

- dealing with specialists in areas where the manager is not an expert.

Managing project changes

Managers will also have a problem if the project changes during its life. Project changes may be forced onto a project in many ways:

- Changes in the environment may mean that the project needs to be adapted in order to achieve a better environmental fit

- There may be internal changes that impact on activities in the value chain, resources available, production techniques etc.

- The project sponsor may change one of the project constraints such as the scope of the project.

When changes are enforced on the project the project manager should revisit the project initiation document. This needs to be updated for the new changes. Resources may need to be re-allocated, timings may need to be adjusted, projected benefits may need to be reappraised etc.

The project manager needs to reconsider whether goals and objectives can still be achieved and whether a new pathway is required in order to do this. It may be that a new business plan needs to be agreed with the project sponsor if the project will be significantly different to the one that was originally planned.

The problem could be treated as a slippage problem and similar control actions could be taken such as fast tracking or crashing the project.

For changes to constraints the project manager could consider negotiating with the project sponsor rather than simply accepting the changes. Project sponsors will often attempt to make changes to constraints but one of the skills that a project manager needs is to be able to resist these. Even small changes over time can result in large changes overall and the project manager needs to be confident in the original business plan and objectives for the project. One compromise that a project manager may seek is to suggest that the changes are considered as a new or follow on project that can be planned and managed once the originally planned project is complete.

6   Project monitoring and control

Project control has three elements:

- setting targets

- assessing performance against these targets

- taking action if the targets are not being met (the project is out of control).

Setting targets

Performance measurements can include:

- Expenditure (cost).
- Schedule (time) performance – avoiding schedule slippage is a key objective.
- Scope measures – both product scope and project scope.
- Functional quality.
- Technical quality performance.
- Issue management performance.
- Client satisfaction measures.

> **Performance measures**
>
> **Monitoring the project**
>
> Performance measurements can include:
>
> - Expenditure (cost) – starts with the establishment of budgets and as the project progresses, decisions regarding procurement, design, development, deployment, etc., will be assessed with respect to their impact on expenditures. Actual expenditures will be compared to a baseline, and any variances will be reported to management for corrective action.
> - Schedule (time) performance – refers to the timely completion of project deliverables as compared to a baseline schedule defined in the project plan. The schedules will identify all of the project's stages, phases and activities assigned to each team member, mapping them to a timeline that measures key milestones (dates) that are used to keep track of work progress. Avoiding schedule slippage is a key objective.
> - Scope measures – are primarily concerned with product scope (the set of functions and features that characterise the product or service) and project scope (work that must be accomplished to deliver the product/service with the specified functions and features). Scope is measured based upon the degree of compliance of baseline product/service features and functions with proposed project deliverables (the means used for their delivery).
> - Functional quality – refers to the quality or correctness of the products, and/or services, features/functions delivered as a result of the project.
> - Technical quality performance – refers to the technical infrastructure that provides the foundation for product and service delivery. In the case of an IT project, such indicators as system availability, downtime, problem resolution, and response time and network utilisation would measure technical quality performance.

> - Issue management performance – refers to the identification and resolution of issues or exceptions that are impacting the successful delivery of the project. Issues can be related to communications, human resources, contracts, product/service features and functions, etc. The purpose of issue management is to ensure that all matters requiring resolution, decisions or direction are addressed as soon as possible to avoid negative consequences on project objectives and deliverables (cost, schedule, scope or products/services).
>
> - Client satisfaction measures – include client perceptions on various aspects of achieving a high degree of client satisfaction with implementation support or with operational products/services.
>
> Phase boundaries are key points at which a number of aspects of the project can be reviewed.
>
> - Is the business case for the project still valid?
>
> - Is the project meeting its objectives?
>
> - Has the risk situation altered?
>
> - Should the project progress to the next phase?

Assessing performance

A well-constructed plan with clear deliverables should make it very easy to track progress. The project manager should set up mechanisms whereby the team regularly reviews what tasks have been completed or delayed and what the impact is on the rest of the plan.

This process is aided by specific project gateways. This will be review points that are planned for critical points in the project. The reviews will also ensure that the business case which justified the project is still valid at this stage.

If problems are identified then project control measures and corrective action will be necessary.

Threat identification

The following can threaten the success of a project. Identifying these in advance can help reduce the risk of slippage and other potential problems:

- Poor management

- Poor planning

- Lack of control mechanisms

- Unrealistic deadlines

- Insufficient budget

- Moving targets.

Threat identification and slippage reduction

The following can threaten the success of a project. Suggestions are included as to how to minimise the slippage involved with those threats:

- Poor management – many project leaders will be from technical backgrounds and they may not have the proper management skills for controlling large projects. Project leaders should be properly trained so that they have managerial skills as well as technical skills.

  They should not be given large critically important projects until they have proved themselves on smaller exercises.

- Poor planning – managers have not made use of the various planning methods available: network analysis, PERT, Gantt charts. They have not broken the project down into its various activities and estimated a time and cost for each.

- Lack of control mechanisms – it is essential to be able to monitor the progress of projects, otherwise it is impossible to decide whether they will meet cost and time budgets. Reporting mechanisms and review dates should be set out in advance.

- Unrealistic deadlines – there is often pressure from users for projects to be completed quickly. Project teams, particularly if they have had to win the job competitively, may have suggested times that are unrealistic. Project managers must look critically at the deadlines. They should identify the critical activities of the project and ensure that these do not slip.

- Insufficient budget – too few people are employed on the project, inadequate hardware is bought, the cheapest (not the best) solutions are always sought. Of course, organisations cannot ignore costs and should try to get good value for money. However, it is important to be objective about what a given cost budget can produce by way of project outcomes. If money is tight, it might be better to do a smaller project thoroughly than a larger one poorly.

- Moving targets – the project specification keeps changing as the project progresses. This will certainly add costs and delay to the project. Users' requirements should be thoroughly examined and the analyst should check understanding before the project is started. Techniques such as structured walkthroughs and prototyping will help here.

KAPLAN PUBLISHING

Test your understanding 4

Printplus Inc is a printing company that has recently begun implementing a new computerised job costing system. The project manager who had started the project is now no longer with the company. You have been asked to step into the role of the project manager and complete the task of implementing the new system.

Required:

(a) Briefly describe the key factors that you will need to review in order to get to grips with the current status of the project.

(b) Identify possible threats to timely completion of the project, and state briefly how they can be minimised.

Project control

Controlling the project means:

*   taking early corrective action when needed

*   balancing project effort

*   looking for where effort can be reduced

*   making changes early rather than late.

Measurement of all relevant variables is important both for management information and also for the specification of 'what kind' and 'how much' corrective action is necessary.

Examples of corrective action include:

*   'fast tracking' – a project management technique used to ensure that projects are completed within the shortest time possible, often by doing some activities in parallel that would normally be done in sequence (such as design and construction)

*   'crashing' – project crashing is a method for shortening the project duration by reducing the time of one or more of the critical project activities to less than its normal activity time. The object of crashing is to reduce project duration while minimising the cost of crashing

*   adding additional resources (people, money, time, etc.)

*   scope reduction

*   adopting higher risk but potentially more efficient approaches

*   employee motivation.

Some corrective actions tend to be more tactical, and some more strategic.

7 Project completion

The final stages of a broadly successful project can be most rewarding. It is at this stage that people can finally see the realisation of plans and objectives.

Project success and failure

Successful project management can be defined as having achieved the project objectives and benefits:

- Within the allocated time period
- Within the budgeted cost
- At the desired performance or specification level
- While utilising the assigned resources effectively and efficiently
- With customer confirmation of expectations
- Without disturbing the main work flow of the organisation.

Reasons why projects succeed:

- Project sponsorship at executive level
- Good PID and business case
- Strong project management
- The right mix of team players
- Good decision making structure
- Good communication
- Team members are working toward common goals.

Reasons for projects' failure:

- Failure to align project with organisational objectives
- Poor scope
- Unrealistic expectations
- Lack of executive sponsorship
- Lack of true project management
- Inability to move beyond individual conflicts
- Internal politics.

The barriers to project management success are:

- Project complexity
- Customer's special requirements and scope changes
- Organisational structural and systemic resistance
- Project risks
- Changes in technology.

A Post Project Review (PPR)

This happens at the end of the project and allows the project team to move on to other projects. It can often be the last stage of the project, with the review culminating in the sign-off of the project and the formal dissolution of the project team. The focus of the post-project **review is on the conduct of the project itself**, not the product it has delivered. The aim is to identify and understand what went well and what went badly in the project and to feed lessons learned back into the project management standards with the aim of improving subsequent project management in the organisation.

It typically involves:

- disbanding the team and 'tying up loose ends'
- performance review
- determination of lessons learnt
- formal closure by the steering committee.

Contents of a post project review (PPR)

- Acceptance by client – the outputs of the project should be successfully transferred to the project's clients or users. It is important at this stage to follow the **dissemination plan**.

- Review of outputs against goals – the project team should be able to illustrate that the project has delivered its planned outputs and that outcomes can reasonably be expected to flow from them. It is important at this stage to follow the **evaluation plan**.

- Disbanding the team and 'tying up loose ends' – it is important to ensure that all project activities are satisfactorily completed and project teams should be gradually wound down. It is important at this stage to follow the **exit and sustainability plan**.

- Performance review – for large projects this may be a useful way of identifying issues and concerns that could be relevant to other projects. Key areas to review include the following:
  - Technical performance review (was scope of project achieved?).
  - Cost/budget performance.
  - Schedule performance.
  - Project planning and control.
  - Team relationships.
  - Problem identification.
  - Customer relationships.
  - Communication.
  - Risk evaluation and assessment of risk management policies.
  - Outstanding issues.

> - Lessons learnt that relate to the way the project was managed should contribute to the smooth running of future projects. A starting point for any new project should be a review of the documentation of any similar projects undertaken in the past.
>
> - Formal closure by the steering committee – the project steering committee cannot disband until the project's outcomes are seen as achieved, or the project is classed as unsuccessful.

Post Implementation Review (PIR)

A PIR is an **essential component** of the benefits management process. A post-**implementation review focuses on the product delivered** by the project. It usually takes place a specified time after the product has been delivered. This allows the actual users of the product an opportunity to use and experience the product or service and to feedback their observations into a formal review. The post-implementation review will focus on the product's fitness for purpose. The review will not only discuss strategies for fixing or addressing identified faults, but it will also make recommendations on how to avoid these faults in the future. In this instance these lessons learned are fed back into the product production process. Without a PIR, a business cannot demonstrate that its investment in the project was worthwhile.

PIRs can sometimes be an **on-going** element of project management that may be used at project gateways to examine changes implemented to date.

 Comparing the PPR and PIR

For most projects, a PIR is undertaken when there has been sufficient time to demonstrate the business benefits of the new project. For a major programme of change there may be several PIRs over time. The review will normally involve the project manager, senior management representatives and, where used, internal benefits management experts.

The PPR and PIR are related but have different objectives. The PPR is a one-off exercise at the end of a project with the key objective of learning lessons and feeding them into the organisation's project management processes and procedures for the benefit of future projects.

The objective of the PIR is to ensure that the maximum benefit is obtained for the organisation through the new project, and to make recommendations if the benefits are not obtained. Every project is different, but it is typical to perform a PIR two to twelve months after completion of the project.

The PPR focuses on the performance of the project, whilst the PIR focuses on the performance of the product of the project.

A PIR would typically involve the following analysis:

- the achievement (to date) of business case objectives (effectively a gap analysis)

- costs and benefits to date against forecast

- areas for further development

- consistency of the project with the overall business strategy

- the effectiveness of revised business operations (functions, processes, staff numbers etc.)

- stakeholder satisfaction (both internal and external).

Post-implementation review of an IT system

When appraising a new IT system after changeover, comparison should be made between predicted and actual performance (variance analysis). This might include:

- Throughput speeds

- Number of errors or queries

- Cost of processing

- Amount of downtime.

The review would also need to cover whether users' needs had been met.

The review should not be performed too soon after the new system goes live, or 'teething problems' and lack of user familiarity will distort the results.

Recommendations should be made where appropriate to improve the system's future performance.

The review should also make wider recommendations on improving systems development and project planning and management processes.

Test your understanding 5

At what stage of the project life cycle should the following events take place?

- Review progress to date against agreed performance measures and targets

- Compare project costs and benefits to create a financial rationale for the project

- Determine what project staff will be needed, when they will be needed and what roles each staff member will play

- Evaluate why expected project benefits have not accrued

- Make enabling changes to facilitate the achievement of proposed business changes.

8 Chapter summary

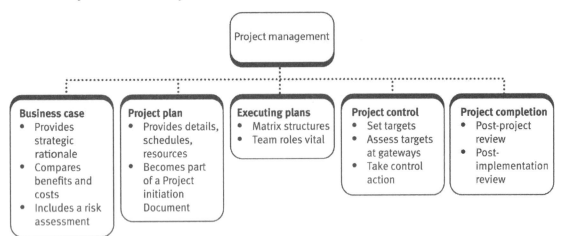

Project management

Business case
- Provides strategic rationale
- Compares benefits and costs
- Includes a risk assessment

Project plan
- Provides details, schedules, resources
- Becomes part of a Project initiation Document

Executing plans
- Matrix structures
- Team roles vital

Project control
- Set targets
- Assess targets at gateways
- Take control action

Project completion
- Post-project review
- Post-implementation review

Test your understanding answers

Test your understanding 1

Law suit

The risk here appears to be of low likelihood – the business has not suffered such an event in the past. However, the potential impact is high – the law suit could completely wipe out the $6m NPV (especially if the event has led to a death). The risk of a lawsuit should be dealt with by taking out indemnity insurance. The risk is then transferred to the insurance company.

1   **Pool closure**

2   The risk of a pool closure appears to be high as this has occurred on several other instances in the past. A new pool which suddenly has to close could have a potentially high impact on the business – newly acquired customers may never return to the pool. This risk is serious and since a provision of a pool is clearly essential for the sports centre, the risk must be avoided instead. It may mean that the pool is not built until the cause in other centres has been investigated and cured or perhaps new contractors or builders need to be used.

Income fraud

This risk may be highly likely given that there is likely to be a high degree of cash handling in the business. However, the sums involved are likely to be small and therefore the potential impact is low.

1   The risk of fraud requires risk reduction techniques – this is exactly the type of risk that a good internal control system would be designed to prevent.

2   **Bad weather**

3   This risk is unlikely to have a high impact or high likelihood. Schools are likely to have programmed lessons well in advance and students would be expected to continue participation even when the weather is poor.

Bad weather will always be a risk when dealing with outdoor activities and is probably best accepted and the lost revenues factored into the initial forecasts.

Professional skill:
The key evaluation skills will be in ensuring that your assessment is justified. No marks would be awarded for simply stating whether a risk is of high or low likelihood. Instead your opinion needs to be backed by relevant opinions of the organisation and its environment.

Test your understanding 2

In creating a business case document it is important that all potential benefits are identified and scaled. However, there is a temptation to overstate the scale of benefits in order to improve the likelihood of project appraisal. This is typically done when making a financial appraisal of the project.

In this project it would appear that many of the benefits of the project have been overstated:

- The extra returns from an increase in market share are unlikely to be quantifiable and very unlikely to be placed at the financial side of the scale. These are likely to be a **measurable** benefit only and should not be included in the financial appraisal.

- The savings from staff motivation will be very difficult to measure or quantify. These may be an **observable** benefit and should not be included as a financial one.

- The reduction in customer response times might be either measurable or even **quantifiable**. However, it would be very difficult to give this a financial value, and again this should be removed from the financial appraisal.

So in the financial appraisal the project manager would only be left with the saving from the redundancy (a clearly financial benefit) and the project costs. This would represent a net financial cost of $60,000.

This does not mean that the project would be rejected. It simply represents the net financial cost of the project that should be measured up against other factors such as the non-financial benefits, the project risks, the project drivers etc.

Professional skill:

Scepticism needs to be shown in challenging the opinion of the manager that all of the benefits are financial benefits. You cannot sit on the fence here, you need to be very definite and explain why your opinion might differ from hers.

Test your understanding 3

Advantages

- The key advantage of a matrix structure is effective coordination of multi-disciplinary teams through the project teams. This should ensure that decisions will require less amendment when implemented as all perspectives have been incorporated from the beginning.

- Matrix structures allow project teams to be created and changed relatively easily and quickly, giving extra flexibility to respond to market developments.

- Employees will also benefit from the matrix approach as they will learn new skills and have to adapt to solving a range of problems outside their functional specialisms.

Disadvantages

- The main problem with matrix structures involves clarifying responsibilities and demands made on employees. Employees may feel stressed and confused when conflicting demands are made by functional and project managers.

- This is usually resolved by having frequent meetings between functional and project heads, taking up time that could be used more effectively elsewhere. In some organisations functional heads have felt that their authority is diluted and project heads given priority.

- Linked to the above, staff appraisal becomes more difficult with a matrix structure.

Test your understanding 4

(a) The following key factors should be considered in reviewing the current status of the project.

- **Time.** The progress reports on the project should be reviewed, to determine whether or not the project is currently on target for completion within the expected time. An assessment should be made as to whether the remaining tasks can be completed by the original deadline.

- **Resources.** It will be important to identify the resources that have been allocated to the project. Resources include both human resources and computer equipment/time. Having established what resources have been made available, an assessment will have to be made of how sufficient or effective these are for achieving the project goals.

- **Cost.** The original budget for the project should be reviewed in the context of the actual costs incurred to date. A sensible estimate of the further costs that will be incurred in completing the project should then be made.

- **Quality.** The project plan should be reviewed to find out whether or not any quality standards were agreed for the intermediary stages of the project. If they were, it will be important to establish whether or not these standards are being met.

(b) The following may be identified as key threats to completion of the project on time.

Possible threat	Minimise by
Poor management of time	• Discuss stage and completion deadline with the project team.
	• Stress the importance of completion targets.
	• Regular progress reports and progress meetings.
Poor planning	• Using planning tools such as Gantt charts or CPA.
Lack of control mechanisms	• Set milestones. • Ensure progress reporting throughout the project.
Unrealistic deadlines	• Identify critical activities and the critical path. • Negotiate deadlines with stakeholders.
Insufficient budget	• Focus cost compromises on least critical areas. • Negotiate injection of resources to complete on time.

Test your understanding 5

Reviewing progress to date against agreed performance measures and targets is part of project control. The aim is to determine (at a pre-determined project gateway) whether or not the project is out of control and corrective action is needed.

Comparing project costs and benefits to create a financial rationale for the project should be part of the business case document and is an element of project initiation. The financial rationale should help the project manager to gain approval for the project.

Determining what project staff will be needed, when they will be needed and what roles each staff member will play should be part of the project plan (and project initiation document). It should not be part of the business case document and should not be done until the project has been approved.

Evaluating why expected project benefits have not accrued would be part of a post-implementation review. A review would take place into why the project isn't providing the benefits that were planned for as part of the original business case.

Making enabling changes to facilitate the achievement of proposed business changes would be part of the project execution. Change owners would perform the tasks and the project manager would be responsible for overseeing these, motivating the owners, liaising with benefit owners etc.

Note:

The aim of this question is to ensure that you understand the different components of the project life cycle. You would not get this type of question in an examination, but you could get a question on any of the individual stages and it is important that you understand the types of activities that could be taking place at each stage.

Financial decision making

Chapter learning objectives

Upon completion of this chapter you will be able to:

- discuss how advances in information technology are transforming the finance sector and the role and structure of the finance function within organisations

- evaluate alternative structures for the finance function using business partnering, outsourcing and shared or global business services

- determine the overall investment requirements of a business

- assess and advise on the alternative sources of short and long-term finance available to the organisation to support strategy and operations

- discuss from a strategic perspective, the continuing need for effective cost management and control systems within organisations

- review and justify decisions to select or abandon competing investments or projects applying suitable investment appraisal techniques

- evaluate methods of forecasting, budgeting, standard costing and variance analysis in support of strategic planning and decision making

PER

Two of the PER performance objectives (PO9 and 11) are that you advise on alternative sources of finance and evaluate and review the financial viability of investment decisions. You identify, measure, and advise on the financial risks to the organisation. Working through this chapter should help you understand how to demonstrate these objectives.

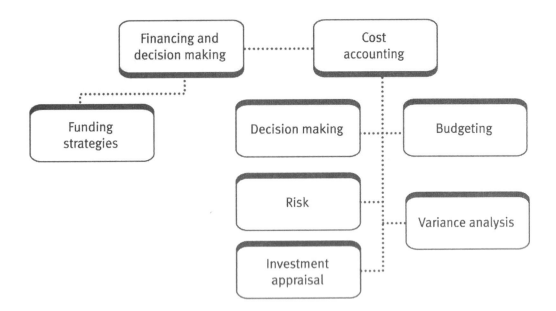

1 The relationship between strategy and finance

As with areas such as process redesign and information technology, finance can play a vital role in developing strategies and in putting them into action.

Strategic choice and financial analysis		

For example, the role of finance plays a key role in making strategic choices. In applying Johnson, Scholes and Whittington's strategy evaluation tests a decision maker might have the following financial concerns and therefore carry out accompanying financial analysis:

Aspect	Key concerns	Financial analysis
Acceptability	Achieving acceptable returns to shareholders	• Cash flow forecasts to ensure dividend growth requirements can be met
		• NPV
		• ROCE
		• Valuation of real options
		• Cost-benefit analysis
		• Ratio analysis (e.g. dividend yield, growth)
	Risk	• Sensitivity
		• Break-even
		• Ratio analysis (e.g. gearing, dividend cover)

Feasibility	Resources	• Cash flow forecast to identify funding needs • Ability to raise finance needed • Working capital implications • Foreign exchange implications
Suitability	Getting the best returns from alternatives	• Return on Investment • Comparison of alternatives • Profit margins

Financial objectives of stakeholders

Financial strategy often focuses on shareholder wealth. But there are financial expectations from other stakeholders which must also be considered.

Financial expectations of stakeholders

It is generally accepted that the strategic objective of a profit-seeking organisation is the long-term goal of maximising the wealth of the owners (usually shareholders) of the organisation.

- Shareholder view – the only responsibility for business is to make money for shareholders – the market is the best way to allocate scarce resources.

- Stakeholder view – the achievement of shareholder value is only possible if other stakeholders are (at least) kept satisfied.

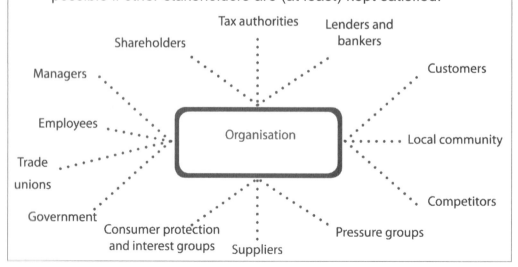

Typically:

- lenders expect profits, positive cash flow, growth and debt reduction

- employees expect increased wages and benefits as well as stable employment and growth

- creditors and suppliers expect payment within invoice terms and growth

- customers expect timely and complete delivery of services and products with increasing value and quality at appropriate pricing

- shareholders expect the continuance of the business enterprise and a fair financial return as payment of risk bearing and the use of their capital.

It is no longer enough to be profitable and have positive cash flow to be judged successful. All of the company's stakeholders require the company to perform within a narrow band of predetermined expectations. Failure to fall within the band of expected performance can, and will, result in:

- reduced access to funding (both debt and equity)

- loss of employee morale and de-motivation of staff

- loss of customers and suppliers

- shareholder revolt.

The role of the finance function

The role of the finance function has developed into a much broader scope than simply the provision and checking of financial information. A finance function will typically perform the following functions within an organisation:

- accounting – recording and assimilating financial transactions

- funding – ensuring that there is adequate funding available and that this is obtained at the lowest possible cost

- compliance – ensuring that transactions comply with necessary legislation and regulatory guidance

- management and control – supporting organisational decision making and monitoring and supporting the achievement of organisational objectives

- strategy and risk – monitoring and managing financial risk and supporting strategic choices from a financial perspective

The finance function and the role of the accountant

Over the past decade the role of the finance function, and hence the role of the accountant, has changed. Traditionally, the accountant and finance function focused on three key roles: collecting money from customers, paying suppliers, and reporting financial performance to the business. However, some of those tasks have now become automated whilst business expectations of the accountant have been increased significantly.

The accountant can now be expected to be involved in areas such as:

- Gaining competitive advantage in capital markets.

- Forward-looking decision support, sensitivity and scenario planning.

- Providing quantitative and qualitative analysis.

- Finding areas for cost efficiency.

- Improving the quality of information and decision making.

In this way the value of the finance function has been transformed and it is now becoming a strategic partner to the business. New skills and practices are needed from the function. It needs to be more forward looking. It needs to be proactive rather than reactive. It needs to become a centre of excellence as a shared service for the business. The finance function needs to be focused on creating value for the business – just like any other business unit.

An organisation in which the finance function provides timely, useful information to management is likely to achieve better business performance than in others where this is not the case. Likewise, if the finance function can identify opportunities for cost savings, this can support, develop or improve an organisation's competitive position.

Organisations are recognising this value and the role of the accountant has transformed as the role of the finance function has transformed. In the past there were often organisational boundaries (and sometimes physical ones too) between the accountant and the rest of the organisation. The finance function was kept apart and rarely worked with other functions or with clients.

Today, in modern organisations, this has changed. Accountants are no longer just the counters of information but they are also the providers and analysts of information. The accountant will now typically be involved in all aspects of the strategic planning process, such as:

- Analysing the competitive position, the organisational environment, the benefits and problems from different strategic options etc. In this way, the accountant will play a key role in the strategy formulation of the organisation. For example, if an organisation is considering an overseas expansion the accountant will be expected to provide information on current and potential market sizes, the size and spending power of rivals, the expected returns from the project, the cost of the strategy, the cost of finance, and many other aspects that will help determine whether or not the strategy is pursued.

- The accountant will then be involved in the implementation of the strategy. IT systems may need to be evaluated, process redesigns will have to be costed and potential marketing channels evaluated. The accountant is likely to work in many cross-functional, matrix teams in order to aid in the implementation of strategy. So the physical and organisational barriers between the accountant and the rest of the business will disappear.

- The accountant can also add value to their organisation by measuring the performance of activities, managers and other employees within the organisation. This can help assess strategies as they progress. This can be a vital control mechanism (as seen when project management was considered) and allows the organisation to do things like take corrective action, move to contingency plans or abandon projects and strategies.

Structure of the finance function

The roles of the finance department are not always performed in-house or by every finance department that might exist within a business. Just as examined for any other process, activity or function within an organisation, finance departments may consider the use of different structures brought about from elements such as:

- outsourcing,

- shared services, or

- business partnerships.

More details

The least valued activities within the finance function might be outsourced. Determining which functions are least valued could be done through techniques such as Harmon's process-strategy matrix (studied elsewhere in this study text). It may be that some of the accounting tasks are seen to be highly complex but not of great strategic value. For example, tasks such as payroll provision are often outsourced to business partners. This has become so common that the payroll process is becoming very commoditised and there needs to be a very strong argument for not outsourcing the activity.

An organisation with many finance departments spread across, say, its divisions, may not have all functions performed in each division. Shared services are often implemented in the management and control activity in areas such as treasury management. This will allow the organisation to, for example, net off cash surpluses in one part of the company with deficits in another in order to avoid the use of overdrafts and their associated costs. For global businesses shared services can be used to manage foreign exchange transactions in order to reduce the amount of inter-group foreign exchange transactions and to net transactions off against each other.

Business partnering is particularly common in smaller organisations. A group of smaller organisations might, for example, create a partnership for funding. Small organisations often lack the size necessary to access the most flexible and low cost sources of finance. By partnering they may be able to achieve this size. This would allow the partnership to access cheaper finance and allow each partner organisation to share in this benefit and reduce its finance costs.

The influence of information technology

Information technology is facilitating the redesign of the finance function in that it can:

- communicate information more quickly

- more easily connect different parts of the business

- reduce the cost of communicating information with business partners

- more readily identify areas for improvement

- be used to extrapolate and forecast more easily

- gather external information and alternatives more quickly and easily

- provide more information on available B2B options for elements such as outsourcing.

2 The finance function and process automation

2.1 Impacts on the finance function of increased automation

Technology and software developments are driving an increase in process automation across the finance function. Routine and transactional areas such as balancing ledger accounts and extracting trial balances and accounting summaries have been automated since computerised accounting packages came on to the market many years ago.

As technology continues to develop, more areas of finance are becoming automated or are likely to become automated.

> **Illustration 1 – New technology impacting expenses.**
>
> The process of dealing with staff expenses has long been inefficient and unnecessarily complicated. New technology businesses like **Certify** or **Rydoo** allow staff to photograph receipts instantly on their mobile device, this uploads the receipt which is synchronised with their software account. The details are extracted, categorised and where required can be submitted for approval immediately. Exceptions can be flagged and reports can be generated showing line by line detail along with supporting receipts and mileage maps. Approved expenses can then be automatically reimbursed to the employee. The information from all employees is available in instant reports, allowing improved analysis and control.
>
> The process still involves human input but the software enabled automation of the compilation and submission of expenses, as well as the removal of manual receipts and the need for physical verification saves staff time and improves the efficiency of the process whilst also significantly improving the management information available.

2.2 Skills required by the future finance professional

Accountants and **finance professionals** in the future will see basic routine, transactional work reduced with a shift to higher-level skills. The following skills are anticipated to be fundamental to future accountants:

- **Analytical skills** – much of the data produced will come from automated processes and data specialists. Accountants will add value through analysing this data in the business context for meaning and insight

- **Business acumen** – having a wide understanding of all aspects of a business and the environment they are in is crucial to effective decision-making and the ability to provide insight to other functions

- **Judgement** – making decisions, evaluating data sources and applying knowledge to make sound judgements will be a key higher-level skill

- **People skills** – interpersonal skills including the ability to communicate, empathise and understand people will be increasingly important as accountants occupy more central business partnering roles, rather than just producing accounts and reports for others

- **Leadership** – accountants have a unique central position in organisations. This is necessary to be able to understand and question the numbers and information they are given. This provides them with a wider understanding of the entire business and sees accountants increasingly occupying senior executive positions in companies.

Illustration 2 – Automation. Where machines will replace humans.

A 2017 **McKinsey** report, investigated occupational activities where machines would be most likely to replace humans.

The report summarised that roles involving routine repetitive programmable tasks such as **data collection, data processing and repetitive physical activities are most at risk.**

The following is a summary of the extent to which various role types were believed to be automatable:

Data collection – 64%

Data processing – 69%

Applying expertise – 18%

Stakeholder interactions – 20%

Managing others – 9%

As these numbers illustrate some relatively basic areas associated with today's finance professional are likely to disappear, at least partially. Other areas with higher level skills are likely to become much more significant.

2.3 The automation paradox

Increased **automation** of routine tasks takes them out of human control. This can result in the loss of these skills on a practical level, as the automated process takes over and is relied upon.

However atypical events can undermine an automated process as they are built by humans using code and algorithms that cannot accommodate all possible permutations. In this situation, where manual control is required, the deskilling of humans can see organisations unable to cope and therefore slow to respond.

Retaining expertise and ensuring knowledge and understanding of the basic functions of accounting systems and how they operate will be a challenge for the modern finance professional.

For example, the basic process of manually maintaining ledger accounts and balancing them off is fundamental to every bookkeeping course yet it is a task seldom undertaken by accountants today. Modern accounting systems perform multiple checks and balances automatically. Yet this underpinning knowledge is essential to ensure a full understanding of how the system functions and means an accountant can step in should the system fail.

3 Not-for-profit organisations

Organisations such as charities and trade unions are not run to make profits, but to benefit prescribed groups of people.

Financial objectives of 'not-for-profit' organisations

Since the services provided are limited primarily by the funds available, their financial aim is:

- to raise the maximum possible sum each year (net of fund-raising expenses)
- to spend this sum as effectively as possible on the target group (with the minimum of administration costs

Short term targets for NFPs

Not-for-profit organisations will normally set targets for particular aspects of each accounting period's finances, such as the following.

- Total to be raised in grants and voluntary income.
- Maximum percentage that fund-raising expenses represents of this total.
- Amounts to be spent on specified projects.
- Maximum permitted administration costs.

The actual figures achieved can then be compared with these targets and control action taken if necessary.

Funding strategies for NFPs

Most non-profit organisations need their core costs to be covered.

Core costs are the expenditure budgets that are not connected with the levels of activity undertaken by an organisation.

They are:

- the costs that will always need to be funded, regardless of the number of projects and
- are usually fundamental to the organisation's survival, even if they cannot be directly associated with any specific outcome.

Further examples of core costs

Core costs can be placed under three headings:

Management	<ul><li>Costs associated with governance board meetings, etc.</li><li>User engagement and consultation</li><li>Monitoring and evaluation</li><li>CEO and associated staff</li></ul>
Research and development	<ul><li>Innovation – costs associated with developing new activities and ways of operating (before they attract funding)</li><li>Quality assurance</li><li>Staff training and development</li></ul>
Support services	<ul><li>IT, telephone, postage and fax</li><li>Finance and audit</li><li>Income generation (including fundraising)</li><li>Marketing for the organisation</li><li>Premises</li><li>Travel and subsistence</li><li>Personnel</li></ul>

An organisation can only look ahead with confidence when the fundamental core costs are securely funded.

Creating a core funding strategy has different forms at each stage of a non-profit-seeking organisation's evolution.

- Infancy – tends to be heavily dependent on one funding source, which can limit independence.

- Growth phase – if funded by a multitude of projects and many donors it is prone to the pitfalls of mission creep (the expansion of a project or mission beyond its original goals, often after initial successes) and inefficiency.

- Maturity and maintenance – funding should be derived from a constantly changing mix of sources.

Core funding for NFPs

For a non-governmental organisation (NGO), protecting the core funding is the responsibility of the trustees. This requires more than ensuring that the annual accounts do not show an unrestricted deficit, all NGOs need to have a long-term plan as to how the core funds will be met for years ahead. A core funding strategy is a forward thinking, evolving document. It is more than a policy.

An NGO's CEO, Fundraising Director/Manager and the Finance Director/Manager will need to develop the actual strategy and manage its implementation. Each project manager will need to understand how their project budget contributes to the overall strategy.

There are five main elements to core funding.

- Strategic funding – is funding from regular, reliable donors who make an open-ended commitment to an organisation, e.g. institutional donors, wealthy individuals and faith-based communities.

- Apportioning overheads into project budgets – sometimes referred to as the business model, as it is a common formula for determining product pricing. Each project budget is expected to make a contribution towards overheads.

- Self-generated income – is where part of the core costs is funded by activities within its own control – where the donors don't specify how the funds are to be applied, e.g. an endowment, trading, fundraising events, legacy income and membership income.

- Developmental funding – donors agree to invest in the transformation of an organisation's infrastructure for a defined period. They can be described as 'second stage pump primers'.

- Cost minimisation – is astute financial management aimed at reducing core costs to an acceptable minimum. Securing gifts in kind and volunteers are excellent ways of minimising costs, as long as these gifts and the volunteers are effective in ensuring that core activities are delivered.

Test your understanding 1

A museum has previously been government funded and operated as a not-for-profit organisation. However, due to government rationalisation the museum has been forced to become a commercial company. It has achieved initial funding by listing on the country's stock exchange and issuing shares in the newly formed company.

What are the differences in strategic and operational decisions that a financial manager in the museum is likely to experience in the new business?

4 Funding strategies

As well as considering managing for value and the needs of wider stakeholders, financial decision makers must identify:

- which SBUs need funding,
- how funding can support strategic decisions, and
- what type of funding they need.

This will allow them to create unique funding strategies for each business unit.

Funding SBUs and strategic choices

A financial manager should recognise that funding requirements change subject to areas such as where an SBU is in its life cycle, where it lies in the organisation's portfolio (for example, within the BCG matrix) and the strategy that it is pursuing.

Funding strategies in the BCG matrix

Star	**Problem child**
• High growth	• High growth
• High business risk	• Very high business risk
• Use some retained earnings and new equity from investors seeking growth	• Use equity from venture capital
• High reinvestment rate so medium dividends	• Low or zero dividends in the short term
Cash cow	**Dog**
• Low growth	• Low growth
• Medium business risk	• Low business risk
• Use retained earnings (and debt if necessary)	• Use debt until divest
• Large net cash inflows to support dividends	• Zero reinvestment rate so high dividends

Illustration 3 – Matching funding strategies to SBUs

For example, an SBU following a differentiation strategy when it currently sits in a problem child position is likely to need a high level of investment. It will need funding to improve processes, obtain better resources, innovate, market its competitive differences, and to cover short-term losses in performance.

A financial manager must also consider how best to provide this funding.

Both the need for funding and the funding strategy itself would be very different if this was a mature SBU in a cash cow position.

Alternative sources of finance

Financing was covered in detail in FM. A brief summary of alternatives and considerations are given here.

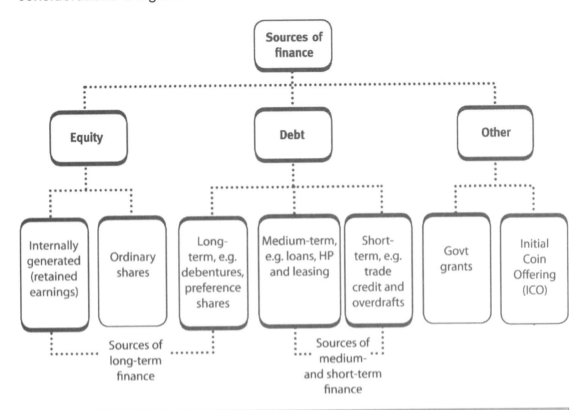

Key sources of internal finance

Internally generated finance is normally more flexible than external finance. However, it is important to remember that it still has a cost. It is an equity source of finance (and therefore will have a 'cost of equity' attached to it) and using internally generated funds instead of, say, paying a dividend to shareholders will mean that the shareholders will require a return on the investment that the organisation is effectively making on their behalf.

The key sources of internally generated finance are as follows:

(1)   Using retained profits

This is achieved by using cash generated within the business (i.e. retaining cash made from trading rather than paying it out as a dividend). This is a cheaper method of raising equity finance than issuing new shares to shareholders as issue costs are avoided, cash is raised more quickly, and it holds the advantage of retaining the existing proportional control of shareholders. It is therefore the most common source of long-term finance for an organisation.

But as a source of equity you should be aware that the cost of this finance is likely to be higher than the cost of debt that may be available to an organisation. Also, in previous studies you may have encountered what is known as the 'clientele effect'. This suggests that shareholders are attracted to particular companies by their history of either paying high dividends or, alternatively, from re-investing high levels of profits and reducing dividends. It will therefore be important that directors are aware of this when making a decision to retain a higher proportion of earnings than in the past as this may upset some shareholders who were expecting a dividend which subsequently does not arise. This may encourage such shareholders to sell their shares and adversely impact on the company's share price.

(2) Better working capital management

As explored later in this chapter, working capital policies can have a significant impact on an organisation's cash flow. Some policies will increase cash flow to the organisation and, therefore, these policies can be used to generate cash for the organisation. These often offer short-term solutions to cash flow problems and are unlikely to be sufficient to fund long-term investments.

Policies can be used to recover debts from receivables more quickly, reduce the investment in inventory or to increase the payment period to payables. For example, if a company with a turnover of $6m p.a. were to decrease its credit policy to customers so that they had to pay after one month instead of after two months, this is likely to increase cash inflow in the year by $500k (i.e. 1/12 × $6m).

These policies, however, may have a detrimental impact on organisational profits. For example, asking customers to pay more quickly may deter them from buying the product so that revenue is impacted as customers turn to rivals with better settlement periods. Or reducing inventory levels may mean that fewer items are available for sale so that, again, revenue is adversely impacted. There may also be business issues. For example, paying suppliers later may mean that they refuse to supply in the future or support other developments such as e-procurement.

(3) Sale of surplus assets

This is another easy source of finance for an organisation and can apply to both non-current assets and to inventories. However, it will be important to consider two elements:

- the asset must truly be surplus to requirements (sale of an asset that is not surplus to requirements may impact on the organisation's ability to operate and function efficiently and effectively),

– the long-term impact must be considered (assets that are not needed now may well be needed in the medium to long term, or they may only be suffering from a seasonal effect. For example, Kaplan requires less building space in January when students are awaiting results, but this is due to seasonality and does not suggest that the buildings should be sold off. It is expensive and disruptive to sell assets now that may be needed again in the short to medium term).

 Initial Coin Offering ICOs

An (ICO) is a means of crowdfunding centred on cryptocurrency, which can be a source of capital for start-up companies. In an ICO, some quantity of the crowd funded cryptocurrency is pre-allocated to investors in the form of "tokens," in exchange for other cryptocurrencies such as Bitcoin or Ethereum, or increasingly for fiat currencies (currency that a government has declared to be legal tender, but it is not backed by a physical commodity). These tokens become functional units of currency if or when the ICO's funding goal is met and the project launches.

The first ICO took place in 2013, with a total of two in that year. By 2014, this had risen to eight ICOs with a combined total value of $30 million. The total value of Initial Coin Offerings breached the barrier of $4 billion globally in 2017, with further growth projected for the coming period. In 2018, ICOs have gained further momentum and are emerging as a workable, alternative form of crowdfunding. Strategically, ICOs continue to crowd out traditional venture capitalist (VC) funding, especially in technology and block chain related start-ups. The continued rise of the ICO in 2018 has even seen the funding technique yield its first "unicorns" (start-ups worth over $1 billion). Telegram and EOS boast an estimated record breaking $1.7 billion and $4.1 billion, respectively.

The mechanism for an ICO is remarkably simple, and so provides a low barrier to entry. ICOs raise money by issuing a 'white paper' that provides details of the concept that the venture intends to build, and details of the tokens that will be issued in exchange for cryptocurrency. The white paper is available via the venture's website, which also provides the mechanism for payment of crypto currency to the venture's account (typically bitcoin or ether). It is now more common for payments to be made into an escrow account, to provide greater assurance of the venture's validity.

Most ICO sites include instructions for how investors should go about buying their bitcoins or ether – the assumption being that they don't already own any cryptocurrency. This is where the regulatory issues arise; because the ICO issues a currency, or token, rather than shares, they have not been considered (by proposers) to be a securities offering, so the associated regulation and controls have not been applied.

Like an Initial Public Offering (IPO), an ICO can be used to raise funds, but unlike an IPO, it is less familiar to regulators. However, the association of ICOs with crypto currencies, in particular Bitcoin and its very rapid growth in value in the last quarter of 2017, has attracted increased scrutiny from regulators around the world. ICOs are increasingly seen as an alternative to classic debt/capital-funding as performed today by Venture Capital/Private Equity firms and banks.

Advantages of ICOs to investors

The fact that ICOs are open to the general public means anyone in the cryptocurrency industry can be involved if they can get funds transferred on time. This means the projects can raise funds in a completely decentralised manner, which is quite important. More investors from all over the world means there is less centralisation, which is what cryptocurrency is all about.

The concept of cryptocurrency ICO means people can help shape the future of the entire business ecosystem. There is a wide range of different projects raising funds through an ICO, and every single project aims to bring something new to the table. Virtually all of these projects raise a lot of money in the process of their ICO taking place. Multi-million dollar projects are very common in the world of cryptocurrency ICOs.

Perhaps the biggest advantage from an investor's perspective is how the tokens can be bought at a low price. Most exchanges will eventually enable trading of these tokens, where they can be sold for a profit if the project is successful. Ethereum-based tokens have a habit of appreciating in value by quite a magnitude. Value gains of over 1,000% over the course of a year or less are quite common, regardless of the projects being finished by that time. From a speculative point of view, cryptocurrency ICOs is more than worth getting involved in. This could ultimately become the downfall of these projects as well, though, but only time will tell if that is the case.

Disadvantages of ICOs to investors

The majority of investors are enthusiasts, rather than people with expertise and an ICO is not regulated or registered. This means users will not be reimbursed if something were to go wrong. This is something a lot of people tend to overlook, even though it has become less of an issue ever since smart contracts were used to lock up ICO funds.

Additionally, not everyone will be able to partake in every ICO. This is especially true on the Ethereum network, as a lot of ICOs sell out in less than 30 minutes. Partaking in such an event means users need to send a transaction at a much higher fee to ensure their transfer is picked up in a network block. This higher cost just to participate in an ICO is not a positive development by any means.

Understanding the risks and issues, perceived and evidenced, around ICOs provides context for the increased regulatory involvement. Investors face risks from fraud – the most consistently identified ICO risk. Publicity about the rapidly increasing values of cryptocurrencies has contributed to the surge in activity, so it's not surprising that ICOs are a potentially easy way for fraudsters to make money.

Money laundering and terrorist financing are also key risks for economies and regulators, who will also have concerns around unregulated ICOs which have potentially serious additional effects to market stability.

There has been an increase in activity from regulators in response to the surge in ICO activity. Regulators have issued consistent warnings of the inherent risks in ICOs and reminders of the need to understand the underlying nature of individual investments. Regulators have taken the view that this needs to be assessed on a case-by-case basis. Where an ICO is classed as a 'security', it would need to satisfy registration and other regulatory requirements, as for any securities offer.

Risks to organisations raising finance

Concerns over ICOs, the potential for increased scrutiny and additional regulation mean that it may be harder, and more expensive, for future start-ups to position an ICO and bring real innovation to market. ICOs are often seen as a route to projects that would not receive funding through traditional financing, but are possibly introducing viable, innovative ideas.

For many, the ICO concept extends the options available for raising finance and accessing a group of participants that appreciate the ideas emerging around blockchain technology. Certainly, many ICOs have enabled start-ups to raise much larger amounts than would have been possible through traditional financing and therefore their viability has been more quickly tested.

The direction so far from regulators is that some ICOs constitute securities offers, and therefore have an associated requirement to fulfil the related regulatory criteria. The possibility that an ICO may be a security will mean additional cost for the promoter and/or a risk that they may wrongly consider that their ICO is not a security and face severe penalties if the regulators judge that it is.

 Refer to the SBL article in ACCA study support resources **"Cryptocurrencies"**

Factors to consider when choosing a financing package

- Cost

- Control

- Availability

- Gearing

- Security

- Cash flow

- Exit routes

Factors to consider when choosing a financing package

(1) **Cost**

- A bank loan is cheaper than an overdraft. Why? Because it is less risky from the bank's perspective. They have a repayment schedule, the loan may be secured, etc.

- Risk to the investor is the main determinant of the cost of the finance.

- Thus debt is usually cheaper than equity finance.

- Short-term loans are cheaper than long-term loans

- The issue costs of debt are also lower than for equity.

(2) **Control**

- Debt does not usually convey voting rights. Neither do preference shares.

- A public issue of shares may change the balance of control.

- A rights issue will not change control, provided existing shareholders take up their rights. In many jurisdictions, companies must offer new shares to existing shareholders first as they have "pre-emption rights".

(3) **Availability**

- Further debt may be restricted by agreements (covenants) in existing loans.

- Could shareholders afford a rights issue of the size suggested?

- Difficult to issue equity if unquoted.

(4) Gearing

- Debt is cheaper than equity but it has a hidden cost – as the level of debt increases the risk faced by the shareholders also increases. Thus their required return and hence the cost to the company will increase. Debt makes the equity more expensive.

- We therefore have two effects of increased gearing – on the positive side the debt is cheap finance, on the negative side the extra risk is bad for the shareholders.

- To see the net effect of gearing we need to look at theories of gearing – general consensus is that there is an optimal level of gearing that is best not exceeded.

(5) Security

- Security is usually needed for debt.

- In a question you could look at the existing statement of financial position for possible assets for security but watch for existing loans as assets may already be taken.

- Ideally assets will be land and buildings – quality assets, thus presenting a problem for service industries.

(6) Cash flow

- A general rule of thumb is to try to match the lifetimes of finance flows and project flows.

- If project cash flows are uncertain, then equity may be better as dividends may be cut if necessary.

- Fixed interest rates make budgeting easier than floating rates.

- Try to avoid loans maturing at the same time.

- In practice a cash flow forecast is essential.

(7) Exit routes

- Could the company repay the finance early? E.g. leases may include penalty clauses.

- Can investors get their money back early if they want to? Difficult if unquoted.

- Venture capitalists want their money back in five to seven years.

Test your understanding 2

Olsen is considering a takeover of a smaller company in the same industry called Albiston. Albiston is currently generating losses but Olsen believes that, although it may take up to two years to turn the business around, significant returns can be made from the acquisition in the long term. The directors have estimated that $10m would be a suitable purchase price, so they are now considering the various financing options available.

Olsen has a very low level of gearing, so the directors are keen to use debt finance to avoid the high issue costs on equity and to attract tax relief on the debt interest. The following two options have been identified:

Option 1 – Loan notes

Olsen has been advised by its investment bankers that it could issue to the public $10 million of 2% coupon loan notes with interest paid annually in arrears. These coupon loan notes have an effective fixed annual charge of 7% p.a. The notes would last for four years and would be redeemed at a 30% premium.

The loan notes would require a fixed and floating charge over the assets of Olsen and Albiston. There would also be some covenants in the loan note agreements.

Option 2 – Bank loan

Alternatively, Olsen's bank has offered a $10 million variable interest rate loan at a variable rate of 8% p.a. Interest would be payable half yearly in arrears and the rate then reset for the next six months. The loan would be repayable in full at par at the end of six years. The loan would also require a fixed and floating charge over the assets of Albiston. There would be extensive covenants in the loan agreement.

Required:

Evaluate the factors that the board of Olsen should consider before deciding upon which source of finance to select.

Professional skill:
Illustrate commercial acumen in exercising judgement on the most appropriate source of finance.

5 The role of cost and management accounting

Cost accounting is an approach to evaluating the overall costs that are associated with conducting business. Generally based on standard accounting practices, cost accounting is one of the tools that managers utilise to determine what type and how much expenses are involved in maintaining the current business model. At the same time, the principles of cost accounting can also be utilised to project changes to these costs in the event that specific changes are implemented.

The role of cost accounting

Cost accounting has many roles in a business, including:

- Inventory valuation – the cost per unit can be used to value inventory in the statement of financial position (balance sheet).

- To record costs – the costs associated with the product need to be recorded in the statement of profit or loss.

- To price products – the business may use the cost per unit to assist in pricing the product. For example, if the cost per unit is $0.30, the business may decide to price the product at $0.50 per unit in order to make the required profit of $0.20 per unit.

- Decision making – the business may use the cost information to make important decisions regarding which products should be made and in what quantities.

From a strategic perspective, we have seen how understanding, minimising and controlling costs can link to a firm's competitive advantage such as a low cost or no-frills strategy. It may also provide a strategic capability to the organisation and create a barrier to entry through the achievement of economies of scale, for example.

Standard cost card

Much of cost accounting is based on the principles of standardisation. It assumes that businesses operate in a stable environment where, for example, a standard amount of materials will be used in the production of each product and that a standard price can be attached to the price of those materials.

Problems with standard costing in modern environments

Standard product costs are associated with traditional manufacturing systems producing large quantities of standard items.

Standard costing may not be appropriate in the modern production environment because:

- Products are often non-standard
- Standards can become quickly outdated
- Production is highly automated
- Often an ideal standard is used
- Modern environments are more concerned with continuous improvement
- Modern managers need more detailed information
- More 'real time' performance measures are needed.

Further explanation

Non-standard products

Standard product costs apply to manufacturing environments in which quantities of an identical product are output from the production process. They are not suitable for manufacturing environments where products are non-standard or are customised to customer specifications.

Standard costs become outdated quickly

Shorter product life cycles in the modern business environment mean that standard costs will need to be reviewed and updated frequently. This will increase the cost of operating a standard cost system but, if the standards are not updated regularly, they will be of limited use for planning and control purposes. The extra work involved in maintaining up-to-date standards might limit the usefulness and relevance of a standard costing system.

Production is highly automated

It is doubtful whether standard costing is of much value for performance setting and control in automated manufacturing environments. There is an underlying assumption in standard costing that control can be exercised by concentrating on the efficiency of the workforce. Direct labour efficiency standards are seen as a key to management control. However, in practice, where manufacturing systems are highly automated, the rates of production output and materials consumption are controlled by the machinery rather than the workforce.

Ideal standard used

Variances are the difference between actual performance and standard, measured in cost terms. The significance of variances for management control purposes depends on the type of standard cost used. JIT and TQM businesses often implement an ideal standard due to the emphasis on continuous improvement and high quality. Therefore, adverse variances with an ideal standard have a different meaning from adverse variances calculated with a current standard.

Emphasis on continuous improvement

Standard costing and adherence to a preset standard is inconsistent with the concept of continuous improvement, which is applied within TQM and JIT environments.

Detailed information is required

Variance analysis is often carried out on an aggregate basis (total material usage variance, total labour efficiency variance and so on) but in a complex and constantly changing business environment more detailed information is required for effective management control.

> **Monitoring performance is important**
>
> Variance analysis control reports tend to be made available to managers at the end of a reporting period. In the modern business environment managers need more 'real time' information about events as they occur.

Despite the limitations that standard costing techniques might have, the remainder of this chapter relies heavily on standard costing principles.

6 Decision making techniques

In this section we look at two areas:

- breakeven analysis

- marginal analysis

Contribution to sales ratios and break-even points

Cost-Volume-Profit (CVP) analysis

CVP analysis makes use of the contribution concept in order to assess the following measures for a single product:

- contribution to sales (C/S) ratio

- break-even point

- margin of safety

(Contribution = selling price less **all** variable costs)

C/S ratio

The C/S ratio of a product is the proportion of the selling price that contributes to fixed overheads and profits. It is comparable to the gross profit margin. The formula for calculating the C/S ratio of a product is as follows:

$$\text{C/S ratio} = \frac{\text{Contribution per unit}}{\text{Selling price per unit}} \quad \text{or} \quad \frac{\text{Total contribution}}{\text{Total sales revenue}}$$

🔑 The C/S ratio is sometimes referred to as the P/V (Profit/Volume) ratio.

Break-even point

The break-even point is the point at which neither a profit nor a loss is made.

- At the break-even point the following situations occur.

    Total sales revenue = Total costs, i.e. Profit = 0

    or

    Total contribution = Fixed costs, i.e. Profit = 0

- The following formula is used to calculate the break-even point in terms of numbers of units sold.

$$\text{Break-even point (in terms of numbers of units sold)} = \frac{\text{Fixed costs}}{\text{Contribution per unit}}$$

- It is also possible to calculate the break-even point in terms of sales revenue using the C/S ratio. The equation is as follows:

$$\text{Break-even point (in terms of sales revenue)} = \frac{\text{Fixed costs}}{\text{C/S ratio}}$$

Margin of safety

The margin of safety is the amount by which anticipated sales (in units) can fall below budget before a business makes a loss. It can be calculated in terms of numbers of units or as a percentage of budgeted sales.

The following formulae are used to calculate the margin of safety:

Margin of safety (in terms of units) Margin of safety (as a % of budgeted sales) = $\dfrac{\text{Budgeted sales – Break-even point sales}}{\text{Budgeted sales}} \times 100\%$

= Budgeted sales – Break-even point sales

Test your understanding 3

A break-down of KP's profit in the last accounting period showed the following:

	$000
Sales	450
Variable costs	(220)
Fixed costs	(160)
Net profit	70

Due to a downturn in market conditions the company is worried that next year may result in losses and would like to know the change in sales that would make this happen.

Required:

Calculate the break-even sales revenue for the business based on its current cost structure. Use this information to determine the percentage fall in sales that would be necessary before the company would begin to incur losses.

(5 marks)

Limitations of break-even analysis

The assumptions of break-even analysis (which also therefore become its weaknesses) are:

- We are only considering the short term.
- There is a constant contribution per unit.
- There is a constant selling price.
- There are constant variable costs per unit and constant fixed costs (so that it ignores stepped fixed costs).
- Sales = production so that there is no stock movement.
- The objective is to maximise profit.

Marginal analysis

Marginal analysis refers to situations where we use contribution to make decisions.

The key is that only costs which vary with the decision should be included in an analysis of the decision.

More details on relevant cost principles

Decision making involves making a choice between two or more alternatives. The decision will be 'rational' and profit-maximising. All decisions will be made using relevant costs and revenues.

'Relevant costs are future cash flows arising as a direct consequence of the decision under consideration.'

There are three elements here:

Cash flows. To evaluate a decision actual cash flows should be considered. Non-cash items such as depreciation and interdivisional charges should be ignored.

Future costs and revenues. This means that past costs and revenues are only useful insofar as they provide a guide to the future. Costs already spent, known as sunk costs, are irrelevant for decision making.

Differential costs and revenues. Only those costs and revenues that alter as a result of a decision are relevant. Where factors are common to all the alternatives being considered they can be ignored; only the differences are relevant.

In many short run situations the fixed costs remain constant for each of the alternatives being considered and thus the marginal costing approach showing sales, marginal cost and contribution is particularly appropriate.

> In the long run (and sometimes in the short run) fixed costs do change and accordingly the differential costs must include any changes in the amount of fixed costs.

Marginal analysis can be used in key areas of decision making such as:

- accepting/rejecting special contracts

- closing/continuation decisions.

Each of these will now be considered in turn.

Accepting/rejecting special contracts

The basic decision rule here is that we should calculate:

Extra revenue received less marginal costs of meeting the special contract.

This would typically mean that items such as fixed costs, contracted costs etc. would be ignored in the decision as they would not be affected by the decision.

Closure or continuation decisions

Part of a business, for example a department or a product, may appear to be unprofitable. The business may have to make a decision as to whether or not this area should be shut down.

The quantifiable cost or benefit of closure

The relevant cash flows associated with closure should be considered. For example:

- the lost contribution from the area that is being closed (= relevant cost of closure)

- savings in specific fixed costs from closure (= relevant benefit of closure)

- known penalties and other costs resulting from the closure, e.g. redundancy, compensation to customers (= relevant cost of closure)

- any known reorganisation costs (= relevant cost of closure)

- any known additional contribution from the alternative use for resources released (= relevant benefit of closure).

If the relevant benefits are greater than the relevant costs of closure then closure may occur. However, before a final decision is made the business should also consider the non-quantifiable factors discussed below.

Other issues to consider

The decision making processes above concentrated on the financial impact of the decisions. Decision makers should also consider qualitative factors such as the impact on customers, competitive advantage and critical success factors etc.

Example of other factors to consider

For example, let's consider the qualitative factors in a make-or-buy decision.

In addition to the relative cost of buying externally compared to making in-house, management must consider a number of other issues before a final decision is made.

- **Reliability of external supplier:** can the outside company be relied upon to meet the requirements in terms of:
    - quantity required
    - quality required
    - delivering on time
    - price stability.
- **Specialist skills:** the external supplier may possess some specialist skills that are not available in-house.
- **Alternative use of resource:** outsourcing will free up resources which may be used in another part of the business.
- **Social:** will outsourcing result in a reduction of the workforce? Redundancy costs should be considered.
- **Legal:** will outsourcing affect contractual obligations with suppliers or employees?
- **Confidentiality:** is there a risk of loss of confidentiality, especially if the external supplier performs similar work for rival companies.
- **Customer reaction:** Do customers attach importance to the products being made in-house?

Non-quantifiable costs and benefits of closure

There are qualitative factors to consider in all of the above marginal decisions. For example, the closure decision might have the following qualitative factors:

- Some of the costs and benefits discussed above may be non-quantifiable at the point of making the shut-down decision:
    - penalties and other costs resulting from the closure (e.g. redundancy, compensation to customers) may not be known with certainty.
    - reorganisation costs may not be known with certainty.
    - additional contribution from the alternative use for resources released may not be known with certainty.
- Knock-on impact of the shut-down decision. For example, supermarkets often stock some goods which they sell at a loss. This is to get customers through the door, who they then hope will purchase other products which have higher profit margins for them. If the decision is taken to stop selling these products then the customers may no longer come to the store.

Test your understanding 4

KRS Ltd is considering whether to administer its own purchase ledger or to use an external accounting service. It has obtained the following cost estimates for each option:

Internal service department

	Cost	Volume
Purchase hardware/software	$320 pa	
Hardware/software maintenance	$750 pa	
Accounting stationery	$500 pa	
Part-time account clerk	$6,000 pa	

External services

	Cost	Volume
Processing of invoices/credit notes	$0.50 per document	5,000 pa
Processing of cheque payments	$0.50 per cheque	4,000 pa
Reconciling supplier accounts	$2.00 per supplier per month	150 suppliers

Determine the cost effectiveness of outsourcing the accounting activities and identify the qualitative factors involved.

Financial reporting implications

The decision making techniques described are more concerned with the impact on cash flow rather than the impact on profits. This is because cash flow is more objective and harder to manipulate than profits

Cash versus profit

In the short term, profits and cash flow are different. There are several reasons for this:

- Some items of cash spending and cash receipt do not affect profits at all. In particular capital receipts and capital payments do not affect profits. A business could earn a profit but spend large sums of money on capital expenditure, so that it makes a profit but has a negative cash flow.

- Profits are calculated after deducting depreciation charges on non-current assets. Depreciation is a notional charge, and does not affect cash flow at all. It is an accounting device for spreading the cost of a non-current asset over its useful life.

- Cash flow is affected by the need to invest in operational working capital. Operational working capital is defined as the working capital a business needs to carry on its day-to-day business operations. It consists of its inventory (inventories) plus its trade receivables minus its trade payables. Investing in working capital affects cash flow, and when the total amount of working capital of a business changes, the profits earned in the period will differ from the operational cash flows.

For accounting purposes, in preparing an income statement there are two possible systems that can be used:

- Cash accounting

- Accruals accounting

These systems will provide different profit figures for the period based on different assumptions about how revenues and costs are recorded in the income statement.

In a system of accruals accounting, revenues and costs are reported in the period where the sale occurs, even if the cash flows for the sale and costs of sale occur in different periods, whereas a system of cash accounting records cash payments and cash receipts as they occur within an accounting period. Cash accounting is an accounting method where receipts are recorded during the period they are received, and the expenses in the period in which they are actually paid. Basically, when the cash is received for a sale, it is recorded in the accounting books as a sale. Its focus is on determining the operational cash flow for the year.

However, cash accounting is not generally accepted as good accounting practice because businesses enter into transactions that are legally enforceable prior to the exchange of cash, but the use of cash accounting does not reflect any transactions which have taken place but are not yet paid for.

Accruals accounting is recognised by law, and businesses are required to use it to measure their profitability for the purpose of external financial reporting.

Therefore, the decisions that an organisation makes may have a different impact on cash flows than they have on profits. This may cause an issue for the business in that shareholders (and many other stakeholders) are not always provided with the cash impact of decisions. Instead the financial reporting that they do receive comes from financial statements that focus on profit rather than cash.

In the long term, the cash impact and the profit impact of a decision should be equal. However, in the short term there is likely to be a difference and shareholders are more likely to react to a change in profit than a change in cash.

Financial reporting implications

If profit is impacted by decisions then it is this that shareholders may focus on. On top of this, if profit is affected then other financial reporting measures may be impacted such as:

- Earnings per share (EPS)
- Price earnings ratio
- Interest cover
- Gearing ratio

In theory, as long as the decision is explained to shareholders this should not impact on their decision making process. However, in practice a reported drop in measures such as EPS and interest cover may lead to shareholders selling their shares, a reduction in the share price in the business and a fall in the value of the business. In the long term, the impact will be smoothed out so that short-term losses will be outweighed by long-term profits if the decision is made on sound decision making principles, but it may lead to shorter-term implications for shareholder wealth.

It should also be noted that from a financial reporting perspective, decisions such as the closure of a business unit will need to be disclosed separately in the financial statements as a discontinued activity. This in turn may influence shareholder perspectives

Therefore, decision makers need to consider this when making decisions. This could be one of the 'other factors' that may be relevant to decisions.

Tax implications

Another factor may be the taxation impact of the decision. Typically the tax impact can be included by forecasting profits and applying the relevant taxation rules. However, there may be other consequences from a taxation perspective such as:

- The decision may move an organisation from one taxation bracket to another
- The decision may change an organisation's eligibility for particular tax reliefs (either positively or negatively)
- A decision may impact on the timing of taxation payments
- Because taxation is based on profits rather than cash there will be timing differences (similar to those considered in the financial reporting implications) that may mean that more taxation is paid earlier rather than later. This in turn may also impact on the attitudes of shareholders and, ultimately, on shareholder wealth.

These factors become further factors for decision makers to consider over and above the simple outcomes from relevant costing or investment appraisal analysis.

Long-term decision making

Some investment decisions may have a longer-term impact and therefore longer-term appraisal techniques will need to be used. These techniques were studied in earlier papers (F5 and F9) and the key points to remember are as follows:

Method:	**Net Present Value (NPV)**
How to calculate:	Use a cost of capital and discount factors to discount future cash flows to give the present value
Best used when:	The project is long and the cost of capital is known
Key advantage:	Gives an absolute estimate of the impact on shareholder wealth
Key disadvantage:	Relies on a reliable cost of capital estimate

Method:	**Payback period**
How to calculate:	Determine how quickly the original cash injection is recovered
Best used when:	The project is short and/or cash is in short supply
Key advantage:	Provides a minimum target for project life
Key disadvantage:	Requires a target/benchmark

Method:	**Accounting Rate of Return (ARR)**
How to calculate:	Divide average profits by the initial investment
Best used when:	The project has profit targets to meet
Key advantage:	A simple calculation based on readily available information
Key disadvantage:	Profits are easily manipulated

Method:	**Internal Rate of Return (IRR)**
How to calculate:	Determine the cost of capital that provides a zero NPV
Best used when:	The project is long and the cost of capital has not yet be determined
Key advantage:	Tells us the highest acceptable cost of capital
Key disadvantage:	It is not useful for comparing projects

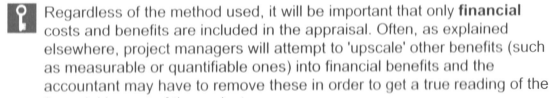 Regardless of the method used, it will be important that only **financial** costs and benefits are included in the appraisal. Often, as explained elsewhere, project managers will attempt to 'upscale' other benefits (such as measurable or quantifiable ones) into financial benefits and the accountant may have to remove these in order to get a true reading of the financial impact of the project.

Problems when focusing on only financial returns

The project appraisal methods which follow focus purely on the financial rewards of a project. However this should not be the only decision criteria that an organisation employs. Examining only financial costs and benefits can lead to the following problems:

- non-financial costs or benefits might outweigh the financial ones. Earlier in the chapter we discussed other types of benefits such as observable and measurable benefits which are ignored in financial calculations.

- managers may be encouraged to use 'creative' calculations of benefits in order to have them classified as financial benefits.

- costs may be removed from the forecasts in order to 'overstate' the case for the project.

- managers may include slack in their forecasts in order to show enough benefit to achieve the project approval but without having onerous targets.

- projects with no financial benefits would automatically be rejected.

7   Dealing with risk and uncertainty in decision making

Forecasting and decision making often include an element of risk or uncertainty. Because they look to the future they often involve estimates of future costs and benefits. We need to consider how risks and uncertainty can be built into the decision making process.

Risk vs uncertainty

When making decisions, a decision maker will aim to account for risk but may struggle to account for uncertainty.

- Risk – quantifiable – there are a number of possible outcomes and the probability of each outcome is known. For example, based on past experience of digging for oil in a particular area, an oil company may estimate that they have a 60% chance of finding oil and a 40% chance of not finding oil. More risk typically means that the outcomes are more volatile and that the possibility of favourable outcomes is lower.

- Uncertainty – unquantifiable – there are a number of possible outcomes but the probability of each outcome is not known. For example, the same oil company may dig for oil in a previously unexplored area. The company knows that it is possible for them to either find or not find oil but it does not know the probabilities of each of these outcomes. More uncertainty typically means that the outcomes themselves become more unpredictable.

Managing uncertainty

Decision making involves making decisions now about what will happen in the future. Events in the future can be predicted, but managers can rarely be 100% confident that these predicted future events will actually arise. As actual results emerge managers are likely to discover that they have achieved better or worse results than those predicted originally.

In an earlier chapter we considered scenario planning, which is one way in which uncertainty can be managed. It is common in practice to consider three possible outcomes; the most likely outcome, the pessimistic (worst possible) outcome and the optimistic (best possible) outcome. This may be supplemented with sensitivity analysis on each outcome. An organisation should then make itself better prepared to deal with uncertainty by ensuring that it is as flexible as possible, reducing operational gearing, ensuring easy access to finance for unexpected funding needs, constantly monitoring its environment for signals of uncertain events becoming more certain etc.

This is a way of preparing for and recognising uncertainty but it does not in itself reduce uncertainty.

Managers might also act to reduce uncertainty itself by doing things like diversifying their investments. If for example, there is uncertainty over which country might have the highest economic growth over the next 5 years then an organisation might invest in a number of countries with strong potential in order to diversify away some of the uncertainty. The diversification can help reduce other uncertainties such as exchange rate uncertainties and possibly even competitive uncertainties.

Environmental testing such as market research may also help reduce uncertainty. An organisation should be constantly monitoring and testing its environment, as discussed in chapter 3 of this text. This may convert uncertainty into risk (which is much easier to manage).

Managing risk

There are many ways in which risk can be dealt with in decision making. The most common technique is to attach probabilities to the potential range of outcomes and calculate expected values from this information.

Probabilities and expected values

 An expected value summarises all the different possible outcomes by calculating a single weighted average. It is the long run average (mean).

The expected value is not the most likely result. It may not even be a possible result, but instead it finds the average outcome if the same event was to take place thousands of times.

Expected value calculations

The following illustrates how calculations may be performed when using expected values.

Expected value formula

$$EV = \Sigma px$$

where x represents the future outcome

and   p represents the probability of the outcome occurring

Example

A company expects the following monthly profits:

Monthly profit	Probability
£10,000	0.70
£20,000	0.30

Calculate the expected value of monthly profit.

Solution

Monthly profit	Probability	px
£10,000	0.70	7,000
£20,000	0.30	6,000
		13,000

Expected profit is £13,000 per month.

Test your understanding 5

A company's sales for a new product are subject to uncertainty. It has determined a range of possible outcomes over the first two years.

Year 1

Sales	$m	%
High	40	60
Low	20	40

Year 2

Sales	$m	%
High	80	90
Low	30	10

(if year 1 sales are high)

Sales	$m	%
High	30	20
Low	10	80

(if year 1 sales are low)

Required:

Calculate the expected sales for each year.

Advantages and disadvantages of EVs

Advantages:

- Takes risk into account by considering the probability of each possible outcome and using this information to calculate an expected value.

- The information is reduced to a single number resulting in easier decisions.

- Calculations are relatively simple.

Disadvantages:

- The probabilities used are usually very subjective.

- The EV is merely a weighted average and therefore has little meaning for a one-off project.

- The EV gives no indication of the dispersion of possible outcomes about the EV, i.e. the risk.

- The EV may not correspond to any of the actual possible outcomes.

Decision trees and multi-stage decision problems

A decision tree is a diagrammatic representation of a decision problem, where all possible courses of action are represented, and every possible outcome of each course of action is shown. Decision trees should be used where a problem involves a series of decisions being made and several outcomes arise during the decision-making process.

Decision trees force the decision maker to consider the logical sequence of events. A complex problem is broken down into smaller, easier-to-handle sections. The financial outcomes and probabilities are shown separately, and the decision tree is 'rolled back' by calculating expected values and making decisions. It is important that only relevant costs and revenues are considered, and that all cash is expressed in present value terms.

Decision tree illustration

Consider the following multi-stage decision:

A company is planning on drilling for oil. It can either drill immediately (at a cost of $50m) or carry out some preliminary tests (at a cost of $10m). Alternatively, the company could sell the rights to the site to another company for $40m.

If it decides to drill now there is a 55% chance that it will find oil and extract it (with a value of $150m).

If further tests are carried out first there is a 70% chance that they will indicate the presence of oil. The sales rights would then be worth $65m. Alternatively, the company could drill for oil itself at a cost of $50m. There is then an 80% chance that oil extraction (worth $150m) is successful.

If further tests are carried out and indicate that no oil is present the value of any sales rights would fall to $15m. The company could still decide to drill for oil itself, but there is only a 20% chance that it would successfully find and extract oil at that point.

A decision tree of the problem would look as follows:

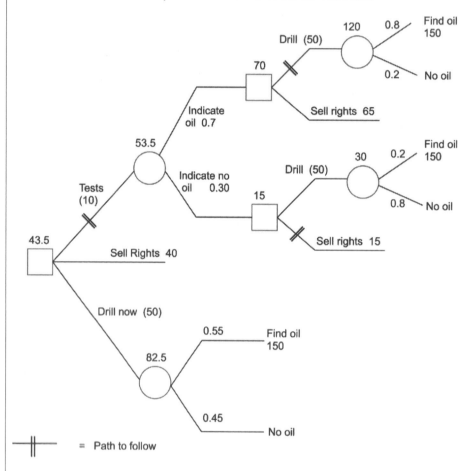

Explanation

It is easier to start at the bottom of the tree. The first box shows the first decision to be made – to test, to drill or to sell the rights. If we follow the 'drill' line/branch, we come to a 'chance' point (represented by a circle). This shows that if we drill there are two possible outcomes – there is a 55% chance that we find oil and make a positive net return of $150m. There is also a 45% chance that no oil is found and that no return is made. The figure on the circle of $82.5m is the expected value calculated from these two outcomes. However, the drill line has a cost of $50m so that the overall net expected return would be $32.5m – and it is this figure that should be used to compare the drill option against the other options.

The middle branch of the tree shows the expected value from selling the rights – $40m.

The top branch shows the analysis of the testing decision. It can be seen that there are many more possible outcomes and also further decisions to be made based on whether or not the tests indicate the presence of oil. Lines that have a double cross marking on them show the best choice to be made based on expected values.

Advice

The company should undertake geological tests. If the tests indicate that oil is present then a drilling programme should be carried out. However, if the tests indicate that there is no oil then the company should sell the drilling rights.

This strategy will maximise expected returns at £43.5m.

Benefits and problems

The main value of a decision tree is that it maps out clearly all the decisions and uncertain events and exactly how they are interrelated. They are especially beneficial where the outcome of one decision affects another decision. For example in the above, the probability of eventual success changes depending on the test outcomes. The analysis is made clearer by annotating the tree with probabilities, cash flows, and expected values so that the optimum decisions (based on expected values) can be clearly seen.

However, drawing a tree diagram is only one way of undertaking a decision. It is based on the concept of expected value and as such suffers from the limitations of this technique. For example, in this scenario, if the test drilling proves positive, the tree indicated the company should drill, as opposed to selling the rights. However, if it does, then there is a 20% chance of it losing £50 million. A risk-averse company may well decide to accept the safer option and sell the rights and settle for £65 million.

8 Budgeting

As part of 'strategy in action', a business will create plans for each SBU, product, function etc. These plans are often in the form of budgets. The budget sets out the short-term plans and targets necessary to fulfil the longer-term strategic plans and objectives.

The budgets will also play a vital role in reviewing and controlling strategic plans. They will be used to identify and investigate variances and to highlight when a plan or process is 'out of control'.

Budgets are distinct from forecasts. A forecast is a prediction of a future outcome. A budget is a plan (usually in financial terms) that looks to use and/or achieve that forecast.

Approaches to budgeting

A periodic budget shows the costs and revenue for one period of time, e.g. a year and is updated on a periodic basis, e.g. every 12 months. However, there are many different ways in which a budget might be prepared.

Rolling budgets

A rolling budget is a 'budget continuously updated by adding a further accounting period (month or quarter) when the earliest accounting period has expired' (CIMA Official Terminology). Rolling budgets are also called 'continuous budgets'.

The strategic role of rolling budgets

When budgeting in conditions subject to rapid financial change rolling budgets can play a key strategic role for organisations. When a budget is prepared, the forecasts on which it is based might be uncertain due to the probability of significant financial changes during the budget period. For example:

- The forecast rate of cost inflation/price inflation might be high
- The business might be affected by changes in an exchange rate, such as the sterling/US dollar rate and the exchange rate might be extremely volatile and subject to large movements within relatively short periods of time

When there is a large amount of uncertainty in the budget, it might be appropriate to prepare rolling budgets at regular intervals, in order to have plans that are reasonably realistic and achievable.

Rolling budgets in practice

For years, senior managers at REL Consultancy Group handled budgeting and revenue forecasting much the way most other companies do. As year-end approached, they would evaluate performance, set sales targets for the upcoming year and then work to see that everyone met or exceeded the goals.

Unfortunately, the process didn't always produce the intended results.

'Invariably,' recalls Stephan Payne, president of the London-based global management consulting firm, 'one of the account directors would land a couple of good clients early in the year and make his annual budget well before the year closed. More often than not, he'd then take his foot off the gas and coast.' To make the budgeting process more timely and relevant, the firm embraced a more complex, albeit intuitive, approach to financial forecasting – the **rolling budget**. Rather than creating an annual financial forecast that remains static for the year, he and his colleagues now produce an 18-month budget and then update projections every month – in effect, recalculating the whole budget. As the firm's actual sales figures come in each month, directors plug them into their forecasting model in place of what they had projected, then roll the budget forward one more month.

No more free rides

The result: an always-current financial forecast that reflects not only the company's most recent monthly results but also any material changes to its business outlook or the economy. In addition, it provides fewer opportunities for account directors to ride the coattails of past performance.

'Now, even the guy who booked a million dollars' worth of business in one month can't sit still because 30 days later, we're going to have an entirely new forecast,' Payne says, adding, 'It's a dynamic process that makes a lot more sense.'

Although traditional one year budgets are still the norm at most companies large and small, many accountants argue that rolling budgets can be a far more useful tool. Unlike static budgets, they encourage managers to react more quickly to changing economic developments or business conditions. They discourage what is too often a fruitless focus on the past ('Why didn't we meet our numbers?') in favour of a realistic focus on the future. And they produce forecasts that, over the near term, are never more than a few months old, even when companies are rolling them forward on a quarterly basis – the more common approach – rather than REL's monthly basis.

'A static budget simply doesn't reflect the pace of business today,' says Jill Langerman, CPA, president and CFO of the accounting firm Fair, Anderson & Langerman in Las Vegas. 'If at mid-year you add a new product to your line-up, you want to calculate the costs and profit margins associated with that and reflect those calculations in your budget OSC to reflect the impact that it will have on your remaining product lines. That way, you can set an accurate performance target and make informed decisions about whether you're now free to invest more in the remaining product lines or perhaps add a new line. If you're not incorporating these new analyses into your budget, it becomes a rather useless document.'

Implementing rolling budgets doesn't necessarily require any fundamental change in the way a company has been doing its budgets – except, of course, it no longer does the job just once a year. However, companies that decide to step up to rolling budgets may want to take advantage of the decision to make a change and consider what else they can do to improve the process. After all, if a company can get everyone on board to make such a fundamental change, a further nudge to make the process more effective and efficient in other ways may be possible, too.

Taken from:

'Budgets on a roll: recalculating a business's outlook several times a year'

Randy Myers, Journal of Accountancy, December 2001. © 2001. Reprinted with permission of AICPA

Incremental budgeting

 The traditional approach to budgeting is to take the previous year's budget and to add on a percentage to allow for inflation and other cost increases. In addition there may be other adjustments for specific items such as an extra worker or extra machine.

Further explanation

- Fairly small changes are made to the current year's budget. For example, adjustments might be made to allow for a planned increase or decline in sales volume, and for inflationary increases in sales prices and costs.

- A check is then made to ensure that the budget produced in this way meets the performance targets of the organisation. For example, the company might have a target of keeping the operating costs to sales ratio at less than, say, 60%.

In a static business environment, incremental budgets are little more than 'last year's budget plus a percentage amount for inflation'.

Whilst this approach to budgeting is popular due to its simplicity it is not very useful in environments which change quickly and unpredictably.

Zero-based budgeting

Zero-based budgeting (ZBB) is a radical alternative to incremental budgeting. In ZBB, all activities and costs are budgeted from scratch (a zero base). For every activity, managers look at its costs and its purpose, and consider whether there are alternative ways of doing it. Non-essential activities and costs are identified and eliminated by removing them from next year's budget.

Adoption of ZBB

ZBB has been adopted more widely in the public sector than the private, although examples of organisations regularly adopting a full ZBB approach are rare. Full-scale ZBB is so resource-intensive that critics claim that its advantages are outweighed by its implementation costs. However, it is not necessary to apply ZBB to the whole of an organisation; benefits can be gained from its application to specific areas. For example, in the public sector, a decision could be made regarding the overall size of the childcare budget, and ZBB could be applied to allocate resources within that particular field; similarly, in a business organisation, ZBB could be applied to individual divisions on a rotational basis. This selective application ensures that a thorough reappraisal of activities is undertaken regularly, but not so regularly that the process itself is a major drain on organisational resources.

Notwithstanding these criticisms, the main plank of the ZBB approach – the rejection of past budgets as a planning baseline – is being increasingly accepted.

ZBB is more outward looking and considers the environmental changes that the organisation is likely to face. Nonetheless, it is a complex, time-consuming and expensive task.

Activity-based budgeting

Whereas ZBB is based on budgets prepared by responsibility centre managers, ABB is based on budgeting for activities. In its simplest form, ABB is simply about using costs determined via ABC to prepare budgets for each activity.

ABB is useful when overheads are significant within a business, but it relies on the use of Activity Based Costing which may not be used by all organisations.

Test your understanding 6

Scenario

For a number of years, the research division of Z has produced its annual budget (for new and continuing projects) using incremental budgeting techniques. The company is now under new management and the annual budget for 20X4 is to be prepared using zero based budgeting techniques.

Tasks:

(a) Explain the differences between incremental and zero based budgeting techniques.

(b) Explain how Z could operate a zero based budgeting system for its research projects.

The operating divisions of Z have in the past always used a traditional approach to analysing costs into their fixed and variable components. A single measure of activity was used which, for simplicity, was the number of units produced. The new management does not accept that such a simplistic approach is appropriate for budgeting in the modern environment and has requested that the managers adopt an activity-based approach to their budgets for 20X4.

Tasks:

(c) (i) Briefly explain activity-based budgeting (ABB).

(ii) Explain how activity-based budgeting would be implemented by the operating divisions of Z.

Meaningful budgetary control

Budgetary control refers to not only the budget setting process but also to the monitoring of ongoing performance against these budgets. For this second process to be useful the budgets themselves must be accurate, reliable and up to date.

Why budgets may not be useful for control purposes

There are two reasons why this might not be the case. Firstly, it may well be that the organisation's environment has changed but that the budget has not been adapted to reflect this. For example, if a budget is based on a 30% forecasted increase in sales but perhaps a change in legislation means that the product is no longer as attractive and sales are now only forecasted to rise by 5%. In this case the budget should be changed in order to reflect the change in the organisation's environment. Without a change to the budget the organisation would look to be out of control and unnecessary actions and investigations would be implemented.

The second reason why the budget itself may not be useful for control purposes is due to the behavioural aspects of budgeting.

Behavioural aspects of budgets

As mentioned above, one of the purposes of budgets is to achieve motivation. There are therefore a number of factors to consider in relation to this:

- the level of difficulty in the budget,
- the links to the organisation's objectives, and
- the level of staff involvement.

Further details

- the level of difficulty in the budget. Budgets should be realistic and just tough enough so that they do not demotivate by being too difficult or present a lack of motivation by being too easy.

- the links to the organisation's objectives. As already discussed, budgets should be linked to objectives to ensure that they motivate managers and staff to achieve those objectives rather than any other objectives (such as their own).

- the level of staff involvement. Involving staff in budgets provides a responsibility that is often linked to strong motivation. On the other hand, the business must be wary of any slack that managers might want to build into budgets in which they have both an input and a responsibility.

KAPLAN PUBLISHING

Making budgetary control effective

Atrill and McLaney identify a number of characteristics that are common to businesses with effective budgetary control:

- a serious attitude is taken to the system
- clear demarcation between areas of managerial responsibility
- budget targets that are challenging yet achievable
- established data collection, analysis and reporting techniques
- reports aimed at individual managers
- fairly short reporting periods
- timely variance reports
- action being taken to get operations back under control if they are shown to be out of control.

Forecasting in budgets

It will be necessary to forecast the principal budget factor. This will often require a forecast of future sales.

There are a number of ways in which it might achieve this:

- it may use market forecasts of expected growth and build these into the expected growth in its trend (although this assumes that the organisation will grow at the same rate as the market).
- mathematical techniques such as linear regression (often compiled on a spreadsheet) can be used to develop an expected linear growth in the trend (although this assumes that the past behaviour will provide an accurate estimate of the expected change in future behaviour).
- the high-low method could be used to forecast the change (though this would suffer from similar problems to the linear regression model, in that it assumes that the trend is linear and will continue to rise at the same rate in the future).

It may be that the forecast needs to account for seasonality. For example, a sporting venue's hot drinks sales may be higher in the winter than they are in the summer. Time series analysis is a way of building seasonality into forecasts.

9 Variance analysis

An effective part of budgetary control is to calculate and investigate variances from the budget.

Flexed budgets

Before any meaningful comparison can be made the original budget should be 'flexed' to the actual level of performance.

Example of a flexed budget

A company has a standard cost of $8 per unit for materials and expects to produce and sell 20,000 units (ignore any changes to materials stock). It sets a materials budget for the purchasing department of $160,000 in total.

During the year, because of a celebrity endorsement, the product become very popular and actual sales and production are 30,000 units (50% above what was originally expected). The purchasing department has spent $220,000 on materials and is very concerned about the massive overspend in their department.

It makes sense that the materials budget for the purchasing department should not be limited to the original $160,000 as now it will have had to buy a lot of extra materials. So instead the original budget is adjusted (or flexed) to reflect the increase in actual level of activity.

	Original	Flexed budget	Actual	Total Materials Variance
Production (units)	20,000	30,000	30,000	–
Materials budget ($)	160,000	240,000	220,000	20,000 Fav

Variance investigation

Variances arise naturally in standard costing because a standard cost is a long-term average cost. In any period actual costs may be higher or lower than standard but in the long run these should cancel out if the process is under control.

Variances may also arise because of:

- poor budgeting
- poor recording of cost
- operational reasons
- random factors.

It is important to identify the reason for a variance so that appropriate action can be taken. The factors preventing the business entity from achieving its optimal level of performance can be ascertained, whereas the impediments to a successful business can be determined and the corrective measures taken against them.

For control purposes, management might need to establish why a particular variance has occurred. Once the reason for the variance has been established, a decision can then be taken as to what control measures, if any, might be appropriate:

- to prevent the adverse variance continuing in the future, or
- to repeat a favourable variance in the future, or
- to bring actual results back on course to achieve the budgeted targets.

Possible interdependence between variances

In many cases, the explanation for one variance might also explain one or more other variances in which case the variances are inter-related.

For control purposes, it might therefore be necessary to look at several variances together and not in isolation.

Examples of interdependent variances

Some examples of interdependence between variances are listed below.

- Using cheaper materials will result in a favourable material price variance, but using the cheaper material in production might increase the wastage rate (adverse material usage) and cause a fall in labour productivity (adverse labour and variable overhead efficiency).

  A more expensive mix of materials (adverse mix variance) might result in higher output yields (favourable yield variance).

- Using more experienced labour to do the work will result in an adverse labour rate variance, but productivity might be higher as a result (favourable labour and variable overhead efficiency).

- Changing the composition of a team might result in a cheaper labour mix (favourable mix variance) but lower productivity (adverse yield variance).

- Workers trying to improve productivity (favourable efficiency variance) in order to win a bonus (adverse rate variance) might use materials wastefully in order to save time (adverse materials usage).

- Cutting sales prices (adverse sales price variance) might result in higher sales demand from customers (favourable sales volume variance).

The controllability principle

Controllability means the extent to which a specific manager can control costs or revenues or any other item (such as output quality). The controllability principle is that a manager should only be made accountable and responsible for costs and revenues that they can control directly.

In variance reporting, this means that variances should be reported to the managers who are in a position to control the costs or revenues to which the variances relate.

Test your understanding 7

Two directors at manufacturing company Buchan are having a heated disagreement. The company is lucky to be operating in an industry that has seen a boom in demand, but Buchan's sales have fallen. Budgeted sales volume for this year was 28,000 units, but only 21,000 units were actually produced and sold.

This has angered the Purchasing Director (PD) who claims that she bought much better components for the company products which should have helped the products stand out from those of rivals. She also claims to have achieved this whilst spending less than her allocated budgeted spend for the year of $1.4m.

The Sales Director (SD) has defended his sales team. He accepts that sales have fallen but suggests that this can only mean that the purchased components weren't as popular as PD expected. SD had given his team clear instructions to adhere to the recommended selling price of $300 per unit but he argued that the drop in sales volume suggests that this was too high.

The production director was happy to report that there were no variances in usage. The finance director confirmed this and explained that the only variances in the year were in sales and purchasing.

Actual values for sales and material costs in the year were as follows:

Sales	$8,400,000
Materials	$1,365,000

Required:

Evaluate the performance of the sales and purchasing teams.

Professional skill:
Illustrate evaluation skills in assessing the implications of the directors' actions.

10 The strategic role of budgeting, standard costing and variances

Budgets, standard costing and variance analysis are most often seen as control mechanisms. They are used to set targets, measure performance, highlight errors, determine responsibility, and take corrective action to return the system to control.

Control mechanisms

The budgeting process will often begin with the principal budget factor but this factor is often determined by the strategic plan (whether that be to increase sales, react to competitive pressure by cutting cost, improving quality etc.). Changes in the standard cost card might be determined by plans to increase efficiency, improve processes, increase quality etc.

Also, budgets etc. are not just backward looking. Many organisations implement what is known as feedforward control in order to take preventative rather than corrective action.

Feedback happens after the event and discovers that something has gone wrong (or right). It is obviously too late to affect the result that has just happened, but the idea is that if we can understand what went wrong in the previous period, then we can stop the problem from recurring.

Feedforward is the comparison of the results that are currently expected in the light of the latest information and the desired results. If there is a difference, then it is investigated and corrected.

Feedforward is more proactive and aims to anticipate problems and prevent them from occurring. Whereas feedback is based on a comparison of historical actual results with the budget for the period to date, feedforward looks ahead and compares the targets or objectives for the period (possibly determined by the strategic plan) and what actual results are now forecast.

However, budgets, standard costing and variances can also have a forward looking and strategic role in forming an important part in the strategic decision making of the organisation. They will influence decisions on whether to outsource an activity, which business units should be removed from a portfolio, which products need a new competitive strategy, whether an acquisition makes financial sense etc.

Further details

The strategic decision making process will involve identifying alternative courses of action, performing cost/benefit analysis on each course, evaluating qualitative issues and choosing a course of action. Budgeting, standard costing and variance analysis can be used alongside more traditional techniques in order to supplement each stage of this process. For example, qualitative techniques such as SWOT, PESTLE analysis and the Ansoff matrix might be used to identify different courses of action, but variance analysis might highlight trends in performance that can influence this, or changes in the standard cost card might present an opportunity for a new competitive strategy.

The performance measures inherent in these systems can be part of an organisation's big data plans. The data here will be internal. The system can provide data on churn rates, how often customers order, market share, complaint rates, changes in material usage, changes in labour efficiency, comparisons of business units etc. Much of this information can play a vital role in the formulation of future strategy and/or be important drivers for strategic change.

Key factors to consider in using budgets etc. to aid strategic planning are:

- The level of participation in budgets. Budget preparation should involve all levels of management (strategic right the way down to operational) so that there is a move away from both the top-down and bottom-up approach, and a move towards a more collaborative approach. This will ensure that strategic plans are guided and influenced by operational and tactical capabilities (and constraints), as well as gaining many of the other advantages of budgetary participation. However, this process is likely to be more time consuming than traditional budgeting techniques, and it may be difficult to obtain agreement across all levels of management.

- It will be important to ensure that standard costs remain relevant to the future strategic environment. In environments that change more rapidly and unpredictably, this will be difficult to achieve.

- A strong performance measurement system. Performance measures need to be expanded beyond traditional financial and accounting measures. Broader measures on customer performance, innovation, quality etc. need to be provided if management are to take meaningful information from the system which can be used in future strategic decisions.

- Accurate variances with clear responsibilities. Variance investigation should indicate long-term patterns and fundamental changes to either operations or the environment.

Many of these elements have been explored in this chapter.

11 Other quantitative analysis techniques

Businesses may also want to quantify forecasts for budgeting, planning and evaluation purposes. There are a number of quantitative techniques students should be familiar with, such as correlation, linear regression and time series analysis.

In exam scenarios, students must be able to explain and apply those techniques. They also must be able to discuss the suitability, principles, uses and limitations of these techniques.

Linear regression

The high-low method only takes account of two observations – the highest and the lowest. To take account of all observations, a more advanced calculation is needed. It is known as **linear regression,** and uses a formula to estimate the linear relationship between the variables.

Linear regression is a simple statistical tool used to model the dependence of a variable (say, costs) on one or more variables (say, volume). This functional relationship may then be formally stated as an equation, with associated statistical values that describe how well this equation fits the data.

Linear regression equation

The equation of a straight line is:

$$y = a + bx$$

where y = dependent variable
       a = intercept (on y-axis)
       b = gradient
       x = independent variable

and   b = $\dfrac{n\Sigma xy - \Sigma x\Sigma y}{n\Sigma x^2 - (\Sigma x)^2}$

where n = number of pairs of data

and   a = $\bar{y} - b\bar{x}$

Regression analysis is a technique for estimating the line of best fit, given a series of data. It is essentially a statistical technique, based on the concept of 'drawing the line that minimises the sum of the squares of the deviations of the line from the observed data' (so it is sometimes referred to as the 'least squares' method). The regression line of y on x is used when an estimate of y (the dependent variable) is required for a given value of x (the **independent** variable).

Linear regression analysis can be used to make forecasts or estimates whenever a linear relationship is assumed between two variables, and historical data is available for analysis. Two such relationships are:

- **A time series and trend line.** Linear regression analysis is an alternative to calculating moving averages to establish a trend line from a time series. (Time series is explained later in this chapter.) The independent variable (x) in a time series is **time**. The dependent variable (y) is **sales, production volume** or **cost**.

- **Total costs, where costs consist of a combination of fixed costs and variable costs** (for example, total overheads, or a semi-variable cost item). Linear regression analysis is an alternative to using the high-low method of cost behaviour analysis. It should be more accurate than the high-low method, because it is based on more items of historical data, not just a 'high' and a 'low' value. In this case:

  - The independent variable (x) in total cost analysis is the volume of activity.

  - The dependent variable (y) is total cost.

  - The value of a is the amount of fixed costs.

  - The value of b is the variable cost per unit of activity.

When a linear relationship is identified and quantified using linear regression analysis, values for 'a' and 'b' are obtained, and these can be used to make a forecast for the budget. For example, a sales budget or forecast can be prepared, or total costs (or total overhead costs) can be estimated, for the budgeted level of activity.

 Illustration 4 – Linear regression

X Co is forecasting its sales for the four quarters of 20X5. It has carried out a linear regression exercise on its past sales data and established the following:

$$a = 20$$

$$b = 0.7$$

The equation of the regression line is therefore:

$$y = 20 + 0.7x$$

When x is number of the quarter and y is the sales value in $000s. Calculate the sales for each of the quarters in 20X5.

Solution

		$000
Quarter 1	y = 20 + (0.7 × 1) =	20.7
Quarter 2	y = 20 + (0.7 × 2) =	21.4
Quarter 3	y = 20 + (0.7 × 3) =	22.1
Quarter 4	y = 20 + (0.7 × 4) =	22.8

Regression analysis is based on sample data. If we selected a different sample, it is probable that a different regression line would be constructed. For this reason, regression analysis is most suited to conditions where there is a relatively stable relationship between the variables.

Illustration 5 – Marcus Aurelius

Marcus Aurelius is a small supermarket chain that has 6 shops. Each shop advertises in their local newspapers and the marketing director is interested in the relationship between the amount that they spend on advertising and the sales revenue that they achieve. She has collated the following information for the 6 shops for the previous year:

Shop	Advertising expenditure	Sales revenue
	$000	$000
1	80	730
2	60	610
3	120	880
4	90	750
5	70	650
6	30	430

She has further performed some calculations for a linear regression calculation as follows:

- the sum of the advertising expenditure (x) column is 450

- the sum of the sales revenue (y) column is 4,050

- when the two columns are multiplied together and summed (xy) the total is 326,500

- when the advertising expenditure is squared (x^2) and summed, the total is 38,300, and

- when the sales revenue is squared (y^2) and summed, the total is 2,849,300.

Calculate the line of best fit using regression analysis:

Advertising expenditure	Sales			
$000	$000			
x	y	xy	x^2	y^2
80	730	58,400	6,400	532,900
60	610	36,600	3,600	372,100
120	880	105,600	14,400	774,400
90	750	67,500	8,100	562,500
70	650	45,500	4,900	422,500
30	430	12,900	900	184,900
450	**4,050**	**326,500**	**38,300**	**2,849,300**

$$b = \frac{n\Sigma xy - \Sigma x\Sigma y}{n\Sigma x^2 - (\Sigma x)^2}$$

$$= \frac{6 \times 326{,}500 - 450 \times 4{,}050}{6 \times 38{,}300 - 450^2}$$

$$= \frac{136{,}500}{27{,}300} = 5$$

$$a = \bar{y} - b\bar{x}$$

$$a = \frac{4{,}050}{6} - 5 \times \frac{450}{6} = 300$$

The regression equation is $\quad y = 300 + 5x$

Mathematical interpretation

If x = 0, then y = 300 and then each time x increases by 1 y increases by 5.

Business interpretation

If no money is spent on advertising then sales would still be $300,000. Then for every additional $1 increase in advertising sales, revenue would increase by $5.

Forecasting

The regression equation can be used for predicting values of y from a given x value.

Interpolation and extrapolation

(1) If the value of x is within the range of our original data, the prediction is known as **interpolation**.

(2) If the value of x is outside the range of our original data, the prediction is known as **extrapolation**.

In general, interpolation is much safer than extrapolation.

Test your understanding 8 – Marcus Aurelius, continued

Marcus Aurelius has just taken on 2 new stores in the same area. The predicted advertising expenditure is expected to be $150,000 for one store and $50,000 for the other.

(a) Calculate the predicted sales revenues.

(b) Explain the reliability of the forecasts.

Limitations of simple linear regression

(1) Assumes a linear relationship between the variables.

(2) Only measures the relationship between two variables. In reality, the dependent variable is affected by many independent variables.

(3) Only interpolated forecasts tend to be reliable. The equation should not be used for extrapolation.

(4) Regression assumes that the historical behaviour of the data continues into the foreseeable future. One of the problems of both techniques (linear regression, as well as time series), is that forecasts are based on past data. Sudden changes in the market will not be immediately reflected in the forecasts. Thus there may still be a role for the managers to use their experience, intuition, and judgement to amend the forecasts produced by the statistical analysis.

(5) Interpolated predictions are only reliable if there is a significant correlation between the data.

(6) The accuracy of forecasting is affected by the need to adjust historical data and future forecasts to allow for price or cost inflation. When historical data is used to calculate a trend line or line of best fit, it should ideally be adjusted to the same index level for prices or costs. If the actual cost or revenue data is used, without adjustments for inflation, the resulting line of best fit will include the inflationary differences.

When a forecast is made from a line of best fit, an adjustment to the forecast should be made for anticipated inflation in the forecast period.

Illustration 6 – BW

Production overhead costs at company BW are assumed to vary with the number of machine hours worked. A line of best fit, based on 20X4 prices, will be calculated from the following historical data, with costs adjusted to allow for cost inflation over time.

Year	Total production overheads $	Number of machine hours	Cost index
20X1	143,040	3,000	192
20X2	156,000	3,200	200
20X3	152,320	2,700	224
20X4	172,000	3,000	235

Required:

(a) Reconcile the cost data to a common price level, to remove differences caused by inflation.

(b) If the line of best fit, based on current (20X4) prices, is calculated as:

$y = 33,000 + 47x$, where y = total production overhead costs in $ and x = the number of machine hours:

calculate the expected total overhead costs in 20X5 if expected production activity is 3,100 machine hours and the expected cost index is 250.

Solution

(a) As the line of best fit is based on 20X4 prices, use this as the common price level. Costs should therefore be adjusted by a factor:

$$\frac{\text{Index level to which costs will be adjusted}}{\text{Actual index level of costs}}$$

Year	Actual overheads	Cost index	Adjustment factor	Costs at 20X4 price level
	$			$
20X1	143,040	192	× 235/192	175,075
20X2	156,000	200	× 235/200	183,300
20X3	152,320	224	× 235/224	159,800
20X4	172,000	235	× 235/235	172,000

(b) If the forecast number of machine hours is 3,100 and the cost index is 250:

Forecast overhead costs = [$33,000 + ($47 × 3,100 hours)] × (250/235)

= $178,700 × (250/235) = $190,106

Correlation

Regression analysis attempts to find the relationship between a number of variables. Correlation is concerned with establishing how strong the relationship is.

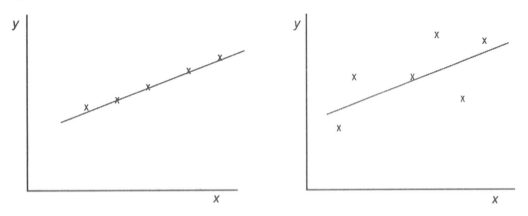

Clearly in the first diagram, the regression line would be a much more useful predictor than the regression line in the second diagram.

In terms of degrees of correlation, two variables might be perfectly correlated, partly correlated, or uncorrelated.

Different types of correlation explained

Perfect correlation

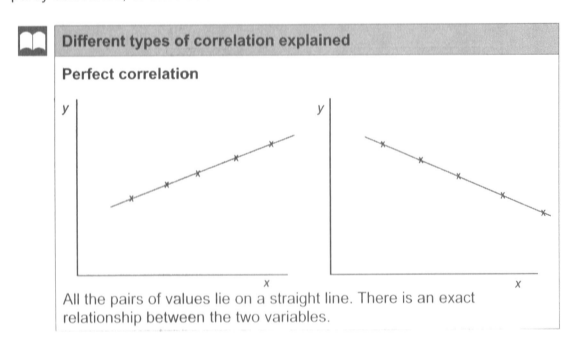

All the pairs of values lie on a straight line. There is an exact relationship between the two variables.

Partial correlation

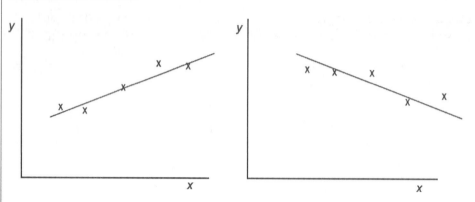

In the first diagram there is not an exact relationship, but low values of x tend to be associated with low values of y, and high values of x tend to be associated with high values of y.

In the second diagram again there is not an exact relationship, but low values of x tend to be associated with high values of y and vice versa.

No correlation

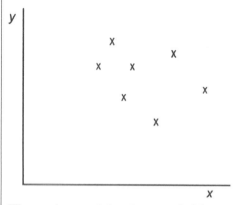

The values of the two variables seem to be completely unconnected.

Positive and negative correlation

Correlation can be positive or negative.

Positive correlation means that high values of one variable are associated with high values of the other and that low values of one are associated with low values of the other.

Negative correlation means that low values of one variable are associated with high values of the other and vice versa.

The correlation coefficient

The degree of correlation can be measured by the Pearsonian correlation coefficient, r (also known as the product moment correlation coefficient).

$$r = \frac{n\sum xy - \sum x \sum y}{\sqrt{\left(n\sum x^2 - \left(\sum x\right)^2\right)\left(n\sum y^2 - \left(\sum y\right)^2\right)}}$$

The calculation of correlation coefficients can be useful in telling us how strongly two sets of data are related to each other – for instance, factory costs in relation to production levels or sales volumes in relation to advertising spend – so that we can decide whether the data can be used to help us forecast.

r must always be between –1 and +1.

If r = 1, there is perfect positive correlation. The data points lie exactly on a straight line of positive gradient.

If r = 0, there is no linear correlation.

If r = –1, there is perfect negative correlation (again the data points lie on a straight line, but with a negative gradient).

For other values of r, the meaning is not so clear. It is generally taken that if r > 0.8, then there is a strong positive correlation and if r < –0.8, there is a strong negative correlation.

However more meaningful information can be gathered from calculating the coefficient of determination, r^2.

Test your understanding 9 – A Co

A Co is assessing the impact of advertising on customer perceived quality of its products.

If the correlation coefficient between variables X (advertising spend) and Y (customer perceived quality) is 0.85, which TWO of the following comments are correct?

A   Values of Y increase as values of X increase

B   Y decreases by 0.15 for every increase of 1 in X

C   Y increases by 0.85 for every increase of 1 in X

D   The link between X and Y values is very strong

E   The link between X and Y values is linear

F   Increases in X cause corresponding increases in Y

The coefficient of determination

This measures how good the estimated regression equation is, designated as r^2 (read as r-squared). The higher the r-squared, the more confidence one can have in the equation. Statistically, the coefficient of determination represents the proportion of the total variation in the y variable that is explained by the regression equation. It has the range of values between 0 and 1.

For example, the following statement "factory overhead is a function of machine hours with $r^2 = 0.80$," can be interpreted as "80% of the total variation of factory overhead is explained by the machine hours and the remaining 20% is accounted for by something other than machine-hours". The 20% is referred to as the **error term**.

> **Test your understanding 10 – Coefficient of determination**
>
> The correlation coefficient (r) for measuring the connection between two variables (x and y) has been calculated as 0.6.
>
> **How much of the variation in the dependent variable (y) is explained by the variation in the independent variable (x)?**
>
> A   36%
>
> B   40%
>
> C   60%
>
> D   64%

Limitations of correlation

(1)   Correlation could be misleading used on sample data. Because an apparent correlation in a sample is not necessarily present in the population from which the sample came from. It could be only due to chance coincidence – a random sampling error. This is why a correlation must be accompanied by a significance test to assess its reliability.

(2)   Correlation and causality are not the same thing. Although a correlation demonstrates that a relationship exists between two variables, it does not automatically imply that one causes the other. Just because X and Y are correlated in some way does not mean that X causes a change in Y, or vice versa.

For instance, if we look at two variables, 'sales of sunglasses' and 'ice cream sales', we know intuitively that there's no way one variable has a cause-and-effect impact on the other. However, both sunglasses sales and ice cream sales will have greater numbers in summer months, so they will be strongly correlated with each other.

(3)   A correlation coefficient of '0' could fail to detect an obvious relationship if it is not a linear one. For example, the correlation coefficient is also 0 in this case:

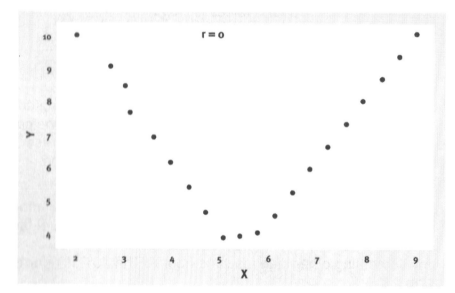

The correlation coefficient will only detect linear relationships. Just because the correlation coefficient is near 0, it doesn't mean that there isn't some type of relationship there.

Time series analysis

Using time series analysis in order to forecast future figures in a budget is a favourite examination topic in the Management Accounting (MA) paper.

In the Performance Management (PM) paper, candidates must be able not only to use the time series techniques to forecast future trends and seasonal variations, but also understand the weaknesses of time series analysis and the problems of using historical data to predict the future.

Time series forecasting methods are based on analysis of historical data. They make the assumption that past patterns in data, such as seasonality, can be used to forecast future data points. This means that its future predictions are more curved than linear.

Definition

A time series is a set of values for some variable (e.g. monthly production) which varies with time. The set of observations will be taken at specific times, usually at regular intervals. Examples of figures which can be plotted as a time series are:

- monthly rainfall in London

- daily closing price of a share on the Stock Exchange

- monthly sales in a department store.

Time series analysis takes historic data and breaks it down into component parts that are easier to extrapolate (predict future values of). In particular, it will isolate the underlying trend.

The basic pattern of a time series can be identified by plotting the recent points of the values on a graph:

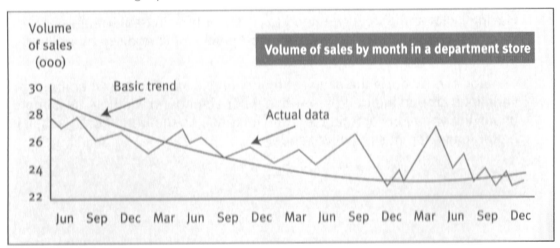

Characteristic time series components

Analysis of time series has revealed certain characteristic movements or variations: the components of the time series. Analysis of these components is essential for forecasting purposes.

The four main types of component are as follows:

- The **basic trend** (long-term): The basic trend refers to the general direction of the graph of a time series over a long interval of time once the short-term variations have been smoothed out. This movement can be represented on the graph by a basic trend curve or line.

- **Cyclical variations** (medium-term): Cyclical variations refer to medium-term oscillations or swings about the basic trend. These cycles may or may not be periodic; they do not necessarily follow exactly similar patterns after equal intervals of time. In business and economic situations movements are said to be cyclical if they recur after time intervals of more than one year. A good example is the trade cycle, representing intervals of boom, decline, recession, and recovery.

- **Random variations** (short-term): Random variations are the sporadic motions of time series due to chance events such as pandemics, floods, strikes, elections, etc. By their very nature, they are unpredictable and therefore cannot play a large part in any forecasting, but it is possible to isolate the random variations by calculating all other types of variation and removing them from the time series data. It is important to extract any significant random variations from the data before using them for forecasting.

- **Seasonal variations** (short-term):

  Seasonal variations are the identical, or almost identical, patterns which a time series follows during corresponding intervals of successive periods. Such movements are due to recurring events such as the sudden increase in department store sales before Christmas. Although, in general, seasonal movements refer to a period of one year, this is not always the case and periods of hours, days, weeks, months, etc. may also be considered, depending on the type of data available.

  Having isolated the trend we need to consider how to deal with the seasonal variations. We will look at two models – the additive model and the multiplicative model.

  The additive model is the simplest model and is satisfactory when the variations around the trend are within a constant band width. If, as is more usual, the variations around the trend increase as the trend itself rises, it is better to use the multiplicative model.

The additive model – finding the seasonal variations

The additive model we will use expresses variations in absolute terms with above and below average figures being shown as positive or negative.

The four components of a time series (T = trend; S = seasonal variation; C = cyclical variation; R = random variation) are expressed as absolute values which are simply added together to produce the actual figures:

Actual data (time series) = T + S + C + R

For unsophisticated analyses over a relatively short period of time cyclical variations (C) and random variations (R) are ignored. Random variations are ignored because they are unpredictable and would not normally exhibit any repetitive pattern, whereas cyclical variations (long-term oscillations) are ignored because their effect is negligible over short periods of time. The model therefore simplifies to:

Actual data = T + S

The seasonal variation is therefore the difference between the computed trend figure and the original time series figure. Thus:

S = Actual – T

Illustration 7 – The additive model

The seasonal variations can be extracted by subtracting each trend value (using the moving averages method) from its corresponding time series value.

Quarter	Original time series (sales, $'000)	Underlying trend	Seasonal variation (S)
	(a)	(b)	(a) – (b)
3	94	100	(6)
4	127	102	25
1	84	106	(22)
2	106	111	(5)

Test Your Understanding 11 – Eastoft Feeds and Fertilisers

Eastoft Feeds and Fertilisers Co uses a number of standard raw materials for its product range. Product F4's main raw material is 'EF1'. The average price per tonne for this material, which is subject to seasonal change, for each quarter during 20X5 is given below. The material is in short supply.

20X5	Q1	Q2	Q3	Q4
Average price per tonne	$40	$44	$64	$76
Seasonal variation	–$4	–$8	+$4	+$8

Use the following table to determine the underlying trend in the average price of raw material 'EF1'.

20X5	Q1	Q2	Q3	Q4
Average price per tonne				
Seasonal variation				
Trend				

Assuming a similar pattern of price movements was to continue, complete the following table to determine the likely purchase price per tonne for each of the 4 quarters of 20X6.

20X6	Q1	Q2	Q3	Q4
Trend (increase of $8 per quarter)				
Seasonal variation				
Forecast price per tonne				

Seasonal variations and the multiplicative model

Some exam questions may give the trend figures and seasonal variations but, instead of the seasonal variations being given in absolute figures as in the additive model that we have used so far, the seasonal variations may be given as percentage figures. This is the case if the **multiplicative model** is used for the time series analysis.

In order to find the forecast figures in this case, simply multiply the trend figure by the seasonal variation percentage and either add it to the trend or deduct it from the trend.

Illustration 8 – The multiplicative model

Given below are the estimated trend figures for a company's sales for the next four quarters:

20X3	Trend
	$
Quarter 1	560,000
Quarter 2	580,000
Quarter 3	605,000
Quarter 4	632,000

The seasonal variations using the multiplicative model have been calculated as:

Quarter 1	+ 15%
Quarter 2	+ 10%
Quarter 3	– 5%
Quarter 4	– 20%

Calculate the forecast sales figures for each of the next four quarters.

Solution

Quarter 1	$560,000 + (560,000 × 0.15) =	$644,000
Quarter 2	$580,000 + (580,000 × 0.10) =	$638,000
Quarter 3	$605,000 – (605,000 × 0.05) =	$574,750
Quarter 4	$632,000 – (632,000 × 0.20) =	$505,600

Note: in some questions, these same seasonal variations may have been given as 1.15, 1.10, 0.95 and 0.80.

Forecast sales would then be determined as:

Quarter 1	$560,000 × 1.15 =	$644,000
Quarter 2	$580,000 × 1.10 =	$638,000
Quarter 3	$605,000 × 0.95 =	$574,750
Quarter 4	$632,000 × 0.80 =	$505,600

Test Your Understanding 12 – IST Co

In IST Co, this year sales amount to $1,325,000. Analysis of recent years show a growth trend of 2% per annum. The seasonal variation has been estimated as follows:

- Quarter 1   +$12,000
- Quarter 2   +$18,000
- Quarter 3   –$25,000
- Quarter 4   –$5,000

You have been asked to forecast the sales for each quarter of next year:

Quarter	$
1	
2	
3	
4	
Year	

Advantages and disadvantages of time series analysis

Advantages	Disadvantages
• Identifies seasonal variations	• Complicated
• Can be non-linear	• 'Seasons' may change
• Accurate	• Based on historical data
	• Less useful in the long term

There are a number of problems with using time series analysis in order to estimate or forecast future results.

- The main problem is the inherent weakness of extrapolation. In order to estimate the trend for the future, the trend line is extended on the graph and the figures read off. However, although the time series has moved in that particular manner in the past, it does not necessarily mean that it will continue to do so in the future.

- The seasonal adjustments used to find the forecast for the future are also based upon historic figures that may well already be out of date. There is no guarantee that the seasonal variations will remain the same in the future. If the time series has a large residual or random variation element, then this will make any forecasts even less reliable.

Conclusions on quantitative techniques

Different forecasting techniques have been explored here (and there are many more in the real world). **Linear regression** is most relevant when there is a linear relationship between the variables, **time series analysis** is most appropriate when seasonal variations cause curved forecasts.

The reliability of a forecasting method can be established over time. If forecasts turn out to be inaccurate, management might decide that they are not worth producing, and that different methods of forecasting should be tried. On the other hand, if forecasts prove to be reasonably accurate, management are likely to continue with the same forecasting method.

12 Chapter summary

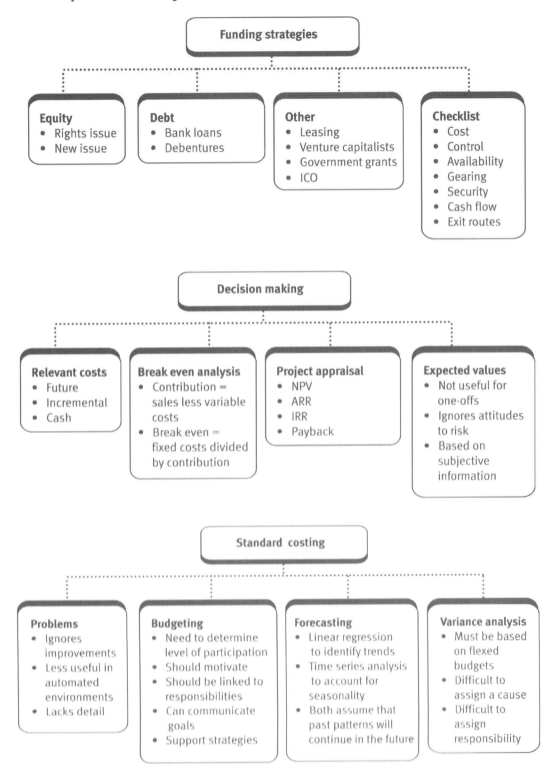

Funding strategies

Equity
- Rights issue
- New issue

Debt
- Bank loans
- Debentures

Other
- Leasing
- Venture capitalists
- Government grants
- ICO

Checklist
- Cost
- Control
- Availability
- Gearing
- Security
- Cash flow
- Exit routes

Decision making

Relevant costs
- Future
- Incremental
- Cash

Break even analysis
- Contribution = sales less variable costs
- Break even = fixed costs divided by contribution

Project appraisal
- NPV
- ARR
- IRR
- Payback

Expected values
- Not useful for one-offs
- Ignores attitudes to risk
- Based on subjective information

Standard costing

Problems
- Ignores improvements
- Less useful in automated environments
- Lacks detail

Budgeting
- Need to determine level of participation
- Should motivate
- Should be linked to responsibilities
- Can communicate goals
- Support strategies

Forecasting
- Linear regression to identify trends
- Time series analysis to account for seasonality
- Both assume that past patterns will continue in the future

Variance analysis
- Must be based on flexed budgets
- Difficult to assign a cause
- Difficult to assign responsibility

Test your understanding answers

Test your understanding 1

Strategic and operational decisions

The major change in emphasis will be that decisions will now have to be made on a largely commercial basis. Profit and share price considerations will become paramount. Examples of where significant changes might occur are:

- financing decision: The firm will have to compete for a wide range of sources of finance. Choices between various types of finance will now have to be made, e.g. debt versus equity

- dividend decision: The firm will now have to consider its policy on dividend payout to shareholders

- investment decision: Commercial rather than social considerations will become of major importance. Diversification into other products and markets will now be possible. Expansion by merger and take-over can also be considered

- threat of take-over: If the government completely relinquishes its ownership it is possible that the firm could be subject to take-over bids

- other areas: Pricing, marketing, staffing, etc., will now be largely free of government constraints.

Test your understanding 2

There are a number of differences between the sources of finance that the directors at Olsen should consider.

There appears to be differences in the covenants. Whilst the loan notes involve some covenants the bank covenants are extensive. This may limit Olsen's ability to increase dividends, raise further debt or issue new shares without the banks approval. This would make the bank loan less attractive for Olsen.

In terms of availability the bank loan appears to be a definite offer from Olsen's bank. The loan notes, however, may not be fully subscribed – particularly if investors are wary of buying debt in a company that is making losses. There will also be higher issues costs associated with the loan notes which would make them less attractive to Olsen.

There is a difference in the length of the finance options. An acquisition is a long-term investment, particularly in this scenario where it will take a couple of years for Olsen to turn Albiston around. Olsen should therefore aim to secure finance over the longest period possible. The bank loan has a longer period of six years and would be better for this purpose.

The loan notes appear to be cheaper, with an annual cost of 7% compared to the bank loan cost of 8% p.a. However, it may be that if interest rates fall in the future the bank loan would become more attractive in terms of cost (and vice versa). Olsen needs to consider market expectations on the future of interest rates in the economy. If interest rates are expected to fall then the bank loan may become cheaper in the long term.

In terms of cash flow, the loan notes would appear to be preferable (at least in the short term). The coupon interest is much smaller and most of the cost is attributed to the redemption on premium which doesn't arise for four years. As Albiston will be making losses for a couple of years it would be preferable to delay debt repayments and interest for as long as possible. The bank loan is also less attractive as its interest payments are made six monthly which will put added pressure on cash flows.

There is a discrepancy in the terms of the security required for each source of finance. The loan notes will be secured on the assets of both Olsen and Albiston whilst the bank loan will only use Albiston's assets as security. This means that if the acquisition was to fail (which is a possibility given the losses experienced at Albiston) then with the bank loan Olsen would not have to make any further capital injections.

Overall, there are a lot of factors that the board should take into account. However, the bank loan appears to be less risky and has a longer period and therefore it would appear to be a more attractive source of finance.

Professional skill:

It is the final paragraph which covers the necessary professional skill. The answer is showing a clear understanding of the key issues to be considered when determining the best solution for Olsen. This displays strong commercial acumen.

Test your understanding 3

Firstly we need to calculate the break-even sales revenue.

Because we haven't been given any information on units, we must have to use the contribution sales revenue technique:

$$\text{C/S ratio} = \frac{\text{Total contribution}}{\text{Total sales revenue}} = \frac{(450 - 220)}{450}$$

$$= 0.511 \text{ (or } 51.1\%)$$

$$\text{Break-even point (in terms of sales revenue)} = \frac{\text{Fixed costs}}{\text{C/S ratio}}$$

$$\text{Break-even point (in terms of sales revenue)} = \frac{\$160{,}000}{0.511}$$

$$\text{Break-even point (in terms of sales revenue)} = \$313{,}000$$

Now that we know the break-even position we can calculate the margin of safety (this is what is required in the second element of the question).

$$\text{Margin of safety (as a \% of budgeted sales)} = \frac{\text{Budgeted sales} - \text{Break-even sales}}{\text{Budgeted sales}} \times 100\%$$

$$\text{Margin of safety (as a \% of budgeted sales)} = \frac{450 - 313}{450} \times 100\%$$

$$= 0.3044 \text{ (or } 30.44\%)$$

This tells us that for the company to fall into a loss making position its sales next year would have to fall by over 30.44% from their current position.

Test your understanding 4

Annual internal processing costs

Hardware and software	$320
Hardware/software annual maintenance	$750
Accounting stationery	$500
Part time accounts clerk	$6,000
	———
Total	$7,570
	———

Annual outsourcing costs

Processing of invoices/credit notes	$2,500	5,000 × $0.50
Processing of cheque payments	$2,000	4,000 × $0.50
Reconciling supplier accounts	$3,600	150 × $2 × 12
	———	
Total	$8,100	
	———	

It would not be cost effective to outsource the accounting activities. The present costs of $7,570 would rise to $8,100 p.a.

Qualitative factors include:

- predicted volumes – higher volumes will make outsourcing more expensive

- the quality of supply – will the external supplier make more errors?

- security of information.

Test your understanding 5

Year 1

Expected value = ($40 × 60%) + ($20 × 40%) = $32m.

Year 2

Expected value = [($80 × 90%) + ($30 × 10%)] × 60% + [($30 × 20%) + ($10 × 80%)] × 40%

= [$75 × 60%] + [$14 × 40%] = $50.6m

Test your understanding 6

(a) An incremental budget starts off with last year's budget or last year's actual results and adds on a certain percentage to take account of expected inflation and/or any expected changes in the level of activity. It is a very simple, quick and cheap budget to produce, but it does not promote a questioning attitude. Activities are undertaken without thought. They are simply incorporated into the next budget because they were in the last budget and nobody has given any thought as to whether the activity is still really worthwhile.

With ZBB, each manager sets out what he or she wishes to accomplish over the forthcoming period. For each activity they want to undertake, they look at different ways of achieving the objective and they look at providing the service at different levels. They estimate the costs and benefits and the activity only takes place if the benefits exceed the costs. Also once all the activities have been evaluated, they can be ranked against each other and the company's resources directed to the best activities.

(b) The managers/researchers responsible for each project should decide which projects they wish to undertake in the forthcoming period. These projects will be a mixture of continued projects and new projects. For the projects which have already been started and which the managers want to continue in the next period, we should ignore any cash flows already incurred (they are sunk costs), and we should only look at future costs and benefits. Similarly, for the new projects we should only look at the future costs and benefits. Different ways of achieving the same research goals should also be investigated and the projects should only go ahead if the benefit exceeds the cost. Once all the potential projects have been evaluated if there are insufficient funds to undertake all the worthwhile projects, then the funds should be allocated to the best projects on the basis of a cost-benefit analysis.

ZBB is usually of a highly subjective nature. (The costs are often reasonably certain, but usually a lot of uncertainty is attached to the estimated benefits.) This will be even truer of a research division where the researchers may have their own pet projects which they are unable to view in an objective light.

(c)   (i)   Activity-based budgeting is where the budget is based upon a number of different levels of activity, i.e. on a number of different cost drivers, rather than being based on just one level of activity such as machine hours or output in units.

The activity-based budget will be based upon the number of units of the cost driver multiplied by the cost per unit of cost driver. The cost driver is that factor which actually causes the cost and therefore should lead to a more accurate budget as the budgeted cost will be based on the thing that should influence that cost. The alternative is to use absorption costing and assume that all overheads vary with output or machine hours or labour hours or that they are fixed.

(ii)   Z may employ an outside specialist such as a management consultant who will investigate the business and determine what activities the business undertakes during the course of its operations.

The consultant will discuss matters with the staff and the process will normally be time consuming. For each activity, efforts will be made to determine the factor which is most closely related to the costs of that activity, i.e. the cost driver. The investigation may bring to light non-value-added activities which can then be eliminated. It should improve the understanding of all those involved as to the true relationship between cost and level of activity.

Managers would then estimate the expected incidence of their cost drivers and multiply by the budgeted cost driver rate to get the budget for the forthcoming period. ABB would be more complicated than a traditional budget and the overheads would be broken down into many activities such as set-up costs, materials, handling costs, etc rather than expenses such as rent, heating, depreciation, etc.

With ABB the majority of the overhead costs would be perceived as variable rather than fixed. Of course it is not necessary to employ an outside consultant. The company may feel that they have their own managers with sufficient skills and time to undertake the exercise.

Test your understanding 7

The PD does appear to have reduced the overall spending on materials but this is not a true analysis of his team's performance as the original target was for the production and sales of 28,000 units but only 21,000 units were produced. Therefore the materials budget should be adjusted to provide a 'flexed' budget of $1,050,000.

This is then compared to the actual cost of $1,365,000 to provide an adverse variance of $315,000. This can be fully attributed to the increased cost of components purchased. This could reflect very poorly on PD.

However, it is important to remember that many variances are interrelated. Subject to strategic impacts on areas such as competitive advantages gained through product design, this variance may be acceptable to the board if it subsequently leads to an overall positive impact on profits for Buchan if a positive impact on sales is generated.

The overall sales variance is neutral. The actual sales price was $400 which, when compared to the budgeted sales price of $300 provides a favourable variance of $2.1m. It would therefore appear that the sales team have ignored SD's advice to adhere to the recommended selling price and have instead increased it by $100. This may have been due to the sales team expecting to be able to sell the product at a higher price due to the usage of the better component used in production.

However, the sales price variance is wiped out by the sales volume variance. Buchan will have lost market share as the market has continued to expand. It shows that the decision to increase the selling price was a poor one and that the sales department are greatly at fault for the downturn in Buchan's performance. It may be that, had the sales team maintained the selling price at $300 actual sales volume may have been above the 28,000 units budgeted for and that PD's purchasing decision may have been vindicated.

Due to the interdependence between these variances it is difficult to determine who exactly is to be blamed for the downturn in Buchan's performance. Nonetheless, it can be said that SD's failure to control the sales team's actions on adhering to the recommended selling price reflects poorly on him.

Professional skill:

Evaluation skills can be illustrated by linking together the cause and effect of the directors' actions. For example, highlighting that the increase in sales price will lead to a fall in sales volume. Or that a rise in sales volume may have vindicated PD's decision.

Test your understanding 8 – Marcus Aurelius, continued

(a)

	$000
Sales revenue = $300k + (5 × $150k) =	1,050
Sales revenue = $300k + (5 × $50k) =	550

(b) The second prediction is the more reliable as it involves interpolation. The first prediction goes beyond the original data upon which the regression line was based and thus assumes that the relationship will continue on in the same way, which may not be true.

Test your understanding 9 – A Co

A and D

The correlation is positive and hence values of Y typically increase as values of X increase.

Numerically, its 'r' value is close to 1 and hence the link between X and Y values is very strong.

We can never deduce cause and effect from any correlation coefficient, however large, so (F) is incorrect as are the numerical comments in (B) and (C).

(E) is incorrect because a linear relationship between ranks of values does not necessarily imply one between the values themselves.

Test your understanding 10 – Coefficient of determination

A

Coefficient of determination = r^2 = 0.6 × 0.6 = 0.36 = 36%

Test Your Understanding 11 – Eastoft Feeds and Fertilisers

Trend:

20X5	Q1	Q2	Q3	Q4
Average price per tonne	$40	$44	$64	$76
Seasonal variation	–$4	–$8	+$4	+$8
Trend	$44	$52	$60	$68

Forecast:

20X6	Q1	Q2	Q3	Q4
Trend (increase of $8 per quarter)	$76	$84	$92	$100
Seasonal variation	–$4	–$8	+$4	+$8
Forecast price per tonne	$72	$76	$96	$108

Test Your Understanding 12 – IST Co

Next Year's sales = $1,325,000 × (1 + 2%)

Next Year's sales = $1,351,500

Next Year's quarterly sales = $1,351,500 / 4 = $337,875 per quarter

- Quarter 1   sales = $337,875 + $12,000 = $349,875

- Quarter 2   sales = $337,875 + $18,000 = $355,875

- Quarter 3   sales = $337,875 – $25,000 = $312,875

- Quarter 4   sales = $337,875 – $5,000 = $332,875

Quarter	$
1	$349,875
2	$355,875
3	$312,875
4	$332,875
Year	$1,351,500

Managing strategic change

Chapter learning objectives

Upon completion of this chapter you will be able to:

- evaluate different types of strategic change and their implications

- assess implications of change in an organisation using Balogun and Hope Hailey's contextual features

- manage change in an organisation using Lewin's three stage model

- analyse opportunities for organisational improvement using the four view POPIT (people, organisation, processes and information technology) model.[3]

- discuss how talent management can contribute to supporting organisation strategy

PER

One of the PER performance objectives (PO3) is that you contribute to the wider business strategy of your organisation through your personal and team objectives. You identify innovative ways to improve organisational performance – which may include making or recommending business process changes and improvements. Working through this chapter should help you understand how to demonstrate that objective.

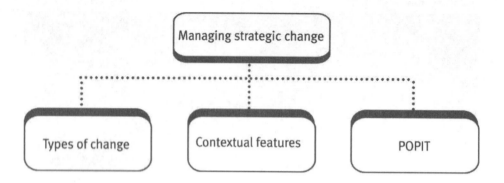

1   Strategic change

Across many parts of this study text it has been suggested that an organisation may have to change its strategy. This may be forced upon it by changes in its environment or it may be a deliberate attempt to do things such as placing the organisation in a new competitive position. This chapter examines how strategic change can be managed in order for it to be achieved successfully.

Types of strategic change

Change can be classified by the extent of the change required, and the speed with which the change is to be achieved:

Incremental	**Evolution**	**Adaptation**
Speed of change		
	Revolution	**Reconstruction**

Big Bang   Transformation   Realignment

Extent of change

📖 **Further explanation**

Explanation of the axes

Transformation	This entails changing an organisation's culture. It is a fundamental change that cannot be handled within the existing organisational paradigm.
Realignment	This does not involve a fundamental reappraisal of the central assumptions and beliefs.
Incremental change	This can take a long period of time, but results in a fundamentally different organisation once completed.
Big Bang change	This change is likely to be a forced, reactive transformation using simultaneous initiatives on many fronts, and often in a relatively short space of time.

Explanation of the types of change

Adaptation	This is the most common type of change. It is slow and gradual and is based on the existing culture, processes and competencies.
Reconstruction	This is a much quicker change, often brought about by sudden external pressures such as a new competitor innovation or a change in the regulatory environment. The change may also be motivated by a sudden downturn in financial performance. The organisation may launch many initiatives at the same time, rather than aim for the gradual approach associated with an adaptation.
Evolution	In anticipation of the need for future change an organisation will aim to change its culture over time. Johnson, Scholes and Whittington suggest that this can be the most challenging type of change as there is no immediate need for it but it will be vital to the long-term success of the organisation. It might be best supported by a switch to a more learning organisation with a clear commitment to sustained change.
Revolution	This involves rapid and fundamental change within an organisation. It may follow a period of strategic flux and the organisation is likely to be facing extreme external pressure for change. Culture within the organisation is likely to have to significantly adapt to new processes, products, markets and objectives. Without this change in culture the change (and the organisation) will usually fail. Many new initiatives are likely to be launched simultaneously in order to reverse the organisation's direction.

Illustration 1 – Strategic change

Strategic change is by definition far-reaching. We speak of strategic change when fundamental alterations are made to the business system or the organisational system. Adding a lemon-flavoured Coke to the product portfolio is interesting, maybe important, but not a strategic change, while branching out into bottled water was – it was a major departure from Coca-Cola's traditional business system.

Selecting an approach to strategic change

As explained in an earlier chapter, within incremental change there may be a danger of strategic drift, because change is based on the existing paradigm and routines of the organisation, even when environmental or competitive pressure might suggest the need for more fundamental change.

In selecting an approach to strategic change, most managers struggle with the question of how bold they should be. On the one hand, they usually realise that to fundamentally transform the organisation, a break with the past is needed. To achieve strategic renewal it is essential to turn away from the firm's heritage and to start with a clean slate. On the other hand, they also recognise the value of continuity, building on past experiences, investments and loyalties. To achieve lasting strategic renewal, people in the organisation will need time to learn, adapt and grow into a new organisational reality.

The 'window of opportunity' for achieving a revolutionary strategic change can be small for a number of reasons. Some of the most common triggers are:

- competitive pressure – when a firm is under intense competitive pressure and its market position starts to erode quickly, a rapid and dramatic response might be the only approach possible. Especially when the organisation threatens to slip into a downward spiral towards insolvency, a bold turnaround can be the only option left to the firm.

- regulatory pressure – firms can also be put under pressure by the government or regulatory agencies to push through major changes within a short period of time. Such externally imposed revolutions can be witnessed among public sector organisations (e.g. hospitals and schools) and highly regulated industries (e.g. utilities and telecommunications), but in other sectors of the economy as well (e.g. public health regulations). Some larger organisations will, however, seek to influence and control regulation.

- first mover advantage – a more proactive reason for instigating revolutionary change, is to be the first firm to introduce a new product, service or technology and to build up barriers to entry for late movers.

Test your understanding 1

Briefly explain the four types of strategic change in an organisation.

2 The influence of organisational culture on change

Transformational change will often require a fundamental change in the organisational culture. A new brand (symbol) may be required, the level of organisational flexibility may need to be changed (controls), new routines may have to be employed etc. So that the cultural web (studied elsewhere in this text) may need to be re-examined and changed.

Many organisations find that some elements of the cultural web are easier to change than others. For example, it may be easier to change the formal organisational structure than it is to change long established routines and habits.

3 What is culture?

Organisational culture is an important concept since it has a widespread influence on the behaviours and actions of employees. It represents a powerful force on an organisation's strategies, structures and systems, the way it responds to change and ultimately, how well the organisation performs.

Handy described culture as:

'the way we do things around here'

By this Handy means the sum total of the **belief, knowledge, attitudes, norms** and **customs** that prevail in an organisation.

4 Levels of culture

According to Edgar Schein (1992)

Culture exists at three different levels:

1   **Artefacts**. These are the things that can be seen, heard and observed. This is largely the view of the organisation that the public experience. It can include items such as:

   —   Dress codes. Is the dress code formal or informal, for example are uniforms worn?

   —   Patterns of behaviour. This is the way people within the organisation are seen as acting.

   —   Physical symbols. This could include logos and branding.

   —   Office layout. This includes the facilities and furnishings.

2   **Espoused Values**. These can be identified from stories and the opinions of those within the organisation. It can include items such as:

- Language. This is the way people communicate both within and outside the organisation.

- Behaviour. This shows what the people in the organisation feel is important.

- How people justify what they do. These values can be deep rooted, many will take for granted that their behaviour is acceptable without questioning it.

3   **Basic assumptions**. These beliefs are so deeply embedded in a culture that members are no longer consciously aware of them. They can include:

- Beliefs on environmental issues. If this is important, it will be part of every aspect of the work done.

- How people should be treated. This will include human relations policies, customer relationships etc.

As you go through the levels, the elements become less visible and more ingrained. At the third level, those within the organisation may not even be aware of their beliefs, they have become so fundamentally part of their way of being.

For an organisation, understanding this helps them to anticipate problems with their culture and allows them to see how difficult it may be to change. Changing level one items, such as dress codes or office layouts, is relatively easy, but changing values and beliefs can be very difficult. This may also lead to differences between the levels, for example what the organisation says and does may be different to how it is perceived by the outside world. The public may view certain acts as superficial and often do not believe that the underlying beliefs of the organisation have really changed.

The organisational iceberg

The idea of hidden elements in culture is often referred to as the organisational iceberg.

The iceberg describes two levels at which culture operates:

- Formal aspects (visible) above the water

- Behavioural aspects (hidden) below the water.

The elements of culture above the surface would include:

- goals

- technology

- procedures

- structure

- skills.

The hidden elements represent the larger part of the iceberg which is below the water, and that would include:

- attitudes
- style
- communication patterns
- values
- feelings
- beliefs.

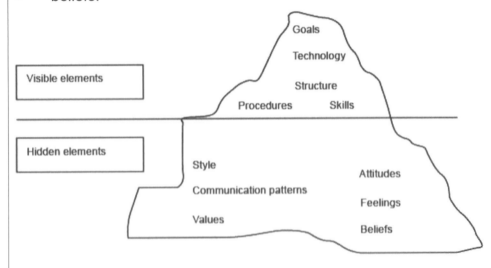

The diagram shows that what the public, customers, suppliers and others outside of an organisation see is only a small part of the picture. Much of what makes the organisation what it is, is intangible or hidden from view. It suggests that it is really only possible to fully understand the workings and culture of an organisation from within.

 Using the "Cultural Web" to map change

The concept of the cultural web is a useful device for mapping out change but its real worth is in the fact that we can identify which elements of culture need to change. Questions to ask include:

Stories	
	• What core belief do the stories in my place reflect?
	• How pervasive are these beliefs (through the levels of the organisation)?
	• Do stories relate to: strengths or weaknesses, successes or failures, conformity or mavericks? Who are the heroes and villains?
	• What norms do the mavericks deviate from?

Routines and rituals	• What behaviour do routines encourage? Which would look odd if changed?
	• What are the key rituals? What core beliefs do they reflect?
	• What do training programmes emphasise?
	• How easy are the rituals/routines to change?
Organisational structures	• How mechanistic/organic are the structures in my organisation?
	• How flat/hierarchical are the structures? How formal/informal are they?
	• Do structures encourage collaboration or competition?
	• What types of power structure do they support?
Control systems	• What is most closely monitored/controlled in my organisation?
	• Is emphasis on reward or punishment? Are there many/few controls?
	• Are controls related to history or current strategies?
Power structures	• What are the core beliefs of the leadership in my organisation?
	• How strongly held are these beliefs (idealists or pragmatists)?
	• How is power distributed in the organisation?
	• What are the main blockages to change?
Symbols	• What language and jargon are used in my place of work?
	• How internal or accessible are they?
	• What aspects of strategy are highlighted in publicity?
	• What status symbols are there?
	• Are there particular symbols that denote the organisation?
Overall	• What is the dominant culture? How easy is this to change?

However, any change to organisational culture has potential to come up against levels of resistance from staff – staff who have a lot of power from their current organisational role, for example, may be very reluctant to give up this power. A change leader therefore needs to examine how this resistance might be overcome.

Test your understanding 2
Which element of the cultural web is explained by the following?
'The processes in place to monitor what is going on.'
A   Organisational structures
B   Power structures
C   The paradigm
D   Control systems

Why is culture important?

Culture is that invisible bond, which ties the people of a community together. It refers to the pattern of human activity. The importance of culture lies in its close association with the way of living of the people. The different cultures of the world have brought in diversity in the ways of life of the people inhabiting different parts of the world.

Culture is related to the development of one's attitude. The cultural values of an individual have a deep impact on his/her attitude towards life. They shape an individual's thinking and influence his/her mindset.

- It gives an individual a unique identity.

- The culture of a community gives its people a character of their own.

- Culture shapes the personality of a community. This includes the language that a community speaks, the art forms it hosts, its staple food, its customs, traditions and festivities comprise the community's culture.

Advantages of having a strong culture

An organisation's culture has a significant bearing on the way it relates to its stakeholders (especially customers and staff), the development of its strategy and its structure. A strong culture will:

- facilitate good communication and co-ordination within the organisation.

- provide a framework of social identity and a sense of belonging.

- reduce differences amongst the members of the organisation.

- strengthen the dominant values and attitudes.

- regulate behaviour and norms among members of the organisation.

- minimise some of the perceptual differences among people within the organisation.

- reflect the philosophy and values of the organisation's founder or dominant group.

- affect the organisation's strategy and ability to respond to change.

Disadvantages of having a strong culture

A strong culture that does not have positive attributes in relation to stakeholders and change is a hindrance to effectiveness. Other disadvantages of a strong culture are:

- Strong cultures are difficult to change, beliefs which underpin culture can be deep rooted.

- Strong cultures may have a blinkered view which could affect the organisation's ability or desire to learn new skills.

- Strong cultures may stress inappropriate values. A strong culture which is positive can enhance the performance of the organisation, but a strong culture which is negative can have the opposite effect.

- Where two strong cultures come into contact e.g., in a merger, then conflicts can arise.

- A strong culture may not be attuned to the environment e.g., a strong innovative culture is only appropriate in a dynamic, shifting environment.

Influences on culture

The structure and culture of an organisation will develop over time and will be determined by a complex set of variables, including:

Size	How large is the organisation in terms of turnover, physical size and employee numbers?
Technology	How technologically advanced is the organisation either in terms of its product, or its productive processes?
Diversity	How diverse is the company either in terms of product range, geographical spread or cultural make-up of its stakeholders?
Age	How old is the business or the managers of the business? Do its strategic level decision makers have experience to draw upon?
History	What worked in the past? Do decision makers have past successes to draw upon? Are they willing to learn from their mistakes?
Ownership	Is the organisation owned by a sole trader? Is there a small number of institutional shareholders or are there large numbers of small shareholders?

When analysing an organisation, look for clues given as to the culture of the organisation using these main areas, although there are many other influences, including the leadership style adopted.

Other influences on culture

As well as the main influences on culture listed above, there are other, more subtle influences:

- The degree of individual initiative – is it encouraged or are decisions always referred upwards?

- The degree of risk tolerance – are managers only allowed to follow low-risk strategies?

- Clarity of direction – is there a clear focus; are these clear objectives and performance expectations?

- The degree of integration between groups – are different units encouraged to work together? Are management aloof or approachable; is communication clear to lower level staff?

- The reward system – are individuals rewarded for succeeding, i.e. are rewards based on performance criteria?

- Conflict tolerance – are employees encouraged to air grievances?

- Communication patterns – is there a formal hierarchy or an informal network?

- Formalisation of clothing and office layout – are there strict rules over this?

- The kind of people employed – are they graduates, young, old, etc.?

5 Resistance to change

Resistance to change is the action taken by individuals and groups when they perceive that a change that is occurring is a threat to them.

Resistance is 'any attitude or behaviour that reflects a person's unwillingness to make or support a desired change'.

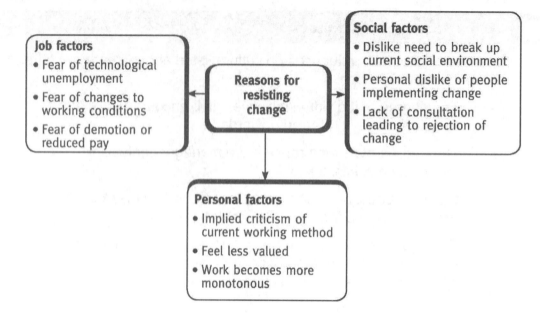

Resistance may take many forms, including active or passive, overt or covert, individual or organised, aggressive or timid. For each source of resistance, management need to provide an appropriate response.

Reasons for resisting change

According to Kotter and Schlesinger (1979) there are four reasons that explain why certain people resist change:

- Parochial self-interest (some people are concerned with the implication of the change for themselves and how it may affect their own interests, rather than considering the effects for the success of the business).

- Misunderstanding (communication problems; inadequate information).

- Low tolerance to change (certain people are very keen on security and stability in their work).

- Different assessments of the situation (some employees may disagree on the reasons for the change and on the advantages and disadvantages of the change process).

Test your understanding 3

Your organisation is going through a big upheaval and you are not very pleased – in fact you are quite worried.

What could your manager do or say to increase your resistance?

KAPLAN PUBLISHING

6 Overcoming resistance

Lewin

Kurt Lewin developed a simple model for achieving successful change and overcoming resistance in three steps:

- Unfreezing – create the initial motivation to change by convincing staff of the undesirability of the present situation.

- The change process itself – mainly concerned with identifying what the new behaviour or norm should be. This stage will often involve new information being communicated and new attitudes, culture and concepts being adopted.

- Refreezing or stabilising the change – ensuring that the new process and systems become a natural part of the organisation's culture (implying reinforcement of the new pattern of work or behaviour through changed rewards systems etc.).

> **Further details**
>
> **Unfreezing**
>
> The first element of the model is to break down and remove the current resistance to change. Staff need to be convinced that the current system is not successful and needs to change. Failures in the current culture, whether that be in its structure, people's routines or organisational controls etc. need to be examined and explained. The benefits of a proposed new system need to be clearly communicated to staff – this may require some of the strong leadership styles explored in the next part of this chapter.
>
> The aim is to motivate staff to make the change and to reduce their level of resistance. Their attitudes are 'unfrozen', they are no longer 'stuck in their ways', and they are now willing to make the change.
>
> **Changing**
>
> The new system and the associated changes can now be implemented. Again, this may require hands-on leadership and it will most certainly require good communication. Some change will have to be supported by additional training and resources.

Refreezing

The new system now needs to become part of the organisational culture. It needs to feel natural to staff. This may require a new reward structure linked to the new system, new rules/controls, new targets etc. Organisations will create new stories around the success of the change, they should aim to celebrate successes and communicate to staff how the expected benefits are being achieved. This should help imbed the change as part of the old culture. The aim is to ensure that staff do not fall back on old habits and want to return to the old culture and way of doing things.

Some argue that the refreezing step is outdated in contemporary business due to the continuous need for change. They find it unnecessary to spend time freezing a new state when chances are it will need to be re-evaluated and possibly changed again in the immediate future. However, without the refreezing step, there is a high chance that people will revert back to the old way of doing things. Taking one step forward and two steps back can be a common theme when organisations overlook the refreezing step in anticipation of future change.

Lewin's force field analysis

Lewin also emphasised the importance of force field analysis. He argued that managers should consider any change situation in terms of:

- the factors encouraging and facilitating the change (the driving forces)

- the factors that hinder change (the restraining forces).

If we want to bring about change we must disturb the equilibrium by:

- strengthening the driving forces

- weakening the restraining forces

- or both.

The model encourages us to identify the various forces impinging on the target of change, to consider the relative strengths of these forces and to explore alternative strategies for modifying the force field.

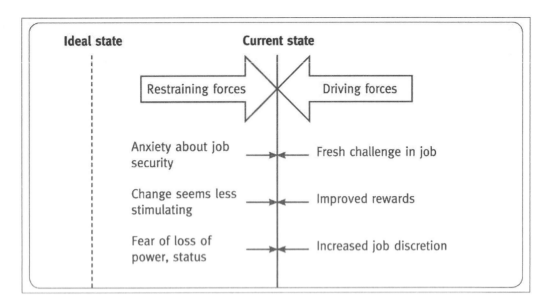

Test your understanding 4

WW is a company specialising in industrial paint manufacturing. It has recently experienced significant growth in turnover and has opened two new factories to help it cope with the additional demand.

The managers of WW have become concerned that their current accounting software is no longer adequate for their needs. The current system is a basic one, which is mainly designed to record transactions and produce financial statements at the end of each period. Given the growth in the business, the managers of WW now need additional information, such as the production of monthly management reports and the ability to accurately cost each unit of their products.

The current accounting system does not support these functions, meaning the accounting department is required to produce the information manually, which is both complex and time-consuming.

WW's managers are concerned that this delay in obtaining management information may be putting the firm at a disadvantage in the marketplace.

The managers are therefore currently considering the purchase of a new, more complex, accounting package that will easily allow the production of the management accounting information that they need.

WW has a small accounting department with six members of staff. All of these staff members have been employees of the company for many years. The current accounting package has been in use within WW for the last seven years.

Required:

Explain how WW could manage the changeover to the new accounting package.

Leadership styles

Kotter and Schlesinger believe that successful change is achieved through strong leadership. They set out the following change approaches to deal with resistance:

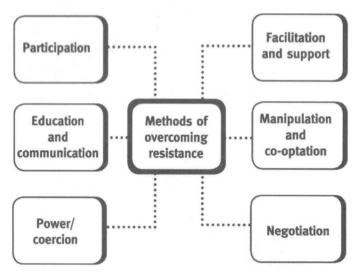

Explanation of the Kotter and Schlesinger styles

- Participation – aims to involve employees, usually by allowing some input into decision making. This could easily result in employees enjoying raised levels of autonomy, by allowing them to design their own jobs, pay structures, etc.
- Education and communication – used as a background factor to reinforce another approach. This strategy relies upon the hopeful belief that communication about the benefits of change to employees will result in their acceptance of the need to exercise the changes necessary.
- Power/coercion – involves the compulsory approach by management to implement change. This method finds its roots from the formal authority that management possesses, together with legislative support.
- Facilitation and support – employees may need to be counselled to help them overcome their fears and anxieties about change. Management may find it necessary to develop individual awareness of the need for change.
- Manipulation and co-optation – involves covert attempts to sidestep potential resistance. The information that is disseminated is selective and distorted to only emphasise the benefits of the change. Co-optation involves giving key people access to the decision-making process.
- Negotiation – is often practised in unionised companies. Simply, the process of negotiation is exercised, enabling several parties with opposing interests to bargain. This bargaining leads to a situation of compromise and agreement.

When to use each style

Strategies: addressing resistance to change			
Approach/ style	**Situations used**	**Advantages**	**Disadvantages**
Education + Communication	Where there is a lack of or inaccurate information and analysis.	If persuaded, people will help with the implementation of change.	Can be time consuming if many people are involved.
Participation + Involvement	Where initiators do not have all information to design change, and where others have power to resist.	Participants are committed to implementing change including their relevant contribution.	Can be very time consuming with possibly inappropriate changes made.
Facilitation + Support	Where resistance comes from adjustment problems.	Best approach for adjustment issues.	Can be time consuming, expensive and still fail.
Negotiation + Agreement	Where one group will lose out and has power to resist.	Can be an easy way to avoid major resistance.	Can be too expensive if it leads to general compliance.
Strategies: addressing resistance to change			
Approach/ style	**Situations used**	**Advantages**	**Disadvantages**
Manipulation + Co-optation	Where other tactics won't work or are too costly.	Can be a relatively quick and inexpensive solution to resistance.	Can lead to future problems if people feel they have been manipulated.
Explicit + Implicit Coercion	Where speed is essential, and the change initiators possess considerable power.	It is speedy and can overcome any kind of resistance.	Can be risky if it leaves people angry at the initiators.

Test your understanding 5

A manager is in charge of a team that has been given the task of introducing a new management reporting system into regional offices. There is considerable resistance to the changes from the office managers, and comments that you have heard include the following:

- I have more important work priorities to take up my time.

- I'm used to the old system.

- The new system is too complicated.

- The new system will create more paperwork.

- The new system will make me more accountable.

- My job in the new system is not clear.

How would you try to deal with this resistance to change?

7   The context for change (Balogun and Hope Hailey)

For change to be successful, implementation efforts need to fit the organisational context. There is no simple 'off the shelf' approach that will work for all organisations. Balogun and Hope Hailey suggest that there are a number of **contextual features** that should be considered before an implementation approach (for example a style of leadership) for the change is determined:

- time

- scope

- preservation

- diversity

- capability

- capacity

- readiness

- power

Explanation of the model

Contextual features can be seen as existing within an overall change kaleidoscope. This was developed by Julia Balogun and Veronica Hope Hailey to help managers design such a 'context sensitive' approach to change.

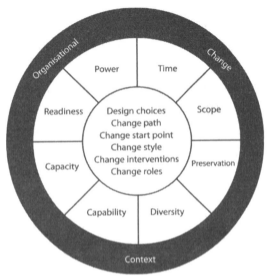

The kaleidoscope has three rings:

- The outer ring relates to the wider strategic change context.

- The middle ring relates to specific contextual factors that need to be considered when formulating a change plan.

- The inner circle gives a menu of choices and interventions ('design choices') available to change agents.

Contextual features

- **Time** – is there time for longer-term strategic development or does the firm have to react quickly to a crisis?

- **Scope** – how much of the organisation will be affected? Is the change best described as realignment or transformation?

- **Preservation** – which aspects of working, culture, competences and people need to be retained?

- **Diversity** – the need to recognise that different departments (e.g. marketing and R&D) may have different sub-cultures.

- **Capability** – whether abilities exist to cope with the change. These can be on an individual, managerial or organisational level.

- **Capacity** – are resources (e.g. money, managerial time) available to invest in the change process?

- **Readiness** – are staff aware of the need for change and are they committed to that change?

- **Power** – how much authority and autonomy do change agents have to make proposed changes?

Each of these factors can be assessed as positive, negative or neutral in the context of change. Positive features facilitate change and negative ones restrict change.

Design choices

Design choices represent the key features of a change management approach:

- **Change path** – clarifying the types of change in terms of timescales, the extent of change and the desired outcomes.

- **Change start point** – where the change is initiated (e.g. top-down or bottom up).

- **Change style** – which management style should be adopted (e.g. collaborative, participative, directive or coercive)?

- **Change interventions** – which mechanisms should be deployed (e.g. education, communication, cultural interventions)?

- **Change roles** – assigning roles and responsibilities (e.g. leadership, use of consultants, role of change action teams).

8 Changes to the business system

For change to be implemented successfully it needs to be co-ordinated across the entire business system. The POPIT (or four-view) model provides details of the key aspects that should be considered in managing changes within any business system:

Expandable Text

The business system's success will depend upon:

- **People:** staff need to have the right skills and motivation to carry out the tasks. They need to understand tasks and their roles within the organisation. Staff need to be developed to support business changes and resistance to change has to be managed and overcome. This will involve understanding and sometimes shifting the organisational culture.

- **Organisation:** success must be organised. Job roles need to be clearly defined and understood, lines of command and communication need to be effective, the organisational structure needs to support the organisational strategy, there needs to be flexibility in changing environments and bureaucracy needs to be kept to a minimum. Organisational support will be an important link between the other elements of the business system.

- **Processes:** these must be well defined, efficient, documented and understood. Those of high strategic importance and complexity should have undergone process improvement. Opportunities for improvement in other areas must have been explored in order to maximise efficiency and support the organisational strategy.

- **IT:** IT needs to support the changes that are taking place within the system. It needs to provide the relevant information at the point that it is needed. IT can replace some manual tasks and improve the efficiency of others. IT may facilitate organisational changes, process changes and staff development and it therefore binds all of the other elements together. IT must be exploited in order to maximise business benefits.

These elements must all be considered, planned and co-ordinated if business system changes (such as process redesigns) are to be successful. A failure in one area will often restrict the success in other areas. For example, organisations that are resistant to change and have bureaucratic structures often fail to make successes out of IT innovations and process redesigns.

For example, Kodak created digital photography but the senior management were reluctant to exploit it as they knew that it would destroy their film-based business model. 10 years before digital photography became widespread Kodak knew of the threat. But the organisation and the people did not support the IT and processes that existed within Kodak to exploit this technology. Ultimately this meant that digital photography was exploited by rivals and Kodak failed as a business, despite the fact that Kodak was the organisation who initially created the technology.

It will be important that all four elements work together and are considered in achieving successful business changes. An organisation's capabilities are often derived from and driven from success in having these four elements working together successfully.

When to use the model

The model can be used in a number of ways:

- Identifying weaknesses in systems.

- Identifying opportunities for system improvements.

- Identifying areas that are not working well together.

- Ensuring that all aspects of business change are considered when making process redesigns.

- Ensuring that project managers do not become too blinkered and ignore all organisational consequences. For example, many project managers become overly focused on creating an excellent process (covered elsewhere in this text) but forget that the process will only be successful if the people in the organisation have the skills to use it properly.

In an examination, it may well be used in the review stage of a project to help identify problems that have occurred because not all consequences were considered.

Test your understanding 6

An organisation has carried out an 18 month project to redesign the way in which it manages its upstream supply chain. It has well established e-procurement systems that have been in place for over five years and which are well integrated with existing suppliers.

The project manager (formerly part of the procurement team) carried out a plan to introduce a wider variety of suppliers who were willing to provide more flexible order quantities and provide better pricing and inventory information. The procurement process was redesigned to ensure that activities were in place that forced procurers to consider these suppliers and their information when making procurement decisions. All procurers were retrained and new 'super-procurers' were created as champions of the new process. These super-procurers had strong links to strategic management and were seen as a vital element in implementing, facilitating and supporting the new process. The presence of these super-procurers encouraged procurers to support the change and also gave a potential new level of employment for staff to aim at.

However, the new process has been in place for two months and has come under widespread criticism. Procurers complain that it is difficult to accumulate and assimilate the necessary information from the new system. Procurers suggest that this information is not provided via the current e-procurement system and the lack of links to these new suppliers means that the information often has to be obtained via email and subsequently becomes cumbersome and difficult to pull together. Senior management have complained that procurement costs have increased and there appears to be little or no expectation of a payback from the organisation's high initial investment. Customers have complained about low inventory levels and delayed orders and some major customers are now threatening to take their business elsewhere. It has subsequently been found that in the last few days procurement staff have reverted to the old procurement system.

Required:

Use the POPIT model to briefly consider the element(s) of the business system that appear to have been responsible for the failure of this project.

> **Professional skill:**
>
> Illustrate evaluation skills in assessing the problems within the business system.

Talent management

One aspect of the POPIT model is people. There is growing evidence that people are a key determinant of organisational success. An organisation's staff can help differentiate the organisation from rivals, can make an organisation more flexible, can help make strategic change quicker and more successful, and can ensure ongoing improvement within an organisation.

The key to making this a success is talent management.

 Talent management is an organisation's commitment to identify, recruit, engage, retain, and develop the most talented and superior employees valued by the organisation.

Key elements of talent management are that:

- people are seen as a major source of competitive advantage, and their training and development is seen as an investment, not a cost

- staff are recruited based on potential and cultural fit (rather than past experience or qualifications)

- learning is seen as essential and embedded in the organisation as a means of coping with change and ensuring that strategic objectives are met

- employees have the expectation that they will learn and change and retrain as necessary as strategy demands

- the development and training of their staff is seen as a key part of a manager's role

- changes outside the organisation are reflected in changes to training, controls and rewards

- human resource implications are considered as part of strategic planning

- information is shared about talented employees and their potential career paths across the organisation. This enables various departments to identify available talent when opportunities are made or arise

- tracking the career paths of employees and managing available opportunities for talented employees

9 Chapter summary

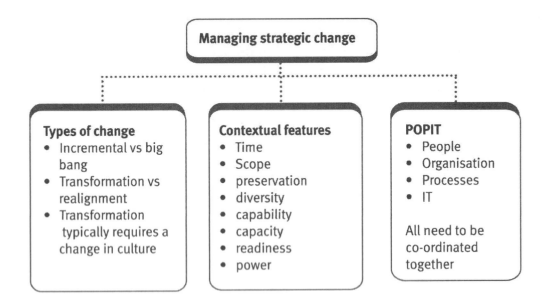

Managing strategic change

Types of change
- Incremental vs big bang
- Transformation vs realignment
- Transformation typically requires a change in culture

Contextual features
- Time
- Scope
- preservation
- diversity
- capability
- capacity
- readiness
- power

POPIT
- People
- Organisation
- Processes
- IT

All need to be co-ordinated together

Test your understanding answers

Test your understanding 1

- Adaptation is change that can be accommodated within the current paradigm (the current organisational beliefs and assumptions) and occurs incrementally. This is the most common form of change in organisations.

- Reconstruction is the type of change that may be rapid and can involve a good deal of upheaval in an organisation, but which does not fundamentally change the paradigm.

- Evolution is a change in strategy that requires paradigm change, but over time.

- Revolution is change that requires rapid and major strategic and paradigm change, perhaps in circumstances where pressure for change is extreme, e.g. if profit decline or a take-over threatens the continued existence of the firm.

Test your understanding 2

D   Control systems

Control systems include internal controls, performance measurement and reward structures.

Test your understanding 3

Managers can increase resistance by:

- failing to be specific about a change
- failing to explain why change is needed
- not consulting
- keeping people in the dark
- creating excess work pressure
- expecting immediate results
- not dealing with fears and anxieties
- ignoring resistance.

Test your understanding 4

Lewin's model suggests that, in order to be successful, WW will need to follow three stages in the changeover to a new accounting package.

Unfreeze

Staff need to be convinced of the need for the new accounting package. This could be difficult within WW for several reasons:

- WW's six employees have used the current accounting system for many years. This may mean that they are 'stuck in their ways' and unwilling to learn the new skills required for the new system.

- In addition, currently management accounting information can only be produced after a time-consuming and complex process. If a new system improves the efficiency of this process, employees may fear that they will become redundant.

- To help with this, WW needs to convince them of the superiority of the new system. For instance, it appears that it will make the production of management reports much faster, easing the workload for the employees.

- WW also needs to communicate well with its employees. Resistance is often caused by a fear of the unknown. Managers could discuss with staff the level of training that they will be given on the new system and attempt to allay any fears they may have about potential redundancies.

- Finally, WW's managers could also stress to staff members that it will benefit the business as a whole. The current system may cause WW to be less competitive in the marketplace, which could threaten the business as a whole.

Change

This involves actually moving staff onto the new accounting system. This stage will involve training all members of the accounting department on how to use the new system. Enough time must be allowed for employees to be reasonably comfortable with the new system before the changeover is made.

Communication is also vital here – employees must know when the new system will be installed and what will be expected from them. For example, what new reports will the managers expect from the system and when they will need to be prepared.

Refreeze

Finally, WW's managers must ensure that employees do not slip back into old habits and start using the old systems again. Clearly, if the old accounting system is entirely replaced by the new one, it should be easy to ensure that staff members do not continue to use the original accounting system. However, employees may still continue preparing the management reports manually.

To avoid this, managers could refuse to accept reports in the old, manual format – instead requiring that they be produced from the new system. Staff could be rewarded for using the new system and penalised if the old methods are still used.

Test your understanding 5

Change introduced through the use of power or manipulation is likely to add to anxiety. Education and communication will rarely succeed on their own when introducing major change. However, they are useful as a support for a negotiation or participation approach. The negotiation approach requires the existence of organised representatives and a formal procedure that is suitable for some items such as change in employment terms but would be inadvisable for other items of changing procedures, organisational changes, decentralisation, etc. In these cases, participation offers the best opportunity of allaying staff anxieties by involving them early in the change process and continuing that involvement through to completion.

Test your understanding 6

In this project it would appear that people were well organised. Procurers were retrained, the process was explained and there appeared to be a willingness for change. The new job role of super-procurer appeared to provide a potential level of motivation to the staff.

The change also appeared well organised. There was good communication as well as support from senior management. The super-procurers would help to organise staff and the project manager would organise the process. The fact that super-procurers had links to senior management would allow for any ad hoc changes required to be implemented when and if necessary.

The process was redesigned and there is no evidence in the scenario of any problems in this area. It appears that the existing process was well understood (the project manager had formerly worked as a procurer) and strong investment objectives in terms of broadening the supplier base and procurement flexibility.

But it is in the area of information technology (IT) where the business system appears to have failed. The project continued with a five year old system without any modifications for the new process. No integration appears to have been made to the system for the new suppliers and instead procurement staff are left with two incompatible systems (an integrated e-procurement system for existing suppliers and an email system for new suppliers).

The project manager has lost focus on a key element in the business systems and this appears to have been a key reason for the project failure.

Professional skill:
Each element of the business system needs to be assessed for success or failure. Your opinion as to whether it was a success or failure is largely irrelevant – what matters most is that you can justify your opinion based on evidence from the scenario.

Other employability and digital skills

Chapter learning objectives

This chapter contains an overview of the other employability and digital skills syllabus area. This is relevant for all ACCA Applied Skills (except LW) and Strategic Professional exams.

1 Purpose of chapter

This chapter explains the content included within the other employability and digital skills syllabus area. A similar syllabus area is included in all Applied Skills (except LW) and Strategic Professional level syllabi.

ACCA exams utilise software and technology similar to those used in the modern workplace. By studying ACCA exams, candidates will be equipped with both technical syllabus knowledge and practical, applied software skills. The other employability and digital skills syllabus area is included within the syllabus to acknowledge this acquired skillset.

2 Content of the other employability and digital skills syllabus area

The other employability and digital skills syllabus area is outlined in the syllabus and study guide. It consists of the following:

1   Use computer technology to efficiently access and manipulate relevant information.

2   Work on relevant response options, using available functions and technology, as would be required in the workplace.

3   Navigate windows and computer screens to create and amend responses to exam requirements, using the appropriate tools.

4   Present data and information effectively, using the appropriate tools.

By using a computer-based examination (CBE), the ACCA has enabled the use of word processing, spreadsheet, screen navigation and data processing functionalities to become part of their assessment range. This replicates the skills used in the modern workplace, whether in accounting practice, in industry or outside of accountancy altogether.

Whilst sitting an exam, candidates will be using the functionality of the CBE software in a variety of ways e.g. to prioritise information within the question data provided, to organise and present their answers in a manageable fashion, to use shortcuts and software functionality to increase efficiency. Skills garnered in the workplace can be used in the examination and vice versa.

This reflects that exams offered at Applied Skills and Strategic Professional are designed to be relevant and accessible to all students. The delivery mode and assessment types require students to demonstrate similar skills to those required in the modern workplace. Offering computer-based exams (CBE) at all levels gives students the opportunity to focus on the application of knowledge to scenarios, using a range of tools – spreadsheets, word processing and presentations. This not only allows students to demonstrate their technical and professional skills, but also their use of the technology relevant to the modern workplace. CBEs, therefore, offer the candidate an examination delivery method that allows them to demonstrate their knowledge and skills with the technology they are most familiar with, in the classroom or at work.

3 CBE support and the ACCA Exam Practice Platform

ACCA candidates can access the ACCA's Exam Practice Platform to practice attempting questions using the CBE software. It is imperative that candidates are familiar with the software before attempting the exam.

The link to the SBL Exam Practice Platform access gateway can be found here:

https://bit.ly/33PTfbW

This requires a MyACCA login to access the platform.

Support, access to other papers, tutorial videos and CBE advice can be found here:

https://www.accaglobal.com/gb/en/student/exam-support-resources.html

4 Contents of the CBE and Exam Practice Platform

On entering the Exam Practice Platform, candidates will access their dashboard, as follows:

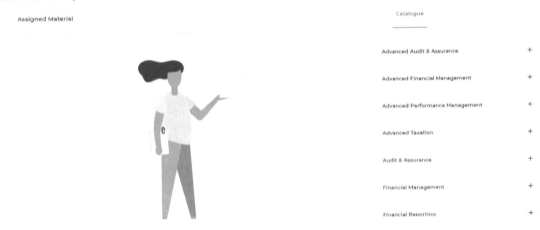

Candidates should click their appropriate paper in the right hand side menu. There they will be able to 'assign' content to their workspace. Candidates can assign a blank workspace or ACCA official resources (which include past papers presented using the CBE software for the candidates to attempt) to their workspace.

This will be added to the candidate's 'Self-Assigned Material' listing as below:

When working within the assignment the candidate will use response options to provide their answer.

The **Response Options** are where the candidate will attempt their answers.

There are up to three types of response option provided, dependent upon the specific syllabus a candidate is studying. Not every option will appear in each exam. Check the exam practice platform for examples of the responses that are commonplace within your exam.

The response options are:

– the word processor,

– the spreadsheet, and

– the slides.

The candidate must determine which of the response options is the most suitable for their specific answer.

These replicate the functionality of widely used software packages. The ACCA has developed this software, for use during home question practice and under exam conditions, to replicate the practical skill sets and work-based behaviours adopted by various industries throughout the world. By studying the ACCA qualification, candidates will improve, not only on their technical knowledge and understanding, but also on skills applied on a daily basis within their work environments. Candidates should practise questions using the CBE platform to ensure they are familiar with the various functions available within their specific examination.

Word Processor

The word processor response option, when relevant, will appear as follows:

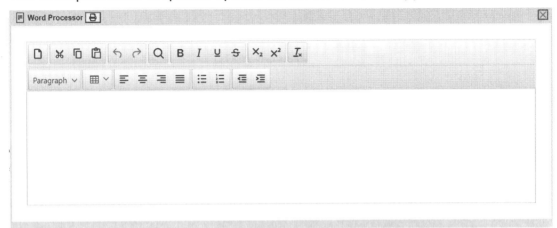

This resource has the following advantages and disadvantages:

Advantages	Disadvantages
It is easier to continue typing without entering new cells or becoming concerned about cell width	It cannot automatically perform calculations
Answers can be more easily split into paragraphs to make them more visually appealing and easier to mark	Numerical tables can be difficult to label and align
Bullet points can be used to present lists	
Text can be easily aligned and justified	
Superscript and subscript can be easily added to express terms such as 4^2, for example	

It is, therefore, best suited to discursive answers where candidates are asked, for example, to discuss, analyse or evaluate issues from a scenario or calculation.

The word processing software application could be used in the workplace within the writing of meeting agendas, meeting minutes, external letters, marketing output, briefings, audit reports, textbooks and instructional documentation.

Spreadsheet

The spreadsheet response option, when relevant, will appear as follows:

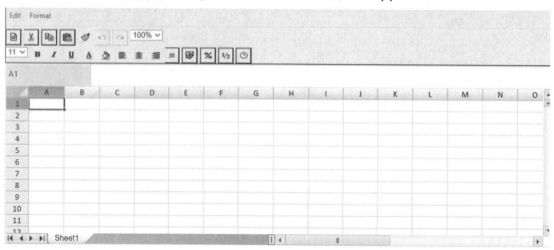

The spreadsheet software uses the same functionality as other commonly used spreadsheet software. Basic formulae functionality, such as SUM, power functions (e.g. SQRT) and the use of brackets are all reproduced within the ACCA software. Candidates are advised to practise questions using the software so that they are familiar with the functions available and how they can be utilised to the candidate's advantage through improved efficiency.

This resource has the following advantages and disadvantages:

Advantages	Disadvantages
This can quickly and easily perform calculations (e.g. using sums for totals or formulae for calculations)	Text will carry over beyond one cell and may go across and beyond the page width making answers difficult to follow (and mark)
Data within tables can be easily aligned	Bullet points are difficult to use
Shortcut icons can be used to quickly round figures, change numbers to percentages etc	
Tables can easily and quickly be copied when calculations need to be reperformed (e.g. for sensitivity analysis, tax calculations for more than one person, financial statements for more than one company etc.)	
Column width can be adjusted to label length	

It is, therefore, best suited for performing calculations within the examination e.g. NPVs, tax computations, goodwill calculations.

Spreadsheet software is ubiquitous in the modern workplace. It has the capacity to record, store and organise huge swathes of data and information relating to all aspects of a business. Examples of only a few of its possible practical applications include the preparation of management and financial accounts, operational controls and record-keeping e.g. expense claims, data analytics, project appraisals, sample size selection and tax computations.

Slides

The slides response option, when relevant, will appear as follows:

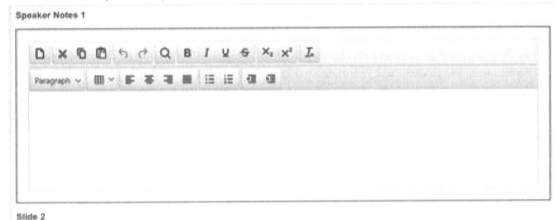

This resource has the following advantages and disadvantages:

Advantages	Disadvantages
Key messages are easier to see	There is limited space and ability to contain detail outside of the speaker notes
Tables can be easily added	It cannot automatically perform calculations
Speaker notes can be added for the detail	
Bullet points can be used to provide lists	
Titles can be given more prominence	

This is best suited for requirements that ask for presentations. This is not a common response option and is not applicable to most papers. Expect to see it within SBL.

The simple, aesthetically pleasing visual information provided by slide software is effectively used in the workplace when material is required to be shared with a wider audience. Slide software will be used during sales pitches, job interviews, presentations, key note speeches and product launches.

Be sure to address the requirement when preparing the slides. Keep the slide content focused on the requirement as it is important to remember that each slide needs to create immediate impact, be quick and easy to read for the audience and presented in a clear concise way.

As a general guide, each slide prepared should contain between three and five brief bullet points focusing on the requirement and outlining the content to the audience.

Slides should be produced with accompanying notes, to explain the bullet points in more detail. These notes must be directly linked to the points made on the slide, so a note per bullet point is a good guide.

It a critical to remember that these are the speaker's notes and you may be preparing this presentation for another senior manager. Therefore, they must be able to understand how the notes link to and explain the bullet points.

5   Chapter summary

The CBE software will replicate the work that is performed by accountants in a typical workplace. It will be used across the syllabus to support a candidate's answer by providing suitable response options for different types of answers.

These response options will be most suitable in the following instances (when available):

–   For discursive answers: it is best to use the word processing option

–   For calculations: it is best to use the spreadsheet option

–   For presentations: it is best to use the slides option

Practice case study – Question

MAGNA – PRESEEN

1   INTRODUCTION

Magna is a large distributor of children's toys and games. It is based in Essland and designs, manufactures, markets, and distributes a wide variety of family oriented products. Essland is a developed economy with a high level of income per capita.

The business started 83 years ago with one simple family board game called Magna but now produce a wide range of board games, toys and mobile games.

The company is structured into three divisions, one for each of its main product lines – Board games, Toys and Mobile Gaming

Magna have a September year end

It is currently October 20X4

2   INDUSTRY INFORMATION

OVERVIEW AND CHALLENGES

The toy and gaming industry in Essland is large but rapidly changing with a large number of foreign and domestic companies all competing for a share of the market.

Board games are still popular, despite being seen as 'old fashioned' by some and demand has dropped significantly from the 'hey-day' 20-30 years ago, but have stabilised in the last ten years.

The overall board game market is reasonably static; however, the popularity of individual games can vary significantly, with some traditional board games being family favourites for decades. New board games are being created regularly to try to become the next big hit, and whilst some succeed, many new games fail to capture the public's imagination.

Toys are a huge market in Essland and globally, with total toy sales in Essland approximately $1,700m in 20X4. As with board games, some toys have been popular for decades (e.g. toy cars, dolls, building blocks), whilst other toys become a 'must have' craze for a short period before often fading just as quickly.

The toy market is very seasonal, with holiday periods particularly important for toy companies. Getting your marketing or key product launch wrong before a big holiday season can be disastrous for any toy company – both financially and in terms of reputation.

The industry has seen a big shift towards mobile gaming in recent years as the improved technology and increased popularity of smartphones has led to the launch of more complex and better games for mobile phones – often rivalling those only available on expensive game consoles just a few years ago.

Many small and independent developers create mobile games and have been very successful. The main problems are making new games popular and well known in an increasingly crowded marketplace and how to monetise the product. Many customers expect mobile game apps to be 'free' and developers who charge for their games will often have difficulty in selling their game when other similar products are free. Many developers rely on in-game adverts and/or in-game purchases (of bonuses, additional game features, etc.) to make revenue from their product.

Total industry sales in Essland

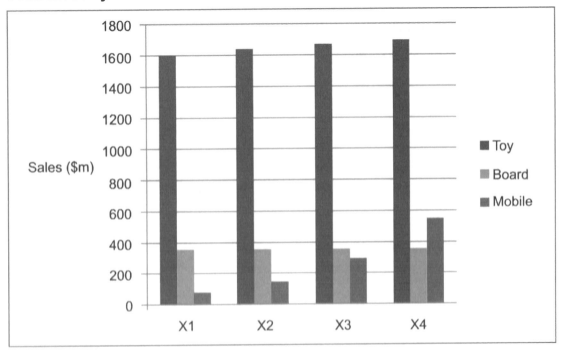

CUSTOMERS

Whilst the end user of toys are usually children, it is generally adults who buy the toys (normally as a gift or reward). Therefore, often a toy needs to make itself attractive to both the child and the buying adult. Some companies do this by advertising the 'educational' value of the toy or the 'life-skills' it will build. Other companies just focus on making their toys as appealing to the child as possible, relying on 'pester-power' that the adult will then buy a toy that the child really wants.

Board games attract a very wide range of customers, from young children up to adults. There has been a growth in recent years in adults playing board games in regular 'game nights' between couples and friends. Board games are also popular with many families trying to increase 'family time' and reduce 'screen time', particularly for children.

3   COMPANY INFORMATION

OWNERSHIP & BOARD STRUCTURE

Magna has both an Executive Board and a Supervisory (non-executive) Board. Both elements attend regular board meetings

Ami Patel – Managing director

Dena Alexiou – Production director

Fred Jones – Operations director

Raj Patel – Marketing director

Paul Simpson – Finance director

Marilyn Catz – Chairwoman and leader of the supervisory board

Vern Lewis – Bank representative on the supervisory board

Sean Batton – Employee representative, member of the supervisory board

Grace Khan – Shareholder representative, member of the supervisory board

MAGNA'S DIVISIONS AND PRODUCTS

Board game division

This is the oldest division within the group and represents the original business idea when the company set up 83 years ago. The business started with one simple family game called Magna (from which the company takes its name), which involved moving magnetic pieces around a reinforced cardboard game board. The game became very popular and provided the finance needed for the development of other board games.

Today, Magna produces around 70 different types of board games designed to be popular for many market segments. Sales volumes, however, currently are only a small percentage of the levels reached 20 years ago, when board games were a popular gift and means of family entertainment. Today there are many substitute products and greater opportunities for expending family time together. Magna has also faced a great influx of foreign competition with global brands and global marketing budgets.

The board division is run by the great-granddaughter of the original company founder. She also sits on Magna's supervisory board, though the family now own less than 20% of the company's issued share capital. But other shareholders are reassured by the ongoing family involvement in the business.

Toy division

This division has operated for over 20 years. Magna took a decision to produce some toys overseas and sell them through its existing network of retail customers. This was a very popular strategy and sales levels have been at a consistent high level for a number of years. The toy division's products include a number of core toy lines, including dolls, action figures, toy vehicles, clothing and accessories for children of all ages. Magna often links up with successful film and book franchises to produce 'character' themed toys.

Product life cycles can be short. Magna ensures regular updates of its product lines and has invested heavily in product development to ensure that, in common with its three biggest domestic rivals, consistently high sales volumes have been maintained for a number of years.

Mobile gaming division

This is Magna's newest division. Marketing director Raj Patel had the idea of creating mobile applications that were versions of Magna's current board games. The mobile games would have the same name as the original board game in order to build on the loyalty and branding built up in the past by the board game division. The mobile game would be available on a range of mobile devices and tablets.

Creating the mobile games involves a considerable upfront investment and so far only two mobile games have been developed. Initially there was a heavy investment in finding the best way to leverage the game brands and some initial attempts had to be terminated and written off. The best model was then found to be one where the mobile games are free to download but there are in-app purchases that are aimed at quickly recovering Magna's initial investment.

Both mobile games that are currently on the market have now proven to be very popular downloads on the most commonly used mobile platforms. There are plans for four more mobile games to be launched in the next 6 months and each game is expected to have a payback period of less than three months.

PRODUCTION AND SALES

Traditionally, Magna produced their own toys and games in Essland and were a large employer, however as competition increased, particularly from foreign companies there was pressure to decrease costs in order to remain competitive. This led to closures of Essland based factories and Magna moved their manufacturing overseas.

Magna closed its last factory in Essland five years ago. Magna's toys are now produced in Magna-owned manufacturing facilities in Ayland, Beeland and Ceeland as well as through independent toy manufacturers located in Geeland. All four of the countries where Magna's products are made would be classed as 'developing' economies.

Magna has always had a strong presence in Essland, based on their over 80 year history and respected brand name, making it a 'safe brand' for parents to buy from. However, Magna have found it more difficult to expand overseas, with just 6 percent of Magna's current revenue generated outside of its home nation.

Magna has also found itself very reliant on a small number of key customers; during the most recent financial year about half of Magna's sales were made through three main retail customers. The Board realise this is risky but are confident they have an excellent relationship with all main customers.

RISKS TO MAGNA

The Board of Magna have identified the following as key risks:

–   Decline of core Board Game market

–   Loss of a major customer

–   Inability to adapt to changing market conditions and the growth of video/mobile gaming

–   Reputational damage from a safety issue linked to a Magna game or toy

4. MAGNA WEBSITE EXTRACT

Magna prides itself on having the highest standards of corporate ethics as well as investing a great deal in end customer care.

Magna are passionate about creating the highest quality games and toys in Essland. When you buy a Magna toy or game you know you have a safe, quality product that will last for many years of family fun and happy memories.

Magna knows you want only the best, and that's what our service needs to provide. Our staff are valued and treated as part of the Magna family, because we feel when staff feel welcomed and valued, so do the customers.

Here at Magna, we are all kids at heart and want to have fun! We encourage our designers and developers to push the boundaries of their imagination – because when they have fun, they create the best products you to have fun!

5 FINANCIALS

Key financial data for Magna's divisions

Board game division

Year ended 30th September	X1	X2	X3	X4
Sales revenue ($m)	15	14	13	13
Net profit ($m)	2	1	1	1

Toy division

Year ended 30th September	X1	X2	X3	X4
Sales revenue ($m)	480	482	485	488
Net profit ($m)	101	98	100	97

Mobile gaming division

Year ended 30th September	X1	X2	X3	X4
Sales revenue ($m)				6
Net profit ($m)				(6)

END OF PRESEEN

MAGNA – QUESTION

Magna is a large distributor of children's toys and games. It is based in Essland and designs, manufactures, markets, and distributes a wide variety of family oriented products. Essland is a developed economy with a high level of income per capita.

Magna uses a consultancy firm, DPP, to provide ad-hoc reports on potential business strategies and issues. You are Aki Bacuna, a recently qualified accountant seconded to the team of DPP, which is responsible for preparing reports for Magna. You report to a senior partner called Mark Johnstone.

Mark Johnstone wants you to help in preparing sections of a report requested by Magna. In order to help you in this task he has provided you with a number of pieces of information from various sources:

Exhibit 1: Press Release

Exhibit 2: Extract from draft Magna Emergency Board Meeting Minutes

Exhibit 3: New business operation proposal

Exhibit 4: Email trail on outsourcing social media marketing

The case requirements are included in the tasks shown below:

EXHIBIT 1

PRESS RELEASE FROM MAGNA:

Magna Recalls Various Products Because of Possible Health Risk

FOR IMMEDIATE RELEASE – 1st November 20X4

Magna is voluntarily recalling approximately 500,000 Willies Roadster products as identified by the product codes listed in the Appendix to this release. It is also recalling 18 million Alexa Charm products, also identified in Appendix 1.

This recall of the Willies Roadster products is based on a recent finding that these products have been painted using a lead-based paint. There is a potential risk to consumers from lead-based paint, as lead is a highly toxic material. This recall is in part necessary since Clover Productions, a Geeland subcontractor responsible for the production of these toys for Magna, violated Magna's ethical and safety policies and utilised paint from a non-authorised third party supplier.

The Alexa Charm products include a small set of magnets which, if swallowed, could pose physical harm to small children. Although this is not the intended purpose of the Alexa Charm and the risk to children is small, Magna has taken the risk seriously and has acted immediately in the interests of its loyal customer base.

Magna is not aware to date of any customer complaints or illnesses related to its recalled products. However, Magna offers an unreserved apology to parents and a promise that enhanced safety checks will be implemented in all of Magna's production facilities around the world. At present safety checks are limited to raw material testing but these will be expanded to include checks on finished goods leaving all manufacturing facilities used by Magna (both owned and subcontracted).

The recalled products were distributed to stores nationwide in Essland. The only products recalled are those identified in Appendix 1.

Magna has notified retailers and is taking this voluntary action as a precautionary measure. This recall is being conducted with the knowledge of the Consumer Product Safety Commission (CPSC).

Consumers who have purchased or received any of the products identified in Appendix 1 are urged to return them to the store where they were purchased for an exchange or full refund.

Appendix 1 – details of recalled products:

Product name	Product Code
Willies Roadster Wild Game Pack	104-GBE-2049Y
Willies Roadster Mega Collectors Pack	198-GBE-2064B
Girls love Alexa Charms	96458-GTR-10457
Alexa Charm Teenage Special	84520-GYJ-69874
Alexa Loves Charms	12368-GFD-78621

EXHIBIT 2

Extract from Magna Emergency Board Meeting Minutes

15th January 20X5

In attendance:

Dena Alexiou (DA) – Production director

Grace Khan (GK) – Shareholder representative, member of the supervisory board

Fred Jones (FJ) – Operations director

Marilyn Catz (MC) – Chairwoman and leader of the supervisory board

Sean Batton (SB) – Employee representative, member of the supervisory board

Raj Patel (RP) – Marketing director

Vern Lewis (VL) – Bank representative on the supervisory board

Paul Simpson (PS) – Finance director

Discussion of supplier issues and the product recall

FJ: I've called this meeting between the supervisory board and the executive board to discuss the situation with Clover Productions. I feel that it is my duty as part of the executive board to try to salvage some sort of relationship with Clover. This is what I have been working to achieve ever since we issued the press release for the product recall.

MC: I was unaware that you were doing this. Why would you feel the need to do that?

FJ: Clover Productions is responsible for 30% of Magna's annual toy production and it is demanding an apology from Magna for what it perceived to be accusations concerning its product safety. If such an apology is not forthcoming, Clover's Managing Director has told me that future orders would not be secure.

PS: Well, given that Clover was responsible for the recall of 18.5 million toys I'm not convinced that this would be any great loss.

DA: Actually, of the 18.5 million toys recalled, only 0.5 million were contaminated by paint. The other 18 million were recalled as a result of a flaw in Magna's own product design, not through a manufacturing flaw at Clover.

SB: That's true, but it would have been a heavy administrative burden if we had separate announcements for every type of recall.

RP: And very confusing for our consumers and retail customers too.

DA: It was simply unfortunate if stakeholders assumed that Clover was at fault for the entire recall.

GK: I'm amazed that I'm only finding out about the true reasons for the recall now. I would have insisted on changes to the press release announcement had I known. Who approved the press release?

MC: I did. It's my role to protect the share price not the reputation of overseas suppliers. Fred, can you confirm whether other suppliers could be found to take over Magna's orders from Clover if necessary.

FJ: It probably wouldn't be too difficult to find other toy suppliers, but I feel that the right thing to do would be to apologise to Clover. At Magna we pride ourselves on our honesty.

BP: Acting as an ethical company is one of the things that our research shows that our customers value about us.

GK: I think shareholders have always thought that Magna had strong ethical principles but I'm not sure who they would react if they knew how Magna had handled this situation

SB: Transparency and honesty should underpin all of Magna's actions.

VL: Fred, can you fill us in on the design faults leading to the recall.

FJ: No regular reports were produced by the design team for the executive board relating to the levels of quality compliance and other control issues. The head of design, Katy Keane, has an excellent reputation and has been with Magna for many years. She does her own recruiting and team management and is given a lot of autonomy in how the design team operate. The executive board therefore tended to just accept that the design team was effective.

VL: What about the involvement of internal audit in checking the design team's controls?

FJ: Magna's internal audit team spends the majority of its time checking the relevance of financial controls and suggesting cost reductions rather than product design.

GK: Fred, are any more recalls likely in the light of what has happened recently?

FJ: I can't rule it out, since so many toys sold by Magna include magnets. As far as I am aware, these toys are all undergoing significant testing now by the design team.

MC: I suggest that instead of a direct apology, a statement be made to appease Clover, explaining how important product safety is to Magna and the value of transparency and honesty.

FJ: Let's hope that this is enough.

GK: I think that this decision needs further investigation. I think that we should get some outside, independent advice on how to proceed here.

EXHIBIT 3

New business operation proposal – Mobile gaming division

Dena Alexiou and Raj Patel both feel that Magna has moved on to greater success since it closed down its last in-house production facilities. Outsourcing production has allowed the company to focus more on branding, product refreshment and consumer satisfaction as well as providing access to a much greater production capacity and the ability to gain from supplier efficiencies and competitiveness.

Raj Patel, Dena Alexiou and Chloe Slater, the head of the mobile gaming division, have looked at three business processes within the division that they believe are candidates for outsourcing. There are a number of agencies in the market to which Magna could easily outsource any of these nominated activities. Details of the activities are provided below:

Game design and production

In mobile game design it is important to reflect the gameplay, look and characters from the original board games, but at the same time take account of modern game playing approaches and the need to offer a range of different timed versions (for example, short games that may last less than 5 minutes to longer, multi-hour games that can be returned to at will). Experienced, skilled designers are employed by Magna and these staff are supported by a heavy investment in state-of-the-art technology.

It is also vital to get the balance right between immediately available free items, upgrade items that can be gained through repeat plays and premium items that must be purchased via in-app payment systems. Magna has found that getting this balance right is the key to a game's success. It is often this element that will generate repeat business for the game, impact on reviews and recommendations (a critical success factor for any mobile game) and encourage users to download other games in the division's portfolio.

In-app payment systems

This is a system for taking payments from players who want to buy in-game items such as premium characters, extra playing time or customisable layouts. The system needs a high level of security in order to protect users' information.

Typically, users have set up payment mechanisms on the gaming platform and therefore Magna actually only deals with the platform holder rather than the gamer. Payments are made to Magna in bulk at regular intervals. The main task for Magna staff is in determining activity level and price, all of which is stored on Magna's servers. These are matched to the platform holder's records and payment is typically received within two or three days.

Post-production testing

Finished mobile games must be tested across a number of platforms and a number of devices. This task is made difficult, as the number of devices on which the game must operate can be vast and can constantly change as new devices and new software comes on to the market.

However, any post-production problems can be quickly solved via game updates delivered quickly to the key game platforms. Gamers can leave feedback on these platforms if they are experiencing problems or if the game won't download and/or work on their device.

Magna's team have found that providing updates can be done relatively quickly and there is little impact on consumer demand, but the process takes up a lot of resource which could be better spent on game development.

EXHIBIT 4

Email trail on outsourcing social media marketing

Johnstone, Mark

From:	Raj Patel
Sent:	Monday, 18th Dec 20X5, 1:28 pm
To:	Mark Johnstone
Subject:	Outsourcing social marketing

Hello Mark,

I know that we are commissioning DPP to do a report for us. As part of this could you also look at the email below that I received from my nephew.

He's recently graduated in computer sciences and reckons that he'd be more 'on the ball' and up-to-date with social trends than our current e-marketing team. He thinks he could double our advertising 'uptake'. This refers to the number of users who see an advert for one of our mobile games whilst using social networks and then subsequently download and use the game.

At the moment we get an uptake rate of around 0.1%. This is for around 25million advert views. It isn't a great source of revenue for us at the minute, but each user spends an average of $6 per annum after downloading the game and making in-app purchases. We spend around $0.005 for each advert view.

My nephew has made a proposal for us to outsource this form of advertising to him. I didn't feel that ethically I was in the best position to make this decision for the business so I thought it'd be better to get your firm's independent decision on this.

Anyway, I look forward to receiving your report on this and the other matters that we discussed.

Raj

------Original message----------------

From: Ali Patel

Sent: Monday, 18th Dec 20X5, 11:45 am

To: Raj Patel

Subject: The best marketing deal ever

Heh Raj.

It was good to see you at mama's at the weekend. Hope you got home ok.

I was telling you about my skills in social marketing and you asked me to send you some plans.

I think I could double your current uptake using all the skills I picked up at college. We learnt some stuff that I think your company would be blown away with.

I'm also very cheap as I want to use this to make my name in this game. So, I'd only cost $50,000 a year for doing this. This would cover all costs for all advert views.

Let me know what you think.

Cya soon.

Ali

TASK 1

Marilyn Catz is of the opinion that an apology should not be made to the Geeland supplier, Clover, and the true reasons behind the toy recall should be kept secret. She recognises that although all recalled toys had been made in Geeland, by Clover Productions, they were not fully responsible for the recall.

The safety of toys in Essland is overseen by The Consumer Product Safety Commission (CPSC) which, following the recall, held a meeting on the safety of goods made in Geeland. Magna paid a substantial fine to the CPSC for marketing, importing and selling non-compliant toys and Marilyn Catz is convinced that Magna has therefore taken sufficient responsibility for the recall. Magna was congratulated on its crisis response by several media publications in Essland.

Marilyn Catz is more concerned with the impact on consumer confidence than on the relationship with one of its many suppliers. She believes that Magna should make a public statement that reassures the public as to Magna's strong focus on product safety. She has asked DPP to present in its report to Magna, some advice on the communication issues relevant to this product recall.

Required:

(a)   Referencing the facts presented, determine whether or not Magna should disclose publicly the true causes of the product recall. You should refer to the principles of ethical decision-making.   **(14 marks)**

Professional skills marks are available for illustrating commercial acumen relevant to this decision.   **(4 marks)**

(b)   Referencing the product recalls already made, prepare a public statement which Marilyn Catz can present to address the following areas:

(i)   The reasons for the recall, incorporating the principles of transparency and honesty.   **(6 marks)**

Professional skills marks for demonstrating communication skills in ensuring that the statement is satisfactory to both the stakeholders of Magna and Marilyn Catz.   **(4 marks)**

(ii)   An explanation of the importance of product safety for Magna.

(6 marks)

(Total: 34 marks)

TASK 2

Marilyn Catz, the Chairwoman of Magna, is considering whether one of the reasons that the recent product recall occurred is that the company is too diversified. It operates too many divisions, imports from too many countries and sells too many products.

Marilyn Catz wants to evaluate whether the business portfolio should be narrowed by removing one of its business units. However, she is unsure on how this would impact on the company's future corporate strategies. She has asked DPP to present a report on the following:

Required:

(a) Prepare a draft report for the board which evaluates the current performance and contribution of each of the three current divisions in the Magna portfolio and assesses their relative significance to the company's future strategy.   **(20 marks)**

Professional skills marks are available for illustrating evaluation skills in assessing potential implications for Magna for the issues relevant to this decision.   **(4 marks)**

Fred Jones, Magna's Operations Director, disagrees with Marilyn Catz about the company's activities being too diversified and that this caused the product recalls. He instead has argued that the company is focused on the wrong areas of control.

He thinks that there is too much time and attention in keeping the supervisory board happy and in having too many meetings where issues get discussed but rarely get actioned. He argues that time and resources would be better spent on internal controls and arrangements. He believes that if more time was spent in actually ensuring that the business was operating as it should, it would automatically remove for too many 'time wasting' meetings. Fred Jones has asked DPP to prepare a report on the following issues:

Required:

(b) Critically appraise the internal control and internal audit arrangements at Magna, identified within the sources of information provided to you.   **(10 marks)**

(c) Explain how a two-tier board differs from a single tier board and explain the disadvantages to Magna of operating a two-tier board system.   **(8 marks)**

(Total: 42 marks)

TASK 3

Dena Alexiou and Raj Patel want the Magna boards to consider a move towards further outsourcing, particularly in the new mobile gaming division. Dena believes that the early failures in product launches were caused by Magna's lack of technical expertise in the market as well as a lack of understanding of what the customer wanted and how the products should have been marketed.

Raj Patel also wants DPP's advice on the proposal to outsource its social media marketing. This is not something that Magna has considered outsourcing, as it is too strategically important to the success of the games division and the mobile gaming division. But if Magna was financially much better off from doing so, then Raj believes that the Board of Magna would consider it. Raj has asked for some briefing notes which he can use to present to the board on the following:

Required:

(a) Evaluate whether the processes identified by Dena and Raj should be outsourced by Magna. **(9 marks)**

Professional skills marks are available for illustrating analysis skills relevant to this decision. **(4 marks)**

(b) Calculate the potential financial benefit from outsourcing social media marketing and evaluate the other factors that Magna should consider in making this decision. **(7 marks)**

Professional skills marks are available for illustrating professional scepticism related to the offer from Ali Patel. **(4 marks)**

(Total: 24 marks)

END OF QUESTION

Practice case study – Answer

◈ Tutorial Notes

At the Professional Level, it is not always possible to publish suggested answers which comprehensively cover all the valid points which candidates might make. Credit will be given to candidates for points not included in the suggested answers, but which, nevertheless, are relevant to the requirements. In addition, in this integrated case study examination, candidates may re-introduce points made in other questions or parts of questions as long as these are made in the specific context of the requirements of the question being answered.

The suggested answers presented below inevitably give much more detail than would be expected from most candidates under examination conditions, and include most of the obvious points evidenced from the case information. The answers are therefore intended to provide a structure of the approach required from candidates, and cover the range and depth of knowledge relating to each task which might be demonstrated by the most well prepared and able candidates.

1   Answer

Task 1

(a)   Approach for addressing the ethical issue

Step 1: What are the facts of the case?

The facts are that Magna was forced to recall 18.5 million toys, mainly due to their own design issues. These design issues were however, not mentioned by the CEO in the announcement accompanying the recall. The only explanation given was that a supplier in Geeland had used lead paint, in contravention of their agreement with Magna. In fact, this was the reason for the recall of only 0.5 million of the toys. The supplier, Clover Productions, is now angry that they have been blamed for the entire recall and has threatened to stop supplying Magna unless an apology is issued.

Step 2: What are the ethical issues in the case?

The ethical issues are whether to disclose the information publicly, thereby being fair to the supplier and honest about Magna's own role in the recall or to conceal the information, thereby preserving Magna's image as a company which dealt well with a crisis at least in the short term.

Step 3: What are the norms, principles and values relevant to the case?

The company is bound by the norms and expectations of its stock exchange and it should have the highest standards of corporate ethics, particularly valuing its reputation for customer care. This means that it owes an implicit and explicit duty of care to both its customers and its shareholders. As a company that seemingly values its reputation as a well-governed organisation, it is also bound by the underlying principles of corporate governance that include integrity, honesty and transparency. Health and safety issues are also very important in all manufacturing and Magna should ensure that all of its toys are compliant with the highest health and safety standards.

Step 4: What are the alternative courses of action?

Alternative 1 is to disclose the information about the causes of the recall to the shareholders, public and other stakeholders. Alternative 2 is to seek to suppress the information within the company and hope that there is no leak.

Step 5: What course of action is most consistent with the norms, values and principles identified in step 3?

The information is material to a number of parties' better understanding of why the recall was necessary. The suppliers, retail customers, consumers, the Consumer Product Safety Commission and the shareholders would all benefit from clarification of the information. Disclosure would seem to be the most appropriate course of action notwithstanding the potentially unfortunate consequences for Magna of this information leaking out. However, disclosure may result in damage to reputation which will be harmful to shareholder value.

Step 6: What are the consequences of each possible course of action?

If the company makes the disclosure, there is a risk that reputational damage would be high. The CPSC may take action if it feels that Magna was dishonest with customers or itself as a regulatory body. It is unclear if the reason for the recall changing would affect the fine however. Clover Productions, if it feels the 'apology' is sufficient would presumably continue to manufacture Magna's toys and so production would not be threatened. This would benefit retail customers and shareholders unless they decided they no longer wished to associate with Magna due to the incorrect announcement in the first instance.

If the company were to suppress the information, then each person in possession of the knowledge would be faced with their own ethical dilemma. Not only that, Clover Productions may choose to publicise the true facts so as not to lose other customers and Magna would be forced to confirm the real reasons for the recall or be exposed as compromising the truth.

Step 7: What is the decision?

Alternative 1 is that the company should make a full and detailed disclosure, probably with an acceptance of full responsibility for the recall of 18 million of the toys. This would be consistent with the company's claimed ethical values and also with the important core values of corporate governance (integrity, transparency, etc.).

Alternative 2 is to leave the situation as it is, take all necessary measures to replace the supplier and hope that the scandal 'blows over'.

This would be a very risky option as the cost to the company's reputation and to the directors personally, if the information was ever to emerge, would be significant. It would also be against the letter and spirit of the core values of corporate governance. It would be unlikely to protect shareholder value in the longer term, is the least ethical of the options and so should be avoided.

It is recommended that Magna follow Alternative 1 and disclose the full facts of the recall in a public statement.

(b)   **Magna Public Statement**

Magna Public Statement

by Marilyn Catz, CEO of Magna

Willie Roadster Product recall

As has been widely reported in the media, Magna recently saw the need to recall a great many toys as a precautionary measure since it was discovered they were not up to our usual high standard of manufacture. As CEO I wish to take this opportunity to give some more details on the recall and also give our many stakeholders reassurance that Magna continues to pledge its commitment to the 'highest standards' of ethical performance. In particular we are dedicated to ensuring full compliance with regulation in all jurisdictions, the safety and care of all those relying on Magna's products, transparency and above all honesty in our communication with stakeholders.

It has now become apparent that the majority of the toys in the recall were actually at fault because of a design problem originating at Magna. As a board of directors our position is one of default disclosure. If we find our organisation to be at fault we must be open and honest with stakeholders about that. This level of transparency is one of the underlying principles of good corporate governance which of course we uphold.

The high level of honesty we are committed to offer our stakeholders necessitates not only a full and transparent disclosure of product safety issues but also a public reinforcement of our confidence in our Geeland suppliers who continue to produce top quality toys in partnership with our organisation.

The importance of product safety at Magna

As chief executive officer, you will understand that it is my job to lead the company and to protect stakeholder interests. These are responsibilities I take very seriously, particularly those interests of customers who purchase and enjoy our toys. Product safety is particularly important at Magna as we are producing goods for children whose wellbeing simply cannot be compromised.

It is for this reason that the decision for a precautionary recall of so many toys was made. Although we are confident in the safety of goods we produce, we refuse to take even the slightest risk with customer safety. However difficult and inconvenient the recall may be, it is our duty to ensure 100% product safety and if we cannot do that, we must take action.

Following the recall, we have put extra safety checks in place, adding in more quality checks to finished goods to complement extensive quality control on raw materials already carried out.

We hope this statement has reassured customers, suppliers and shareholders alike that Magna remains committed to supplying excellent quality toys both now and in the future.

About Magna

Magna is a large distributor of children's toys and games. It is based in Essland and designs, manufactures, markets, and distributes a wide variety of family oriented products.

Task 2

REPORT

Performance and contribution of Magna's division

To: The board of directors of Magna

From: DPP

Date: Today

Introduction

The evaluation of the performance and position of each of the business divisions within Magna is explored using the Boston Consulting Group (BCG) matrix. The key issues follow.

Board game division

The board game division has shown a decline in revenue across the last four years. This corresponds with the industry growth chart which reflects that the market as a whole is declining. Much of this decline can be attributed to the product going out of fashion and the rise in the number of substitute entertainment options.

Magna has a small share of the market. Industry sales levels are around $350m and Magna's sales are only $13m giving the company a market share of around 4%. Magna's sales have been attacked by larger international rivals and it is unlikely that there is much scope for Magna to take these rivals on as they have better brands and bigger marketing budgets.

The board game division would be classified as a dog in the Boston box. Typically, dogs are business units that should be divested. They have poor prospects of improving and are unlikely to contribute much to future business strategies. However, at Magna, this strategy may not be the best way forward. Firstly, this is the original business idea from which the company takes its name. The division is run by the great-granddaughter of the original founder and a removal of the division could cause concern not only in terms of the image of the business but also in providing assurance to some shareholders. On top of all this, the board game division provides the branding and reputation upon which Magna plans to build the mobile gaming division. It would therefore appear unwise to dispose of this division, at least in the short- to medium-term, despite its relatively weak financial performance and market position.

Toy division

This part of the business appears to be very successful for Magna. The division would appear to have a high market share as it has achieved consistently high sales levels for a number of years. This can also be inferred from the chart of industry sales; industry sales appear to be around $1.7bn and Magna accounted for $488m of this (consistent with previous years) which would give Magna a market share of around 29%.

However, growth in the market would appear to be low. The industry sales chart shows little growth in the industry and Magna's sales have also shown only 0.6% growth in the last year. Magna recognises that products have short life cycles and, although product ranges are regularly refreshed, it is likely that sales of new products are merely compensating for declines in older products rather than creating new growth for the division.

In terms of the Boston box, the division can be classified as a cash cow. This is reflected by the fact that the division accounts for almost all of the company's profits and it is likely that any cash reserves built up by the business are attributable to this division.

This would suggest that the division should be exploited – the returns in this division should be used to fund the strategies and investment required in the other business units. However, it should be noted that there is a high degree of product investment required in the toy division in order to refresh the product lines. It will be important that any fund extraction from the division does not harm this. It might also be necessary for the division to invest in marketing in order to overcome the potential reputational damage that may result from the recent product recalls.

Mobile gaming division

The mobile gaming division appears to have entered a high growth market. Mobile gaming is attractive to consumers as it is easily accessible and can fill various lengths of entertainment time. It is likely that as consumers move away from traditional board games they will switch to substitutes such as mobile gaming. The industry growth chart shows the market approximately trebling its sales over the last three years and there is no indication that this growth will slow down in the short term.

Magna has a very small share in the market. It is new to the market and only 2 of its 70 board games have been developed for mobile gaming. With $8m of sales in a market with sales approximating $550m, Magna's market share is less than 2%.

The mobile gaming division is therefore likely to be a 'problem child' for Magna. It is making losses and is in a poor market position. It will take significant investment in order for market share to increase and recent write-offs and failures might indicate that Magna does not have the ability to compete well in the market. On that basis it may be better to divest of the division.

However, the initial problems are not uncommon with new product developments and the problems do appear to have been overcome. Magna has now found a business model which works for the division. New product launches are planned and have a break-even period of only a few months, which means that the division is likely to very quickly to turn into profitability. It should easily be able to overtake the profits made in the board game division and the market growth indicates that there is great scope for high revenue and profit growth in the future.

Overall

It would appear unwise to divest of any of the business units. The toy division should lend some financial support to the mobile gaming division to support continued product development and growth in this division. The board game division should be retained (at least in the short- to medium-term) in order to provide the platform for product development in the high growth mobile gaming division.

Parts b and c

REPORT

Performance and contribution of Magna's division

To:	Fred Jones, Operations Director, Magna
From:	DPP
Date:	Today

Introduction

This report aims to explain the deficiencies in Magna's internal controls systems and the disadvantages of a two-tier board system.

Deficiencies in Magna's internal controls

Tests only carried out on Raw Materials

Magna has not carried out tests on finished toys imported from any of its suppliers located in the four producing countries. Quality control is limited to raw materials testing. This has led to the situation in which the faulty toys were not identified before reaching the final customer. If the faulty toys had been discovered before they left the factory, the recall and all of its associated costs could have been avoided.

No regular reports to the board from the design team

The design team appears to operate as an isolated unit and does not report to the operations board on any control issues. This means the operations board is not familiar with the design process or the measures in place to prevent design errors being made. The operations board has been unable to step in to prevent a crisis and has only become aware of the design issues once the toys were in circulation. If the design team had to explain themselves more fully to the board and prove that sufficient controls were in place, the recall may have been avoided.

The head of design has unfettered power

It would appear that the head of design reports to no-one. This means that if there are issues with her work they are not dealt with on a timely basis. It also means she may take excessive risks or cut corners, safe in the knowledge that no one will call her to account. She may recruit unsuitable team members and then cover up their inadequacies. The lack of checks on the work of the head of design has no doubt contributed to the recall being necessary.

The board assumes the design team is effective

The operations board takes no interest in the work of the design team, choosing instead to assume they are effective since the head of design has been in post a long time. This means not only that unfettered power is unchecked but that senior managers lack the basic understanding of how the team operates. Problems occurring are not picked up leading to the recall and the potential of further recalls in the future.

Internal audit is limited in its scope

Internal audit is limited to looking at financial controls and cost cutting meaning it has not detected any issues with the design team. Although financial controls and cost cutting are important in a company like Magna, an effective internal audit function should have a wider scope. If it had included the controls over the design team in its remit, issues may have been picked up sooner.

Magna's two-tier board system

Single and two tier boards

Single tier describes a situation where the board structure is a unitary board (consisting of executive and non-executive directors together).

In a two tier, structure, the operations (or management) board of executive directors has responsibility for creating and implementing corporate policy and strategy. The supervisory board of non-executives provides advice and checks on behalf of a wider group of stakeholders. The supervisory board typically includes, for example, representatives from major banks that have historically been large providers of long-term finance to companies (and are often major shareholders). The supervisory board does not have full access to financial information, is meant to take an unbiased overview of the company, and is the main body responsible for safeguarding the external stakeholders' interests. The presence on the supervisory board of representatives from banks and employees (trade unions) may introduce perspectives that are not present in some single tier boards. For example, many members of the supervisory board would not meet the criteria under corporate governance guidelines in some countries for being considered independent.

Disadvantages of two tier board structure in Magna

The main disadvantage of the two-tier structure in Magna is that the supervisory board, which is responsible for communicating with the stakeholders and therefore making the announcement by Marilyn Catz concerning the recall, was not in possession of all the facts. This may be because Ms Catz did not fully brief them but in a single tier she would not have the opportunity to neglect to tell the full story since operational directors would be present at meetings and involved in decision making.

A further problem is the lack of awareness of what is happening in Magna at an operational level. Fred Jones is busy dealing with the potential loss of a main supplier and yet the members of that board have no idea of the issues which caused the situation. Until Fred Jones requests an emergency meeting with the supervisory board, the lack of communication is a real problem limiting the effectiveness of the decision made.

This lack of communication will also create problems in terms of the additional bureaucracy to share relevant facts between the two boards to facilitate understanding. This will clearly affect the speed of decision making at Magna, its ability to react to events such as the product recall and ultimately its reputation and market value.

Members of the supervisory board appear to lack basic knowledge of the operations of Magna, as evidenced by the bank representative's questions on the design team and internal audit. This lack of knowledge will not only make strategic decision making very difficult for Magna's executive board but also ultimately have a negative effect on the motivation of supervisory board members, manifesting itself in a feeling of isolation and lack of authority on behalf of its members.

Conclusion

There are many issues in the internal control system that need to be rectified and it is recommended that action is taken as soon as possible. In terms of the structure of the company's board, whilst there are many disadvantages to a two tier board system, the importance of the company's stakeholders means that it is unlikely that a move to a single tier system could be negotiated.

Task 3

(a) Process outsourcing

> **NB – Harmon's Process Strategy Matrix has been used to provide structure to this answer. Any suitable, common sense approach would also have been appropriate.**

Paul Harmon has proposed a process-strategy matrix that considers the strategic importance of the process on one axis and the complexity of the process on the other. This leads to four quadrants for which Harmon suggests different generic process solutions. Harmon suggested that only processes which are complex but which are not strategically important should be outsourced.

The location of each of the three Magna processes considered for outsourcing are assessed against this criteria.

Game design and production

This is a complex process. It requires experienced skilled staff and state-of-the-art technology. This would make it a candidate for outsourcing.

However, the process appears to be a strategically important process. This process generates repeat business, impacts on the number of downloads and influences reviews.

Processes which are complex and strategically important should not be outsourced. Harmon suggests instead that this type of process should be focused on and improved internally. These processes are fundamental to the mobile gaming division's success and improvements in this area should lead to improvements in the success of the division.

In-app payment systems

This is not a complex process. It involves marrying up Magna's sales records to those of the platform provider. This should be a simple process that is not resource intensive.

The process is also unlikely to be strategically important. It will not be a differentiator given that game users have set up accounts with the platform provider and pay through the platform provider. Therefore, a payment for one game will be no different to a payment for another.

Harmon suggests that processes that are not strategically important or complex should require little resources and minimum effort. There is little value to be had from outsourcing such simple processes.

Post production testing

This process does not appear to be strategically important. Updates can be used to quickly solve any problems and have little impact on consumer demand.

The process does seem to be a complex one. There are many devices which require compatibility and the list of devices constantly changes. It is unlikely that Magna has access to all of these devices or the skills to keep up to date with the changes happening in the market.

This process is a definite candidate for outsourcing. Agencies can be used to perform the testing and these agencies are likely to be more used to dealing with a wide range of devices. It would also add an extra layer of confidence in the quality of the product if it is tested externally. Outsourcing the process would free up Magna staff time to focus on more strategically important processes.

Overall

Only the post production testing process should be considered for outsourcing. In-app payment systems require little resources and game design and production is too strategically important to consider for outsourcing.

(b) **Social media marketing**

Current estimated revenue from advert views = 0.1% × 25m × $6 = $150,000

Current estimated cost of advert views = 25m × $0.005 = $125,000

Current estimated profit from advert views = $150,000 – $125,000 = $25,000 per annum

Estimated revenue from increased advert views = 2 × $150,000 = $300,000

Ali Patel's fee = $50,000

Revised annual profit = $300,000 – $50,000 = $250,000

Increase in profit from using Ali Patel = $250,000 – $25,000 = $225,000

Using Ali Patel to perform this task would increase profit almost tenfold. This appears to be a very attractive financial offer, but there are many other issues that should be considered before using Ali for this work.

These figures have ignored any redundancy costs that may be incurred within Magna if existing staff who carry out this role are no longer required. Alternatively, Magna may still retain some of these costs and this has not been accounted for in the above calculations.

- The value may be significantly higher over time as more games are developed (which may increase the take-up) or more than 25m views are generated by Magna.

- The value will have a higher value if considered over more than a one year time frame – though the time value of money would then need to be considered.

- Ali Patel has never carried out this work before. There is no evidence (other than from his own statements) that his knowledge will be better than the experienced staff already employed within Magna. Many of Magna's existing staff are likely to have similar qualifications and some may be as recently qualified as Ali Patel.

- There is no way to confirm Ali Patel's estimates. He claims he could double take-up but there is no evidence to support this. Perhaps if he was used on a trial basis for a number of weeks evidence on his ability to double take-up.

- His fee also appears to be an unrealistic cost of employing adverts. It is likely that much of these costs will be variable in nature as Magna must pay the social media companies for hosting each advert. It is unclear whether the $50,000 fee paid to Ali Patel will cover such costs.

Overall, Ali Patel's offer looks to be very lucrative. But his lack of experience and the lack of evidence to support his estimates would mean that the rewards may not actually accrue to Magna. It is recommended that Magna maintains its existing social marketing plan but perhaps Ali Patel could be trialed on a short-term parallel basis.

Marking guide

Task 1 (a)

Technical marks

Up to 2 marks for each relevant point, ensuring that the student has made points on both sides of the argument. Ethics MUST be included to score full marks (Up to a maximum of 14 in total.)

Professional skills marks

How well has the candidate demonstrated Professional skills as follows:	Not at all	Not so well	Quite well	Very well
Commercial acumen relevant to the decision	The candidate has not shown or applied commercial awareness	The candidate is aware of some commercial factors but has not employed it well to the scenario.	However, the candidate has not exercised judgement in determining the best way forward for Magna.	The candidate has shown a strong insight of commercial awareness and applied it to the scenario. The candidate has also exercised judgement in determining the best way forward for Magna.
	0	1.33	2.66	4

Task 1 (b)

Technical marks

(i) 2 marks for explanation of recall. 2 marks for each well explained point on transparency and honesty. Must be applied, definitions only maximum 1 mark each. Total: 6 marks

(ii) 2 marks for each well explained point on product safety. Must be applied to the case. Total: 6 marks

Professional skills marks

How well has the candidate demonstrated Professional skills as follows:	Not at all	Not so well	Quite well	Very well
Demonstrating strong communication in ensuring that the statement solves the key issues arising from the product recall.	The candidate uses poor, unprofessional language and statements are ambiguous and/or illogical.	The candidate's language is professional but lacks clarity. The candidate repeats themselves and arguments are unpersuasive.	The candidate's language is occasionally complex and/or unprofessional Statements are occasionally not persuasive.	The candidate uses a professional tone and language. The candidate uses positive and authoritative language which is unambiguous and persuasive.
	0	1.33	2.66	4

Task 2a

For each business unit:

- Up to 4 marks for an assessment of growth and market share.
- Up to 4 marks for an assessment of the position in the company portfolio and the division's future strategy.
- Maximum marks per division = 7.
- (Up to a maximum of 20 marks)

Professional skills marks

How well has the candidate demonstrated Professional skills as follows:	Not at all	Not so well	Quite well	Very well
Evaluation skills relating to the decision.	The candidate has failed to use an appropriate structure and has therefore not identified or applied relevant criteria to the position of the business units within Magna's portfolio.	The candidate has used a relevant structure, but the assessment is unsupported by relevant information from the case study. The future strategy is not evaluated or justified.	The candidate has used a relevant structure, and the analysis is supported by relevant information from the case study. However, the future strategy is not evaluated or justified and there is limited demonstration of reflection of the findings.	The candidate has used a relevant structure, and the assessment is supported by relevant information from the case study. The future strategy is evaluated and the candidate has shown strong reflection of their findings.
	0	1.33	2.66	4

Tasks 2b and 2c

Technical marks

(b)   2 marks for each criticism up to a total of 10 marks.

(c)   2 marks for explaining how a two-tier board differs from a single tier board. 2 marks for evaluating each disadvantage of a two-tier system up to a maximum of 6 marks. (Up to a maximum of 8 in total.)

Task 3

Technical marks

(a)   3 marks for an analysis of each process. Total: 9 marks.

(b)   3 marks for calculating the impact on annual profits. 4 marks for an evaluation of other issues. Total: 7 marks.

Professional skills marks

How well has the candidate demonstrated Professional skills as follows	Not at all	Not so well	Quite well	Very well
3 (a) Analytical skills relating to the impact on the Magna business.	The candidate has failed to apply any relevant criteria or analysis to the decision.	The candidate may have used a relevant model, but the assessment is unsupported by relevant information from the case study.	The candidate built relevant analysis supported by relevant information from the case study, but the plan for each process is unclear.	The candidate assessment is supported by relevant information from the case study and a clear plan is proposed for each process.
	0	1.33	2.66	4
3 (b) Professional scepticism relating to the offer from Ali Patel.	The candidate has taken Ali Patel's numbers at face value and has failed to challenge them at all.	The candidate has not questioned and challenged Ali Patel's lack of experience or the lack of evidence for his estimates.	The candidate has challenged both Ali Patel's lack of experience OR the reliability of his estimates and suggested that these cannot be taken at face value.	The candidate has considered both Ali Patel's lack of experience AND the reliability of his estimates and suggested and justified why these cannot be taken at face value.
	0	1.33	2.66	4

KAPLAN PUBLISHING

Supplementary Questions and Answers

1   Concepts of strategy

Question 1: David Gould

David Gould set up his accounting firm, providing accounting services to small businesses, in 20X6. Within three years his fee income was in excess of £100K a year and he had nearly 100 clients most of whom had been gained through word of mouth. David recognised that these small or micro businesses, typically employing ten or fewer people, were receiving less than satisfactory service from their current accountants. These accounting firms typically had between five and ten partners and operated regionally and not nationally. Evidence of poor service included limited access to their particular accountant, poor response time to clients' enquiries and failure to identify opportunities to save clients' money. In addition bad advice, lack of interest in business development opportunities for the client and poor internal communication between the partners and their staff contributed to client dissatisfaction. David has deliberately kept the costs of the business down by employing three part-time accountants and relying on his wife to run the office.

David had recently met Ian King who ran a similar sized accounting firm. The personal chemistry between the two and complementary skills led to a partnership being proposed. Gould and King Associates, subject to securing the necessary funding, is to be launched in September 20Y0. David is to focus on the business development side of the partnership and Ian on the core services provided. Indicative of their creative thinking is David's conviction that accounting services are promoted very inadequately with little attempt to communicate with clients using the internet.

He is also convinced that there are real opportunities for the partnership to move into new areas such as providing accountancy services for property developers, both at home and abroad. Ian feels that the partnership should set up its own subsidiary in India, enjoying the benefits of much cheaper accountancy staff and avoiding the costs and complications of outsourcing their core accounting services. Ian sees fee income growing to £2 million in five years' time.

David has been asked by his bank to provide it with a business plan setting out how the partnership intends to grow and develop.

Required:

(a)   Write a short report for David explaining the key features that you consider to be important and that you would expect to see in the business plan for the Gould and King partnership that David has to present to his bank.   **(15 marks)**

There is considerable evidence that small firms are reluctant to carry out strategic planning in their businesses.

(b)   Evaluate the advantages and disadvantages for Gould and King Associates in creating and implementing a strategic plan.

(10 marks)

(Total: 25 marks)

2   Strategic analysis

Question 2: Dunvegan Ltd

Dunvegan Ltd is a forestry company operating in the UK, mainly in Scotland. In addition to forests at various stages of maturity, the company also owns many hectares of undeveloped land.

So far Dunvegan Ltd's timber has consisted almost exclusively of spruce trees which produce softwood used extensively in building work. Spruce sells for the equivalent of about £200 per cubic metre. However, genetic engineering has produced a remarkable new tree which has the growth characteristics of spruce, but which produces hard wood with the appearance and qualities of mahogany. This species, the Maho spruce, should grow quite happily in Scotland and produce worthwhile crops after ten years, each Maho spruce tree producing about 2 cubic metres. Currently, mahogany sells for the equivalent of £900 per cubic metre.

The company which developed the Maho spruce has ensured that the trees are sterile and has also successfully applied for worldwide patents on the genetic material. Seedlings are available only from that company at a cost of £200 each.

Dunvegan Ltd is considering whether to invest in Maho spruce. Land already owned by the company would be used (market value £1,000/hectare) and the company's planting and drainage equipment would be assigned temporarily to the project. Because the seedlings are so expensive, relatively light planting would be used at 1,500 seedlings per hectare. Annual maintenance and security would be £1,000/hectare for each of the ten years of the project. Dunvegan Ltd is considering planting 1,000 hectares with Maho spruce.

In the UK Dunvegan Ltd has three main competitors; mahogany is also imported from four countries in the tropics where it is a valuable export. Some of the wood is from managed plantations, but some is from natural forest. Recently the price of mahogany has been rising as supplies become short and plantations have to be renewed. Dunvegan Ltd's accountant has read an article in a recent edition of Lumber About, the monthly trade paper of the timber business, in which the economic effects of the Maho spruce were discussed. If around 3,000 – 4,000 hectares were planted in the UK, then the price of mahogany would be £500 per cubic metre at the end of ten years. If around 2,000 hectares only were planted, then the price would be £800 per cubic metre. The break-even price is estimated to be £639/cubic metre.

Required:

From the viewpoint of an independent consultant, write a report to the directors of Dunvegan Ltd on the proposed Maho spruce plantation.

(25 marks)

Question 3: CSC Clothing

The Clothing Supply Company (CSC) is seen as a market leader in the design and manufacture of garments such as knitwear and weatherproof clothing for outdoor sports. The company is over a hundred years old and is based in rural islands of Scotland where it originally used to make and supply hill farmers with outdoor working clothes. CSC prides itself on the use of traditional fabric designs, the craftsmanship of its garment workers and the fact that it buys much of its cloth from local weavers, so supporting the local economy.

In recent years CSC has achieved a degree of dominance over other specialist Scottish clothing manufacturers. The CSC product range now enjoys an international reputation based not only on design and the quality of handmade tailoring but also on the attractive and well known brand name, which is perceived to be associated with the country lifestyle of wealthy society leaders. CSC garments are distributed to and sold at premium prices through the best department stores in London, New York and Tokyo and are especially popular with overseas tourists visiting the United Kingdom.

CSC had been a family-owned business until 1997 when it was sold to the KZ Corporation, a Pacific Rim-based multinational conglomerate involved in shipbuilding, construction and consumer electronics. The KZ Corporation is keen to maximise what it sees as the global brand potential of CSC and to justify what some KZ managers see as the excessively high price paid to the owner's family for their controlling shares in CSC.

To address these issues, the vice-president of global operations at KZ has commissioned a strategy study to identify ways in which CSC can be integrated into the KZ Corporation.

Required:

(a)   Analyse the extent to which international location might determine the competitive position of the Clothing Supply Company.

(16 marks)

(b)   The strategy study was concerned at the relatively high production cost of CSC clothing products and believed that costs could be substantially reduced by moving production to South East Asia. Evaluate the risks and opportunities presented by this suggestion.

(9 marks)

(Total: 25 marks)

Question 4: A University

A University which derives most of its funds from the government provides undergraduate courses (leading to bachelors' degrees) and post-graduate courses (leading to masters' degrees). Some of its funds come from contributions from student fees, consultancy work and research. In recent years, the University has placed emphasis on recruiting lecturers who have achieved success in delivering good academic research. This has led to the University improving its reputation within its national academic community, and applications from prospective students for its courses have increased.

The University has good student support facilities in respect of a library, which is well-stocked with books and journals and up-to-date IT equipment. It also has a gymnasium and comprehensive sports facilities. Courses at the University are administered by well-qualified and trained non-teaching staff that provide non-academic (that is, not learning-related) support to the lecturers and students.

The University has had no difficulty in filling its courses to the level permitted by the government, but has experienced an increase in the numbers of students who have withdrawn from the first year of their courses after only a few months. An increasing number of students are also transferring from their three-year undergraduate courses to other courses within the University but many have left and gone to different universities. This increasing trend of student withdrawal is having a detrimental effect on the University's income as the government pays only for students who complete a full year of their study.

You are the University's management accountant and have been asked by the vice-chancellor (who is the chief executive of the University) to review the withdrawal rate of students from the University's courses.

(Candidates do not require any knowledge of University admission and withdrawal processes to answer this question.)

Required:

Assess the University's value adding activities, and advise the vice-chancellor how this analysis will help to determine why the rate of student withdrawal is increasing. **(25 marks)**

3 Performance analysis

Question 5: MW and FS

Background

MW and FS are both supermarket chains which operate in different parts of a country. Both are listed on the country's Stock Exchange. MW operates in the north of the country while FS stores are located predominantly in the south. Recently the Chairman of FS has approached the Chairman of MW and suggested that MW may wish to present a takeover bid for FS. The Chairman of FS has indicated that such a bid would be favourably received by his Board of Directors and would pre-empt a bid being made by other less desirable predators in the industry. According to the Chairman of FS, there would need to be some staff rationalisation and about 10% of the total number of stores of the combined group would need to be sold as a result of demands which would be made by the country's competition regulatory organisation. However, he believes that there would be increased profitability for the combined group as a whole which would lead to improved shareholder value. At this stage, no public announcement of the possible takeover has been made and all the information relating to it is being treated as strictly confidential.

MW

MW was established over 100 years ago by Mr W. His son (KW), who is now over 70 years old, is the Chairman of the company. The W family has maintained strong control over the business and still owns nearly 40% of its shares. The main principle established by Mr W was that of offering quality products at a reasonable price and this principle has been rigidly maintained throughout the company's history.

Organisationally, MW stores are split into two operating areas – the North West and the North East – although it is controlled from its Head Office by KW and his management team. Each individual store is managed locally by a Store Manager and an assistant. In addition, there are supervisors, till checkout staff, store keepers and shelf stackers working in each store. Other skilled trade staff are also employed including butchers, bakers and fishmongers.

Recent results have shown that MW has increased its sales by 8% and its net profit by 15% over the previous year. MW has become a popular share as a result of the company's ability to cut its operating costs and increase its profitability each year.

KW follows the sound principles of business development established by his father. He prefers to rely on a capital structure which is low geared and has generated organic growth rather than undertaking large takeovers. The last time MW undertook a takeover was 25 years ago when it bought six supermarkets. If a bid is made for FS then it is most likely that KW will wish to offer a share exchange rather than pay any cash. He is acutely aware of competition in the industry within the country and has been advised by the Finance Director that there are two other main competitors which may put forward counter-bids if MW makes an offer for FS.

FS

FS's stores operate within the South West and South East of the country. Approximately 55% of its shares are held by ten major institutional shareholders who have been disappointed in recent performance. These institutional shareholders have been impressed by the success of MW and instructed the Chairman to begin takeover negotiations with KW.

Performance of both companies for the last financial year

For simplicity, the data supplied below represents the average for each store in the relevant area. All stores for each company are built to a standard layout. On average, FS stores are 20% smaller in terms of area than MW stores.

	MW		FS	
	North West $ million	North East $ million	South West $ million	South East $ million
Turnover	10.0	8.0	6.0	5.0
Cost of sales (excluding wages)	4.0	3.0	2.0	1.8
Overheads				
Salaries	1.0	1.0	0.7	0.6
Non-supervisory wages	1.0	0.7	0.7	0.6
Other overheads	1.0	1.1	1.1	0.9
Local taxes	1.0	0.8	0.7	0.6
Net profit	2.0	1.4	0.8	0.5

Additional information

Per store:	MW		FS	
	North West	**North East**	**South West**	**South East**
Total square metres	6,000	6,000	4,800	4,800
Average number of customer visits	0.3 million	0.25 million	0.15 million	0.1 million
Managers and supervisors	15	12	14	12
Total staff	69	56	56	51

The profit attributable to ordinary shareholders in the last financial year was $225 million for MW and $200 million for FS. Inventory is held centrally by each company in its own secure warehouse. It is issued on a daily basis to each store. On average, each MW store has an inventory turnover of 2 days while each FS store has an inventory turnover of 3.5 days.

Required:

(a) Analyse MW's strategic position. **(10 marks)**

(b) In your capacity as Management Accountant for MW, prepare an initial briefing report for the board's consideration prior to any combination of the two businesses which compares the performance of the two businesses. Your report should include an analysis of the data provided in the scenario by making whatever calculations you think appropriate. **(12 marks)**

(Total: 22 marks)

4 **Strategic choice**

Question 6: News Reel Inc

News Reel Inc was incorporated in 1958 and has been wholly owned by members of the Xiang family since that date. The board of directors consists solely of family members. The company manufactures newsprint for sale in the newspaper and magazine industry at a single site in Hoyan Province, to the north west of Eastlandia. Eastlandia is a small island, approximately 200 kilometres off the coast of the mainland continent. In terms of the paper industry, News Reel may be regarded as a small to medium-sized manufacturing company.

The company profile

Markets

The company's major customer has for many years been the Eastlandian Evening Star (EES), for which it is the sole supplier of newsprint. The contract is renewable each year and the price is determined on a cost plus basis.

Historically the EES contract has made up about 30% of the company's revenue, but during the economic recession other business has suffered significantly. As a result the EES contract made up 40% of total revenue in News Reel's last accounting year.

The remaining 60% of sales was mainly to magazines and free newspapers published and circulated across Eastlandia. Frequently orders have been won by News Reel's willingness to provide small quantities of newsprint from short production runs and its promise of prompt delivery.

Raw materials

The major raw material for News Reel is pulp. Rather than rely on the major pulp manufacturers, which import timber from Canada and Scandinavia, the company is supplied exclusively under short-term contracts from a privately-owned Eastlandian mill, Quickpulp Inc, which possesses local softwoods.

In recent years News Reel purchases have accounted for 8% to 10% of Quickpulp Inc's revenue. Whilst these supplies of pulp are slightly more expensive than those that can be purchased from the larger manufacturers, they have the advantage of short and certain delivery times, enabling News Reel to carry negligible inventories of raw materials.

Production

News Reel makes a single product, reels of newsprint. The company's manufacturing operations have been built up over time; as a result a small proportion of its operating non-current assets are replaced each year. Given the scale of its activities, the business is not as capital intensive as many of its larger competitors in the industry; consequently it has a higher proportion of labour costs per tonne of output than the industry average.

In fact, News Reel struggles to compete when tendering for major orders as it uses more pulp per tonne of output than would be the case if it could operate large scale, modern machinery. In compensation however, set-up costs are much lower, and this enables small production runs to be accommodated, ensuring greater flexibility in production scheduling. Due to weak trading volumes the company has only been operating at 70% of productive capacity this year, and a similar level of 30% surplus capacity is expected next year.

The competitive environment

The Eastlandian paper industry is dominated by ten listed companies, whose operations are primarily based on the mainland continent. All produce both commodity newsprint and a variety of branded paper products for specialist markets.

There are also a number of smaller companies, of a similar size to News Reel, which mainly specialise in niche markets. A new phenomenon affecting all sectors has been the growth of low-cost, low-quality recycled paper, supported by subsidies from some foreign governments for their own producers.

The paper industry has been affected significantly by the recession, with most companies operating with excess capacity. This in turn has led them to cut margins when tendering for contracts. The following are the features of the competitive environment:

- Depressed pulp and paper prices (a reflection of their historic value).

- The failure of one or two small operators and downsizing by survivors as they rationalise their operations.

- An increased tendency towards diversification.

A strategic dilemma

The chairman of News Reel has recently been informed that the EES has been acquired by a multinational and that when the existing commitment expires at the end of this year, the contract to supply newsprint will be put out to tender on an annual basis.

He has also been told that the terms of the new contract will be that all newsprint which the EES requires next year will be supplied by the successful bidder at a predetermined tender price per reel. The bids have to be submitted by 30 November and the successful bid will be announced a month later. The contract will not be awarded solely on the basis of price, but this is likely to be a major factor. At the board meeting to discuss these developments the following views were expressed:

The marketing director

'It has long been my view that we have been over-dependent on EES as a customer. Even if we do win the contract next year, there is no guarantee that we will be able to retain it in the future. In my view it is therefore essential that we seek out new markets and new products.

'In particular we are too small to be a commodity producer of newsprint without the EES contract. We need to develop into niche markets within the paper sector by producing differentiated branded products.

'In fact there is currently an opportunity for us. A small local firm, MedicNote Inc, is currently looking for a buyer. It has been very profitable, specialising in exploiting the growing demand in the market for pharmaceutical paper products, but it has experienced severe cash flow problems recently due to overtrading.'

The production director

'I agree with the need to diversify, but making newsprint is what we are good at. We have no experience in other markets. I have just been told that Quickpulp shareholders are looking to sell the company due to recent losses arising from weak world pulp prices. In my opinion this represents an ideal opportunity to secure pulp supplies at a low cost. I am also in favour of more modern large scale machinery in order to drive down marginal costs. This will enable us to compete in the long run in our core activity.'

The finance director

'Even if an acquisition strategy is felt to be appropriate, it is very difficult to evaluate the feasibility of the two options in precise monetary terms as much will depend on the prices of the two businesses. In my judgement News Reel is sufficiently liquid to fund one or other of the options suggested but, given current uncertainties, it would be difficult to raise finance for both of them.'

Required:

As a management consultant you have been commissioned to prepare briefing notes for the directors of News Reel covering the following areas:

(a) Analyse the company's current strategic position.   **(14 marks)**

(b) Evaluate the future strategic options available to the company by appraising:

- the potential growth strategies that the company could pursue,

and

- the particular diversification/acquisition strategies suggested.

(24 marks)

Question 7: Qualispecs

Qualispecs has a reputation for quality, traditional products. It has a group of optician shops, both rented and owned, from which it sells its spectacles. Recently, it has suffered intense competition and eroding customer loyalty, but a new chief executive has joined from one of its major rivals Fastglass.

Fastglass is capturing Qualispecs' market through partnership with a high street shopping group. These shops install mini-labs in which prescriptions for spectacles are dispensed within an hour. Some competitors have successfully experimented with designer frames and sunglasses. Others have reduced costs through new computer-aided production methods.

Qualispecs has continued to operate as it always has, letting the product 'speak for itself' and failing to utilise advances in technology. Although production costs remain high, Qualispecs is financially secure and has large cash reserves. Fortunately, the country's most popular sports star recently received a prestigious international award wearing a pair of Qualispecs' spectacles.

The new chief executive has established as a priority the need for improved financial performance. Following a review she discovers that:

(i)   targets are set centrally and shops report monthly. Site profitability varies enormously, and fixed costs are high in shopping malls

(ii)   shops exercise no control over job roles, working conditions, and pay rates

(iii)   individual staff pay is increased annually according to a pre-determined pay scale. Everyone also receives a small one-off payment based on group financial performance.

Market analysts predict a slowdown in the national economy but feel that consumer spending will continue to increase, particularly among 18 to 30 year olds.

Required:

(a)   Produce a corporate appraisal of Qualispecs, taking account of internal and external factors, and discuss the key strategic challenges facing the company. **(20 marks)**

(b)   Corporate appraisal offers a 'snapshot' of the present. In order to focus on the future there is a need to develop realistic policies and programmes. Recommend, with reasons, strategies from your appraisal that would enable Qualispecs to build on its past success. **(5 marks)**

(Total: 25 marks)

Question 8: T Plc

Introduction

T plc is a well-established company providing telecommunications services both nationally and internationally. Its business has been concerned with telephone calls, the provision of telephone lines and equipment, and private telecommunication networks. T plc has supplemented these services recently by offering mobile phones, which is an expanding market worldwide.

The company maintains a diverse customer base, including residential users, multi-national companies, government agencies and public sector organisations. The company handles approximately 100 million calls each working day, and employs nearly 140,000 personnel.

Strategic development

The Chairman of T plc stated within the latest Annual Report that there are three main areas in which the company aims to develop in order to remain a world leader in the telecommunications market. He believes that the three main growth areas reflect the evolving nature of the telecommunications market and will provide scope for development. The areas in which development is planned are:

- expansion of the telecommunications business in the national and overseas markets, both by the company acting on its own and through partnership arrangements with other suppliers

- diversification into television and multi-media services, providing the hardware to permit telephone shopping from home and broadcasting services

- extension of the joint ventures and strategic alliances which have already been established with companies in North America, Europe, India and the Far East.

The Chairman explained that the company is intent on becoming a world leader in communications. This will be achieved through maintaining its focus on long-term development by improving its services to customers, developing high quality up-to-date products and being innovative, flexible and market-driven. His aim is to deliver a world-class service at competitive cost.

Financial information

Comparative statistics showing extracts from the company's financial performance in its national telecommunications market over the last two years are as follows:

	Last year $ million	Previous year $ million
Turnover	16,613	15,977
Profit before interest and tax	3,323	2,876
Capital employed	22,150	21,300

The Chairman expressed satisfaction with the increase in turnover and stated that cost efficiencies were now being generated following completion of a staff reduction programme.

Business opportunities

The Chief Executive of T has stated that the major opportunities are:

- encouraging greater use of the telephone

- provision of advanced services and research and development into new technology, including the internet and systems integration

- the increasing freedom from government control of worldwide telecommunication services.

An extensive television and poster advertising campaign has been used by the company. This was in order to penetrate further the residential market by encouraging greater use of the telephone with various charging incentives being offered to residential customers.

Markets and competition

The company is currently experiencing an erosion of its market share and faces increasingly strong competition in the mobile phone market. While T plc is the leader in its national market, with an 85% share of the telecommunications business, it has experienced a reduced demand for the supply of residential lines in the last five years as competition has increased. The market for the supply of equipment in the national telecommunications market is perceived to be static.

Industry regulation

The government has established an industry regulatory organisation to promote competition and deter anti-competitive behaviour. As a result of the activities of the regulator and aggressive pricing strategies, it is anticipated that charges to customers will remain constant for at least the next three years.

Required:

(a) Evaluate the telecommunication industry in which T plc is operating. **(10 marks)**

(b) Briefly evaluate the market development opportunities available to T plc. **(8 marks)**

(Total: 18 marks)

5   Methods of strategic development

Question 9: Pelatihan

Introduction

Pelatihan is a privately-owned training college, which specialises in providing courses in business subjects. Pelatihan was founded in 1992 by its current Chief Executive, who is a qualified lawyer. Pelatihan grew rapidly to become one of the largest and most highly regarded colleges in A, an Asian country.

The general situation in A

The last two decades have been a period of rapid social change for the residents of A. The country's economy has developed from being mainly based on subsistence agriculture (that is, agriculture carried out with the aim of feeding the farmer and his/her family), to being much more progressive in all respects. The population is now fairly well educated, with literacy levels much higher among the under-20 age group than in the older population.

This is partly as a result of government policy (introduced in the 1970s) aimed at making education to age 16 available to all citizens of A. While subsistence agriculture has declined sharply, commercial agriculture still contributes about 40% of the country's Gross National Product (GNP). The fastest developing sectors are manufacturing, food production, tourism, financial services and retail.

A is now regarded as a developed Asian economy, with a well-established business and financial community. A is home to many large industrial and commercial corporations, many of which operate globally. Recently, the economy of A has been growing at a rate of about 15% each year. This is better than the growth rates in neighbouring countries. A has a stable, democratic, political system. Its government has been in power for the last six years. A general election is expected at some time in the next two years, and the government is concerned that the main opposition party may be elected. Unlike a number of other countries in the region, A has no recent history of violent unrest or terrorist activity.

The business training market in A

The business training industry is dominated by three major colleges (of which Pelatihan is one).

There are also a number of smaller colleges. The estimated market shares are shown below.

Market shares %	Pelatihan	Koulos	Opleid	Smaller colleges
Finance & Accounting (F&A) courses	40	18	30	15
Marketing courses	15	40	15	30
Law courses	35	30	25	10
Human Resource Management (HRM) courses	20	25	40	15
Other courses	–	40	20	40

Pelatihan has grown to its current size by means of organic growth. Both Koulos and Opleid, on the other hand, have made several acquisitions of smaller colleges in the last five years. Indeed, there have been rumours of a possible merger between Koulos and Opleid, but there is no evidence to support this. Koulos was founded in 1990 by a group of academics from a university. Opleid was founded in 1994 by an ex-director of Koulos, to specialise in Finance courses. Opleid has since recruited a number of experienced tutors from elsewhere in the industry, including an ex-director of Pelatihan.

An independent survey, reported in the press in early 20X1, made the following comments about the market:

"The business training industry in A is very buoyant in most sectors. Demand for courses in Law and HRM is rising quite rapidly, while the market for Finance courses is also growing (though at a slower rate). Marketing is the only sector in decline, possibly as a result of the growth in online 'e-learning' courses provided by The Marketing Institute."

'The Marketing Institute' (mentioned in the comment) is the professional body responsible for the development of marketing professionals in A. It is not a college. Currently it is the only professional institute in A to offer its own courses, whether online or 'face-to-face'. Other institutes are known to be considering the provision of online courses. Koulos is known to be developing online courses, though Pelatihan has no plans to do so.

The structure and performance of Pelatihan

The Board of Directors of Pelatihan now consists of the Chief Executive and four other directors. They are all senior tutors. Each of the four directors is responsible for a 'faculty' of the college, each of which provides courses in a specialist professional area.

The courses provided by Pelatihan range from one day 'insight' or 'update' courses, on a theoretical or practical topic, to much longer courses leading towards exams for academic and professional qualifications. Courses for diplomas, degrees and professional qualifications require students to attend the college for up to 60 days in any one year. Pelatihan does not provide any full time courses and does not provide any student accommodation.

Almost all the students on one day courses have their courses paid for by their employers. Some students on longer courses are also funded by their employers, but approximately half pay their own tuition fees. The college does not discriminate on price between employer-funded students and those who pay their own fees on individual courses. However, some large employers receive a discount for 'bulk purchase' of places on courses.

The performance of the college during its most recent financial year is summarised in Table 1.

Table 1

Comparison of results

Year ended 30 September 20X1	Actual	Budget
Sales revenue (A$ Million)		
Finance and Accounting (F&A) faculty	4.2	4.5
Marketing faculty	0.8	1.0
Law faculty	4.0	4.0
HRM faculty	3.1	3.5
Total for Pelatihan	12.1	13.0
Profit (before interest and tax) (A$ Million)		
Finance and Accounting (F&A) faculty	0.6	1.0
Marketing faculty	(0.1)	0.5
Law faculty	0.6	1.0
HRM faculty	0.4	1.0
Corporate and central costs	(1.4)	(1.2)
Total for Pelatihan	0.1	2.3
Staff numbers (equivalent full time employees)		
Finance and Accounting (F&A) faculty	23	*
Marketing faculty	6	*
Law faculty	26	*
HRM faculty	18	*
Corporate and central costs	14	*
Total for Pelatihan	87	*

Student day numbers **		
Finance and Accounting (F&A) faculty	2030	2000
Marketing faculty	410	450
Law faculty	2100	2000
HRM faculty	1150	1500
Total for Pelatihan	5690	5950

* No budget was set for staff numbers

** A student day is one student attending for one day

The recent board meeting of Pelatihan

At a recent board meeting, the following issues were raised:

- The directors responsible for the F&A and Marketing faculties each raised concerns about a small number of large employer organisations which represent a significant proportion of their faculty's business. These organisations are starting to demand discounts in excess of 20%. This is far higher than the discounts given to other corporate customers. The director of the Law faculty said that one of the law firms she deals with often books up to half of the places on a course, but now demands a discount of 20%.

- The director responsible for the Law faculty reported that two of her tutors had recently resigned, in order to take up positions with Koulos.

- The Chief Executive expressed concern at the poor financial performance of Pelatihan, when compared to the budget for 20X0-X1. He asked for a volunteer to take responsibility for financial planning and control for the new financial year. The director of the F&A faculty said that he could not help, as he was too busy teaching students and dealing with clients. There was no volunteer, so the Chief Executive reluctantly agreed to continue overseeing the work of the three finance staff.

Required:

(a) Analyse the product portfolio of Pelatihan. In the light of this matrix and the information contained in Table 1, comment on the performance of the business. **(13 marks)**

(b) Analyse the company's overall position. **(12 marks)**

(Total: 25 marks)

Question 10: WG plc

Introduction

WG plc was formed four years ago following the merger of two large pharmaceutical companies. Prior to the merger the two companies had been competitors: they believed that by combining forces the shareholders of each company would benefit from increased profits arising from the rationalisation of manufacturing facilities, distribution networks, and concentration of resources towards more focused research and development.

With operating outlets in Europe, Asia, the United States of America and Africa, WG plc regards itself as a global company. It employs approximately 50,000 people worldwide and has developed a wide portfolio of products. Its profits before tax last year increased by 20% and represented approximately 35% of turnover. The company declared that its earnings and dividends per share in the same period each increased by 15% over the previous financial year.

All manufacturers of pharmaceutical products claim that their pricing policies need to be set at a level to achieve high profitability in order to attract funds from investors. They argue that this is necessary to meet their high research and development commitments. In recent years, WG plc and other pharmaceutical manufacturers have encountered public and governmental challenges to their high levels of profitability.

WG plc encounters strong competition from other world-class pharmaceutical manufacturers, but these are few in number. High research and development costs present a major obstacle to potential competitors tempted to enter the industry.

Mission and objectives

The directors of WG plc have defined their overall corporate mission as being to 'combat disease by developing innovative medicines and services and providing them to healthcare organisations for the treatment of patients worldwide'.

The directors have confirmed their main objective is to sustain profitability while achieving the company's overall mission. They have also explained that WG plc aims to work towards eliminating those diseases for which the company is engaged in providing treatments. Achievement of the profitability objective is continually threatened by patents coming to the end of their lives. Patents give the sole right to make, use and sell a new product for a limited period.

Product development

A large proportion of the company's turnover in recent years has been derived from one particular drug. The patent for this drug expires next year and it is expected that its sales at that time will represent no more than 10% of total turnover. Four years ago, the sales of this drug produced almost half the company's entire turnover.

A new product, Coffstop, has now completed its rigorous development phases and is being marketed to pharmaceutical stores throughout the world by WG plc. It is in competition with a similar drug, Peffstill, produced and marketed by a direct competitor of WG plc. Medical research and opinion has concluded that Coffstop is generally more effective than Peffstill in treating the condition for which they are intended. Both drugs are available over the counter from pharmacies. The directors of WG plc are optimistic that Coffstop will become very popular because of its improved effectiveness over other market products.

Market development

WG plc has experienced slow growth in its mature markets of Western Europe, North America and Japan. These markets contribute 80% of overall turnover but their governments have reduced expenditure on pharmaceutical products in recent years. The company has encountered a rapid sales increase in its expanding markets of Eastern Europe, South America, the Asia Pacific region, India, Africa and the Middle East. The directors of the company hold the view that increasing population growth in these markets is likely to provide substantial opportunities for the company over the next two decades.

Research and development

Almost 15% of WG plc's turnover last year was spent on research and development. WG plc has the largest research and development organisation of all pharmaceutical companies worldwide.

Much research is sponsored by national governments and world health organisations. A major piece of research which has recently been undertaken relates to new treatments for malaria as the disease is now demonstrating some resistance to existing treatments. WG plc has established a 'donation programme' for the new drug in virulent areas for the disease. This means that the company is donating batches of the drug to the health organisations in these areas. The cost of this programme is offset by the sales of the new drug in other areas of the world by making it available to people proposing to travel to the regions where malaria is widespread.

Required:

(a) Evaluate the nature and importance of the market threat which WG plc would face if it failed to provide sufficient resources for product development. **(10 marks)**

(b) Discuss the practical issues which the directors of WG plc would need to consider if the company entered a strategic alliance with a competitor for the joint development of future pharmaceutical products. **(10 marks)**

(Total: 20 marks)

6 Organising for success: structure and processes

Question 11: Multinational company

A multinational company which makes and sells consumer durables is reviewing the future organisational structure of its European operations, which employ over 100,000 people.

Development of the company

The company has expanded rapidly in the late 1940s and 1950s. Separate marketing companies were established in all the main European countries to serve the distinctive needs of the markets in each individual country, with some manufacturing facilities in the larger countries. Some exports to other smaller European markets had also been made. A divisional structure was adopted which permitted considerable freedom to individual country managers, who were responsible for all operations in their country. They could decide what models to design, make and sell, the marketing and pricing strategy, and the sourcing.

The industry background

There has been progressive integration of European economies, making cross-border transactions easier. The consumer durable industry has also become much more competitive and cost-conscious, and is faced with considerable overcapacity. New product models can no longer be justified for one country only, but are designed for sale in all countries, and made in one or two chosen plants (possibly in Eastern Europe, with cheaper labour) to serve all markets.

The company now

Although the country-based divisional structure is still in place, most key decisions are now taken at European Head Office. These include the selection of new models to make and sell, and the plants at which these models are to be made, whether these are existing plants or new plants in cheap labour areas.

Local markets are still distinctive with different taxation, distribution costs and pricing structures. Individual country managers still set country selling prices, although comparisons of prices across Europe reveal considerable anomalies. Manufacturing facilities are still operated in major countries, even though it is difficult to justify continuing investment without government subsidy.

Required:

Discuss the potential problems of the present country-based divisional structure and its effectiveness as Europe becomes more integrated and cross-border transactions become easier.

Recommend, with reasons, whether the present divisional organisational structure should be retained, and if this is not supported, recommend an alternative.

(25 marks)

Question 12: QS Software – Part 1

QS is a small software design company, set up in May 20X0 by two graduates, John Jones and Sam Smith. Since it started, it has built a strong local reputation, working with a range of small- to medium-sized businesses to design and develop software applications. It also occasionally advises businesses on hardware installation. It also runs a retail shop, where it constructs and sells custom-made computers to individuals and undertakes repairs and maintenance in a workshop located behind the shop. The design and development team are located above the shop.

Organisation chart

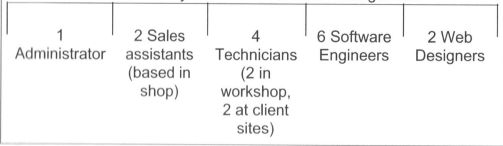

John Jones: Business development and marketing
Sam Smith: Systems and technical management

| 1 Administrator | 2 Sales assistants (based in shop) | 4 Technicians (2 in workshop, 2 at client sites) | 6 Software Engineers | 2 Web Designers |

Both owners recognise that the quality of products and services is vital in such a highly competitive market and, to date, QS has managed to maintain a high quality of customer service by focusing only upon individual customers and small- to medium-sized businesses.

New business opportunity: Regal Global Advertising (RGA)

In August 20X6, John Jones met an old university friend who was working as the IT manager of a large local marketing company called Regal Global Advertising (RGA). It emerged that RGA was looking to invest in setting up a new customer database and website. RGA was also considering re-investing in new hardware throughout the organisation, which would require an on-going maintenance facility. The customer database and website would need to be in place and fully operational by 30 May 20X8.

On returning to the office, John began to put together an outline tender document and an outline project plan. However, Sam Smith, the other partner, was reluctant to take on such a large project as they had no previous experience of managing work on this scale and, more importantly, they already had sufficient work with existing clients for the foreseeable future. John's response to Sam's concerns of maintaining quality for existing customers was: 'Don't worry, we'll fit it in around everything else – there's plenty of time to get it all done'. As John was responsible for new business, which in the past had always been successful, Sam agreed to allow the tender to progress.

John Jones and Sam Smith both have ambitions to develop QS into a major software company, and they are already considering how they should be planning the structure of the organisation to cope with the demands of growing and succeeding in the competitive software industry.

They believe that the future success of the company will depend primarily on the initiative and ingenuity of the IT specialists that the company employs. They are hoping that within a few years, they will be able to take more of a 'back seat' role in the management and direction of the company.

Their ideas about organisation structure have been influenced by the analysis by Mintzberg of an organisation into five elements.

Required:

(a) Analyse the current organisational structure of QS and identify any advantages and disadvantages this structural form might have in the business environment in which QS operates.

(12 marks)

(b) Consider how the organisational structure should be developed in the future.

(8 marks)

(Total: 20 marks)

Question 13: Nikki Photocopiers

Nikki Photocopiers manufactures and sells photocopiers to businesses throughout Europe. The market is highly competitive with major global players present.

Despite earlier success, the firm has recently seen a downturn in its performance as typified by the following customer ratings in **European Business Photocopier Magazine**:

	Rating (last year's rating in brackets)
Value for money	2nd (1st)
Features	2nd (3rd)
Reliability	3rd (2nd)
Servicing and maintenance	7th (5th)

Last year the firm introduced a customer relationship management (CRM) software system so the fall in the service rating was a surprise. Before this survey had been published the directors had planned to redesign research and production processes but, based on this feedback, decided to look at the customer servicing and maintenance process first. Outsourcing was rejected as an option and the focus was placed on reengineering the process instead.

Current process

CURRENT PROCESS

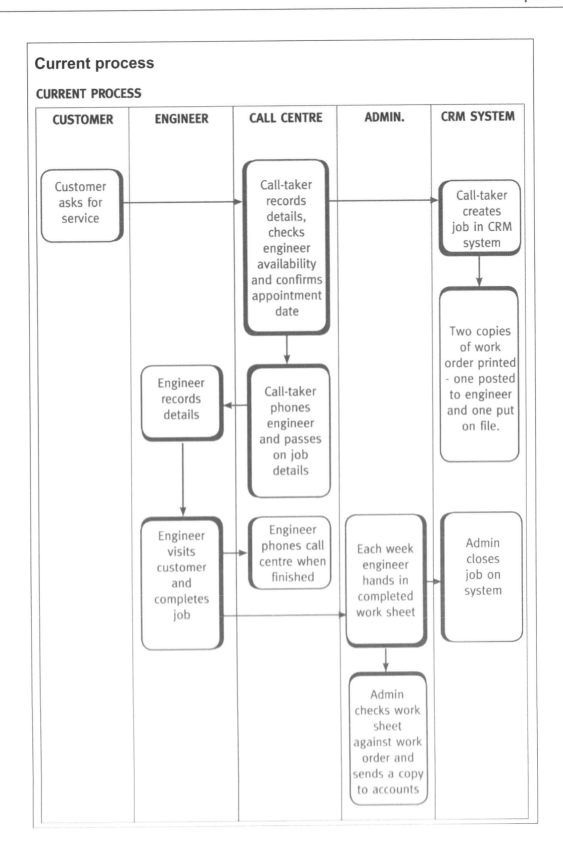

CUSTOMER	ENGINEER	CALL CENTRE	ADMIN.	CRM SYSTEM
Customer asks for service		Call-taker records details, checks engineer availability and confirms appointment date		Call-taker creates job in CRM system
				Two copies of work order printed - one posted to engineer and one put on file.
	Engineer records details	Call-taker phones engineer and passes on job details		
	Engineer visits customer and completes job	Engineer phones call centre when finished	Each week engineer hands in completed work sheet	Admin closes job on system
			Admin checks work sheet against work order and sends a copy to accounts	

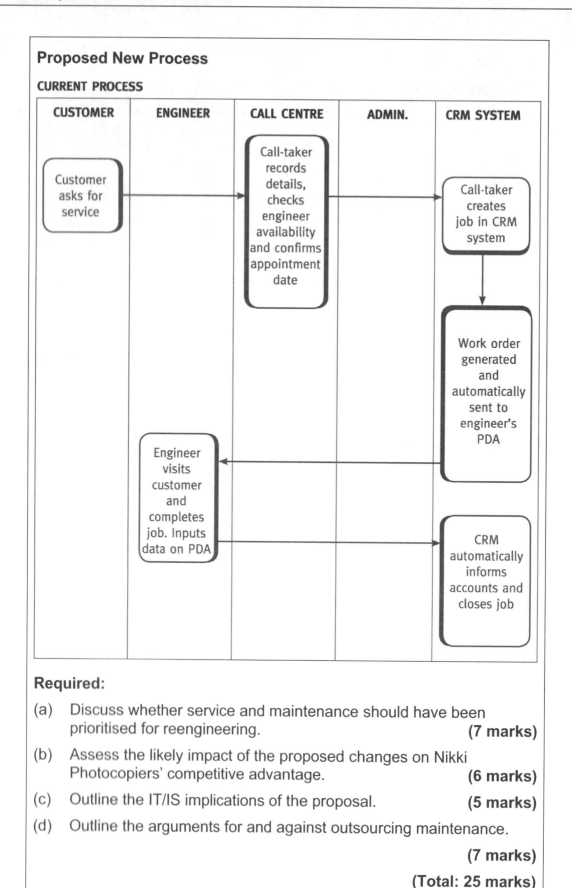

Proposed New Process

CURRENT PROCESS

CUSTOMER	ENGINEER	CALL CENTRE	ADMIN.	CRM SYSTEM

Customer asks for service

Call-taker records details, checks engineer availability and confirms appointment date

Call-taker creates job in CRM system

Work order generated and automatically sent to engineer's PDA

Engineer visits customer and completes job. Inputs data on PDA

CRM automatically informs accounts and closes job

Required:

(a) Discuss whether service and maintenance should have been prioritised for reengineering. **(7 marks)**

(b) Assess the likely impact of the proposed changes on Nikki Photocopiers' competitive advantage. **(6 marks)**

(c) Outline the IT/IS implications of the proposal. **(5 marks)**

(d) Outline the arguments for and against outsourcing maintenance.

(7 marks)

(Total: 25 marks)

7 E-business

Question 14: SDW

The SDW Company has been trading for one year. It provides rail travel services between three major cities in the country in which it operates.

Mr M, the majority shareholder and managing director, is keen to expand its operations and, in particular, to use the internet as the major selling medium. He has discovered, for example, that doubling sales on the internet usually results in no additional costs. However, doubling sales using a call centre normally results in a doubling of staff and an increase in costs.

All tickets are currently sold via the company's call centre. The company has an internet site although this is used for publicity only, not for sales or marketing. Competitors currently use a mixture of selling media, although detailed information on the success of each medium is not available to the SDW Company.

Mr M has asked you, as a qualified management accountant, to assist him in upgrading the company's internet site and, in particular, show how this will help to reduce operating costs.

Required:

(a)　Advise Mr M on how to establish and implement an appropriate internet strategy for the SDW Company. **(13 marks)**

(b)　Discuss the key customer-orientated features of an internet site, showing how these can be used to meet the objective of cost reduction required by Mr M. **(12 marks)**

(Total: 25 marks)

Question 15: RBT

RBT manufactures tractors, harvesting machinery and similar farm equipment. It operates from one integrated office and factory near the capital of the country in which it is based. Due to restricted demand and the cost of manufacture of individual items, all equipment is manufactured to specific orders from clients. No inventories of finished goods are maintained although inventories of spare parts are available for sale.

The farm equipment is sold to farm owners by one of 20 sales representatives. The general procedure for making a sale is for the representative to visit the farm owner to discuss the owner's requirements. Basic price and model specification information are obtained from printed manuals that the representative carries. The representative then telephones the RBT office and confirms with production staff that the order can be made, checks the price and receives an estimated delivery date. An order confirmation is written out and the representative moves on to the next appointment. The farmer pays for the equipment on receipt.

As the country in which RBT operates is large, representatives cannot often visit RBT's office, so their price and model specification manuals may be out of date.

The board of RBT is considering the introduction of a new information system. Each representative will be given a portable PC. Information on such things as products and prices will be kept on an intranet and downloaded by telephone line when needed by the representative. Access to production managers and sales representatives will also be made via the intranet. The voice telephone system will be discontinued and email is thought to be unnecessary.

Required:

(a) Evaluate the proposed use of the intranet within the RBT Company showing whether it would provide an appropriate communication channel for the sales representatives. Suggest ways in which any problems you have identified with the new systems may be resolved.

(b) Identify and evaluate any information systems that can be used to provide clients with information on the progress of their orders with RBT while they are being manufactured.

8   Using IT successfully

Question 16: MACOMP

Introduction

MACOMP is a small manufacturer of replacement machine components for machinery used in the mining and oil exploration industries. It is based in an African country, Zedland. It was formed in 1952, as a partnership between two engineers, and incorporated in 1977.

MACOMP now employs 120 staff, and has an annual turnover equivalent to one million US dollars. MACOMP is proud to offer the very highest levels of customer service. Much of the machinery used by MACOMP's customers is quite old and, as a result, components are no longer available from the original equipment manufacturers (OEMs), most of which are large multinational companies. MACOMP mostly supplies parts directly to the end-users but also receives a small but significant proportion of its business from OEMs, who then supply the components to their customers.

The current business model

MACOMP has always run its business in a very traditional way. The sales manager receives most orders by telephone or fax. The order specifies the OEM part number that the component is to replace. If MACOMP has previously supplied that component, the sales manager checks the price list and tells the customer the price. MACOMP holds very low levels of finished goods inventory, and then only of the most commonly ordered components.

Where MACOMP needs to make a component for the first time, an MACOMP 'estimator' (a qualified engineer, responsible for producing an estimate of the material and labour involved in manufacturing the item) obtains the original drawings of the component, either from MACOMP's extensive archives or from the OEM. The estimator then produces detailed engineering drawings, a list of materials and parts required, and an estimate of the labour hours likely to be used at each stage of the manufacturing process. The estimate is passed to a costing clerk in the accounts department who calculates the likely product cost (labour, materials and overheads), adds a 'mark-up' of 50%, and advises the sales manager of the price. If the customer accepts the price, an order is passed to the production department, which schedules and completes the work. If the actual cost of production is significantly different from that estimated, the price list is amended to reflect the actual manufacturing cost.

Very occasionally, a customer sends (or brings in) an old component, which cannot be traced back to an OEM. The sales manager gives the component to an estimator, who dismantles the component and produces the necessary engineering drawings and estimate. This process is called 'reverse engineering', and is common in the component manufacturing industry. Reverse engineering currently accounts for about 5% of MACOMP's business.

When an order is fulfilled, the component is delivered to the customer, together with an invoice. Most customers pay within 30 days, by cash or cheque. MACOMP does not have a problem with bad debts. An increasing proportion of MACOMP's business is now transacted in US dollars, as African currencies tend to be unstable.

MACOMP prides itself on the personal service it provides. The close contact it has with its customers means that MACOMP receives a significant amount of repeat business. MACOMP has never advertised its services, but grew significantly until 20X9 as a result of 'word of mouth' recommendations by satisfied customers. MACOMP, however, has not experienced growth for the last two years, although turnover and profit have remained stable.

MACOMP uses only very basic Information Systems (IS), and reports its performance using a simple comparison between budget and actual, which is produced using a spreadsheet package. MACOMP's accounting system is not automated, and transactions are recorded in traditional ledgers.

Project E: Computerised accounting and e-commerce systems

The sales manager of MACOMP has noticed that customers are increasingly mentioning that they would like to be able to order online. He knows that there has been a significant growth in business-to-business (B2B) e-commerce in recent years. The sales manager has recognised that in order to grow and to make a move into e-commerce possible, MACOMP's accounting system will have to be updated to a computerised one.

Having spoken to a number of potential suppliers, the sales manager has now received a proposal from SSS, a local company, to supply tailored 'off-the-shelf' systems for both accounting and e-commerce.

The sales manager believes that, following implementation of the new systems e-commerce could lead to an increase in the company's turnover of 10% each year for the foreseeable future. However, the sales manager thinks that a cautious approach should be taken and that the system may only lead to strategic advantages for around 5 years, after which time competitors are likely to have caught up and developed similar systems.

The sales manager also thinks that any increase in indirect costs as a result of this higher volume of business will be fully offset by a reduction in administration workload as a result of the new computerised accounting system. The mark-up on products sold by e-commerce will be the same as at present (that is, 50%).

Required:

(a) Briefly explain how e-commerce has impacted on the way business is conducted and briefly discuss how a new Information Systems (IS) strategy might impact upon corporate and business strategies. **(12 marks)**

(b) Assess how the e-commerce investment could benefit the activities of MACOMP. **(13 marks)**

(Total: 25 marks)

9 E-marketing

Question 17: Marketing

Prendips is a national company which has been built up over many years primarily through an acquisition strategy. It now has three distinct subsidiaries in the UK and group head office is assessing how each subsidiary's product should be marketed. The three subsidiaries are as follows:

- ABC Inc makes and sells machine parts which are used in the manufacture of 10 pin bowling machines.

- DEF Ltd sells fridges, freezers and cookers to the general public.

- GHI Inc manufactures and sells kids jelly sweet candy.

Discuss how the marketing mix could be used to sell each of the subsidiary's products. **(12 marks)**

10   Project management

Question 18: QS Software – Part 2

(Part 1 of this question was covered in an earlier part of this chapter and should be read before attempting this part of the scenario.)

QS was awarded the contract to undertake the project at the end of October 20X7.

Project scope

The project was to be completed by 30 May 20X8, 30 calendar weeks after the award of the contract, with the design and delivery of a customer database, which could be utilised by the customers through access to a re-designed website. In addition, there was an option to extend the contract for a further 12 months for systems maintenance. This would be negotiated and finalised only after successful project completion and systems performance evaluation.

Project resources

Sam Smith was assigned the role of project manager, with responsibility for managing the delivery of the final project to RGA. It was planned that three of the software engineers and one of the workshop technicians would work full-time on the project. However, due to QS already being committed to other jobs, Sam allowed these core staff to be released from the RGA work when necessary. Other QS staff were to be assigned temporarily to the RGA project as and when they were needed.

John Jones agreed to act as liaison between the project team and the IT manager of RGA, as he considered it to be his project, having won the contract. However, John would not be directly involved in the day-to-day activities of the project.

Sam was not happy about being responsible for team management and co-ordination. He preferred the technical work to managing people and had little experience of team leadership and delegation. No contract undertaken by QS previously had required this level of project management.

Project progress

Phase one of the project began one week late, due to one software engineer working on another job. It was agreed at this point by Sam and John that, to save time, the purchase of the hardware could be brought forward. However, the first stage payment had not yet been made and the purchases had to be made by extending the overdraft facility. John was confident that the first key payment milestone would be reached and the financial concerns would be short-lived.

The website and customer database were completed on time, but prototype construction had to be delayed, as Sam allowed the technician to work on other jobs during this time. (Sam was not fully aware of all the details of the project plan as he had not been involved at the planning stage, and he and John rarely saw each other. Sam himself was often absent visiting other clients.) The first stage deadline was missed. Although technically the project was progressing as planned, the main concern for Sam Smith was the availability of staff to complete key stages. Although other existing work being carried out by QS was small in comparison to the RGA project, these customers also required a quality service and commitment to deadlines. The second stage deadline was in danger of being missed.

In March, the IT manager from RGA contacted John Jones to demand an explanation for the project delays. He was also concerned that so few staff of QS were working on the project, in particular the lack of visibility of the project manager. The IT manager demanded a meeting with both Sam and John to review the current project status. John also spoke to QS's bank manager who was concerned about the current overdraft facility.

A small business adviser was assigned from the bank to assist QS for the remainder of the project.

Project review meeting – 2 April 20X8

John called an emergency meeting with Sam, the other key project team members and the small business adviser. The main issues which arose from the meeting were as follows.

- The designers were concerned that they did not know which work to prioritise.

- The project team members were not aware of any deadlines for the RGA project, as no one had shown them a project plan or schedule of work.

- Sam argued that he was not a trained project manager and could not be expected to manage such a large undertaking and be responsible for all of the other smaller jobs in progress.

- The cash resources of the business were in a critical state. QS could not afford to miss another stage deadline or lose the lucrative maintenance contract.

Required:

Identify the problems currently being encountered by Sam in managing the project team of the RGA Project. **(13 marks)**

Recommend ways in which the managers of QS could improve the management of the project team. **(12 marks)**

(Total: 25 marks)

11   Financial decision making

Question 19: Spartan

It is easier to revise sources of finance and ratios using a question.

Spartan Inc. is a medium-sized manufacturing company that plans to increase capacity by purchasing new machinery at an initial cost of $3m. The following are the most recent financial statements of the company:

Statement of profit or loss for the years ending 31 December

	20X6	20X5
	$000	$000
Turnover	5,000	5,000
Cost of sales	3,100	3,000
Gross profit	1,900	2,000
Administration and distribution expenses	400	250
Profit before interest and tax	1,500	1,750
Interest	400	380
Profit before tax	1,500	1,370
Tax	330	400
Profit after tax	770	970
Dividends	390	390
Retained earnings	380	580

Balance sheets (statements of financial position) as at 31 December

	20X6		20X5	
	$000	$000	$000	$000
		6,500		6,400
Non-current assets				
Current assets				
Inventories	1,170		1,000	
Debtors	850		900	
Cash	130		100	
		2,150		2,000
Total assets		8,650		8,400

Equity and liabilities		
Share capital		
Ordinary shares ($1 each)	3,500	3,500
Reserves	500	120
	4,000	3,620
10% Loan notes 2011	3,500	3,500
Current liabilities	1,150	1,280
Total equity and liabilities	8,650	8,400

The investment is expected to increase annual sales by 5,500 units. Investment in replacement machinery would be needed after five years. Financial data on the additional units to be sold is as follows:

Selling price per unit	$500
Production costs per unit	$200

- Variable administration and distribution expenses are expected to increase by $220,000 per year as a result of the increase in capacity.

- In addition to the initial investment in new machinery, $400,000 would need to be invested in working capital.

- The full amount of the initial investment in new machinery of $3 million will give rise to capital allowances on a 25% per year reducing balance basis. The scrap value of the machinery after five years is expected to be negligible.

- Tax liabilities are paid in the year in which they arise and Spartan Inc. pays tax at 30% of annual profits.

- The Finance Director of Spartan has proposed that the $3.4 million investment should be financed by an issue of loan notes at a fixed rate of 8% per year.

- Spartan uses an after-tax discount rate of 12% to evaluate investment proposals. In preparing its financial statements, Spartan uses straight-line depreciation over the expected life of fixed assets.

- Average data for the business sector in which Spartan operates is as follows:

  - Gearing (book value of debt/book value of equity) 100%

  - Interest cover 4 times

  - Current ratio 2:1

  - Inventory days 90 days.

Required:

(a) Suggest alternative sources of finance that Spartan could use, outlining the advantages and disadvantages of each.

(b) Analyse and comment on the recent financial performance of the company.

(c) Calculate the effect on the gearing and interest cover of Spartan Inc. of financing the proposed investment with an issue of loan notes and compare your results with the sector averages.

Question 20: Bits and Pieces

Bits and Pieces (B&P) operates a retail store selling spares and accessories for the car market. The store has previously only opened for six days per week for the 50 working weeks in the year, but B&P is now considering also opening on Sundays. The sales of the business on Monday through to Saturday averages at $10,000 per day with average gross profit of 70% earned.

B&P expects that the gross profit % earned on a Sunday will be 20 percentage points lower than the average earned on the other days in the week. This is because they plan to offer substantial discounts and promotions on a Sunday to attract customers. Given the price reduction, Sunday sales revenues are expected to be 60% more than the average daily sales revenues for the other days. These Sunday sales estimates are for new customers only, with no allowance being made for those customers that may transfer from other days.

B&P buys all its goods from one supplier. This supplier gives a 5% discount on all purchases if annual spend exceeds $1,000,000. It has been agreed to pay time and a half to sales assistants that work on Sundays. The normal hourly rate is $20 per hour. In total five sales assistants will be needed for the six hours that the store will be open on a Sunday. They will also be able to take a half-day off (four hours) during the week. Staffing levels will be allowed to reduce slightly during the week to avoid extra costs being incurred.

The staff will have to be supervised by a manager, currently employed by the company and paid an annual salary of $80,000. If he works on a Sunday he will take the equivalent time off during the week when the assistant manager is available to cover for him at no extra cost to B&P. He will also be paid a bonus of 1% of the extra sales generated on the Sunday project.

The store will have to be lit at a cost of $30 per hour and heated at a cost of $45 per hour. The heating will come on two hours before the store opens in the 25 'winter' weeks to make sure it is warm enough for customers to come in at opening time. The store is not heated in the other weeks.

The rent of the store amounts to $420,000 per annum.

Required:

(a) Calculate whether the Sunday opening incremental revenue exceeds the incremental costs over a year (ignore inventory movements) and on this basis reach a conclusion as to whether Sunday opening is financially justifiable. **(12 marks)**

(b) Discuss whether the manager's pay deal (time off and bonus) is likely to motivate him. **(4 marks)**

(c) Briefly discuss whether offering substantial price discounts and promotions on Sunday is a good suggestion. **(4 marks)**

(Total: 20 marks)

Question 21: Teemo

The holding company of Teemo, a manufacturer, has had a shake-up at all levels of Teemo's organisation. A new board has been appointed as well as many new senior managers. The newly-appointed Managing Director of Teemo has lots of experience in the industry but very little accounting knowledge. She has received a variance report for Month 6, which is shown below:

Month 6 Variance Report

	Favourable $	Adverse $	$
Expected profit on actual sales			38,000
Production variances			
Materials price		6,300	
Materials usage		6,000	
Labour rate	5,400		
Labour efficiency		2,400	
Variable overhead expenditure	–	–	
Variable overhead efficiency		1,200	
Fixed overhead		4,000	
	5,040	19,900	14,860
Actual profit			11,140

The previous managing director was focused on cost control and was less concerned about the performance of the sales department. The new MD has asked the new finance director to provide some idea of the performance of the sales team and to explain the variance report to her so that she can make a judgement on the performance of the company over the last month. She would like to know what the budgeted contribution was before she makes a judgement on the overall performance.

The finance director has gathered together the following information prior to preparing his report:

(1) Teemo produces one type of product. It operates a standard marginal costing system.

(2) The standard unit cost and price of the product is as follows:

Month 6 Variance Report

	$	$
Selling price		250
Direct material (5 kg at $20)	100	
Direct labour (4 hours at $10)	40	
Variable overheads	20	160
		___
Contribution		90
		___

(3) The variable overhead absorption rate is based on direct labour hours. The company has budgeted fixed overheads of $70,000 per month.

(4) Budgeted sales and production levels are 1,000 units per month.

(5) 1,200 units were actually produced and sold in month 6.

(6) The actual direct materials purchased and used was 6,300 kg costing $132,300 and the actual direct labour hours worked were 5,040 hours.

Required:

Prepare a report for the Managing Director of FX that explains and interprets the Month 6 variance report.   **(14 marks)**

Question 22: Cost accounting

The following question is aimed at improving the recall of some of the brought forward cost accounting techniques which may appear in this exam.

Traditional costing

An organisation budgets to produce and sell 3,800 units of a product in the forthcoming year. The amount of capital investment attributable to the product will be $600,000 and the organisation requires a rate of return of 15% on all capital invested.

Further details concerning the product are as follows:

Direct material cost per unit	$14
Direct labour cost per unit	$19
Variable overhead cost per unit	$3
Machine hours per unit	8

Fixed overhead is absorbed at a rate of $11 per machine hour.

Required:

Determine the selling price per unit of the product which will achieve the specified return on investment.

Activity-based costing

A small accountancy firm provides three services as follows:

	Statutory audit	Tax services	Other services
Budgeted services	50	100	400
Budgeted labour hours per service	18	2	4
Average number of reviews per service	3	0.5	2

Other services include services such as pension planning, business consultancy and business valuations.

The budgeted activity cost for reviews was $55,000.

Required:

If an ABC system is used by the accountancy firm, determine how much review cost is attached to each statutory audit service. Comment briefly on the suitability of an ABC system to a firm of accountants.

Decision making

A company manufactures two models of a pocket calculator: The basic model sells for $5.50, has a direct material cost of $1.25 and requires 0.25 hours of labour time to produce. The other model, the Scientist, sells for $7.50, has a direct material cost of $1.63 and takes 0.375 hours to produce.

Labour, which is paid at the rate of $6 per hour, is currently very scarce, while demand for the company's calculators is heavy. The company is currently producing 8,000 of the basic model and 4,000 of the Scientist model per month, while fixed costs are $24,000 per month.

An overseas customer has offered the company a contract, worth $35,000, for a number of calculators made to its requirements. The estimating department has ascertained the following facts in respect of the work:

- The labour time for the contract would be 1,200 hours.

- The material cost would be $9,000 plus the cost of a particular component not normally used in the company's models.

- These components could be purchased from a supplier for $2,500 or alternatively, they could be made internally for a material cost of $1,000 and an additional labour time of 150 hours.

Required:

Determine whether the company should accept the proposed new contract.

Dealing with risk and uncertainty

A firm of consultants provides regular service work for a large client based in the east of the country. The client is now expanding to the west of the country and has asked the firm of consultants to bid for the consultancy work that would be needed for this area. The contract is referred to as the West Contract.

The consultancy firm has determined that it makes $60 contribution per labour hour from existing work for this client and it would expect this level of contribution to continue if it wins the new West Contract. The work could be carried out from the existing office (although there is likely to be around an extra $4,000 in administrative costs), but the firm believes that without a commitment to the west of the country there is only a 60% chance of winning the contract. The cost of preparing the bid from the existing office is $20,000.

If the bid is won there is an expectation of gaining 1,000 hours of consultancy work from the client for each of the next three years (when the contract is typically re-opened for tender). The cost of preparing the bid would rise to $30,000.

However, if the consultancy firm was to make a commitment to having a physical presence in the west of the country they expect to be able to gain a further 3,000 hours of work from other clients. Work for these other clients would be expected to make a contribution of $80 per hour.

The physical presence in the west would also increase the firm's chance of winning the West Contract by 20%. It would, however, involve setting up an office in the west (i.e. renting space and hiring staff etc.) which has an expected cost of $750,000 and has no expected residual value in three years' time (the time period over which the firm evaluates all new strategic proposals).

Required:

Determine the best course of action for the firm. Ignore the time value of money.

Variance analysis

The following data relates to the budget for a company producing a product in March:

Budgeted production and sales	1,750 units
Standard cost per unit:	
	$
Direct materials	6.00
Direct labour	3.00
Variable production overhead	0.75
Fixed production overhead	2.50
	12.25
Standard sales price	18.25
Standard profit per unit	6.00
Number of units produced and sold in March	1,800 units
Actual sales revenue	$32,300

Required:

Calculate the sales price and sales volume profit variance. What would be the sales volume contribution variance if standard marginal costing were used?

Question 23: MN plc

MN plc has a rolling programme of investment decisions. One of these investment decisions is to consider mutually-exclusive investments A, B and C. The following information has been produced by the investment manager.

	Investment decision A £	Investment decision B £	Investment decision C £
Initial investment	105,000	187,000	245,000
Cash inflow for A: years 1 to 3	48,000		
Cash inflow for B: years 1 to 6		48,000	
Cash inflow for C: years 1 to 9			48,000
Net present value (NPV) at 10% each year	14,376	22,040	31,432
Ranking	3rd	2nd	1st
Internal rate of return (IRR)	17.5%	14%	13%
Ranking	1st	2nd	3rd

Required:

(a) Prepare a report for the management of MN plc which includes:

- a statement of the reasons for differences between NPV and IRR rankings – use investment A to illustrate the points you make;

- a brief summary which gives MN plc's management advice on which project should be selected. **(9 marks)**

(b) One of the directors has suggested using payback to assess the investments. Explain to him the advantages and disadvantages of using payback methods over IRR and NPV. Use the figures above to illustrate your answer. **(7 marks)**

(Total: 16 marks)

Question 24: Ski Runs

A landowner in an area of the country which has high mountain peaks proposes to develop a number of ski runs down the side of a mountain. The runs will be approximately 5 km long, dropping 1,000 metres from the mountain's summit to a car park. Two alternative strategies (each giving the same capacity) are being considered for the development:

Investment levels

Low investment, involving the construction of a series of tows to haul skiers from the car park to the summit: the initial cost of constructing the tows will be $250,000 and tow motors will have to be replaced after five years at a cost of $50,000; operating costs will be $90,000 per year (fixed) and $3.50 per skier (variable).

High investment, involving the construction of a cable-car system giving a non-stop ride to the summit: the initial cost of constructing the lift will be $1,200,000; operating costs will be $30,000 per year (fixed) and $1 per skier (variable).

The regional tourist board will subsidise the initial construction cost of the development (using either strategy) by providing a loan for half the value of the initial construction cost. The loan is at an interest rate of 4% repayable over six years on an annuity basis. The tourist board requires (as a condition of the loan) that a flat fee of $8 is charged for each skier towed/lifted to the summit.

Number of skiers

The number of skiers using the runs will be dependent on the quality of snow cover. The better the snow cover, then the more runs it will be possible to open and the longer will the runs be able to stay open. The landowner forecasts that in any ten-year period, and assuming an $8 fee, the seasons will be as follows:

Quality of snow cover	Number of seasons	Number of skiers
Good	3	60,000
Moderate	4	40,000
Poor	3	5,000

Business risks

The landowner has stated:

'Although the quality of snow cover is unpredictable for any one year, we can determine the expected outcome for an average year using probabilities and base our investment appraisal and business plan on that.'

A business adviser has commented on this statement as follows:

'The whole problem about winter sports in this country is the variability and unpredictability of snow cover. On average, conditions are as good as anywhere on the continent. However, if your first three seasons are poor then this could have a devastating effect on project viability.'

Financial returns

The landowner's cost of money is 12% per annum and in appraising investments he considers cash flows over a ten-year period only. He has ignored fixed costs from the assessment due to their nature, but included the cost of the loan repayments as a relevant cash flow.

His calculations are as follows:

Time		Cash flow		12% DF	NPV	
		Low	High		Low $000	High $000
0	Construction	(250.0)	(1,200.0)	1	(250.0)	(1,200.0)
0	Tourist Board loan	125.0	600.0	1	125.0	600.0
1–10	Fee income	284.0	284.0	5.650	1604.6	1604.6
1–10	Variable costs ($3.50/$1 × 35.5)	(124.3)	(35.5)	5.650	(702.3)	(200.6)
5	Replacement motors	(50.0)		0.567	(28.4)	
1–6	Loan repayments	(23.8)	(114.5)	4.111	(97.8)	(470.7)
	NPV				651.1	333.3

Note on loan repayments: 4% 6 yr annuity factor = 5.242. Annual repayments = 125/5.242 = 23.8.

On this basis the landowner has decided to make the low level of investment.

Required:

(a) Explain and briefly assess the landowner's financial appraisal of the project. Your answer should include an explanation on why finance-related cash flows (loan drawdowns, interest payments and loan repayments) are normally excluded from project appraisal exercises, and identify the circumstances when such cash flows are included in the appraisal. **(13 marks)**

(b) Explain the full range of risks and uncertainties involved in the project at the outset. Explain how these can be incorporated and allowed for in appraisal of the project. **(12 marks)**

(Total: 25 marks)

12 Managing strategic change

Question 25: Y

Y is one of the five main high street banks in the country. Since banking deregulation in the late 1980s, Y, like other banks, has been facing increasing competition, first from other existing financial institutions but more recently from new entrants who have started to offer deposit accounts and a number of other financial services.

In seeking to respond to these competitive threats, the bank's senior management has started to implement a number of changes. These involve a significant restructuring of the organisation with the removal of a number of layers of management, and a consequent reduction in staffing levels in most divisions. The closure of a number of high street branches is also planned.

The telephone-banking arm is being substantially enlarged and a major investment in IT is being undertaken. The effect on staff will be considerable. A programme of voluntary redundancy and redeployment is planned and, given the demand for new skills, a considerable amount of training will need to be carried out. Despite clear evidence of the threat of the future of the bank, the plans set forth by management are meeting resistance from the workforce. The banking unions in particular seem determined to obstruct the changes wherever possible.

Required (with reference to the above scenario)

(a) Explain why the implementation of organisational change often proves to be so difficult. **(12 marks)**

(b) Advise Y's management about the ways in which change can be facilitated. **(13 marks)**

(Total: 25 marks)

Question 26: BHH Clothing

The European clothing industry is a mature industry characterised by the following:

- Powerful retailers resulting in high pressure on manufacturers' margins.

- Increasing globalisation resulting in many manufacturers switching production to cheaper locations outside Europe to reduce their cost base.

- Increasing competition from Chinese manufacturers due to their lower costs, an improving reputation for quality and the relaxation of quotas.

Retailers buy on three criteria and put pressure on manufacturers to improve each of the following:

- Design/quality

- Cost/price

- Speed to market/lead times.

BHH is a clothing manufacturer based in Europe, making ladies and girls' clothing aimed at the medium/high price segments of the market. The majority are sold under retailers' own labels. BHH's competitive strategy to date has been to differentiate through close collaboration with clients, good designs and hand finishing of garments. Historically BHH has resisted the pressure to source garments from cheaper countries outside of Europe but falling margins have lead directors to question this stance.

Issues were brought to a head recently when BHH lost Forum, a major customer, despite offering a 4% price cut. Forum claimed that they could get similar garments supplied much cheaper by companies that use Chinese factories to make them. Two other large customers are also putting pressure on BHH to cut prices without compromising quality.

At a recent board meeting directors decided that the only way forward was to keep design and finishing in Europe but outsource the manufacture of the basic garment to China. Unfortunately news of this decision leaked out to the workforce before the board could make a formal announcement, causing widespread unrest amongst employees, some of whom have worked for BHH for over twenty years. There is thus now the threat of strike action to try to resist feared redundancies.

Required:

Apply the change kaleidoscope model to BHH as follows:

(a) Examine the wider strategic context for change by assessing the main environmental influences and considering the alternative strategies available to BHH.   **(10 marks)**

(b) Analyse, information permitting, the contextual features that the directors must consider.   **(10 marks)**

(c) Discuss the design choices available to manage the change process and make recommendations.   **(5 marks)**

(Total: 25 marks)

Suggested solutions

Question 1: David Gould

(a) Writing a business plan is a critical stage in moving an idea for a business into a reality. The reality includes presenting a convincing case to potential financers of the business, be they banks or venture capitalists. The key ingredients include clearly saying what you plan to do and why people should want to buy your particular service. Experts warn of starting with a detailed cash flow and then working backwards to make the numbers fit. You should regard the business plan as a management tool and not simply a sales document. Again, the advice is to make credible and achievable projections; it is better to exceed low targets than fail to achieve over-ambitious ones. Many business plans are based on deeply flawed research. Key to your business success will be the size of your target market. There is much evidence to suggest that it is the make-up of the team presenting the plan and their commitment rather than the business idea itself that will determine whether the necessary financial support is made.

Clearly, you need to say how much money you require and why. Again the advice is not to be afraid to ask for large amounts if your business requires it. Linked to how much you want is a clear statement of the return the investor or lender will get – how much of the equity are you willing to give or what security can you offer the lender? Figures are important and you need projected cash flows, profit and loss accounts and balance sheets for at least three years ahead. Potential investors and/or lenders are likely to be impressed by a plan which clearly indicates where the major risks are to be found and the strategies available to handle such risks.

There needs to be a clear statement of the major steps and milestones on the way to achieving your goals. Where are you now, where do you intend to be and how are you going to get there. One expert argues there are three elements of the plan itself – an executive summary pulling together the key points in your proposal, secondly the plan itself and finally an 'elevator pitch', a one paragraph description that explains the business in the time it takes to go up in a lift.

In summary, your business plan should contain an executive summary as explained above, the objectives of the business, including key financial targets and the philosophy of the business, the target market and relevant forecasts, the range of products/services, the marketing strategy linked to the target markets, resource availability, people and organisation involved, performance measurement to measure progress towards stated objectives and a summary of financial information.

One final point is to remember that no business plan ever was carried out exactly! In many ways it is the quality of the thinking the plan includes and the actual process through which it is developed that will determine success.

(b) Clearly, there is a link between the ability to write a business plan and the willingness, or otherwise, of small firms to carry out strategic planning. Whilst writing a business plan may be a necessity in order to acquire financial support, there is much more question over the benefits to the existing small business, such as Gould and King, of carrying out strategic planning. One of the areas of greatest debate is whether carrying out strategic planning leads to improved performance. Equally contentious is whether the formal rational planning model is worthwhile or whether strategy is much more of an emergent process, with the firm responding to changes in its competitive environment.

One source argues that small firms may be reluctant to create a strategic plan because of the time involved; small firms may find day-to-day survival and crisis management prevents them having the luxury of planning where they mean to be over the next few years. Secondly, strategic plans may also be viewed as too restricting, stopping the firm responding flexibly and quickly to opportunities and threats. Thirdly, many small firms may feel that they lack the necessary skills to carry out strategic planning. Strategic planning is seen as a 'big' firm process and inappropriate for small firms. Again, there is evidence to suggest that owner-managers are much less aware of strategic management tools such as SWOT, PESTEL and mission statements than their managers. Finally, owner-managers may be reluctant to involve others in the planning process, which would necessitate giving them access to key information about the business. Here there is an issue of the lack of trust and openness preventing the owner-manager developing and sharing a strategic plan. Many owner-managers may be quite happy to limit the size of the business to one which they can personally control.

On the positive side there is evidence to show that a commitment to strategic planning results in speedier decision making, a better ability to introduce change and innovation and being good at managing change. This in turn results in better performance including higher rates of growth and profits, clear indicators of competitive advantage. If Gould and King are looking to grow the business as suggested, this means some strategic planning will necessarily be involved.

Question 2: Dunvegan Ltd

Report

To   The Directors of Dunvegan Ltd Independent Consultant

From   Today

Date   Proposed Maho spruce plantation

Subject Introduction

I have been asked to give advice on the proposal to plant 1,000 hectares of land with Maho spruce.

Political

Mahogany currently comes from four countries in the tropics. As it is a valuable export, these countries can be expected to be willing to sell mahogany irrespective of local political changes.

In the UK, however, there is growing concern about the deforestation of the tropics and suspicion about the source of many hardwoods. It is possible that the UK or EC will tighten import legislation.

Locally-grown, renewable mahogany substitute should be favoured in this ecologically-aware age.

Economic

Mahogany is principally used for building (window frames etc.) and furniture (veneers). Both of these industries are very sensitive to the health of the economy. It is difficult to predict the economic health of the country ten years hence and so the project will have considerable risk and uncertainty.

Social

If home-owning continues to grow, it is to be expected that demand for high-quality materials will also grow. As mentioned under the political paragraph, using tropical hardwoods could become socially unacceptable and it would appear that the Maho spruce should provide a politically acceptable substitute.

However, some people may object to using genetically-engineered material.

Technological

Although Maho spruce has been patented, there is no reason why other manufacturers could not develop similar products. That would drive down the cost of seedlings (a major cost of the undertaking) and hence the price that would eventually have to be achieved to make the investment pay.

The industry competitive position

The industry competitive position can be analysed in terms of rivals, buyers, suppliers, substitutes and potential new entrants to the market.

Rivals

The potential rivals are the other UK forestry companies and the suppliers from the tropics.

Whether other UK forestry companies will decide to compete is a very complex decision and is discussed below.

The foreign suppliers, which depend on their hardwood for valuable foreign currency, are likely to retaliate with price cuts when they perceive Maho spruce as a threat.

Buyers

It is likely that there are many relatively small buyers of hardwood. If so, there will be little pressure from them.

Suppliers

The main supplier to Dunvegan Ltd is the supplier of the seedlings. At the moment there is only one supplier and this would normally place that company in a very strong position.

However, the supply pattern here is unusual. Once 1,000 hectares are planted, the supplier has no power at all over this project as no further supplies are needed for it.

Future projects would need to be evaluated in the light of supplier attitudes at the time.

New entrants

New entrants into the forestry industry are unlikely, but there is some risk if the crops become more lucrative and land is set aside from normal agricultural use (EC regulations). Much will depend on the perceived economies of the industry.

Substitutes

Maho spruce is an excellent substitute for mahogany. Substitutes for Maho spruce might be other genetically-engineered trees with more attractive or cheaper timber. Substitutes maturing more quickly would be particularly serious as they would capture the market and drive down prices before Dunvegan's timber had matured.

Financial forecasts

If the present price of mahogany and mahogany substitutes is maintained, then the project will produce a positive net present value.

If the price falls by more than about 30% to below £639, then the project will produce a negative net present value.

Competitor reaction

As mentioned above, it is likely that the foreign suppliers will cut their prices so as to keep earning foreign exchange. The reaction of UK forestry companies will depend on their estimates of future prices and supplies.

If the price of mahogany is expected to fall to £500, then the plantation should not be undertaken as there would be a negative NPV. If the price is expected to fall to no less than £800 then the project would produce a positive NPV.

However, Dunvegan Ltd's competitors will have carried out similar calculations. Their break-even points must be very similar to Dunvegan Ltd's as the NPV calculation is dominated by the initial price of the seedlings and the final price of the timber.

The competitors can also be assumed to have read the economist's article in the trade journal.

All the players are faced with an investment paradox.

(a) If a player believes that the others will invest, then investing is not worthwhile as the timber price will fall to an uneconomic level. (Of course, if they all believe this, no one will invest and the price would stay high.)

(b) If a player believes that the others will not invest, then investing is worthwhile as the price would stay high. (Of course, if they all believe this, all will invest and the price would fall.)

Conventional financial analysis is of little further help here. It is crucial to try to find out the true intentions of the competition or to try to limit their scope for competition.

It is in the interests of the producers of the Maho spruce to bring stability to their market. If everyone is afraid to invest, then that company will get no revenue. An agreement with the supply company to limit the sale of seedlings each year would ensure that the prices remained higher and that investment would be worthwhile.

Size of investment

The proposed investment is large, especially as there are many important factors which could change over the project's life: the project is high risk even if not using innovative technology.

Risk could be reduced by planting over several years rather than 1,000 hectares at one time. That way the economics of the investment could be monitored and decisions taken about each slice of investment. Naturally, this approach would delay the maturity of some of the crop. There is a risk that this would reduce the final income (if mahogany prices were to fall) but prices could also rise (strong reaction against natural mahogany, economic upturn). Delaying planting could also reduce the initial price of seedlings as other bioengineering companies launch new products.

Summary

In so far as environmental factors can be judged, it would seem that Maho spruce should be a popular product. The main risk arises from technological advances which could produce similar cheaper timber. However, the economics of the project are very dependent on the future price of Maho spruce timber, its substitutes and the reactions of rivals.

Question 3: CSC Clothing

(a) The extent to which location has historically determined the competitive advantage of CSC and the extent to which it will do so in the future are issues of crucial importance to KZ. A historical analysis of location provides a deeper understanding of CSC's strategic position, and an analysis of the extent to which it is still relevant will assist KZ as it contemplates shifting CSC production and exploiting the CSC brand image.

The debate about **location and comparative advantage** is both long standing and ongoing. However, the work of **Porter (Competitive Advantage of Nations)** presents us with a useful framework in which to consider the attributes of advantage.

Porter identifies **four interlocking elements which form a 'diamond' of location-based advantage.** These four elements can be used to analyse the position of CSC as follows:

– **Factor conditions**. These are the resource inputs needed by the business and in particular the inherited factors of natural resources – climate, labour and the evolution of knowledge and skills. CSC grew out of a business which originally both made and supplied outdoor clothing to Scottish hill farmers thus reflecting the influence of a climate and a geography which demanded tough weatherproof clothing (influences – quality and fitness for purpose) and developed the knowledge and skills to design and manufacture such clothing.

– **Intense home market demand conditions,** led by sophisticated and numerous independent buyers, drive firms to innovate continually and improve their products. Over time, CSC has been required to meet the demanding product requirements of the Scottish hill farmers which means that its products have evolved features of superior weatherproofing and durability. Although the products may today be bought by people who will never venture on a mountain in winter, they are nevertheless buying into what is seen to be a product ownership image associated with the product's history and design attributes (similar to buying an off-road, four-wheel drive vehicle for use within a city environment).

- **Related and supporting local industries**, which through mutual support and collaboration enhance competitive potential, for example through design synergies achieved by close co-operation between firms operating within the value chain. CSC has enjoyed the support of local weavers which allows integration of cloth requirements such as supply and delivery, quality attributes and, in particular, the traditional pattern design used in the garment fabrics.

- **Intense local demand rivalry** which leads to the emergence of firms with strong competitive characteristics, in other words, the home market hones competitive skills which promote domination in worldwide markets. This appears to be the case within CSC's home market where CSC first emerged as the market leader among a number of competing Scottish firms within this specialist garment business.

Porter also identifies other factors, such as the **role of government,** which might assist through intervention – industry support in research and development, or more often non-intervention – creating a business environment which promotes competition. CSC has evolved through a one-hundred-year period of relative business stability and freedom from either intervention or subsidy.

Finally, there is always an element of chance within business success stories. CSC has achieved its success through a process of product development (moving from simple garments for farmers to garment-based products for sports such as shooting and fishing), and market development (using existing products in new markets – creating a fashion niche image). Both opportunities have in part been made possible by the chance adoption of its basic products by the rich and famous, which in turn has made the products prestigious and therefore ones which the not-so-rich and famous wish to acquire.

(b)　CSC could reduce its product costs by moving garment production from Scotland to South East Asia. However, it is doubtful to what extent this move has a strategic fit with the competitive strategy adopted by CSC. The CSC strategy is based on **focused differentiation**, that is, creating a perception of high value to the customer and charging a high price for it – by implication such a strategy will lead to **niche market segmentation**. In this case, the niche is a global one which targets similar customers with similar aspirations worldwide (other product examples, Rolex, Gucci) and is independent of cultural differences.

This is the context within which KZ must decide its production policy for CSC. The **decision cannot be cost-based alone** and subsequently made in isolation of the values, needs and requirements of the customers of CSC and their associated patterns of buyer behaviour. CSC products are not bought on the basis of price, but on the basis of buyers seeking to acquire reflected status associated with the product.

The fact that each garment is handmade in Scotland, using traditional materials and design, is a key part of what the customer is buying into. CSC recognises this and its integrated marketing strategy reflects this – price, product concept, distribution channels (the best stores) and promotion are all in balance. Although it may be possible to maintain product quality by moving production away from Scotland KZ would run a major risk of destroying the CSC product concept and hence the differentiation element which allows the adoption of a premium pricing approach.

Question 4: A University

Value activities consist of all those activities a firm undertakes, from the moment of initial purchase of raw materials and other inputs, to the moment of final receipt of payment from the customer. Value chain analysis (VCA) looks at each of the processes that make up the chain of activity and asks both how important it is in a given company's production or service activity, and how the company compares in that respect to its competitors. The value chain model divides an organisation's activities into nine generic activities, five primary activities and four support activities.

To review the withdrawal rate of students from the University's courses a clear statement of the University's objectives and what they are trying to achieve needs to be drawn up by the management team. The management accountant will then analyse the primary and support activities in the University's value chain and identify areas that are causing the greatest level of concern.

Primary activities

- **Inbound logistics** – are the activities concerned with handling the inputs. From the University's point of view the analysis will cover:

  - the intake of students, e.g. whether entry requirements have changed. A lowering of standards may lead to students being unable to cope with the work, while a raising may find students' expectations of the course is not fulfilled. An increase in the intake could lead to more revenue but less individual attention for students with short-term problems.

  - the courses offered and whether they have changed over the period of increased withdrawal.

- **Operations** – concerned with the transformation of the inputs and will look in detail at:

  - how the University compares with competitor institutions – do they have similar withdrawal rates in the first year? If not, then the University needs to determine what it is doing differently and what it must do to improve the service. A review of the students that leave might show a pattern to the transfers, e.g. students leaving to go to particular universities.

  - the calibre of staff – are the lecturers able to communicate effectively and do they show an interest in helping the students in their studies? Also, does their treatment of students vary between the first year and subsequent years?

- **Outbound logistics** – are concerned with the finished product, i.e. the skills and abilities of the graduates after completing their courses and the perception of the customers – the government and employers.

- **Marketing and sales** – are responsible for communication with the customers, e.g. advertising and promotion. The analysis should assess what attracts the students and why an increasing number believe that the course is not living up to their expectations.

- **Service** – covers all of the activities that occur after graduation and includes arranging milk rounds, job fairs and other links to potential employers. The management accountant should analyse the types of contact with the graduate and the retention rates for students moving on to other courses in the University.

Support activities

- **Procurement** – is the process of purchasing inputs. Areas that will be analysed include the efficiency and adequacy of the supplies and the level of administrative support provided to the lecturers and students.

- **Technology development** – covers not just machines and processes, but also know-how. Improved technology development may be employed in delivering course material to students. Technology may also be used in undertaking marketing research into the attractiveness of types of courses to prospective students.

- **Human resource management** transcends all primary activities. It includes all the activities involved in the recruitment, training, development and remuneration of staff.

- **Infrastructure** – which supports the entire value chain, includes the systems of planning, finance, quality control and estate management.

Managing the linkages

- **Primary-primary.** Inter-departmental co-operation between, say, inbound logistics and marketing to ensure that prospective students are given sufficient information about courses.

- **Support-primary.** Computer-based operations, involving co-operation between information technology and lecturers. For example, teaching aids and course notes made available.

- **Support-support.** Computer-based information systems automatically monitoring recruitment policies.

The VCA analysis will help to determine why the rate of student withdrawal is increasing and to decide how individual activities might be changed to improve the value of the University's offerings. Because of the linkages it is important that the organisation's activities are not dealt with in isolation. Choices will have to be made about the relationships and how they influence strategic capability e.g. the recruitment of staff with more teaching rather than research experience might have a positive effect on the students' experience but a negative effect on the University's reputation within its national academic community.

Linkages between the University's support and primary activities may also need strengthening, e.g. if some of the lecturers are lacking in communication skills it could be a direct result of management style or a failure of human resources policy. Any inadequacies in support will have a detrimental effect on lecturers, which may be a contributory factor leading to the problems of student withdrawal facing the University.

Question 5: MW and FS

(a) **MW's strategic position**

When developing a strategic plan it is useful to undertake a SWOT analysis. At the current time MW is seeking to enhance its shareholder value, its main objective. Therefore the SWOT analysis can be used to identify how the business can build on its strengths and take corrective action for its weaknesses. This in turn will increase both profitability and market share for MW.

Strengths

- Secure financial base.

- Well established in the North.

- Increased share price and profitability.

Weaknesses

- Prior experience in takeovers is limited.
- Lack of experience in managing the takeover process itself.
- Not maximising use of capital resources.
- Not much opportunity for further organic growth in the North.
- The company cultures will be different, so will require integration.

Opportunities

- Takeover will mean improvements in both competitiveness and market share.
- An increase in gearing will mean that the company will make increased use of debt, in turn resulting in lower costs, as debt is cheaper than equity.
- Takeover of FS will mean expansion into the South.

Threats

- Staff morale may fall when stores are sold after the takeover takes place.
- The bid cost may rise if competitors are also interested in purchasing FS.
- If MW does not do the takeover, it risks stagnation in its own market.
- The family shareholding will be diluted if the takeover goes ahead.
- Another competitor could purchase FS, meaning that MW would see a reduction in its competitiveness as well as losing market share.

(b) **Assessment of FS**

It is immediately apparent from the calculations that the FS stores do not reach the level of absolute profitability enjoyed by MW. They do, however, have better gross profit to turnover levels. This means that MW is more efficient in terms of its overhead costs. If the takeover goes ahead shareholder value will be enhanced providing MW is able to achieve overall the same ratio of gross profit to turnover that FS currently achieves. Also, in order to increase shareholder value the net profit to turnover ratio of MW will need to be achieved within the new company, by carrying out efficiency improvements within FS.

Inventory turnover is a good example of where MW currently has greater efficiency than FS, as FS holds inventory for 75% longer on average, meaning there is a potential to reduce costs by putting MW's policies in place.

Looking at the sales, gross profit and net profits per customer, it is apparent that FS uses premium pricing in comparison with MW. For example, if a comparison is made between the sales of northwest MW and the southwest FS stores the following calculation can be made:

$$\text{Volume of customers} = \frac{\$10 \text{ million}}{\$6 \text{ million}} \times 0.15 \text{ million} = \frac{0.25 \text{ million customers}}{\text{(MW pricing policies)}}$$

This compares to 0.3 million customers of MW in the northwest, so reinforcing the fact that the higher sales and profits are a result of premium pricing.

In FS stores the gross profit to turnover is higher than in MW stores, whilst the profit per square metre of FS stores in the southwest is comparable to the northeast MW stores, but lower in the southeast. Also net profit per square metre is lower for the FS stores. This demonstrates that the increased gross profit to turnover ratio of FS is achieved by premium pricing and not efficient use of space. This means that this is another area where MW could add shareholder value, by increased efficiency in the use of floor space in FS stores.

It is also apparent from the calculations that the staff of MW generate more turnover per employee than those of FS. This again supports the fact that, if MW's efficiency can be implemented in FS stores, this will result in increased shareholder value. This lower level of turnover per employee could be caused by the fact that FS staff get paid less than MW employees doing the same job, meaning that staff morale could be low. I feel that this should also be looked at within the different geographical areas of MW, as at the present time there is a difference in salaries between those working in the northwest and the northeast.

Calculations based on data provided in the scenario

	MW		FS	
	North West	North East	South West	South East
Gross profit	$6 million	$5 million	$4.0 million	$3.2 million
GP %	60%	62.5%	67%	64%
NP %	20%	17.5%	13.3%	10%
GP/sq. mtr.	$1,000	$833	$833	$667
NP/sq. mtr.	$333	$233	$167	$104
Sales/customer visit	$33.33	$40	$40	$50
GP/customer visit	$20	$25	$27	$32
NP/customer visit	$6.67	$7	$5.30	$5
Turnover/employee	$145k	$143k	$107k	$98k
Salaries/supervisor	$66.7k	$83.3k	$50k	$50k
Wages/employee	$18.5k	$16k	$16.k	$15k

Question 6: News Reel Inc

(a) Strategic position analysis

There are a number of tools that can be used to analyse a company's position such as the value chain, PESTEL or 5 Forces analysis. The first of these models analyses the internal position of the business whereas the other models focus on its external position and prospects. The models can be brought together in a SWOT analysis and it is this model that will be used to assess News Reel's position.

Key strategic strengths

– News Reel is a focused differentiator. It stands out (differentiates) on its flexibility and delivery times. This has been arrived at by having less automated production, flexible suppliers and flexible production methods. This should allow the company to gain a competitive advantage and adapt quickly to changes in customer needs.

– Despite being a family owned business, News Reel's past performance has allowed it to accumulate cash and put itself in a strong financial position. It has created a cash reserve sufficient enough to finance an acquisition and allow the company to partake in the opportunities available to it.

– News Reel's reputation and association with EES will further enhance its competitive position and may create a barrier to entry to some foreign rivals.

Key strategic weaknesses

– News Reel is very dependent on EES who make up 40% of the company's revenue. The contract is up for renewal and the loss of such a significant proportion of income could seriously affect the company's viability.

– The company's core market is mature. There is unlikely to be further growth in sales of reels of paper. News Reel needs to seek out new markets and or new products.

– In order to achieve its competitive advantage of flexibility, News Reel has had to accept higher costs of production. Unfortunately this will require higher selling prices which may be difficult to sustain in a tough economic climate.

Key strategic opportunities

Key opportunities for acquisitions have been identified by the company and these will be explored in more detail later. Other opportunities for the business might include expansion into the mainline continent or developing recycled paper. These will also be explored in more detail later. But overall there are a number of opportunities that News Reel could pursue.

Key strategic threats

- The economic downturn in Eastlandia is a threat to New Reel. During such times customers might abandon differentiators and switch to cheaper suppliers in order to cope with falling sales.

- In the longer term, technological changes such as the growth of news aggregators and ereaders might reduce the need for such large volumes of paper products that provide news and entertainment.

- New competition from the mainland may enter the market. They are likely to be bigger than News Reel and have economies of scale which can further drive down selling prices.

- Recycled paper may be more culturally acceptable and in some instances cheaper than traditional paper reels. This substitute could win customers away from News Reels traditional market.

Overall strategic position

News Reel has a strong history and a strong competitive position. But it is over-reliant on one product and one customer in a maturing market. As its market continues to change its strategic position is likely to worsen. It therefore needs to seek out new opportunities in order to secure the long-term future of the business.

(b) **Future strategic options**

Appropriateness of strategic diversification

There are a number of strategic options open to News Reel, but not all of them will satisfy the three criteria of being feasible, suitable and acceptable. Ansoff summarised strategic growth options into four categories and these are explored below.

Market penetration

This involves gaining market share by enhancing a competitive advantage through competitive strategies such as cost leadership and differentiation. Cost leadership is unlikely to be feasible for News Reel due to its low economies of scale (when compared to rivals) and flexible production methods. It would also appear that News Reel has already differentiated the business well and there would be few opportunities for further differentiation. Market penetration would therefore be an unsuitable strategy.

Product development

News Reel could attempt to develop a recycled paper range. However it is likely to lack skills and experience in this area as well as sufficient supply and production facilities. They are also likely to encounter more developed and reputable competitors who will have potentially developed barriers to entry through customer tie-ups and branding. Furthermore, it would appear that the demand for recycled paper is in the low-cost, low-quality sector, which would not suit News Reel's competitive advantage.

Overall, both the feasibility and suitability of a product development strategy can be questioned.

Market development

Market development could be achieved through expansion into the mainland continent. However News Reel is likely to experience similar competitive problems as those experienced in product development as there will be established rivals with better reputations and lower costs. Also, the mainland market is likely to be experiencing similar maturity to the Eastlandian market with the same long-term threats. It would therefore appear to be neither suitable nor acceptable for the long-term future of the business.

Diversification

Feasible acquisitions have been identified by the company and these appear to be acceptable to the board. As already discussed, News Reel needs to change its strategic position and diversification would appear to be the most suitable way to achieve this.

Acquisition of Quickpulp

This is a form of backward integration. News Reel would take control of a supplier and it is likely that it would source more materials from this supplier.

Quickpulp seems eager to sell and News Reel may therefore acquire the business at a favourable price. It is also appealing to the production director as this is a way to secure supplies and possibly drive down production costs in order to compete better and win more tenders.

But the suitability of this strategy must be questioned. It is likely Quickpulp is willing to sell because it is experiencing the same market maturity and downward pressure on prices that News Reel is experiencing. In effect, an acquisition of Quickpulp would only deepen News Reel's problems and make the company more entrenched in an industry that is mature and that News Reel should be looking to remove itself from in the long-term. News Reel would still be reliant on EES and face the same competitive threats that it is currently experiencing. Buying Quickpulp would also increase the exit barriers from the industry if News Reel was to attempt an exit in the future.

Furthermore, News Reel's key competitive advantage is its flexibility. However, tying itself in with a supplier would potentially reduce flexibility and destroy News Reel's competitive advantage.

Overall, it would be advised that News Reel avoids an acquisition of Quickpulp.

Acquisition of Medicnote

An acquisition of Medicnote also appears feasible and acceptable to the board. Once again it is looking for a buyer and its overtrading difficulties might again mean that News Reel can make the acquisition at a favourable price.

But Medicnote would appear to be much more suitable as an acquisition than Quickpulp. It is experiencing growing demand, is very profitable and is in a unique, specialised market position. It is also a move away from a reliance on EES and the problems that News Reel is experiencing in its current market.

This acquisition is likely to remove a number of News Reel's weaknesses (mature market, over-reliance on EES) and avoid some of the future threats (such as social and technological changes which may make newsprint obsolete). Overall it appears to be feasible, suitable and acceptable and it is recommended that News Reel pursues an acquisition of Medicnote

Question 7: Qualispecs

(a) **Corporate appraisal**

A corporate appraisal is an overview of an organisation's current position. It leads on from the internal and external analysis undertaken as part of the business planning process.

As the company works towards achieving its objectives, the corporate appraisal is a summary of the company's:

- strengths within the organisation relative to competitors
- weaknesses within the organisation relative to competitors
- opportunities available from the external environment
- threats from the external environment.

The company must develop a strategy which:

- capitalises on the strengths
- overcomes or mitigates the impact of weaknesses
- takes suitable opportunities
- overcomes or mitigates the threats.

In the case of Qualispecs:

Strengths

– Reputation for quality

Quality is a major reason why people buy products, and continuing to build on this reputation will ensure customers continue to buy Qualispecs's products.

– Financially secure/large cash reserves

Qualispecs does not need to rush into the implementation of new strategies. It can take its time to ensure strategies chosen are appropriate for the business and implemented effectively. It also has funds to invest in new ventures without having to raise external funds.

– Backing of a famous sports star

This helps to improve the image of Qualispecs's products which in turn should result in higher sales, particularly amongst the younger market that might be influenced by the sports star.

– New Chief Executive

The group has a new Chief Executive who has joined from a rival, Fastglass. Fastglass has been a successful and innovative company and the Chief Executive may be able to bring new ideas and provide a fresh approach.

– Established group with many stores

The group has a good basic infrastructure including many stores and experienced staff. This allows them to implement new strategies quickly and easily.

Weaknesses

– Slower dispensing of spectacles

Customer service is worse than competitors in this respect and may be a reason for the reducing customer loyalty.

– Less trendy products than competitors

Some competitors have successfully sold designer frames. These are likely to be stylish and trendy compared to Qualispecs' traditional products. Qualispecs may need to update products more often with the latest designs.

– Smaller product range than competitors

Some competitors have a wider product range than Qualispecs. This provides more choice which may attract customers and also gives competitors the opportunity to upsell products, i.e. selling prescription sunglasses at the same time as standard spectacles.

– Older production methods causing higher costs

This will either cause prices to be higher than competitors or margins to be less. In either case competitors have a distinct advantage.

– Varying performance around the group

Little action is being taken to improve performance of poorly performing stores causing varying performance around the group. This indicates a weakness in internal control systems and perhaps also in development and training programmes.

– Little autonomy for shops

Without autonomy there is little a shop manager can do to improve local operations. In London, for instance, pay may need to be higher to attract the right staff. With no local control over pay levels, shop managers may find it hard to employ good staff and hence improve their business.

This lack of autonomy may also be demotivating to managers. Responsibility was one of the major factors outlined by Hertzberg in his motivation theory as a way to motivate staff.

– No incentive to improve for staff

The use of group-based bonuses means that people cannot be rewarded for good individual performance. Therefore, individuals have little incentive to improve.

Opportunities

Note: Opportunities should be in relation to the market as a whole.

They therefore need to be available to all competitors in the market.

– To adopt new technologies to reduce costs (see earlier)

– To stock a wide range of up-to-date products (see earlier)

– Consumer spending will continue to increase

Despite a slowdown in the economy, consumer spending is likely to increase suggesting an increasing market size in the future. There is therefore further opportunity for all competitors to increase sales.

– Targeting 18 to 30 year olds

The 18 to 30-year-old age group offers a particular opportunity since its spending is likely to increase especially quickly. There is therefore an opportunity to understand this group's needs and to target it specifically.

- Develop a partnership with a high street shopping group

Fastglass has already done this successfully and Qualispecs could follow suit. There are likely to be limited suitable partners so Qualispecs must act quickly before other firms make arrangements with the best partners.

Threats

- Intense competition/eroding customer loyalty

Existing competitors are adopting new strategies with great success (e.g. Fastglass developed joint ventures). This has resulted in Qualispecs's customers moving to competitors, thus reducing profits. This is likely to be a continued threat to Qualispecs who needs to respond.

- Downturn in the economy

In the long term, if the downturn continues it will affect all industries and consumer spending will be likely to fall as people become more defensive in their spending habits.

Key strategic challenges

In summary, the key strategic challenges are to:

- Improve the current lack of clear generic strategy ('stuck in the middle')

Examining Michael Porter's Generic Strategies, Qualispecs appears to have neither a cost leader advantage, a differentiation nor a focus on any particular niche. While traditionally quality has been its focus, new innovations from competitors have eroded its position as the highest quality spectacle retailer. In the long run it will find it hard to compete effectively if it does not rectify this.

- Be more innovative in product and market development

Competitors have successfully developed new strategies while Qualispecs has done very little. This has seen it lose business to competitors. To be successful in the future it needs to update its product range regularly and be more innovative in developing new strategies (e.g. joint ventures).

- Improve performance on a divisional basis by updating internal policies and procedures

Current policies and procedures are demotivating staff and causing varying divisional performance.

(b) **Strategies to move the business forward**

Note: Detailed tools for generating strategic options are discussed in chapter 6. At this stage you were expected to use your common sense.

Competitive strategy

Given the key strength of Qualispecs as having a reputation for quality spectacles, and its current weakness in the cost of products produced, it would appear logical for Qualispecs to refocus activities on quality by producing very high quality spectacles (modern design, hard-wearing, up-to-date features) with a high-quality service (fast dispensing, knowledgeable staff).

Current product/current market

Qualispecs would benefit from consolidating its current strengths and refocusing on quality. It should invest in new technology in order to reduce costs which will enable it to be competitive. This also capitalises on its significant cash reserves.

It needs to improve its internal processes to ensure that staff are motivated through a good incentive scheme, quality training and by being given autonomy. This will capitalise on its skilled workforce and overcome the weakness in the way it is managed.

Current market/new products

Product development is a vital new strategy for Qualispecs to follow. Its competitors have been successful in doing this. One aspect of providing a high quality service is being able to offer a wide range of products to meet varying customer needs. Qualispecs may need to invest more in Research and Development and implement new product development programmes.

New market/current products

A joint venture strategy with a retailer who competes based on quality (e.g. Marks and Spencer) would both build on the reputation of Qualispecs and also introduce it to a new group of customers who will buy its products through association with the retail group. The retail group may also have outlets in other parts of the country (or even internationally) which would allow Qualispecs to expand its markets.

Diversification

There appears no need at present to diversify. The disadvantages of operating in new markets with new products (e.g. lack of experience and reputation) outweigh any possible advantages.

Question 8: T Plc

(a) PEST Analysis

The following external factors are relevant to T plc:

Political factors

T plc currently dominates its national telecommunications market with an 85% share of the market. The company will be under political pressure from the national government to reduce its dominance by opening up the national telecom market to competition and reducing prices for telecom products charged to consumers.

The government has appointed an industry regulator to be directly involved in the control of the telecom industry and T plc no doubt will be under close scrutiny. Political forces will be a major factor affecting the operations and plans of T plc.

Economic factors

There are three main economic elements that T plc needs to consider. These are:

– Shareholder wealth

   T plc's shareholders are a major stakeholder group who will have economic objectives of profit maximisation and rising share value.

– The contribution of the telecommunications industry to the national economy.

   The telecommunications industry plays a major role in contributing towards economic growth and prosperity. T plc has a responsibility to develop new technology and to provide a reliable, value for money service to its users.

– The economies of foreign countries.

   The economic conditions in each foreign country T plc operates in should be considered e.g. foreign currency exchange rates and national economic boom and slump cycles.

Social factors

Telecommunication products are social products used by people for many reasons. The company should ensure that it understands the social role of the industry and provides a reliable service. The company should also portray itself as socially responsible, have a set of social objectives and keep in close contact with the consumers e.g. by producing a range of services for elderly citizens who are more dependent on telephones for obtaining help when needed.

Technical factors

The telecommunications industry is a high-tech industry that is currently very dynamic. T plc is the market leader in the industry and must be innovative to maintain its competitive advantage. The company must invest in research and development to ensure it has a constant supply of new products in the years ahead to replace those going into the decline stage of their product life cycle.

(b) **Strategy evaluation**

By relating products to markets, Ansoff identified four main strategies for achieving long-term growth. Using this model the potential market opportunities are as follows:

Market penetration strategies

T plc currently has 85% of its national market. There is little scope for obtaining any growth by increasing its market share. Most households and businesses will have a conventional telephone line so some of the company's products will be at the maturity stage of their life cycle offering little prospect of growth. Some market growth might be achieved by getting existing customers to use the telephone more.

A market penetration strategy only offers limited growth prospects.

Product development strategy

This strategy involves introducing new products in existing markets. T plc has already achieved a good track record for new product development and with continued investment in research and development should maintain its momentum. There is a lot of market opportunity in the industry for this strategy, for example further developments in mobile phone and Internet technology.

Market development strategy

T plc has pursued a successful strategy of expanding into foreign markets with existing products. It currently has operations in North America, Europe, India and the Far East. In T plc's latest annual report, the Chairman refers to developing these markets further. Tremendous opportunities exist in additional developing countries such as those in Africa where the company currently has operations.

Diversification strategy

This involves introducing new products to new markets and is a high-risk strategy. T plc is a large profitable company with a prospector (innovative) culture. The company should evaluate carefully the risk of any diversification strategy and if opportunities exist they should be considered e.g. digital television technology.

The company should pursue all four strategies with the main emphasis on product development and market development, as these exploit the company's main strengths of expertise in research and development, and growth in foreign markets.

Question 9: Pelatihan

(a) **Assessment of the company's performance**

The product portfolio

The Boston Consulting Group Matrix (BCG) categorises products (or SBU's) according to their market growth on the one hand, and their relative market share on the other.

Finance and Accounting

According to BCG, Finance and Accounting courses would be classified as a cash cow, having a relatively high share of what is a lower growth market according to the independent survey. Since the survey states that the market is growing at a slower rate than Law and HRM this will make it less attractive to new entrants. This SBU should not therefore need cash to defend its position, but instead be able to provide funds to finance other areas of the business.

Marketing

According to BCG, Marketing would be classified as a dog product, having a relatively low share of a low growth (and hence unattractive) market. The market is actually in decline according to the survey. This would normally imply a product with few prospects which should be discontinued in the long term.

Law

According to BCG, Law would be classified as a star product, having a high share of a high growth (and hence attractive) market. A star needs to be defended since new entrants will be attracted to the market and potentially steal Pelatihan's market share.

HRM

According to BCG, HRM would be classified as a problem child having a relatively low share of a high growth (and hence attractive) market. To continue with a problem child and grow market share, cash will need to be taken from other SBUs and invested.

Overall Portfolio Evaluation

On first glance Pelatihan's portfolio appears balanced with Finance and Accounting courses generating cash to fund HRM and Law. Only Marketing has a questionable future, with competition from online courses forcing the market into decline. However, the BCG appraisal is simplistic and Pelatihan's profits are significantly below budget suggesting there are issues with the present portfolio.

Strengths and Weaknesses of Pelatihan's performance

Strengths:

Performance of law and finance

The Law SBU has achieved its sales revenue target of $4m. As a 'star' with 35% of the market in a buoyant sector, this is encouraging for Pelatihan. The competition in this market is strong, with Koulos and Opleid having 30% and 25% of the market respectively. These other colleges are likely to try to increase market share going forward and Pelatihan will need to defend its position in order to safeguard Law as a future cash cow (when demand slows).

Student day numbers (defined as one student attending for one day) are up on budget in both the Law faculty (5% above budget) and the Finance faculty (1.5% above budget). This would suggest that Pelatihan has been successful in attracting students to these courses (despite the fact that these additional days have not translated into extra revenue.) This may be due to the fact that both Law and Finance are areas where 'update' courses will be popular as legislation or accounting standards change. All qualified personnel in country A could potentially be targeted to attend such courses.

HRM on the other hand, has seen a student day reduction of 23% against budget. Despite this, corresponding revenue is only down by 11.4% or $0.4m. Budgeted revenue per student day in this faculty was $2333 and a figure of $2696 has actually been achieved. The increasing demand for HRM courses as mentioned in the independent survey may explain why Pelatihan has been able to charge more per student day than budgeted. However, since this is a problem child SBU, requiring significant investment, Pelatihan will need to work on attracting more students on to courses to bring actual days in line with the budget.

Revenue from each faculty

Pelatihan is not overly dependent on any one sector for revenue, however Finance represents the biggest contributor at 34.7% (budget 34.6%). Since finance is the Cash Cow, the generation of extra revenue is a positive. The percentage of revenue coming from marketing (the dog SBU) has fallen to 6.6 (budget 7.7) which shows a good strategic direction is being taken in order to become less reliant on this product.

Efficiency of each faculty

The finance faculty staff are the most efficient, with 88 student days per staff member. This is a relative strength and is further borne out by the mix statistics which show that the finance faculty teaches 36% of Pelatihan's student days with only 32% of the staff. Since Pelatihan is the market leader in Finance and Accounting, building on such economies of scale is essential. Finance, as a cash cow SBU, needs to provide funding for the other faculties and the staff efficiency would seem to give good grounding for this to occur.

The law faculty, with rapidly rising demand has also been able to generate a relatively high number of student days per staff member at 81 (against an average of 75).

Weaknesses

Overall performance

Overall sales revenue is down 6.9% or $0.9m against budget. The marketing sector is the worst performer, missing the target by 20% (which explains $0.2m of the total shortfall).

This is disappointing since presumably the online courses offered by The Marketing Institute were considered when the budget was set and more student days would appear to have been lost than envisaged at that time (marketing student days are down 9% on budget).

The discounts being demanded by large employer organisations could be an explanation for the loss of expected marketing revenue as well as the 6.6% fall against budget of finance faculty revenue.

Budgeted profit before interest and tax ($2.3m) is all but wiped out in Pelatihan's actual results. An overall margin of 17.7% was expected but in reality only 0.8% was achieved. The weaknesses which have led to this result are explored further below.

Cost control

There are significant weaknesses in cost control in each faculty with all 4 exceeding budgeted costs despite revenue targets not being hit (this weakness can also be seen in the 16.7% increase in central costs over budget). Overall sales revenue is down 6.9% as mentioned above but for this to translate into a 96% drop in expected profits is indicative of total inefficiency.

What is unclear from the analysis is why, in a mainly fixed cost business, such massive increases in cost should have occurred at all. The problem is compounded by the fact the CEO has been unable to find a senior member of staff willing to take responsibility for financial planning and control. An investigation into the reasons for such high costs is therefore unlikely.

Profit margins

The marketing faculty, classified as a 'dog' by the BCG is loss making despite an expected 50% PBIT margin. All other margins are significantly lower than the budgeted figures with HRM falling from 28.5% in the budget to 12.9% in the actual results. This does suggest that the problems with cost control span the entire organisation.

Revenue per staff member

Staff members are seemingly unable to generate as much revenue as expected. Despite the director of the Finance faculty spending so much time teaching students and dealing with clients, staff in his SBU are 6.6% below budget in terms of revenue per staff member.

Mix of days/staff and revenue

Inefficiencies can be seen in the marketing faculty, employing 8% of the staff to generate only 7% of Pelatihan's revenue and student days and also the Law division, using 36% of the staff to generate 33% of the revenue. Pelatihan should consider using 'multi skilled' tutors who can teach across faculties to try and increase utilisation of all staff.

Revenue and costs per student day

The finance and marketing faculties have both experienced adverse variances in terms of revenue per student day, presumably due at least in part to the excessive discounts demanded by corporate clients. The law faculty has also seen a 5% adverse variance in pricing however, and it may be that the competition from Koulos and Opleid has been stronger than expected, driving prices down.

The cost per student day is of real concern, particularly in the marketing faculty where it is double that budgeted. The HRM faculty has also failed to control costs, with cost per student day 41% higher than expected. Action will need to be taken immediately to deal with the problems faced by this division.

Reliability of budgets

Finally, it is worth mentioning that there may be a weakness in the budget itself. With no senior member of staff willing to take on responsibility for it, it is possible that the targets set were not realistic in the current climate, or that mistakes have been made (for example the budgeted cost per student day in Marketing which does appear low compared to the other faculties and has led to the almost 100% adverse variance mentioned earlier).

(b) **Overall strategic position and performance of Pelatihan**

Strengths

Pelatihan is one of the largest and most highly regarded colleges in country A. Its brand name will be a significant strength and should serve to attract students to enrol on its courses. Pelatihan has a stronger position in the Finance and Accounting and Law markets due to its superior market share.

Pelatihan is operating in country A which has a well-educated younger population and a stable government likely to continue its investment in training. The fact that many of Pelatihan's students are funded by employers gives Pelatihan some security in respect of demand levels. Employers are more likely to pay for 'block' training or see staff through to the end of a qualification despite economic conditions. They will also provide significant student numbers in many instances (as is the case in the Law faculty).

Country A is much more stable than many of its neighbours with no history of violence or unrest. This is likely to be attractive to overseas students who cannot access training in unstable home nations.

The structure of Pelatihan is divisionalised with four senior tutors each heading up a faculty and the CEO overseeing the entire operation. This will create focus, with each 'expert' director making decisions tailored to their market. The fact that Pelatihan has grown organically (as opposed to via acquisition like Koulos and Opleid) will further add to the cohesiveness of its structure and the ability to present a uniform culture with none of the integration problems likely to be faced by other acquisitive competitors.

The economy of A is growing at 15% a year. This means increasing numbers of organisations requiring training are present. Since Pelatihan doesn't specialise in one sector, it is able to cater to the training requirements of all organisations. Companies which do not require accountancy or legal training may still take advantage of HRM courses or marketing. Pelatihan's broad product range is however, also present in its biggest competitors.

Weaknesses

Pelatihan has a major weakness in financial planning and control, with inaccurate budgets and no real understanding of why the 07/08 results are so far below budget. In such a highly competitive industry this is a serious problem, leading to poor decision making across the organisation.

Pelatihan provides similar products to its main competitors and this lack of differentiation makes it difficult for Pelatihan to compete on anything other than price. Pelatihan's pricing strategy is being threatened by a small number of employer organisations demanding discounts in excess of those usually offered. The inability to negotiate and build up ongoing relationships with clients to protect against such demands is a weakness.

Most of Pelatihan's costs will be fixed (for example, staff costs and premises) and this exposes the business to great risk if revenue falls. Any such fall (for example through discounts) will impact immediately on profit.

Pelatihan would appear to be less innovative than its main competitors. The introduction of e-learning by the Institute of Marketing has been enough to push the marketing sector which Pelatihan operates in into decline. Koulos is known to be developing on online courses but despite this, Pelatihan has no plans to do likewise.

There are staff issues within Pelatihan. Firstly, the loss of staff from the law faculty to join a main competitor signals a lack of loyalty amongst what should be, in a training organisation, the biggest asset of the business (namely tutors). Without the reputation of talented tutors, Pelatihan will find it difficult to attract students and it is also the case that students may follow tutors to their new employer further weakening Pelatihan's position.

The second staff issue is apparent from the inability of the CEO to find a volunteer amongst his senior colleagues to take over the financial planning and control of the organisation (a weakness highlighted above). The director of the finance faculty, an obvious choice for the role, claims to be too busy dealing with clients despite having a relatively large contingent of 23 staff. To leave the CEO (a lawyer) in charge of this particular area would appear to be unwise, particularly for an organisation which presumably employs many qualified accountants, the director of finance being just one, who could take on the role.

Opportunities

Firstly, Pelatihan could choose to invest in the Law and HRM faculties in line with the findings of the BCG matrix. Demand for courses in both areas is rising rapidly and Pelatihan will need significant investment to maintain its current leading market share in Law and build up its relatively low market share in HRM.

Online courses are a potential area for investment and have already proved successful for the Marketing Institute in country A. It is likely to be the case in the future that provision of such courses becomes 'expected' by students and moves very quickly from being a core competence to a threshold competence. Pelatihan needs to begin investing now, in all faculties to bring this kind of training into its organisation. Online courses could enable them to sell courses to overseas students, allowing market development without the costs associated with setting up new colleges.

Since Pelatihan has staff and premises, it could look to provide other courses and increase the utilisation of both. For example, there may be a demand for bespoke training courses which Pelatihan, with a talented tutor team, could easily provide. It may even be possible to carry out these courses at client premises, saving even more costs. Such courses, if successful, would impact greatly on revenue without a corresponding increase in costs. Koulos and Opleid both have a significant share of the 'other' course market (40% and 20% respectively) and Pelatihan could use its reputation as a highly regarded training provider to cross over into this market.

Pelatihan is one of the three dominant training organisations in country A, however there are smaller colleges operating in every one of Pelatihan's sectors. An opportunity may arise to purchase one or more of these smaller colleges, particularly if they have a significant share of the 'other' courses market (small colleges hold 40% market share). Although Pelatihan has never grown this way before, it would provide a quick entry into a potentially lucrative market.

Country A has a growing economy and no history of violence or terrorist attacks. Many neighbouring countries are not so stable and since Pelatihan does not currently offer full time courses or accommodation, it could attempt to attract students from neighbouring countries by offering both.

A strategy to increase the utilisation of tutors could be devised with teaching across faculties becoming part of the culture at Pelatihan. Finally, developing relationships (and contracts) with corporate clients so that they are not in a position of power to demand high discounts is an opportunity Pelatihan should try to exploit.

Threats

A is a developed Asian country whose government has been in power for six years and has been responsible for making education more widely available as well as supporting the development of new industries. A general election is however coming up and there are fears that the opposition party may be elected. This could change the position of training companies significantly if they no longer have the support of the ruling party, they may find that taxes increase or their market contracts.

There are threats to the Finance and Marketing faculties from a small number of corporate clients who are demanding high discounts. This is also apparent in the Law faculty where one particular client books up to half the places on a course but demands a 20% discount. If Pelatihan does not offer these discounts there is a very real chance that clients will be lost to the competition, since, as already mentioned, the product itself is unlikely to be differentiated and price will be the main bargaining tool.

As well as the potential loss of clients, more tutors could be lost to competitors. The Law faculty operates in a fast growing market and at present Pelatihan is the market leader. Koulos is however only 5% behind in terms of market share and since students will often follow popular tutors to a new training organisation, there is a possibility that Pelatihan will lose its market leader position as a result of this loss of staff.

Provision of online courses by the Marketing Institute is probably the reason why the marketing sector has gone into decline. Koulos operates in all four of Pelatihan's sectors and is already in the process of developing online training. There is a risk that the provision of online training by a competitor pushes the other 'traditional' sectors into decline, leaving Pelatihan with very little to fall back on.

In addition, there are rumours of a possible merger between Koulos and Opleid. If this were to go ahead, Pelatihan would lose its market leader position in both the law and finance faculties. The new merged operation would be able to exploit significant economies of scale and Pelatihan would find it impossible to compete.

Finally, poor financial control and ultimately, disappointing performance against budget may be enough to damage Pelatihan's reputation.

Question 10: WG plc

(a) Product development

For any company to retain its position as market leader, it must introduce a continual stream of new products, services or ideas to replace those that are declining. WG plc holds a position as one of the leaders in the global pharmaceutical industry, so it is important that it is able to introduce new products to replace existing ones when patents expire. Because the development phase in the pharmaceutical industry is very long and very risky, it is important that WG plc invests regularly in a programme of research and development (R&D). This will help to ensure that it has new products and services that will meet both its profitability objective and its aim of developing innovative medicines and services.

It has been a well-established idea for many years that products and services follow a 'life cycle' that affects the current rate of sale and, more importantly, has significant implications for the strategic options for the future. The theory breaks the economic life of a product into a number of stages. Being aware of the fact that a product has a life cycle can become the foundation for policies and practices aimed at building up the market. The best advantage it gives is in the launching of a new product.

The **Boston Consulting Group (BCG) matrix** attempts to relate critical strategic issues to the different phases of the product life cycle. Using the rate of market growth and relative market share, the matrix classifies products as either cash cows, stars, problem children or dogs. It is likely that, at any time, companies will have products in all these categories. The position of the product or service within the matrix has implications for the cash flows of the company and it is therefore important that the managers monitor the position continuously. They must recognise that products that are currently classified as cash cows will eventually become dogs and cease to generate cash. To avoid having too many products in a low growth and low market share category, it is essential that steps are taken to ensure that the company is always developing new products that have the potential to become stars. For companies like WG plc it is imperative that adequate resources are allocated to R&D in the strategic plan.

An example of the effects of the stages in the life cycle and in the Boston matrix can be illustrated by one of WG plc's products. Four years ago one particular drug produced almost half of its turnover. Because the patent expires next year, it is expected that sales will drop to represent no more than 10% of turnover. This type of problem makes the company vulnerable to competition in the dynamic environment of the pharmaceutical industry. It is essential for WG plc to be continually developing new products, if it is to retain its dominant position in the industry.

Almost 15% of WG plc's turnover last year was spent on research and development. They have the largest research and development organisation of all pharmaceutical companies worldwide. It is clear that the managers have taken a decision to allocate resources to research activities to ensure that the company retains its competitive advantage. They are also determined to produce and develop new and innovative medicines and services worldwide to enable the company to achieve its corporate mission and objectives.

If the company did not provide the necessary resources to fund R&D, it is likely that the number of new products would not keep up with demand and the company would lose its dominant position in the pharmaceutical industry. This could lead to competitors enjoying increases in their sales, market share and, possibly, profits at WG plc's expense. R&D is evidently the source of WG plc's competitive advantage and so sufficient resources must be allocated to this activity if the company is to retain its current dominance in the pharmaceutical industry.

(b) **Strategic alliances**

Strategic alliances play an important part in global strategies where competitors lack a key success factor for some market. It may be distribution, a brand name, a selling organisation, the technology, R&D capability or manufacturing capability. The pharmaceutical industry requires large inputs of both technical expertise and resources, as R&D activities are crucial to the success of the companies. There are many practical issues that the directors of WG plc would need to consider if the company entered a strategic alliance with a competitor for the joint development of future pharmaceutical products.

If the strategic alliance is an informal arrangement it can be implemented faster and be more flexible. As conditions change and people change, the alliance can be adjusted. The problem with this type of arrangement is that with low exit barriers and commitment, there may be a low level of strategic importance and a temptation to pull out when difficulties arise.

A formal joint venture involving equity and legal documentation, on the other hand, has a different set of problems. When equity sharing is involved, there are issues about control, return on investment and achieving a fair percentage of the venture. A major concern is whether or not such a permanent relationship will be equitable in the face of uncertainty about the relative contributions of the partners and the eventual success of the venture. Before the commencement of the strategic alliance it is important that an equitable and agreed method of contributing to and sharing the venture's outputs is finalised.

Basically there are usually two sets of systems, people, cultures and structures that need to be reconciled, so it is essential that the control and management of the venture is discussed and finalised to minimise the possibility of serious disputes during the collaboration. It may be necessary to allocate special managers to the collaboration, but there will still be issues that arise in relation to the fundamental loyalty and commitment of the staff that participate in the venture. The main areas for the directors of WG plc to consider are the extent of the alliance in terms of markets and products and the sharing of costs and expenses between the two participants. It is important that these are agreed so that the position is clear to both parties.

One of the main issues facing the directors of WG plc is likely to be the input of resources, both intangible and physical. The intangible assets such as skill, expertise and patents are likely to be the cause of more disputes than the capital and machinery in an organisation. It may be necessary to share confidential and sensitive information that might prove to be difficult before trust is built up between the parties involved at both the personal and corporate levels. To enhance the chances of a successful strategic alliance, both sides must gain. They should protect and enhance the assets and skills being contributed and not let a partner take over.

The directors should also consider the effect on competitors and regulatory bodies to avoid any legislation or regulations that will affect the alliance adversely. By recognising that there may potential problems in this area, it may be possible to minimise the impact of them.

All of these practical issues will need to be agreed by the directors from the outset if the alliance is to be successful. However, if the companies are able to manage this effectively, a strategic alliance provides the potential of accomplishing a strategic objective or task quickly, inexpensively and with a high prospect for success. It should result in major benefits.

Question 11: Multinational company

The company currently operates with two different structures:

*   A centralised structure with the European Head Office maintaining responsibility for product design, manufacturing and the product range.

*   A decentralised structure based on national divisions within Europe, with each division's managers being responsible for setting the selling prices of each product and the distribution of products.

This organisation, using joint responsibility, has the following weaknesses:

*   Conflict and resentment between head office managers and divisional managers will arise because some decisions are imposed on divisional managers whilst they must make others. It is likely that when things go wrong, managers spend a lot of time blaming each other instead of trying to solve problems.

*   Divisional managers are likely to be de-motivated by the removal of their authority over the years as the European Head Office has taken over responsibility for decisions they used to have.

*   As European business practice becomes more integrated and greater harmonisation between countries occurs, there will be less benefits that can be obtained from having a divisional structure based on different countries. Duplication of work will result, particularly associated with marketing. Further integration within Europe is likely to result in a single European Currency, harmonisation of taxes and pricing within Europe becoming more uniform.

Recommendation

The company should restructure and reconfigure itself as a divisional structure based on related product groups. The company is quite large with over 100,000 employees in Europe.

The company should be divided into three or four product divisions comprising about 30,000 – 35,000 employees with head office retaining responsibility for administration. Each division should be responsible for product design, production decisions and marketing for the whole of Europe. Each division can be further sub-divided into small product groups each having its own management team.

The structure will have the following benefits:

*   Each division can be established as an investment centre with its own performance targets. This will enable head office to monitor each division and, at the same time, will enable divisional management to make their own decisions.

- Head Office will be less involved in all operational decisions allowing decisions to be made by divisional managers who know about their product range.

- Each division will be more involved in all operational decisions allowing decisions to be made by divisional managers, who know about their product range.

- Each division will be large enough to benefit from economies of scale. This will ensure that inefficiencies of having too many small national divisions can be eliminated.

- The managers of each division will be motivated to ensure that their division operates effectively and economically, as the performance of their division can be benchmarked against its competitors.

- It will be easier to divest a division at a later time if required or add a division should an acquisition or merger be made.

- The European Head Office can be reduced in size because some of its current responsibilities will be taken over by the divisions.

It should be emphasised that this is a strategic structural change and will take time to accomplish. It will need the support of the company's managers and employees and its success will depend upon the integration of the European business environment. If this does not take place the current structure should be retained with minor improvements.

Question 12: QS Software – Part 1

(a) **Organisational structure**

The formal structure of QS, as described in its organisation chart can be analysed as follows.

(i) Departmentation is primarily on a functional basis, although it also reflects product categories (web, software, hardware, repairs). The management partnership is also functionally divided.

(ii) The overall configuration is what Mintzberg calls a 'simple structure'.

– The strategic apex (the partners) exercises direct control over the operating core: sales assistants, technicians, software engineers and web designers.

– Other functions are pared down to a minimum. There is no middle line or technostructure, and only a one-person support staff (the administrator).

(iii) The organisation is flat, with (as far as we know) only two levels of hierarchy.

The advantages of QS's structure for its environment may be summarised as follows.

- It has short lines of communication and authority, with direct connection between the strategic apex and operating core. This should lead to responsiveness to client demands and environmental changes (e.g. developments in web-based technologies), as decisions can swiftly be made in response to upward communication and feedback.

- Mintzberg suggested that simple structures are suited to dynamic environments, because they are able to co-ordinate by direct supervision.

- Clients requiring individual products or services are likely to benefit from the clarity of the functional departments (and their distinct locations).

The disadvantages of QS's structure for its environment may be summarised as follows.

- Direct supervision from the strategic apex may become dysfunctional where the span of control and the number of tasks to be supervised gets too large. The two owners may not be able to supervise the complex multiple tasks required if QS wins the RGA contract.

- QS does not (as far as we know) have alternative co-ordination mechanisms in place. In order to co-ordinate project work (such as the RGA contract), some element of matrix organisation will be required, with software engineers, web designers, administrators and managers working together on the project team.

- Functional organisations can create vertical barriers to the 'horizontal' expectations of customers who require multi-functional expertise on a project (Peters).

(b) **Developing the organisation**

Mintzberg identified five basic parts or elements within an organisation:

- There is a strategic apex, consisting of the managers who make the key policy decisions.

- There is an operating core, consisting of the employees who do the basic operational work of making goods or providing services for customers.

- The middle line consists of the middle managers who link the strategic apex to the operating core.

- There is a technostructure, which consists of the technical experts and analysts who plan and control the work of others in the organisation (such as accountants).

- Finally, there are support staff who provide internal services, such as building cleaning and maintenance, car fleet management and legal services.

Mintzberg suggested that the organisation structure for any organisation will depend on the extent to which one or more of these elements dominates within the organisation. For example, if the strategic apex is dominant, the organisation will tend to be entrepreneurial. If the technostructure is strong, the organisation might be a 'machine bureaucracy' focusing primarily on improving deficiency. When the middle line is strong, the organisation will tend to be diversified and conglomerate in nature. When the operating core is strong, for example in a hospital or in schools, the organisation will lean towards professional proficiency in its operations.

It would appear that the owners of the company want to allow their IT specialists a large degree of initiative, suggesting that professional proficiency will be an important feature of the company. It is not totally clear, however, whether the owners plan to create a strong middle line (consisting perhaps of IT specialists-cum-managers), or whether they expect to retain a fairly large amount of management control themselves.

If the owners intend to develop a strong middle line over time, it might be expected that the company will expand through diversification and innovation, retaining an emphasis on proficiency in developing IT software.

 Question 13: Nikki Photocopiers

(a) Whether service and maintenance should have been prioritised for reengineering.

Critical success factors for Nikki should include the following:

- Production cost

- Quality control

- Value for money

- Features

- Reliability

- Servicing and maintenance.

Servicing is just one of a number of key areas that could be a candidate for reengineering.

Using Harmon's strategy/process matrix, servicing would be classified as follows:

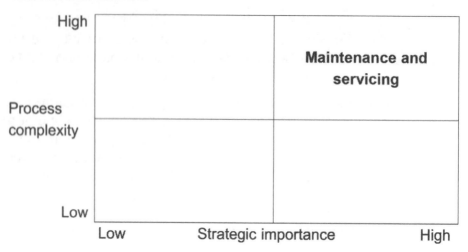

Processes that lie at the upper-right are complex, dynamic and of high strategic importance. These are usually the processes that provide the organisation with its competitive advantage and should be nurtured accordingly.

The main arguments for reengineering servicing and maintenance first are as follows:

– It has seen the largest fall in the magazine ratings.

– Nikki has its worst score in the ratings in this respect.

– The new CRM system does not appear to be generating the benefits it should have.

It could be argued, however, that value for money should have been targeted first, with its implications for pricing and production, as falling from being rated 1st to 2nd has major implications for competitive advantage. A fall from 5th to 7th in servicing is unlikely to be the main factor in Nikki Photocopiers' decline.

(b) Impact of the proposed changes on competitive advantage.

We are not given enough information in the scenario to classify the firm's competitive strategy as either differentiation or cost leadership. However, the process change can be explained in terms of its impact on cost and/or quality as follows:

Quality improvements

- By avoiding having to explain issues over the phone, there is less chance of the engineer being misinformed about the nature of the customer's problem. The likelihood of them turning up without relevant components and having to pay more than one visit is thus reduced.

- The system allows for more detailed customer requirements to be sent to the engineer than could be communicated effectively by phone.

Cost savings

- A cut in administration input and the elimination of the role of call-takers could lead to job cuts and cost-savings.

- Invoices will be able to be prepared instantly rather than at the end of each week. This should result in quicker cash receipts from customers and improved cash flow, thus reducing financing costs, for example.

- Savings in postage and printing costs as the system becomes more paper-free.

(c) **IT/IS implications**

The main IT/IS implications of the proposal are as follows:

Software – the CRM system

- The proposal involves the CRM system automatically generating work orders and sending details to engineers' PDAs. Furthermore, details are automatically sent to accounts once the job is done.

- While none of these are technically difficult, it is not known whether the current system has these capabilities. If not, then additional add-on applications (either off-the-shelf or bespoke) may have to be purchased.

- Even if present, new templates may have to be designed and training given to call-takers and engineers on filling them in correctly.

Hardware – using PDAs

- Presumably new PDAs (and associated software) will have to be bought and training given to engineers on their use.

- An automatic phone system where calls are made between PDAs and the CRM system may also be needed.

(d) **Should maintenance be outsourced?**

Arguments for outsourcing maintenance:

- Photocopiers are relatively simple machines, so it is likely that external firms will have the expertise to be able to maintain them.

- External firms may have economies of scale – for example, having more engineers makes it possible to see customers sooner.

Arguments against outsourcing maintenance:

- The most suitable processes for outsourcing are repetitive and transaction-intensive. Maintenance may have aspects of the former but does not fit the latter criterion.

- Dealing with customer queries is a critical success factor so should be kept in-house.

- Also there is a high risk of damaging the firm's reputation and goodwill if problems are not handled properly.

- The process of maintenance may generate useful information for designing new/improved photocopiers.

On balance, the critical nature of service and maintenance means it should be kept in-house.

Question 14: SDW

(a) **Establishing the website**

Before Mr M tries to establish an internet strategy, he should look at his overall business strategy. In doing this he should find answers to a number of questions, such as:

- Is he only going to continue to operate between three domestic cities?

- How far does he want to expand both internally (in the home market as indicated) and beyond (internationally)?

- Does he have the capacity to take on more bookings should they arise?

- Is he aiming at a different market sector?

- Does he have a business plan?

Checking this strategy is essential because the IT strategy must be seen to support the overall strategy of the company and not drive it. In the case of the SDW Company, this does not appear to be an issue; the owner wishes to develop an e-commerce facility on the internet site. However, care must be taken to ensure that the site does not cause unnecessary disruption to other systems within the company.

Having determined his business strategy, he needs to look at his IT strategy. Would an internet site for bookings be part of his overall IT strategy or simply an add-on? Piecemeal implementation could affect other areas of his business systems.

The SDW Company already has an internet site, so development of any new site must take this into account along with the overall requirements of the business. Expert advice needs to be obtained as to whether or not to amend this site or design a new one. Experts in web design may have to be employed if this expertise is not available in-house.

Additional care will be required in implementing the IT, for example in ensuring that no incompatible systems are introduced. The IT systems being used in the new internet site must be able to connect to the existing call centre systems. Similarly, the initial focus of the site must be on selling seats on the company's trains; other services may be offered later, but establishing the core business first is essential.

Deciding on e-commerce may have an impact on other parts of the business. For example, setting an objective of a given percentage of business through the internet will decrease percentages of business in other areas. Within the SDW Company, there will (hopefully) be a fall in the use of the call centre. This change must be anticipated and planned for. Staff in the call centre must be kept informed concerning the setting up of the internet site, and then assurances given regarding job prospects and training, either within the call centre or other areas of the company. Where reductions in staffing are required, it is better to obtain these naturally rather than by compulsory redundancies.

Mr M should also attempt to obtain information on competitors' sites (and more broadly, sites relevant to the travel industry), to assess particularly their design and ease of use. This would be relatively easy to do – he could even visit the sites himself. This would not tell him how successful the sites were, although some companies boast about the use of their sites in published information. Some travel operators even offer discounted fares for booking this way. He should be careful that any claims are verifiable, and not just another way of attracting publicity. It may be possible to commission some survey information to obtain potential customers' views on booking through a website.

Given the need for security and the current lack of in-house knowledge, setting up an e-commerce system will require specialist assistance, either by recruitment or outsourcing the writing and monitoring of the site.

The services to be offered through e-commerce must also be determined. Decisions regarding services will have a direct impact on the writing of the website, as the authors will need to ensure that the required services can be made available. As already noted, the initial focus must be on travel bookings. Additional services and products may be made available after this core business activity has been satisfied.

Whichever method of writing the website is chosen, budgets must be set for this activity and agreed at board level. If necessary, a cost-benefit analysis will be required, partly to justify the cost of writing the site and partly to show the potential benefits from using the website rather than a call centre.

Implementation issues

The charges (if any) for providing services to customers must also be determined. If e-commerce is to be encouraged, then some discount or other benefit can be expected to attract customers to this service. Given that this method of booking results in lower costs than when booking via a call centre, then the SDW Company can pass on these cost savings to its customers.

Prior to the e-commerce service being made available, it will have to be advertised. The board will need to decide where to advertise and how much the advertising budget will be. Possibilities will include mail-shots to existing customers, perhaps by email, and advertising on the websites of other organisations.

One of the aims of the provision of e-commerce is to try to remain competitive. A review of competitors' and other online sites is advisable to help determine the content and structure of the SDW Company site. This review may also help to identify other areas where competitors currently have an advantage so that the board can address this.

(b) **Features of internet sites focusing on cost reduction**

The site must, of course, be very easy to use. SDW should specify simple instructions on a site that is easy to understand and quick to load. The omission of detailed graphics and providing an 'uncluttered' site will also decrease programming costs.

Incentives to book online such as obtaining loyalty benefits, cheaper prices or being able to book earlier (which may not be available on offline bookings) could be offered. Although this may not save costs on the internet, it will provide overall cost savings by decreasing reliance on the call centre, thus limiting the number of staff employed.

Removing reliance on other more expensive selling media, such as the call centre, removes not only salary costs but also accommodation, pension, equipment and similar costs. Focusing on one booking medium becomes easier to support as only one cost structure is required.

Providing appropriate support to customers within the website which does not involve additional human contact. For example, provision of FAQs, a good help system and advice on each stage of the booking process. Customers are encouraged to resolve their own problems, which limits intervention from expensive staff.

Provision of other information on the website to attract customers to it, for example details of company performance or similar information already available within the organisation. Placing the information on the website is relatively inexpensive given that the information is already required in-house. Setting up web-specific information would be more expensive.

Innovative uses of internet technology, for example suggesting destinations on a limited budget rather than customers specifying where they want to go. Providing these ideas as unique selling points will attract more customers to the website, again limiting reliance on other media.

Question 15: RBT

Intranet

An intranet is an internal company information system where a wide variety of internal information can be posted for access by staff members. Internal information often includes company news, telephone directories, standard forms, copies of rules and procedures, and so on. In this case of the system under consideration by RBT, the intranet would hold up-to-date information on products and prices, so that sales representatives can download this information to their laptops from customer's premises and other remote locations.

Advantages

The proposed new system has the following advantages over the old system:

(1) **More regularly updated information**

An intranet site is very easy and cheap to update, and product and price information can be kept fully up-to-date by head office. The downloaded product information will therefore be much more up-to-date than the old printed materials, and a better customer service can be provided. All the latest products would be made available to customers and customers would always be given the correct prices.

(2) Reduced costs of producing price lists/brochures

Regular price lists and brochures will no longer be required, and the production and printing costs of paper-based products should be reduced.

Disadvantages

The intranet site has the following disadvantages compared with the old system:

(1) Slower communication with the production department

Since the telephone system will be discontinued, the sales people will not have access to production staff to resolve any queries or difficulties with customers. This would be a serious weakness in the system. Good communications between sales and production staff must be maintained.

Solutions

Possible solutions to this problem include:

(i) Email system

Email might provide an efficient way for sales representatives to communicate directly with the production staff, although controls would need to be in place to ensure that the production staff respond promptly to email queries they receive.

(ii) Maintain telephone access

Voice telephone access offers immediate communication. A salesperson can get in contact with a member of the production staff and get an immediate reply. Maintaining telephone access for certain queries would be a useful way of ensuring very quick communication where needed.

(iii) Access to production scheduling system

Allowing salespeople access to the production scheduling system over the intranet would allow them to estimate delivery date themselves thus reducing the need for direct contact between production and sales.

(2) Less personal communication with production department

The intranet is a very impersonal way to communicate with people. It does not allow for two-way conversation, whereas personal contact may be required to resolve difficult issues.

Solution

Both email and a voice telephone system are more personal forms of communication than the intranet. The voice telephone system in particular allows a two-way conversation to take place so that more difficult issues can easily be resolved.

(3) Rejection of new technology

The sales people may dislike the new technology that they are required to use. At present they do not use IT significantly in their work, and so new skills may be required. Many new systems also have 'teething problems' on implementation, which may also make users dislike the new system.

Solutions

(i) **Training**

Training will be required so people know how the system works and can get the best use from it.

(ii) **Consultation**

Consulting users early in the development process is an excellent way of getting user buy-in to the new system. It will also ensure the system is practical from a day-to-day usage point of view.

(iii) **Testing**

Testing systems well prior to implementation will help avoid the teething problems which may be encountered, particularly if the end users are involved since they know better than anyone else the way the system will be used in practice.

(4) Up-front costs

The proposed new system will require significant up-front costs both in terms of developing the new systems and training staff. Given the relatively small number of sales representatives (just 20) the investment may not be financially justified.

Solution

A cost benefit analysis can be undertaken to ascertain whether the costs of the investment are justified.

(5) Information systems – order progress

Manufacturing system – order tracking

As part of the manufacturing process, progress on orders will need to be recorded. The information recorded will include work done, work still to do and the expected completion date. This information might already exist within the current system or it may need to be input into a database which can be accessed by clients.

EDI or extranet

Using electronic data interchange the customer would be able to log on to RBT's systems to directly access the production data.

An extranet is an extension of an intranet. External parties are allowed to log onto the intranet site and use it to access sections of the intranet. The intranet site would need to be connected to the manufacturing system/database so that up-to-date information is available.

Advantages

(1) Clients could access information themselves. This could save staff time and resources in RBT, since there will be fewer customer queries to deal with.

(2) An extranet would be relatively easy to provide if the manufacturing system is already linked to the intranet for the benefit of the salespeople.

(3) Other information could also be provided to customers (such as past order information, account balances and so on).

Disadvantages

(1) There would be a loss of personal contact with customers. The salesperson would not have as many opportunities to make contact with customers in order to build an ongoing relationship. As a consequence, they might identify fewer sales opportunities or find it harder to make a sale because they are less trusted by the customer.

(2) External parties would be accessing internal systems. There is a danger that hackers will get into parts of the system that are confidential, and a risk that important information is stolen or damaged. It could also increase the possibility of viruses being brought in which could damage internal systems.

Internet

Alternatively the RBT could put tracking information on a database which is connected to the company's web site. Clients would then be able to access their information through this site.

Advantages

(1) Labour cost savings, as described for an extranet.

(2) Customers will be familiar with the internet and so find it easier to use than an extranet or internal system accessed via EDI. It also means they will not have to dial in directly to the company's internal network, saving them time and effort.

(3) There is less opportunity for hackers or viruses to enter the internal systems using a website on the internet, since they are not directly accessing internal systems.

(4) Other information could also be provided to customers on the internet site.

Disadvantage

The company may not currently have an internet site. This could be a significant extra expense, in terms of designing, creating and maintaining the site.

Question 16: MACOMP

(a) Benefits of e-business

E-commerce refers to all transactions between an organisation and external parties using electronic media. It is more than just buying using the internet.

The main ways that e-commerce has impacted on the way business is conducted are:

(1) Sales have been made in new markets since geographical limitations have been removed by e-commerce. Orders via a website can be placed from anywhere in the world and thus organisations are able to expand their businesses cheaply and easily.

(2) Business is being conducted much more quickly, with instant orders and purchases possible via e-commerce. Next day delivery is common in many cases or at least 'estimated delivery times' from orders being placed.

(3) Costs are being reduced through e-procurement. Orders to suppliers can be directly triggered once inventory reaches a certain level. This saves time and reduces the risk of 'stock out' as well as inventory holding costs.

(4) Suppliers have been made to compete on price since e-procurement software can check prices automatically through the internet and configure purchase orders to the cheapest suppliers. This means business is conducted in a more competitive way than ever before.

(5) Business can be conducted via online catalogues when one business is purchasing or selling from another (B2B). Quotes and estimates can be communicated via the internet which means that customer service has in many cases improved. Queries are dealt with immediately and there is an automatic 'audit trail' in terms of order information.

Information systems strategy is concerned with seeking strategic advantage from Information Technology (IT). For MACOMP, a new Information Systems strategy might impact upon corporate and business strategies in the following ways:

Impact on Corporate Strategy – IS strategy should be long term in nature and so impact on the overall strategy of the organisation. The board of directors may look at how information systems could support existing strategies, for example expansion of component manufacturing in MACOMP or how it could help develop entirely new directions for the company, for example a move into second hand component sales via the internet.

It is important that IS strategy is demand-led and so environmental analysis already carried out at a corporate level will be useful. Via PESTLE and 5 forces, the company can identify opportunities which could be exploited by a new information systems strategy.

Impact on Business Strategy – The strategy of the strategic business unit (SBU) will be affected by a new Information Systems strategy. The organisation will consider objectives at the business level, for example how the processes undertaken by managers in the OEM sales business could be speeded up in MACOMP. It will then look at what information would be needed for this to happen and how that information will need to interconnect and interact with other information in the organisation.

The reverse engineering SBU is likely to need standard order information from the customer and the ability to input measurements and 'draw' straight onto the system. Estimates can then be carried out much more efficiently.

Overall, IS strategies must be capable of delivering tangible benefits and ultimately enhanced profits.

(b)   **Impact on the value chain**

The proposed e-commerce business will impact on every activity in MACOMP. Using Porter's value chain, the benefits to each part of the organisation can be evaluated.

Primary Activities:

Inbound Logistics – MACOMP builds components for old machinery. In order to establish which raw materials will be required for a part not made before, a qualified engineer either searches MACOMP's archives for drawings or obtains them from the Original Equipment Manufacturer (OEM). This is only the beginning of the costing process carried out by the engineer who must then pull together an estimate to be approved by the customer. An e-commerce system would allow archives to be held on the system, possibly with links to OEM archives as well. The internet would be a key resource to see if components were being supplied by competitors and at what price. MACOMP could therefore ensure a competitive quote or even access drawings from other sources.

If the parts required for each component were listed on the system, together with supplier details, it is possible that automatic orders for raw materials could be generated once a customer accepts a quotation. It would also be possible to give customers prices for components made previously by MACOMP immediately; price lists could be available via email for example.

Sales and Marketing – MACOMP has not experienced growth for the last two years and this could be down to a lack of advertising and a reliance on 'word of mouth'. If MACOMP invests in an e-commerce system and has its own website, growth is likely to result from potential customers searching the internet for suppliers. At present, with no internet presence, such potential buyers do not know that MACOMP exists. A website would be advertising in itself and could be used to inform customers about MACOMP's core values and mission statement as well as answer 'frequently asked questions'.

Service – If customers are given access to a website and an email address, they will be able to submit queries to MACOMP. Dealing with customer enquiries on a timely basis will enable MACOMP to maintain the personal service they pride themselves on. In addition, it will be possible to maintain customer mailing lists online and to communicate on a regular basis with those businesses that have purchased components from MACOMP.

Secondary Activities

Procurement – As previously mentioned MACOMP will be able to save money with e-procurement, automatically searching the internet for the cheapest supplier of raw materials and therefore forcing suppliers to compete on price.

Information Technology – MACOMP's accounting systems are not automated and transactions are recorded in manual ledgers. Investment in a computerised system means that MACOMP can implement internal controls, reduce the risk of human error and become more competitive as a result. The quality of management information produced on an IT system will far outclass anything the company has at present.

Order processing could move to being systems based so that sales staff can trace the progress of orders on the customer's behalf.

HRM – In the future, MACOMP is likely to need fewer employees since much of the manual work will be done automatically on the system. Currently, MACOMP has 120 staff who, if they are retained may find they have more time to work on growing the business as their 'manual' workload decreases.

Infrastructure – The e-commerce system may bring beneficial changes to the culture and structure of MACOMP, allowing it to be more flexible. Since far more information will be available on the system, it may be possible to alter working practices and gain competitive advantage. New roles could be created looking after overseas customers for example, who are now able to order via the internet.

> The strategic and competitive benefits of the new e-commerce system to MACOMP can be seen throughout all of the business's activities. In the long term, these benefits will enable costs to be cut and efficiencies to be exploited. Ultimately, MACOMP will be able to provide a better service to more customers.

Question 17: Marketing

ABC Ltd – selling machine parts

These goods are likely to be supplied to order rather than from stock. Technical performance and reliability of the product are likely to be of primary importance. Price may be of secondary performance. There is likely to be only a small number of customers and therefore the company will only require a small sales team. Promotion and advertising are likely to be of minor importance and distribution is likely to be direct to the customer.

The company should concentrate resources in improving product performance (more regular quality controls, newer machines, well trained labour etc.) than on promotion. Economies of scale may be possible to reduce costs and selling prices.

DEF Ltd – selling consumer durables

This market is very competitive with both large national stores and local specialists competing for market share. However, most products will have a manufacturer's retail price which most companies will stick to in order to avoid price wars (even timing special sale periods to coincide with competitors). The division will sell direct to the public so place is not a vital concern for the marketing mix. The important factors are likely to be product and promotion. Consumers will be interested in areas of the product such as its efficiency, power, size etc. which the company cannot really change as it does not manufacture the product. However DEF can augment the product with areas such as guarantees and installations. With so much competition, promotion of the products will be important. Promotion should be made through adverts in newspapers, direct mailing and the use of trade in policies.

In such a competitive market, the company should concentrate its marketing on promotion and augmenting the product so that it is seen to be different from that of competitors (who are selling the same basic product).

GHI Ltd – producing and selling kids jellies

The first decision the company has to make is the place that it sells its goods. There are three possible options: through supermarkets, through independent traders (corner shops etc.) or directly to the public. There are disadvantages in all three strategies: supermarkets are powerful and will demand lower prices, independent traders are likely to give a lower volume, and selling direct to the public would involve setting up a network of retail shops which would be very expensive. It is suggested that the company aims to sell to supermarkets as this is likely to give a higher volume and agreements can be made for national coverage. If the company decides it wants to sell to supermarkets then it will have to compete for shelf space. It is therefore recommended that it follows a strategy of price penetration i.e. starts off at a low price to stimulate demand and then builds the price up as brand loyalty and awareness increase. The product should be designed to be colourful and jolly to appeal to kids.

The company should focus on place and price within its marketing mix and promotion is seen as a less important factor within the mix.

Question 18: QS Software – Part 2

(a) **Project management problems**

Successful management of a project team requires:

- clarity about the project's scope and objectives, and about exam member roles within it

- up-to-date awareness of (changing) project plans and feedback on current progress in regard to defined gates and milestones

- focused commitment and availability to the project (including visibility to stakeholders)

- the encouragement of multi-directional communication between team leader and members

- leadership skills: particularly in team-building, motivation and negotiation.

Sam apparently has the following key problems in these areas:

(1) He lacks clarity about the project's objectives and milestones. Not having been involved in the planning stage, and not being in direct contact with the RGA IT manager, he appears to be unaware of the project plans and crucial stage deadlines. He has therefore been unable to brief his team, who in turn have problems prioritising, co-ordinating and scheduling work.

(2) He lacks focused commitment and availability to the project, having to divide his time between RGA and other clients. This is reflected in his lack of 'visibility' to key project stakeholders (particularly the IT manager of RGA), which causes concern about the level of commitment and resource being devoted to the project. It is also likely to convey confused priorities to his team members – especially since he supports this by allowing core staff to be released from RGA work 'when necessary'.

(3) He lacks the skills and orientation for project team management. He is 'not happy' about his role as team manager/co-ordinator, as his preference is for technical work and he has little experience of people management or project management on this scale.

(4) There appears to have been little communication between team members, or between the team (as represented by Sam) and other stakeholders, either in the form of project plans or team meetings. This makes it difficult for the team to co-ordinate work, monitor progress and solve problems. It also makes it difficult for them to feel committed to the project – especially given the mixed messages from Sam.

(5) The unclear and dysfunctional project management structure exacerbates these problems. John Jones considers it to be 'his' project and therefore adopts the role of liaison between the project team and RGA – even though this is the project manager's (Sam's) role, and he himself has no day-to-day involvement in the work. John fails to communicate regularly or effectively with Sam.

(b) **Improving project management**

Recommendations for improvement in the team management, which should take effect from this point on, are as follows:

(1) Sam should be empowered to take up the project manager's role. He should be the one to be in regular contact with the client (in the person of the IT manager of RGA) – not John. Sam is already in the best position to appreciate the scheduling priorities and conflicts of the technical team, so he is in the best position to negotiate with the client. However, this requires that he also receives more information on the project scope and objectives, plans, progress and adjustments.

(2) Sam needs to dedicate his time to the RGA project and ensure that he is more 'visible' to the key project stakeholders (as a symbol of QS's commitment of resource to the project). There is genuine conflict with QS's objective of maintaining quality to other clients, but RGA must be classed as QS's key account – quite apart from the costs of continuing delays. If Sam is unwilling or unable to devote the time to RGA, QS should consider shifting the project management role to John – or to a contracted project manager.

(3) Sam needs to deploy project team members in a more focused fashion. He cannot afford to release RGA team members over the next seven or eight weeks: instead, he may have to negotiate delays with other clients. Alternatively, he may be able to sub-contract work or to hire additional specialist staff on a short-contract or freelance basis. RGA's own IT staff might also become more involved (e.g. in testing and installation).

(4) QS staff working on RGA should be regarded as a dedicated temporary project team, focusing solely on RGA work, collaborating and communicating on a regular basis. Sam should attempt, even at this stage, to do some 'team building' to enhance the team's commitment to the project, through a project re-launch (involving comprehensive briefing on the client, project scope, project plans and so on), team meetings and other techniques.

(5) Communication mechanisms should be set up to ensure regular, multi-directional flow of information about plans, adjustments and progress. Daily team review meetings might be held at QS, with regular progress reports, liaison with the IT manager of RGA and stakeholder reviews.

Question 19: Spartan Inc.

(a) **Retained earnings** – the most important form of finance in practice for both smaller and larger businesses. However, while retained earnings may seem an easy source of finance for a company, there is a danger that if it does not achieve an adequate internal return on these retained earnings, it may become the subject of a take-over bid from another company that considers that it could manage the capital of the business more effectively. This does not apply to Spartan because they do not have sufficient funds to finance the growth.

Equity – is the net value of a company after deducting its liabilities from its assets. However, in financing language, equity is usually taken to be the share capital in the business, and a slice of equity can be sold to raise money either to invest in the business or for shareholders to realise some cash for themselves, or a mix of these. Spartan has already issued shares but could release some more. The potential benefits are:

–   raise money without the burden of interest payment or compulsory capital repayment (although dividend payments will be required)

–   Spartan can bring strategic partners into the company, which can help with credibility

–   the new shareholders may well participate in further rounds of financing

–   they can provide expertise, e.g. as non-executive directors.

Further sources of equity include:

–   Personal resources, friends and family.

–   Corporate venturing – where a major company invests in a smaller one, to gain access to innovation and ideas.

–   Government-sponsored funds.

Grants – Grants are available for all sorts of projects, although the main targets are businesses involved in:

–   innovation

–   research

–   export

–   heritage and arts

–   technology and training and

–   those based in 'disadvantaged' areas.

The biggest disadvantage is identifying what grants are available, and completing the paperwork required.

Loans – there are many types:

- Regular institutional loan – from banks, etc. – money is advanced for a specific purpose and is repayable over a fixed period at a fixed or variable rate. The maximum loan amount will be based on available security (often personal) and the ability to 'service' (pay) interest and capital repayments. It may be possible to negotiate stepped payments and capital repayment holidays. The lender will want to see credible financial forecasts, especially cash flow projections.

- 'Soft' loans – from government sponsored funds – a number of loan funds have been established, financed by a mix of public and private money, to help certain defined industry sectors or regions. These loans are usually unsecured, and the terms are often easier than regular loans.

- Mezzanine funds – available from various sources including banks, venture capital firms and specialist mezzanine loan providers. This type of debt sits between equity and regular loans (hence the name). The loan is unsecured, and in return for the increased risk the interest rate will be higher and typically the lender will require the right to buy shares in the company on favourable terms (known as 'equity kicker', warrants, or share options).

The advantages and disadvantages are outlined below:

Advantages	Disadvantages
• Generally, short-term borrowing (less than one year) is cheaper than longer-term borrowing.	• Although debt is attractive due to its cheap cost, its disadvantage is that interest has to be paid.
• Debt interest is corporation tax deductible (unlike equity dividends) making it even cheaper to a taxpaying company.	• If too much is borrowed then the company may not be able to meet interest and principal payments and liquidation may follow.
• Debt interest is corporation tax deductible (unlike equity dividends) making it even cheaper to a taxpaying company.	• The level of a company's borrowings is usually measured by the capital gearing ratio (the ratio of debt finance to equity finance) and companies must ensure this does not become too high.

• Arrangement costs are usually lower on debt finance than equity finance and once again, unlike equity arrangement costs, they are also tax deductible.	• Many lenders will require assets to be pledged as security against loans – good quality assets such as land and buildings provide security for borrowing – intangible assets such as capitalised research and development expenditure usually do not.
• With long-term borrowing, if the borrower does not breach the debt covenants, the finance is assured for the duration of the loan.	• This risk is at its highest on overdraft borrowing where the bank can call in the overdraft 'on demand'. • Some types of debt finance are only available to large listed companies.

Outside of equity, loans and grants, the following sources of finance should be considered – although these will not be suitable for Spartan's investment.

Overdraft – a facility to borrow up to a prescribed amount for a defined period (usually one year renewable).

Factoring or invoice discounting – a factoring agent, usually a bank subsidiary, pays a company up to 85% of the invoice value when the invoice is originated, i.e. when the goods or services are delivered by the company. The balance is paid, less fees, when the customer settles the invoice.

Leasing, HP, contract purchase – all forms of loan where the security given is over the asset purchased.

(b) **Ratio calculations**

	Calc	20X5	Calc	20X6
ROCE	1,750/7,120	24.6%	1,500/7,500	20%
Net profit margin	1,750/5,000	35%	1,500/5	30%
Asset turnover	5,000/7,120	0.70	5,000/7,500	0.67
Current ratio	2,000/1,280	1.56	2,150/1,150	1.87
Quick ratio	1,000/1,280	0.78	980/1,150	0.85
Inventory days	365 × 1,000/3,000	122 days	365 × 1,170/3,100	138 days

Receivable days	12 × 900/5,000	2.2 months	12 × 850/5,000	2 months
Sales/working capital	5,000/720	6.9	5,000/1,000	5.0
Debt/equity	3,500/3,620	96.7%	3,500/4,000	87.5%
Interest cover	1,750/380	4.6	1,500/400	3.75

The return on capital employed of Spartan has declined as a result of both falling net profit margin and falling asset turnover: while comparable with the sector average of 25% in 20X5, it is well below the sector average in 20X6. The problem here is that turnover has remained static while both cost of sales and investment in assets have increased.

Despite the fall in profitability, both current ratio and quick ratio have improved, in the main due to the increase in inventory levels and the decline in current liabilities, the composition of which is unknown. The current ratio remains below the sector average, however. The increase in both inventory levels and inventory days, together with the fact that inventory days is now 53% above the sector average, may indicate that current products are becoming harder to sell, a conclusion supported by the failure to increase turnover and the reduced profit margin. The expected increase in sales volume is therefore likely to be associated with a new product launch, since it is unlikely that an increase in capacity alone will be able to generate increased sales. There is also the possibility that the static sales of existing products may herald a decline in sales in the future.

The decrease in receivables days is an encouraging sign, but the interpretation of the decreased sales/working capital ratio is uncertain. While the decrease could indicate less aggressive working capital management, it could also indicate that trade creditors are less willing to extend credit to Spartan, or that inventory management is poor.

The gearing of the company has fallen, but only because reserves have been increased by retained profit. The interest cover has declined since interest has increased and operating profit has fallen. Given the constant long-term debt, the increase in interest, although small, could indicate an increase in overdraft finance.

Ratio analysis offers evidence that the financial performance of Spartan Inc. has been disappointing in terms of sales, profitability and inventory management. It may be that the management of Spartan see the increase in capacity as a cure for the company's declining performance.

(c) The current gearing of Spartan Inc. = 100 × (3.5m/4m) = 87.5%

Total debt after issuing $3.4m of debt = 3.5m + 3.4m = $6.9m

New level of gearing = 100 × (6.9m/4m) = 172.5%

Current annual loan note interest = $350,000 (3.5m × 0.1)

Current interest on overdraft = 400,000 – 350,000 = $50,000

Annual interest on new debt = $272,000 (3.4m × 0.08)

Expected annual interest = 400,000 + 272,000 = $672,000

Current profit before interest and tax = $1.5m

Current interest cover = 3.75 (1.5m/0.4m)

Assuming straight line depreciation, additional depreciation = $600,000 per year

Expected profit before interest and tax = 1.5 + 1.43 – 0.6 = $2.33m

Expected interest cover = 3.47 (2.33/0.672)

This is lower than the current interest cover and also assumes no change in overdraft interest.

Thus, Spartan's gearing is expected to rise from slightly below the sector average of 100% to significantly more than the sector average. Spartan's interest cover is likely to remain at a level lower than the sector average of four times, and will be slightly reduced assuming no change in overdraft interest.

Question 20: Bits and Pieces

(a) The decision to open on Sundays is to be based on incremental revenue and incremental costs:

	Ref	$	$
Incremental revenue	(W1)		800,000
Incremental costs			
Cost of sales	(W2)	335,000	
Staff	(W3)	45,000	
Lighting	(W4)	9,000	
Heating	(W5)	9,000	
Manager's bonus	(W6)	8,000	
Total costs			(406,000)
Net incremental revenue			394,000

Conclusion

On the basis of the above it is clear that the incremental revenue exceeds the incremental costs and therefore it is financially justifiable.

(W1) Incremental revenue

Day	Sales	Gross profit	Gross profit	Cost of sales
	$	%	$	$
Average	10,000	70.0%		
Sunday (+60% of average)	16,000	50.0%	8,000	8,000
Annually (50 days)	800,000	50.0%	400,000	400,000
Current results (300 days)	3,000,000	70.0%	2,500,000	
New results	3,800,000	65.8%	2,500,000	

(W2) Purchasing and discount on purchasing

Current annual purchasing is $18,000 × 50 = $900,000

Extra purchasing from Sunday trading is $800,000 − $400,000 = $400,000

New annual purchasing is ($900,000 + $400,000) × 0.95 = $1,235,000

Incremental cost is $1,235,000 − $900,000 = $335,000 (a $65,000 discount)

(W3) Staff costs

Staff costs on a Sunday are 5 staff × 6 hours × $20 per hour × 1.5 = $900 per day Annual cost is $900 × 50 days = $45,000

(W4) Lighting costs

Lighting costs are 6 hours × $30 per hour × 50 days = $9,000

(W5) Heating costs

Heating cost in winter is 8 hours × $45 per hour × 25 days = $9,000

(W6) Manager's bonus

This is based on the incremental revenue $800,000 × 1% = $8,000 (or $160 per day)

Tutorial note

Only relevant cash flows should be taken into consideration when making this decision, i.e. the future incremental cash flows that occur as a result of Sunday opening. Prepare a summary of the relevant cash flows and reference in workings, where required.

(b) The manager's rewards can be summarised as follows:

Time off

This appears far from generous. The other staff are being paid time and a half and yet the manager does not appear to have this option and also is only being given time off in lieu (TOIL) at normal rates. Some managers may want their time back as TOIL so as to spend time with family or social friends; others may want the cash to spend. One would have thought some flexibility would have been sensible if the manager is to be motivated properly.

Bonus

The bonus can be calculated at $8,000 per annum (W6); on a day worked basis, this is $160 per day. This is less than that being paid to normal staff; at time and a half they earn 6 hours × $20 × 1.5 = $180 per day. It is very unlikely to be enough to keep the presumably better qualified manager happy. Indeed the bonus is dependent on the level of new sales and so there is an element of risk involved for the manager. Generally speaking higher risk for lower returns is far from motivating.

The level of sales could of course be much bigger than is currently predicted. However, given the uplift on normal average daily sales is already +60%, this is unlikely to be significant.

(c) When new products or in this case opening times are launched then some form of market stimulant is often necessary. B&P has chosen to offer substantial discounts and promotions. There are various issues here:

 – Changing buying patterns: It is possible that customers might delay a purchase a day or two in order to buy on a Sunday. This would cost the business since the margin earned on Sunday is predicted to be 20% points lower than on other days.

 – Complaints: Customers that have already bought an item on another day might complain when they see the same product on sale for much less when they come back in for something else on a Sunday. Businesses need to be strong in this regard in that they have to retain control over their pricing policy. Studies have shown that only a small proportion of people will actually complain in this situation. More might not, though, be caught out twice and hence will change the timing of purchases (as above).

 – Quality: The price of an item can say something about its quality. Low prices tend to suggest poor quality and vice versa. B&P should be careful not to suggest that lower prices reflect lower quality and hence damage the reputation of the business.

Question 21: Teemo

REPORT

To: The Managing Director of Teemo

From: Management Accountant

Date:

Subject: Month 6 Variance Report

This report aims to explain and interpret the Month 6 variance report.

Original planned profit

As can be seen from the original standard cost card, the original plan was to sell the product for £250. With a cost per unit of £160 (made up of material, labour and overhead costs), a contribution of £90 was planned for each unit.

Teemo budgeted to produce and sell 1,000 units so total contribution was expected to be £90,000. Budgeted fixed overheads (which could include items such as rent and insurance) were expected to be £70,000 so that a profit of £20,000 was the company's original target.

As actual profit was only £11,140 there must have been some deviation (or 'variance') away from the original plan. The variance report aims to explain why and where this has occurred.

Variances

There have been a number of deviations away from the original plan and each one is split into a different variance on the variance report.

Volume variance

Teemo sold 200 units more than was budgeted. So at a contribution of £90 per unit this should have created an extra £18,000 of profit. This is the 'volume variance' so that the expected profit on actual sales of 1,200 units was £38,000. This may have been caused by the fall in selling price (see next variance).

Sales price variance

The sales price variance is negative as it has been deducted from the expected profit – it has had an 'adverse' affect on profit. This tells us that the actual selling price of the product must have been below the original budgeted price of £250.

As 1,200 units were sold and the variance totals £12,000, the reduction in price must have been £10 per unit. So the actual selling price must have been reduced to £240 per unit. Without further investigation we do not know why the price was lowered, it could have been a deliberate marketing strategy or a reaction to similar moves by rivals.

Materials price variance

This is another adverse variance – in order to have an adverse affect on profit the price per kg of material (budgeted to be £20/kg) must have increased. The company spent £132,300 on 6,300 kg of material which gives an actual price of £21/kg. This £1/kg increase for the 6,300 kg purchased has caused the £6,300 adverse variance. This might have been caused by an uncontrollable change in market price or a switch of supplier.

Materials usage variance

Teemo originally planned to use 5 kg of material on each unit of production. As 1,200 units were produced, 6,000 kg should have been used. 6,300 kg were actually used which gives an adverse variance of 300 kg. At a standard cost of £20/kg, this caused the adverse usage variance of £6,000. This might have been caused by a change in the materials used causing unfamiliarity to staff.

Labour rate variance

A favourable labour rate variance means that there has been a positive effect on profits by a change in the labour rate per hour. £5,040 was saved on the 5,040 hours worked – a saving of £1 per hour. The budgeted rate per hour was £10 so the company must have paid an average rate of only £9 per hour. Perhaps a lower grade of labour was used – which might also explain the adverse materials usage variance.

Labour efficiency variance

Teemo budgeted for each unit to take 4 hours of labour. The total expected time for the 1,200 units actually produced would therefore be 4,800 units. 5,040 hours were actually worked, giving 240 extra hours of labour that weren't expected. At a standard cost of £10 per hour this creates a total adverse variance of £2,400. This would be consistent with the use of a lower grade of labour who may take longer to complete the task.

Variable overhead expenditure variance

There was no variance here which means that the planned expenditure on variable overheads per hour (£5) and the actual cost per hour must have been the same.

Variable overhead efficiency variance

Variable overhead efficiency is linked to the labour efficiency variance (and will have an identical cause). Because labour worked 240 hours more than expected, the company's machines, for example, will have had to have been operated for an extra 240 hours – this gives an extra cost to the company. At a standard cost of £5 per hour for variable overheads, the total extra cost will be £1,200.

Fixed overhead variance

The adverse fixed overhead variance tells us that Teemo spent £4,000 more than the £70,000 originally budgeted on these costs. More detailed analysis is not possible without a detailed breakdown of the individual elements of the fixed overheads, but this could be caused by extra system costs of monitoring new staff, materials wastage etc.

Overall

The variance report highlights that the main cause of the downturn in profits was the cost overruns – especially on materials. The next step should be to investigate why these variances occurred.

Question 22: Cost accounting

Traditional costing

The variable cost per unit of the product is $36 per unit (direct material $14 + direct labour $19 + variable overhead $3 = $36).

The total (full) cost of the product is $124 per unit (variable cost $36 + fixed overhead (8 hours × $11) = $124)

The red return from investment in the product is:

= $600,000 × 15% = $90,000

The required return per unit sold = $90,000/3,800 units = $23.68

The required selling price = $124.00 full cost + $23.68 = $147.68

Activity-based costing

The most appropriate cost driver for reviews would be the number of reviews per service.

Total number of reviews = (50 × 3) + (100 × 0.5) + (400 × 2) = 1,000

Cost per review = $55,000/1,000 = $55

The review cost for statutory audit services = $55 × 3 = $165.

Activity-based costing was originally developed for manufacturing industries. But it has now gained widespread use in many service organisations such as hospitals, accountancy practices, banks and insurance companies. It is just as important for these businesses to control costs, maximise the use of resources and improve pricing as it is in a manufacturing business.

An accountancy practice would seem to satisfy much of the criteria that make ABC relevant and useful to an organisation in that:

- indirect costs are high relative to direct costs (accountancy firms will have high levels of indirect overheads such as administrative costs, rent, depreciation, insurance etc. and very low direct costs such as material), and

- services are complex and are often tailored to customer specifications (and therefore, unlike in traditional costing, it would not be very useful to have one sole cost driver [such as direct labour hours] for all services).

Decision making

In view of its scarcity, labour is taken as the limiting factor.

The decision on whether to make or buy the component has to be made before it can be decided whether or not to accept the contract. In order to do this the contribution per labour hour for normal production must first be calculated, as the contract will replace some normal production.

	Basic		Scientist	
	$	$	$	$
Selling price		5.50		7.50
Materials	1.25		1.63	
Labour	1.50		2.25	
	——		——	
		2.75		3.88
		——		——
Contribution		2.75		3.62
		——		——
Contribution per direct labour hour (@0.25/0.375 hours per unit)		11.00		9.653

Therefore, if the company is to make the component it would be better to reduce production of the 'Scientist' model, in order to accommodate the special order.

The company should now compare the costs of making or buying the component.

An opportunity cost arises due to the lost contribution on the Scientist model.

Special contract:	Manufacture of Component
	$
Materials	1,000
Labour ($6 × 150 hours)	900
Opportunity cost (150 hours × $9.6533)	1,448
	——
Production cost	3,348
	——

Since this is higher than the bought-in price of $2,500 the company would be advised to buy the component from the supplier if they accept the contract.

The contract can now be evaluated:

	$	Contract contribution $
Sales revenue		35,000
Material cost	9,000	
Component	2,500	
Labour ($6 × 1,200)	7,200	
	———	18,700
Contribution		16,300
Contribution per direct labour hour		$13.58

Since the contribution is higher than either of the existing products, the company should accept the contract assuming this would not prejudice the market for existing products.

Because the contribution is higher for the 'Basic' model, it would be wise to reduce production of the Scientist model. However, the hours spent on producing the Scientist model per month are 4,000 units × 0.375 hours −1,500, and so the contract would displace 80% of the production time of the Scientist model. The recommendation assumes that this can be done without harming long-term sales of the Scientist model (the scenario suggests that the demand for the product is high and therefore there would be no lost sales of the product in the long term).

As the customer is overseas, this seems a reasonable assumption. However, before finalising the decision there are many other factors that should be considered such as:

- whether all costs have been considered (for example, extra delivery costs for the overseas customer)

- the potential impact of any foreign exchange rate movements

- whether this will be a one-off contract or whether it will open the door for more profitable work with this customer

- the value of the experience and impact on overseas reputation of beginning to export the product

- the level of competition for the contract

- the extra administration involved in dealing with a foreign customer (such as dealing in a foreign language and performing reasonable credit checks etc.

- the potential impact on existing customers who buy packages of basic and scientific models

Dealing with risk and uncertainty

There in a number of possible outcomes that need to be considered here and the expected value for each of these needs to be considered.

The value of the contract with the existing client is:

= 3 years × 1,000 hours × $60 per hour contribution = $180,000.

If the firm remains in the east, there will be an extra $4,000 in administrative costs and a bid fee of $20,000 giving two possible net outcomes from the bid as follows:

The contract can now be evaluated:

	Probability	Net outcome
Win the bid	60%	$156,000
Lose the bid	40%	($24,000)

The expected value for this is

= (60% × 156,000) + (40% × –24,000) = $84,000

If the organisation moves to the west it will win additional work alongside the contract with a value of:

= 3 years × 3,000 hours × $80 per hour contribution = $720,0000

But moving to the west would mean that there would be a required investment of $750,000 and the bid preparation cost would be $30,000. The net outcome of losing the bid would therefore be:

= 720,000 – 750,000 – 30,000 = ($60,000)

This would give two possible net outcomes from the bid as follows:

	Probability	Net outcome
Win the bid	80%	$180,000
Lose the bid	20%	($60,000)

The expected value for this is:

= (80% × 180,000) + (20% × –60,000) = $132,000

There is no advantage of moving to the west unless the contract bid is also made (if the firm moves to the west without bidding and winning the contract it will lose $30,000). On the basis of expected values, the best course of action is to move to the west and bid for the contract (this provides an expected value of $132,000 as opposed to only $84,000 if the bid is made from the existing eastern office).

But there are many other factors that the firm should consider before finalising its decision. Some of these are discussed below.

The expected value technique used has a number of issues. For example, it ignores the range of possible outcomes when the decisions are compared. Staying in the east has a range of –$24,000 to $156,000, but moving to the west opens the firm up to the possibility of a much higher loss of $60,000. If the firm is very risk averse then this may help decide in favour of remaining in the east. Also, the technique used is based on subjective probabilities and some sensitivity to these should be determined. Finally, the expected value technique is best used for long-term recurring decisions rather than for one-off decisions such as this.

The firm should also consider whether failing to move to the west and match the client's needs might lead to the loss of existing work with this client – especially if the door is opened to a competitor in the west to build a relationship with the client. Also, the possibility of further work from the client as it expands in the future might open up even greater opportunities for the firm.

There may also be some synergies possible from having offices in two locations such as having better access to staff or offering staff secondments between offices. It may also be that new clients won in the west may be able to provide extra work for the eastern office.

But there may also be problems with operating in the west such as the ability of the firm's organisational structure to cope with having offices in more than one location. Or it may be that the money tied up in the investment may have been better used for other strategies or opportunities.

Overall, it would appear that moving to the west has a strong financial logic. But major strategic decisions such as this should be evaluated against much wider criteria than a simple expected financial outcome.

There is no advantage of moving to the west unless the contract bid is also made (if the firm moves to the west without bidding and winning the contract it will lose $30,000). On the basis of expected values, the best course of action is to move to the west and bid for the contract (this provides an expected value of $132,000 as opposed to only $84,000 if the bid is made from the existing eastern office).

But there are many other factors that the firm should consider before finalising its decision. Some of these are discussed below.

The expected value technique used has a number of issues. For example, it ignores the range of possible outcomes when the decisions are compared. Staying in the east has a range of –$24,000 to $156,000, but moving to the west opens the firm up to the possibility of a much higher loss of $60,000. If the firm is very risk averse then this may help decide in favour of remaining in the east. Also, the technique used is based on subjective probabilities and some sensitivity to these should be determined. Finally, the expected value technique is best used for long-term recurring decisions rather than for one-off decisions such as this.

The firm should also consider whether failing to move to the west and match the client's needs might lead to the loss of existing work with this client – especially if the door is opened to a competitor in the west to build a relationship with the client. Also, the possibility of further work from the client as it expands in the future might open up even greater opportunities for the firm.

There may also be some synergies possible from having offices in two locations such as having better access to staff or offering staff secondments between offices. It may also be that new clients won in the west may be able to provide extra work for the eastern office.

But there may also be problems with operating in the west such as the ability of the firm's organisational structure to cope with having offices in more than one location. Or it may be that the money tied up in the investment may have been better used for other strategies or opportunities.

Overall, it would appear that moving to the west has a strong financial logic. But major strategic decisions such as this should be evaluated against much wider criteria than a simple expected financial outcome.

Variance analysis

	$
Sales price variance:	
Units sold should have sold for	32,850
(1.800 units × $18.25 per unit)	
(actual sales revenue)	32,300
	———
Sales price variance	550 (A)
	———

	Units
Sales volume variance	
Actual sales volume	1,800
Budgeted sales volume	1,750
	———
Sales volume variance	50
	———
× standard profit per unit	× $6
	———
Sales volume profit variance	$300 (F)
	———

If marginal costing is used, the contribution per unit is $8.50 ($18.25 – 6.00 – 3.00 – 0.75)

Sales volume variance	Units
Actual sales volume	1,800
Budgeted sales volume	1,750
	———
Sales volume variance	50
	———
× standard profit per unit	× $8.50
	———
Sales volume contribution variance	$425 (F)
	———

Question 23: MN plc

(a)

To:	The Management
From:	The Management Accountant
Subject:	Investment projects A, B and C
Date:	1 July 2006

The investment manager has analysed three mutually-exclusive investment opportunities A, B and C.

Reasons for differences between NPV and IRR rankings:

There are two main reasons that NPV and IRR rankings differ:

(1) The magnitude of the cash flows.

(2) The timing of the cash flows.

Magnitude of cash flows

Imagine we were faced with a choice between the following two projects:

Project A₁	Year	Cash flow
		£
	0	(105,000)
	1	48,000
	2	48,000
	3	48,000

Project A₂	Year	Cash flow
		£
	0	(105)
	1	49
	2	49
	3	49

The cash flows in Project A₁ are approximately 1,000 times bigger than those in Project A₂. Hence the NPV of Project A₁ will be approximately 1,000 times bigger than the NPV of Project A₂. The NPV of Project A₁ is £14,376, but the NPV of A₂ will be just over £16.86. NPV would therefore suggest that Project A₁ should be preferred.

Consider the IRRs of A₁ and A₂. In Project A₂ the return is £48,000 p.a., whereas project A₂ yields £49 p.a. The relative percentage return from Project A₂ is thus higher than that of Project A₁. Hence A₂ has a greater IRR than A₁.

The inconsistency in ranking has been caused by the magnitude of the figures.

Timing of cash flows

The actual time periods when the cash is generated can produce conflicting results.

Again consider two projects:

Project A₁	Year	Cash flow
		£
	0	(105,000)
	1	48,000
	2	48,000
	3	48,000

Project A₂	Year	Cash flow
		£
	0	(105,000)
	1	130,000
	2	0
	3	0

The NPV of Project A₂ is £13,170 (130 × 0.909 – 105).

This NPV is lower than the NPV of Project A₁.

The magnitude of the cash sums is very similar in both projects.

If we consider how the NPVs of the two projects reduce as the discount rate rises.

The NPV of A_1 will fall rapidly as the cash flows in the years 2 and 3 very quickly reduce in present value terms. The NPV of this project becomes zero at a 17.5% discount rate.

The cash in Project A_2 is all received in the first year. This cash sum is only £130,000, compared to cash in flows of £144,000 in Project A_1. However the value of the year 1 cash flow remains strong even as the discount rate rises.

Indeed, at a discount rate of 17.5% the NPV of A_2 is still positive at £5,630 ($130 \times 1/1.175 - 105$).

Hence the IRR of Project A_2 MUST be greater than 17.5%. Again there has been a conflict in the rankings, this time because of the timing of the cash flows.

These examples should illustrate that it is just as important to consider WHEN the cash flows arise as to consider HOW MUCH the cash flows are. It is very important to obtain cash in the early years of a project whilst it holds a high present value.

Comparison of opportunities A, B and C

The capital outlay in Project C is much greater than the other two projects. Cash inflows are generated for 9 years.

At a low cost of capital this project is worth the most to the company. The cash in years 6 to 9 maintains a high value when discount rates are low. However, this project is very sensitive to increases in discount rates. As the cost of capital rises the NPV of Project C declines rapidly. This is illustrated in the graph at the beginning of the report.

Project A is less sensitive to increases in discount rates. All its cash is received in years 1 to 3. These maintain a strong value as the discount rate increases. Project A could be said to be the least risky of the three choices if interest rates are volatile.

Which project should be selected?

The company has a cost of capital of 10%. At this rate Project C produces an NPV of £31,432. This is of higher benefit to MN plc than either projects A or B. Hence this project should be selected.

Assumptions: cash flows are known and certain. The cost of capital is known. Taxation and inflationary aspects have been ignored. If MN plc is very risk averse, Project A may be considered as its NPV is more robust to increases in the cost of capital than Projects B or C.

If you require any further information on this matter, please do not hesitate to contact me.

Signed: Management Accountant

(b) The payback period is the time that elapses before the initial cash outlay is recovered.

The paybacks in the example are:

	Assuming even cash flows	Assuming year end Cash flows
Project A	2 years 2 months	3 years
Project C	3 years 10 months	4 years
Project B	5 years 1 month	5 years

Advantages of payback

(1) **Exposure to risk.** It is widely recognised that long-term forecasting is less reliable than short-term forecasts. Projects with short paybacks tend to be less risky than projects with long paybacks. A project with a one-year payback is less risky than a project with a 10-year payback. Management can have very little confidence in forecasts of events ten years from now.

(2) **Liquidity.** Investment opportunities often require significant capital outlay. It may be important to recover this capital expenditure quickly for the company to maintain a strong position. Payback illustrates how quickly the capital can be recovered.

(3) **Simple measure.** The payback period is not a complicated measure. Technical expertise is not required to understand the meaning of payback.

(4) **Not subjective.** Payback period uses cash flows. Some investment appraisal methods use the rather more subjective measure of accounting profit (the accounting rate of return).

Disadvantages of payback

(1) The time value of money is ignored. Each of the projects being considered by MN plc generates £48,000. Payback period fails to recognise that as time elapses the present value of this cash diminishes. It would be possible to overcome this problem by calculating a discounted payback period.

(2) Cash flows after the payback are ignored. Option C has a payback of a little over five years. This information does not reveal that Project C continues to generate cash for four further years.

(3) Not a measure of absolute profitability. Payback fails to indicate HOW MUCH each project is worth. It seems naïve to select a project on the basis of payback without considering the amount of benefit received.

In the example Project A has a payback of just over two years, however its NPV is only £14,376.

Project C yields an NPV of £31,432 – more than double A's NPV. Payback period ignores this fact.

Question 24: Ski Runs

(a) The landowner has used a net present value (NPV) technique. This is the best technique to use for a project which is expected to last so far into the future. It means that the time value of money will be accounted for and that an estimate of the overall benefit (in current terms) of each investment can be used. The project with the highest NPV should be the project which is chosen for investment. This explains why the landowner has suggested that the low level of investment is the best decision.

The key elements of the calculation are:

(1) **Fee income**

This has been calculated on the basis of expected values (if 3 out of 10 seasons will be good, for example, this represents a 30% probability.

Expected number of skiers per year = [(30% × 60,000) + (40% × 40,000) + (30% × 5,000)] = 35,500

Expected fee income = 35,500 * $8 = $284,000

(2) **Annual costs**

The variable costs have rightly been included and calculated properly. But there is no reason to ignore fixed costs. It would be relevant to ignore fixed costs if they were not affected by the investment and were the same for each project. But that is not the case in this scenario. This is a fundamental cost for this project. It is one of the key differentiators between the investments – making the high investment might mean a higher initial lay out, but the landowner would benefit from fixed costs which are $60,000 per annum lower.

At a discount factor of 5.650 (for 10 years at 12%), the present value of the fixed costs would be $508,500 for the low investment but only $169,500 for the high investment. This would change the whole nature of the decision because the NPV of the low investment would fall to $142,600, whilst the high level investment would become $163,800. It would mean that the project decision would change and that the high investment is the better project path to follow.

(3) **Loan repayments/finance cost**

Discounting a project's operating flows at the investor's cost of capital allows for the meeting of finance costs of the investment (at that cost of capital) out of the inflows before giving the investor a benefit, as measured by the NPV.

An alternative approach would be to prepare a 'loan statement', showing year by year the interest clocking up, cash inflows and loan/interest payments, reaching a final net balance at the end of the project.

Including the finance cash flows with the operating cash flows in an NPV calculation would be a combination of these two approaches and would be a waste of time, if the finance cost of the investment was equal to the rate at which the flows were being discounted. This is because the NPV of the finance flows at this rate would, by definition, be 0 (see tutorial illustration below).

However, if the specific finance for the project is not part of the investor's general funds, with a cost at a rate differing from that used in the NPV calculation, it should be regarded as a separate set of cash flows to be included within the NPV calculation. In the case of the skiing project, half of the finance is provided by means of a subsidised loan from the Tourist Board, at 4%. Discounting these flows at the landowner's cost of capital, 12%, would actually result in a positive NPV, representing the benefit gained by receiving a loan at below average cost.

Tutorial Illustration:

For example, suppose a loan of $400,000 was taken out at an interest rate of 10%, with annual interest payments and the principal to be repaid after two years:

Time		Finance flow	10% Discount Factor	NPV
		$000		$000
0	Drawdown	400	1	400.0
1	Interest	(40)	0.909	(36.4)
2	Interest	(40)	0.826	(33.0)
3	Repaid	(400)	0.826	(330.6)
	NPV			0

(b) Virtually all the data used in the assessment of the project NPVs could be subject to variation, or risk. The most significant variable is probably the quality of snow cover, which in turn affects level of demand, and an attempt has been made to quantify this variability.

Other potential variables are costs, both initial and subsequent capital expenditure and annual operating costs. The discount rate (cost of capital) and fees may also be subject to variation and may have to be changed if anticipated demand levels are not realised at the original fee set.

The extent to which variability can be built into the project appraisal depends upon whether it can be expressed in quantifiable terms. If possible values for the variable can be predicted, with relative likelihoods (probabilities) then the approach may be to:

– use an expected value within one NPV calculation; or

– calculate several NPVs based upon the different values to give a range of possible outcomes.

The advantage of the first approach is that it will give a precise decision; however, that decision will be based upon a value that will often not coincide with an actual possible value. It is instead a long-run average value that may not be appropriate for a one-off situation.

The second approach will allow the investor to review all possible actual outcomes, and their likelihoods, in order that he can make a decision based upon his own risk-return preferences. This will be affected, inter alia, by the size of the investment relative to the investor's wealth and the amount he can afford to lose.

If the degree of uncertainty of an input variable cannot be reasonably quantified, the variability cannot actually be built into the NPV computation itself. However, sensitivity analysis may be used to assess the extent to which the value could change from that used in the NPV computation before it changes the decision – i.e. before it turns a positive NPV negative or vice versa.

Information about the sensitive variables in a problem will help the investor to make an informed decision.

Question 25: Y

(a) Resistance to change in organisations can be considered according to whether the resistance comes from individuals, groups or the organisations themselves.

Individual level

At the individual level, the following reasons/causes have been noted as factors involved in resistance: fear of the unknown, well-formed habits, threats to economic interest/status and the threat of inconvenience. In the case of Y, there is much for employees to fear. Several will be afraid that, in the longer term, they may lose their jobs. Some will fear that they may have to move from one job to another or from one department to another. For some, this will be quite an upheaval, although others may welcome the change. Some will fear that the change may bring a loss of status in the organisation, especially those in middle management whose jobs are to go. Redeployment to another job may include a protected salary, but delayering will inevitably result in a loss of status for some employees. Then there are the problems with learning new skills. Some employees will fear that they might not make the grade and be reluctant to take on retraining.

Group level

At group level there will be collections of individuals who see their position threatened and who will combine to resist any threats to their position. The middle management groups in Y in particular will feel threatened and will be looking to their trade union to protect their interests. There may well be calls for industrial action to attempt to prevent delayering from taking place, or at least to win for the managers affected the highest possible severance pay or redeployment terms.

Even where individuals are not members of a trade union, it is possible for groups of employees, including managers, to collude informally to resist change. This may be achieved by such measures as withholding information or by not being wholly co-operative with those seeking to implement change.

Organisational level

At the level of the organisation, a number of factors will operate to make the change process difficult. These include the existing structure and culture of the organisation, the existing investment in resources, and past contracts and agreements with various stakeholders within the organisation. For example, many state industries that have been privatised in recent years have required flatter, more organic, organisational structures; it is hard to change from a 'role' culture to a 'task' culture to cope with competition in the open market and hard to renegotiate the terms of the contracts with stakeholders, such as the trade unions.

(b) A useful way of looking at the problem of resistance to change is via the simple framework formulated by American social psychologist, Lewin.

Lewin's framework suggests that change, or lack of it, is the result of disequilibrium or equilibrium between two sets of opposing forces. One set he refers to as 'driving' forces, because they act to encourage and facilitate change, and the other as 'restraining forces' because they act in the opposite direction and seek to maintain the status quo.

Any attempt to bring about change, therefore, requires ways and means of overcoming resistance to change. This may be achieved in a variety of ways, but it is apparent that what is required is either a further strengthening of the forces for change or a reduction in the power of restraining forces.

Using this framework we can see that the major driving force for change is the increasing competition brought about by changes in the industry environment. There is little that Y can do about this except to respond to it by becoming leaner and more effective. The reduction in management levels should help to cut costs, and the strengthening of the telephone banking division should help the bank's competitiveness, as should the investment in IT and training.

The spur to change is the threat of the new competition, and management should seek to communicate the message to managers and other employees more effectively. We cannot tell from the scenario just what attempts have been made to communicate to the workforce either the seriousness of the bank's situation, or the rationale behind senior management's plans to combat this situation. To the extent that the need for the planned action has not been properly communicated it follows that this must be an early priority for the senior management team. Communication, along with other means such as education, participation, consultation, manipulation and coercion are part of a typology of methods advocated by theorists such as Kotter and Schlesinger for assisting in the management of a/the change process.

It may be that communication is not sufficient and that a process of education is required. In this day and age the senior managers should tread carefully. Bank employees generally have a high level of education and it would not help the case for change if management underestimated this. Nevertheless, in trying to persuade employees that the plans management have drawn up are in the best interests of all, there may be a place for the education of some staff members to management's point of view.

A method associated with communication and education is that of facilitation and support. Y management may be able to alleviate fears of some individuals by the use of counselling and group discussion.

Another way of reducing resistance to change is that of involving all employees from the start of the change process. By putting the problem the bank is facing to employees in a series of face-to-face meetings, and offering the possibility of participation in the decision-making and planning process, it may be possible to get more employees to buy into the planned changes. The problem in the case of Y is that senior management may already have made decisions without consultation. This kind of participation exercise is also time-consuming.

Given that the decisions have been made and that resistance has already been encountered it may well be that the best way forward now is through a process of negotiation with representatives of the workforce. In the case of Y it is probable that trade union officials will represent the employees' side. Through a process of negotiation and bargaining it may be that the union can gain sufficient concessions from management, in terms of built-in safeguards and appropriate compensation for its members. The bank could then be allowed to proceed without further hindrance.

An alternative approach is the less ethically based use of manipulation and co-optation. Manipulation involves seeking to persuade people by the use of partial and misleading information while co-optation involves 'buying people off' by the promise of some kind of reward for going along with the proposed changes. Through these methods are used, they are not the kinds of methods that professional people would involve themselves with.

If all else fails, however; senior management may find that the use of explicit and implicit coercion is the only way forward. This may involve mass redundancies without right of appeal. This method would be one of last resort since the image of the bank would suffer and the morale of the remaining workforce would be badly affected.

Question 26: BHH Clothing

(a) **The strategic context**

The key environmental issues are as follows:

– High customer power.

– The threat from low cost competitors.

Both of these threats are likely to increase rather than decrease.

The options available to BHH include the following:

(1) The main advantages of the current plan are that they should reduce cost without compromising quality. Furthermore BHH keeps the higher-skilled value-added finishing aspects in-house. This should help BHH manage the threat from low-cost competitors but does not address the problem of high customer power.

(2) Keep manufacturing in Europe but focus on improving production efficiency to reduce costs. This could involve implementing TQM, better use of IT, improved throughput, eliminating processes that do not add value and improving employee motivation and output. This could be planned as part of a BPR project but is likely to be just a short-term fix. In the longer term the threat from lower-cost Chinese manufacturers will still need to be addressed.

(3) BHH could shift both manufacturing and finishing overseas, focusing mainly on the customer relationship and design aspects. This should reduce costs further but would lose the differentiating factor that comes from high quality finishing.

(4) BHH could seek to sell goods under its own brand name to reduce customer power. However, this will require substantial investment to develop the BHH brand in the market.

(5) BHH could seek to vertically integrate forwards and open its own retail outlets. Again, the problem for BHH would be the major investment required.

(6) BHH could manufacture higher volume garments overseas but seek to make and deliver small batches of more exclusive lines with shorter lead times. This would allow BHH to be more responsive to market trends, thus reducing the risk of "fashion miss" (i.e. producing items that consumers do not want). The offer of reduced lead times may be difficult for Chinese firms to match and so would enhance BHH's strategy of differentiation. This would also reduce the scale of redundancies facing BHH.

Summary

Given its lack of brand strength, BHH has to move at least some of its manufacturing overseas to respond to the serious environmental threats it faces. Major change is thus unavoidable. However, the directors may wish to consider option 6 above as a way of reducing the impact of the change process.

(b) **Contextual features**

The key contextual features are as follows:

- **Time** – Given the recent loss of Forum and the threat from other retailers, BHH has to act quickly to develop a response. The time context is close to being a crisis rather than allowing an incremental approach. Time must thus be viewed as a strong driver of change but as a negative aspect in terms of how easy that change will be.

- **Scope** – A significant proportion of manufacturing must be outsourced but design and finishing should continue as before without major changes. On balance the scope aspect is best described as realignment rather than transformational.

- **Preservation** – It is vital that design, customer service and finishing skills are retained, despite other production staff (presumably) being made redundant. A major threat is that current employee unrest will result in key staff looking for new jobs elsewhere. The existing culture may need to be refocused firmly on high quality and customer responsiveness.

- **Diversity** – While there is likely to be a difference in sub-culture between production and design, only the latter will really be impacted by the change. Furthermore, there is likely to be a strong sense of unity within BHH due to them all being based in the same location and the length of time many employees have worked together. Given that the change will primarily impact production workers, diversity is unlikely to be a problem. (Note: were BHH to switch to short lead-time, small-batch production, then the change would be more widespread, in which case diversity would be a more major consideration).

- **Capability** – Given that management have so far resisted the industry trend to outsource production, it is likely that BHH does not have staff who are experienced in change and change management.

- **Capacity** – Given falling margins it is probable that BHH does not have significant funds to invest in the change process. However, the move to outsourcing will not require significant funds. Instead there will be pressure on management time to locate and screen potential suppliers. There is insufficient information available to determine whether or not this will be a problem.

- **Readiness** – A major problem facing management is that staff have discovered some aspects of the change without being properly informed. The negative implications have thus been blown out of proportion, resulting in threatened strike action. Staff are thus likely to oppose any changes rather than support them.

- **Power** – There is insufficient information to determine how much authority and respect change agents have to implement proposed changes. It is clear however, that employee representatives are key players in the change process.

(c) **Design choices**

Key recommendations are as follows:

- **Change path** – The most pressing problem is to avoid strike action and to reassure staff about the actual changes proposed. Only then can management look to address the details of how, when and where production should be outsourced.

- **Change start point** – The crisis nature of the problem necessitates a top-down approach initially where senior management need to regain control of event.

- **Change style** – Once the immediate problem of staff unrest is addressed, management should adopt a participative approach to involve employee representatives in deciding how and where redundancies should be made, whether some staff could be retrained and what support will be offered to staff who lose their jobs.

- **Change interventions** – Initially the key mechanism is likely to be communication and education to convince employees that only production staff involved in making the basic garments might lose jobs. As stated above participation will be key to successful change management.

– **Change roles** – Given the lack of experience of change, BHH may wish to employ the services of external consultants. Either way it is vital that change action teams are set up, including designers, finishers and production staff. BHH could also consider including representatives from key customers to improve BHH's chances of keeping their accounts. Certainly consultants should be used to investigate potential Chinese suppliers.

KAPLAN PUBLISHING